Darwinism, Design, and *Public Education*

Rhetoric and Public Affairs Series

Darwinism, Design, and *Public Education*

❈ ❈ ❈

edited by
John Angus Campbell
Stephen C. Meyer

Michigan State University Press
East Lansing

Michigan State University Press
East Lansing, Michigan 48823-5245

Printed and bound in the United States of America.

09 08 07 06 05 04 2 3 4 5 6 7 8 9 10

LIBRARY OF CONGRESS CATALOGING-IN-PUBLICATION DATA

Darwinism, design, and public education / edited by John Angus Campbell, Stephen C. Meyer.
    p. cm. — (Rhetoric and public affairs series)
Includes bibliographical references.
    ISBN 0-87013-670-4 (casebind : alk. paper) — ISBN 0-87013-675-5 (pbk. : alk. paper)
    1. Evolution (Biology)—Study and teaching. 2. Intelligent design (Teleology)—Study and teaching. I. Campbell, John Angus. II. Meyer, Stephen C. III. Series.
    QH362.D37 2003
    576.8'071—dc22

                                2003020507

Cover design by Brian Gage, www.briangagedesign.com
Book design by Sans Serif, Inc.

"DNA Strands That Are Magnified 75 Times" © Philip A. Harrington, Getty Images; "Double Helix Model" © Jason Reed, Getty Images; "Darwin Portrait" Berlin Photograph of Charles Darwin, courtesy of the University of Oklahoma History of Science Collections; "Trilobite Fossil" drawing provided by J. Y. Chen.

Visit Michigan State University Press on the World Wide Web at:
www.msupress.msu.edu

Contents

Acknowledgments

No book of this scope can be completed without the help of many skilled people. We wish to thank Walt and Ginny Hearn, Paul Nelson, Steve Dilley, and Anna Jennings for their invaluable assistance in editing and compiling this book. We would also like to thank Dan Roosien and Annette Tanner at Michigan State University Press for their skill and efficiency in bringing this book through the editorial process. Finally, we must gratefully acknowledge series editor Marty Medhurst. Marty's invitation to expand a 1998 special issue of the journal *Rhetoric and Public Affairs* gave us the opportunity to develop a comprehensive book project exploring the pedagogical, legal, and scientific issues raised by the controversy over biological origins. The resulting work would not have come to fruition without him.

We dedicate this book to Brooke and Elaine.

John Angus Campbell and Stephen C. Meyer
October 2003

Why Are We Still Debating Darwinism?
Why Not Teach the Controversy?

John Angus Campbell

❉ ❉ ❉

From the Scopes trial in 1925 through the action of the Kansas State Board of Education in 1999, the teaching of evolution in public schools has been a flashpoint in American education.[1] As in all long-standing controversies, positions harden and disputants speak chiefly to rally their own supporters. The debate ebbs and flows in public awareness until a local school board's decision catapults it once again into the lead story or back onto page one.

Many suppose that the debate over teaching evolution in public schools has gone on so long that it is going nowhere. But all things historical are hostage to change. Although its implications are not yet fully evident, something new has happened in the debate over the teaching of evolution. The advent of a modern scientific theory of intelligent design (ID) and a scholarly research community advancing this theory (the ID movement) have reenergized and are now redefining the character of this once-stalled controversy.[2] ID is a science, a philosophy, and a movement for educational reform.

As science, ID is an argument against the orthodox Darwinian claim that mindless forces—such as variation, inheritance, natural

selection, and time—can account for the principal features of the biological world.

As a philosophy, ID is a critique of the prevailing philosophy of science
that limits explanation to purely physical or material causes.

As a program for educational reform, ID is a public movement to make
Darwinism—its evidence, philosophic presuppositions, and rhetorical
tactics—a matter of informed, broad, and spirited public discussion.

ID in all its senses has clear implications for the teaching of science, particularly biology, in the public schools—irrespective of one's view of the
merits of the contemporary design argument. A central claim of the ID
movement is that if science education is to be other than state-sponsored
propaganda, a clear and principled distinction must be drawn between empirical science and the materialist philosophy that drives contemporary
Darwinian theories of biological origins.[3]

As critics of ID are quick to point out, design arguments are not new.
The basic insight on which such arguments rest is one side in an ancient
philosophic controversy. That is, the complexity of the world order, particularly as seen in the study of life, appears to have been produced by intelligence or mind rather than by self-sufficient material forces. In ancient
times, Heraclitus, Empedocles, Democritus, and Anaxamander upheld the
self-sufficiency thesis, while Plato and Aristotle argued for mind.[4]

Why this argument should reemerge just now is easy to understand. At
a time when contemporary cosmology speaks of "anthropic fine-tuning"
and biology seeks to understand the "code of life" and the design of "molecular machines," the rise of the design hypothesis is as appropriate to our
time as were the ideas of "natural selection" and "survival of the fittest" to
the period of capitalist expansion and industrialization during the mid-
nineteenth century.[5] "Information" and the nonmaterial products of intelligence are part of our daily speech, as is evident by our use of such terms
as *software, programs, gigabytes,* or *RAM* and our questions about the "compatibility" of computers and printers.

What is new about the theory of intelligent design is the shock it ad-
ministers through its creative restatement, in contemporary scientific
terms, of an old and presumably extinct intellectual tradition. The origin of
biological novelty was thought to have been identified, if not precisely by
Darwin in 1859, then at least by neo-Darwinians in their 1940s synthesis.
Yet design theorists insist that natural selection acting on random genetic
mutation does not account for the fundamental morphological innovations
in the history of life—whether novel organs, body plans, or cellular ma-

chines. Instead, they insist that actual design, not just a natural process mimicking design, is responsible for the complex features and systems found in living things. Though this view may not be new, the evidence and modes of analysis that design theorists use to advance it clearly are.[6]

Thus, the ID movement has only recently come into public awareness. Nevertheless, such awareness is growing rapidly as a result of the books and public speaking of Berkeley law professor Phillip Johnson; the book *Darwin's Black Box* by Lehigh University biochemist Michael Behe; William Dembski's *The Design Inference;* Jonathan Wells's *Icons of Evolution;* Paul Nelson's *On Common Descent;* and the scientific and philosophical essays of Stephen Meyer in anthologies such as *Science and Evidence of Design, Mere Creation,* and *Debating Design: From Darwin to DNA.* The growth of this intellectual movement has recently attracted prominent news stories in the *New York Times, Los Angeles Times, Wall Street Journal,* and the *National Post* (of Canada) as well an extensive two-part critique in the *New York Review of Books.*[7] Additionally, a recent Zogby poll shows strong support for the educational agenda of the design movement. Nearly 78 percent of those surveyed by Zogby favor including information about the scientific case for intelligent design in the public school science curriculum alongside standard Darwinian accounts of life's origins.[8] Congress has also expressed its support for teaching students about the scientific controversies that exist concerning biological evolutionary theory. The report language in the 2001 federal No Child Left Behind Act urges schools to adopt a science curriculum that "help[s] students to understand the full range of scientific views that exist" about controversial subjects "such as biological evolution" and "why such topics may generate controversy." Additionally, the Ohio State Board of Education recently adopted a provision in their state science standards requiring students to know why "scientists today continue to investigate and critically analyze aspects of evolutionary theory." While the Ohio State Board's decision did not mandate the teaching of intelligent design, it does require that students know about scientific criticisms of contemporary evolutionary theory. It also allows local school districts and teachers to present the theory of intelligent design if they so choose. One local school district, the Patrick Henry School District, has already announced its intention to teach students about the theory.[9]

Even so, many of the technical arguments of design theorists are not yet well known. The aim of this volume, *Darwinism, Design, and Public Education,* which itself has "evolved" or (if one prefers) was "redesigned" from a special issue of the journal *Rhetoric and Public Affairs,* is not to advocate the

theory of ID. Instead, this volume seeks to introduce science educators to
the arguments of the design theorists and to those of prominent critics of
ID, so that educators may consider the merits of the main pedagogical argument of this volume, namely, that science teachers would do well to
"teach the controversy" or "controversies" over contemporary evolutionary theory.

Teachers who do so will advance public understanding of both the nature and rhetoric of science.[10] By the "rhetoric of science," I mean the
study of the argumentative tactics employed by scientists not only in their
scientific writing but also in their public and educational pronouncements.
The rhetoric of science also seeks to identify presumptive substance and to
detect probable weaknesses (or obfuscation) in a scientific argument or discourse.[11] In addition, the rhetoric of science seeks to foster civility in public discourse. On this score, it is important to remember John Stuart Mill's
observation that in any controversy where the stakes are high, even the
best people may present bad arguments with the best of intentions and,
conversely, that those who do not prevail in public opinion may yet make
many good arguments.[12]

Organization of the Volume

With this in mind, *Darwinism, Design, and Public Education* will seek to advance public discussion of science education by presenting arguments for
and against a more inclusive, controversy-based biology curriculum. In
order to do this, the book will also present arguments for and against both
contemporary Darwinism and the theory of ID itself.

Darwinism, Design, and Public Education is divided into four parts and appendixes. The first part of the volume presents three essays arguing for a
more inclusive approach to science education—indeed, one that would encourage science educators to teach students about scientific challenges to
Darwinian theory and about the challenge posed to Darwinism by advocates of the theory of intelligent design. The second part includes several
essays that provide scientific critiques of contemporary evolutionary theories or textbook presentations of these theories. The third part presents essays that develop the scientific case for intelligent design. The fourth part
offers responses, chiefly critical, to the essays in the first three parts of the
volume. The appendixes present both supporting documents about the
controversy over the teaching of evolution in the public schools (including
the transcript of a recent hearing of the U.S. Commission on Civil Rights

and an essay by Donald Kennedy) and a technical supplement to the case by Stephen C. Meyer, Marcus Ross, Paul Nelson, and Paul Chien on the Cambrian explosion.

Part I

Part I, "Should Darwinism Be Presented Critically and Comparatively in the Public Schools?: Philosophical, Educational, and Legal Issues," sets the agenda for the book. The question considered throughout the volume is "Should public school science teachers be free to teach the controversies over biological origins?" In my opening essay, "Intelligent Design, Darwinism, and the Philosophy of Public Education," I argue that teaching Darwin's theory of natural selection comparatively is the mode Darwin himself followed in the *Origin*. It is the traditional method used in the humanities, it is used to teach values, it is explicitly sanctioned by Mill's *On Liberty,* and it fosters student interest in science. Further, it helps teach the skills of analysis and critical deliberation that are central to democratic citizenship. In "Intelligent Design Theory, Religion, and the Science Curriculum," Warren A. Nord argues that liberal education in a pluralistic democracy requires the inclusion of competing points of view, including design theory in science classes, "not because it is a better or more reasonable theory than its naturalistic counterparts . . . [but] because we disagree about whether it is a better theory." That disagreement is of such a kind that educators are obligated to teach students about it. Throughout the essay, Nord develops his thesis: "By refusing to take seriously contending interpretations of nature, we teach science, in effect, as a matter of authority. Students typically come to accept its claims as a matter of faith in the scientific tradition rather than as a matter of critical reason."

The first part concludes with "Teaching the Controversy: Is It Science, Religion, or Speech?" In this essay, David DeWolf, Stephen C. Meyer, and Mark E. DeForrest argue that the law allows, and good pedagogy requires, public school biology teachers to "teach the controversies" over biological origins. They examine several proposed curricular changes that would rectify what they regard as the current imbalance in the biology curriculum. Their hypothetical teacher, John Spokes, would like to correct errors in present biology texts, expose students to evidential challenges to evolutionary theory, and discuss alternative theories of biological origins.[13] The authors ask, "Does the law allow him to do so?" They argue that it does, by showing that exposing students to an evidentially based critique of standard theories and to a similarly evidentially based case for alternatives constitutes good science. They also show that presenting ID as an alternative theory does not constitute an establishment of religion. They suggest instead that refusal to allow Spokes to teach his subject in this more open way could well constitute a form of legally prohibited viewpoint discrimination.

Part II

The logic of the remainder of this volume follows directly from the educational and legal controversy that DeWolf, Meyer, and DeForrest address from the practical concerns of their hypothetical teacher, John Spokes. A teacher considering whether to "teach the controversy" will face practical pedagogical issues about the type of material that would be permissible, or desirable, to present.

In their legal essay, they ask a question: what exactly can Spokes (or any other public high school teacher) teach? Can teachers correct errors in the biology texts, including those that exaggerate the evidential support for Darwinism? Similarly, can teachers expose students to scientific critiques of neo-Darwinism and related evolutionary theories? If so, can they also tell students about alternative theories of origins, including specifically the theory of intelligent design? DeWolf, Meyer, and DeForrest argue that teachers may legally critique neo-Darwinism and present ID as an alternative. But this raises practical questions for science educators. First, what are the scientific critiques of textbooks or neo-Darwinism that students should know about? Second, what is the theory of intelligent design and what evidence, if any, supports it? And third, what scientific (or philosophical) critiques of design theory should students and educators know about?

The remainder of the book is organized mainly around these three questions to help science educators "teach the controversy" if they should so choose and to help policymakers assess the merits of the pedagogical argument made for this approach in Part I. Thus, Part IV includes not only substantive critiques of the scientific case in Parts II and III but also critiques of the pedagogical proposal—that is, the "teach the controversy" approach advocated in Part I.

Part II, "Scientific Critique of Biology Textbooks and Contemporary Evolutionary Theory," first seeks to establish that there are many errors in present biology texts, errors that in some cases overstate the evidential support for neo-Darwinism and chemical evolutionary theory. Part II also seeks to establish the existence of a significant evidential challenge to reigning evolutionary theories, even if that challenge goes almost unreported in basic texts. In short, it seeks to show that there is an evidential challenge to contemporary evolutionary theory that students need to know about. (Additional aspects of this challenge are addressed in Part III in the articles that also make a positive case for intelligent design.)

In the first essay in Part II, Stephen C. Meyer and Michael Newton Keas identify an important error of omission, not only in textbooks, but also in most public discussions of evolutionary theory. Their essay, "The Meanings of Evolution," describes the multiple separate meanings associated with the term *evolution*. They recommend that teachers clearly define the separate meanings of that word and distinguish those meanings that enjoy strong evidential and scientific support from those that seem controversial or less conclusively established.

David Berlinski's "The Deniable Darwin" shows how, contrary to popular reports, qualified researchers do in fact have serious scientific objections to Darwin's theory. Berlinski uses probability theory to take exception to almost every major claim advanced for the explanatory power of Darwinian natural selection.

Turning specifically to the textbook issue, Jonathan Wells's essays, "Haeckel's Embryos and Evolution: Setting the Record Straight" and "Second Thoughts about Peppered Moths" (both published previously in science, or science education, journals), illustrate the pedagogically convenient errors tolerated in textbooks—in the case of Haeckel, for over a hundred years—by a science education regime that lacks motivation to correct its errors.

In "Where Do We Come From? A Humbling Look at the Biology of Life's Origin," Massimo Pigliucci summarizes the status and prospects of current origin-of-life research. He critiques many current texts for their overly sanguine discussion of chemical evolutionary theories of the origin of life. (Pigliucci is not a design theorist; his trenchant critique of ID is presented in Part IV.)

Finally, developing further the difficulties identified by Pigliucci and expanding on the Wells examples, Gordon C. Mills, Malcolm Lancaster, and Walter L. Bradley explore in "Origin of Life and Evolution in Biology Text Books: A Critique" how current developments in biochemistry and origin-of-life studies contradict many current textbook presentations of chemical evolutionary theory.

Part III

In Part III, "The Theory of Intelligent Design: A Scientific Alternative to Neo-Darwinian and/or Chemical Evolutionary Theories," design theorists seek to bring the comparative or controversy-centered model set forth in

Part I to a critical point of development. They defend the comparative explanatory power of their theory with evidence from biochemistry, molecular biology, developmental biology, genetics, and paleontology. Here, design theorists argue their theory provides a better explanation of familiar biological phenomena—such as the information stored in DNA and proteins, molecular homologies, the complex structure of molecular machines, and the pattern of appearance in the fossil record—than do competing neo-Darwinian or chemical evolutionary theories.

Stephen C. Meyer initiates this line of argument in "DNA and the Origin of Life: Information, Specification, and Explanation." He contends that intelligent design provides a better explanation than competing chemical evolutionary models for the origin of the information present in large biomacromolecules such as DNA, RNA, and proteins. Meyer shows that the term *information* as applied to DNA connotes not only improbability or complexity but also specificity of function. He then argues that neither chance nor necessity, nor the combination of the two, can explain the origin of information starting from purely physical-chemical antecedents. Instead, he argues that our knowledge of the causal powers of both natural entities and intelligent agency suggests intelligent design as the best explanation for the origin of the information necessary to build a cell in the first place.

In "Design in the Details: The Origin of Biomolecular Machines," the biochemist Michael J. Behe sets forth a central concept of the contemporary design argument, the notion of "irreducible complexity." Behe argues that the phenomena of his field include systems and mechanisms that display complex, interdependent, and coordinated functions. Such intricacy, Behe argues, defies the causal power of natural selection acting on random variation, the "no end in view" mechanism of neo-Darwinism. Yet he notes that irreducible complexity is a feature of systems that are known to be designed by intelligent agents. He thus concludes that intelligent design provides a better explanation for the presence of irreducible complexity in the molecular machines of the cell.

In "Homology in Biology: Problem for Naturalistic Science and Prospect for Intelligent Design," Paul Nelson and Jonathan Wells reexamine the phenomenon of homology, the structural identity of parts in distinct species such as the pentadactyl plan of the human hand, the wing of a bird, and the flipper of a seal, on which Darwin was willing to rest his entire argument. Nelson and Wells contend that natural selection explains some of the facts of homology but leaves important anomalies (including many so-called molecular sequence homologies) unexplained. They argue that intelligent design explains the origin of homology better than the mechanisms cited by advocates of neo-Darwinism.

Next, Stephen C. Meyer, Marcus Ross, Paul Nelson, and Paul Chien, in "The Cambrian Explosion: Biology's Big Bang," show that the pattern of fossil appearance in the Cambrian period contradicts the predictions or empirical expectations of neo-Darwinian (and punctuationalist) evolutionary theory. They argue that the fossil record displays several features—a hierarchical top-down pattern of appearance, the morphological isolation of disparate body plans, and a discontinuous increase in information content—that are strongly reminiscent of the pattern of evidence found in the history of human technology. Thus, they conclude that intelligent design provides a better, more causally adequate, explanation of the origin of the novel animal forms present in the Cambrian explosion. Meyer and his coauthors also note that (whatever its explanation) this dramatic event in the history of life is, with very few exceptions, not discussed in American basic biology texts.

With his colleagues having established an evidential basis for considering an inference to intelligent design, William A. Dembski provides a summary of his theory of design detection. In "Reinstating Design within Science," Dembski argues that advances in the information sciences have provided a theoretical basis for detecting the prior action of an intelligent agent. Starting from the commonsense observation that we make design inferences all the time, Dembski shows that we do so on the basis of clear criteria. He then shows how those criteria, complexity and specification, reliably indicate intelligent causation. He gives a rational reconstruction of a method by which rational agents decide between competing types of explanation, those based on chance, physical-chemical necessity, or intelligent design. Since he asserts we can detect design by reference to objective criteria, Dembski also argues for the scientific legitimacy of inferences to intelligent design.

Part IV

In Part IV, "Critical Responses," several prominent scientists and scholars critique either the substantive arguments for intelligent design or the case for exposing students to these arguments, or both. Though most responses are sharply critical, a few support more inclusive science education and a few support some of the substantive scientific claims of ID advocates.

Phillip Johnson, the one ID proponent included among the respondents, supports both.

In the first response, Celeste Michelle Condit offers a spirited critique of Meyer's argument to design based upon the presence of information in DNA. She also dismisses ID as unscientific and defends a Darwinism-only approach to science education (though perhaps one taught less dogmatically than at present). She bases her critique in part on her studies of public controversies over genetic engineering. She also offers advice on how religion might take itself more seriously by relinquishing any claim to be an empirical discourse and warns of the dangers of religion in the public sphere, particularly in the classroom.

David Depew critiques the basic idea of design in biology as framed by the design theorists, though he acknowledges, with the ID authors, that a robust debate about the mechanisms of evolution is currently under way within biology. Depew notes, however, that Darwinism is not Darwin's science alone but a family of theories often holding very different views of the mechanisms and tempo of evolutionary change. He thus faults the ID proponents in Part III, specifically Michael J. Behe, for failing to acknowledge the promise of other fully naturalistic proposals—in particular, self-organizational models—that he believes can explain the origin of biological information and complexity. The concluding section of his essay suggests a provisional openness toward a larger role for deliberation in the science classroom.

Bruce H. Weber critiques Behe's notion of "irreducible complexity" and challenges Behe's claim that no intermediate structures have been reported in the literature. On matters of educational policy, Weber has recently developed a university course in which the ID model and the Darwinian model are contrasted and critiqued.

Massimo Pigliucci then provides a pointed response to Dembski's argument for "specified complexity" and offers a clear account of the meanings of design in biology. He shows why he believes that inferences to intelligent agency rest on bad science and faulty logic. Pigliucci has long maintained that, since only Darwinism is science, only Darwinism should be taught in public schools.

Philosopher Michael Ruse, whose testimony was instrumental in Judge Overton's decision in the Arkansas creation–science case, defends himself against the charge of inconsistency leveled in my essay in Part I. He reiterates the soundness of the fundamental tenets of neo-Darwinism and of his view that "professional Darwinism" is science and ID is not.

Eugene Garver urges that only Darwin's theory should be taught in the public schools and taught "dogmatically and intelligently." Garver critiques the central contentions of the "teach the controversy" model, including the notion that any important connection exists between the teaching of science and the democratic practices of the larger society.

Though William Provine disagrees with the substance of the case for ID, he does favor a more inclusive approach to teaching the controversy. He thus disagrees with the educational proposals of both Eugene Garver and Alvin Plantinga (see below). Provine argues that living organisms only appear designed. He reaffirms that this appearance can be fully explained by neo-Darwinian theory. Unlike many prominent neo-Darwinians, however, Provine encourages teachers to tell their students about scientific criticism of neo-Darwinism as well as the arguments for intelligent design. Having repeatedly invited Phillip Johnson for debates before his classes at Cornell, Provine is critical of science educators who refuse to debate the merits of Darwinism in the classroom.

In sharp contrast to Garver, who favors teaching only Darwinism, and Provine, who favors teaching both Darwinism and design, Alvin Plantinga challenges the propriety of teaching Darwinism at all. Plantinga argues that, in a pluralistic culture, elementary fairness and justice require that public schools cannot teach as true what its citizens hold—as part of their basic beliefs—to be false.

John Lyne reflects on the Darwinian debate from his experience in graduate and undergraduate teaching in the humanities and calls attention to how theories of the nature of things, no matter how scientific, always carry implicit worldview commitments.

Steve Fuller, while expressing caution on all metaphysical positions, sees no greater danger in ID than in Darwinism. On educational and cultural levels, he sees a positive role for ID, lending his support to the ID critique of Darwinism and to its effort to bring about a productive alliance between science and democratic culture.

Brig Klyce and Chandra Wickramasinghe (Wickramasinghe was a witness for the defense in the Arkansas creation-science case in the early 1980s) illustrate the pluralism of the design perspective in that, while they reject the idea of a designer, they also reject neo-Darwinist theory and fully accept the ID critique of conventional Darwinian science. They also support the "teach the controversy" model. Following the earlier lead of Sir Fred Hoyle, Klyce and Wickramasinghe make a positive case for space-borne spores as the basis for the development and differentiation of life on Earth.

In a concluding essay, ID godfather Phillip Johnson engages Stanley Fish's critique of liberalism. He suggests that open discussion of the theory of intelligent design would advance pluralism and liberal political ideals in general.

By design, we chose respondents who would provide mainly negative assessment and critique of ID. The only exceptions are Phillip Johnson, who helped launch the ID movement; Alvin Plantinga, who has long questioned the rationality of Darwinism on philosophic grounds; and Steve Fuller, whose positive response seems more directed to the democratic implications of the ID view of science and society than to the philosophic or scientific merits of its argument.[14]

Appendixes

The appendixes present (A) the transcript of a briefing held before the United States Commission on Civil Rights Schools and Religion Project on 21 August 1998, in Seattle; (B) a short essay by Donald Kennedy, former president of Stanford University; and (C, D, and E) technical evidence supporting the case made by Meyer, Ross, Nelson, and Chien in "The Cambrian Explosion: Biology's Big Bang."

The briefing (appendix A) consisted of a panel on curriculum entitled "Curriculum Controversies in Biology." The two panelists were Stephen C. Meyer, a senior fellow of the Discovery Institute, and Eugenie Scott, who for many years has headed the National Center for Science Education. The testimony of Meyer and Scott, and their responses to the extensive questions posed by the commissioners, particularly on the issue of possible viewpoint discrimination in the current science curriculum, provides a clear contrast between the philosophic assumptions and educational practices advocated by the two principal sides in this dispute.

Donald Kennedy's essay (appendix B) summarizes the rationale for the "Darwin only" position presented in the National Academy of Science's booklet *Teaching About Evolution and The Nature of Science*, which was written by a group of research scientists and high school teachers headed by Kennedy.

Appendixes C, D, and E provide information and analysis supporting the paleontological arguments made by Meyer, Ross, Nelson, and Chien in their essay, "The Cambrian Explosion: Biology's Big Bang."

An Objection to the Organization of This Volume

Clearly, even with a preponderance of negative responses, this volume gives greater voice to the arguments of the ID advocates and to those advocating discussion of ID in the public school curriculum. To some, this may seem unbalanced and even gratuitous. And indeed, from one perspective, the best plan for this volume might have been to assign equal space to each side. The problem with that approach, as Darwin himself was quick to realize, is that novelty requires time and repetition to sink in.[15] Darwin's uphill battle to distinguish his own position in the public mind and in the understanding of his peers from that of his predecessors is our warrant for giving greater space (in Parts I–III), but far from an unchallenged right of way (Part IV), to ID, the less familiar side in the current debate. Darwin, as in the case of contemporary defenders of ID, was not introducing a new idea for the first time but was attempting to establish his own explanation of the old and long discredited idea of "evolution." Darwin's challenge was to get his colleagues and the public to see how his proposed mechanism ("natural selection") put the whole argument for evolution on a very different footing from the arguments advanced by his grandfather, Erasmus Darwin, Jean Chevalier Lamarck, Robert Chambers, and Herbert Spencer.

Like Darwin's theory, as perceived by his peers and by the public in 1859, the contemporary argument for design is also a restatement of an old position. A key challenge for ID advocates is to distinguish their position, grounded in the information sciences and the method of "inferring to the best explanation," from its predecessors. Even as reviewers of the *Origin* identified it with earlier and discredited theories, so one will find in this volume respondents whose evaluation of intelligent design echoes the language of Darwin's initial reviewers.[16] The critical reaction here of the majority of respondents underscores the propriety of the organizational plan of this volume, providing balance to the dispute in a manner that is contextual and qualitative, not merely quantitative. Since Darwinism long ago replaced design as the established paradigm in science, readers of this volume are presumed to have learned Darwin's argument in school, as did their fathers and mothers, grandparents, and even great-grandparents.[17] For most readers, these pages will provide a first encounter with an alternative to the established paradigm by qualified authors who believe that Darwinism is false and wish to see it replaced. Our procedure of presenting the theory of intelligent design in detail and in the words of its defenders, even at the expense of not providing equal space for objections from the established theory, is one that Darwin's contemporary, John Stuart Mill, in that other classic of 1859, *On Liberty,* recognized as just and equitable when evaluating an idea that has been marginalized and generally rejected.[18] It is a tribute to the quality of the respondents whose critiques appear in Part IV that, necessarily brief as are their comments, they omit no objection to ID whether considered as science, as philosophy, or as a program for educational reform.

Two Additional Matters

Two additional considerations, the claim of ID to be science and the timing of this volume—why revisit this dispute?—deserve comment.

Is Intelligent Design Science?

However one weighs the claim that design theory is not, and cannot be, science—a decisive claim for some—that claim should be considered both in light of the design arguments advanced in Part III and in light of the historical character of the philosophy of science. Pronounced as is the parallel between Darwinism and design, at least in audience reaction and burden of proof, the parallel is nowhere more pronounced and symmetrical than on the charge that ID is not science. Various initial readers of Darwin's theory rejected it as science and regarded his book as an example of theorizing unrestrained by evidence.[19] John Herschel, an intellectual mentor whom Darwin highly respected, crushingly rejected the idea of natural selection.[20] Louis Agassiz characterized Darwin's theory "as a scientific mistake, untrue in its facts, unscientific in its method and mischievous in its tendency."[21] In his subsequent editions and particularly in his private letters, Darwin took pains to convince his readers that what he was offering was substantive science and not wish fulfillment.[22]

Darwin's hostile or skeptical readers were, in a way, correct. What Darwin was presenting was not just an argument for evolution by natural selection but a revolution in scientific method.[23] In 1859, few would have questioned whether design arguments were scientific; then, inferences to design in books on "natural philosophy" were commonplace and unremarkable. The book from which Darwin learned scientific method and logic, Herschel's *Preliminary Discourse,* legitimated the design inference as one of the highest motives for studying science.[24] By his careful attention to it in the *Origin,* Darwin certainly treated design as a potentially warranted scientific inference.[25]

A present reader, however, may conclude that ID is not and cannot be science because it draws an inference to an unobservable, nonmaterial cause. Yet that reader has no greater certainty (to be consistently comparative about it) than the most ardent ID advocate that such a conclusion will be acceptable to scientists or philosophers of science in a hundred years— or for that matter, in twenty-five years, ten years, or next week. If the *Origin* provides any basis for surmise, it is within the bounds of historical possibility that a perspective that would at first glance strike today's best scientific and philosophic minds as the height of the ridiculous may eventually be accepted.

Not that novel arguments in science or in life are necessarily good, any more than traditional or familiar ones are necessarily bad. Ernst Mach clearly held scientific views that Max Planck judged as reactionary, and it was these same "reactionary" views that nurtured Einstein's imagination and helped him formulate his epochal and notably counterintuitive theory of relativity (or to give it its proper name, the theory of invariance).[26] Views of science judged, for whatever reasons, as unacceptable to the scientific regime of a particular country or time have repeatedly shown themselves to be capable, under the right circumstances or in the right minds, of generating science as good as, or better than, the "legitimate science" of many an established paradigm.[27] As Darwin might have said, the rejection of novelty by a science establishment with a deep cultural and metaphysical investment in an alternative point of view seems to be part of some more general rhetorical law.

In any case, as Thomas Kuhn pointed out, debate about the methodological rules of science often forms part of the practice of science, especially during times when established paradigms are being challenged.[28] Those who reject the "teach the controversy" model on the grounds that ID violates the current rules of scientific practice only beg the question. The present regime of methodological rules cannot prevent controversy for the simple reason that those rules may themselves be one of the subjects of scientific controversy. Why not let students know about these debates as well? In the current context, that means letting students know that some scientists and philosophers (see, for example, Stephen C. Meyer's conclusion in his essay "DNA and the Origin of Life") challenge the convention of methodological naturalism and its prohibition on explaining phenomenon by reference to intelligent causes.

I have already mentioned the important role of computers and concepts from the information sciences in creating a climate of opinion that has fostered a reemergence of design language in science.[29] Clearly, the theoretical imagination of our time is neither that of Darwin's nor that of the neo-Darwinian synthesis of the 1940s. But why, even given that fact, is it productive to revisit what, at least in outline, must seem to be a very familiar debate? The issue needs reconsideration because science education, like science itself, must be constantly subject to revision in light of the demands of new generations of students and of new scientific knowledge. Indeed, advances in molecular biology, paleontology, and the information sciences have placed traditional questions of design on a new footing.

The Changing Roster of Disputants

An additional reason for revisiting the dispute is that the disputants have changed. The ID movement, comprising as it does academics, scientists, philosophers, humanist educators, and interested laypeople, is certainly not the same, except for purposes of histrionic exaggeration, as the young-earth, six-literal-days "creation science" of the past. Who is the designer? Who knows? ID advocates, unlike creation-science advocates, sign no confession of faith, nor could they gain agreement among themselves on one credo, were anyone foolish enough to suggest it. In the ambience of ID's "broad tent" and amid lively disagreements on just about every fundamental issue except the need to critique Darwinism and to affirm the detectability of design in nature, one will find persons of many philosophic perspectives and metaphysical commitments.

Given the fundamental changes that have overtaken the parties to this dispute, the dispute itself must be reconsidered.

The changes now reframing this historic debate are both intellectual and social. The appearance of Thomas Kuhn's 1962 treatise, *The Structure of Scientific Revolutions,* sparked an intellectual revolution, which he himself called "a paradigm shift," in both the philosophy of science and the social understanding of science.[30] Contrary to the positivist climate that characterized science at the opening of the twentieth century—which *Sputnik* revitalized and carried to the U.S. public schools well into its latter decades—in the early twenty-first century science is now acknowledged to be a highly interpretive enterprise.

The current interpretive understanding of science has developed through roughly three broad stages. In the heroic age of modern science, the seventeenth century, Bacon argued that theories emerged inductively from data.[31] We see remnants of this view of science even in Darwin's

Origin, where he spoke of how he began his species research "by patiently accumulating and reflecting on all sorts of facts which could possibly have any bearing on it." During all that time of fact collecting, he refrained chastely from any theorizing. "After five years' work I allowed myself to speculate on the subject."[32]

In the era of positivism, from the mid-nineteenth century through the mid-twentieth, theorizing was recognized as having a far more central role in science than Bacon gave it, but theory evaluation was still thought to be unproblematically data-determined.[33] Huxley, for example, kept trying to think of crucial experiments that would prove Darwin's theory up or down.[34] Darwin politely discouraged him, arguing that Huxley did not grasp that his argument was comparative.[35]

In the neo-positivist era, roughly from the 1940s until Kuhn, theory evaluation and explanation were thought to be pretty much what Huxley took them to be: formulaic. Karl Popper taught that one could test a scientific theory by making predictions and then determining by observation whether the predictions confirmed or falsified one's theory.[36] Similarly, Carl Hempel argued that successful explanation occurred when one could deduce an event or phenomenon from a set of specified initial conditions and laws.[37] Both of these models, for all their partial truths and separate and collective strengths, portrayed testing theories and formulating explanations as something that could take place without considering the merits of competing theories and explanations. More recent developments in the philosophy of science, from Imre Lakatos's "Falsification and the Methodology of Scientific Research Programs" to Peter Lipton's *Inference to the Best Explanation,* have stressed the comparative and competitive nature of theory evaluation.[38]

A key development in understanding theory evaluation since Hempel and Popper has thus been the realization that science rests on argument, that much of the substance of science hinges on which theory among a group of competitors can provide the best interpretation of a set of data.[39] It is in this sense—the sense of the comparative value of explanation and argument within the complex interrogation of nature we call science—that contemporary scientific theory has added its discriminating color to the terms *scientific reason* or *scientific method* or just plain *science.* Because theory evaluation is now understood to be a comparative process, the argumentative back-and-forth recognized under the ancient disciplines of dialectic and rhetoric has now been elevated within science to a dignity it has not enjoyed since the overturn of Aristotelian science in the seventeenth century.[40] Though some have contended that recognition of the role of informal argument amid the rigors of science makes science "mere rhetoric," it does nothing of the kind.[41] Rhetoric itself included logic, nor is there anything "mere" about knowing enough to participate meaningfully in a scientific discussion or, as a citizen bystander, knowing enough to know what the argument is about.[42]

The implications of these developments in the philosophy of science for the education of tomorrow's scientists are anything but academic or abstract. For a modern scientist, early education in comparative argument, and persuasive communication forms a core of foundational skills indispensable for future achievement—irrespective of the content of tomorrow's theories. A contemporary scientist must know not only how to put a hypothesis forward but how to put it across.[43] A scientist gets grants.[44] Having gotten them and done the experiments, the researcher must interpret the results, show what has been discovered, draw out its implications, and show why funding for more experiments, or experiments of a new kind, is now necessary. In addition, the scientist must defend his or her work against possible counterfindings of other independent peers working in the same field, sharing the same love of truth and competing for the same research dollars, promotions, prizes, and recognition. In today's world, nature never speaks but with a human voice and never more authoritatively than after argumentation between research rivals leaves no refuge but consensus—if sometimes grudgingly and if only for now.[45]

Training in argument, essential for the education of tomorrow's scientists, is no less important for tomorrow's citizens. One has only to think of the stressful necessity that modern medicine routinely places on laypeople to challenge expert advice and seek a second or third opinion to realize that lay skepticism of natural science is a practical reality in our world—and on balance a good thing.[46] What better place than the biology class to understand the appropriateness of skeptical questions directed toward scientific authority and to learn how, from asking such questions in medical contexts, lives have been saved, and in research contexts, new discoveries made?

Nor is the thesis persuasive that critique must be postponed until the student achieves mastery.[47] Jerome Groopman tells the story of how he and his wife, though both doctors and reluctant to challenge the opinion of fellow professionals, twice did so and thereby saved the life of their son. He also cites the story of a couple that, with no formal medical education at all, made a similar challenge with similar results.[48] The presentation of science and the critique of scientific reasoning, including the possibilities for error in fact, inferences, or theories, need to be taught simultaneously. Science, over and over again having proven itself indispensable to society, by that very feat has underscored the need for critical thinking about science to be integrated into the fabric of scientific education.[49]

The Merits of Comparison, Criticism, and Competition

By showing that scientific reasoning is not one but many and does not stand alone but on a continuum with the reasoning of common life, the critical comparative model makes science education more rigorous and socially responsive than the Darwin-only model and at the same time addresses legitimate concerns of an increasingly informed, skeptical, and impatient public. The debate over educational vouchers continues. The home-schooling movement originated by religiously conservative parents has grown and diversified to include nonreligious parents fed up with the inability of schools to teach values or even to teach, placing increasing pressure on public education.[50] Whether public education can sufficiently reform itself to win the confidence of the people whom it is supposed to serve is an open question—and the debate about biological origins, while far from the whole, is an important part of it. The science that generated the debate over evolution has changed. So has the society that continues the debate. There is hope for a fresh beginning. What for Hannah Arendt was the political equivalent of grace is, just possibly, not in vain.[51]

In the late 1950s, at the height of positivism in science and under the urgency of national defense, the idea that a value-neutral science—even if it touched on questions of ultimate beginnings, endings, and the narrative that governed meanings—could be taught unproblematically seemed reasonable to many thoughtful people.[52] Those who dissented were regarded as a fringe minority whose opinions had already been assigned to history's dustbin and whose opposition would abate with the spread of education and indoor plumbing. In the years since *Leave It to Beaver* and "Duck and Cover," those who dissent from Darwin's master narrative, or variants thereof, have grown in number and self-confidence. Many turn out to be remarkably well educated and not particularly rural. A more important fact is that at the dawn of the twenty-first century the United States is clearly and robustly a pluralistic culture, becoming more diversified and energetic in its pluralism all the time.[53]

Many complain, "But teaching evolution is not an issue in Europe, or even in Canada; the issue is peculiar to the United States." And perhaps it is. But the implication that we are invited to draw from this statement, that as Europe now is, so America is destined to become, or that Americans should be ashamed of themselves for not regarding the teaching of evolution as do Europeans, is as an argument as patronizing and uninformed as it is self-defeating. America has always been different from Europe both in its cultural pluralism and in the seriousness of its religious engagement. Yet these differences have not prohibited America from participating in the scientific or technological leadership of the world.

That Americans, with their diverse cultural backgrounds and worldviews (whether religious or secular), should disagree about an issue as fundamental as biological origins—that they should disagree for scientific, philosophical, or religious reasons (or even a mixture of all of these)—should neither surprise nor shame us. Nor should such disagreement paralyze our educational system as it seeks to educate students about the theory of Darwinian evolution, the scientific evidence relevant to adjudicating it, and possible competing interpretations of such evidence. Americans have often found ways to accommodate the pluralism of perspective that is inherent to our democratic culture. With the recognition that science, no less than politics or religion, necessarily involves the assessment of competing perspectives and interpretations, the pluralism that we have often incorporated into other modes of American life may now find a welcome home in the sometimes ideologically charged environment of our public school science classrooms.

There are three, and only three, options before us: teach evolution as Eugene Garver suggests, "dogmatically and intelligently"; avoid teaching it at all, as Alvin Plantinga suggests; or teach it in the spirit of the humanities as the current reigning, though contestable, theory and thereby honor in science education the integrity of informed dissenting opinion that grounds our American tradition of unity in diversity within politics, religion, and culture.

Notes

1. Edward J. Larson, *Summer for the Gods: The Scopes Trial and America's Continuing Debate Over Science and Religion* (New York: Basic Books, 1997); Edward J. Larson, *Trial and Error: The American Controversy over Creation and Evolution* (Oxford: Oxford University Press, 1989).

2. Nancy Pearcey, "We're Not in Kansas Anymore," *Christianity Today* (22 May 2000): 42–50; Nancy Pearcey, "Intelligent Design," *Touchstone: A Journal of Mere Christianity* 12 (July/Aug. 1999): 25–28.

3. For a good account of the engagement of ID scholars with other scholars on these issues, see Jon Buell and Virginia Hearn, eds., *Darwinism: Science or Philosophy? Proceedings of "Darwinism: Scientific Inference or Philosophical Preference"* (Richardson, Tex.: Foundation for Thought and Ethics, 1994). Also, an excellent conference entitled "Naturalism, Theism and the Scientific Enterprise: An Interdisciplinary Conference," held at the University of Texas, Austin (20–23 Feb. 1997), sponsored by the Philosophy Department of the University of Texas and organized by Robert Koons, brought together over a hundred scholars from the natural sciences, humanities, theology, philosophy, and law. Principal speakers were Michael Ruse, Darwin scholar and philosopher of science, University of Guelph; Alvin Plantinga, University of Notre Dame, critic of philosophic naturalism; Frederick Grinnell, University of Texas Southwestern Medical Center, philosopher of science; and Phillip Johnson, University of California School of Law, leader of the ID movement. Proceedings of the conference may be accessed at http://www.dla.utexas.edu/depts/philosophy/faculty/koons/ntse/ntse.html.

4. David J. Depew and Bruce H. Weber, *Darwinism Evolving: Systems Dynamics and the Genealogy of Natural Selection* (Cambridge: MIT Press, 1997), chap. 2, esp. pages 36–42; J. P. Moreland, *Christianity and the Nature of Science* (Grand Rapids, Mich.: Baker Books, 1994), 214–15.

5. M. A. Corey, *God and the New Cosmology: The Anthropic Design Argument* (Lanham, Md.: Rowan and Littlefield, 1993); John D. Barrow and Frank J. Tipler, *The Anthropic Cosmological Principle* (Oxford: Oxford University Press, 1986); Jeremy Campbell, *Grammatical Man: Information, Entropy, Language and Life* (New York: Simon and Schuster, 1982).

6. On the relation of Darwin's thesis to the neo-Darwinian synthesis, see Peter J. Bowler, *Evolution: The History of an Idea* (Berkeley: University of California Press, 1984), 296–300; Leah Ceccarelli, "A Rhetoric of Interdisciplinary Scientific Discourse: Textual Criticism of Dobzhansky's Genetics and the Origins of Species," *Social Epistemology* 9: 91–112.

7. Phillip E. Johnson, *Darwin on Trial* (Downers Grove, Ill.: InterVarsity Press, 1997); Phillip E. Johnson, *Reason in the Balance: The Case Against Naturalism in Science, Law, and Education* (Downers Grove, Ill.: InterVarsity Press, 1995); Phillip E. Johnson, *Defeating Darwinism by Opening*

Minds (Downers Grove, Ill.: InterVarsity Press, 1997); Phillip E. Johnson, *Objections Sustained: Subversive Essays on Evolution, Law, and Culture* (Downers Grove, Ill.: InterVarsity, 1998); Michael Behe, *Darwin's Black Box: The Biochemical Challenge to Evolution* (New York: Free Press, 1996); William A. Dembski, *The Design Inference: Eliminating Chance through Small Probabilities* (Cambridge: Cambridge University Press, 1998); William A. Dembski and James M. Kushiner, eds., *Signs of Intelligence* (Grand Rapids, Mich.: Brazos Press, 2000); Jonathan Wells, *Icons of Evolution* (Washington, D.C.: Regnery, 2000); Paul Nelson, *On Common Descent* (Chicago: University of Chicago Evolutionary Monograph Series, forthcoming 2004); Michael J. Behe, William A. Dembski, and Stephen C. Meyer, *Science and Evidence of Design* (San Francisco: Ignatius, 2000); William A. Dembski, ed., *Mere Creation: Science, Faith and Intelligent Design* (Downers Grove, Ill.: InterVarsity Press, 1998); William A. Dembski and Michael Ruse, *Debating Design: From Darwin to DNA* (Cambridge: Cambridge University Press, forthcoming); James Glanz, "Darwin vs. Design: Evolutionists' New Battle," *New York Times,* 8 Apr. 2001; Teresa Watanabe, "Enlisting Science to Find the Fingerprints of a Creator," *Los Angeles Times,* 25 Mar. 2001; Gregg Easterbrook, "The New Fundamentalism," *Wall Street Journal,* 8 Aug. 2000; George Sim Johnston, "Designed for Living," *Wall Street Journal,* 15 Oct. 1999; Elizabeth Nickson, "God's Two Books: Nature and Scripture," *National Post of Canada,* 5 May 2001.

8. The Zogby poll may be viewed at http://www.reviewevolution.org. Among the new books on ID is Robert Pennock, *Intelligent Design Creationism and Its Critics: Philosophical, Theological, and Scientific Perspectives* (Cambridge: MIT Press, 2001).

9. "Ohio Plan Would Teach Evolution Debate," *New York Times,* 15 Oct. 2002, A15.

10. "Special Issue on the Intelligent Design Argument," *Rhetoric and Public Affairs* 1 (winter 1998).

11. For an excellent exposition of the central features of the rhetoric of science, see Marcello Pera, *The Discourses of Science,* trans. Clarissa Botsford (Chicago: University of Chicago Press, 1994).

12. John Stuart Mill, *On Liberty* (Harmondsworth: Penguin Books, 1980). On good people making bad arguments, see pages 116–17; on an aspect of truth being found on the side that may not prevail, see pages 108–15. "It is always probable that dissentients have something worth

hearing to say for themselves, and that truth would lose something by their silence" (111).

13. That there is a problem with contemporary textbooks has been documented by a study commissioned by the American Association for the Advancement of Science (AAAS). "According to a new study, not one of 10 widely used high school biology textbooks is acceptable overall. . . . The textbooks are so bad, the study's authors say, that the best advice they can offer to schools faced with a decision about buying new biology books is: Don't." AAAS spokesperson George Nelson said, "They present the content in a disconnected way . . . [and they] camouflage the important ideas with details and trivia." In general, the books focus too much on details and pay scant attention to overall concepts unifying these details into an understandable picture. From "Biology Textbooks Miss Big Picture," *Boston Globe,* quoted in the *Commercial Appeal,* Memphis, Tenn., 28 June 2000. Clearly the kind of debate over evolution that ID would encourage, as set forth in the various essays in this volume, would not only address this problem on a conceptual level but would help to provide the broad cultural support necessary to bring about reform.

14. Alvin Plantinga, *Warrant and Proper Function* (Oxford: Oxford University Press), 216–38.

15. Francis Darwin, ed., *The Life and Letters of Charles Darwin,* vol. 2 (New York: D. Appleton, 1911). To Lyell, 6 June 1860: "I can only hope by reiterated explanations finally to make the matter clearer" (111).

16. Anonymous, "Darwin on the Origin of Species," *North American Review* 90 (Apr. 1860): 475.

17. Larson, *Trial and Error,* introduction and chap. 1.

18. Mill, *On Liberty.* "On any of the great open questions just enumerated, if either of the two opinions has a better claim than the other, not merely to be tolerated, but to be encouraged and countenanced, it is the one which happens at the particular time and place to be in a minority. That is the opinion which for the time being, represents the neglected interests, the side of human well-being which is in danger of obtaining less than its share" (111).

19. Adam Sedgwick, "Objections to Mr. Darwin's Theory of the Origin of Species," *Spectator* (24 Mar. 1860), reprinted in David Hull, *Darwin and His Critics* (Cambridge: Harvard University Press, 1973), 155–70; Samuel Haughton, "Biogenesis," *Natural History Review* 7 (1869): 23–32, reprinted in Hull, *Darwin,* 217–27.

20. Darwin, *Life and Letters,* vol. 2. To Lyell, 12 Dec. 1859: "[Natural selection] 'is the law of higgeldy-piggeldy.' What this exactly means I do not know, but it is evidently very contemptuous. If true this is a great blow and discouragement" (37).

21. Louis Agassiz, "Prof. Agassiz on the Origin of Species," *American Journal of Science* 30 (July 1860): 154. Agassiz also observed, "I must protest now and forever against the bigotry spreading in some quarters, which would press upon science doctrines not immediately flowing from scientific premises and check its free progress" (from Agassiz's *Essay on Classification* [1859], 71–72, cited in Hull, *Darwin,* 446).

22. Changes in the various editions of the *Origin* are numerous. See Morse Peckham, ed., *The Origin of Species by Charles Darwin: A Variorum Text* (Philadelphia: University of Pennsylvania Press, 1959). See especially chapter 7, which Darwin added chiefly to rebut the objections of St. George Jackson Mivart, and chapter 15, the final chapter. Among the many friends and later readers to whom Darwin patiently explained his doctrine were Joseph Hooker, Charles Lyell, and Thomas Henry Huxley. See John Angus Campbell, "The Invisible Rhetorician: Charles Darwin's 'Third Party' Strategy," *Rhetorica* 7 (winter 1989): 55–85, esp. note 24. On the extreme doubts about the explanatory adequacy of natural selection, see Lyell's letter to Huxley, 17 June 1859, in Frederick Burkhardt and Sydney Smith, eds., *The Correspondence of Charles Darwin,* vol. 7 (Cambridge: Cambridge University Press, 1985), 305–7.

23. Michael T. Ghiselin, *The Triumph of the Darwinian Method* (Berkeley: University of California Press, 1969).

24. John F. W. Herschel, *A Preliminary Discourse on the Study of Natural Philosophy* (Chicago: University of Chicago Press, 1987). "The testimony of natural reason . . . places the existence and principal attributes of a Deity on such grounds as to render doubt absurd and atheism ridiculous" (7).

25. See especially chapters 6–8 in Charles Darwin, *On the Origin of Species* (Cambridge: Harvard University Press, [1859] 1964). Darwin's attention in these chapters to objections and to the appearance of design, particularly in organs of special complexity (see pages 186–94), shows in particular the seriousness with which he took design as a rival scientific hypothesis.

26. Steve Fuller, *Thomas Kuhn: A Philosophical History of Our Times* (Chicago: University of Chicago Press, 2000). "Mach highlighted fundamental objections to Newtonian mechanics that remained just as potent as when

they were first made nearly two centuries earlier, but had been suppressed from the professional training of physicists. The most famous of these objections pertained to the existence of absolute space and time, the ether, atoms, and even mass itself. Indeed Einstein credited Mach with keeping them alive long enough so as to suggest the need for what became relativity theory" (123).

27. One thinks of the rejection of the earth-centered view in the ancient world and of evolution itself, as well as of the contemporary ambiguous relation of alternative medicine or folk medicine to established medicine. Further, there is the ambiguous relationship of Goethe's science to established science and of the solid contributions of "idealist" or "essentialist" science, which in the hands of Linnaeus immeasurably advanced botany or in those of Cuvier helped establish the reality of past extinctions. Mill put the principle well: "Even in natural philosophy, there is always some other explanation possible of the same facts; some geocentric theory instead of heliocentric, some phlogiston instead of oxygen" (*On Liberty,* 98). For a good discussion of the scientific contributions of schools of thought operating from very different metaphysical premises, see Timothy Lenoir, *The Strategy of Life: Teleology and Mechanics in 19th-Century German Biology* (Chicago: University of Chicago Press, 1989). A suggestive recent example comes from the inventor of the DNA sequencer, Leroy Hood. Hood recently resigned his prestigious post at the University of Washington and delivered a stinging indictment that the blinkered department-centered specializations of universities make them unfit for contemporary biological research. In founding a new Institute for Systems Biology, he proposes to bring together biologists, computer scientists, engineers, physicists, and mathematicians. His research aim is to break with academic biology, take a systems approach, and by using computers look at the structure and behavior of cells or organisms and simulate their behavior as Boeing aircraft does an airplane. His research agenda seems markedly suggestive of what an ID program of scientific research might look like. Andrew Pollack, "Scientist At Work: Leroy Hood; A Biotech Superstar Looks at the Bigger Picture," *New York Times,* 17 Apr. 2001.

28. Thomas S. Kuhn, *The Structure of Scientific Revolutions,* 2nd ed. (Chicago: University of Chicago Press, 1970), 92–110.

29. Freeman Dyson, *Infinite in All Directions* (New York: Harper and Row, 1988). Dyson notes the reemergence of design in contemporary science and says a good word on behalf of the symmetry between the

anthropic principle in cosmology and design in biology: "The argument from design still has some merit as a philosophic principle. I propose we allow the argument from design the same status as the Anthropic Principle, excluded from science but tolerated in metascience" (297).

30. Kuhn, *Structure of Scientific Revolutions;* see also Fuller, *Thomas Kuhn.*

31. Michel Malherbe, "Bacon's Method of Science," in *The Cambridge Companion to Bacon,* ed. Markku Peltonen (Cambridge: Cambridge University Press, 1996), 75–98.

32. Darwin, *Origin,* 1.

33. I use the term *positivism* in a broad sense to include the founding of the positivist program of thought by August Comte (1798–1857), especially his influential view that society progresses through theological, metaphysical, and positive stages of existence. I also include under the label "positivist" the specific school of twentieth-century positivists, the Logical Empiricists.

34. For Huxley's approach to science and how it differed from Darwin's, see Mario A. Digregorio, *T. H. Huxley's Place in Natural Science* (New Haven, Conn.: Yale University Press, 1984), 34–50.

35. Burkhardt and Smith, *Correspondence,* vol. 7 (letter of 2 June 1859), 301.

36. Karl R. Popper, *Logic of Scientific Discovery* (New York: Harper Torchbooks, 1965), 265–81.

37. Carl G. Hempel, *Aspects of Scientific Explanation* (New York: Harper and Row, 1965).

38. I. Lakatos and A. Musgrave, eds., *Criticism and the Growth of Knowledge: Proceedings of the Colloquium in the Philosophy of Science, London 1965* (Cambridge: Cambridge University Press, 1970), 91–195; Peter Lipton, *Inference to the Best Explanation* (New York: Routledge, 1991).

39. For a model of science based on argument, grounded in the analogy between scientific and legal argument, see Stephen Toulmin, *Human Understanding: The Collective Use and Evolution of Concepts* (Princeton, N.J.: Princeton University Press, 1972), 239–41.

40. Marcello Pera and William R. Shea, *Persuading Science: The Art of Scientific Rhetoric* (Canton, Mass.: Science History Publications, 1991), 29–37.

41. For an authoritative explication and defense of the legitimate role of rhetoric/dialectic in science, see Pera, *Discourses;* see also Lawrence J. Prelli, *A Rhetoric of Science: Inventing Scientific Discourse* (Columbia: University of South Carolina Press, 1989); Alan G. Gross, *The Rhetoric of Science* (Cambridge: Harvard University Press, 1996); Charles Taylor,

Defining Science: A Rhetoric of Demarcation (Madison: University of Wisconsin Press, 1996); Jeanne Fahnestock, *Rhetorical Figures in Science* (Oxford: Oxford University Press, 1999).

42. Eugene Garver, *Aristotle's Rhetoric: An Art of Character* (Chicago: University of Chicago Press, 1994); see also Pera, *Discourses,* esp. chaps. 2 and 3.

43. Thomas F. Gieryn, *Cultural Boundaries of Science: Credibility on the Line* (Chicago: University of Chicago Press, 1999), 23–34; Margaret C. Jacob, ed., *The Politics of Western Science: 1640–1990* (Atlantic Highlands, N.J.: Humanities Press, 1990), 1–18, 81–102.

44. Leslie Stevenson and Henry Byerly, *The Many Faces of Science* (Boulder, Col.: Westview Press, 2000), 133–41.

45. Pera, *Discourses,* 31–36.

46. Jerome Groopman, *Second Opinions: Stories of Intuition and Choice in the Changing World of Medicine* (New York: Viking, 2000), 9–37.

47. John Dewey opposed teaching science in a manner that reduced it to mere memorization and recitation, stripped of its critical component. See John Dewey, "The Relation of Science and Philosophy as a Basis of Education," in *John Dewey on Education: Selected Writings,* ed. R. D. Archambault (Chicago: University of Chicago Press, 1964), 19; Jürgen Habermas speaks tellingly to this point when he observes, "Uncritical mastery of existing disciplines offers no hope that learners will suddenly undergo a change in attitude, becoming skeptical and analytical about ideas, or they will suddenly be able to criticize after having hidden this virtue away for so long" (in Robert E. Young, ed., *Critical Theory of Education: Habermas and Our Children's Future* [New York: Columbia University Teachers College Press, 1990], 33). See also Martin Eger, "A Tale of Two Controversies: Dissonance in the Theory and Practice of Rationality," *Zygon* 23 (1988): 291–325.

48. Groopman, *Second Opinions,* chap. 1.

49. Stevenson and Byerly, *The Many Faces of Science,* 226–30.

50. Dissatisfaction with public schools, of course, takes many forms, including a desire for greater intimacy or bonding with one's children and concerns for safety, as well as dissatisfaction with prevailing public education. See Peter T. Kilborn, "Learning at Home, Students Take the Lead," *New York Times,* 24 May 2000. See also Linda Tagliaferro, "More Families Opt for Home Schooling," *New York Times,* 5 Dec. 1999.

51. Hannah Arendt, *The Human Condition* (New York: Doubleday Anchor Books, 1959), 212–23.

52. For an excellent discussion, see the introductory and concluding chapters of Larson, *Trial and Error*.

53. Elmore Leonard, "With or Without Prayer: One More Hail Mary Story," *New York Times Magazine*, 27 May 2000, 84–85. In the same number, see Jennifer Egan, "Where Meditation Is Going," 86–88. See also Edward Larson and Larry Witham, "The More They Learn the Less They Believe," *Nature* 394 (June 1998): 313.

❈ Part I

*Should Darwinism Be Presented Critically
and Comparatively in the Public Schools?
Philosophical, Educational, and Legal Issues*

Intelligent Design, Darwinism, and the Philosophy of Public Education

John Angus Campbell

❉ ❉ ❉

Intelligent design (ID) is hardly a new idea from the standpoint of either science or philosophy. Long before William Jennings Bryan, Billy Sunday, or the Christian Coalition were on the scene, before the canon of Scripture was closed—or parts of it even opened—the issues now raised by advocates of intelligent design were being debated by foundational figures of Western thought.[1] Whether Western science would look to Heraclitus and Democritus or to Plato and Aristotle for its philosophy of science has been one of the longest running issues in our tradition.[2] From the ancient world to Aquinas; from the middle ages to Paley; from Paley to Cuvier, Lamarck, and Darwin; to our own century and to such figures as Teilhard de Chardin, Stephen Hawking, and the latest speculations on "the anthropic principle" in cosmology, the idea that nature manifests the kind of order one associates with mind rather than with material self-sufficiency has found advocates as well as detractors among scientists and philosophers of science.[3]

Darwin had his first encounter with a philosophy making strong claims for the material self-sufficiency of nature when, as a medical student at Edinburgh, he pursued extracurricular studies under anatomist-zoologist Robert Grant. Grant was the first scientist Darwin had met who praised the genius of Lamarck, whose evolutionary views were analogous to those Darwin knew from the works of his grandfather, poet-philosopher Erasmus Darwin.[4] Grant's refusal to give Darwin credit for his independent discovery that the so-called ova of a bryozoan *Flustra* species were in fact the eggs of another species turned Darwin away in disgust from Grant's evolutionism and (already alienated from medicine) from professional science in general.[5]

As a divinity student at Cambridge, Darwin gained an in-depth exposure to the opposite view of nature, one that made strong claims for the role of an intelligent designer. In a more congenial and leisurely atmosphere, where Darwin was among young men of his own class, he developed a close friendship with the Reverend John Stephens Henslow, professor of botany. Under Henslow's direction, Darwin participated in Henslow's non-credit science courses and weekly informal science discussions at Henslow's home and read William Paley's *Evidences of Christianity* and *Natural Theology*. Quick to take a hint from his new mentor, whom he admired both as a man and as a teacher, Darwin read John Herschel's *Preliminary Discourse*, a major work in the philosophy of science, which presented design—indeed, the being of a designer—not only as a legitimate inference from science but as a motive to its study.[6] Darwin also read Wilhelm von Humboldt's *Personal Narrative*, which, along with Henslow's own unfulfilled travel lust, fired Darwin with a desire to travel as a naturalist and eventually led to his appointment as naturalist aboard the *Beagle*.[7] Although Darwin's study of design was done in the context of his preparation for the Anglican priesthood, his education was truly liberal.

Darwin learned the standard arguments for design through dialectical engagement with their opposite. Rehearsing its reader through the proofs of design, Paley's *Natural Theology*—in the spirit and with the easy charm of a Michael Behe—urged the reader to think seriously of the claims for self-organization and of the evidentiary difficulties in addressing them.[8] Paley's *Evidences of Christianity* taught Darwin about Hume's case against miracles. Darwin learned from Paley how to chip away at large objections through accumulating small probabilities on the other side, a procedure Darwin would later use to great effect in his evolutionary works.[9] In fact, the only part of the academic instruction Darwin received at Cambridge that he claimed was permanently valuable to him was his study of Paley's design arguments. The design model gave Darwin a valuable set of questions with which to approach the study of the natural world and a motive, both scientific and religious, for pursuing them. Of this model, Darwin observed in his *Autobiography:* "The logic of this book [Paley's *Evidences*], and as I may add of *Natural Theology* gave me as much delight as did Euclid. The careful study of these works, without attempting to learn any part by rote, was the only part of the Academical Course which as I then felt and as I still believe, was of the least use to me in the education of my mind. I did not at that time trouble myself about Paley's premises; and taking these on trust I was charmed and convinced by the long line of argumentation."[10]

Herschel's *Preliminary Discourse* similarly inspired Darwin; Herschel, he said, "filled me with a burning zeal to add something to the noble structure of natural science." It might also be added that Herschel gave him his sense of scientific method as a performing art—a delicate amalgam of induction, deduction, hypotheses, and practical experience—that informed everything he wrote as a scientist.[11] Although Darwin's epochal *Origin* challenged the design hypothesis as formulated by Paley and endorsed by Herschel (Darwin was disappointed when Herschel called natural selection "the law of higgledy piggledy"), the design model structures the rhetoric of Darwin's *Origin* at every turn and continues to provide the grammar of well–known Darwin defenders from Stephen Jay Gould to Richard Dawkins and Daniel Dennett.[12]

If the design hypothesis was central in motivating Darwin to the study of science, it was no less important in shaping the development of his evolutionary ideas, which began possibly as early as the last leg of the *Beagle* voyage and were certainly in place by the early months of 1837 following his return in October 1836.[13] No one can read Darwin's transmutation notebooks without being impressed with how he tested his nascent evolutionism against the counterview of ID.[14] Throughout his notebooks, Darwin worked to make his ideas seem an extension of the accepted scientific and religious premise that the organic sphere is part of a system of divinely designed laws. The theistic premise of received science is present in the very first entry of his first transmutation notebook. There, taking his title *Zoonomia* from his grandfather's encyclopedic medical work, Darwin also took his grandfather's distinction between asexual and sexual reproduction and his grandfather's deistic belief in a creator. He used both to argue that sexual reproduction, because it engenders variation, is the divinely ordained law by which biological structures are adapted to a world of change.[15] Though Darwin's notebooks are filled with miscellaneous snippets of information and telegraphic sentences and fragments, whole sections show clearly how he argued to make his various theories clear and persuasive to an anticipated audience who saw, as he did (but in a more radical way), the whole of nature as a system of designed laws. In Darwin's notebooks as well as in the full development of his argument in his *Sketch* of 1842 and his *Essay* of 1844, one finds ample evidence of the same premise.[16]

Nowhere is the public and scientific character of the design argument, and its centrality to Darwin's thinking, more clearly manifest than in the structure of his own mature argument. The tone and context of that argument are set in the opening pages of his 1859 book. The flyleaf of the first edition of the *Origin* boasted two dedicatory citations from works of natural theology, one from Cambridge polymath and historian-philosopher of science William Whewell, that events in the natural world are "brought about not by insulated interpositions of Divine power . . . but by the establishment of general laws."[17] The other citation was from Bacon's famous *Advancement of Learning*, urging that no one can be too well read "in the book of God's word, or in the book of God's works."

In the second edition of the *Origin*, Darwin added a third citation, this one from Bishop Butler's classic warhorse against skepticism, the *Analogy of Revealed Religion*. Butler reversed the commonsense progression from "natural" to "supernatural" and argued that the "natural" depends upon and illustrates the supernatural, which is ontologically prior. With implicit approval, Darwin cited Butler's claim that "what is natural as much requires and presupposes an intelligent agent to render it so, i.e., to effect it continually or at stated times, as what is supernatural or miraculous does to effect it for once." In the sixth, final, and least expensive edition of the *Origin*, Darwin added an "advertisement" after his table of contents: "An admirable, and, to a certain extent, favourable Review of this work, including an able discussion on the Theological bearing of the belief in the descent of species, has now been separately published by Professor Asa Gray as a pamphlet. . . . It is entitled 'Natural Selection not inconsistent with Natural Theology.'"[18]

In each chapter of the *Origin*, Darwin employs the concept of intelligent design as a foil in order to make the case for the modification of species by means of natural (rather than intelligent) selection. Chapter 1, "Variation Under Domestication," never mentions God or creation but instead invites the reader to recall what he or she knows already about how domestic plants and animals are intelligently designed by skillful breeders. Citing a famous breeder (Youatt), Darwin secularized a quasi-supernatural image when he presented selection as "the magician's wand, by means of which he [the breeder] may summon into life whatever form and mould he pleases." By the end of the chapter, a reader begins to see how breeders working on nature recapitulate a process conceivably like nature's own and, as Darwin showed in the case of domestication in primitive societies, may not even require conscious art.[19]

Chapter 2, "Variation Under Nature," raises the question of design directly. In the fifth sentence of his first paragraph, Darwin affirmed that, difficult as the concept of a "species" might be to define, "[g]enerally the term includes the unknown element of a distinct act of creation." Later in the chapter, Darwin deconstructed the design argument through what today we would call a study in the sociology of scientific knowledge. Having pointed out how no two experts agreed on where a variety left off and a species began—and this on long-studied common European forms—he proceeded to show how the fixed features on which the design inference then depended were in fact an artifact of the social production of knowledge. Taking the case of "a young naturalist" first learning his trade, Darwin showed that the whole business of this person, his whole status in the scientific fraternity, depended on his coming up with distinct features by which to separate one species from another. Small variations—so central to Darwin's explanation of species change—naturally and on principle, Darwin argued, tended to be overlooked in this schema because they were a nuisance. Noting that greater numbers of varieties are produced by the larger genera, Darwin nicely substituted for the "magic wand" metaphor of chapter 1 the up-to-date image of a factory, referring to the larger genera as "the manufactory of species."[20] Change in animate forms is not just something that happened in the past. It is ongoing in the activity of breeders working with variation and continues in nature to turn out new forms, as we can infer from the fact that the largest families produce the most numerous varieties and subspecies.

In chapter 2, Darwin begins his epistemological critique of the design-based thinking of his time. He contrasted the naturalistic economy of his assumption that a species "is a more or less permanent variety," and a variety "an incipient species," with the apparent extravagance assumption of the fixity of species: "On the other hand, if we look at each species as a special act of creation, there is no apparent reason why more varieties should occur in a group having many species, than in one having few."[21]

In chapter 3, "Struggle for Existence," Darwin's evocation of design is again direct and explicit. The chapter begins by using the very language of reverent enthusiasm characteristic of Paley and the tradition of natural theology:

> How have all those exquisite adaptations of one part of the organisation to another part, and to the conditions of life, and of one distinct organic being to another being, been perfected? We see these beautiful co-adaptations most plainly in the woodpecker and missletoe [*sic*]; and only a little less plainly in the humblest parasite which clings to the hairs of a quadruped or feathers of a bird; in the structure of the beetle which dives through the water; in the plumed seed which is wafted by the gentlest breeze; in short, we see beautiful adaptations everywhere and in every part of the organic world.[22]

In the body of the chapter, Darwin brilliantly introduced the Malthusian logic of differential reproduction, operating on random variation under changing conditions and over lengths of time, to turn what had been the rhetorical questions of the received design-based perspective into the dialectical questions of his evolutionary science. At the end of the chapter, Darwin invited the reader to use this new knowledge to provide a theoretically sophisticated answer to the reverent questions with which the chapter began. What could one do, Darwin asked, to extend the range of a plant just a little farther beyond its present farthest limit? One would have to give it some variation that would enable it better to survive in its conditions of life. Although Darwin reminded the reader that we do not know exactly what the needed variations would be, the lesson of the chapter is not humility at our ignorance, as Darwin insisted, but a dawning awareness of the potential power of a new mode of explanation.[23]

In chapter 4, "Natural Selection," Darwin turned the design argument against itself as a way of making the case for natural selection—and for philosophic naturalism. In an eloquent and lengthy paragraph that begins, "As man can produce and certainly has produced a great result by his methodical and unconscious means of selection, what may not nature effect?" Darwin invested nature analogically with the attributes of the breeder. In a long series of contrasts that read something like an altar call in which an evangelist magnifies the power of God and the littleness of humans—"Man can act only on external characters: nature cares nothing for appearances, except in so far as they may be useful to any being"—Darwin drove home the point that he had been preparing in his stair-step opening chapters. The reader's new knowledge, the knowledge of Malthusian laws plus variation, inheritance, and time, is undergirded, summarized, and communicated through the metaphoric vehicle of an intelligent designer (the breeder); this is made evident in the gorgeous personification completing the sequence of Darwin's contrasts between nature and humans: "It may be said that natural selection is daily and hourly scrutinising, throughout the world, every variation, even the slightest; rejecting that which is bad, preserving and adding up all that is good; silently and insensibly working, whenever and wherever opportunity offers, at the improvement of each organic being in relation to its organic and inorganic conditions of life."[24]

Not least of the points of interest in this passage is its suggestion that the process he has in mind, for all its randomness, may have been divinely guided. Darwin's codiscoverer of natural selection, A. R. Wallace, interpreted the passage this way and for that reason begged Darwin to drop it.[25] Darwin's American defender Asa Gray took this passage as his hint and "baptized" the *Origin* by building an entire theological defense around it.[26]

Striking as is this personification, it must be said immediately that Darwin did not depend merely on "metaphor" to convey his central concept. Although it is territory that only the most intrepid readers will frequent, in the middle of chapter 4 (which Darwin noted in a letter to his publisher was "the key-stone of my arch") Darwin presented a detailed hypothetical taxonomic tree illustrating how the key principle of "divergence from character" followed from the process of variation, inheritance, and natural selection.[27] Neither the tree nor Darwin's exposition is overtly figurative. Yet it is when Darwin was being least metaphoric that his contrast with ID is most potent and interesting.

What is most revolutionary about Darwin's *Origin* is not simply his case for natural selection as the explanatory mechanism of evolution or his case for evolution itself. The other, and equally important, revolution going on within his argument for species change is his case for naturalism, which slides insensibly between an innocent methodological precept and a prior metaphysical commitment. If one masters the argument centered on Darwin's taxonomic tree in chapter 4, one gains a piercingly clear vision of organic development unfolding without plan but according to natural law, while at the same time one gains more than enough scientific material for a complete materialist worldview.[28]

The first step in Darwin's case for metaphysical naturalism—the belief that reality coincides with what is accessible to the methods of the natural sciences—was taken in his flyleaf citations, all of which identified the ordinary mode of divine activity with natural laws. Implicitly and in chapter 2

explicitly, Darwin was laying the foundations for a revolutionary philosophy of science. Though space here prevents a thorough exposition, when
Darwin was having a difficult time with an explanation or when he was
particularly keen on the reader's realizing the consequences of a refusal to
accept an explanation, he would sometimes draw on the reader's partial
commitment to naturalism to negotiate yet further commitments. At some
points Darwin would simply equate naturalistic explanations—evolutionary case histories with the blanks filled in by an "it must have been" story
line—with reality itself.[29]

A good example of the terminus of that process where methodological
naturalism teeters on the edge of metaphysical naturalism—and theism
seems ready to dissolve into materialism—appears toward the end of chapter 5, "Laws of Variation." Darwin noted the presence of stripes on colts
and said of those who refuse to recognize in these stripes the descent of the
modern horse from an ancestor common to the hemionus, quagga, and
zebra that they "reject a real for an unreal, or at least for an unknown,
cause. It [their rejection of genetic descent] makes the works of God a
mere mockery and deception."[30]

On the one hand, this passage gestures toward a materialism in which
being, as opposed to active superintendence of nature, let alone intervention in it, is the only activity left for "God." On the other hand, the passage
suggests that Darwin sought to reinterpret, not abolish, traditional religious
language. At the least, the passage is an example of sections, found
throughout the *Origin,* that cry out for interpretation and hint at what we
can only call Darwin's theology of nature.[31] Does the passage mean that
Darwin thought it appropriate to refer to God in a scientific work and to biological structures as "works of God"? Or is all of this a manner of speaking
or rhetorical strategy aimed at putting God-talk on a course toward ultimate extinction? These are open interpretive questions arising from the
language of the text.[32]

Chapters 6–8 in the *Origin,* "Difficulties on Theory," "Instinct," and "Hy-
bridism," form a unit focused on addressing objections. Pertinent for our
concern with reemerging arguments for design today is Darwin's welcom-
ing of readers' objections and his attempt to find resources, not only from
nature but also from a reader's own perceptual resources, to overcome
these objections. Though Darwin never formally taught school, an opening
line in chapter 6 acknowledges the legitimacy of different perspectives—
one of the defining marks of a master teacher as traditionally understood
in the context of a liberal education: "Long before having arrived at this

part of my work, a crowd of difficulties will have occurred to the reader. Some of them are so grave that to this day I can never reflect on them without being staggered." There is also, in the remainder of the line, the mark of a master dialectician/rhetorician: "but, to the best of my judgment, the greater number are only apparent, and those that are real are not, I think, fatal to my theory."[33]

In these three chapters, Darwin was not arguing simply for the competence of variation and natural selection to account for particular structures and to answer particular difficulties; he was at the same time leading readers to accept his philosophic premise of unlimited naturalism.[34] Much of the logic of these chapters develops lines of argument already in place by chapter 4, indeed implicit already in chapter 1. Whether dealing with structures of extreme perfection such as the eye or seemingly imperfect or trivial structures such as the tail of the giraffe, Darwin's approach was to pose an objection and then present a real or hypothetical sequence of intermediate stages capable of making a step-by-step evolutionary explanation plausible. As Darwin explained in these four chapters, the combination of imperfection of the geological record and extinction of transitional grades in the intense competition shaping the process of divergence of character traits would make transitional structures scarce; an important lesson a reader would learn was to get along without evidence.

Put positively, a reader learned to make inferences based on what Darwin argued were parallel cases. Darwin pointed out, for example, that the flying lemur, or *Galeopithecus,* is unique; it had once been classed falsely among the bats but now stood alone in its class. To show how it may have been formed from its nonflying relatives, Darwin took the example of squirrels, where we do have a series of gradations from those that merely jump well to those that jump farther and to those that glide; that sequence illuminated all the graduated modifications in allied structures necessary to his argument.[35] After Darwin's argument, a reader understands how the lemur could have been formed, having been shown that variations in analogous or the same organs do occur in another mammal.

Central to the intellectual excitement of these chapters is the way Darwin seemed constantly to put his theory at risk and then rescue it. On the extreme perfection of the eye, Darwin began, "To suppose that the eye . . . could have been formed by natural selection, seems, I freely confess, absurd in the highest possible degree." Then he continued, "Yet reason tells me. . . ." A reader is given not a particular lineage leading to the eye of the eagle, the focus of the argument, but a narrative explaining how organs of sight in nature range from nerves sensitive to light all the way through more complex structures, right up to the eye of the eagle. What is so instructive about Darwin as teacher in these arguments is the way he stated his theory as something at risk, not as a necessary or initially "natural" way of seeing nature, and then tried to reason, cajole, and sometimes almost pray the reader over to his side. Again and again in the structuring of Darwin's argument, a reader sees the role of theory, inference, and constructive contrast with the design hypothesis: "Let this process go on for millions and millions of years; and during each year on millions and millions of individuals of many kinds; and may we not believe that a living optical instrument might thus be formed as superior to one of glass, as the works of the Creator are to those of man?"[36]

Space limitations require us to discuss only briefly chapters 9–12, two on the imperfection of the geological record and two on geographical distribution. Here Darwin wrestled with arguments against his theory where the evidence in his favor was admittedly thinnest. Like the preceding suite of chapters, 9–12 are of enormous instructive value in enabling a reader to grasp (or gasp at) the meaning of *inference* and the warranting of inference in science. The final sentence of chapter 9, truly a Darwinian signature line, serves to illustrate how much of his argument pertained to the conventions that were to govern interpretation of the evidence: "On this view, the difficulties above discussed are greatly diminished, or even disappear."[37]

Chapter 13, "Mutual Affinities of Organic Beings: Morphology: Embryology: Rudimentary Organs," concludes Darwin's presentation of his case. By this point, a conscientious reader has mentally rehearsed the argument presented in the first four chapters many times in a variety of distinct yet related contexts, from the barnyard to the fragmentary recesses of the fossil record. In the first part of the chapter, the naturalistic theme first introduced in chapter 2, about the natural meaning of classification, is enforced with emphasis. The resemblance of organic beings "is evidently not arbitrary like the grouping of the stars in constellations."[38] What the grouping of organisms illustrates, Darwin claimed, is genetic descent. Even if a reader rejects Darwin's argument, at this point in the book, she or he can scarcely help feeling its force. Moving on, although he did not use Theodosius Dobzhansky's words, Darwin clearly emphasized Dobzhansky's key point: nothing in morphology, embryology, or rudimentary organs makes sense without the premise of genetic descent, that is, evolution.

Chapter 14, "Recapitulation and Conclusion," is the peroration to what, as Darwin justly affirmed, had been "one long argument."[39] The central change in the status of the design argument is well captured late in the chapter in one of the most famous of Darwin's images. Having rehearsed basic objections to his theory and his responses to them, Darwin set forth his vision, encompassing several sciences, of what difference the perspective he had offered would make to the study of natural history. Any reader interested in illustrations of "paradigm shift" can scarcely do better than to read Darwin's account of questions for research opened up by his theory and the alleged dead ends of research on any other assumption. What interests us now, however, is the way Darwin used an example of design to challenge the conventional meaning of design:

> When we no longer look at an organic being as a savage looks at a ship, as at something wholly beyond his comprehension; when we regard every production of nature as one which has had a history; when we contemplate every complex structure and instinct as the summing up of many contrivances, each useful to the possessor, nearly in the same way as when we look at any great mechanical invention as the summing up of the labour, the experience, the reason, and even the blunders of numerous workmen; when we thus view each organic being, how far more interesting, I speak from experience, will the study of natural history become![40]

In this passage, the advocate of intelligent design becomes a "savage" in the sense that Darwin used the term in his account of the *Beagle* voyage to describe the people of Tierra del Fuego. For Darwin, the Tierra del Fuegans were technically human animals, unwashed, without arts or clothes, and able intellectually to do little more than knock a limpet against a rock.[41] Though, of course, a ship is a product of intelligent design, from the view of the "savage" in Darwin's interpretation, the ship seems to be a miraculous creation, and the unenlightened "people" who gape at it are too degraded in mind even to recognize the artful process of its construction as manifest in occasional imperfections of its design or execution.

Darwin's message through this image seems to be that his account, via the analogy with the art of domestic breeding, has set a new standard for civilized scientific understanding appropriate to a technological age. The design hypothesis is now not just outdated but is a form of intellectual barbarism. Such is the invective under which design advocates have had to labor since Darwin's time.

Exactly how far Darwin wished to press the naturalist theme, with which the *Origin* is laced, is a legitimate and lively subject of disagreement. Certainly Darwin gave his readers a great deal of theological window dressing. In the first edition, the famous and eloquent final line read, "There is grandeur in this view of life with its several powers, having been breathed into a few forms or into one; and that, whilst this planet has gone cycling on according to the fixed law of gravity, from so simple a beginning endless forms most beautiful and most wonderful have been and are being evolved."[42] By the second edition, "breathed" had become "breathed by the Creator."[43] In a letter to his friend Hooker, Darwin confessed to having "truckled to public opinion [when he] used the Pentateuchal term of creation."[44] As for his advertisement for Asa Gray's pamphlet, Darwin emphatically but privately rejected its argument that variations had been providentially guided along certain lines, and—although he promoted the pamphlet—he ridiculed those who believed it.[45] But Darwin used Gray knowingly and, depending on one's view, with either metaphysical magnanimity or cynicism to bring others around to an evolutionary worldview that affirmed the sufficiency of a fully natural process as the explanation for those features of life that had previously required explanation by reference to the activity of a designing intelligence.

In fact, it was at Darwin's urging, with his money and under his direction, that Gray's initially anonymous essays in the *Atlantic Monthly* were gathered into a pamphlet and distributed free of charge to leading scientific and religious figures and to various magazines.[46] Though he plainly said in his *Autobiography* that he held Christianity to be a "damnable doctrine" and repudiated the argument to design ("We can no longer argue that . . . the beautiful hinge of a bivalve shell must have been made by an intelligent being, like the hinge of a door by man"), he may have continued to believe in at least a version of the design argument. Indeed, at times he suggested that the laws of nature that produce evolutionary change might themselves have been designed.[47]

Thus, he acknowledged "the extreme difficulty or rather impossibility of conceiving this immense and wonderful universe, including man . . . as the result of blind chance or necessity." Like all Darwinian statements that seemed to favor ID or to reconcile evolution with it, that argument was inherently unstable and subject to a gradual slide into an all-pervasive naturalism: "This conclusion was strong in my mind . . . when I wrote the *Origin* . . . and . . . since that time . . . it has very gradually . . . become weaker." Developing the "weaker" theme, Darwin went on to ask how much confidence we ought to place in the reasoning of a mind that has "been developed from a mind as low as that possessed by the lowest animal . . . when it draws such grand conclusions?" Darwin seemed genuinely unaware of the irony of his point applied to his own thought, which suggests his adherence to a metaphysical naturalism grown dogmatic. Or perhaps not. One paragraph after proclaiming his theism, Darwin concluded, "The mystery of the beginning of all things is insoluble by us; and I for one must be content to remain an Agnostic."[48]

It is tempting to conclude that, in the end, Darwin's naturalism was immune from the annoying doubt to which only his theism was subject. Donald Flemming seems to have gotten it right when he observed, "The grin of a theodicic Cheshire Cat hangs over the last line of the *Origin*. But that is all, the cat has fled."[49] Nevertheless, one of the liveliest debates in contemporary Darwin scholarship revolves around how much we should see Darwin as remaining in the orbit of some form of traditional theism and how much we should see him as the author of what Daniel Dennett has called a "universal acid" of naturalist skepticism concerning traditional values, beliefs, and norms.[50]

Whether Darwin continued to believe in some kind of a deity and whether Darwinism can be reconciled with a meaningful form of theism remain topics of intense scholarly debate. Nevertheless, one thing seems clear: Darwin formulated his thesis of undirected evolution against the backdrop of science-based design arguments and he understood and defended his own theory as an alternative to these design arguments as promulgated by leading thinkers such as Paley, Herschel, Cuvier and others. He offered natural selection as an alternative explanation for, among other things, the exquisite adaptation of organisms to their environments and for "organs of extreme perfection"—features of living things previously thought to point unequivocally to the activity of a designing intelligence. As Stephen C. Meyer puts it in two later essays, Darwin understood natural selections as a kind of "designer substitute."

ID and the Mission of Science Education in a Democratic Society

It follows from our previous discussion that in order to understand Darwin's argument, to say nothing of the contemporary controversy that it continues to generate, students need to understand Darwinism's dialectical opposite: the intelligent design hypothesis. Further, with so many conflicting interpretations of key scientific and philosophical issues (both longstanding and now emerging), one would think that teaching about the argument of the *Origin*, and its opposites, would be a biology teacher's delight. How better to show the contested character of science, its periodic "paradigm shifts," its conventions of argument, its use and interpretation of evidence, its connection to culture, its polemics, and its relationship to values and larger questions of meaning and purpose than through examining Darwin's text—or through presenting its tensions through age-appropriate secondary readings and discussions? What better plan could there be for giving students the opportunity to "earn their evolutionism" (as Darwin gave his readers the opportunity to earn theirs) than by having them compare the objections posed to Darwin's arguments in his time—as set forth in his text or in updated examples from contemporary science—with similar objections now being set forth by the advocates of ID?

Or so one might naively assume.

Rather than seeing an educational opportunity of the first order in the questions raised by contemporary critics of Darwinism and ID advocates, leaders of the scientific establishment have portrayed all dissent as yet another head of the hydra of "fundamentalism." A good example of this reaction can be seen in a recent essay by Donald Kennedy. Kennedy, president emeritus of Stanford and professor of environmental science, is one of the authors of a pamphlet on teaching evolution published by the National Academy Press. His essay in the *Chronicle of Higher Education* focuses attention on a need for evolution to be taught more widely than it currently is: "it is disheartening that in many parts of the United States, high-school science classes do not teach about evolution at all, or discuss it only briefly."[51] Kennedy raises a number of excellent points.

First, citing Dobzhansky's famous maxim that nothing in biology makes sense except in the light of evolution, Kennedy points out that "evolution is as basic to the rest of biology as atomic structure is to physics." Although design scholars challenge Dobzhansky's maxim, they do not dispute that a thorough knowledge of evolution and of neo-Darwinism is central to understanding the discourse of contemporary biology. Various versions of ID and various versions of evolutionary naturalism have shared a complex yin/yang relationship for the 2,500 years of Western intellectual history. Facets of both are vibrantly in play in Darwin's seminal text.[52] In insisting that a knowledge of evolution is necessary if high school students are to achieve scientific literacy, Kennedy is on the mark.

Second, Kennedy and his colleagues at the National Academy of Sciences (NAS) have set a worthy example in the time and attention they have devoted to improving the quality of high school teaching. Their effort to disseminate knowledge of evolution underscores a need for closer cooperation between university scholars and teachers on the front line of education, all of whom face exceptional challenges in teaching controversial material in whatever field.

Third, Kennedy not only notes that "evolution is not an easy topic to teach well" but perceptively identifies two reasons, intrinsic to the subject, why that is so. One difficulty is "that the theory of evolution depends largely on inference," and another is that the term *theory* has different meanings in popular and learned discourse. In popular discourse, as Kennedy notes, *theory* often means "little more than an idea"; in science, however, "a theory is an explanation supported by a variety of observations and tests." As pointed out in the previous section, a host of productively contested issues about "theory" and "inference" are robustly at play in Darwin's text.

Finally, Kennedy notes the importance for science educators to approach the religious convictions of students with sensitivity. Referring to what he has learned from his own encounters with educators who disbelieve in evolution on religious grounds and noting particularly a debate he had with two such teachers on *The News Hour with Jim Lehrer,* Kennedy observes, "Perhaps the most useful lesson of these and other discussions is how important it is for scientists to treat religious conviction with respect." Despite the excellence of these points, Kennedy's essay is on balance disquieting.

First, consider Kennedy's philosophy of education. The NAS booklet was necessary, Kennedy affirms, because "in the United States, religious opposition to teaching evolution is deeply rooted and growing stronger." Rather than consider, in a dialectical spirit, how those disaffected with evolution might be engaged, Kennedy reacts defensively. The aim of the NAS pamphlet is "[t]o help teachers confront the objections of fundamentalist Christians." Here Kennedy's essay raises a serious question of educational philosophy. Is it the business of teachers as representatives of the state to "confront" the worldviews of students with an eye to straightening them out, however mistaken, from the standpoint of the majority, those worldviews may be?

How does one apply that principle? And where does one place a limit on it? Should not biology teachers also "confront" Christian Science students with the truth of the germ-theory of disease or Jehovah's Witness students with the true facts about blood transfusion? And what of the creation accounts of Native Americans, belief in which is sometimes connected with negative attitudes toward anthropologists?[53] Why only certain beliefs? Why not belief in astrology? Or faith healing? And how many other scientifically "false" beliefs are common to the culture? Perhaps there should be an official government list—and science teachers should be charged to confront them also. Given Kennedy's educational principle, education by confrontation, what prevents such a list from being drawn up?

However appropriate confrontation may be for maintaining discipline in the classroom—as, for example, when a student is disruptive or when the teacher has evidence of cheating—confrontation hardly seems an appropriate spirit for presenting subject material that, for all its scientific content, also centers on the great traditional human questions of origin, destiny, and purpose. Such questions, by their very character, are controversial in the classroom because they are controversial in the larger culture.

Kennedy's language also seems to place an ideological condition on teaching evolution. Are only biology teachers who subscribe to some authoritative version of evolution qualified to teach it? Or is it possible that evolution could be well taught even by teachers who have questions about it, the way Adam Smith might be well taught by a socialist or Marx by a free-enterpriser or Milton by an atheist? Second, Kennedy's tendency to label individuals with reservations about the received neo-Darwinian theory as opponents of teaching evolution (or even science) is clearly inaccurate. Kennedy comments favorably on his encounter with one of the other discussants on the *News Hour*. "One creationist was a very thoughtful young teacher from a Christian high school, who professed admiration for the NAS booklet and said that he had no problem with crediting small biological changes to evolution, but that he thought evolutionists hadn't given satisfactory accounts of big biological changes." How do "thoughtful[ness]," "admiration for the booklet," possibly even use of it to explicate the received view in his classes constitute opposition to teaching evolution? From Kennedy's description, it sounds as though this teacher was simply unconvinced; he did not believe that the processes explaining microevolution were adequate to account for macroevolution. As long as his students understood what the processes of variation, inheritance, and natural selection were and why they were accepted by the larger scientific community as an explanation for the development of unlimited biological novelty, what of it? Having learned reflection from their reflective teacher, some of this teacher's students may go on, as did Darwin in a similar milieu, to discover that they think differently, while others may, on further reflection, decide that their teacher was right to begin with. Here Kennedy appears less concerned with the effective teaching of evolution than with getting teachers who might read the NAS booklet, and especially students, to subscribe to the received theory. Clearly scientific literacy in a modern democratic society requires that students *understand* the theory of evolution. But does it also require that students believe the theory? Is a pedagogical policy designed to produce intellectual assent, even belief, consistent with our liberal traditions?

Third, Kennedy incorrectly equates all attempts to challenge the theory, or to modify the way it is taught—central aims of the ID movement—with a sectarian religious agenda. Kennedy is quick to point to *Edwards v. Aguillard,* in which the court held that an Arkansas state law requiring that evolution be taught only in conjunction with creation science constituted "an impermissible endorsement of religion." Yet as David DeWolf and his colleagues make clear in a subsequent essay, there are clear legal, scientific, and methodological differences between the theory of intelligent design and creation-science. Further, the recent unanimous decision by the Ohio State Board of Education requiring students to learn about scientific criticism of evolutionary theory clearly illustrates that the public, and its leaders, increasingly understand the difference between using science to teach religion and allowing teachers to use critical questioning to teach science. Many leading and philosophically informed science educators (none of whom are associated with the ID movement) are now making very similar points.

For example, in a series of major essays, William Cobern has offered an unsparing critique of the philosophy of science that informs most science teaching.[54] Drawing on deep and well-established literature in the field of science education, Cobern describes most science teaching as based on "the myth of school science"—an amalgam of "classical realism, philosophical materialism, strict objectivity, and hypothetico-deductive method."[55] Along with various colleagues of his, he has begun to outline an alternative philosophy and curricular strategy. While a thorough discussion of Cobern's views is beyond the scope of this essay, we will mention a number of important points that he raises.

First, Cobern critiques the positivist dichotomy between knowledge and belief that characterizes most presentations of the nature of science in the school curriculum and emphasizes that all science requires presuppositions and assumptions. Cobern repeatedly stresses that these assumptions are pedagogic keys to making students partners in their own learning. In an essay coauthored with Cathleen C. Loving, "Defining 'Science' in a Multicultural World: Implications for Science Education," Cobern and Loving argue for the integrity of science as a way of knowing. They also argue for the importance of presenting it in the context of an epistemic pluralism that avoids—and indeed critiques—relativism. Cobern critiques the often heard justification for teaching Darwinism dogmatically—that the theory is not controversial among scientists—by emphasizing the overlooked, and highly relevant, educational point that it is very controversial among students and with the larger culture. Cobern stresses that the controversial character of evolutionary theory among students has implications for their *learning* of it as well as for the way it is taught.[56] Cobern points out that many students simply do not believe in evolution—and that they are not likely to learn much about it either unless they learn more about what a theory is, how a theory comes to gain credibility, and how science relates to other great questions of life. Cobern argues that if science educators want to make teaching evolution a futile exercise, the current approach (even when supplemented with more, and clearer, presentation of facts such as those manifest in Kennedy's otherwise welcome pamphlet) will do the job. Only frank, open, historically and critically informed dialogue between students and teachers about how scientific theories are constructed and how they relate to the rest of life—in short, science taught as a fully invested branch of a liberal, humanistic education—will facilitate the higher order learning required for students to understand evolution.

Cobern is not alone in his advocacy of the presentation of historically grounded understandings of opposite points of view to teach Darwin's theory. In an essay entitled "Learning about Evolution: A Special Case of Intentional Conceptual Change," Cobern's science education colleagues, Sherry Southerland and Gale Sinatra underscore the difficulty of teaching evolution when students perceive it to conflict with their prior beliefs.[57] Rather than "confront" students in the spirit of Kennedy's approach, Southerland and Sinatra challenge the reigning educational model and urge an approach that enlists the "intentional beliefs" of the students about the nature of scientific knowledge and their willingness to question ideas (both their own and those commonly received as scientific) in the process of learning about evolution. Their approach includes role-playing, dramatizing the controversy, and the use of controversial readings in natural history accompanied by small group discussions.

In a paper similarly exploring "Knowledge, Belief, and Understanding in Science Education," Colin Gauld recommends that "[i]n the case of issues which are expected to be controversial, understanding the alternative positions of various stakeholders can be a prelude to the students choosing between them." Thus, he suggests that "care should be taken to ensure students understand the various positions before encouraging them to make a choice based on what they think is reasonable evidence."[58] He, as well as Southerland and Sinatra, emphasize teaching students skills in argumentation and discussion, encouraging them to critique both the knowledge claims of science and of commonsense reasoning, and enabling them to understand competing perspectives.

That professional science educators, none of whom are associated with ID (and for all we know may be critical of it) would come to the same conclusions as ID advocates about how best to teach evolution is not surprising. The idea of teaching in *utramque partem* is arguably the oldest idea in our common educational tradition. Darwinism and design theory are clearly opposed philosophically and scientifically; however, considered from an educational standpoint each competing perspective is half of an ancient, unbreakable dialectical pair. The entangled roots of this pair run deep in our common tradition of education, science, theology and philosophy. Whatever the rising or waning fortunes of either hypothesis during one or another historical period, these two perspectives are sisters. They will likely continue their complex antagonistic relation into distant futurity—if for no other reason than that each requires knowledge of the other to define and explain itself.

Thus, contra Kennedy, the issue is not the intrusion of religion into scientific matters. The issue is the educational importance of acknowledging the scientific, philosophic, and theological questions raised by Darwinian evolution as matters for critical awareness, understanding, and individual judgment in the spirit of consumer protection. That evolutionary theories entail metaphysical commitments and make philosophic assumptions is a truth not in philosophic dispute. If scholars know this, why shouldn't the public be informed? And their children? The work of Cobern, Loving, Southerland, Sinatra, Gauld, and their colleagues suggests that science education, like science itself, may soon be self-correcting.

Indeed, biology education needs an overhaul such as this since the philosophical and worldview issues arising from the teaching of evolution are not likely to go away any time soon. There are several reasons for this.

First, and most important, these issues will not go away because, as pointed out earlier, they are part of Darwin's text and part of his continuing legacy. The structure of Darwin's argument, in every chapter of the *Origin* without exception, is given as a debate or dialogue with various kinds of "design" arguments—from outright immediate young-earth creation, which Darwin along with most of his audience rejected, to more sophisticated versions, at least one of which he may have recommended. Certainly it is not the business of pressure groups with special agendas to set the

science curriculum. By the same token, it is not the business of science educators to pronounce on metaphysical issues or pretend that they do not
exist or have been resolved by empirical research. When Kennedy comments, "Few scientists would object to creationist views expressed only
from the pulpit," he is less reassuring than perhaps he intended to be about
the neutrality of his colleagues toward such questions. Clearly he seems
less informed than he ought to be about the general theological content in
the *Origin*—and of the continuing philosophic disputes it engenders.

Second, if the opposition to evolution from popular religion sets the
United States apart from other countries where evolution is more widely
taught, the reason is closely connected with other historical differences
that make our culture unique. Though Thomas Jefferson was certainly no
orthodox Christian, when he sponsored the disestablishment of the Anglican Church in Virginia he inadvertently fertilized the ground that later
would nourish our long-standing dispute about evolution.[59] Left to survive
or perish according to their ability to garner support from the voluntary
gifts and free association of individuals, and unencumbered by association
with the state, democratically organized forms of religion became central to
the American national character.[60] Tocqueville noticed the depth of religious belief in America and its institutionally independent form; he
counted our religious faith as one of the great bulwarks of the celebrated
American experiment in democratic freedom and civic order.[61]

It is hardly remarkable that large, impersonal, state-sponsored science,
which has grown exponentially since World War II, should inherit something of the historic American distrust of centralized authority. That is particularly true when representatives of that authority use it to teach a grand
master-narrative encompassing everything that is, including humanity's
place in the scheme of things. And should we not distrust teaching young
students to cultivate passive unquestioning minds concerning the assumptions, methods, and conclusions of so-called scientific authority?[62] In a country where religion is taken seriously and rests on a popular and independent
foundation, science teaching of the totalistic kind that Kennedy seems to
have in mind stirs up the deep American suspicion of authority once re-
served for state-sponsored hierarchies, whether temporal or spiritual.

Finally, philosophical and theological issues will not go away because
suspicion that Darwinian evolution is ideologically rooted is justified. Darwinism's lack of ideological neutrality has been documented in meticulous,
up-to-date, and indisputable detail.[63] Kennedy is particularly sensitive to
this issue, as indicated by his response to another panelist on the *News Hour*

show. Unlike the discussant who approved of the NAS pamphlet while dissenting from it, another guest on the program, "a dean at a fundamentalist Christian university," was not at all impressed with the NAS booklet; he said that "evolutionists were 'brainwashing' their students while supported by tax dollars." Kennedy "found particularly telling his charge that many evolutionary biologists are atheists; the claim that scientists (and thus science) are inherently anti-religious is a perennial feature of the creationist case."

By coincidence, a few weeks prior to the appearance of Donald Kennedy's essay in the *Chronicle of Higher Education,* historian Edward Larson (winner of a Pulitzer Prize for his book *Summer for the Gods,* exposing the antisouthern "Inherit the Wind" myth surrounding the Scopes Trial) and coauthor Larry Witham reported on the second phase of their study duplicating a famous survey done in 1914 and again in 1933 by James Leuba on the religious beliefs of American scientists.[64] In 1914, Leuba found that "58 percent of 1,000 randomly selected U.S. scientists expressed disbelief or doubt in the existence of God, and that this figure rose to near 70 percent among the 400 'greater' scientists within his sample." When Leuba repeated his study in 1933, he found that "these percentages had increased to 67 percent and 85 percent, respectively." When Larson and Witham repeated Leuba's 1914 study in 1996, they found "little change from 1914 . . . 60.7 percent express[ed] disbelief or doubt." When Larson and Witham repeated the second phase of Leuba's 1914 survey among "greater scientists," they found the rate of belief "lower than ever—a mere 7 percent of respondents." Leuba, as Larson and Witham note, "attributed the higher level of disbelief and doubt among 'greater scientists' to their 'superior knowledge, understanding, and experience.'"

Of the first stage of the Larson and Witham study, Oxford University scientist Peter Atkins had remarked, "You clearly can be a scientist and have religious beliefs. But I don't think you can be a real scientist in the deepest sense of the word because they are such alien categories of knowledge." Atkins's comment helped motivate Larson and Witham to redo the second stage of Leuba's 1914 survey of "greater" scientists. They selected as their sample group the distinguished organization of which Kennedy is a member:

Our chosen group of "greater" scientists were members of the National Academy of Sciences (NAS). Our survey found near universal rejection of the transcendent by NAS natural scientists. Disbelief in God and immortality among NAS biological scientists was 65.2 percent and 69 percent respectively, and among NAS physical scientists, it was 79 percent and 76.3 percent.

Of particular significance to our present concerns was this finding: "Biological scientists had the lowest rate of belief (5.6 percent in God, 7.1 percent in immortality), with physicists and astronomers slightly higher (7.5 percent in God, 7.5 percent in immortality)."

Larson and Witham's concluding observation could not be more pertinent to Kennedy's claim of religious neutrality for evolution:

As we compiled our findings, the NAS issued a booklet encouraging the teaching of evolution in public schools, an ongoing source of friction between the scientific community and some conservative Christians in the United States. The booklet assures readers, "Whether God exists or not is a question about which science is neutral." NAS President Bruce Alberts said: "There are many outstanding members of this academy who are very religious people, people who believe in evolution, many of them biologists."

Our survey suggests otherwise.[65]

Active hostility toward conventional theism (or, for that matter, philosophic theism) is almost a hallmark among evolutionary biologists and their philosophic allies. Daniel Dennett, William Provine, Richard Dawkins, E. O. Wilson, Richard Lewontin, and Stephen Pinker, to name a few, may not be household words, but they are hardly obscure figures in their respective fields.[66] Only six months before Kennedy's editorial appeared, William Provine, professor of the history of biology at Cornell, gave the 1998 keynote address at the Darwin Day celebration at the University of Tennessee. In his address, Provine asserted that evolution had buried any gods worth having and that "evolution is the greatest engine of atheism ever invented."[67] If, as Kennedy says, it is part of the creationist case to imply that evolution is irreligious, we find here solid agreement between opposed camps.

Militant atheism is an overt and inescapable inference of the evolutionist case as set forth by many of evolution's most distinguished public defenders. Those who recommend temporizing positions are met, at best, by "mild amusement" from their peers.[68] To pretend that evolutionary science, as understood by the vast majority of its most accomplished advocates, is religiously neutral will advance neither the public understanding of science nor the public discussion of the values and assumptions that inevitably inform its teaching.[69]

Intelligent Design, American Pluralism, and Teaching the Controversy

Donald Kennedy's position on evolution—to respond to all dissent on the part of students with "confrontation," and to regard any attempt to question evolution as a form of opposition to authoritatively certified truths of science—is hardly unique to him. Kennedy mirrors a philosophy of education still widely practiced and often articulated by many official spokesmen for science. It stands in sharpest contrast not with American "fundamentalism" but with the philosophy of education common to academics in the humanities. The tension between these two approaches has been carefully documented in a study by Martin Eger on the contrast between assumptions governing the teaching of science and assumptions reigning in the humanities. Eger's little-known essay is titled "A Tale of Two Controversies: Dissonance in the Theory and Practice of Rationality."[70]

Eger documents how, following the precepts of Mill's *On Liberty,* contemporary educational theorists Clive Bell and Lawrence Kohlberg have urged the importance of critical questioning as the ground of reason.[71] According to that line of thought, it is not enough that a person have a correct moral belief if that belief, and the orientation that underpins it, abides in the individual's mind as a prejudice. The important point is for the individual to be able to defend his or her beliefs. In geometry, it is not enough for an individual to know the answer to a problem without knowing how to perform the proofs; in ethics, it is not enough to know what is right and wrong without being able to say why. Clearly this position, that students be able to defend their ethical commitments, is closely connected with a second position: that students be able to consider alternatives, even radical, immoral, or socially unacceptable alternatives to present ethical practices.

Why teaching along those lines would create friction with parents should be clear. Such classroom practice, supported by the disciplinary theory, places a wedge between the moral education offered by the home and the moral education offered by the school. The parental burden—to encourage the child to develop a moral point of view, subscribe to particular ethical precepts, and follow prescribed models of conduct—is undermined when the school urges students to question those precepts and consider alternatives to those models. It can hardly be a source of delight to educational theorists or classroom teachers that such practice has placed schools and families at odds for over a decade. As Eger documents, the reason why educators, backed by the power of the state and the courts, insist on an educational program guaranteed to be controversial and divisive is because fundamental issues are at stake.[72] Following Mill, it is a fundamental and settled conviction of educators that reason is a better alternative to decision-making than tradition or prejudice and that critical questioning and the consideration of alternatives are the defining characteristics of reason in ethical decision-making and values clarification.

Clearly, much in the pedagogical program could be improved. From the standpoint of ethical reason in the tradition of Aristotle and Edmund Burke, before one can reason about ethics one must first have a foundation of prior experience—or reason has nothing to work with. Burke's comment that through "just prejudice" an individual's virtue becomes part of that person's habit is as true now as it always was. To reason well on ethics one must have experience. But as Burke also remarked, when one reflects on traditional conduct, one will often discover its rationale and reaffirm the "just prejudice" along with the reason for its existence.[73] Many objections to ethics programs in public schools could be addressed by expanding what constitutes a good reason to include using "common sense" and respecting the advice of parents, spiritual leaders, experienced persons, and the testimony of traditional moral precepts. Defects of ethics programs, however serious, are, within age-appropriate limits, remediable, and their principle is worth defending. The pluses of an ethics education program are that it is based on argument; it offers training in seeing and discovering opposite points of view; and it encourages students to find and weigh evidence, to offer reasons, and to think for themselves.

In the teaching of science, particularly in biology, Eger finds a remarkably contrasting model. When it comes to science pedagogy, the advocates of contemporary neo-Darwinism sound like the parents complaining about the morally corrosive effects of the ethics curriculum. Philip Kitcher and Michael Ruse, two prominent defenders of orthodox Darwinism, urge that the very idea of exposing scientifically untrained minds to questions regarding a choice between evolution and "creationism" is a dereliction of educational duty. As Ruse puts it, "Teaching scientific creationism will stunt abilities in all areas. . . . Thus I say keep it out of the schools."[74]

What is of interest in these two cases is their agonistic symmetry. The mark of reason in one model is the criterion of unreason in the other. For educational ethicists, the giving of reasons for every belief differentiates reason from unreason. For educational theorists of science, the unquestioning mastery of a prior system is the precondition for proper understanding. In ethics, consideration of unorthodox or conventionally unacceptable alternatives (for instance, that dishonesty might be the best policy) is to be met without prejudice. In science, by contrast, even permitting the bare impression that there might be some arguments in favor of creationism—or in the present case, of ID—is a dereliction of educational responsibility.

Again, for ethical reasoning, training of the mind requires that students realize that something can be said in favor of almost any position. For science, any argument in favor of alternatives to current neo-Darwinian orthodoxy is false—in advance—and education consists in recognizing that fact, whether one knows the reason why or not.

Before the work of Thomas Kuhn focused attention on the logic of scientific revolutions, before the rise of the "rhetoric of science" movement, one might have claimed that the methods one follows in "science" and the methods one follows in ethics and the humanities are completely different. That position will no longer wash, and everyone conversant with contemporary work in the history and philosophy of science knows it.[75] Darwin himself pointed out that the kind of reasoning presented in the *Origin* is the reasoning of everyday life, and it was on that standard he would have his argument judged.[76] Anyone doubting that Darwin was right—that "science" (for all its emphasis on universality) follows methods of deliberation parallel to those of law, ethics, or practical reason—should read Marcello Pera's *Discourses of Science.*

We now come to the crux of the matter as set forth in Eger's essay and to the potential educational pertinence of ID. The impasse between present programs for teaching critical reason in ethics and the outright deliberate prohibition of critical questions in the teaching of Darwinism represents a fundamental incoherence in the model of reason presented in public schools. What kind of thinking has led to this impasse? The impasse has been created by the myth of "two cultures" and a positivist folktale of a unique "scientific method" hermetically sealed off from ordinary life and the demands of practical reason, value, and philosophic perspective. The challenge before us now, as parents, teachers, academics, people of all faiths or of none, is to use what we know to develop alternatives to the present system. That system, which produces needless social conflict, is politically unsustainable, intellectually bankrupt, and ethically indefensible.[77]

As Richard Rorty has pointed out in *Achieving Our Country,* the time has come for new thinking on the part of American progressives—and by extension, on the part of all Americans of good will.[78] Ordinary citizens as well as academics have an important role to play in developing a revitalized

progressive politics, by developing creative new policies and bold unorthodox citizen-coalitions to help bring them about. Communication scholars
and science educators could play a major role in exposing and offering concrete alternatives to disastrous public policies that continue to block accurate public understanding of science. Those who wish to return biology to
its true Darwinian roots as a liberal study should not be stigmatized as big-
ots. It is not enough for academics to understand that positivism is false or
wrong. The point is to enter the political arena with concrete alternatives,
and through civic discourse improve science education and the public understanding of science.

Speaking as a citizen and drawing on what I have learned as a rhetorical
educator and rhetorician of science, I offer three suggestions to help move
the discussion forward:

First, the starting point for discussion of reform of science teaching
should be Eger's diagnosis of a fundamental incoherence in American education. If Eger has demonstrated anything, it is that scientism has not
served science education well. It has separated science from its history and
roots in liberal education and wedded it to a dogmatic materialist ideology
incompatible with the values of a democratic and pluralistic culture. The
answer to dealing with philosophic or theological problems posed by the
teaching of biology is not, as currently mandated in California, to have science apparatchiks tell dissenting students that belief in the God of traditional theism is private and subjective with no basis in objective reality.[79]
Of course, science teachers should not teach (in the sense of inculcating)
"theism," or naturalism, or pantheism—except as philosophies relevant to
the scientific subjects at hand and contested by other philosophies.[80]

But to discuss relevant presuppositions and possible philosophical implications of scientific theories, and to point out how different scientists and
philosophers of science draw different conclusions about design in nature,
would seem to be nothing other than basic liberal education and common
sense.[81] At present, such a thought is very controversial.

Second, parents and concerned citizens need to be brought into the discussion about science education in some venue other than the courts.
Laypeople have not been well served by experts in this matter. Philip
Kitcher in his otherwise excellent essay on Darwin, "Persuasion," does not
hesitate to justify lying to the public for its own good if that is what it takes
to conceal the antitheistic implications of the Darwinian paradigm.[82]
Michael Ruse—whose style, person, and writings are a delight—invented
the rationale of the Overton decision in the Arkansas creation-science trial

to fit the criteria for a winning case as specified by his American Civil Liberties Union (ACLU) handlers. His position is a laughingstock among his professional peers and an ethical and conceptual embarrassment to his profession. Although he has staunchly defended his actions in the Arkansas case, to his great credit he has published an anthology of basic documents about the case and its philosophic aftermath in which he has allowed the weakness of his own defense to shine through in the devastating clarity of his colleagues' unanswered rebuttals.

As I have written in a review of Ruse's *But Is It Science?* the philosophy of science offered in his deposition and in his testimony on the stand is at odds with his published work.[83] When speaking to a learned audience in the German Democratic Republic (GDR) the month before his deposition in Little Rock, Ruse ridiculed demarcationism, made particular fun of Sir Karl Popper (an arch-demarcationist), acknowledged the philosophical and theological issues raised by Darwin's theory, and emphasized the intimate and undemarcatable association between science and culture. A few weeks later in Little Rock, Ruse strongly defended demarcationism. He invented a five-point version of it beautifully contrived to meet the demands of his immediate rhetorical situation, whatever the cost to his consistency as a philosopher. The ACLU was correct in both assumptions they made about him and the judge in the case: Ruse could be depended on to fill in the philosophic details for the legal strategy they had already decided on before he arrived in Little Rock, and Judge Overton would find his testimony persuasive.[84]

Anyone who wishes to learn more about what Michael Ruse thinks about science and its relation to culture and religion could scarcely do better than to read his magisterial *Monad to Man,* the thesis of his GDR lecture expanded to just under a thousand pages.[85] If one is interested in a very different subject—his cultural politics—one should read his deposition in the Arkansas case. His *Monad* book affirms in meticulously documented detail a philosophy of science at odds with every major point of his deposition. No progressive science educator and no advocate of the teaching philosophy of ID could hope to surpass Ruse in documenting the religious functions that Darwinism has performed from the nineteenth century to the present. His book is an authoritative guide for showing how easily an all-encompassing worldview grounded in "science" becomes a cult, complete with shrines and its own iconography.

As Ruse aptly notes, "Not only has evolution functioned as an ideology, as a secular religion, but for many professional biologists that has been its

primary role."[86] Venue relativism—positivism for the masses and construc-
tivism for the elite—is an unstable position rhetorically, philosophically,
and ethically. In a welcome development, Ruse seems to have publicly dis-
avowed the defining tenet of the demarcationist position offered in his
Arkansas testimony. "I think that philosophically one should be sensitive to
what I think history shows, namely, that evolution . . . akin to religion involves making certain a priori or metaphysical assumptions, which at some
level cannot be proven empirically."[87]

Third, the innovative pedagogical ideas of Cobern, Southerland, and
others and new pedagogic experiments should be tried. Recently, I learned
of a new course being offered for the first time at Michigan State University. The course seems to be well designed to address interpretive questions
raised by evolutionism and to provide a good model for the kind of approach that could work well in high schools. The course, "Critical Analysis
of Controversies in Evolution," is taught by James Smith, an evolutionary
biologist. Its units include a class discussion entitled "Is Behe Correct? Is
Darwin Correct?" Part of the assignment for that session reads, "Summa-
rize the evidence used to support and refute Behe's concept of Intelligent
Design." Coming as the unit does after earlier ones in which the details of
Darwinism and evolutionism are carefully studied, Smith's syllabus shows
how learning real science can be part of a truly liberal education.[88]

Nothing as situationally sensitive as teaching can hope to find a single
model equally appropriate to all contexts. What is needed as our culture
moves out from beneath the epistemic tyranny of positivism and as we
begin to repair the deep social damage that tyranny has done to science (in
its conduct, teaching, and public understanding) is to recover the capacity
to think clearly about public education.

A model for presenting controversial material without teachers either
"confronting" dissenting students with the "correct" answer or backing
down from teaching the best current evidence and theories is given in Gerald Graff's *Beyond the Culture Wars: How Teaching the Conflicts Can Revitalize
American Education.*[89] Though his book is not aimed at the teaching of science and his insights, like those of James Smith and others, would need to
be adapted for high school courses, Graff's perspective is profoundly consonant with the central insight of contemporary scholarship in the history
and philosophy of science. Science is, among other things, a series of controversies over great scientific questions as well as an activity that is deeply
enmeshed in culture and informed by contestable philosophic assumptions. Graff is clear that "teaching the conflicts has nothing to do with

relativism or denying the existence of truth." Quite to the contrary, Graff emphasizes the importance of critical examination of difference as truth's first and best line of defense: "The best way to make relativists of students is to expose them to an endless series of different positions which are *not* debated before their eyes. Acknowledging that culture [read science] is a debate rather than a monologue does not prevent us from energetically fighting for the truth of our own convictions [or from defending the received view]. On the contrary, when truth is disputed, we can seek it only by entering the debate—as Socrates knew when he taught the conflicts two millennia ago."[90]

Donald Kennedy is right. Not to know the theory of evolution is to be scientifically illiterate. Beyond that, not to know evidential challenges to the theory, that the theory requires assumptions, carries philosophic implications, is open to different interpretations, and in the end is subject to the attrition of time and the inevitable convulsion of scientific revolution is also to be scientifically illiterate.

Notes

1. R. G. Collingwood, *The Idea of Nature* (Oxford: Oxford University Press, 1976); Giorgio de Santillana, *The Origins of Scientific Thought: From Anaximander to Proclus 600 B.C. to A.D. 500* (New York: Mentor Books, 1961); Werner Jaeger, *The Theology of the Early Greek Philosophers* (Oxford: Oxford University Press, 1947); F. M. Cornford, *From Religion to Philosophy: A Study in the Origins of Western Speculation* (New York: Harper Torchbooks, 1957), esp. 144–59; Daniel O'Connor and Francis Oakley, eds., *Creation: The Impact of an Idea* (New York: Charles Scribner's Sons, 1968), esp. 1–28; Alexander P. D. Mourelatos, ed., *The Pre-Socratics: A Collection of Critical Essays* (Garden City, N.Y.: Doubleday Anchor Books, 1974); Frederick Copleston, S. J., *A History of Philosophy,* vol. 1. *Greece and Rome,* Pt. 1 (Garden City, N.Y.: Image Books, 1993), 89–92 and esp. 96–97; R. Hooykaas, *Religion and the Rise of Modern Science* (Grand Rapids, Mich.: William B. Eerdmans, 1978), esp. 1–7.

2. S. Sambursky, *The Physical World of the Greeks,* translated from the Hebrew by Merton Dagut (New York: Collier Books, 1962), 126–28; Benjamin Farrington, *Greek Science* (Baltimore: Penguin Books, 1963), 58–65, 144–48; F. M. Cornford, *Before and After Socrates* (Cambridge: Cambridge University Press, 1972), chap. 1, esp. pages 25–28, and chap. 4, esp. pages 99–109. See Collingwood, *Idea of Nature,* esp. the

introduction, pages 155–57, and conclusion. See also Daniel O'Connor, "Two Philosophies of Nature," in O'Connor and Oakley, *Creation,* 15–28; G. S. Kirk, "Natural Change in Heraclitus," in Mourelatos, *Pre-Socratics,* 189–96; W. K. C. Guthrie, "Flux and Logos in Heraclitus," in Mourelatos, *Pre-Socratics,* 214–28. The utility of the concept of mind and of form suggesting mind for morphology is well noted by E. S. Russell, *Form and Function: A Contribution to the History of Animal Morphology* (Chicago: University of Chicago Press, 1982), 1–16.

3. For the key role of the biblical idea of a divine creator in the development of Western science, see O'Connor and Oakley, *Creation;* see also David C. Lindberg and Ronald L. Numbers, *God and Nature: Historical Essays on the Encounter between Christianity and Science* (Berkeley: University of California Press, 1986). On medieval science and on the continuities and discontinuities between medieval and modern science, see A. C. Crombie, *Medieval and Early Modern Science,* vol. 1, *Science in the Middle Ages: V–XIII Centuries* (Cambridge: Harvard University Press, 1963), esp. 172–74; A. C. Crombie, *Medieval and Early Modern Science,* vol. 2, *Science in the Later Middle Ages and Early Modern Times: XIII—XVII Centuries* (Cambridge: Harvard University Press, 1963), 285–333. For the changing view of material self–sufficiency and design since the rise of modern science, see Richard S. Westfall, *Science and Religion in Seventeenth-Century England* (New Haven, Conn.: Yale University Press, 1958); Allen G. Debus, *Man and Nature in the Renaissance* (Cambridge: Cambridge University Press, 1978), 99–100 and chaps. 7 and 8; E. A. Burtt, *The Metaphysical Foundations of Modern Science* (Garden City, N.Y.: Doubleday Anchor Books, 1954), esp. 25–35, 303–25; Hooykaas, *Religion,* 7–28, 161–62; John C. Greene, *The Death of Adam: Evolution and Its Impact on Western Thought* (Garden City, N.Y.: Mentor Books, 1961), esp. 11–24; Charles Coulston Gillispie, *Genesis and Geology: The Impact of Scientific Discoveries Upon Religious Beliefs in the Decades before Darwin* (New York: Harper and Row, 1959), esp. chaps. 1 and 8. For the impact of material self-sufficiency on the idea of "form" in biology in the nineteenth century, see Timothy Lenoir, *The Strategy of Life: Teleology and Mechanics in Nineteenth-Century German Biology* (Chicago: University of Chicago Press, 1982), esp. the introduction and chap. 1; Russell, *Form and Function,* esp. chap. 13. For a contemporary statement of similar critiques, see Hans Jonas, *The Phenomenon of Life: Toward a Philosophical Biology* (Chicago: University of Chicago Press, 1982), 38–63; Stanley N. Salthe, *Development and Evolution: Complexity and Change in Biology*

(Cambridge: MIT Press/Bradford Books, 1993). For an account of the interrelation of Christianity and science, see Nancy R. Pearcey and Charles B. Thaxton, *The Soul of Science: Christian Faith and Natural Philosophy* (Wheaton, Ill.: Crossway Books, 1994). For an account of continuing philosophic issues in this relation, see J. P. Moreland, *Christianity and the Nature of Science: A Philosophical Investigation* (Grand Rapids, Mich.: Baker Book House, 1994); Ernst Benz, *Evolution and Christian Hope: Man's Concept of the Future, from the Early Fathers to Teilhard de Chardin*, trans. Hanz G. Frank (Garden City, N.Y.: Doubleday Anchor Books, 1968); Stanley Jaki, *Chance or Reality and Other Essays* (Lanham, Md.: University Presses of America, 1986); John Polkinghorne, *The Faith of a Physicist* (Princeton, N.J.: Princeton University Press, 1994); Arthur Peacocke, *Theology for a Scientific Age: Being and Becoming Natural, Divine, and Human* (Minneapolis: Fortress Press, 1993). Contemporary perspectives on self-organization and Darwinism, with a critique of the idea of design, can be found in David J. Depew and Bruce H. Weber, *Darwinism Evolving: Systems Dynamics and the Genealogy of Natural Selection* (Cambridge: MIT Press, 1997); see also Stuart A. Kauffman, *The Origins of Order: Self-Organization and Selection in Evolution* (Oxford: Oxford University Press, 1993); Michael Ruse, *Monad to Man: The Concept of Progress in Evolutionary Biology* (Cambridge: Cambridge University Press, 1996); Robert J. Richards, *Darwin and the Emergence of Evolutionary Theories of Mind and Behavior* (Chicago: University of Chicago Press, 1987). For a careful, philosophically informed study of "design," "God," and "the anthropic principle" as they relate to modern cosmology and physics, see John Leslie, *Universes* (London: Routledge, 1989); M. A. Corey, *God and the New Cosmology: The Anthropic Design Argument* (Lanham, Md.: Rowman and Littlefield, 1993). A helpful debate on key issues in contemporary cosmological thought and whether its tendency is theistic or atheistic is William Lane Craig and Quentin Smith, *Theism, Atheism and Big Bang Cosmology* (Cambridge: Cambridge University Press, 1995). See the lucid exposition of these issues with special attention to contemporary Darwinism in Robert C. Koons, "A New Look at the Cosmological Argument," *American Philosophical Quarterly* 34, no. 2 (1997): 193—211. See also Dean Overman, *A Case Against Accident and Self-Organization* (New York: Rowman and Littlefield, 1998); Michael J. Denton, *Nature's Destiny: How the Laws of Biology Reveal Purpose in the Universe* (New York: Free Press, 1998).

4. Gavin de Beer, ed., *Charles Darwin and Thomas Henry Huxley: Autobiographies* (Oxford: Oxford University Press, 1983), 26.

5. Janet Browne, *Charles Darwin, Voyaging: A Biography* (Princeton, N.J.: Princeton University Press, 1995), 80–88.

6. Darwin, in de Beer, *Charles Darwin and Thomas Henry Huxley*, 31–33, 35–38; John F. W. Herschel, *A Preliminary Discourse on the Study of Natural History* (Chicago: University of Chicago Press, 1987), 16–17, 37–38.

7. Darwin, in de Beer, *Charles Darwin and Thomas Henry Huxley*, 38; Browne, *Voyaging*, 133.

8. William Paley, *Natural Theology: Or, Evidences of the Existence and Attributes of the Deity, Collected from the Appearances of Nature* (Boston: Gould and Lincoln, 1863), esp. 1–13.

9. Edward Manier, *The Young Darwin and His Cultural Circle: A Study of Influences Which Helped Shape the Language and Logic of the First Drafts of the Theory of Natural Selection* (Dordrecht, Holland: D. Reidel, 1978), 70–73. For a critique of Hume's argument against design, see Elliott Sober, *Philosophy of Biology* (Boulder, Colo.: Westview, 1993). For a critique of Hume's reasoning on the related issue of miracle, see Sandy Zabell, "The Probabilistic Analysis of Testimony," *Journal of Statistical Planning and Inference* 20 (1988): 327–54. For a meticulous and friendly summation of Hume's case in the context of eighteenth-century Christian apologetics, see Lloyd F. Bitzer, "The 'Indian Prince' in Miracle Arguments of Hume and His Predecessors and Early Critics," *Philosophy and Rhetoric* 31 (1998): 175–230.

10. Darwin, in de Beer, *Charles Darwin and Thomas Henry Huxley*, 32–33.

11. Ibid., 38; Herschel, *Preliminary Discourse*, esp. Part II, chaps. 4–7.

12. Francis Darwin, ed., *The Life and Letters of Charles Darwin*, vol. 2 (New York: D. Appleton, 1911), to Charles Lyell, 12 Dec. 1859: "What this exactly means I do not know, but it is evidently very contemptuous. If true this is a great blow and discouragement" (37); John Angus Campbell, "Scientific Revolution and the Grammar of Culture: The Case of Darwin's Origin," *Quarterly Journal of Speech* 72 (1986): 351–76; John Angus Campbell, "Of Orchids, Insects, and Natural Theology: Timing, Tactics, and Cultural Critique in Darwin's Post-*Origin* Strategy," *Argumentation* 8 (1994): 63–81; John Angus Campbell, "The Comic Frame and the Rhetoric of Science: Epistemology and Ethics in Darwin's *Origin*," *Rhetoric Society Quarterly* 24 (1994): 27–50.

13. M. J. S. Hodge, "Darwin and the Laws of the Animate Part of the Terrestrial System (1835–1837): On the Lyellian Origins of His

Zoonomical Explanatory Program," *Studies in the History of Biology* 7 (1983): 106; David Kohn, "Theories to Work By: Rejected Theories, Reproduction, and Darwin's Path to Natural Selection," *Studies in the History of Biology* 4 (1980): 67–170.

14. John Angus Campbell, "Scientific Discovery and Rhetorical Invention: The Path to Darwin's Origin," in *The Invention and Persuasion in the Conduct of Inquiry,* ed. Herbert W. Simons (Chicago: University of Chicago Press, 1990), esp. 62–78.

15. Paul H. Barrett, Peter J. Gautry, Sandra Herbert, David Kohn, and Sydney Smith, eds., *Charles Darwin's Notebooks, 1836–1844: Geology, Transmutation of Species, Metaphysical Enquiries* (Ithaca, N.Y.: Cornell University Press, 1987), 167–74; Kohn, "Theories," 83–95; Campbell, "Scientific Discovery," 58–68; also John Angus Campbell, "On the Way to the Origin: Darwin's Evolutionary Insight and Its Rhetorical Transformation," Van Zelst Lecture in Communication (Evanston, Ill., 1990), esp. 14–21; Manier, *The Young Darwin,* chaps. 9 and 10; Dov Ospovat, *The Development of Darwin's Theory: Natural History, Natural Theology, and Natural Selection, 1838–1859* (Cambridge: Cambridge University Press, 1981), 60–86.

16. Gavin de Beer, ed., *Evolution by Natural Selection* (Cambridge: Cambridge University Press, 1958), 45–46.

17. All citations concerning variations among the various editions of the *Origin* are from Morse Peckham, ed., *"The Origin of Species" by Charles Darwin: A Variorum Text* (Philadelphia: University of Pennsylvania Press, 1959), 40.

18. Ibid., 40, 57.

19. Single individual citations from the *Origin* will be from Charles Darwin, *On the Origin of Species: A Facsimile of the First Edition with an Introduction by Ernst Mayr* (Cambridge: Harvard University Press, 1964), 31, 34–36.

20. Ibid., 44, 50, 51, 56.

21. Ibid., 52–53, 55.

22. Ibid., 60–61.

23. Ibid., 77–79.

24. Ibid., 83, 84.

25. A. R. Wallace to Darwin, 2 July 1866, in Francis Darwin, ed., *More Letters of Charles Darwin,* vol. 1 (New York: D. Appleton, 1903), 267–70.

26. Jane Loring Gray, ed., *The Letters of Asa Gray,* vol. 1 (Boston: Houghton, Mifflin, 1893), 321; A. Hunter DuPree, ed., *Darwiniana by Asa Gray* (Cambridge: Harvard University Press, 1963), 46, 51–71, 72–142.

27. Darwin, *Life and Letters*, vol. 1, 5 Apr. 1859, 510–11; Darwin, *Origin*, 111–25.

28. Campbell, "Comic Frame," esp. 41–46.

29. For a good account of the difference between "how possibly" versus "how actually" thinking in evolutionary biology and for how virtually the whole of the *Origin* is one long "how possibly" argument, see Robert O'Hara, "Homage to Clio, or, Toward an Historical Philosophy for Evolutionary Biology," *Systematic Zoology* 37 (1988): 142–55.

30. Darwin, *Origin*, 167.

31. Although I cannot here give full documentation, by my count, excluding the flyleaf citations, there are 108 references to "creation" or related terms for the action of God in the first edition of the *Origin*—including the term *mystery*. Here I give only the chapter, the raw number, and characteristic terms: Introduction = 3 "mystery of mysteries, created"; chap. 1 = 0; chap. 2 = 3 "created, creation"; chap. 3 = 0; chap. 4 = 3 "creation, created"; chap. 5 = 12 "creation, created"; chapter 6 = 7 "created, creation"; chap. 7 = 1 "endowed"; chap. 8 = 13 "endowed, specially acquired or endowed, mysterious"; chap. 9 = 1 "created"; chap. 10 = 2 "act of creation, gratuitous mystery"; chap. 11 = 12 "creation, created"; chap. 12 = 11 "independent creation, theory of creation"; chap. 13 = 11 "Creator, Plan of the Creator"; chap. 14 = 29 "special endowment, suddenly created, independent acts of creation."

32. For an excellent discussion of theological thought in Darwin's work, see Neal C. Gillespie, *Charles Darwin and the Problem of Creation* (Chicago: University of Chicago Press, 1982).

33. Darwin, *Origin*, 171.

34. For a more detailed analysis of the strategy of these chapters, see Campbell, "Comic Frame," 41–46.

35. Darwin, *Origin*, 180–81.

36. Ibid., 186, 189.

37. Ibid., 311.

38. Ibid., 411.

39. Ibid., 459.

40. Ibid., 486.

41. Charles Darwin, *Journal of Researches into the Geology and Natural History of the Various Countries Visited by H.M.S. Beagle*, 1st ed. facsimile reprint (New York: Hafner, 1952), 226–30, 234–37.

42. Darwin, *Origin*, 490.

43. Peckham, *Variorum,* 759.

44. Darwin, *Life and Letters,* vol. 2, 29 Mar. 1863, 202–3.

45. John Angus Campbell, "The Invisible Rhetorician: Charles Darwin's 'Third Party' Strategy," *Rhetorica* 7 (winter 1989): 60–63; Darwin, *More Letters,* vol. 1, 163–64, 190–93.

46. Campbell, "Invisible Rhetorician," 72–73.

47. Darwin, in de Beer, *Charles Darwin and Thomas Henry Huxley,* 50–51.

48. Ibid., 54.

49. Donald Flemming, "The Centenary of the Origin of Species," *Journal of the History of Ideas* 20 (1959): 442–43.

50. Daniel C. Dennett, *Darwin's Dangerous Idea: Evolution and the Meanings of Life* (New York: Simon and Schuster, 1995), 61–84.

51. Donald Kennedy, "Helping Schools to Teach Evolution," *Chronicle of Higher Education* (7 Aug. 1998), Opinion Page: A48.

52. Browne, *Voyaging.*

53. Leslie Alan Horvitz, "Indians and Anthropologists Are Battling Over Old Bones," *Washington Times,* 18 Nov. 1996.

54. William W. Cobern, "Point: Belief, Understanding, and the Teaching of Evolution," *Journal of Research in Science Teaching* 31 (1994): 583–90; Cobern, "Science Education as an Exercise in Foreign Affairs," *Science and Education* 4 (1995): 287–302; Cobern, "The Nature of Science and the Role of Knowledge and Belief," *Science and Education* 9 (2000): 219–46; William W. Cobern and Cathleen C. Loving, "Defining 'Science' in a Multicultural World: Implications for Science Education," *Science and Education* 85 (2000): 50–67.

55. Cobern, "The Nature of Science and the Role of Knowledge and Belief," 233.

56. Cobern, "Science Education as an Exercise in Foreign Affairs," 290–94.

57. Sherry A. Southerland and Gale M. Sinatra, "Learning about Biological Evolution: A Special Case of Intentional Conceptual Change," in *Intentional Conceptual Change,* ed. Gale M. Sinatra and Paul R. Pintrich (New York: Academic Press, 2003).

58. Colin Gauld, "Knowledge, Belief, and Understanding in Science Education" (paper presented at the sixth International History, Philosophy, and Science Teaching Conference, Denver, Colo., November 2001), 5.

59. For an extremely valuable discussion of this point, see George M. Marsden, *The Soul of the American University: From Protestant Establishment to Established Nonbelief* (New York: Oxford University Press, 1994), 327–30. Marsden draws particular attention to Walter Lippmann's

probing reflection on the Scopes trial in *American Inquisitors* and how
Lippmann grasped the Jeffersonian tension in Bryan between refusal
to support with one's tax dollars an abhorrent system of ideas and majority rule.

60. Arthur Schlesinger Jr., "The Age of Alexander Campbell," *Restoration
Review* 1 (1959): 136–51.

61. Alexis de Tocqueville, *Democracy in America*, trans. George Lawrence
(Garden City, N.Y.: Doubleday Anchor Books, 1969), 287–300. The
parallel between those Euro-centric thinkers of de Tocqueville's day
and those of our own time who deplore American religiosity—always
from the standpoint of a materialist metaphysic—has to rank as one of
the great continuities of American intellectual history. "But our
pedants find it an obvious mistake; constantly they prove to me that all
is fine in America except just that religious spirit which I admire; I am
informed that on the other side of the ocean freedom and human hap-
piness lack nothing but Spinoza's belief in the eternity of the world and
Cabanis' contention that thought is a secretion of the brain. To that I
have ready no answer to give, except that those who talk like that
have never been in America and have never seen either religious peoples or free ones" (Tocqueville, *Democracy in America*, 294).

62. Stuart W. Leslie, "Science and Politics in Cold-War America," in *The
Politics of Western Science: 1640–1990*, ed. Margaret C. Jacob (Atlantic
Highlands, N.J.: The Humanities Press, 1992), 199–233; Ruse, *Monad to
Man*.

63. Ruse, *Monad to Man*.

64. Edward J. Larson, *Summer for the Gods: The Scopes Trial and America's
Continuing Debate over Science and Religion* (New York: Basic Books,
1997); Edward Larson and Larry Witham, "The More They Learn The
Less They Believe," *Nature* 394 (June 1998): 313. See also story in the
Washington Times, 30 July 1998.

65. Larson and Witham, "The More They Learn."

66. The case of Stephen Jay Gould, the obvious name missing from this list,
is instructive. Gould's position on the worldview issue is politic. Unlike
Dawkins and Dennett, Gould does not make a career of bashing theists.
In his "Nonoverlapping Magisteria: Science and Religion Are Not in
Conflict, for Their Teachings Occupy Distinctly Different Domains," *Natural History* (Mar. 1997), Gould leaves science to deal with reality and
religion and philosophy to address everything else. For a philosophic
critique of the stance embodied in this position, see Craig and Smith,

Theism; Polkinghorne, *Faith;* Koons, "Cosmological Argument"; and Leslie, *Universes.* In this note, I can point out only that design theorists do not cede "reality" to metaphysical naturalism, content themselves with epistemic apartheid, and call it a day. The ID argument is, and has always been, that reality in all its fullness—including the physical nature studied by science—manifests marks of an intelligent designer. Theoretic reflection on design and purpose is not the property of some special domain set apart from science but an implication, however contestable, from the study of science. Gould understands this. By confining science to physical "reality" and "reality" to that which is known by the methods of the natural sciences, he makes metaphysical materialism coincident with all truly reliable knowledge. Gould's is a kinder, gentler version of the same materialist episteme he holds in common with Dawkins and Dennett. In this episteme, any affirmation of a creative intelligence in nature is a personal, aesthetic preference.

Gould's politic and lulling way of handling theists is usefully placed in perspective by the candor of his Harvard colleague Richard Lewontin in "The Demon Haunted World," *New York Review of Books,* 9 Jan. 1997,: "It is not that the methods and institutions of science somehow compel us to accept a material explanation of the phenomenal world, but, on the contrary, that we are forced by our *a priori* adherence to material causes to create an apparatus of investigation and a set of concepts that produce material explanations, no matter how counter-intuitive, no matter how mystifying to the uninitiated. Moreover, that materialism is absolute, for we cannot allow a Divine Foot in the door" (31).

In light of Lewontin's candor, the remarkable thing is not the emergence of the ID movement but the length of time it has taken scholars who are neither materialists nor fundamentalists to catch on. Clearly, until we have the kind of thorough, open and critical kind of science education that progressive science educators are calling for, the most outrageous and extreme bits of positivist folklore will be blandly presented to the public as the epitome of moderation and common sense.

Interestingly, in his *Chronicle* essay, Kennedy points with pride to a 1984 National Academy of Sciences statement: "Science and religion represent different ways of knowing: Science is engaged in testing through experiments and research whereas [religious] belief rests on spiritual convictions that, by their nature, resist such challenges." The perspective of Kennedy and his colleagues, with its simple, untroubled, and thoroughly positivistic dichotomy between reason defined as objective, observational science and faith understood as subjective experience, is a textbook example of what Cobern and other science educators have identified as "the myth of school science." As Cobern notes, "The more appropriate dichotomy is that epistemology . . . requires both reason *and* faith versus reason *or* faith. All forms of knowledge including empirically demonstrated knowledge require some form of foundation that is not itself empirically demonstrable in any non-tautological fashion. Some will resist the use of the word 'faith,' but I think it is fair to say that we have 'faith' in these presuppositions. Faith and reason operate together, which suggests that there is no unambiguous epistemic distinction between knowledge and belief." Cobern, "The Nature of Science and the Role of Knowledge and Belief," 234.

67. http://fp.bio.utk.edu/darwin/frmain.html.
68. Scott Field, "Of Souls and Skyhooks," *Trends in Ecology and Evolution* (July 1998): 296.
69. That high school science textbooks are far from neutral on these larger issues of meaning and purpose connected with the teaching of evolution is readily evident. See Stephen C. Meyer, "Don't Ask, Don't Tell in Biology Instruction," *Washington Times,* 4 July 1996. Meyer instances the following two examples as far from atypical. (1) "Each animal phylum represents an experiment in the design of body structures to perform the tasks necessary for survival. Of course there has never been any kind of plan to these experiments because evolution works without either plan or purpose. . . . Evolution is random and undirected" (quoted in Kenneth Miller and J. Levine, *Biology* [Englewood Cliffs, N.J.: Prentice Hall, 1993], 658). (2) "By coupling undirected purposeless variation to the blind uncaring process of natural selection Darwin made theological or spiritual explanations of the life processes superfluous. Together with Marx's materialist theory of history and society and Freud's attribution of human behavior to influences over which we have little control, Darwin's theory of evolution was a crucial plank in the platform of mechanism and materialism—of much of science, in short—that has since been the stage of most western thought" (quoted in Douglas J. Futuyma, *Evolutionary Biology,* 3rd ed. [Sunderland, Mass.: Sinauer Associates, 1986], 3).
70. Martin Eger, "A Tale of Two Controversies: Dissonance in the Theory and Practice of Rationality," *Zygon* 23 (1988): 291–325.

71. Ibid., 292–301.
72. Ibid., 293–98.
73. Peckham, *Variorum,* "It has recently been objected that this is an unsafe method of arguing; but it is a method used in judging of the common events of life, and has often been used by the greatest natural philosophers" (748).
74. Eger, "Tale," 299.
75. For an excellent account of how thoroughly contentious and argumentative science is at the very highest levels, see David L. Hull, *Science As a Process: An Evolutionary Account of the Social and Conceptual Development of Science* (Chicago: University of Chicago Press, 1988).
76. Peckham, *Variorum,* "It has recently been objected that this is an unsafe method of arguing; but it is a method used in judging of the common events of life, and has often been used by the greatest natural philosophers" (748).
77. For "social conflict," see Eger, "Tale"; for "politically unsustainable," see Edward J. Larson, *Trial and Error: The American Controversy Over Creation and Evolution* (Oxford: Oxford University Press, 1989). Having surveyed the career of the teaching of evolution since the Scopes trial and in light of the Arkansas decision, Larson, a lawyer and legal scholar, concludes in his final chapter that laws in fundamental opposition to the values and beliefs of the people cannot ultimately be sustained. By "intellectually bankrupt" I mean that an old and thoroughly discredited philosophy of science—positivist demarcationism—is presented to the courts and to the people to justify the present teaching of evolution, and another and opposed philosophy of science is presented to professional peers. By "ethically indefensible" I mean that the present system requires fundamental deception about the obvious metaphysical implication of Darwinism as drawn by the overwhelming number of scientists who understand it best.
78. Richard Rorty, *Achieving Our Country: Leftist Thought in Twentieth-Century America* (Cambridge: Harvard University Press, 1998), 99–107. I endorse Rorty's trenchant critique of the ills of the postmodern university and his call for academics to form alliances with others outside the university and to become politically active. I support a "Bigger Tent" American pragmatism than does Rorty. In *Fundamentalism and American Culture: The Shaping of Twentieth-Century Evangelicalism: 1870–1925* (New York: Oxford University Press, 1980), historian George Marsden makes some suggestive observations on how large Big Tent pragmatism really

is in his comments on two of the most outstanding representatives of this broader American tradition: William Jennings Bryan and Billy Sunday. "[Bryan] abandoned, in the spirit of American pragmatism, not only the fine points of theology but also any attempt to present a theoretical defense of Christianity and relied on the evidence of practical results" (134). And "At his ordination examination for the Presbyterian ministry in 1903, [Billy Sunday's] characteristic response to questions on theology and history was 'That's too deep for me,' or 'I'll have to pass that up.' 'I don't know any more about theology than a jack-rabbit knows about ping-pong, but I'm on my way to glory'" (130).

79. Kevin Padian, "The California Science Framework: A Victory for Scientific Integrity," *National Center for Scientific Education Reports* 9 (1989): "At times some students may insist that certain conclusions of science cannot be true because of certain religious or philosophic beliefs that they hold. . . . It is appropriate for the teacher to express in this regard, 'I understand that you may have personal reservations about accepting this scientific evidence, but it is scientific knowledge about which there is no reasonable doubt among scientists in their field, and it is my responsibility to teach it because it is part of our common intellectual heritage'" (20).

80. See comments on James Smith's course in the final section of this essay.

81. For an exceptionally lucid and well–balanced account of the philosophic issues, and typical mistakes made on all sides of the contemporary evolution debate, see Del Ratzsch, *The Battle of Beginnings: Why Neither Side Is Winning the Creation-Evolution Debate* (Downers Grove, Ill.: InterVarsity Press, 1996), esp. chaps. 8–13.

82. Philip Kitcher, "Persuasion," in *Persuading Science: The Art of Scientific Rhetoric,* ed. Marello Pera and William R. Shea (Conton, Mass.: Science History Publications, USA, 1991), 19.

83. Michael Ruse, ed., *But Is It Science? The Philosophic Question in the Creation/Evolution Controversy* (Amherst, N.Y.: Prometheus Books, 1996); John Angus Campbell, "But Is It Science? The Philosophical Question in the Creation/Evolutionary Controversy," *Social Epistemology* 12 (1998): 157–65.

84. Ruse, *But Is It Science?*. See Ruse's sections "Who Is Responsible for Legal Strategy?" and "What Is the Witness's Responsibility?" 389–92, and Philip L. Quinn's rebuttal, "Creationism, Methodology and Poli-

tics," 395–99. The candor of Richard Lewontin on the role of expert opinion in such cases is again a breath of fresh air. What ultimately is revealed by our long-standing American debate over evolution, Lewontin notes, is "a deep problem of democratic self-governance" ("Demon Haunted World," 32). As Lewontin sees it, we simply have to trust the testimony of experts in judicial proceedings involving science. "Anyone who has ever served as an expert witness . . . knows that the court may spend an inordinate time 'qualifying' the expert, who, once qualified, gives testimony that is not meant to be a persuasive argument, but an assertion unchallengeable by anyone but another expert" (32). Though Lewontin sees our current situation with regard to evolution from a rhetorical point of view, he cites Plato's *Gorgias,* and in so doing reveals, perhaps inadvertently, an underlying uncertainty about the compatibility of at least his understanding of science with democracy. Lewontin criticizes his late friend Carl Sagan for "believ[ing] like the Evangelist John, that the truth shall make you free. But they are wrong. It is not the truth that makes you free. It is our possession of the power to discover the truth. Our dilemma is that we do not know how to provide that power" (32). In Lewontin's materialist soteriology, only the elite few are capable of freedom. Theologically, Lewontin is a gnostic. Politically, for that very reason and to that extent, he is an antidemocrat. Here Abraham Lincoln, that great ID theoretician of our national experience, being at once more optimistic toward God and more pessimistic toward humans, offered better grounds for hope that ordinary people could understand what they needed to from experts. At least on the metaphysics informing (or in Lewontin's case, constituting) his science, Lincoln's great maxim is very much to the point: while some of the people will be fooled all of the time, and some of the people will be fooled some of the time, all of the people will not be fooled all of the time. How long the remainder will be fooled by Michael Ruse or by Donald Kennedy or by Stephen Gould is plainly not as long as without the ID movement—an intellectual movement with potentially very broad public support.

Is science compatible with democracy? It certainly was in Lincoln's time. Whether the materialist metaphysic that currently masquerades as science is likewise compatible has yet to be shown—and is far from obvious. Whatever real problems there may be with science and democratic governance, without materialist metaphysics (as Darwin might say) the problem is greatly diminished, or rather disappears.

85. Michael Ruse, "The Ideology of Darwinism," in *Abhandlungen Der Akademie Der Wissenschaften Der DDR* (Berlin: Akademie-Verlag, 1983), 233–56.

86. Ruse, *Monad to Man*, 530.

87. Michael Ruse (speech given at the annual meeting of the American Association for the Advancement of Science, Boston, Mass., 1993).

88. My information comes from an e-mail communication from Levi Derek Boldt, Smith's graduate teaching assistant.

89. Gerald Graff, *Beyond the Culture Wars: How Teaching the Conflicts Can Revitalize American Education* (New York: W. W. Norton, 1992).

90. Ibid., 15.

Intelligent Design Theory, Religion, and the Science Curriculum

Warren A. Nord

❈ ❈ ❈

The Great Temptation of educators is to teach students nothing but the truth—as they understand it, of course. When this happens, however, education is reduced to training or socialization or indoctrination, even if they turn out to be right. Properly understood, education requires the ability to think critically, to reason one's way through conflicting evidence and arguments. Students must learn about contending ways of making sense of the world if they are to be educated.

We disagree deeply in our culture (and, more specifically, in our intellectual life) about how to make sense of nature; we disagree about the relationship of science and religion; we disagree about evolution. This being the case, we are obligated to educate students about the alternatives rather than simply train them in any particular approach to making sense of the world, even if we educators, we scientists, are confident that it is the right one.

I am not going to argue that students should be required to learn about intelligent design (ID) theory because it is a better or more reasonable theory than its naturalistic counterparts. I don't know whether it is. Instead, I am going to argue that some study of ID theory should be included in the curriculum because there is substantial disagreement about whether ID is a better theory and the disagreement is of such a kind that educators are obligated to teach students about it.

Before tackling ID theory, however, I want to say a little about the nature of a liberal education and why the study of religion must be included in the K–12 curriculum. I realize that its advocates typically argue that ID theory should be taken seriously as a scientific theory, not as theology. Nonetheless, I want to locate my topic in a larger context in a way I hope will prove to be helpful.[1]

I

There are, I think, three compelling arguments for requiring serious study of religion in public schools (and public universities)—what I will call the educational argument, the civic or justice argument, and the constitutional argument. I would like to emphasize that these arguments are secular arguments. I have no religious agenda. I also note that these arguments are meant to stake out common ground on which we might stand together in constructing a system of public education. My conception of education is, I believe, the least controversial position all things considered.

Before I sketch these arguments, let me say just a little about how seriously religion is now taken in public schools. Over the last decade, I have reviewed eighty-two high school textbooks in a variety of disciplines (including the sciences) and the national contents standards in eleven subject areas (again, including the sciences) for their treatment of religion.[2] I suspect that few readers will be surprised to learn that religion is rarely taken seriously in the texts or in the standards. Among the standards, only the civics and history standards take religion seriously—though civics texts are abysmal in their treatment of religion. History texts, by contrast, have a good deal to say about religion—at least in the context of distant history. But, like the history standards, the texts have less and less to say about religion as they approach the last several centuries. This isn't all that surprising in that our civilization has become increasingly secular over the last several centuries, though I think both the texts and the standards fall well short of giving religion its due in the modern world.

While history texts say a fair amount about religion in the context of ancient, medieval, and early modern history, they are, nonetheless, fully secular texts in the sense that they interpret history in exclusively secular categories. Within the Jewish, Christian, and Islamic traditions, by contrast, history is understood as the working out of God's purposes; indeed, God intervenes in history at various times and in various ways. Even if one is a liberal and reads such intervention mythically rather than in terms of literal history, there is still a religious meaning to history that the texts ignore. That is, history texts teach students how to think in secular ways about religion; they do not teach students religious ways of thinking about history.

To see why this is important let me draw a distinction between teaching about subjects, on the one hand, and teaching disciplines, on the other. Approaching history as a subject, we might interpret it in a variety of ways, religious as well as secular. But schools don't teach the subject of history, they teach the discipline of history. They teach students to make sense of history as contemporary secular historians make sense of it. And so it is with other "subjects" of the curriculum. Schools don't teach students about the subject of economics, for example, a subject about which there is an extensive and rich religious literature; instead, they teach the discipline of neo-classical economic theory, according to which people are self-interested utility-maximizers and the economic domain is the scene of competition by atomistic individuals for scarce resources—a view found in no religious tradition.

Now, it is often thought that a liberal education is one that requires students to study a variety of subjects. No doubt this is right so far as it goes, but a good liberal education must also require that students learn about various ways of making sense of those different subjects. Indeed, it will introduce students to the major ways that humankind has developed for making sense of the world.

I don't have the space to flesh out all of the reasons for this conception of liberal education. Let me simply say that if students are to think critically when we disagree, they must learn about the alternatives. One can't think critically about what it means to be a Democrat unless one also understands something about what it means to be a Republican; one can't think critically about capitalism unless one understands something of the alternatives to capitalism.

If this is the case, then public education is profoundly illiberal in failing to include religious interpretations of the subjects that comprise the curriculum. Indeed, it actively discourages critical thinking by failing to provide students any critical distance on the secular ways of thinking and living that they are taught to accept uncritically in their various courses.

It is not enough—it is nowhere near enough—to teach students about religion in the context of history. In fact, doing just this conveys the idea that religion is a thing of the past. The curricular conversation should reflect to some considerable extent our contemporary cultural conversations about history, psychology, economics, politics, morality, sexuality, and nature—conversations in which we hear, if we listen with any care, a variety of religious as well as secular voices. To filter those religious voices out of the curricular conversation is a profoundly illiberal act. I will put it in this way: we don't educate students about most subjects; rather, we train them to think in secular ways about them.

This, then, is the educational argument: when we disagree deeply about subjects of importance, students must learn about the contending ways of thinking about them. As the literary critic Gerald Graff puts it, we must "teach the conflicts."[3]

Second, it is politically unjust to leave religious voices out of the curriculum. Consider an analogy. We would be rightly appalled if a public school taught only the views of Republicans (or Democrats), ignoring the opposing party. As I have suggested, there are educational reasons for teaching students about both political parties: doing so enables them to think in informed and critical ways about the world of politics. But there are also civic reasons, reasons of justice, for doing so. Public schools must take the public seriously. They cannot become the political or ideological tool of any particular faction of the public. As a matter of justice, public schools must be built on common ground. But the only way to find common ground when we disagree—as we do about politics—is to include all of the contending political voices in the curricular conversation. We treat each other with respect, as a democracy requires, when we listen to each other, when we teach the conflicts.

Consider another analogy. A generation ago texts and curricula said virtually nothing about women, blacks, and members of minority subcultures. Hardly anyone would now say that this was just, a matter of benign neglect as it were. We now—most of us—realize that this was a form of discrimination, of educational disenfranchisement. And so it is with religious subcultures; religious parents are now, in effect, educationally disenfranchised; their ways of thinking and living aren't taken seriously. The curricular silencing of religious cultures is, in effect, an act of political oppression.

Third, it is unconstitutional to ignore religion. It is, of course, uncontroversial that it is permissible, constitutionally, to teach about religion in public schools when done properly. No Supreme Court justice has ever held otherwise. But I want to make a stronger argument.

For the past fifty years the Court has been clear that public schools must be neutral in matters of religion—in two senses. Schools must be neutral among religions (they can't favor Protestants over Catholics or Christians over Jews); and they must be neutral between religion and nonreligion. Schools can't promote religion; they can't proselytize; they can't conduct religious exercises. Of course, neutrality is a two-edged sword. Just as schools can't favor religion over nonreligion, neither can they favor nonreligion over religion. As Justice Hugo Black put it in the seminal 1947 *Everson* ruling, "State power is no more to be used so as to handicap religions than it is to favor them."[4] Similarly, in his majority opinion in *Abington Township v. Schempp* (1963), Justice Tom Clark wrote that schools can't favor "those who believe in no religion over those who do believe." And in a concurring opinion, Justice Arthur Goldberg warned that an "untutored devotion to the concept of neutrality" can lead to a "pervasive devotion to the secular and a passive, or even active, hostility to the religious."[5]

Of course, this is just what has happened. An "untutored" and naive conception of neutrality has led educators to ban smoking guns, explicit hostility to religion, when the hostility has been philosophically rather more subtle—though no less substantial for that.

No doubt many of the particular claims made by scientists and secular scholars can be reconciled with most traditional Western religions; it is at the level of theories and, still more deeply, of philosophical presuppositions or worldviews that they are often in tension or conflict; we teach students to interpret experiences and evidence in secular rather than religious ways.

There is no such thing as a neutral point of view. The only way to be neutral, when all ground is contested ground, is to be fair to the alternatives, taking everyone seriously. That is, given the Court's long-standing interpretation of the Establishment Clause, it is mandatory for public schools to require the study of religion if they require the study of disciplines that cumulatively lead to a "pervasive devotion to the secular"—as they do.

I hope it is clear now why I suggested that my arguments define common ground amid our differences about religion. That is, the educational, civic, and constitutional arguments are each inclusive; they each require that everyone be taken seriously. And, in turn, they provide a reason for everyone to support public education—for everyone's voice will be included in the curricular conversation.

II

So how do we be religiously neutral? What would a politically just, liberal education look like regarding religion? Needless to say, a great deal depends on the age and maturity of students. I'm not going to say anything about elementary education but simply sketch the two-prong approach that should characterize the high school curriculum.

First, students should learn something about religious ways of thinking about any subject that is religiously controversial in the relevant courses. So, for example, an economics text should include a chapter in which secular social scientific ways of understanding human nature, values, and the economic domain of life are contrasted with religious alternatives. Indeed, every text should provide students with historical and philosophical perspectives on the subject at hand, establishing connections and tensions with other disciplines and domains of the culture—including religion. A liberal education is a conversation, not a sequence of disciplinary monologues.

I am not arguing for a "balanced-treatment" or "equal-time" requirement in particular courses. Economics courses need not become courses in moral theology. In any case, given their competence, economics teachers are not likely to be prepared to deal with a variety of religious ways of approaching their subject. At most, they can provide a minimal fairness.

A robust fairness, by contrast, is possible only if students are required to study religious as well as secular ways of making sense of the world in some depth in courses devoted to the study of religion. Indeed, a good liberal education should require at least one-year-long high school course in religious studies (with other courses, I would hope, available as electives). The primary goal of such a course should be to provide students with a sufficiently intensive exposure to religious ways of thinking and living to enable them actually to understand religion (rather than simply know a few historical facts about religion). It should expose students to scriptural texts, but it should also use primary sources that enable students to understand how contemporary theologians and writers within religious traditions make sense of those subjects in the curriculum—morality, sexuality, history, psychology, economics, and nature—that they will be taught to interpret in secular categories in their other courses.

Obviously, major reforms in teacher education are necessary if religion is to be taken seriously across the curriculum, as is a new generation of textbooks sensitive to religion. No doubt many will find such reforms unlikely. Of course, several decades ago textbooks and curricula said little about women and minority cultures. Several decades ago, few universities had departments of religious studies. Now multicultural education is commonplace, and most universities have departments of religious studies. Things change.

III

All right, now let's hone in on religion and science. First, I note the extraordinarily lively conversation among scholars and intellectuals in our culture about the relationship of religion and science. Too often the media version of this conversation reduces it to a polarized battle over evolution between fundamentalists and all the rest of us reasonable folk. But there are at least ten or twenty, not just two, religious positions on evolution; there are theologically liberal as well as fundamentalist responses to neo-Darwinism. And, of course, the evolution question is only one of many about the relationship of science and religion.

So what does it mean to be (liberally) educated against the background of this cultural conversation? What does civic justice require? What is constitutionally required? Well, if students are to think critically, if schools are to treat different cultural traditions with respect, if education is to be religiously neutral, then, when we disagree, as we do about the relationship of religion and science, students should learn about the nature of the disagreement; they should hear the contending voices; they should be taught the conflicts.

No doubt students don't need to learn about every cultural controversy, only the important ones. But this is clearly an important one—one might even say that it is of cosmic importance. I won't belabor this point.[6]

The curriculum must initiate students into our cultural conversation. But where in the curriculum should this take place? The usual answer is that students should learn about science in science classes and religion somewhere else—probably in a social studies class. Of course, there are no social studies courses now where students can learn anything about religious ways of interpreting nature. But even if there were, this wouldn't absolve science texts and courses of the responsibility to be part of the conversation.

Why? The purpose of high school science courses should not be to train scientists but to educate students by initiating them into our ongoing cultural conversation about how to make sense of the world. Science texts do not now convey to students anything of the controversial nature of this

conversation. We typically teach science as one more disciplinary monologue that students must listen to uncritically. By refusing to take seriously
contending interpretations of nature we teach science, in effect, as a matter
of authority, and students typically come to accept the claims of science as
a matter of faith in the scientific tradition rather than of critical reason.

Science texts typically include a perfunctory chapter on scientific
method, but these chapters never include any substantive discussion of the
relationship of religion to scientific method; indeed, rarely do they say anything about religion at all. When they do, it is usually to affirm a two-
worlds view, according to which science and religion are conceptual apples
and oranges. (This is also the official view of the National Association of Biology Teachers and the National Academy of Sciences.)[7] Because they are
assumed to be incommensurable activities, the authors of science texts are
presumably absolved of the responsibility to say anything about religion.
Of course, the two-worlds view of the relationship is deeply controversial
and itself needs critical discussion. In any case, the nature of the relationship is a theological or philosophical problem of a kind that can't be settled
scientifically. Simply to proclaim the two-worlds solution is an act of intellectual imperialism.

Science texts should include a substantive chapter on the various ways
of relating science and religion in our contemporary cultural conversation,
and when they deal with religiously controversial topics (like evolution, or
the origins of life, or the Big Bang, or ecology, or the relationship of the
brain and the mind), they must tell students enough about the conversation to enable them to make some sense of it. Texts must alert students to
the fact that they are about to study something religiously controversial.
The point isn't to convert science courses into theology courses; it is to locate scientific interpretations of nature in the context of our larger cultural
conversation; it is to transform a monologue into a discussion.

If students are to think critically, they must learn what is controversial—
and why. They must know something of the contending alternatives. It is
also tremendously important, however, that the alternatives are not presented in the abstract, but in context. So, for example, creation science,
theories of intelligent design, theological accounts of evolution, and neo-
Darwinism aren't simply items on a cafeteria line that students should be
free to choose depending on their tastes. If they are to make educated
judgments about the alternatives, they should understand how widely held
the different views are and within which scientific and religious traditions.
Which are consensus views, which are controversial views, and for whom?

And what can advocates of each view say in defense of that view or in criticism of its competitors? I have elsewhere called the relevant governing principle "The Principle of Cultural Location and Weight." This principle seems to me to be of enormous importance, yet it is rarely followed. In general, if students are to make informed and reasoned judgments, they must have some sense of where alternative theories acquire their authority, of what traditions are they a part, and how controversial they are within those traditions and within our culture.

Clearly, there is no constitutional problem with teaching students about religious interpretations of nature (neutrally) in public schools, though one might wonder whether this is permissible in science courses. The Supreme Court's *Edwards v. Aguillard* (1987) decision has often been read to ban teaching about religion in science courses. In *Edwards,* the Court struck down Louisiana's "balanced-treatment" act, which required that students be taught creation science if they were taught "evolution science." Why was the act unconstitutional? The purpose of the act, Justice William Brennan wrote for the Court, was to shore up fundamentalist Christianity, and this violated the neutrality required by the Establishment Clause—and he cited a paper trail of comments from Louisiana legislators that made it clear that their purpose was to promote conservative Christianity.[8]

Now the Court has traditionally held that a religious purpose need not invalidate a law so long as there is also a good secular purpose for it. Justice Brennan could find no secular purpose for the Louisiana law, but, of course, there might well be a good secular purpose in requiring students to learn something about religious ways of interpreting nature. I have argued that a good liberal education requires it. If students are to think in an informed and critical way about matters of controversy and importance (like the origins of the universe and life), they must be sensitive to religious alternatives to secular ways of making sense of nature and the world and the various ways in which science and religion are understood to relate to each other.

Indeed, because the Establishment Clause itself requires public schools (as governmental agencies) to be religiously neutral and because the only way to make sense of neutrality is in terms of fairness to the contending alternatives, schools must teach students about various religious ways of making sense of nature if they teach ways of thinking about the world that are critical of religion.

Everyone agrees that science is critical of fundamentalism, but the scientific and educational establishments typically argue that there is no conflict

between science and religion properly understood, true religion. But this is
itself a theological judgment, and a controversial one at that. In any case,
should it be permissible for schools to undermine conservative religion so
long as we can reconcile science and one variety of liberal theology? Is this
neutral among religions—as the Establishment Clause requires? Of course,
some liberal theologians also have difficulty with neo-Darwinism and its
purposeless conception of nature. By keeping students ignorant not just of
creationism and conservative religion but of liberal ways of integrating science and religion, science education nurtures a secular mentality and profoundly biases the thinking of students.

Clearly, religious neutrality doesn't give religious folks a veto over evolution. Rather, neutrality requires that students learn about modern science (including, of course, neo-Darwinism) and various religious ways of
conceiving nature.[9]

Now I cannot see any principled reason why it should be permissible to
teach about religion in a social studies class but not in a science class when
religion is relevant to the subject under discussion and is not introduced
gratuitously but serves the purposes of a genuinely liberal education. In
fact, I do not find anything in Justice Brennan's ruling in *Edwards,* or in
any other Supreme Court ruling, that would prohibit this. Hence, I take it
that with the proper purposes, where we teach about religion is an educational rather than a constitutional question.

It is also worth noting that the National Science Education Standards
provide at least a small opening for the discussion of religion. The seventh
of eight proposed content standards requires that science education "give
students a means to understand and act on personal and social issues" such
as health, sexuality, and the environment, all areas of our social life where,
the standards acknowledge, religious beliefs and values are relevant. Moreover, because science provides no moral direction, "understanding science
alone will not resolve local, national, or global challenges."[10] Perhaps,
then, science should be studied in tandem with ethics and religion?

The eighth content standard requires that students learn that "science
reflects its history and is an ongoing, changing enterprise." Indeed, "scientists are influenced by societal, cultural, and personal beliefs and ways of
viewing the world. Science is not separate from society but rather science is
a part of society." Consequently, students should learn the role "that science has played in the development of various cultures." Not surprisingly,
then, teachers need to be able to make "conceptual connections" to "other
school subjects."[11] Arguably, the implication of these claims is that science

should be taught not as a disciplinary monologue but in cultural context, developing conceptual connections to other areas of the curriculum and other domains of our culture, perhaps even including religion, as part of a good liberal education.

That said, I remain skeptical that science texts will ever devote any substantial space to the discussion of religious alternatives. This, together with the fact that science teachers are unlikely to be educated to understand the variety of religious ways of making sense of nature, means that the "natural inclusion" of religion in science courses will never yield more than a nominal fairness, and there will be a need for a course in religious studies that deals with religious interpretations of nature, among other things, in depth.

IV

Of course, advocates of ID theory typically claim that it is a scientific theory—at least when science is freed of its philosophical commitment to naturalism. Its critics in the scientific establishment argue that because it appeals to supernatural causes it is thinly veiled religion. The first point I want to make is that even if ID theory is a religious theory, this does not mean, given my argument so far, that it shouldn't be discussed as an alternative to naturalistic theories in science courses.

The fact that ID theory is controversial provides a reason for including it in the discussion, for it is, I have argued, the task of a liberal education to teach the conflicts. It is true that not all controversies warrant a place in the curriculum; they must be important controversies. But I think it fair to say that it is important both scientifically and religiously to know if there is scientific evidence for design in nature—and, perhaps, for the existence of God. The religious importance of ID theory is relevant to whether it is discussed in science texts and courses because, as I have argued, as part of a liberal education science courses must participate in curricular conversation with other disciplines and other domains of our culture.

But, of course, there is a huge difference between mentioning ID theory as a religious theory and taking it seriously as a scientific theory, engaging it, exploring what can be said for and against it scientifically, considering it a contender for the truth. Do we include ID theory in the conversation only as a theory held by some theologians and philosophers?

Let me suggest two arguments for taking ID theory seriously as science. First, what should be taken seriously as science is in part, at least, a matter

of what good scientists take seriously, rather than a matter of a priori doctrines about the nature of science. On this argument, it seems relevant to
ask how many scientists take the theory seriously. What is their standing
within establishment science? What kinds of research have they done? To
what extent can the theory be integrated into accepted science? To what
extent is it an ad hoc theory? Does it grow honestly grow out of the evidence rather than out of prior ideological or religious commitments? (And,
correlatively, does establishment science grow honestly out of the evidence
rather than out of prior ideological or philosophical commitments?)

As an outsider, I don't feel particularly competent to address these questions, though it appears to me that the scientific and philosophical sophis-
tication of ID theorists puts them in a quite different class from astrologers
and old-fashioned creation scientists.

My more fundamental argument is philosophical.[12] Modern science has
prided itself on its openness to new evidence and to the potential falsification of its theories. There is, nonetheless, a kind of scientific fundamentalism in which methodological naturalism functions much as does Scripture
for religious fundamentalists: just as fundamentalists are not open (in principle) to scientific evidence that falsifies Scripture, so methodological naturalists are not open (in principle) to nonnaturalistic evidence, claims, or
theories that might be taken to falsify established science.[13] There is, no
doubt, a good reason why scientists should adhere to a methodological
naturalism: science owes much of its progress over the past several centuries to the fact that it has excluded supernatural causes and design from
its explanations. As a result, most scientists have developed a faith—that is,
a trust—that methodological naturalism will, in the long run, prove adequate to the task of discovering the basic structure of nature and answering
every question about it.

But unless the nature and limitations of this methodological naturalism
are themselves the subject of discussion, unless methodological naturalism
is itself open to potential falsification, this commitment will be, in effect, an
uncritical faith—and surely there is some risk in uncritically trusting that
all of reality can be explained in naturalistic categories. (Of course, naturalism is deeply controversial among even secular intellectuals in dealing with
some aspects of reality—the mind and morality, for example.)

Now it may be that a measure of faith is essential to the practice of any
intellectual tradition (I suspect that it is), but public schools should not be
in the business of nurturing faith, whether it be in religion, politics, economics, or science. A liberal education should encourage critical thinking,

and this can only be done when we are willing to lay bare and question our fundamental assumptions. Certainly one of the most important of these assumptions is the adequacy of scientific method as presently conceived. When (if at all) might it need revision? In what intellectual contexts is the use of (traditional) scientific method controversial?

ID theory—like natural theology more generally—nicely points to one of the fundamental problems in our intellectual life: the all too uncritical compartmentalization of knowledge in academic disciplines. Methodological naturalism and the old two-worlds view of science and religion force science and religion into separate procrustean beds when, arguably, they are (admittedly somewhat strange) bedfellows. This is, as I have suggested, a problem with regard to virtually every discipline. Economists are not about to give up their commitment to methodological naturalism either, and academic historians are unlikely to see any evidence of God's hand in the movement of history given their methodological commitments.

My argument, then, is not that ID theory must be included in science courses because it is good science or because it is a better theory than neo-Darwinism or because science must be separated from methodological naturalism. Rather, it is that each of these claims is part and parcel of deep and important controversies in our cultural and intellectual life, and students must be taught the conflicts.

So, for the educational, political, and constitutional reasons I have mentioned, it cannot be the proper task of public schools to encourage, much less uncritically encourage, students to accept neo-Darwinism and methodological naturalism, secular rather than religious interpretations of nature—or of any subject—when we deeply disagree. Of course, students must learn what the great majority of scientists take to be good science, but they must also learn where the points of controversy are and something about the alternatives. They must learn something of the important and lively conversation about the relationship of science and religion going on in our culture. And still more generally, they must learn about the potential points of overlap, tension, and conflict between secular and various religious ways of making sense of all of the subjects of the curriculum, science included.

Notes

1. For background and more extensive discussions of some of the themes in this chapter, see Warren A. Nord, *Religion and American Education:*

    Rethinking a National Dilemma (Chapel Hill: University of North Carolina Press, 1995); Warren A. Nord and Charles C. Haynes, *Taking Religion Seriously across the Curriculum* (Alexandria, Va.: ASCD Press, 1998).

2. See Nord, *Religion and American Education*, chap. 4; Nord and Haynes, *Taking Religion Seriously.*

3. See Gerald Graff, *Beyond the Culture Wars* (New York: Norton, 1992).

4. *Everson v. Board of Education*, 330 U.S. 1, 16 (1947).

5. *Abington Township v. Schempp*, 374 U.S. 203, 225, 306 (1963).

6. The important point here is that the curriculum should be driven by what is important in the larger culture rather than what is important in the disciplines only.

7. See the National Association of Biology Teachers, "Statement on Teaching Evolution," (www.nabt.org/oldsite/evolution.html) (n.d.); the National Academy of Sciences, *Teaching about Evolution and the Nature of Science* (Washington, D.C.: National Academy Press, 1998), 58.

8. *Edwards v. Aguillard*, 482 U.S. 578 (1987).

9. The fact that there are many religious ways of conceiving nature is sometimes used to argue that it is impractical, if not impossible, to include them all in the discussion. But there are not so many different kinds of religious alternatives. In any case, it would seem to be educationally and constitutionally important to approximate fairness rather than to disregard it completely.

10. National Research Council, *National Science Education Standards* (Washington, D.C.: National Academy Press, 1996), 107, 197–98, 199.

11. Ibid., 107, 201, 59.

12. Here I owe a great deal to Phillip Johnson, though my more fundamental debt is to the philosopher E. M. Adams. For Johnson, see "Evolution on Trial: The Establishment of Naturalism," in *First Things* (Oct. 1990), and *Reason in the Balance: The Case Against Naturalism in Science, Law and Education* (Downers Grove, Ill.: InterVarsity Press, 1995). For Adams, see *Religion and Cultural Freedom* (Philadelphia: Temple University Press, 1993).

13. I develop this argument at much greater length in *Religion and American Education*, 179–87.

Teaching the Controversy:
Is It Science, Religion, or Speech?

David DeWolf, Stephen C. Meyer, and
Mark E. DeForrest

❉ ❉ ❉

One can hardly imagine a more contentious issue in the American culture wars than the debate over how biological origins should be
taught in public schools. On the one hand, the National Academy of Sciences, the National Center for Science Education, and the American Civil
Liberties Union have insisted that any departure from a strictly Darwinian
approach to the issue constitutes an attack on science and even an unconstitutional intrusion of religion into the public school science curriculum.
On the other hand, many parents and religious activists have long rebelled
against what they perceive as a dogmatic attack on their religious beliefs.
Beginning in the 1970s, such activists sought to promote a Bible-based
curriculum—known as scientific creationism—as either a complement or
an alternative to the standard Darwinist curriculum advocated by the National Academy of Sciences and others. So the battle lines were drawn.

When confronted with a conflict between establishment science and religious fundamentalism, most lawyers have assumed that the law clearly
favors the former. Although the creationists won some battles in state legislatures during the 1980s, they clearly lost the war in the courts. In

McLean v. Arkansas Board of Education and *Edwards v. Aguillard,* the courts ruled that teaching "scientific creationism" or "creation-science" would have resulted in an unconstitutional advancement of religion.[1] Media reports have portrayed all subsequent local controversies as reruns of those earlier battles, some even invoking imagery from the Scopes trial in the 1920s.[2]

Such reports have served to obscure rather than illuminate the legal issues that school boards and their lawyers now increasingly face. Not only are the legal issues surrounding the *Edwards* decision more complex than often reported, but the challenge to the Darwinian curriculum in public education has changed. Now, in the early years of the new century, school board lawyers are far less likely to confront a religion-based challenge to the current biology curriculum than they are to face a situation resembling the one portrayed in the following hypothetical example:

> John Spokes has taught biology for several years at a public high school. He has devoted several class periods to Darwin's theory of evolution and its key concepts, such as natural selection, random mutation, and descent with modification.[3] He also has discussed how the theory of chemical evolution explains the origin of the first life starting from simple chemicals. Spokes provided a standard textbook treatment of these theories, explaining that the evolutionary process is "random and undirected" and occurs "without either plan or purpose," as some textbooks phrase it. [4]
>
> Recently, however, Spokes has encountered increasing criticism of his teaching. Some parents complain that his lectures selectively present the scientific evidence. This disturbs Spokes, and he agrees to read publications critiquing contemporary Darwinian and chemical evolutionary theory. To his surprise, Spokes finds himself impressed with much of what he reads. Articles document serious errors in textbook presentations, errors that overstate the evidential case for neo-Darwinian and chemical evolutionary theory.[5] Other scientific articles suggest that textbooks commit many errors of omission, errors that understate the evidential difficulties with neo-Darwinian claims. Spokes learns for instance about the so-called Cambrian explosion, a term describing the sudden appearance of most of the major animal phyla (or body plans) in the Cambrian period (530 million years ago), in clear contradiction to Darwinian expectations about the fossil record. Spokes also notices that scientists writing in technical journals openly discuss the challenge that these data pose to the neo-Darwinian prediction of gradual step-by-step change.[6] Yet Spokes knows that most introductory biology texts do not even mention the Cambrian explosion, let alone that it might challenge contemporary Darwinism.

Spokes's reading about the Cambrian explosion sensitizes him to another issue, one of definition. He begins to suspect that textbooks have created confusion by using the term *evolution* as though it were a unitary concept, even though it can refer to everything from the universal common ancestry thesis to small-scale change to large-scale innovation via a strictly mindless material mechanism.[7] Moreover, technical literature suggests that although Darwin's mechanism of natural selection acting on random variations explains small-scale "microevolutionary" changes (such as the beak size and shape of the Galapagos finches), it fails to explain the large-scale "macroevolutionary" transformations required to build novel organs, body plans, and morphological structures.[8] Spokes learns about scientists who accept "evolution" in one or more of the senses described above but who do not accept the classical Darwinian explanation of *apparent* design. He notices that many scientists now question whether natural selection (and other similarly naturalistic mechanisms) can explain all instances of "apparent design." Some of these scientists argue that certain features of living systems, such as "irreducibly complex" molecular machines in cells or the "information content of the DNA molecule," suggest *real* design by an intelligent agent. Though not altogether congenial to his own way of thinking, Spokes finds these ideas provocative and fascinating. He admits that the scientists advancing these ideas have excellent credentials and appeal to scientific evidence, not to religious authority.[9]

Spokes finds himself in a quandary. He is unsure how to incorporate what he has read into the way he teaches his high school students. For one thing, he is not politically naive. He has read statements issued by the National Academy of Sciences, the National Association of Biology Teachers, and the American Association for the Advancement of Science, statements that urge him to ignore any criticism of Darwinism as unscientific and religiously motivated.[10] He realizes he may be accused of "attacking science" or "teaching creationism" or even "bringing religion into the science classroom." Still, he finds it troubling that his students learn nothing of important differences of opinion among scientists, and he is confident that, regardless of anyone else's motivation, his motivation is only to "teach the controversy" and to discuss scientific evidence and how it is variously interpreted by different scientists.[11]

Spokes decides that, at a minimum, he must modify his presentation to reflect the additional information and diversity of scientific opinion that he has encountered. In addition to presenting the standard biological and chemical evolutionary theory, he plans four changes in his pedagogy.

First, he wants to correct the blatant factual errors in his textbook that overstate the evidential case for neo-Darwinian and chemical evolutionary theory.

Second, he intends to tell students about the evidential challenges to these theories that current textbooks fail to mention.

Third, he wants to define the term *evolution* without equivocation and to distinguish clearly between those senses of the term that enjoy widespread support among scientists and those that remain controversial, even if only among a minority of scientists.

Finally, he wants to tell his students that a growing minority of scientists do see evidence of real, not just apparent, design in biological systems. Wisely, Spokes decides to bring his plan to his principal, and ultimately to the school board, to be sure he is on safe ground. Is he?

Although this portrait of Spokes is hypothetical, the issues it raises are not.[12] An increasing number of teachers around the country have begun to implement similar changes in their own biology curriculum, often, though not always, creating controversy.[13] School boards, fearing both ideological strife and costly litigation, have seldom known how to react to these teachers. On the one hand, forbidding any dissent from Darwinian theory smacks of censorship. On the other hand, even school board members sympathetic to such changes assume that federal law forbids science educators to deviate from an exclusively Darwinian curriculum. In short, many school boards do not know what the law allows.

This discussion will attempt to clarify what the law does allow teachers to teach in their biology classrooms. In the process, it will answer three key questions necessary to deciding the legal status of Spokes's proposed curriculum. These are:

Is It Science? Are Spokes's intended changes in his biology curriculum scientific? Is his plan to correct and critique textbook presentations of neo-Darwinism scientific? Are the alternative theories that Spokes wants to present, including the theory of intelligent design, scientific?

Is It Religion? Does Spokes's plan to correct and critique textbook presentations of neo-Darwinism constitute an establishment of religion? Does Spokes's plan to expose his students to evidence of design and design theory qualify as teaching religion? Does the First Amendment prevent the presentation of this point of view?

Is It Speech? Do Spokes's plans to correct and critique textbook presentations of neo-Darwinism, and to expose students to the alternative theory of intelligent design, enjoy protection under the First Amendment, either in the prohibition of viewpoint discrimination or as an exercise of academic freedom?

Before addressing those questions, however, we must first place them in a broader historical context.

I. A Brief History of the Origins Controversy
A. Classical Science-Based Design Arguments

Prior to publication of the *Origin of Species* by Charles Darwin in 1859, many Western thinkers, for more than 2,000 years, had answered the question "How did life arise?" by invoking the activity of a purposeful designer or creator. Design arguments based on observations of the natural world were made by Greek and Roman philosophers such as Plato and Cicero, by Jewish philosophers such as Maimonides, and by Christian thinkers such as Thomas Aquinas.[14]

The idea of design also figured centrally in the modern scientific revolution (1500–1700).[15] As historians of science have often pointed out, many of the founders of early modern science assumed that the natural world *was* intelligible. They assumed that it had been designed by a rational mind. In addition, many individual scientists—Johannes Kepler (1571–1650) in astronomy, John Ray (1627–1705) in biology, Robert Boyle (1627–1691) in chemistry—made specific design arguments based on empirical discoveries in their respective fields.[16] The design tradition attained an almost majestic rhetorical quality in the writings of Sir Isaac Newton (1642–1727), who made elegant and sophisticated arguments based on biological, physical, and astronomical discoveries. Writing in the General Scholium to his *Principia*, Newton suggested that the stability of the planetary system depended not only on the regular action of universal gravitation but also on the precise initial positioning of the planets and comets in relation to the sun. As he explained: "[T]hough these bodies may, indeed, continue in their orbits by the mere laws of gravity, yet they could by no means have at first derived the regular position of the orbits themselves from those laws. . . . [Thus] [t]his most beautiful system of the sun, planets, and comets, could only proceed from the counsel and dominion of an intelligent and powerful Being."[17] Or as he wrote in the *Opticks:* "How came the Bodies of Animals to be contrived with so much Art, and for what ends were their several parts? Was the Eye contrived without Skill in Opticks, and the Ear without Knowledge of Sounds? . . . And these things being rightly dispatch'd, does it not appear from Phænomena that there is a Being incorporeal, living, intelligent, omnipresent."[18]

Despite the objections of some enlightenment philosophers, notably David Hume (1711–1776), science-based design arguments continued well into the early nineteenth century, especially in biology. William Paley's

(1743–1805) *Natural Theology,* published in 1803 (several years after Hume's criticism of the design argument), is the most notable example. Paley's work had cataloged a host of biological systems that suggested the work of a superintending intelligence. He argued that the astonishing complexity and superb adaptation of means to ends in such systems could not originate strictly through the blind forces of nature, any more than could a complex machine such as a pocket watch.[19]

B. Darwin and the Eclipse of Design

Acceptance of the design argument finally began to abate during the late nineteenth century with the emergence of increasingly powerful materialistic explanations of apparent design, particularly Charles Darwin's theory of evolution by natural selection.[20] Darwin argued in 1859 that living organisms only *appeared* to be designed. To make this case, he proposed a concrete mechanism, natural selection acting on random variations, that could explain the adaptation of organisms to their environment as well as other evidences of apparent design, without actually invoking an intelligent or directing agency. Darwin saw that natural forces would accomplish the work of a human breeder and thus that blind nature could come to mimic, over time, the action of a selecting intelligence: a designer. If the origin of biological organisms could be explained naturalistically, as Darwin argued, then explanations invoking an intelligent designer were unnecessary and even vacuous.[21]

Even so, natural selection as a causal mechanism had a mixed reception in the immediate post-Darwinian period. As historian of biology Peter Bowler has noted, classical Darwinism entered a period of eclipse, in part because Darwin lacked a theory of the origin and transmission of new heritable variation. By the late 1930s and 1940s, however, when developments in a number of fields helped to clarify the nature of genetic variation, natural selection was revived as the main engine of evolutionary change.[22] The resuscitation of the variation/natural selection mechanism by modern genetics and population genetics became known as the neo-Darwinian synthesis. According to the new synthetic theory of evolution, the mechanism of natural selection acting on random variations (especially small-scale mutations) sufficed to account for the origin of novel biological forms and structures. Small-scale microevolutionary changes could be extrapolated indefinitely to account for large-scale macroevolutionary development. With the revival of natural selection, the neo-Darwinists would assert, like Darwinists before them, that they had found a "designer substitute" that could explain the appearance of design in biology as a result of the action of a wholly natural mechanism.[23] As Harvard evolutionary biologist Ernst Mayr has explained, "[T]he real core of Darwinism . . . is the theory of natural selection. This theory is so important for the Darwinian because it permits the explanation of adaptation, the 'design' of the natural theologian, by natural means."[24]

C. Problems with the Neo-Darwinian Synthesis and the Reemergence of Design

In the late 1960s, the modern synthesis that emerged during the 1930s and 1940s began to unravel in the face of new developments in paleontology, systematics, molecular biology, genetics, and developmental biology. Since then a series of technical articles and books—including *Evolution: A Theory in Crisis* (1986) by Michael Denton; *Darwinism: The Refutation of a Myth* (1987) by Søren Løvtrup; *The Origins of Order* (1993) by Stuart A. Kauffman; *How the Leopard Changed Its Spots* (1994) by Brian C. Goodwin; *Reinventing Darwin* (1995) by Niles Eldredge; *The Shape of Life* (1996) by Rudolf A. Raff; *Darwin's Black Box* (1996) by Michael Behe; *The Origin of Animal Body Plans* (1997) by Wallace Arthur; *Sudden Origins: Fossils, Genes, and the Emergence of Species* (1999) by Jeffrey H. Schwartz—has cast doubt on the creative power of neo-Darwinism's mutation/selection mechanism. As a result, a search for alternative naturalistic mechanisms of innovation has ensued with, as yet, no obvious success or consensus. So common are doubts about the creative capacity of the selection/mutation mechanism, neo-Darwinism's designer substitute, that prominent spokespersons for evolutionary theory must now periodically assure the public that "just because we don't know *how* evolution occurred, does not justify doubt about *whether* it occurred."[25] As Niles Eldredge wrote as early as 1982, "most observers see the current situation in evolutionary theory—where the object is to explain how, not if, life evolves—as bordering on total chaos."[26] Or as Stephen Gould wrote in 1980, "the neo-Darwinism synthesis is effectively dead, despite its continued presence as textbook orthodoxy."[27]

By now, scientists writing in technical journals across the subdisciplines of biology have questioned neo-Darwinian theory on many evidential and theoretical grounds, including:

1. The neo-Darwinian mechanism of natural selection acting on random variations does not seem sufficient to produce:

(a) novel specified genetic information;[28]

(b) "irreducibly complex," "functionally integrated" molecular machines and systems (such as bacterial motors, signal transduction circuits, or the blood-clotting system);[29]

(c) novel organs and morphological structures (such as wings, feathers, eyes, echo location, the amniotic egg, skin, nervous systems, and multicellularity); and[30]

(d) novel body plans.[31]

2. Many significant mechanisms of evolutionary change do not depend on random mutations as the neo-Darwinian mechanism requires but instead seem to be directed by preprogrammed responses to environmental stimuli.[32]

3. The pattern of sudden appearance, missing transitional forms, and "stasis" in the fossil record—as seen in the Cambrian explosion, the "marine Mesozoic revolution," and the "big bloom" of angiosperm plant life, for example—do not conform to neo-Darwinian expectations about the history of life.[33]

4. Evidence from developmental biology suggests clear limits to the amount of evolutionary change that organisms can undergo, casting doubt on the Darwinian theory of common descent and suggesting a reason for morphological stasis in the fossil record.[34]

5. Many homologous structures (and even some proteins) derive from non-homologous genes, while many dissimilar structures derive from similar genes, in both cases contradicting neo-Darwinian expectations.[35]

6. The (inferred) developmental programs among the metazoan animals of the Cambrian period are strikingly dissimilar (or "not conserved"), contrary to neo-Darwinian expectations.[36]

7. The genetic code has not proven to be "universal," contrary to neo-Darwinian expectations based on the theory of universal common descent.[37]

Further, biochemists and origin-of-life researchers have challenged the standard Oparin/Miller chemical evolutionary theory for the origin of the first life for many reasons, including:

1. Geochemists have failed to find evidence of the nitrogen-rich "prebiotic soup" required by the standard chemical evolutionary model.[38]

2. The remains of single-celled organisms in the very oldest rocks testify that life emerged more quickly than the standard model (or any other model) envisions or can explain.[39]

3. Geological and geochemical evidence suggests that prebiotic atmospheric conditions were hostile, not friendly, to the production of amino acids and other essential building blocks of life.[40]

4. In virtue of (3), experiments such as Stanley Miller's, allegedly simulating the origin of prebiotic building blocks have no relevance to actual early earth processes.[41]

5. Origin-of-life researchers lack plausible explanations for the origin of the specified information in DNA necessary to build essential proteins.[42]

6. Origin-of-life researchers lack plausible explanations for the origin of the functionally integrated information-processing system present in even the simplest cells.[43]

High school and college biology textbooks have almost universally failed to report these and other difficulties found in recent technical literature.[44] Instead, standard textbooks continue to affirm both neo-Darwinian and chemical evolutionary theory unequivocally and without qualification. Moreover, as noted in the Spokes example, many texts continue to include significant factual errors, either of omission or commission. Although Spokes is hypothetical, the problems in the texts are not.[45]

II. May Spokes Teach Criticism?

It may seem obvious that there can be no rationally defensible grounds for preventing teachers from exposing students to well-documented scientific critiques of a theory or obsolete textbook material. Nevertheless, teachers like Spokes often feel reluctant to break with textbook orthodoxy and expose students to articles and other supplementary materials documenting problems with neo-Darwinism or its textbook presentation. Their reluctance is understandable. Many official spokespersons for an exclusively Darwinist curriculum now treat any criticism of neo-Darwinian (or chemical evolutionary) theory as tantamount to an attack on science itself. Others assume that criticism necessarily derives from religious motives, equating any critique with advocacy of "creationism."

That rhetorical strategy fails for several reasons. First, it implicitly equates a particular theory of biological origins, albeit a long dominant one, with the science of biology itself. In no other field would such a self-serving rhetoric stand unchallenged for long. Imagine Freudians equating psychology with the Freudian theory of the mind or advocates of phlogiston equating their theory with the field of chemistry itself. Science has long been characterized by theoretical competition among multiple, competing hypotheses and explanations. Science requires criticism as well as the articulation and defense of reigning theories. Thus, biologists who seek to insulate their preferred theories from critique by rhetorical gerrymandering—that is, by equating dominant evolutionary theories with science itself and then treating all criticism of such theories as "unscientific"—are themselves acting in a profoundly unscientific manner.

Note, second, the list of evidential difficulties cited above. Each can be found in standard scientific journals: *Paleobiology, Developmental Biology, Natural History.* Of course, some religiously motivated creationists may want to make polemical use of evidential difficulties. Yet that does not mean that scientific critique of neo-Darwinism necessarily conceals a religious motive—if motive is even germane to deciding the scientific legitimacy of such critique. In any case, the pedagogical issue is not the motive of the critics but the existence of empirical critiques of neo-Darwinian and chemical evolutionary theory that textbooks do not report to students. Our teacher, Spokes, wants to eliminate that disparity between textbook presentations and current scientific discussion of the issue. Such a proposal hardly constitutes "religious" or "unscientific" activity.

To illustrate this point more concretely, consider an example mentioned above. Origin-of-life researchers now acknowledge that Stanley Miller's famous experiment simulating the production of amino acids under allegedly prebiotic early earth conditions does not support chemical evolutionary theory. Origin-of-life scientists, including Miller himself, now admit that no evidence supports the strongly "reducing" mixture of gases that Miller assumed in his 1953 experiment.[46] Indeed, considerable geochemical evidence now contradicts that assumption.[47] If simulation experiments are rerun with a more realistic mixture of gases, they do not produce amino acids in any appreciable yields. Yet few introductory biology textbooks report any of these scientific developments.[48]

If Spokes reports these developments, can anyone credibly maintain that he has acted in an "unscientific" or "religious" manner? Instead, Spokes's critics act in a most illiberal way. By stigmatizing critique as either "unscientific" or "religious," advocates for the exclusive presentation of orthodox evolutionary theories discourage teachers from teaching students what scientists actually know and report in their technical journals and encourage instead the presentation of a simplistic caricature of scientific method and origins research.

Of course, some Darwinist advocacy groups have expressed concern that providing critique of, as well as evidence and arguments for, orthodox evolutionary theories would confuse students.[49] But clearly students are not well served by presenting a false picture of agreement where in fact there is controversy. Even a prominent Darwinist, Will Provine, has complained that the failure to present the controversy makes science education deadly dull and robs it of interest that might motivate students.[50] Granted, textbook presentations in many fields fail to capture the richness and detail of front-line research. But errors of fact in biology texts do not seem to reflect mere oversimplifications. Many errors are egregious and easy to correct, and they almost universally overstate the evidential support for orthodox evolutionary theories. Thus, there is every reason to encourage Spokes to speak to students about the existence of evidential criticism of neo-Darwinism in the scientific literature and to correct textbooks where they are clearly in error.

The question of the legitimacy of Spokes's intended curricular change brings up another issue. Recall that he does not intend merely to expose students to scientific critique of neo-Darwinism. He also now intends to teach them about an alternative theory—known as the theory of intelligent design or design theory (sometimes abbreviated simply design)—that directly challenges a key proposition of both neo-Darwinian and chemical evolutionary theory, namely, the denial of actual design in biology. Of course, if the neo-Darwinian mechanism cannot explain the origin of apparent design, as many biologists have argued, some scientists will quite reasonably want to reconsider the possibility of actual (that is, intelligent) design as an alternative explanation. Not surprisingly, many scientists have done exactly that, and teachers like Spokes will increasingly want to tell their students about this development in science.

Nevertheless, Spokes's desire to teach about design raises additional issues. Some have argued that design theory does not qualify as a scientific theory. Others have maintained that it constitutes an establishment of religion, or at least a religious theory. To assess the legality of Spokes's decision requires making an assessment of the scientific and religious status of design theory. Before we can do that, we will review the main tenets and features of the theory.

III. A Brief Introduction to
Contemporary Design Theory

Since the 1980s, a growing number of scientists have asserted that, contrary to neo-Darwinian orthodoxy, nature displays abundant evidence of real, not just apparent, design. These scientists, known as design theorists, advocate an alternative theory of biological origins known as the theory of intelligent design. They have developed design theory in such books as *Darwin's Black Box, The Mystery of Life's Origin, Of Pandas and People, Mere Creation,* and *The Design Inference,* as well as in articles in scientific and technical journals.[51] Design theory holds that intelligent causes rather than undirected natural causes best explain many features of living systems. During recent years, design theorists have developed both a general theory of design detection and many specific empirical arguments to support their views.

A. A Theory of Intelligent Design

Developments in the information sciences have recently made possible the articulation of criteria by which intelligently designed systems can be identified by the kinds of patterns they exhibit. In *The Design Inference,* mathematician and probability theorist William Dembski notes that rational agents often infer or detect the prior activity of other designing minds by the character of the effects they leave behind. Archaeologists assume, for example, that rational agents produced the inscriptions on the Rosetta Stone. Insurance fraud investigators detect certain "cheating patterns" that suggest intentional manipulation of circumstances rather than "natural" disasters. Cryptographers distinguish between random signals and those that carry encoded messages. Dembski shows that recognizing the activity of intelligent agents constitutes a common and fully rational mode of inference.[52]

Dembski then explicates the criteria by which rational agents recognize the effects of other rational agents and distinguish them from the effects of natural causes. He argues that systems or sequences that have the joint properties of "high complexity" (or low probability) and "specification" invariably result from intelligent causes, not from chance or physical-chemical laws.[53] As it turns out, these criteria are equivalent (or "isomorphic") to the notion of specified information or information content. Thus, Dembski's work suggests that "high information content" indicates prior intelligent activity. This theoretical insight comports with common, as well as scientific, experience. Few rational people would, for example, attribute hieroglyphic inscriptions to natural forces such as wind or erosion; instead, they would immediately recognize the activity of intelligent agents. Dembski's discussion shows why: Our reasoning includes a comparative evaluation process that he represents with a device he calls "the explanatory filter." The filter outlines a formal method by which scientists (as well as ordinary people) decide among three different types of explanations: chance, necessity, and design. His "explanatory filter" constitutes, in effect, a scientific method for detecting the effects of intelligence.[54] (Dembski's essay, "Reinstating Design within Science," in the Part III of this volume describes his theory and method of design detection in more detail.)

B. Design Theory: An Empirical Basis?

In addition to making use of a formal theory articulating criteria by which intelligent causes can be detected in the "echo of their effects," design theorists point to specific empirical evidence of design, both in biology and physics. They argue that biological organisms in particular display distinctive features of intelligently designed systems. Many now see especially striking evidence of design in biology, even if much of it is still reported by scientists and journals that presuppose a neo-Darwinian perspective.

For example, in *Darwin's Black Box,* biochemist Michael Behe shows that neo-Darwinists have failed to explain the origin of complex molecular machines in living systems. Behe examines the tiny rotary engines that turn the whiplike flagella of certain bacteria. He shows that the intricate machinery in this molecular motor—including a rotor, a stator, O-rings, bushings, and a drive shaft—requires the coordinated interaction of approximately forty complex protein parts.[55] The absence of any one of these proteins would result in the complete loss of motor function. To suggest that such an "irreducibly complex" engine emerged gradually in a Darwinian fashion strains credulity. Natural selection selects functionally advantageous systems. Yet motor function ensues only *after* all necessary parts have independently self-assembled: an astronomically improbable event.

Thus, Behe insists that Darwinian mechanisms cannot account for the origin of molecular motors and other "irreducibly complex" systems that require the coordinated interaction of multiple, independent protein parts. Instead, he notes that we know of only one cause sufficient to produce functionally integrated, irreducibly complex systems: intelligent design. Whenever we encounter irreducibly complex systems and we know how they arose, invariably a designer played a causal role. Thus, Behe concludes on the basis of our knowledge of present cause-and-effect relationships (in accord with the standard uniformitarian method employed in the historical sciences) that the molecular machines and complex systems we observe in cells can be best explained as the result of an intelligent cause.[56] In brief, molecular motors *appear* designed because they *were* designed. (Behe's essay, "Design in the Details: The Origin of Biomolecular Machines," in Part III makes this case in more detail.)

Behe is not alone in his conclusions. Consider the case of Dean Kenyon. For nearly twenty years, Kenyon was a leading evolutionary theorist who specialized in origin-of-life biology. While at San Francisco State College in 1969, he coauthored *Biochemical Predestination*, a book that defined evolutionary thinking on the origin of life for over a decade. Kenyon's theory attempted to show how complex biomolecules such as proteins and DNA might have "self-organized" via strictly chemical forces.[57] Yet as Kenyon reflected more on developments in biochemistry and molecular biology, he began to question whether undirected chemistry could really produce the information-rich molecules found in even "simple" cells.

Discoveries in molecular biology during the 1950s and 1960s showed that DNA contained the assembly instructions or information necessary to build proteins in the cell. These instructions function in much the same way as software in a machine code. As Richard Dawkins notes, "The machine code of the genes is uncannily computer like."[58] Or, as software innovator Bill Gates notes, "DNA is like a computer program, but far, far more advanced than any software we've ever created."[59] Further, the information in DNA displays both the complexity and specificity of function that, according to Dembski's theory, indicate design.[60] As a result of such evidence, Kenyon and other scientists (notably Charles Thaxton, Walter Bradley, and Roger Olsen) and philosophers of science have concluded that the "specified complexity" or high information content of DNA—like the information in a computer program, an ancient scroll, or a newspaper article—had an intelligent source.[61] (In Part III, Stephen C. Meyer's essay, "DNA and the Origin of Life: Information, Specification, and Explanation," develops this argument in more detail.)

Some scientists and philosophers of science also have argued that the fossil record has also provided new support for design. Fossil studies reveal a biological "big bang" near the beginning of the Cambrian period 530 million years ago. At that time, more than twenty separate major groups of organisms, or phyla (including most of the basic body plans of modern animals), emerged suddenly without clear precursors. Although neo-Darwinian theory requires vast periods of time for the step-by-step development of new biological organs and body plans, fossil finds have repeatedly confirmed a pattern of explosive appearance and prolonged stability in living forms. Moreover, the fossil record also shows a "top-down" hierarchical pattern of appearance in which major structural themes or body plans emerge before minor variations on those themes. Not only does this pattern directly contradict the "bottom-up" pattern predicted by neo-Darwinism, but as Stephen C. Meyer, Marcus Ross, Paul Nelson, and Paul Chien argue in their essay, "The Cambrian Explosion: Biology's Big Bang," in Part III, it also strongly resembles the pattern evident in the history of human technological design. For this and other reasons, they argue that intelligent design best explains the fossil evidence associated with the Cambrian explosion.[62]

Other scientists now see evidence of design in phenomena previously thought to provide unequivocal support for naturalistic evolutionary theories.[63] For example, in their essay, "Homology in Biology: Problem for Naturalistic Science and Prospect for Intelligent Design," Paul Nelson and Jonathan Wells argue that the phenomenon known as homology poses a severe challenge to the theory of universal common descent but supports the theory of intelligent design.

In sum, design theorists have begun to marshal an impressive array of empirical evidence from a variety of subdisciplines of biology to support their perspective and to challenge standard evolutionary theories for the origin and development of life.[64]

Of course, the legal and educational point at issue is not whether design theorists are right in their scientific claims but whether their work may be discussed in science classrooms of public high schools. Setting aside for the moment concerns about the constitutional issues raised by the possible religious implications of design theory, teachers and school boards must assess whether information about the work of scientists such as Behe, Kenyon, Thaxton, Bradley, Meyer, Chien, Wells, Dembski, and others has a legitimate place in a public school biology classroom.

The discussion above demonstrates that, right or wrong, the work of such scientists is clearly germane to the topic of biological origins. As noted, Darwin's theory (and other naturalistic origins theories) sought explicitly to explain the appearance of design in biology without reference to an actual designer.[65] Thus, it is misleading to suggest, as many do, that Darwinism and design theory address two different subjects: one scientific and the other religious. Rather, both Darwinism and design theory represent competing answers to the same question: How did living forms (with their appearance of design) arise and diversify on Earth? At present, many biology texts explain the evidence and arguments *for* the efficacy of natural selection and random variation, neo-Darwinism's designer substitute.[66] Good science education requires that students learn and understand such evidence and arguments. Yet if well-credentialed scientists now dispute the adequacy of the neo-Darwinian mechanism (and other similarly materialistic theories) and some now publicly advocate the (actual) design hypothesis, surely their work is relevant to a discussion of the scientific issues raised by neo-Darwinian theory. At the very least, knowing the evidence and arguments *for* design will help students to understand the full intellectual significance of neo-Darwinism in its current context.[67] More important, exposure to information about design will help correct the current imbalance in the presentation of this issue in current biological texts.

IV. But Is It Science?
Darwinism, Design, and Demarcation

Of course, critics of design theory generally do not dispute the data (as opposed to the interpretation) that design theorists marshal in support of their view, nor do they disagree that some evidence might be interpreted to support the idea of design. They argue instead that the very notion of intelligent design is inherently unscientific, that design theory does not qualify as science according to established definitions of the term. To justify that claim, critics cite various definitional or demarcation criteria that purport to define science and distinguish it (providing "demarcation") from pseudoscience, metaphysics, or religion.[68] Those kinds of arguments have previously played an important role in deciding the scientific, and consequently legal, status of creation science. Moreover, they continue to cast doubt on the scientific status of other alternatives to strictly naturalistic origins theories, including design theory.

A. *McLean v. Arkansas* and the Definition of Science

In 1982, a federal judge adopted a five-point definition of science as part of his finding that a law requiring Arkansas public schools to teach "creation science" alongside standard neo-Darwinian theory was unconstitutional.[69] Although there are decisive differences between design theory and creation science, critics of design theory often rely upon the *McLean* criteria to establish definitional or methodological norms.[70]

In *McLean*, Judge William Overton ruled that the Arkansas law violated the First Amendment's Establishment Clause.[71] He based his decision not only on the Establishment Clause but on a finding that so-called creation science does not qualify as science.[72] He reasoned that because creation science does not qualify as science, it constituted religion. In making his determination, Judge Overton relied on the expert testimony of Darwinian philosopher of science Michael Ruse. In their testimony, Ruse and other expert witnesses asserted a five-point definition of science that provided allegedly normative criteria for determining whether a theory qualifies as scientific. According to Ruse, any theory that failed to meet those five criteria could not be considered to be "scientific." According to Ruse, for a theory to be scientific it must be: (1) guided by natural law; (2) explanatory by natural law; (3) testable against the empirical world; (4) tentative in its conclusions; and (5) falsifiable. Ruse further testified that creation science—in part because it invoked the singular action of a creator as the cause of certain events in the history of life—could never meet those criteria. Thus, he concluded that creationism might be true, but it could never qualify as science. Judge Overton ultimately agreed, adopting Ruse's five demarcation criteria as part of his opinion.[73]

Although the case was in some ways superseded by the subsequent ruling of the U.S. Supreme Court in *Edwards v. Aguillard,* the *McLean* case, and the philosophy of science that underwrites it, poses an implied challenge to the scientific status of all theories of origin (including design theory) that invoke singular, intelligent causes as opposed to strictly material causes.[74] If design theory does not qualify as science, as Ruse testified and the court ruled concerning creation science, then, at least as a pedagogical matter, design theory does not belong in the science classroom.

B. The Demise of Demarcation Arguments

Notwithstanding the favorable reception that Michael Ruse enjoyed in Judge Overton's courtroom, many prominent philosophers of science, including Larry Laudan and Philip Quinn (neither of whom supported creation science's empirical claims), soon repudiated Ruse's testimony on the grounds that, as Laudan argued, it "canoniz[ed] a false stereotype of what science is and how it works."[75] These philosophers of science insisted that Ruse's testimony seriously misrepresented contemporary thinking in the philosophy of science about the status of the demarcation problem.[76] It now seems clear for several reasons that the philosophy of science provides no grounds for disqualifying nonmaterialistic alternatives to Darwinism as inherently "unscientific."

First, as Laudan noted, many philosophers of science have generally abandoned attempts to define science by reference to abstract demarcation criteria. They have found it notoriously difficult to define science generally via the kind of methodological criteria that Ruse and the court promulgated in the *McLean* case—in part because proposed demarcation criteria have inevitably fallen prey to death by counterexample.[77] Well-established scientific theories often lack some of the presumably necessary features of true science (for example, falsifiability, observability, repeatability, and use of lawlike explanation), while many poorly supported, disreputable, or "crank" ideas often meet some of those same criteria.

Consider, for example, the criteria of falsifiability and tentativeness, two key and related litmus tests in the 1981 *McLean* trial.[78] Although Ruse asserts that all truly scientific theories are held tentatively by their proponents and are readily falsifiable by contradictory evidence, the history of science tells a very different story. As distinguished historian and philosopher of science Imre Lakatos showed in the 1970s, some of the most powerful scientific theories have been constructed by those who stubbornly refused to reject their theories in the face of anomalous data. For example, on the basis of his theory of universal gravitation, Sir Isaac Newton made a number of predictions that did not materialize about the position of planets. Nevertheless, rather than rejecting the notion of universal gravitation, he refined his "auxiliary assumptions" (for example, the assumption that planets are perfectly spherical and influenced only by gravitational force) and left his core theory in place. As Lakatos showed, the explanatory flexibility of Newton's theory in the face of apparently falsifying evidence turned out to be one of its greatest strengths. Such flexibility emphatically did not compromise universal gravitation's "scientific status," as Ruse's definition of science would imply.[79]

On the other hand, the history of science is littered with the remains of failed theories that have been falsified not by the airtight disproof of a single anomaly but by the judgment of the scientific community concerning the preponderance of data.[80] Are such falsified, and therefore falsifiable, theories (for example, the flat earth, phlogiston, geocentricism, and flood geology) more scientific than successful theories (such as Newton's was in, say, 1750) that possess wide-ranging explanatory power?

As a result of such contradictions, most contemporary philosophers of science have come to regard the question "What distinguishes science from nonscience?" as both intractable and uninteresting. Instead, philosophers of science have increasingly realized that the real issue is not whether a theory is "scientific" according to some abstract definition but whether a theory is true—that is, warranted by the evidence. As Laudan explains, "If we would stand up and be counted on the side of reason, we ought to drop terms like 'pseudo-science' . . . they . . . do only emotive work for us."[81] As Martin Eger has summarized, "[d]emarcation arguments have collapsed. Philosophers of science don't hold them anymore. They may still enjoy acceptance in the popular world, but that's a different world."[82]

Second, even if one assumes for the sake of argument that criteria could be found to demarcate science in general from nonscience in general, the specific demarcation criteria used in the *McLean* case have proven incapable of discriminating the scientific status of materialistic and nonmaterialistic origins theories. Laudan notes, for example, that Judge Overton's opinion made much of creation science's inability to be tested or falsified.[83] Yet, as Laudan argues, to make the claim that

> creationism is neither falsifiable nor testable is to assert that Creationism makes no empirical assertions whatever. That is surely false. Creationists make a wide range of testable assertions about matters of fact. Thus, as Judge Overton himself grants (apparently without seeing its implications), the creationists say that the earth is of very recent origin . . . they argue that most of the geological features of the earth's surface are diluvial in character . . . they assert the limited variability of species. They are committed to the view that, since animals and man were created at the same time, the human fossil record must be paleontologically co-extensive with the record of lower animals.[84]

Laudan notes that though creation scientists "are committed to a large number of factual . . . claims," available evidence contradicts their empirical claims. As he explains, "no one has shown how to reconcile such claims with the available evidence—evidence which speaks persuasively to a long earth history, among other things. In brief, these claims are testable, they have been tested, and they have failed those tests."[85]

Yet, Laudan notes, if creationist arguments have been shown to be false by empirical evidence (as Ruse and other expert witnesses at the Arkansas trial no doubt believed), then creation science must be falsifiable.[86] But if it is falsifiable, by Ruse's own criterion, it qualifies as scientific.

Similar problems have afflicted Ruse's other demarcation criteria. For example, insofar as both creationist and evolutionary theories make historical claims about past causal events, both theories offer causal explanations that are not explained by natural law. The theory of common descent, a central thesis of the *Origin of Species,* does not explain by natural law. Common descent explains by postulating hypothetical historical events (and a pattern of events) that, if actual, would explain a variety of presently observed data. The theory of common descent makes claims about what happened in the past—namely, that unobserved transitional organisms existed forming a genealogical bridge between presently existing life forms.[87] Thus, on the theory of common descent, a postulated pattern of events, not a law, does the main explanatory work. Similarly, as Laudan observes, scientists often make "existence claims" about past events or present processes without knowing the natural laws on which they depend. Laudan notes, "Darwin took himself to have established the existence of [the mechanism of] natural selection almost a half century before geneticists were able to lay out the laws of heredity on which natural selection depended."[88]

Thus, Ruse's second demarcation criterion would require, if applied consistently, classifying *both* creation science and classical Darwinism (as well as much of neo-Darwinism) as unscientific. According to Laudan: "If we took the *McLean* Opinion criterion seriously, we should have to say that . . . Darwin [was] unscientific; and, to take an example from our own time, it would follow that plate tectonics is unscientific because we have not yet identified the laws of physics and chemistry which account for the dynamics of crustal motion."[89]

Third, analyses of the demarcation problem have suggested that naturalistic and nonnaturalistic origins theories (including both Darwinism and design theory) are "methodologically equivalent," both in their ability to meet various demarcation criteria and as historical theories of origin. As noted above, Laudan's critique suggests that when the specific demarcation criteria promulgated in the *McLean* case are applied rigidly, they disqualify both Darwinism and various nonmaterialistic alternatives.[90] Yet as his discussion of falsification suggests, if certain criteria are applied more liberally, both theories may qualify as scientific.

More recent studies in the philosophy of science have confirmed and amplified Laudan's analysis.[91] They suggest that philosophically neutral criteria that can define science narrowly enough to disqualify theories of creation or design without also disqualifying Darwinism and/or other materialistic evolutionary theories on identical grounds do not exist.[92] Either science will be defined so narrowly as to disqualify both types of theory, or science must be defined more broadly, and the initial reasons for excluding opposing theories will evaporate. Thus, materialistic and nonmaterialistic origins theories appear to be methodologically equivalent with respect to a wide range of demarcation criteria—that is, both appear equally scientific or equally unscientific provided the same methodological criteria are used to adjudicate their scientific status (and provided philosophically neutral criteria are used to make those assessments).

Recent work on the historical sciences suggests deep methodological and logical similarities between various origins theories. Philosopher of biology Elliott Sober has argued that both classical design arguments and the Darwinian argument for descent with modification constitute attempts to make inferences to the best explanation.[93] Other work in the philosophy of science has shown that both Darwinism and design theory attempt to answer characteristically historical questions: both may have metaphysical implications or overtones; both employ characteristically historical forms of inference, explanation, and testing; and both are subject to similar epistemological limitations.[94]

C. Majority and Minority Opinions

Accordingly, even many of those who previously wielded demarcation arguments as a way of protecting the Darwinist hegemony in public education, including some prominent advocates of these arguments, have either abandoned or repudiated them.[95] For example, Eugenie Scott of the National Center for Science Education (an advocacy group for an exclusively Darwinist curriculum) no longer seeks to dismiss creation science as pseudoscience or as unscientific; instead, she argues that it constitutes "bad science." Scott no longer repudiates design theory as inherently "unscientific," as she did as recently as 1994; she now argues that it is a minority viewpoint within science.[96] Similarly, during a talk to the American Association for the Advancement of Science (AAAS) in 1993, Michael Ruse himself repudiated his previous support for the demarcation principle by admitting that Darwinism (like creationism) "depends upon certain unprovable metaphysical assumptions."[97] In his more recent scholarship, Ruse has openly argued that evolutionary theory has often functioned as a kind of "secular religion."[98]

D. Novel Paradigms versus Establishment Science: Majority and Minority Perspectives in Science

The demise of demarcation arguments within the philosophy of science has made it difficult for critics of design (or other nonnaturalistic origins theories) to label them unscientific in principle. As Laudan and others have argued, the status and merit of competing origins theories must be decided on the basis of empirical evidence and argument, not upon abstract philosophical or methodological litmus tests.[99] Yet as we have seen, design theorists in particular make extensive appeals to such empirical evidence and argument. Moreover, if, arguably, design theory has both a theoretical basis and evidential support and if it meets abstract definitional criteria of scientific status equally as well as its main theoretical rivals, then it seems natural to ask: On what grounds can design theory now be excluded from public school science curriculum?

Some have claimed that design theory is too new to merit discussion in biology classrooms, and no doubt its newness does partially explain its frequent omission.[100] Nevertheless, the relative novelty of design theory does not justify its exclusion on either legal or pedagogical grounds. Quite the reverse is the case. The law provides no guidelines for determining how long a scientific theory must have existed in order to warrant teaching students about it. Further, good teachers know that exposing students to new (and even controversial) ideas can stimulate student interest and engagement and can lead to greater subject mastery. Nor does science itself have a governing body that can issue binding rulings about such matters. Instead, this constitutes a matter for local teachers and school boards to decide.

Other critics of design theory have asserted another reason for exclusion: its minority status within science. Until design theory wins the support of the majority of scientists, they argue, students should not be exposed to the evidence or arguments for it.[101] Such a view seems profoundly at odds with scientific practice, which itself requires dialogue and debate between scientists, some of whom advocate, from time to time, new interpretations against established views. Those who insist that teachers may present only the majority view on a scientific issue, or that only majority opinions constitute "the scientific perspective," overlook the history of science. Many established scientific theories originally met opposition from the majority of scientists. And science often includes argument between competing theoretical perspectives. As the Supreme Court stated in *Daubert v. Merrell Dow Pharmaceuticals, Inc.*, "Scientific conclusions are subject to perpetual revision. . . . The scientific project is advanced by broad and wide-ranging consideration of a multitude of hypotheses, for those that are incorrect will eventually be shown to be so, and that in itself is an advance."[102]

Since, again, no ruling body in science can determine when a minority scientific interpretation has attracted sufficient support to warrant discussion in the science classroom, the pedagogical debate will necessarily, and properly, devolve to individual teachers and local school boards. In any case, defining permissible science as coextensive with majority scientific opinion erects a more restrictive standard than the law itself now recognizes in deciding the admissibility of expert scientific opinion.

E. Daubert's Redefinition of Science

For seventy years, the exclusion of minority scientific views as evidence was enshrined in *Frye v. United States*.[103] At his trial for murder, James Alphonzo Frye offered systolic blood pressure taken during pretrial questioning—essentially an early, crude type of polygraph—to prove his innocence. In affirming the trial court's refusal to admit the testimony, the D.C. Circuit noted that this form of evidence had not been generally accepted within the appropriate scientific disciplines. It then ruled that the test of reliability—and thus of admissibility—was general acceptance within the scientific community.[104] Although *Frye* was widely followed, it was also criticized.[105]

In 1989, *Frye's* hold on the courts was broken when the Maine Supreme Court abandoned Maine's version of the *Frye* rule. The acceptance of certain "clinical features" by an expert's profession "does not establish the scientific reliability of [the expert's] conclusions." Whether or not an opinion can qualify as scientific is determined by the quantity and quality of empirical support upon which the assertion is based.[106]

Four years later, the U.S. Supreme Court decided *Daubert v. Merrell Dow Pharmaceuticals, Inc. Daubert* arose from a claim that Merrell Dow's drug, Bendectin, had caused birth defects. Noting that the Federal Rules of Evidence are to be liberally construed in favor of admissibility, the Court found that *Frye's* "general acceptance" test was too restrictive; instead, trial courts should admit evidence if it is "supported by appropriate validation—*i.e.,* 'good grounds,' based on what is known." Since the hallmark for science under *Daubert* is "evidentiary reliability," *Daubert* heralds a critical shift in the judicial system's understanding of the nature of science itself.[107] As more states abandon *Frye* in favor of the rule announced in *Daubert*, scientific claims will be evaluated not on the basis of a popularity poll among scientists or by the fulfillment of a set of arbitrary criteria.[108] Instead, the test for scientific legitimacy comes from the validation of the empirical research supporting the evidence.[109]

That trend makes reliance on the current scientific consensus or the demarcation criteria in *McLean v. Arkansas* even more questionable. Since *Daubert* has made the question of scientific legitimacy turn on "evidentiary reliability," the courtroom should be hospitable to competing theories, provided that each theory has an empirical basis.[110] To exclude an interpretation because it has not yet achieved majority support usurps the function that juries ought to serve.[111] By analogy, the debate over origins theory should not exclude at the outset a viewpoint because of its inability to command a majority of scientists; it should be the function of scientific inquiry itself to permit competing theories to argue, on the basis of empirical data, for wider acceptance.[112]

F. An Answer for Spokes

It is hard to conceive of a legitimate objection to Spokes's plan to correct errors in biology textbooks, including both errors of omission and commission. To the contrary, refusing to permit criticism contradicts the scientific commitment to open argument and self-correction. If refusing to permit criticism would be illiberal, refusing to permit the discussion of alternative theories would be illogical. As noted, neo-Darwinism claims to have found a mechanism that can explain the appearance of design in biology without recourse to an actual designer.[113] If that mechanism cannot explain the appearance of design, as many scientists now argue, it is likely that at least some scientists will want to consider actual design as a better explanation. Scientific critique of the mechanism that functions as a designer substitute leads logically to reconsideration of the need for a real designer.

Similarly, students confronted with dissenting opinions about neo-Darwinism will naturally want to ask: Are there any other competing explanations for the origin of biological form? Good science cannot require teachers to refuse to answer such a question. Spokes should be free to say, "Some scientists see evidence of actual design rather than just apparent design; they believe that this hypothesis constitutes a better explanation for certain features of biological organisms." Given the absence of a "scientific magisterium," or a reigning body of scientists to decide empirical disputes by edict, Spokes should be free to present design theory and allow students to consider its merits. Unless some other reason for excluding it can be established, he should feel free to teach the entire scientific controversy, as accurately and fairly as he is able, and permit his students, as potential scientists in the making, to judge for themselves.

Of course, another reason for excluding discussion of design theory has been proffered: the claim that it violates the Establishment Clause.

V. Is It Religion? The Theory of Intelligent Design and the Establishment Clause

The first law review article to address the legality of presenting intelligent design to public school students argues that the theory of intelligent design should not be included in science classroom discussion because to do so would constitute an establishment of religion. In a review of the legal status of a supplementary text that presents the theory of intelligent design, Jay D. Wexler states, at least for the purpose of argument, that design theory may qualify as scientific in character. Nevertheless, he argues that teaching about design would offend the Establishment Clause of the First Amendment because the theory of intelligent design constitutes a religious belief. Thus, he argues, the same limitations apply to teaching design theory as apply to teaching Judaism, Christianity, or Buddhism in the public schools. He notes, "[t]he First Amendment forbids the government from establishing religion; it does not require it to teach science."[114]

This section will proceed in several stages to refute the identification of design theory as a religion. First, we will show that the courts have been reluctant to proffer specific legal definitions of religion, especially ones that can be used to assign the legal burdens of religion to institutions or entities that do not define themselves as religious. Second, we will show that the definitional criteria the courts have enunciated, such as a test adopted by the Ninth Circuit Court of Appeals, do not justify classifying the theory of intelligent design as a religion. Third, we will show that attempts to equate the theory of intelligent design with creation science, and thus to extend legal judgments about the inadmissibility of creation science to design theory, ignore legally relevant differences between them.[115] We will show that neither the ruling in *Edwards* v. *Aguillard* nor a more general reliance on the *Lemon* test can offer any constitutional basis for preventing teachers from teaching students about the theory of intelligent design in public science classrooms.[116]

A. Defining Religion

Just as establishing a general definition of science has proven to be both legally and philosophically problematic, so, too, has the task of finding a general legal definition of religion proven to be challenging for the courts. Nevertheless, given the language of the Establishment Clause, the courts require some criteria by which they can identify religion and decide when to assign the legal benefits or burdens of religion. Unless the courts have some working definition of religion, they cannot decide, for example, whether an organization seeking a tax advantage available to religious organizations (but not to others) should receive it.[117] Similarly, lacking such a definition, they cannot decide when to forbid government aid to religious organizations or to organizations that want to use government funds for religious purposes.[118]

Cases that turn on the definition of religion typically result from a dispute brought by someone who complains that a state's definition of religion is either too narrow (because it does not extend to the complainant, who wants a benefit conferred by religion) or too broad (because the complainant doesn't want a legal burden associated with nonreligious status).[119] The courts have generally shown a willingness to accept a broader conception of religion when complainants seek benefits of religious status under the law, such as exemption from military service.[120] They have tended to favor a more narrow conception of religion when considering the assignment of legal burdens to defendants who deny being engaged in religious activity.[121] Such cases arise when someone accuses a defendant of engaging in a religious activity in order to impose on the defendant the constitutional restrictions that accompany a religious designation.[122] As we shall see, such accusations are rarely successful.[123]

Despite the obvious necessity of having *some* definition of religion, a review of relevant cases shows that the courts have been hesitant to draw precise boundaries.[124] The Ninth, Eleventh, and Second Circuits have all rejected the invitation to craft precise definitions of religion.[125] As the Second Circuit Court of Appeals recognized in *United States v. Kauten*, the meaning of *religion* as a term "is found in the history of the human race and is incapable of compression into a few words."[126] The judges' reluctance may derive, in part, from their recognition of the danger of trying to make theological or philosophical distinctions in the absence of training or authority to do so.[127]

Moreover, scholars have also expressed concern that in making theological and philosophical distinctions about what constitutes religion, and thereby extending or withholding benefits or burdens on that basis, judges will become instruments for the favoring of one theological view over another.[128] Clearly, different religions have different understandings of the nature of religion and religious belief. Judgments about the nature of religion may thus necessarily favor one religious viewpoint over another. For this reason, the courts have been understandably hesitant to devise bright-line definitions of religion, especially where those definitions would too easily allow courts to assign the legal burdens of religion.[129]

A typical example is *Peloza v. Capistrano Unified School District.*[130] Peloza sued the school district that employed him, claiming that by forcing him to teach "evolutionism" and "secular humanism" to his students, his employer had created an "establishment of religion." The court rejected his assertion, finding that neither "evolutionism [n]or secular humanism are 'religions' for Establishment Clause purposes."[131] The court based that finding on "both the dictionary definition of religion and the clear weight of the caselaw" contradicting Peloza's claim. The court also referred to the suggestion by Laurence Tribe that "anything 'arguably non-religious' should not be considered religious in applying the establishment clause."[132]

Similarly, in *Alvarado v. City of San Jose,* a group of citizens brought suit against the city of San Jose, California, alleging that the city's installation of a sculpture of the Aztec god Quetzalcoatl violated the Establishment Clause.[133] The court ruled that the sculpture was not religious in nature. In making its ruling, the court relied on a three-part test to define religion: "First, a religion addresses fundamental and ultimate questions having to do with deep and imponderable matters. Second, a religion is comprehensive in nature; it consists of a belief-system as opposed to an isolated teaching. Third, a religion often can be recognized by the presence of certain formal and external signs."[134]

The court further clarified the test by noting that "formal and external signs" include such practices as "formal services, ceremonial functions, the existence of clergy, structure and organization, efforts at propagation, observance of holidays and other similar manifestations associated with the traditional religions."[135]

B. Applying the Ninth Circuit's Test for Religion

Though the courts have generally resisted formulating definitions of religion, the Ninth Circuit test articulated in *Peloza* and *Alvarado* stands as a clear exception to that rule.[136] Even so, this three-part test clearly provides no grounds for classifying the theory of intelligent design as a religion.

Consider the first part: Design theory does not attempt to address "fundamental and ultimate questions" concerning "deep and imponderable matters."[137] On the contrary, design theory seeks to answer a question raised by Darwin, as well as by contemporary biologists: How did biological organisms acquire their appearance of design? Design theory, unlike neo-Darwinism, attributes this appearance to a designing intelligence, but it does not address the characteristics or identity of the designing intelligence.[138] Of course, design theory is consistent with theism and adds plausibility to the classical design arguments for the existence of God.[139] But that compatibility does not make it a religious belief. As Justice Lewis Powell wrote in his concurrence to *Edwards v. Aguillard:* "[A] decision respecting the subject matter to be taught in public schools does not violate the Establishment Clause simply because the material to be taught 'happens to coincide or harmonize with the tenets of some or all religions.'" According to Powell, interference by the federal courts in the decisions of local and state educational officials is justified "only when the purpose for their decisions is clearly religious."[140]

The second part of the test identifies religion with a *comprehensive* belief system "as opposed to an isolated teaching."[141] Design theory does not offer a theory of morality or metaphysics or an opinion on the prospects for an afterlife. It requires neither a belief in divine revelation nor a code of conduct; nor does it purport to uncover the underlying meaning of the universe or to confer esoteric knowledge upon its adherents. It is simply a theory about the source of the appearance of design in living organisms.[142] It is a clear example of an "isolated teaching," one that has no logically necessary connections to any spiritual dogma or church institution. Design theory has no religious pretensions. It merely tries to apply a well-established scientific method to the analysis of biological phenomena.

The third part of the test concerns the "presence of certain formal and external signs." The court provided a list of such signs, including liturgy, clergy, and observance of holidays.[143] Obviously, design theory has none of these: no sacred texts; no ordained ministers, priests, or religious teachers; no design theory liturgies; no design theory holidays; and no institutional structures like those of religious groups. Design theorists have formed organizations and institutes, but these resemble other academic or professional associations rather than churches or religious institutions.[144]

C. Do Religious Implications Turn a Theory into Religion?

According to the Ninth Circuit's three-part test, design theory should not be classified as religion. To say that, however, does not suggest that evidence for design has no religious or metaphysical *implications*. Design theory argues that a designing intelligence is responsible for the "irreducibly complex" and "information-rich" structures in biological organisms.[145] Students who believe in a creator God may, therefore, find support for their faith from the evidence that supports design theory and may identify the designing intelligence allegedly responsible for biological complexity with the God of their religious belief. Alternatively, students with no religious convictions may find that evidence of design leads them to ask theological questions and to inquire into the identity of such a designing intelligence.

The potential for metaphysical extrapolation, however, does not make design theory a religious doctrine. Nor is this potential unique to design theory. Darwinism and other materialistic origins theories have a similar potential. Nonreligious students may find support for agnostic or materialistic metaphysical beliefs in Darwinian theory. Similarly, a religious student might find a materialistic worldview more plausible as a result of a scientific study of Darwinism. Darwinism, which holds that life evolved through an undirected natural process, implies that common religious beliefs about the origin of life and the nature of human life are, if not false, then implausible.[146] Indeed, a host of prominent neo-Darwinian scientists—from Douglas Futuyma to William Provine to Stephen Jay Gould—have insisted that Darwinism has made traditional beliefs about God and humanity either untenable or less plausible. Consider the following statements by Gould:[147]

"[B]iology took away our status as paragons created in the image of God."[148]

"Before Darwin, we thought that a benevolent God had created us."[149]

"[W]hy do humans exist? . . . I do not think that any 'higher' answer can be given. . . . We are the offspring of history, and must establish our own paths in this most diverse and interesting of conceivable universes—one indifferent to our suffering, and therefore offering us maximal freedom to thrive, or to fail, in our own chosen way."[150]

Contrary to the popular "just-the-facts" stereotype of science, many scientific theories have larger ideological and religious implications.[151] Origins theories, in particular, raise unavoidable philosophical and religious considerations. Theories about where the universe, life, and humanity came from invariably affect our perspectives about human nature, morality, and ultimate reality. As the preceding quotations from Gould have made clear, neo-Darwinian evolutionary theory has implications for such questions.

Darwinism (in both its classical and contemporary versions) insists that living systems organized themselves into increasingly complex structures without assistance from a guiding intelligence.[152] Chemical evolutionary theorists likewise insist that the first life arose, without direction, from brute chemistry.[153] Zoologist Richard Dawkins has dubbed this the "blind watchmaker" thesis. He and other leading evolutionary theorists claim that biological evidence overwhelmingly supports this purposeless and fully materialistic account of creation.[154] Thus George Gaylord Simpson, the leading neo-Darwinist a generation ago, could claim: "Man is the result of a *purposeless* and materialistic process that did not have him in mind. He was not planned."[155]

Accordingly, many major biology texts present evolution as a process in which a purposeful intelligence (such as God) plays no detectable role. Purves, Orians, and Heller state in their text, "the living world is constantly evolving, and that evolutionary change occurs without any 'goals' . . . evolution is not directed." Or as Miller and Levine's popular text asserts, the evolutionary process is "random and undirected" and occurs "without plan or purpose."[156] Some texts even state that Darwin's theory has profoundly negative implications for theism and especially for its belief in the purposeful design of nature. As Futuyma's biology text explains: "By coupling undirected, purposeless variation to the blind, uncaring process of natural selection, Darwin made theological or spiritual explanations of the life processes superfluous."[157]

Nevertheless, the content of a scientific theory, and not its implications, determines its legal status in public school science classrooms. Otherwise, the antitheistic implications of neo-Darwinism (as articulated by some of its chief advocates) would disqualify it from inclusion in the curriculum. As Justice Hugo Black once asked, "[I]f the theory [of evolution] is considered anti-religious, as the Court indicates, how can the State be bound by the Federal Constitution to permit its teachers to advocate such an 'anti-religious' doctrine to schoolchildren?" Of course, Justice Black's question was purely rhetorical, since he did not advocate actually forbidding teachers to teach about Darwinian evolutionary theory.[158] Such an outcome would be unthinkable. Yet if the religious (or antireligious) implications rather than the specific propositional content of theories were at issue, then arguably neither Darwinian theory nor design theory could pass constitutional muster. That result, however, would not only undercut science education but would also violate constitutional precedents. One of the few fixed points in Establishment Clause jurisprudence during the last half century has been that incidental harmonies with religious beliefs do not disqualify secular concepts under the First Amendment.[159]

D. Extending *Edwards v. Aguillard* to Cover Design Theory?

Many critics may concede that general legal definitions of religion (such as the Ninth Circuit test) cannot establish design as a religion for legal purposes. Nevertheless, they would classify design theory as religion on different grounds. Rather than applying a general definition of religion as a legal test, these critics have equated design theory with religion by claiming that the issue is controlled by the Court's holding in *Edwards v. Aguillard.*[160]

In the early 1980s, creationists in Louisiana sought to introduce scientific creationism into the Louisiana public school system. As a result, the Louisiana legislature passed a law titled "Balanced Treatment for Creation-Science and Evolution-Science in Public School Instruction" (the "Act"). The Act did not require teaching either creationism or evolution but did require that when one theory was taught, the other must be taught as well.[161]

Several parents and concerned citizens challenged the constitutionality of the Act in federal court. They argued that the Act violated the First Amendment's Establishment Clause, which prohibits the government from officially endorsing a religious belief. The state responded that the Act did not violate the First Amendment because it had the legitimate secular purpose of strengthening and broadening the academic freedom of teachers. The district court and the Court of Appeals for the Fifth Circuit, however, found that the state's actual purpose was to promote the religious doctrine of creationism (known also as creation science).[162]

The Court, in a majority opinion written by Justice William Brennan, ruled that the Act constituted an unconstitutional infringement on the Establishment Clause of the First Amendment based on the *Lemon* test.[163] This test, which was first enunciated by the Court in *Lemon v. Kurtzman,* consists of three prongs: (1) the government's action must have a secular purpose; (2) the government's action must not have the primary effect of either advancing or inhibiting religion; and (3) the government's action must not result in an "excessive entanglement" of the government and religion.[164] If government action or legislation violates any of these three prongs, it will be deemed unconstitutional under the Establishment Clause.[165]

The first of these prongs has become known as the "purpose prong."[166] The Court found that the Act violated the purpose prong and was therefore unconstitutional for several reasons.[167] First, since the legislative history of the Act constantly referenced the religious views of the legislators, the Court became suspicious of the state's claim that the Act's purpose was to advance academic freedom. Second, the Court found that the intent of the legislator who drafted the Act was to narrow the science curriculum in order to favor a particular religious belief (that is, the creation account as found in the book of Genesis). In support of this finding, the Court noted that the Act's sponsor actually preferred that "neither [creationism nor evolution] be taught." The Court, therefore, concluded that the purpose of the Act was to limit, rather than promote, academic freedom and science education.[168]

The Court also found that the Act did not grant teachers any new "flexibility [in teaching science] that they did not already possess." The Court noted that no Louisiana law barred the teaching of any scientific theory about biological origins. Since teachers were already free to teach scientific alternatives to Darwinian evolution, the Court reasoned that the Act did not expand the academic freedom already enjoyed by teachers in Louisiana.[169]

Having rejected the state's proffered reason for the Act, the Court then uncovered what it regarded as the true intent of the Louisiana law: the promotion of a particular religious view. The Court found that the Act had a "discriminatory preference" for the teaching of creationism because it required the production of curriculum guides for creationism. Further, it found that only creationism was protected by certain sections of the Act and that the Act undercut truly comprehensive science instruction by limiting the theories of origins that teachers could teach to just two: evolution and creationism.[170]

In deciding against the Act, the Court was careful to point out that its decision in no way excluded the teaching of other scientific theories about biological origins. Likewise, the Court left the door open to scientific critiques of Darwinian evolution. In an illuminating section of the majority opinion, the Court even stated that teaching a variety of scientific theories about origins "might be validly done with the clear secular intent of enhancing the effectiveness of science instruction." The Court, however, could not discern such an intent in the legislative history of the Act. Instead, it determined that the primary purpose of the Act was to promote a particular religious doctrine, thereby violating the Establishment Clause.[171]

Many have assumed that the reasoning in *Edwards* can be extended to cover curricular debates about the admissibility of teaching about design theory. Indeed, many have argued that the theory of intelligent design and creation science are effectively indistinguishable for both scientific and legal purposes.[172] Since the court in *Edwards* ruled that creation science promoted a religious viewpoint, many have concluded that teaching public school students about design theory also illicitly promotes a religious viewpoint in the public schools.[173]

E. Legal Differences between Creation Science and Design Theory

Despite claims to the contrary, design theory and scientific creationism differ in propositional content, method of inquiry, and thus in legal status. Recall that in *Edwards v. Aguillard* the Court decided against the legality of scientific creationism because it constituted an advancement of religion. The Court reached this decision in large part because the propositional content of scientific creationism closely mirrors the creation narrative in the book of Genesis.[174] Although philosophers of science now agree that the *scientific* status of an idea does not depend on its source, the Court seems to have assumed that the *legal* status of an idea—and therefore the legal status of any curriculum based on that idea—does depend on its source. Thus, given the Court's reasoning in *Edwards,* the teaching of creation science remains legally problematic.

Nevertheless, the Court's decision does not apply to design theory because design theory is not based on a religious text or doctrine. Design theory begins with the data that scientists observe in the laboratory and nature and attempts to explain such data based on what we know about the patterns that generally indicate intelligent causes. For design theorists, the conclusion of design constitutes an inference from biological data, not a deduction from religious authority.

Further, the propositional content of design theory differs significantly from that of scientific creationism. Scientific creationism is committed to the following propositions:

1. There was a sudden creation of the universe, energy, and life from nothing.
2. Mutations and natural selection are insufficient to bring about the development of all living kinds from a single organism.
3. Changes in the originally created kinds of plants and animals occur only within fixed limits.
4. There is a separate ancestry for humans and apes.
5. The earth's geology can be explained via catastrophism, primarily by the occurrence of a worldwide flood.
6. The earth and living kinds had a relatively recent origin (on the order of 10,000 years ago).[175]

Those six tenets taken jointly define scientific creationism for legal purposes. The Court in *Edwards* ruled that, taken jointly, this group of propositions may not be taught in public school science classrooms—at least not where they are animated by the religious purpose of the Louisiana legislature. Nevertheless, the Court left the door open to some of those tenets being discussed individually.[176]

Design theory, on the other hand, asserts the following:

1. High information content (or specified complexity) and irreducible complexity constitute strong indicators or hallmarks of past intelligent design.[177]
2. Biological systems have a high information content (or specified complexity) and utilize subsystems that manifest irreducible complexity.[178]
3. Naturalistic mechanisms or undirected causes do not suffice to explain the origin of information (specified complexity) or irreducible complexity.[179]
4. Therefore, intelligent design constitutes the best explanation for the origin of information and irreducible complexity in biological systems.[180]

A comparison of these two lists demonstrates that design theory and scientific creationism differ markedly in content. Clearly, then, they do not derive from the same source. Thus, the Court's ruling in *Edwards* does not apply to design theory and can provide no grounds for excluding discussion of intelligent design from the public school science curriculum.

F. A Residual *Lemon* Objection

Some might acknowledge these differences and still claim that teaching about design theory constitutes an advancement of religion. For example, it could be argued that the theory of intelligent design suffers from its own inability to meet the *Lemon* test, which was the basis of the Court's decision in *Edwards*. Just as the Act advocating the teaching of creation science failed to meet the *Lemon* test because the Court found that it expressed a religious and not a secular purpose, one might argue that teaching about design theory would run afoul of the *Lemon* test because advocates for its inclusion in the curriculum have religious, rather than secular, reasons for promoting it. As noted above, many advocates of contemporary design theory do openly acknowledge that evidence for design in nature may have theistic implications.[181] Some also see Darwinian evolution as an implicit challenge to a theistic worldview.[182] Viewing the issue as they do, some advocates for the inclusion of design theory in the curriculum, including teachers, school board members, and parents, may view teaching about the theory of intelligent design as a means of defending, or even promoting, their theistic beliefs.[183] Thus, one might argue that such religiously motivated advocacy disqualifies design theory from consideration in the curriculum under the first prong of the *Lemon* test.

Nevertheless, even the presence of religiously motivated advocacy for design theory in the curriculum does not warrant its exclusion under the first prong of the *Lemon* test—for several reasons.

First, the *Lemon* test does not require that advocates of a government action have *no* religious motivations, only that a government action itself embodies *some* secular purpose.[184] Recall that the majority in *Edwards* rejected the proffered secular purpose of the legislature: the claim that the Act sought to promote academic freedom. It found this claim implausible on the grounds that teachers already had the academic freedom to teach alternative scientific viewpoints. Failing to find a plausible secular purpose for the Act, the Court concluded that the sole motivation of those advocating the Act must have been to advance a religious viewpoint.[185]

By contrast, in the hypothetical example we have posed, John Spokes wants to improve science education and to expose his students to the full range of opinion that exists among scientists about biological origins. Thus, his teaching is clearly motivated by a secular purpose. Moreover, even if Spokes had a religious as well as a scientific purpose for wanting to expose his students to the theory of intelligent design, or even if some of his supporters on the school board had such a purpose, his proposed pedagogy would still meet the first prong of the *Lemon* test. Again, the *Lemon* test does not require that a government action (such as teaching a public school science class) have *only* a secular purpose, but that it have *a* secular

purpose.[186] Insofar as Spokes seeks to inform his students about a variety
of scientific interpretations of existing biological data, or to enhance his
students' critical thinking skills, or to expose students to the method of
multiple competing hypotheses in the historical sciences, his pedagogy
clearly embodies a secular purpose.

Second, since the *Edwards* decision, the constitutional standard for deciding the permissibility of religiously motivated speech has changed. In
Rosenberger v. Rector and Visitors of the University of Virginia, the Court permitted an evangelical Christian student publication group to receive state
funds for an expressly religious publication, despite the claim that such
funding would violate the Establishment Clause.[187] Since other student
groups had received state funds for promoting their viewpoints, the Court
found that the exclusion of a religious viewpoint because of its content
would constitute viewpoint discrimination. Indeed, the Court struck down
the university's refusal to fund the religious group as a violation of the First
Amendment's guarantee of viewpoint neutrality.[188]

Yet if the Court has ruled that the Constitution allows funding religiously
motivated speech—even speech of an explicitly religious character—in order
to prevent viewpoint discrimination, then clearly the Constitution must permit other forms of religiously motivated expression, especially those forms of
expression that address scientific evidence and are (at most) religious only in
their implications. Thus, a teacher or school board that chooses to include
presentations about design theory in the curriculum, in order to prevent an
imbalance in the presentation of scientific perspectives on biological origins,
would enact a secular purpose every bit as compelling as the one the state
university was required to demonstrate in *Rosenberger.*[189]

In any case, no constitutional test has established design theory as a religious viewpoint, much less an establishment of religion. Nor, strictly
speaking, can the *Lemon* test make such determinations. Instead, the courts
use the *Lemon* test to determine when a government action involving religion constitutes an unacceptable advancement of that religion.[190] In *Edwards,* the Court simply assumed that creation science constituted a
religious belief because of its resemblance to the creation narrative in the
book of Genesis and then sought to determine whether the Act constituted
an illicit advancement of that religious belief.[191] Yet as argued above, similar grounds do not exist for classifying design theory as a religious belief.
Given its basis in scientific evidence and its failure to meet other legal criteria of religion, such as those articulated in the Ninth Circuit test, every
presumption militates against such an identification.

G. Back to Spokes

Spokes need not worry about a legal challenge to his decision to expose students to scientific criticism of Darwinian evolution. As the Court's ruling in *Edwards* made explicit, exposing students to critiques of Darwinian theory does not constitute an advancement of religion.[192] Indeed, the refusal to permit any criticism of Darwinism resembles nothing so much as an enshrinement of the very "orthodoxy" that Justice Robert Jackson once declared inconsistent with our Constitution.[193]

Spokes should also have no compunctions about what might seem a more controversial action, namely, his teaching students about alternatives to Darwinism, including the theory of intelligent design.[194] Given the larger theistic implications of design, Spokes might fear censure under the Establishment Clause. Yet if Spokes's actions advance the secular purpose of improving science education, then whatever support design theory might provide to religious belief does not compromise its legal status. In any case, as a good science teacher, Spokes can encourage students not to limit consideration of the scientific evidence based on their metaphysical presuppositions, whether theological or naturalistic.[195] If a student raises the metaphysical implications of a theory as an argument for or against its acceptance, then Spokes can encourage students to address the evidential merits of the competing theories.[196] On the other hand, to deny discussion of an important scientific issue because it causes metaphysical discomfort to some would in effect grant a heckler's veto. The Court has refused to do this.[197]

In his biology class, Spokes can present his students with multiple competing hypotheses, such as classical Darwinism, the neo-Darwinist synthesis, punctuated equilibrium, and design theory. By allowing students to evaluate the evidential merits of each theory, Spokes eschews indoctrination in favor of liberal education. Given the metaphysical implications in play with whatever hypothesis, such a pedagogy more closely honors the intent of the Establishment Clause than the one-sided and dogmatic mode of presentation demanded by the National Center for Science Education and the National Academy of Sciences.[198]

VI. Is It Speech? Design Theory and Viewpoint Discrimination

Suppose the administrators and school board members, after listening to Spokes's presentation, decide to endorse Spokes's curricular changes, including his decision to teach students about the scientific case for design. Would they face legal exposure for doing so? Given the controversy associated with these issues and the widespread (if erroneous) belief that all nonmaterialistic alternatives to Darwinism (such as design theory) constitute religion, many school boards might assume that they should permit teachers to teach only about Darwinism and forbid any discussion of alternative theories, especially design theory. Given widespread misconceptions about the bearing of the Establishment Clause on the biology curriculum, school boards and administrators might assume that restricting teachers in this way represents the safest course legally. The law, however, not only permits Spokes to present alternatives, but it now forbids publicly funded viewpoint discrimination (with certain exceptions that do not apply to this controversy). Moreover, recent cases have provided a strong reaffirmation of the primary responsibility and authority reposed in school boards to decide on their own curriculum: "Someone must fix the curriculum of any school, public or private. In the case of a public school, in our opinion, it is far better public policy, absent a valid statutory directive on the subject, that the makeup of the curriculum be entrusted to the local school authorities who are in some sense responsible, rather than to the teachers, who would be responsible only to the judges, had they a First Amendment right to participate in the makeup of the curriculum."[199] Thus, if a teacher (with the school board's support) elects to broaden the curriculum, the law not only allows but encourages such a course of action.

A more difficult case might arise if a teacher wants to broaden his or her curriculum as Spokes has decided to do, but the teacher's school board or administration opposes his or her pedagogy. Here the authority of the school board to decide curriculum collides with the academic freedom of the teacher. What does the law, and particularly the recent rulings about viewpoint discrimination, have to say in such situations? Do Spokes's proposed changes constitute legally protected speech, or does the authority of the school board trump Spokes's academic freedom?

Several precedents suggest that Spokes's changes do constitute legally protected speech and that even the legitimate rights of school boards to set curricular guidelines do not supersede Spokes's academic freedom in this matter. As noted, the law has strongly affirmed the authority of school boards to establish the curricular guidelines in their school districts. Nevertheless, that authority is not unlimited. As the Court said in *Tinker v. Des Moines Independent Community School District:* "First Amendment rights, applied in light of the special characteristics of the school environment, are available to teachers and students. It can hardly be argued that either students or teachers shed their constitutional rights to freedom of speech or expression at the schoolhouse gate. This has been the unmistakable holding of this Court for almost 50 years."[200] Addressing a situation in which a school board claimed the unfettered right to determine the content of a school library, the Court made the following comments:

> Petitioners [the school board] rightly possess significant discretion to determine the content of their school libraries. But that discretion may not be exercised in a narrowly partisan or political manner. If a Democratic school board, motivated by party affiliation, ordered the removal of all books written by or in favor of Republicans, few would doubt that the order violated the constitutional rights of the students denied access to those books. The same conclusion would surely apply if an all-white school board, motivated by racial animus, decided to remove all books authored by blacks or advocating racial equality and integration. Our Constitution does not permit the official suppression of *ideas.* Thus whether petitioners' removal of books from their school libraries denied respondents their First Amendment rights depends upon the motivation behind petitioners' actions. If petitioners *intended* by their removal decision to deny respondents access to ideas with which petitioners disagreed, and if this intent was the decisive factor in petitioners' [school board's] decision, then petitioners have exercised their discretion in violation of the Constitution. To permit such intentions to control official actions would be to encourage the precise sort of officially prescribed orthodoxy unequivocally condemned in *Barnette.*[201]

Such rulings suggest that school boards that allow teachers (or their libraries) to present only one side of a controversial issue expose themselves to risk of litigation, especially if their decision to do so is "*intended* . . . to deny . . . access to ideas with which [they] disagreed."

A. The *Rosenberger* Revolution

For many years, lawyers and others have assumed that the Establishment Clause superseded the constitutional guarantees of free speech. Nevertheless, the U.S. Supreme Court has more recently emphasized that the First Amendment prohibits the government from regulating speech "based on its substantive content or the message it conveys," even where the content of the speech is religious. Indeed, the Court has described this view of the First Amendment as "axiomatic."[202] The Court has strongly affirmed this principle in several opinions dealing with issues as diverse as civil rights meetings, the funding of a religiously based student publication at a public university, and the use of a public school auditorium by a religious group to show a film.[203] These rulings bear significantly on deciding the relative priority of, and the relationship between, a school board's right to determine curriculum content and a teacher's right to academic freedom.

In the most recent case on viewpoint discrimination, *Rosenberger v. Rector and Visitors of the University of Virginia,* the Supreme Court strongly reaffirmed its previous holdings and held that viewpoint discrimination arising from a misplaced fear of violating the Establishment Clause is itself unconstitutional. Rosenberger, a student at a state university, objected to the university's refusal to grant to his organization's newspaper the same financial subsidy that other campus organizations had received. The university defended its policy by citing the newspaper's evangelical Christian perspective. The university held that any funding of the paper would endorse a religious viewpoint and would thus violate the Constitution. The Supreme Court rejected this argument, holding that if a public institution opens a forum for free speech, it cannot then censor the forum based solely on the viewpoint of the speech expressed.[204]

The Court noted that viewpoint discrimination "is presumed to be unconstitutional." Nevertheless, it argued, when the government itself targets speech simply because of its content "the violation of the First Amendment is all the more blatant." Consequently, the Court found that the government must "abstain" from content-based speech restrictions when the "ideology or the opinion or perspective of the speaker is the rationale for the restriction."[205] The Court affirmed that the government may not engage in content-based suppression of speech even when the public forum where the speech occurs was created by the government in the first place.[206]

The Court's position allowed two exceptions. First, the government may control access to a nonpublic forum based "on subject matter and speaker identity" if the government's action is reasonable considering the forum's purpose and if the action is viewpoint neutral. This means that the government can suppress speech in a nonpublic forum if the speaker wants to discuss "a topic not encompassed within the purpose of the forum" or if the speaker is outside the special class for whom the forum was created.[207] Second, if the government is charged with viewpoint discrimination, it can clear itself of that charge by showing that to permit the speech in question would violate the Establishment Clause.[208]

Neither of these exceptions applies to Spokes's plan to teach his students about design theory. The Court showed itself quite willing to grant wide latitude for even explicitly religious speech or viewpoints in *Rosenberger,* when it articulated an Establishment Clause exception to the general prohibition against viewpoint discrimination.[209] If the Court had meant to include all religious speech within this exception, it clearly could not have reached the decision it did in *Rosenberger.* In any case, as already argued, teaching about design theory does not constitute an establishment of religion.

Moreover, the overwhelming majority of public schools (including presumably Spokes's) already address the subject of biological origins in their science curriculum. Although the courts have limited the free speech rights of teachers in the public school context, teachers do have the right to choose supplementary material that is appropriate to the subjects they have been mandated to teach.[210] Likewise, students may certainly learn about current ideas relevant to the subjects they are studying.[211]

Further, the Supreme Court has found that teachers, students, and parents have a "liberty interest" under the Fourteenth Amendment's Due Process Clause not to be prevented from studying certain subjects.[212] A critical aspect of this liberty interest is academic freedom. Academic freedom allows teachers to present appropriate material to their students without fear of censorship or retribution from the government. Teachers not only need academic freedom to teach effectively, but students need it to explore and develop new ideas. Without academic freedom, education becomes indoctrination.

The Supreme Court recognized this fundamental right to academic freedom in *Epperson v. Arkansas.*[213] In that case, the Court struck down an Arkansas statute that restricted the teachings of biological origins. The statute prohibited, with criminal sanction, the teaching of the theory of evolution in the state's public schools. A teacher challenged the statute, claiming that it violated her academic freedom. The Supreme Court, in rejecting the Arkansas law as unconstitutional, strongly upheld the academic freedom of teachers in the public schools.[214]

The Court found that the First Amendment's guarantees apply to our school systems, where they are "essential to safeguard the fundamental values of freedom of speech and inquiry and of belief." The Court made clear that "the First Amendment 'does not tolerate laws that cast a pall of orthodoxy over the classroom.'" Most significant, the Court found that the government's power to determine school curricula does not give it the power to prevent "the teaching of a scientific theory or doctrine where that prohibition is based upon reasons that violate the First Amendment." The Court even went so far as to assert that "it is much too late to argue that the State may impose upon the teachers in its schools any conditions that it chooses, however restrictive they may be of constitutional guarantees."[215] The same freedoms that allow teachers to present Darwinian evolutionary theory would seem to allow teachers to teach students about the theory of intelligent design, even if their school boards oppose their pedagogy.

Although public schools are not public forums per se, they are publicly funded places where ideas are exchanged.[216] Thus, if public schools or other governmental agencies bar teachers from teaching about design theory but allow teachers to teach neo-Darwinism, they will undermine free speech and foster viewpoint discrimination. At the very least, the government has no affirmative duty to censor teachers who attempt to present alternative viewpoints on scientific issues. Instead, strictly speaking, the Constitution prohibits such censorship or the regulation of speech "in ways that favor some viewpoints or ideas at the expense of others."[217]

B. *Edwards v. Aguillard* Revisited

Some might argue, of course, that court strictures against viewpoint discrimination apply only to "soft" subjects in the humanities such as politics, law, and religion that admit many differing interpretations. Since, they argue, the "hard" sciences do not involve significant subjectivity in interpretation, controversy plays no legitimate role in scientific discourse or education. Thus, teachers have no need to teach both sides of controversial issues in science, and school boards have no reason to respect the right of teachers who do so. Such an objection, however, not only belies a false and antiquated positivistic philosophy of science (certainly the history of science shows many arguments between scientists about the correct interpretation of data), it also contradicts the explicit and specific ruling of the Court concerning the scientific controversy over biological origins.

As noted above, in *Edwards v. Aguillard* the Court affirmed the academic freedom of teachers in public schools to present a variety of scientific theories about biological origins. Indeed, the Court struck down the Louisiana Balanced Treatment Act in large part based on academic freedom considerations. Recall that the Court found disingenuous the Act's proffered secular purpose of promoting academic freedom and that it expressed concern about several specific provisions of the Act that appeared to limit such freedom. In rejecting the proffered purpose of the Act, the Court carefully reaffirmed the academic freedom of teachers to teach alternative scientific (as opposed to Bible-based) theories of origins. The Court noted that the

Louisiana law did not give teachers any more flexibility in teaching about scientific origins theories than they had before the passage of the law. It noted that Louisiana had no statute that prevented teachers from presenting any scientific theory regarding biological or human origins.[218] The Court's language on this point is both instructive and decisive:

> We do not imply that a legislature could never require that scientific critiques of prevailing scientific theories be taught. Indeed, the Court acknowledged in *Stone* that its decision forbidding the posting of the Ten Commandments did not mean that no use could ever be made of the Ten Commandments, or that the Ten Commandments played an exclusively religious role in the history of Western Civilization. In a similar way, teaching a variety of scientific theories about the origins of humankind to schoolchildren might be validly done with the clear secular intent of enhancing the effectiveness of science instruction.[219]

Far from placing its imprimatur on Darwinism as the only permissible scientific theory of biological origins, *Edwards* clearly supports the principle of academic freedom in science education.[220] Further, the *Edwards* case, viewed in the context of recent rulings on viewpoint discrimination, suggests that science teachers, as much as teachers of other subjects, have the academic freedom to structure their presentations of controversial issues to avoid discrimination based on the content of the ideas in question—that is, to avoid viewpoint discrimination.

Thus, following *Edwards,* John Spokes certainly has the academic freedom to present the scientific weaknesses of Darwinism to his students without fear of running afoul of the Establishment Clause. As the Court itself stated, it did not want its ruling in *Edwards* to be construed as a ban on teaching "scientific critiques of prevailing scientific theories." Further, nothing in the *Edwards* decision justifies excluding consideration of design theory in the biology curriculum, unless it could be established that design theory, like creation science, constitutes a religious belief. Quite the contrary, the Court made clear that "teaching a variety of scientific theories about the origins of humankind to schoolchildren might be validly done with the clear secular intent of enhancing the effectiveness of science instruction."[221]

Thus, following *Edwards* and *Rosenberger,* Spokes's proposed curricular changes do give every indication of being constitutionally protected speech. Provided that his school board has already directed him to teach about the general subject of biological origins, Spokes should have the freedom to define how specifically he will do so in accord with his own professional judgment about the merits of relevant scientific ideas and in accord with court dictates about the dangers of viewpoint discrimination. Further, *Rosenberger* suggests that a school board would face far more exposure to litigation by preventing Spokes from implementing his changes than by allowing him to do so. Certainly, a school district that forced a teacher to affirm the truth of Darwinism as a condition of employment would enshrine the type of "officially prescribed orthodoxy" condemned by the Court in *West Virginia Board of Education v. Barnette*.[222] A school board that refused to permit criticism of Darwinism would violate the principles expressed in *Tinker* and *Pico*. But a school board that encouraged an open discussion of the issue, consistent with the best scientific evidence, would reduce the likelihood of litigation by any party.

VII. Conclusion

Until recently, the Darwinian perspective has enjoyed a monopoly over the curriculum in public school biology classes. Nevertheless, various factors have undermined the basis for that monopoly.

First, dissenting scientific opinion about the sufficiency of the neo-Darwinian mechanism as an explanation for the origin of apparent design has broken the Darwinian hegemony in the scientific world.

Second, within the philosophy of science, the failure of demarcation arguments has meant that both Darwinian evolutionary theory and design theory now enjoy equivalent methodological status, thereby denying any legal basis for excluding opposing theories from consideration.

Constitutional precedents have also changed the context of this curriculum debate. In 1986, *Edwards* affirmed the right of teachers to discuss alternative scientific theories of origin in their classrooms. In addition, subsequent cases such as *Rosenberger* have made it more difficult to use the Establishment Clause to limit academic freedom and the rights of free expression.

These changes have begun to affect public perceptions of the curricular debate. For example, recently in Melvindale, Michigan, a Detroit suburb, the school board voted to purchase a number of books (including Michael Behe's *Darwin's Black Box*) that detail specifically scientific challenges to standard materialistic theories of evolution.[223] This seemingly innocuous action provoked the National Center for Science Education (NCSE), a Darwinist lobby in Oakland, California, to issue a creationism "alert" on its website. NCSE director Eugenie Scott has warned that the inclusion of books such as Behe's would have a chilling effect on science education.[224] Such hysteria not only betrays the fear that always accompanies loss of cultural control but represents a clear attempt to suppress controversy rather than to enlist it in the service of science education—as the law not only allows but would now encourage.

When school boards or biology teachers (like John Spokes) take the initiative to teach rather than suppress the controversy as it exists in the scientific world, school board lawyers should encourage rather than resist this more open dialectical approach.

The time has come for school boards to resist threats of litigation from those who would censor teachers like Spokes and to defend their efforts to expand student access to evidence and information about this timely and compelling controversy.

Notes

1. *McLean v. Arkansas Board of Education,* 529 F. Supp. 1255 (E.D. Ark. 1982); *Edwards v. Aguillard,* 482 U.S. 578 (1987).

2. John Gibeaut, "Evolution of a Controversy," *Journal of the American Bar Association* (Nov. 1999): 50–55.

3. Throughout this essay, we will refer to this view as "Darwinian" or "Darwinist." Although in this essay we sometimes carefully distinguish between classical Darwinian, contemporary neo-Darwinian, and chemical evolutionary theories, we also use the term "Darwinian" or "Darwinist" to refer to all purely naturalistic theories of evolution—those that deny any role for a designing intelligence in the history of life. As will be discussed in greater detail below, the central feature of a Darwinist theory is that it regards the apparent design of living things as merely apparent. Moreover, the term *creationism* is misleading because it suggests that those who are opposed to Darwinism base their opposition on a literal reading of the book of Genesis. See discussion in part IV.A.

4. Kenneth R. Miller and Joseph Levine, *Biology,* 4th ed. (Upper Saddle River, N.J.: Prentice Hall, 1998), 658; Charles Darwin, *The Origin of Species* (Harmondsworth, England: Penguin Books, 1968), 130–172; Francisco J. Ayala, "Darwin's Revolution," in *Creative Evolution,* ed. John H. Campbell and J. William Schopf (Boston: Jones and Barlett, 1994), 1, 4–5.

5. Jonathan Wells, "Haeckel's Embryos and Evolution: Setting the Record Straight," *American Biology Teacher* 61 (1999): 345–49; Gordon C. Mills et al., "Origin of Life and Evolution in Biology Textbooks—A Critique," *American Biology Teacher* 55 (1993): 78–83; Jonathan Wells, *Icons of Evolution* (Washington, D.C.: Regnery, 2000).

6. See note 56.

7. Keith Stewart Thomson, "Marginalia: The Meanings of Evolution," *American Scientist* (Sept.-Oct. 1982): 529–31.

8. Indeed, Spokes finds that many distinguished biologists (e.g., Stuart Kauffman, Rudolf Raff, George Miklos, James Valentine) openly acknowledge that small-scale microevolutionary changes cannot be extrapolated to explain large-scale macroevolutionary innovation. As one group of scientists put it, natural selection can explain "the *survival*, but not the *arrival*, of the fittest." Scott Gilbert et al., "Resynthesizing Evolutionary and Developmental Biology," *Developmental Biology* 173 (1996): 357, 361.

9. Michael J. Behe, *Darwin's Black Box: The Biochemical Challenge to Evolution* (New York: Free Press, 1996).

10. National Academy of Science, *Teaching about Evolution and the Nature of Science* (Washington, D.C.: National Academy Press, 1998). "Those who oppose the teaching of evolution in public schools sometimes ask that teachers present 'the evidence against evolution.' There is no debate within the scientific community, however, over whether evolution occurred, and there is no evidence that evolution has not occurred. Some of the details of how evolution occurs are still being investigated. But scientists continue to debate only the particular mechanisms that result in evolution, not the overall accuracy of evolution as the explanation of life's history" (4).

The National Association of Biology Teachers (NABT) issued the following statement on teaching evolution: "The same examination, pondering and possible revision have firmly established evolution as an important natural process explained by valid scientific principles, and clearly differentiate and separate science from various kinds of nonscientific ways of knowing, including those with a supernatural basis such as creationism. Whether called 'creation science,' 'scientific creationism,' 'intelligent-design theory,' 'young-earth theory' or some other synonym, creation beliefs have no place in the science classroom. Explanations employing non-naturalistic or supernatural events, whether or not explicit reference is made to a supernatural being, are outside the realm of science and not part of a valid science curriculum. Evolutionary theory, indeed all of science, is necessarily silent on religion and neither refutes nor supports the existence of a deity or deities" (National Academy of Science, *Teaching about Evolution*, Appendix C, page 129).

"The Commission on Science Education of the American Association for the Advancement of Science, is vigorously opposed to attempts by some boards of education, and other groups to require that religious accounts of creation be taught in science classes" (ibid.).

11. John Angus Campbell, "Intelligent Design, Darwinism, and the Philosophy of Public Education," *Rhetoric and Public Affairs* 1 (1998): 469, 487.

12. Gibeaut, "Evolution," describes one such case. For an additional case, see Daniel J. Pinchot, "Moon Mulls Biblical Biology Three Years after Suit, Board Wants to Get Creation in Classes," *Pittsburgh Post-Gazette*, 29 Aug. 1997. More recently, a biology teacher was reassigned because he taught intelligent design as part of his treatment of the origins issue. See Marjorie Coeyman, "Evolution Gets Dismissed from Some Classes," *Christian Science Monitor*, 16 Aug. 1999.

13. "Creationist Book to Be Used in Burlington—Biology Teacher Questions Evolutionary Theory," *Seattle Times*, 14 June 1999; Barbara Galloway, "Group Asks Alternative to Theory of Evolution; Louisville Activists Say Darwin Camp Has Monopoly," *Akron Beacon Journal*, 13 Feb. 1995; Laurie Goodstein, "Scientists Take New Look at Creationism," *Houston Chronicle*, 10 Jan. 1998; Jennifer Juarez Robles and Matt Helms, "Schools Consider Creationism," *Detroit Free Press*, 11 Nov. 1997; Andrea Schoellkopf, "Proposed Science Curriculum Would Allow Creationism," *Albuquerque Journal*, 29 Oct. 1997.

14. Plato, *The Laws*, trans. A. E. Taylor (New York: Dutton, 1969), 279; Cicero, *De Natura Deorum*, trans. H. Rackham (New York: G. Putnam's Sons, 1933), 217; Aquinas used the argument from design as one of his proofs for the existence of God. See John Hick, *Arguments for the Existence of God* (New York: Herder and Herder, 1971), 1.

15. Neal C. Gillespie, "Natural History, Natural Theology, and Social Order: John Ray and the Newtonian Ideology," *Journal of the History of Biology* 20 (1987): 1.

16. Johannes Kepler, *Harmonies of the World*, trans. Charles Glen Wallis (Amherst, N.Y.: Prometheus Books, [1619] 1995), 170, 240; *Johannes Kepler, Mysterium Cosmographicum [The Secret of the Universe]*, trans. A.

M. Duncan (New York: Arabis Books, [1596] 1981), 93–103; John Ray, *The Wisdom of God Manifested in the Works of the Creation*, 3rd ed., (New York: Arno Press, [1701] 1977); Robert Boyle, *Selected Philosophical Papers of Robert Boyle* (Totowa, N.J.: Barnes and Noble Books, 1979), 172. Kepler's belief that the work of God is evident in nature is illustrated by his statement in the *Harmonies of the World* that God "by the light of nature promote[s] in us the desire for the light of grace, that by its means [God] mayest transport us into the light of glory" (240). See also Morris Kline, *Mathematics: The Loss of Certainty* (New York: Oxford University Press, 1980). "The strength of Copernicus's and Kepler's conviction that God must have designed the world harmoniously and simply can be judged by the objections with which they had to contend" (39).

17. *Newton's Principia*, trans. Andrew Motte and Florian Cajori, rev. (Berkeley: University of California Press, [1686] 1934), 543–44.

18. Sir Isaac Newton, *Opticks* (New York: Dover 1952), 369–70.

19. William Paley, *Natural Theology* (Hartford, Conn.: G. Goodwin, 1821).

20. For a discussion of this methodological shift, see Neil C. Gillespie, *Charles Darwin and the Problem of Creation* (Chicago: University of Chicago Press, 1979).

21. The effort to explain biological organisms was reinforced by a trend in science to provide fully naturalistic accounts for other phenomena, such as the precise configuration of the planets in the solar system (Laplace) and the origin of geological features (Lyell and Hutton). It was also reinforced (and in large part made possible) by an emerging positivistic tradition in science that increasingly sought to exclude appeals to supernatural or intelligent causes from science *by definition*. See ibid.

22. Peter J. Bowler, *Theories of Human Evolution: A Century of Debate, 1844–1944* (Baltimore: Johns Hopkins University Press, 1986), 44–50. Natural selection, as Darwin well understood, could accomplish nothing without a steady supply of genetic variation, the ultimate source of new biological structure. Nevertheless, both the blending theory of inheritance that Darwin had assumed and the classical Mendelian genetics that soon replaced it implied limitations on the amount of genetic variability available to natural selection. This in turn implied limits on the amount of novel structure that natural selection could produce.

23. John Maynard Smith, *The Theory of Evolution*, 3rd ed. (Baltimore: Penguin Books, 1975). "[T]he fact of evolution was not generally

accepted until a theory had been put forward to suggest how evolution had occurred, and in particular how organisms could become adapted to their environment; in the absence of such a theory, adaptation suggested design, and so implied a creator. It was this need which Darwin's theory of natural selection satisfied" (30).

24. Ernst Mayr, foreword to *Darwinism Defended,* by Michael Ruse (Reading, Mass.: Addison-Wesley, 1982): xi-xii.

25. Douglas Futuyma, "Evolution as Fact and Theory," *Bios* 56 (1985). "There is absolutely no disagreement among professional biologists on the fact that evolution has occurred. . . . But the *theory* of how evolution occurs is quite another matter, and is the subject of intense dispute" (3, 8). Of course, to admit that natural selection cannot explain the appearance of design is in effect to admit that it has failed to perform the role that is claimed for it as a designer substitute.

26. Niles Eldredge, "An Ode to Adaptive Transformation," *Nature* 296 (1982): 508.

27. Stephen Jay Gould, "Is a New and General Theory of Evolution Emerging?" *Paleobiology* 6 (1980): 119–20.

28. One of the most significant doubts about the creative power of the mutation/selection mechanism has followed directly from the elucidation of the nature of genetic information by molecular biologists in the 1950s and 1960s. Beginning in the late 1960s, mathematicians and probability theorists who began to analyze this problem found themselves deeply skeptical about the efficacy of random mutation as a means of generating specified information in the time available to the evolutionary process. See symposium volume, Paul S. Moorhead and Martin M. Kaplan eds., *Mathematical Challenges to the Neo-Darwinian Interpretation of Evolution* (New York: A. Liss, 1967), especially papers and comments from M. Eden, M. Shutzenberger, S. M. Ulam, and P. Gavaudan. This problem is discussed extensively in Stephen C. Meyer's essay, "DNA and the Origin of Life: Information, Specification, and Explanation," and in the essay, "The Cambrian Explosion: Biology's Big Bang," Stephen C. Meyer, Marcus Ross, Paul Nelson, and Paul Chien in this volume.

29. Behe, *Darwin's Black Box.*

30. Bernard John and George L. Gabor Miklos, *The Eukaryote Genome in Development and Evolution* (Boston: Allen and Unwin, 1988); A. H. Brush, "On the Origin of Feathers," *Journal of Evolutionary Biology* 9

108   *DeWolf et al.*

(1996): 131–42; H. Allen Orr and Jerry A. Coyne, "The Genetics of Adaptation: A Reassessment," *American Naturalist* 140 (1992): 725–42.

31. K. S. W. Campbell and C. R. Marshall, "Rates of Evolution," in *Rates of Evolution,* ed. K. S. W. Campbell and M. R. Day (Boston: Allen and Unwin, 1987), 61, 66–100; George L. Gabor Miklos, "Emergence of Organizational Complexities during Metazoan Evolution: Perspectives from Molecular Biology, Palaeontology and Neo-Darwinism," *Memoirs of the Association of Australasian Palaeontologists* 15 (1993): 7–41; Scott F. Gilbert et al., "Resynthesizing Evolutionary and Developmental Biology," *Developmental Biology* 173 (1996): 357–72.

32. James A. Shapiro, "Genome Organization, Natural Genetic Engineering and Adaptive Mutation," *Trends in Genetics* 13 (1997): 98–104; J. A. Shapiro, "Natural Genetic Engineering in Evolution," *Genetica* 86 (1992): 99–111; Richard von Sternberg, "Genome Self-Modification and Cellular Control of Genome Reorganization," *Rivista di Biologia/Biology Forum* 89 (1996): 424–53.

33. According to Stephen Jay Gould, "The extreme rarity of transitional forms in the fossil record persists as the trade secret of paleontology. The evolutionary trees that adorn our textbooks have data only at the tips and nodes of their branches; the rest is inference, however reasonable, not the evidence of fossils" ("Evolution's Erratic Pace," *Natural History* [May 1977]: 12, 14). Trilobite specialist Niles Eldredge of the American Museum in New York and one of the authors of the hypothesis of punctuated equilibria, for instance, describes commencing his work on the trilobite genus *Phacops,* sampling Middle Devonian strata across the United States, only to discover to his dismay that the trilobites were not varying smoothly and gradually between species, as theory predicted. See Niles Eldredge, *Reinventing Darwin: The Great Debate at the High Table of Evolutionary Theory* (New York: Wiley, 1995). Indeed, the fossil record as a whole proved so disturbing to traditional Darwinism that Eldredge and Stephen Gould rejected the gradualist neo-Darwinism model of evolutionary change in favor of a theory known as punctuated equilibrium. According to punctuated equilibrium, the fossil record shows long periods of stability "punctuated" by abrupt changes, resulting in entirely new organisms. Punctuated equilibrium reduces the conflict with the fossil record but does so at the cost of abandoning a sufficient explanatory mechanism for the appearance of biological novelty—the very thing that made Darwin's theory initially so attractive as a designer substitute. See D. Raup,

"Conflicts between Darwin and Paleontology," *Field Museum of Natural History Bulletin* 50 (Jan. 1979): 22–29; Jeffrey H. Schwartz, "Homeobox Genes, Fossils, and the Origin of Species," *Anatomical Record* 257 (1999): 15–31 [New Anat.].

34. A. D. Bradshaw, "Genostasis and the Limits to Evolution," *Transactions Royal Society London* 333 Series B (1991): 289–305; Brian K. Hall, "*Baupläne*, Phylotypic Stages, and Constraint: Why There Are So Few Types of Animals," *Evolutionary Biology* 29 (1996): 215–61; Kazuo Kawano, "How Far Can the Neo-Darwinism Be Extended? A Consideration from the History of Higher Taxa in Coleoptera," *Rivista di Biologia/Biology Forum* 91 (1998): 31–52.

35. Gavin de Beer, *Homology: An Unsolved Problem* (London: Oxford University Press, 1971); Michael Denton, *Evolution: A Theory in Crisis* (Bethesda, Md.: Adler and Adler, 1986), 142–56; John Gerhart and Marc Kirschner, *Cells, Embryos, and Evolution* (Malden, Mass.: Blackwell Science, 1997), 125–46; John A. Davison, "Semi-Meiosis as an Evolutionary Mechanism," *Journal of Theoretical Biology* 111 (1984): 725–35; W. J. Dickinson, "Molecules and Morphology: Where's the Homology?" *Trends in Genetics* 11 (1995): 119–21; Stephen J. Gaunt, "Chick Limbs, Fly Wings and Homology at the Fringe," *Nature* 386 (1997): 324–25; Gregory A. Wray and Ehab Abouheif, "When Is Homology Not Homology?" *Current Opinion in Genetics and Development* 8 (1998): 675–80.

36. Wallace Arthur, *The Origin of Animal Body Plans: A Study in Evolutionary Developmental Biology* (New York: Cambridge University Press, 1997); Rudolf A. Raff, *The Shape of Life* (Chicago: University of Chicago Press, 1996); César Arenas-Mena et al., "Expression of the Hox Gene Complex in the Indirect Development of a Sea Urchin," *Proceedings of the National Academy of Sciences U.S.A.* 95 (1998): 13062–67; Barbara C. Boyer and Jonathan Q. Henry, "Evolutionary Modifications of the Spiralian Developmental Program," *American Zoologist* 38 (1998): 621–33; Graham E. Budd, "Does Evolution in Body Patterning Genes Drive Morphological Change—or Vice Versa?" *BioEssays* 21 (1999): 326–32; Eric H. Davidson, "How Embryos Work: A Comparative View of Diverse Modes of Cell Fate Specification," *Development* 108 (1990): 365–89; Gabriel Gellon and William McGinnis, "Shaping Animal Body Plans in Development and Evolution by Modulation of Hox Expression Patterns," *BioEssays* 20 (1998): 116–25; Miodrag Grbic et al., "Development of Polyembryonic Insects: A Major Departure from

Typical Insect Embryogenesis," *Development, Genes, and Evolution* 208 (1998): 69–81.

37. Syozo Osawa, *Evolution of the Genetic Code* (New York: Oxford University Press, 1995); T. Jukes and S. Osawa, "Recent Evidence for Evolution of the Genetic Code," in *Evolution of Life,* ed. S. Osawa and T. Honjo (New York: Springer-Verlag, 1991), 79–95; Syozo Osawa et al., "Recent Evidence for Evolution of the Genetic Code," *Microbiological Reviews* 56 (1992): 229–64; Patrick J. Keeling and W. Ford Doolittle, "A Non-Canonical Genetic Code in an Early Diverging Eukaryotic Lineage," *Embo Journal* 15 (1996): 2285–90; Patrick J. Keeling and W. Ford Doolittle, "Widespread and Ancient Distribution of a Noncanonical Genetic Code in Diplomonads," *Molecular Biology and Evolution* 14 (1997): 895–901; Anee Baroin Tourancheau et al., "Genetic Code Deviations in the Ciliates: Evidence for Multiple and Independent Events," *Embo Journal* 14 (1995): 3262–67.

38. Charles B. Thaxton et al., *The Mystery of Life's Origin* (New York: Philosophical Library, 1984), 42. In the words of Jim Brooks, "the nitrogen content of early PreCambrian organic matter is relatively low (less than .15 percent). From this we can be reasonably certain that: there never was any substantial amount of 'primitive soup' on Earth when ancient PreCambrian sediments were formed; if such a 'soup' ever existed it was only for a brief period of time" (Jim Brooks, *Origins of Life* [Belleville, Mich., USA: Lion Pub., 1985], 118, emphasis omitted).

39. After the 1960s, a series of new fossil finds forced scientists to revise progressively downward their estimates of the time available for chemical evolution on Earth. See J. Brooks and G. Shaw, *Origin and Development of Living Systems* (New York: Academic Press, 1973), 73, 267–305, 361; Brooks, *Origins,* 104–16; Thaxton et al., *Mystery,* 69–72; Klaus Dose, "The Origin of Life: More Questions Than Answers," *Interdisciplinary Science Reviews* 13 (1988): 348–56; Richard E. Dickerson, "Chemical Evolution and the Origin of Life," *Scientific American* (Sept. 1978): 70–86; Andrew H. Knoll and Elso S. Barghoorn, "Archean Microfossils Showing Cell Division from the Swaziland System of South Africa," *Science* 198 (1977): 396–98; Donald R. Lowe, "Stromatolites 3,400-Myr-Old from the Archean of Western Australia," *Nature* 284 (1980): 441–43; Kevin A. Maher and David J. Stevenson, "Impact Frustration of the Origin of Life," *Nature* 331 (1988): 612–14; S. J. Mojzsis et al., "Evidence for Life on Earth Before 3,800 Million Years Ago," *Nature* 384 (1996): 55–59; Leslie E. Orgel, "The Origin of Life—

A Review of Facts and Speculations," *Trends in Biochemical Sciences* 23 (1998): 491–95; H. D. Pflug and H. Jaeschke-Boyer, "Combined Structural and Chemical Analysis of 3,800–Myr-Old Microfossils," *Nature* 280 (1979): 483–85; J. William Schopf and Elso S. Barghoorn, "Alga-Like Fossils from the Early Precambrian of South Africa," *Science* 156 (1967): 508–11; M. R. Walter et al., "Stromatolites 3,400–3,500 Myr Old from the North Pole Area, Western Australia," *Nature* 284 (1980): 443–45.

40. Robert Shapiro, *Origins: A Skeptic's Guide to the Creation of Life on Earth* (New York: Summit Books, 1986); Thaxton et al., *Mystery,* 69–98; Joel S. Levine, "The Photochemistry of the Paleoatmosphere," *Journal of Molecular Evolution* 18 (1982): 161–72.

41. Dose, "Origin of Life"; Shapiro, *Origins,* 98–116; Thaxton et al., *Mystery,* 99–112.

42. Besides design, chemical evolutionary theorists have relied on three general types of explanations for the origin of the specified complexity (specified information) found in DNA: chance, prebiotic natural selection, and self-organization. Numerous problems have been found with each of these explanations:

   1. *Chance-Based Models:* Emile Borel, *Probabilities and Life,* trans. Maurice Baudin (New York: Dover, [1943] 1962), 28; A. G. Cairns-Smith, *The Life Puzzle* (Edinburgh: Oliver and Boyd, 1971), 95; Hubert P. Yockey, *Information Theory and Molecular Biology* (New York: Cambridge University Press, 1992); Michael J. Behe, "Experimental Support for Regarding Functional Classes of Proteins to Be Highly Isolated from Each Other," in *Darwinism: Science or Philosophy?* ed. J. Buell and V. Hearn (Richardson, Tex.: Foundation for Thought and Ethics, 1994), 60–71; Ilya Prigogine et al., "Thermodynamics of Evolution," *Physics Today* (Nov. 1972): 23–28; John F. Reidhaar-Olson and Robert T. Sauer, "Functionally Acceptable Substitutions in Two Alpha-Helical Regions of Lambda Repressor," *Proteins: Structure, Function, and Genetics* 7 (1990): 306–16; Hubert P. Yockey, "A Calculation of the Probability of Spontaneous Biogenesis by Information Theory," *Journal of Theoretical Biology* 67 (1977): 377–98, esp. 380.

   2. *Prebiotic Natural Selection:* Ludwig von Bertalanffy, *Robots, Men and Minds* (New York: G. Braziller, 1967), 82; Christian de Duve, *Blueprint for a Cell: The Nature and Origin of Life* (Burlington, N.C.: N. Patterson, 1991), 187; Dean H. Kenyon, foreword to Thaxton et al., *Mystery,* v–viii; Peter T. Mora, "The Folly of Probability," in *The Origins of Prebiological Systems and of Their Molecular Matrices,* ed. Sidney W. Fox (New York: Academic Press, 1965), 39–64; Peter T. Mora, "Urge and

Molecular Biology," *Nature* 199 (1963): 212–19; Gerard Schramm, "Synthesis in Nucleosis and Polynucleotides with Metaphosphate Esters, in Fox, *Origins of Prebiological Systems,* 309–15.

3. *Self-Organization:* Percival Davis and Dean H. Kenyon, *Of Pandas and People: The Central Question of Biological Origins* (Dallas: Haughton, 1993); Bernd-Olaf Küppers, *Information and the Origin of Life* (Cambridge: MIT Press, 1990), 170–72; Shapiro, *Origins,* 117–31; Yockey, *Information Theory,* 259–93; John Horgan, "The World According to RNA," *Scientific American* (Jan. 1996): 27–30; Dean Kenyon and Gordon C. Mills, "The RNA World: A Critique," *Origins and Design* 17 (1996): 9; Randall A. Kok et al., "A Statistical Examination of Self-Ordering of Amino Acids in Proteins," *Origins of Life and Evolution of the Biosphere* 18 (1988): 135–42; Stephen C. Meyer, "DNA by Design: An Inference to the Best Explanation for the Origin of Biological Information," *Rhetoric and Public Affairs* 1 (1998): 519–56; Stephen C. Meyer, "The Explanatory Power of Design," in *Mere Creation: Science, Faith and Intelligent Design,* ed. William A. Dembski (Downers Grove, Ill.: InterVarsity Press, 1998), 128–134; Robert Shapiro, "Prebiotic Ribose Synthesis: A Critical Analysis," *Origins of Life and Evolution of the Biosphere* 18 (1988): 71–85; Charles B. Thaxton and Walter L. Bradley, "Information and the Origin of Life," in *The Creation Hypothesis: Scientific Evidence for an Intelligent Designer,* ed. J. P. Moreland (Downers Grove, Ill.: InterVarsity Press, 1994), 173–210.

43. Jacques Monod, *Chance and Necessity* (New York: Knopf, 1971), 143; Shapiro, *Origins,* 132–54; K. R. Popper, "Scientific Reduction and the Essential Incompleteness of All Science," in *Studies in the Philosophy of Biology,* ed. F. J. Ayala and T. Dobzhansky (London: Macmillan, 1974), 259; Massimo Pigliucci, "Where Do We Come From? A Humbling Look at the Biology of Life's Origin," *Skeptical Inquirer* (Sept.–Oct. 1999): 21–27.

44. Helena Curtis and Sue N. Barnes, *Invitation to Biology,* 5th ed. (New York: Worth Publishers, 1994); Douglas J. Futuyma, *Evolutionary Biology,* 3rd ed. (Sunderland, Mass.: Sinauer Associates, 1998); Burton S. Guttman, *Biology* (Boston: McGraw-Hill, 1999); Cecie Starr and Ralph Taggart, *Biology: The Unity and Diversity of Life,* 8th ed. (Belmont, Calif.: Wadsworth Pub., 1998); Mills et al., "Origins of Life," 78–83; Jonathan Wells, "Haeckel's Embryos and Evolution: Setting the Record Straight," *American Biology Teacher* 61 (1999): 345–49; Jonathan Wells, "Second Thoughts About Peppered Moths," *Scientist* (24 May 1999): 13.

45. Mills et al., "Origins of Life," 78–83.

46. Antonio Lazcano and Stanley L. Miller, "The Origin and Early Evolution of Life: Prebiotic Chemistry, the Pre-RNA World, and Time," *Cell* 85 (1996): 793; Stanley L. Miller, "The Prebiotic Synthesis of Organic Compounds as a Step Toward the Origin of Life," in *Major Events in the History of Life,* ed. J. William Schopf (Boston: Jones and Bartlett, 1993), 5.

47. For example, Thaxton and Bradley, "Information," 173–210.

48. Miller and Levine, *Biology,* 344; Alton L. Biggs et al., *Biology: The Dynamics of Life* (New York: Glencoe, 1991), 227–28.

49. Eugenie C. Scott, "Keep Science Free from Creationism," *Insight* (21 Feb. 1994): 29; U.S. Commission on Civil Rights, Hearings, Seattle (21 Aug. 1998) http://w1.548.telia.com/~454804688/civilright.html.

50. William B. Provine, Review of *Teaching About Evolution and the Nature of Science,* by the National Academy of Sciences, http://fp.bio.utk.edu/darwin/NASguidebook/provine_1.html.

51. Behe, *Darwin's Black Box;* Thaxton et al., *Mystery;* Davis and Kenyon, *Of Pandas and People;* Dembski, *Mere Creation;* William A. Dembski, *The Design Inference: Eliminating Change Through Small Probabilities* (New York: Cambridge University Press, 1998).

52. Dembski, *Design Inference,* 1–35.

53. Ibid., 36–66. Complex sequences are those that exhibit an irregular and improbable arrangement that defies expression by a simple rule or algorithm. A specification, on the other hand, is a match or correspondence between a physical system or sequence and a set of independent functional requirements or constraints. To illustrate these concepts (of complexity and specification), consider the following three sets of symbols:

"inetehnsdysk]idfawqnz,mfdifhsnmcpew,ms.s/a"

"Time and tide waits for no man."

"ABABABABABABABABABABABABAB"

Both the first and second sequences shown above are complex because both defy reduction to a simple rule. Each represents a highly irregular, aperiodic, and improbable sequence of symbols. The third sequence is not complex but is instead highly ordered and repetitive. Of the two complex sequences, only one exemplifies a set of independent functional requirements—that is, is specified. English has a number of such functional requirements. For example, to convey meaning in English one must employ existing conventions of vocabulary (associations of symbol sequences with particular objects, concepts, or ideas) and existing conventions of syntax and grammar (such as "every sentence requires a subject and a verb"). When arrangements of symbols "match" or utilize existing vocabulary and grammatical conventions (i.e., functional requirements), communication can occur. Such arrangements exhibit "specification." The second sequence ("Time and tide wait for no man") clearly exhibits such a match between itself and the preexisting requirements of vocabulary and grammar. It has employed these conventions to express a meaningful idea.

Indeed, of the three sequences above, only the second manifests both the jointly necessary indicators of a designed system. The third sequence lacks complexity, though it does exhibit a simple periodic pattern, a specification of sorts. The first sequence is complex but not specified, as we have seen. Only the second sequence exhibits both complexity and specification. Thus, according to Dembski's theory, only the second sequence, but not the first and third, implicates an intelligent cause—as indeed our intuition tells us. See Dembski, *Design Inference;* Meyer, "DNA by Design"; Meyer, "DNA and the Origin of Life: Information, Specification, and Explanation," in this volume.

54. Dembski, *Design Inference,* 36–66.
55. Behe, *Darwin's Black Box,* 179, 69–73.
56. Ibid., 3–164, 187–231.
57. Dean H. Kenyon and Gary Steinman, *Biochemical Predestination* (New York: McGraw Hill, 1969), 36, 219–69.
58. Richard Dawkins, *River Out of Eden* (New York: Basic Books, 1995), 17.
59. Bill Gates, *The Road Ahead* (New York: Viking, 1996), 228.
60. Sahotra Sarkar, "Biological Information: A Skeptical Look at Some Central Dogmas of Molecular Biology," in *The Philosophy and History of Molecular Biology: New Perspectives,* ed. Sahotra Sarkar (Boston: Kluwer Academic, 1996), 191.
61. Meyer, "DNA by Design"; Meyer, "Explanatory Power," 113–47.
62. Meyer et al., "Cambrian Explosion"; Robert F. DeHaan and John L. Wiester, "Cambrian Explosion: The Fossil Record and Intelligent Design," in *Signs of Intelligence: Understanding Intelligent Design,* eds. William A. Dembski and James M. Kushiner (Grand Rapids, Mich.: Brazos, 2001), 145–156.

63. Jonathan Wells and Paul Nelson, "Homology: A Concept in Crisis," *Origins and Design* (fall 1997): 12 (arguing that "naturalistic mechanisms proposed to explain homology do not fit the evidence").

64. Ibid.

65. Ayala, "Darwin's Revolution."

66. Miller and Levine, *Biology.*

67. John A. Campbell, "Intelligent Design, Darwinism, and the Philosophy of Public Education," *Rhetoric and Public Affairs* 1 (1998): 469, 481 (proposing that students will learn more about Darwin's theory by studying "intelligent design").

68. "Explanations employing nonnaturalistic or supernatural events, whether or not explicit reference is made to a supernatural being, are outside the realm of science and not part of a valid science curriculum" (National Academy of Science, *Teaching about Evolution,* 127).

69. *McLean* at 1267: "[T]he essential characteristics of science are: (1) It is guided by natural law; (2) It has to be explanatory by reference to natural law; (3) It is testable against the empirical world; (4) Its conclusions are tentative, i.e., are not necessarily the final word; and (5) It is falsifiable."

70. See part V.E.

71. See *McLean* at 1258, 1264. The court specifically found that the Arkansas law "was passed with the specific purpose . . . of advancing religion" (1264). This placed the law directly in conflict with the First Amendment's establishment clause under the *Lemon* test. For a statute to pass constitutional muster under *Lemon* it must have a secular legislative purpose, it cannot either advance or inhibit religion, and it must not foster an excessive entanglement between government and religion. See *Lemon v. Kurtzman,* 403 U.S. 602, 612–13 (1971); *Stone v. Graham,* 449 U.S. 39, 40 (1980). A violation of any of the prongs of the *Lemon* test results in a violation of the Establishment Clause. See *McLean,* at 1258. The court in *McLean* found that the Arkansas law's purpose was to advance religion in the public schools in violation of *Lemon*'s first prong (1264). The court in *McLean* also found that the Arkansas law would result in an impermissible entanglement with religion, violating the third prong of *Lemon* (1272).

72. *McLean,* at 1267–72. The court's language was unambiguous: "Section 4(a) [of the Arkansas Act] lacks legitimate educational value because 'creation science' as defined in that section is simply not science." See generally Robert M. Gordon, "*McLean v. Arkansas Board of Education:*

"Finding the Science in 'Creation Science,'" *Northwestern University Law Review* 77 (1982): 374 (discussing court's finding that creation science is unscientific).

73. *McLean,* at 1272, 1267. In the court's words, these five points are the "essential characteristics of science."

74. *Edwards;* National Academy of Science, *Teaching About Evolution.* See discussion in part V.D.

75. Larry Laudan, "Science at the Bar—Causes for Concern," in *But Is It Science?* ed. Michael Ruse (Amherst, N.Y.: Prometheus Books, 1988), 351, 355: "It simply will not do for the defenders of science to invoke philosophy of science when it suits them . . . and to dismiss it as 'arcane' and 'remote' when it does not"; Philip Quinn, "The Philosopher of Science as Expert Witness," in Ruse, *But Is It Science?* (criticizing expert testimony in *McLean* as "fallacious" and not representative of "settled consensus of opinion in the relevant community of scholars," 367, 384).

76. Laudan, "Science at the Bar"; Quinn, "Philosopher of Science," 367–85.

77. Laudan, "Science at the Bar," 353–55.

78. See discussion in part V.D.

79. Imre Lakatos, "Falsification and the Methodology of Scientific Research Programmes," in *Scientific Knowledge: Basic Issues in the Philosophy of Science,* ed. Janet A. Kouvray (Belmont, Calif.: Wadsworth, 1987), 173, 175, 192 (presenting scientific progress as rational process rather than religious conversions).

80. Ibid., 175.

81. Larry Laudan, "The Demise of the Demarcation Problem," in Ruse, *But Is It Science?.*

82. Jon Buell, "Broaden Science Curriculum," *Dallas Morning News,* 10 Mar. 1989, (quoting unidentified "authority").

83. Laudan, "Science at the Bar," 354.

84. Ibid., 352.

85. Ibid.

86. Ibid., 352–53.

87. Charles Darwin, *On the Origin of Species,* (Cambridge: Harvard University Press, [1859] 1964), 411–34.

88. Laudan, "Science at the Bar," 354.

89. Ibid.

90. Ibid.

91. For example, Stephen C. Meyer, "The Demarcation of Science and Religion," in *The History of Science and Religion in the Western Tradition: An Encyclopedia,* ed. Gary Ferngren et al. (New York: Garland, 2000), 17, 22 ("[I]nsofar as both creationist and evolutionary theories constitute historical theories about past causal events, neither explains exclusively by reference to natural law."); Stephen C. Meyer, "The Nature of Historical Science and the Demarcation of Design and Descent," in *Facets of Faith and Science,* ed. Jitse M. van der Meer (Lanham, Md.: Pascal Centre for Advanced Studies in Faith and Science: University Press of America, 1996), 4; Stephen C. Meyer, "The Methodological Equivalence of Design and Descent: Can There Be a Scientific 'Theory of Creation?'" in Moreland, *The Creation Hypothesis* ("The exclusion of one of the logically possible programs of origins research by assumption . . . seriously diminishes the significance of any claim to theoretical superiority by advocates of a remaining group," 102).

92. Laudan, "Science at the Bar," 354.

93. Elliott Sober, *Philosophy of Biology* (Boulder, Colo.: Westview Press, 1993), finding that creationism and Darwinism both use characteristic approaches and techniques to attempt to explain certain phenomena (27, 56).

94. Meyer, "Demarcation," 91–130; Meyer, "Methodological Equivalence," 99. ("[T]he conjunction of the methodological equivalence of design and descent and the existence of a convention that regards descent as scientific implies that design should—by that same convention—be regarded as scientific too.")

95. Interestingly, there is considerable evidence that some advocates of these demarcation arguments in the Arkansas trial knew them to be inadequate at the time of the trial itself. For example, Barry Gross, a philosopher of science who served as a consultant to the law firm of Skadden, Arps (who represented the ACLU), has written that he informed the ACLU at the time of the trial that the *McLean* criteria were inaccurate and inadequate. Barry R. Gross, "Commentary: Philosophers at the Bar—Some Reasons for Restraint," *Science, Technology and Human Values,* (fall 1983): 36. As he wrote after the trial, "Philosophically, these criteria may have been acceptable sixty or eighty years ago, but they are not rigorous, they are redundant, and they take no account of many distinctions nor of historical cases. The opinion does not state whether they are singly necessary or jointly sufficient. One

would not recommend to graduate school a student who could do no
better than this."

96. U.S. Commission on Civil Rights, Hearings.
97. Speech by Michael Ruse to the Annual Meeting of the American Association for the Advancement of Science,13 Feb. 1993, http://www.leaderv-.com/orgs/am/orpages/or151/mr93tran.html.
98. Michael Ruse, *Monad to Man* (Cambridge: Harvard University Press, 1996), 511–17.
99. Laudan, "Science at the Bar," 351–55.
100. U.S. Commission on Civil Rights, Hearings.
101. Ibid.
102. *Daubert v. Merrell Dow Pharmaceuticals, Inc.,* 509 U.S. 579 (1993).
103. *Frye v. United States,* 293 F. 1013, 1014 (D.C. Cir. 1923), holding that "while courts will go a long way in admitting expert testimony deduced from a well-recognized scientific principle or discovery, the thing from which the deduction is made must be sufficiently established to have gained general acceptance in the particular field in which it belongs."
104. Ibid., at 1013–14.
105. *Daubert,* at 585–86. "In the 70 years since its formulation in the *Frye* case, the 'general acceptance' test has been the dominant standard for determining the admissibility of novel scientific evidence at trial," citing Eric D. Green and Charles R. Nesson, *Problems, Cases, and Materials on Evidence* (Boston: Little Brown, 1983), 649.

One criticism was the court's reliance on professional acceptance by the scientific community as a gauge of legitimate science. A popular evidence casebook summarizes one of the arguments against the *Frye* ruling: "[T]he extent of the acceptance of the technique by peers is not the substantive test of scientific validity; the degree of acceptance is merely circumstantial evidence that the hypothesis has been properly validated by experimentation" (Ronald L. Carlson et al., *Evidence in the Nineties,* 3rd ed. [1991], 289, citing Bert Black, "A Unified Theory of Scientific Evidence," *Fordham Law Review* 56 [1988]: 595, 625, 632).
106. *State v. York,* 564 A.2d 389, 390–91 (Me. 1989). In ruling on the admissibility of a social worker's testimony regarding the behavior of an eight-year-old child, the Maine court found that the guiding principle in evaluating the legitimacy of scientific evidence is "solid empirical research" (at 390).

107. *Daubert,* 582, 587–89, 590. The view of science in *Daubert* was recently strengthened by the Supreme Court's ruling in *Kumho Tire Co. v. Carmichael,* 526 U.S. 137 (1999). *Kumho* extended *Daubert* to apply to the expert testimony of nonscientists offered under Rule 702 (see *Kumho* at 141). The Court expanded the number of criteria which could be considered when evaluating evidence under *Daubert,* but continued to apply its fundamental rule, that scientific reliability should be considered a function of the coherence of the methodology employed, not by whether a view commands majority status in the particular discipline. See *Kumho* at 149, holding that trial judge's duty is to "determine whether the testimony [in question] has 'a reliable basis in the knowledge and experience of [the relevant] discipline'" (quoting *Daubert,* 509 U.S. at 592 [second alteration in original]).

108. *Daubert,* at 594 ("The inquiry envisioned by Rule 702 is, we emphasize, a flexible one"). Examples of cases favoring the *Daubert* rule include *Commonwealth v. Lanigan,* 641 N.E.2d 1342, 1349 (Mass. 1994), adopting *Daubert* test; *Hand v. Norfolk S. Ry. Co.,* No. 03A01–9704-CV-00123, 1998 WL 281946, at *4 (Tenn. App. 1998), following but not officially adopting the *Daubert* test; *State v. Streich,* 658 A.2d 38, 47 (Vt. 1995), applying *Daubert*'s factors; *State v. Anderson,* 881 P.2d 29, 36 (N.M. 1994), citing *Daubert* to support judicially created admissibility considerations. But see *State v. Tankersley,* 956 P.2d 486, 491 (Ariz. 1998), refusing to replace *Frye* with *Daubert* but noting that issue not properly before court; *State v. Copeland,* 922 P.2d 1304, 1310 (Wash. 1996), holding *Frye,* not *Daubert,* test applied to admission of scientific evidence.

109. *Daubert,* at 590; *York,* at 390–91.

110. *Daubert,* at 590.

111. For example, *United States v. Chischilly,* 30 F.3d 1144, 1154 (9th Cir. 1994), holding that judges should not supplant the jury's function of evaluating evidence by "'cross-examination, presentation of contrary evidence, and careful instruction'" of juries (quoting *Daubert,* at 596).

112. A good example of a minority viewpoint that is worthy of scientific debate is Francis Crick's theory that life originated on a distant planet and was "seeded" by a more developed civilization that transported life via unmanned spacecraft. See generally Francis H. Crick and Leslie E. Orgel, "Directed Panspermia," *Icarus* 19 (1973): 341, explaining Francis Crick's "theory that organisms were deliberately transmitted to the earth by intelligent beings on another planet." As one

commentator stated, this theory "remains outside the mainstream of science; however, the mental exercises that Crick entertains both for and against his theory are stimulating and informative" ("A Visit With Dr. Francis Crick, Access Excellence Classic Collection," http://www.accessexcellence.org/AE/AEC/CC/crick.html.

113. See part I.B.

114. Davis and Kenyon, *Of Pandas and People;* Jay D. Wexler, "Of Pandas, People, and the First Amendment: The Constitutionality of Teaching Intelligent Design in the Public Schools," *Stanford Law Review* 49 (1997): 439, 467–68. The First Amendment's establishment clause reads, in part: "Congress shall make no law respecting an establishment of religion." The Establishment Clause has been incorporated by the Fourteenth Amendment, so its prohibition against the establishment of religion applies equally to state and federal governments. See *Everson v. Board of Education,* 330 U.S. 1, 15–16 (1947). To Wexler, the scientific merit of intelligent design is "not . . . a very important question after all" ("Of Pandas," 468). Instead, the only critical question is whether the teaching of intelligent design violates the requirement that schools refrain from teaching religion. Since intelligent design implies the existence of a designer, it is logical to assume "a supreme, supernatural being who designed, coordinated, and created all of nature according to a master plan" (460). For this reason, any attempt to teach intelligent design is inherently religious and therefore must be excluded from the public school system (462–63).

115. Wexler, "Of Pandas."

116. *Edwards; Lemon,* at 612–13.

117. *Texas Monthly, Inc. v. Bullock,* 489 U.S. 1, 25 (1989), striking down tax exemption for religious periodical as nonneutral benefit.

118. *Witters v. Washington Dep't of Servs. for the Blind,* 474 U.S. 481, 489 (1986), holding that state aid to a blind student studying theology was not barred by the First Amendment.

119. *United States v. Seeger,* 380 U.S. 163, 164–65 (1965), seeking exemption from military service obligation for conscientious objections based on religious belief; *Sherbert v. Verner,* 374 U.S. 398, 399–402 (1963), seeking exemption based on religious belief from requirement to work on Saturday to receive unemployment benefits; *Wisconsin v. Yoder,* 406 U.S. 205, 207 (1972), seeking religious exemption from compulsory school attendance statute; *Thomas v. Review Bd. of Ind. Employment Security Div.,* 450 U.S. 707, 709–13 (1981), seeking religious exemption

from requirement to work in armament factory to receive unemployment benefits; *Texas Monthly, Inc.,* at 25, challenging tax exemption for religious periodicals.

120. *Seeger,* at 176. Nevertheless, courts have rejected claims of religious motivation where they find that religious language merely affects a form of fraud. See, for example, *United States v. Meyers,* 95 F.3d 1475, 1481 (10th Cir. 1996), rejecting defendant's claim that he was wrongfully convicted of violating drug laws, in contravention of his right to free exercise of religion, because of his membership in Church of Marijuana.

121. For example, *Grove v. Mead Sch. Dist. No. 354,* 753 F.2d 1528, 1534 (9th Cir. 1985), finding that use of literature text offensive to fundamentalist Christians did not result in promotion of alleged religion of secular humanism; *Brown v. Woodland Joint Unified Sch. Dist.,* 27 F.3d 1373, 1378–83 (9th Cir. 1994), reasoning that teaching students about witchcraft and inviting them to participate in classroom poetry and chanting did not promote "religion" of witchcraft.

122. *Malnak v. Yogi,* 592 F.2d 197, 198–99 (3d Cir. 1979). We may use the term "religious" in a metaphorical sense, such as commenting that a person is "religious" about getting exercise or watching a favorite sporting event. But it requires more than a great deal of passion or commitment to an activity or idea to make something religious for legal purposes. See *Meyers,* at 1481–84.

123. The only successful claim has been *Malnak,* at 198–99, enjoining practitioners from teaching "Science of Creative Intelligence-Transcendental Meditation" to public school students because practices were too closely related to traditional Hindu doctrines. The more common result is to deny the claim that the defendant's belief system operates in a way analogous to religion. See, for example, *Grove,* 753 F.2d at 1537–38; *Brown,* 27 F.3d at 1380–81.

124. Dmitry N. Feofanov, "Defining Religion: An Immodest Proposal," *Hofstra Law Review* 23 (1994): 309, 313, stating that "we need a definition of religion because it determines what is protected and what is not"; see also Steven D. Collier, Comment, "Beyond Seeger/Welsh: Redefining Religion Under the Constitution," *Emory Law Journal* 31, Comment (1982): 973, 975 note 14. "A clear definition of religion is essential to any case based solely on the religion clauses, since the First Amendment claim disappears if 'religion' is not involved" [footnote omitted], citing *Theriault v. Silber,* 453 F. Supp. 254 (W.D. Tex.

1978), *appeal dismissed* 579 F.2d 302 (5th Cir. 1978), *and cert. denied,* 440 U.S. 917 (1979); *United States v. Kuch,* 288 F. Supp. 439 (D.D.C. 1968); *Yoder,* at 215. *Alvarado v. City of San Jose,* 94 F.3d 1223, 1227 (9th Cir. 1996). The court in *Alvarado* described the attempt to define religion both as a general term and for Establishment Clause purposes as a "notoriously difficult, if not impossible, task," citing James M. Donovan, "God is as God Does: Law, Anthropology, and the Definition of 'Religion,'" *Seton Hall Constitutional Law Journal* 6 (1995): 23; *Africa v. Pennsylvania,* 662 F.2d 1025, 1031 (3d Cir. 1981), *cert. denied,* 456 U.S. 908 (1982).

125. *Peloza v. Capistrano Unified Sch. Dist.,* 37 F.3d 517, 521 (9th Cir. 1994); *Smith v. Board of Sch. Comm'rs,* 827 F.2d 684, 690–95 (11th Cir. 1987); United States v. Allen, 760 F.2d 447, 450 (2d Cir. 1985).

126. *United States v. Kauten,* 133 F.2d 703, 708 (2d Cir. 1943).

127. Different religions have different understandings of the nature of religion and religious belief. Protestant theologian Paul Tillich defined religion as being an "ultimate concern" (*The Shaking of the Foundations* [New York: Charles Scribner's Sons, 1948], 57). That definition would expand religion beyond traditional theistic grounds to include any strongly held ideological belief concerning the ultimate meaning and purpose of the universe. The Letter of James in the New Testament states that "religion that is pure and undefiled before God, the Father, is this: to care for orphans and widows in their distress, and to keep oneself unstained by the world" (NRSV Harper Study Bible [Grand Rapids, Mich.: Zondervan Publishing House, 1991] 1:27). The Catechism of the Catholic Church identifies true religion with the teachings of the Catholic and apostolic Church. See *Catechism of the Catholic Church* (London: Geoffrey Chapman, 1999), 870. Some evangelical Protestant theologians have even argued that Christianity itself is not properly thought of as a religion. See Dietrich Bonhoeffer, *The Cost of Discipleship,* rev. ed. (New York: Touchstone, 1995); Karl Barth, *The Epistle to the Romans,* 6th ed. (London: Oxford University Press, 1933). Even the role of God in religion is disputed. Some religious traditions (Christianity, Judaism, Islam) affirm monotheism; some (Hinduism, Jainism, animism) affirm a belief in a multiplicity of deities; and others (Buddhism, Confucianism, Taoism) hold no particular view of God or the gods at all. See Willard E. Arnett, *A Modern Reader in the Philosophy of Religion* (New York: Appleton-Century-Crofts, 1966), 4–5.

128. Val D. Ricks, "To God God's, to Caesar Caesar's, and to Both the Defining of Religion," *Creighton Law Review* 26 (1993): 1053, 1054–55. According to Ricks, "only a few United States Supreme Court cases have mentioned the issue, and none have addressed it directly" (1054, note 20), citing *Thomas v. Review Bd.*, 450 U.S. 707 (1981); *Yoder; Welsh v. United States*, 398 U.S. 333 (1970); *Seeger; Torcaso v. Watkins*, 367 U.S. 488 (1961); *United States v. Ballard*, 322 U.S. 78 (1944); *Davis v. Beason*, 133 U.S. 333 (1890); *Reynolds v. United States*, 98 U.S. 145 (1878). Ricks also refers to the relatively small number of appellate court decisions attempting to define religion, citing *Africa, cert. denied*, 456 U.S. 908 (1982); *Malnak*, Adams, J., concurring; *International Soc'y for Krishna Consciousness, Inc. v. Barber*, 650 F.2d 430 (2d Cir. 1981); *Founding Church of Scientology v. United States*, 409 F.2d 1146 (D.C. Cir.), *cert. denied*, 396 U.S. 963 (1969); *Kauten*.

129. See generally David K. DeWolf, "State Action Under the Religion Clauses: Neutral in Result or Neutral in Treatment?" *University of Richmond Law Review* 24 (1990): 253, 275: "[T]he Court's opinion [in *Seeger*] should be read as demonstrating the Court's recognition that when legal rights are made dependent upon theological categories, a court cannot make a legal determination without at the same time becoming entangled in the most sensitive of theological issues."

130. *Peloza.*

131. Ibid., at 519–21, citing *Smith v. Board of Sch. Comm'rs*, 827 F.2d 684, 690–95 (11th Cir. 1987); *United States v. Allen*, 760 F.2d 447, 450–51 (2d Cir. 1985).

132. Ibid. at 521, note 5, citing *Allen*, at 450–51, quoting Laurence H. Tribe, *American Constitutional Law* (Mineola, N.Y.: Foundation Press, 1978), 827–28. Tribe argues that the balance between the Free Exercise and Establishment Clauses of the First Amendment should be struck by favoring religious liberty rather than by sacrificing religious liberty to the Establishment Clause.

133. *Alvarado*, at 1226.

134. Ibid., at 1228–31. This test was first proposed in *Malnak*, at 207–10, Adams, J., concurring. The Third Circuit adopted the test in *Africa*.

135. Quoting *Africa*, at 1035–36 (internal quotations omitted).

136. *Peloza*, at 520; *Alvarado*, at 1229.

137. *Alvarado*, at 1229, quoting *Africa*, at 1032. Clearly, the debate between Darwinists and design theorists about the origin of apparent design could be characterized as a "fundamental" scientific and philosophical

issue. Nevertheless, neither Darwinism nor design theory seeks to answer "ultimate" metaphysical questions, even though both theories have implications for how such questions are approached (see notes 147–49 and 151–57 and accompanying text).

138. William A. Dembski, *Intelligent Design Is Not Optimal Design* (2 Jan. 2000): http://www.discovery.org/crsc/CRSCdbEngine.php3?id=86.

139. Stephen C. Meyer, "Return of the God Hypothesis," *Journal of Interdisciplinary Studies* 1 (1999): 9.

140. *Edwards,* at 605, Powell, J., concurring, quoting *McGowan v. Maryland,* 366 U.S. 420, 442 (1961).

141. *Alvarado,* at 1229, quoting *Africa,* at 1032.

142. See notes 49–54 and accompanying text.

143. Quoting *Africa,* at 1032.

144. For example, Center for Science and Culture, The Discovery Institute, proposing alternatives to materialism. http://www. discovery.org/crsc.

145. Behe, *Darwin's Black Box,* 203; Meyer, "DNA by Design."

146. See notes 20–21 and accompanying text.

147. Futuyma, *Evolutionary Biology,* 5; William Provine, "Evolution and the Foundation of Ethics," *MBL Science* 3 (1988): 25, 26 ("The implications of modern evolutionary biology are inescapable. . . . [E]volutionary biology undermines the fundamental assumptions underlying ethical systems in almost all cultures, Western civilization in particular"); Stephen Jay Gould, *Ever Since Darwin* (New York: W. W. Norton, 1977), 147.

148. Gould, *Ever Since Darwin,* 147.

149. Ibid., 267.

150. Stephen Jay Gould, *Wonderful Life* (New York: W. W. Norton, 1989), 323.

151. One example is the debate over the most effective polio vaccine: the one developed by Jonas Salk or the one developed by Albert Sabin. The debate over superiority was not only about science but involved controversies over the rights of individual patients versus public health and the proper role of doctors in public policy debates. See generally *Reyes v. Wyeth Lab.,* 498 F.2d 1264, 1294–95 (5th Cir. 1974), holding that marketers of oral polio vaccine may be liable when they failed to warn parents that treatment was necessary; Theodore H. Davis, Jr. and Catherine B. Bowman, "No-Fault Compensation for Unavoidable Injuries: Evaluating the National Childhood Vaccine In-

jury Compensation Program," *University of Dayton Law Review* 16 (1991): 277, 281–85, examining the efficacy of the National Childhood Vaccine Injury Compensation program to compensate victims of mandatory childhood vaccine programs while protecting vaccine manufacturers from liability. Other examples could be easily multiplied, such as the issues of global warming, the effect of electromagnetic radiation on health, and the risks associated with cellular telephones or breast implants.

152. Ayala, "Darwin's Revolution," 4–5.

153. Kenyon and Steinman, *Biochemical Predestination*, 6.

154. Richard Dawkins, *The Blind Watchmaker: Why the Evidence of Evolution Reveals a Universe without Design* (New York: W. W. Norton, 1986), 1–6.

155. George Gaylord Simpson, *The Meaning of Evolution*, rev. ed. (New Haven, Conn.: Yale University Press, 1967), 345.

156. Purves, Orians, and Heller, *Life: The Science of Biology*, vol. 2, *Evolution, Diversity, and Ecology* (Sunderland, Mass.: Sinauer Associates, 2001), 3; Miller and Levine, *Biology*, 658. Miller and Levine have removed this note from the 2002 edition of *Biology*.

157. Futuyma, *Evolutionary Biology*, 5.

158. *Epperson v. Arkansas*, 393 U.S. 97, 113 (1968), Black, J., concurring.

159. *Edwards*, at 605, Powell, J., concurring, arguing that subject matter taught in school does not violate Establishment Clause simply "because the material to be taught 'happens to coincide or harmonize with the tenets of some or all religions,'" quoting *McGowan*, at 442. The language from *McGowan* has been cited with approval in numerous subsequent Supreme Court decisions. See *Hernandez v. Commissioner*, 490 U.S. 680, 696 (1989); *Lynch v. Donnelly*, 465 U.S. 668, 682 (1984); *Bob Jones Univ. v. United States*, 461 U.S. 574, 604 n.30 (1983); *Harris v. McRae*, 448 U.S. 297, 319 (1980); *School Dist. v. Schempp*, 374 U.S. 203, 303 (1963), Brennan, J., concurring.

160. *Edwards*, at 579; Wexler, "Of Pandas," 455–66.

161. *Louisiana Revised Statutes Annotated*, §§ 17:286.1–7 (West 1982).

162. *Edwards*, at 581–82.

163. Ibid., at 582–94.

164. *Lemon*, at 612–13. Although the *Lemon* test has received scholarly criticism and has been qualified by the Court, see *Lynch*, at 679, the Court continues to rely on the test's general framework. See Robert A. Sedler, "Understanding the Establishment Clause: The Perspective of

Constitutional Litigation," *Wayne Law Review* 43 (1997): 1317, 1323. Two exceptions are *Marsh v. Chambers,* 463 U.S. 783 (1983), and *Rosenberger v. Rector and Visitors of the University of Virginia,* 515 U.S. 819 (1995). Neither of these cases, however, deals with the teachings of origins in public schools.

165. *Edwards,* at 583.

166. Ibid., at 585, quoting *Lynch,* at 690 (1984), O'Connor, J., concurring.

167. Ibid., at 591–93. Because the Act violated the first prong, the Court did not address whether the Act also violated the second or third prongs.

168. Ibid., at 587–89 (alteration in original).

169. Ibid., at 587.

170. Ibid., at 588–89.

171. Ibid., at 593, 594.

172. The National Academy of Sciences, *Science and Creationism: A View from the National Academy of Sciences* 7, 2nd ed. (Washington, D.C.: National Academy Press, 1999); Scott, Testimony before U.S. Commission on Civil Rights, Hearing ("I see [intelligent design theory] as a synonym for creation science").

173. Wexler, "Of Pandas."

174. *Edwards* at 596, 603–4; see also *McLean,* at 1264–65: "The evidence establishes that the definition of 'creation science' . . . has as its unmentioned reference the first 11 chapters of the Book of Genesis. Among the many creation epics in human history, the account of sudden creation from nothing, or *creatio ex nihilo,* and subsequent destruction of the world by flood is unique to Genesis."

175. Ronald L. Numbers, *The Creationists* (New York: Alfred A. Knopf, 1992), x.

176. *Edwards,* at 594, noting that "a variety of . . . theories . . . might be validly [taught] with the clear secular intent of enhancing . . . instruction. But because the primary purpose of the . . . Act is to endorse a particular religious doctrine," it advances religion in violation of Establishment Clause. Indeed, the Court recognized that some of these individual tenets may form legitimate topics for scientific discussion, and thus could be included in a valid public school science curriculum. For example, in reference to tenet 3, scientists have increasingly debated whether or not there are limits to morphological change among biological organisms (see note 34). According to the neo-Darwinian synthesis there are no limits whatsoever: all organisms

trace their ancestry back to an original single-celled organism (see note 34). This view is called monophyly or common descent and contrasts with polyphyly, the view that some groups of organisms have separate ancestries. Some scientists now cite evidence from the fossil record, molecular sequence analyses, and developmental biology to support this latter view. Stuart A. Kauffman, *The Origins of Order* (New York: Oxford University Press, 1993); Paul Nelson, *On Common Descent* (forthcoming); Malcolm S. Gordon, "The Concept of Monophyly: A Speculative Essay," *Biology and Philosophy* 14 (1999): 331–48; Christian Schwabe, "Theoretical Limitations of Molecular Phylogenetics and the Evolution of Relaxins," *Comparative Biochemistry and Physiology* 107B (1994): 167–77; G. Webster and Brian Goodwin, "The Origin of Species: A Structuralist Approach," *J. Soc. and Biological Structures* 5 (1982): 15–47; Carl Woese, "The Universal Ancestor," *Proceedings of the National Academy of Sciences U.S.A.* 95 (1998): 6854–59. Similarly, many scientists have expressed increasing skepticism about the sufficiency of the neo-Darwinian mechanisms of mutation and natural selection. See John and Miklos, *Eukaryote* Genome; Raff, *Shape of Life*; G. L. G. Miklos and K. S. W. Campbell, "From Protein Domains to Extinct Phyla: Reverse-Engineering Approaches to the Evolution of Biological Complexities," in *Early Life on Earth, Nobel Symposium No. 84,* ed. Stefan Bengtson (New York: Columbia University Press, 1994), 501–16. Many science teachers will want to discuss these scientific developments with their students.

177. Dembski, *Design Inference,* 1–35; Behe, *Darwin's Black Box,* 39–45.
178. Yockey, *Information Theory,* 334; Werner R. Loewenstein, *The Touchstone of Life* (New York: Oxford University Press, 1999), 15; Meyer, "DNA by Design," ; Meyer, "Explanatory Power," 113–47; Thaxton et al., *Mystery,* 127–65, 188–215.
179. See note 42, discussing three explanations of origins of specified complexity.
180. Meyer, "DNA by Design"; Meyer, "Explanatory Power," 113–47; Behe, *Darwin's Black Box,* 252; Thaxton and Bradley, "Information," 173–210.
181. Stephen C. Meyer, "The Return of the God Hypothesis," *Journal of Interdisciplinary Studies* 1 (1999): 1–38.
182. Phillip E. Johnson, "Darwinism and Theism," in Buell and Hearn, *Darwinism,* 42–50.

183. Brendan Sweetman, "Darwin vs. 'Intelligent Design'—Three Views on the Kansas Controversy Over Teaching Evolution in Public Schools: What Evolution Tries to Explain, and What It Leaves Unanswered," *Kansas City Star,* 22 Aug. 1999.

184. *Lemon,* at 612.

185. *Edwards,* at 581–82, 587, 589.

186. *Lemon,* at 612.

187. *Rosenberger,* at 845–46, plurality opinion.

188. Ibid., at 829, 845–46; see also part VI.A., discussing *Rosenberger* decision.

189. Some would no doubt argue that there is no comparable constitutional protection for religious viewpoints in the public high school environment. On the contrary, the Court has extended the principle of viewpoint neutrality to cover religious speech in the public high schools. See *Westside Community Bd. of Educ. v. Mergens,* 496 U.S. 226, 249 (1990), holding the Equal Access Act, which requires student religious clubs to receive same treatment as secular clubs, meets first prong of *Lemon* test: "Congress' avowed purpose—to prevent discrimination against religious and other types of speech—is undeniably secular."

190. *Doe v. County of Montgomery, Ill.,* 915 F. Supp. 32, 35 (C.D. Ill. 1996), stating that "before the Court analyzes the [offending practice] under the *Lemon* test, however, the Court first must determine whether there is even an issue of religion"; *Fleischfresser v. Directors of Sch. Dist. 200,* 15 F.3d 680, 687 (7th Cir. 1994).

191. *Edwards,* at 591–94.

192. Ibid., at 590–91.

193. *West Virginia Bd. of Educ. v. Barnette,* 319 U.S. 624, 642 (1943): "If there is any fixed star in our constitutional constellation, it is that no official, high or petty, can prescribe what shall be orthodox in politics, nationalism, religion, or other matters of opinion or force citizens to confess by word or act their faith therein."

194. Of course, it would still be objectionable to present a religious theory as such. Although critics of teaching alternatives to Darwin frequently suggest that teaching anything other than Darwinism would require that "all creation stories" be taught, this is a misleading argument. Many myths about the origin of the world, such as the Coyote myth prominent in Native American religions, make no claim to be scientific. See, for example, Robert W. Lannan, "Anthropology and Restless

Spirits: The Native American Graves Protection and Repatriation Act, and the Unresolved Issues of Prehistoric Human Remains," *Harvard Environmental Law Review* 22 (1998): 369, 386 (describing Nez Perce account of "the origins of people in North America" as one where coyote cuts "huge" monster up with knife, then creates various Native American tribes from former monster). While such stories can be taught in other courses in the curriculum, such as literature or social studies, they should not be taught in a class concerned with efforts to identify scientific theories regarding the origins issue.

195. Astonishingly, those who claim that design theory is merely religion disguised as science do not hesitate to enlist religion when it suits their purposes. Eugenie Scott, director of the National Center for Science Education and one of the most frequent champions of a Darwin-only presentation, has suggested that biology teachers invite their students to survey community religious leaders: "A teacher in Minnesota told me that he had good luck sending his students out at the beginning of the semester to interview their pastors and priests about evolution. They came back somewhat astonished, 'Hey! Evolution is OK!' Even when there was diversity in opinion, with some religious leaders accepting evolution as compatible with their theology and others rejecting it, it was educational for the students to find out for themselves that there was no single Christian perspective on evolution. The survey-of-ministers approach may not work if the community is religiously homogeneous, especially if that homogeneity is conservative Christian, but it is something that some teachers might consider as a way of getting students' fingers out of their ears" (Eugenie C. Scott, "Dealing with Anti-evolutionism," *Reports of the National Center for Science Education,* http://www.natcenscied.org/dea1174.htm.

196. To be sure, in this era of interdisciplinary studies, where biology textbooks frequently connect the social implications of biology for environmental or ecological issues, it seems a little strange to treat the metaphysical implications of the origins issue as though they were taboo in the science class. The point to be emphasized, however, is not that the questions are unimportant or inappropriate but rather that the methodology of science proceeds from evidence to conclusions, whereas the methodology of a social studies class permits the assertion of values or human intuition as a starting point for discussion. Thus, a student's argument that naturalistic evolution is true (or untrue) because it matches (or conflicts with) the student's fundamental intuitions

about human nature is appropriate in a philosophy or social studies class, but not in a science classroom, where theories are judged according to their ability to explain evidence. Science isn't afraid of where the truth might lead, but its discussions begin with evidence, not with metaphysics. Thus neither "The Bible says it; I believe it; that settles it" nor "All events have a material cause" is acceptable as a scientific argument.

197. *Reno v. American Civil Liberties Union,* 521 U.S. 844 (1997), striking internet restrictions as violating the First Amendment.

198. As noted earlier, one prominent Darwinist has suggested precisely the kind of balanced approach that is advocated in this article. See Provine, Review of *Teaching About Evolution,* and text accompanying note 54.

199. *Boring v. Buncombe County Bd. of Educ.,* 136 F.3d 364, 371 (4th Cir. 1998).

200. *Tinker,* at 506. Later in the opinion the Court stated: "The District Court concluded that the action of the school authorities was reasonable because it was based upon their fear of a disturbance from the wearing of the armbands. But, in our system, undifferentiated fear or apprehension of disturbance is not enough to overcome the right to freedom of expression. Any departure from absolute regimentation may cause trouble. Any variation from the majority's opinion may inspire fear. Any word spoken, in class, in the lunchroom, or on the campus, that deviates from the views of another person may start an argument or cause a disturbance. But our Constitution says we must take this risk . . . and our history says that it is this sort of hazardous freedom—this kind of openness—that is the basis of our national strength and of the independence and vigor of Americans who grow up and live in this relatively permissive, often disputatious, society.

"In order for the State in the person of school officials to justify prohibition of a particular expression of opinion, it must be able to show that its action was caused by something more than a mere desire to avoid the discomfort and unpleasantness that always accompany an unpopular viewpoint" (at 508–9, citation omitted).

201. *Board of Educ., Island Trees Union Free Sch. Dist. No. 26 v. Pico,* 457 U.S. 853, 870–71 (1982).

202. *Rosenberger,,* plurality opinion, citing *Police Dep't of Chicago v. Mosley,* 408 U.S. 92, 96 (1972) and *Turner Broadcasting System,* Inc. v. FCC, 512 U.S., 622, 641–643 (1994)); see *Lamb's Chapel v. Center Moriches Union*

Free Sch. Dist., 508 U.S. 384, 394 (1993), allowing religious film to be shown on public property after school hours. See also *City Council of Los Angeles v. Taxpayers for Vincent,* 466 U.S. 789, 804 (1984). "The general principle that has emerged from this line of cases is that the First Amendment forbids the government to regulate speech in a way that favors some viewpoints or ideas at the expense of others," citing *Bolger v. Youngs Drug Prod. Corp.,* 463 U.S. 60, 65 (1983); *Consolidated Edison Co. v. Public Serv. Comm'n,* 447 U.S. 530, 535–36 (1980); *Carey v. Brown,* 447 U.S. 455, 462–63 (1980); *Young v. American Mini Theatres, Inc.* 427 U.S. 50, 63, 65, 67–68 (1976), plurality opinion; *Mosely,* at 95–96.

203. *Cornelius v. NAACP Legal Defense and Educ. Fund, Inc.,* 473 U.S. 788 (1985)); *Rosenberger; Lamb's Chapel,* at 394.

204. *Rosenberger,* at 827, 828, 829–30, 839. "More than once we have rejected the position that the Establishment Clause even justifies, much less requires, a refusal to extend free speech rights to religious speakers who participate in broad-reaching government programs neutral in design," citing *Lamb's Chapel,* at 393–94; *Mergens,* at 248, 252; *Widmar v. Vincent,* 454 U.S. 263, 274–75 (1981).

205. *Rosenberger,* at 828, 829, citing *Perry Educ. Ass'n v. Perry Local Educators' Ass'n,* 460 U.S. 37, 46 (1983).

206. *Cornelius,* at 806, discussing government prohibition on speech content regulation in a nonpublic forum.

207. Ibid., citing *Perry,* at 49 and *Lehman v. City of Shaker Heights,* 418 U.S. 298 (1974).

208. *Lamb's Chapel,* at 394, citing *Widmar,* at 271.

209. *Rosenberger,* at 842.

210. *Peloza,* at 522, quoting *Tinker,* at 506–7.

211. *Tinker,* at 512–13.

212. Ibid., at 506–7.

213. *Epperson.*

214. Ibid., at 98–99, 100, 104–6.

215. Ibid., at 104, 105, 107, quoting *Keyishian v. Board of Regents,* 385 U.S. 589, 603, 605–6 (1967).

216. *Mergens,* at 247–50.

217. *Vincent,* at 804.

218. *Edwards,* at 587, 593–94, stating that "the Act does not . . . protect academic freedom, but has the distinctly different purpose of discrediting [evolution theory]" (589)

219. Ibid., at 593–94, citation omitted.

220. Ibid., at 586.

221. Ibid., at 593–94.

222. *Pico*, at 871. See also *Abood v. Detroit Bd. of Educ.*, 431 U.S. 209 (1977), noting that First Amendment principles prohibited union and board of education from requiring any teacher to contribute to support of ideological cause that teacher might oppose as condition of holding job as public school teacher.

223. "Libraries in Michigan District Will Carry Books Questioning Evolution," *St. Louis Post Dispatch*, 12 Feb. 1999; Bruce Chapman, "'Intelligent Design' vs. 'Materialism,'" *Seattle Post-Intelligencer*, 14 Nov. 1997.

224. Nancy Young, "Evolution Challenger Asks Court to Ban Textbook," *Virginian-Pilot*, 26 May 1997.

Part II

Scientific Critique of Biology Textbooks and Contemporary Evolutionary Theory

The Meanings of Evolution

Stephen C. Meyer and Michael Newton Keas

❖ ❖ ❖

"Evolution and the theories of evolution are fundamentally different things," testified zoologist Maynard M. Metcalf, the first expert witness for the defense in the 1925 Scopes trial. Metcalf's observation at the "trial of the century" officially marked the beginning of public discussion of the different meanings of *evolution* for the purposes of science education. "The fact of evolution is a thing that is perfectly and absolutely clear," Metcalf explained, "but there are many points—theoretical points as to the methods by which evolution has been brought about—that we are not yet in possession of scientific knowledge to answer."[1]

Metcalf's statement suggested, as many modern biologists have noted, that the term *evolution* can mean different things. His comment also suggested that not all senses of evolution have the same epistemological standing. We can assert confidently that evolution "has occurred," Metcalf explained, but we may be more uncertain about how it occurred.

Metcalf made this distinction to show the court that critique of evolution in one sense did not necessarily count as critique of evolution in other senses. To assume otherwise would be to commit the logical fallacy of equivocation. He feared that confusion between the fact of evolution and the theory of evolution would justify excluding all teaching about evolution simply because some aspects of evolutionary theory did not have the same degree of confirmation as others.[2]

Of course, science teachers must also avoid equivocation, if only because they don't want to confuse their students. Yet for biology teachers, this may prove difficult—given the many separate meanings that the term *evolution* has come to possess. As Yale biologist Keith Stewart Thomson has shown, the term *evolution* may have more than just two meanings.[3]

Equivocal usage poses a practical difficulty for science teachers. Good science teachers must define terms carefully and use them consistently to avoid conflating different ideas. Good biology teachers must tease apart the distinct ideas associated with evolution to help students to evaluate each idea separately and to distinguish evidence and observations, on the one hand, from inferences and theories, on the other.

Thomson identified at least three distinct meanings associated with evolution in contemporary biology: change over time, common ancestry, and the natural mechanisms that produce change in organisms.[4] This essay will further refine these distinctions and present six distinct meanings. In so doing, we want to help science educators distinguish well-established from less well-established senses of the term *evolution*. We also want to help teachers avoid false controversies over senses of the term that enjoy wide scientific confirmation and support and to help them explain the real controversies that remain over more theoretically contentious propositions.

The following definitions develop and distinguish those multiple meanings, which we propose as guideposts for clear biology instruction.

I.

Principal Meanings of Evolution in Biology Textbooks

1. Change over time; history of nature; any sequence of events in nature.
2. Changes in the frequencies of alleles in the gene pool of a population.
3. Limited common descent: the idea that particular groups of organisms have descended from a common ancestor.
4. The mechanisms responsible for the change required to produce limited descent with modification, chiefly natural selection acting on random variations or mutations.
5. Universal common descent: the idea that all organisms have descended from a single common ancestor.

6. "Blind watchmaker" thesis: the idea that all organisms have descended from common ancestors solely through an unguided, unintelligent, purposeless, material processes such as natural selection acting on random variations or mutations; that the mechanisms of natural selection, random variation and mutation, and perhaps other similarly naturalistic mechanisms, are completely sufficient to account for the appearance of design in living organisms.

Let us look at these six definitions of evolution.

1. *Evolution as Change Over Time.* Nature has a history; it is not static. Natural sciences deal with evolution in its first sense—change over time in the natural world—when they seek to reconstruct series of past events to tell the story of nature's history.[5] Astronomers study the life cycles of stars; geologists ponder the changes in the earth's surface; paleontologists note changes in the types of life that have existed over time, as represented in the sedimentary rock record (fossil succession); biologists note ecological succession within recorded human history, which may have, for example, transformed a barren island into a mature forested island community. Although the last example has little to do with neo-Darwinian evolutionary theory, it still fits within the first general sense of evolution as natural historical progression or sequence of events.

2. *Evolution as Gene Frequency Change.* Population geneticists study changes in the frequencies of alleles in gene pools. This very specific sense of evolution, though not without theoretical significance, is closely tied to a large collection of precise observations. The melanism studies of peppered moths, though currently contested, are among the most celebrated examples of such studies in microevolution.[6] For the geneticist, gene frequency change is "evolution in action."

3. *Evolution as Limited Common Descent.* Virtually all scientists (even many creationists) would agree that Darwin's dozen or more famed Galapagos Island finch species are probably descended from a single continental South American finch species. Although such "evolution" did not occur during the brief time scale of the lives of scientists since Darwin (as in the case of the peppered moth), the pattern of biogeographical distribution of these birds strongly suggests to most scientists that all of these birds share a common ancestor. Evolution defined as "limited common descent" designates the scientifically uncontroversial idea that many different varieties of similar organisms within different species, genera, or even families are related by common ancestry. Note that it is possible for

some scientists to accept evolution when defined in this sense without necessarily accepting evolution defined as universal common descent— that is, the idea that all organisms are related by common ancestry.

4. *Evolution as a Mechanism that Produces Limited Change or Descent with Modification.* The term *evolution* also refers to the mechanism that produces the morphological change implied by limited common descent or descent with modification through successive generations. Evolution in this sense refers chiefly to the mechanism of natural selection acting on random genetic variation or mutations. This sense of the term refers to the idea that the variation/selection mechanism can generate at least limited biological or morphological change within a population. Nearly all biologists accept the efficacy of natural selection (and associated phenomena, such as the founder effect and genetic drift) as a mechanism of speciation. Even so, many scientists now question whether such mechanisms can produce the amount of change required to account for the completely novel organs or body plans that emerge in the fossil record. Thus, almost all biologists would accept that the variation/selection mechanism can explain relatively minor variations among groups of organisms (*evolution* meaning #4), even if some of those biologists question the *sufficiency* of the mechanism (*evolution* meaning #6) as an explanation for the origin of the major morphological innovations in the history of life.

5. *Evolution as Universal Common Descent.* Many biologists commonly use the term *evolution* to refer to the idea that all organisms are related by common ancestry from a single living organism. Darwin represented the theory of universal common descent or universal "descent with modification" with a "branching tree" diagram, which showed all present life forms as having emerged gradually over time from one or very few original common ancestors. Darwin's theory of biological history is often referred to as a monophyletic view because it portrays all organisms as ultimately related as a single family.

In the *Origin of Species,* Charles Darwin argued for his theory of universal common descent on the grounds that it best explained a variety of biological evidences, including fossil succession, biogeographical distribution of species (such as the Galapagos finches), the existence of apparently suboptimal or useless organs, and the existence of homologous structures and embryological similarities in otherwise disparate organisms.

The presumed strength of the case for universal common descent has led many scientists to treat the theory of universal common descent as though it were a fact. Maynard M. Metcalf and more recently Stephen Jay Gould and Michael Ruse have been among prominent advocates of the idea that evolution defined as "universal common ancestry" qualifies as a fact. Each of these advocates articulated this view while serving as an expert witness in a creation-evolution court trial. Yet as one of us (Meyer) has argued in response to Michael Ruse, universal common descent is not, strictly speaking, a fact.[7] As Meyer noted:

> Strictly speaking, common descent is an abductive or historical inference, as Professor Ruse himself acknowledges when he speaks more accurately of "inferring historical phylogenies." As defined by C. S. Peirce, abductive inferences attempt to establish past causes by viewing present effects. (As such, it is more accurate to refer to common descent as a theory about facts, i.e., a theory about what in fact happened in the past.) Unfortunately, such theories, and the inferences used to construct them, can be notoriously underdetermined. As Elliot Sober points out, many possible pasts often correspond to any given present state. Establishing the past with certainty, or even beyond reasonable doubt, can therefore, be very difficult.[8]

Although Darwin's monophyletic view of life's history has reigned as the dominant theory of the history of life during most of the twentieth century, a number of biologists now question that view on evidential grounds. These scientists now see the present diversity and disparity of organisms as having originated from many separate ancestral forms and lines of descent. Those favoring a so-called polyphyletic or multiple separate origins view of life's history now cite evidence from paleontology, embryology, biochemistry, and molecular biology in support of their view.[9]

Evolution in the fifth sense not only specifies that all life shares a common ancestry, it implies that virtually no limits exist to the amount of morphological change that can occur in organisms. It assumes that relatively simple organisms can, given adequate time, change into much more complex or different organisms, and these organisms can in turn be altered by the evolutionary process to become yet new organisms. Thus, evolution in this sense entails the idea of unbounded biological change. That view is now opposed by biologists who see biological change as limited and who favor a polyphyletic view of life's history, in which many lineages of animals or plants arise separately (without genealogical connections) during the history of life.

Because Darwin's monophyletic interpretation of life's history is an inference from biological evidence, instructors should encourage students to understand and examine classical Darwinian arguments for that interpretation rather than simply presenting the interpretation as brute fact. Moreover, since several lines of evidence and many qualified scientists now challenge this theory of the history of life, the evidence for alternate polyphyletic theories of life's history should also be discussed and critically evaluated. Allowing students to see how scientists interpret the same biological evidence differently will help encourage evaluation and critical thinking skills. It will also allow students to understand the method of multiple competing hypotheses that scientists often employ to evaluate their data.

We will return to this fifth meaning of evolution in the last sections of this essay when we critique public statements about how evolutionary theory should be taught in public schools. At present, many public policy (and other) statements about how to teach evolution lapse uncritically into describing evolution (that is, universal common descent) as a fact.

In addition to the five definitions of evolution discussed thus far, an additional definition lies at the core of what evolutionary biology means to most scientists today.

6. *Evolution as the "Blind Watchmaker" Thesis.* The "blind watchmaker" thesis, to appropriate Richard Dawkins's clever term, stands for the Darwinian idea that all new living forms arose as the product of unguided, purposeless, material mechanisms, chiefly natural selection acting on random variation or mutation.[10] Evolution in this sense implies that the Darwinian mechanism of natural selection acting on random variations (and other equally naturalistic processes) completely suffices to explain the origin of novel biological forms and the appearance of design in complex organisms. Although Darwinists and neo-Darwinists admit that living organisms appear designed for a purpose, they insist that such "design" is only *apparent*, not *real*, precisely because they also affirm the complete sufficiency of unintelligent natural mechanisms (that can mimic the activity of a designing intelligence) of morphogenesis. In Darwinism, the variation/selection mechanism functions as a kind of "designer substitute." As Dawkins summarizes the blind watchmaker thesis: "Natural selection, the blind, unconscious, automatic process which Darwin discovered and which we now know is the explanation

for the existence and apparently purposeful form of all life, has no purpose in mind. It has no mind and no mind's eye."[11]

In addition to the theory of universal common ancestry, classical "Darwinism" affirmed this sixth meaning of evolution. As Harvard evolutionary
biologist Ernst Mayr has explained: "The real core of Darwinism, however,
is the theory of natural selection. This theory is so important for the Darwinian because it permits the explanation of adaptation, the 'design' of the
natural theologian, by natural means, instead of by divine intervention."[12]
Or as Mayr put it recently:

> First, Darwinism rejects all supernatural phenomena and causations. The
> theory of evolution by natural selection explains the adaptedness and diver-
> sity of the world solely materialistically. It no longer requires God as creator
> or designer (although one is certainly free to believe in God even if one ac-
> cepts evolution). Darwin pointed out that creation, as described in the Bible
> and the origin accounts of other cultures, was contradicted by almost any
> aspect of the natural world. Every aspect of the "wonderful design" so ad-
> mired by natural theologians could be explained by natural selection.[13]

Further, not just classical Darwinism but contemporary neo-Darwinism
has also affirmed this sixth meaning of evolution. Since the 1940s, the
blind watchmaker thesis has been supported by the neo-Darwinian
synthesis—which combined Mendelian genetics with Darwin's theory of
descent with modification. Neo-Darwinists proposed various types of random mutations as the creative engines giving natural selection the raw genetic material upon which to work. Many biologists before the 1940s had
questioned the adequacy of Darwin's mechanism precisely because they
worried that natural selection did not have an adequate source of variation
upon which to operate. Neo-Darwinists argued that the phenomena of
mutations solved that problem by providing natural selection an unlimited
source of genetic change. Thus, they, like the classical Darwinists before
them, again affirmed the complete sufficiency of the (now) neo-Darwinian
mechanism as an explanation for new living forms on Earth (and the appearance of design that they manifest). As George Gaylord Simpson would
assert in his classic 1967 book, *The Meaning of Evolution:* "Man is the result
of a purposeless and natural process that did not have him in mind. He was
not planned."[14] As a result of the neo-Darwinian synthesis, biologists again
assumed that a completely natural mechanism—natural selection acting on
random mutations—could produce not only *limited* morphological change
(and thus, patterns of limited common descent—evolution #3) but also

unlimited morphological change (and thus the pattern of *universal* common descent—evolution #5). Neo-Darwinists also assumed that the new mutation/selection mechanism could account entirely for the appearance of design in biological systems.

This view is reflected in many high school biology texts. As Kenneth Miller and Joseph Levine long asserted it in their popular text, "evolution works without plan or purpose."[15] Or as Purvis, Orians, and Heller tell students, "the living world is constantly evolving without any goals . . . evolutionary change is not directed."[16] Similarly, Douglas Futuyma, in his widely used college textbook, *Evolutionary Biology,* writes: "By coupling undirected, purposeless variation to the blind, uncaring process of natural selection, Darwin made theological or spiritual explanations of the life processes superfluous."[17] Francisco J. Ayala, president of the American Association for the Advancement of Science (AAAS) and chair of the National Academy of Sciences (NAS) steering committee for its 1999 edition of *Science and Creationism* (see analysis below), likewise speaks of Darwinism as having "excluded God as the explanation accounting for the obvious design of organisms."[18]

The blind watchmaker thesis suggests that the neo-Darwinian mechanism (and other related ones) functions as a designer substitute; it plays the role of creator in the scientific account of biological origins. Thus, clearly, this sixth meaning of evolution does have larger metaphysical or worldview implications. Many philosophical naturalists or materialists find support for their worldview in neo-Darwinian theory for what seems to them good reasons. If neo-Darwinism is true, God's creative activity (whether expressed discretely or gradually) would no longer be necessary to explain the origin of new living forms, since a strictly naturalistic mechanism would suffice. Thus, a strictly naturalistic worldview would seem to provide a simpler account of reality, or at least of biological reality, than a theistic one. Further, if neo-Darwinism is true, then the natural world does not display evidence of actual design, divine or otherwise—as most religious theists affirm. For both of these reasons, neither neo-Darwinism nor other materialistic origins theories taught in the public schools (such as the chemical evolutionary theory of the origin of the first life) are religiously or metaphysically neutral. All strictly materialistic origins theories, if true, have implications that would seem to make a materialistic worldview more plausible than a theistic one and would also contradict some deeply held religious beliefs.

Despite the confidence that many biologists and biology texts display in affirming the blind watchmaker thesis—*evolution* in the sixth sense—many scientists, including many biologists, have increasingly questioned the adequacy of the neo-Darwinian mechanism.[19] Recently, a number of scientists have come to question whether natural selection acting on random variation can create the complex organs, molecular machines, and novel body plans that appear during the history of life. Such so-called macroevolutionary changes in the history of life—for example, the relatively sudden appearance of most extant and extinct animal phyla during the Cambrian explosion 530 million years ago—seem especially difficult to explain via the neo-Darwinian mechanism. As Gilbert, Opitz, and Raff have assessed the situation: "The Modern Synthesis is a remarkable achievement. However, starting in the 1970's, many biologists began questioning its adequacy in explaining evolution. Genetics might be adequate for explaining microevolution, but microevolutionary changes in gene frequency were not seen as able to turn a reptile into a mammal or to convert a fish into an amphibian. Microevolution looks at adaptations that concern only the survival of the fittest, not the arrival of the fittest."[20]

Since the 1970s, many scientists have looked for additional naturalistic (or so-called self-organizational) mechanisms to show how extensive morphological innovation could arise—without, as yet, achieving much consensus or obvious success.[21] Some scientists have questioned the sufficiency of the mutation/selection mechanism without proposing any alternatives. Still other scientists, such as Michael Behe, have proposed an alternative nonnaturalistic explanation for the origin of major innovations in the history of life, namely, the theory of intelligent design. Design theorists in general question the adequacy of the neo-Darwinian mechanism and see evidence of real (that is, intelligent) design, not just apparent design, in biology.

Of course, many defenders of the neo-Darwinian mechanism remain, especially in fields such as population genetics, zoology, comparative anatomy, and molecular biology. Nevertheless, given the diversity of opinion within the scientific community, scientific integrity would seem to require teaching students about the controversy that has emerged among scientists about the blind watchmaker thesis. Further, given the larger metaphysical or worldview implications of that thesis, religious neutrality would also seem to require (a) avoiding the issue of design or purpose altogether, in which case neither classical Darwinism nor neo-Darwinism could be taught (since both make explicit claims about the origin of the appearance of design), or (b) teaching the controversy about the origin of this central feature of biological systems.

II.

1. Educational Policy Statements and Treatment of the "E" Word

We favor exposing students to scientific controversies. Teachers need not conceal the metaphysical or ideological issues that arise in the discussion of scientific theories. By allowing students to discuss and evaluate competing views despite their differing metaphysical implications, teachers may find that their students demonstrate a greater enthusiasm for science itself. By eschewing dogmatic presentations where evidence admits competing views, teachers will promote a scientifically and ideologically responsible curriculum. They may also promote a creative engagement by students that gives them a personal interest in the outcome of ongoing scientific discussions. Such engagement could help reverse the historic decline in student interest in science and in the number of science students, especially biology students, who drop science majors before completing their bachelor's degrees.[22]

Scientifically literate people know that nature has a history, that gene frequencies change, that at least limited common descent among organisms has occurred, and that natural selection has played a significant role in speciation and species modification. These first four meanings of evolution might aptly wear the label "mere evolution." Unsurprisingly, few object to teaching mere evolution. Controversy develops, however, when scientists, teachers, or students want to evaluate evolution critically in the fifth or sixth senses of the term. Spokespersons for neo-Darwinism, which embraces evolution in both the fifth and sixth senses, often suggest that dissenting opinion about evolution in any sense is either ill-informed or intellectually perverse.

Nevertheless, those attempts to exclude scientific dissent often employ ambiguous or shifting definitions of the term *evolution*. Many defenders of evolution #5 and/or #6 will offer evidence and argument for evolution in the first four senses of the term and then treat evolution in the latter two senses as equally well established. In the following section, we will show how educational policy statements and advocates for evolution often equivocate in their discussion of evolution to the detriment of public understanding of the issues facing biologists and biology teachers.

2. "The Fact of Evolution": Conflating Meanings #1–3 with Meaning #5

A recent booklet, *Science and Creationism: A View from the National Academy of Sciences* (1999), defends teaching the subject of biological origins from an exclusively evolutionary perspective.[23] According to *Science and Creationism,* not only do alternative theories (such as intelligent design) fail to qualify as science, but evolution has been established beyond any reasonable doubt. The booklet's introduction argues that the "theory of evolution" is a scientific explanation "so thoroughly tested and confirmed" that it is "held with great confidence" and is "one of the strongest and most useful scientific theories we have." It even claims that evolution is so well established that it can legitimately be described as a fact. As the booklet explains, "Scientists most often use the word 'fact' to describe an observation. But scientists can also use fact to mean something that has been tested or observed so many times that there is no longer a compelling reason to keep testing or looking for examples. The occurrence of evolution in this sense is a fact. Scientists no longer question whether descent with modification occurred because the evidence supporting the idea is so strong."[24]

Those statements aptly illustrate the ambiguity associated with the term *evolution* and the confusion that its unqualified use creates. Precisely which sense of evolution has been "so thoroughly tested and confirmed" that it "is held with great confidence" and can even be regarded as "a fact"? Mere evolution, or evolution #5 and/or #6? The NAS statement never specifies, though presumably it means to affirm the theory of universal common descent, evolution #5.

Indeed, the booklet often employs ambiguous (or shifting) definitions from one sentence to the next. The second-to-last sentence in the quotation asserts that "the occurrence of evolution" is a fact. And, of course, it may well be, depending upon which sense of evolution is meant. The phrase, "the occurrence of evolution," seems to imply evolution in the sense of change over time (evolution #1) or perhaps change in the frequency of expression of alleles (evolution #2). Certainly, evolution in these senses has occurred. Yet the next sentence affirms that "descent with modification" is so well established as to be an unquestioned fact. Throughout the booklet, "descent with modification" is equated with the theory of universal common descent (evolution #5), though technically it could refer either to limited or universal common descent (evolution #3 or #5). In any case, given the booklet's conventions, the last sentence of the quotation seems to affirm a stronger meaning of evolution (evolution #5) than that affirmed in the previous sentence (evolution #1, #2, or possibly #3). Yet the booklet provides no additional justification for affirming this stronger meaning. As such, the passage commits the fallacy of equivocation.

The writers of the NAS booklet do, of course, seem aware that the term *evolution* can refer to different concepts. In particular, they make a distinction between *whether* evolution occurred (that is, the fact of evolution) and *how* (that is, the mechanism by which it occurred). Yet their attempt to clarify definitional matters on such grounds only confuses the issue further, as the following passage illustrates:

> The scientific consensus around evolution is overwhelming. Those opposed to the teaching of evolution sometimes use quotations from prominent scientists out of context to claim that scientists do not support evolution. However, an examination of the quotations reveals that the scientists are actually disputing some aspect of *how* evolution occurs, not *whether* evolution occurs. For example, the biologist Stephen Jay Gould once wrote that "the extreme rarity of transitional forms in the fossil record persists as the trade secret of paleontology." But Gould, an accomplished paleontologist and educator about evolution, was arguing about *how* evolution takes place. He was discussing whether the rate of change of species is slow or gradual or whether it takes place in bursts after long periods when little change takes place—an idea known as punctuated equilibrium.[25]

This passage betrays confusion on several counts. First, scientists can affirm *that* evolution (in several different senses, #1–4) has occurred without necessarily affirming the theory of universal common descent. To say that evolution has occurred does not necessarily imply that enough morphological change has occurred to ensure that all organisms are connected by common ancestry. Thus, a scientist could affirm that evolution (#1–4) has occurred and yet doubt the universal common ancestry thesis. In fact, as noted above, many scientists do now take precisely that position. The simple twofold distinction (between "the" fact and the mechanism of evolution) in the NAS booklet obscures this possibility. There are many alleged "facts" of evolution, and the booklet does not distinguish among them.

Second, the "extreme rarity of transitional forms" does reflect negatively on evolution in the fifth sense—that is, it does seem to provide evidence against universal common descent. True, Stephen Gould does not question universal common descent, but he has reasons other than fossil data (molecular evidence, for example) for accepting the theory. The fossil evidence taken at face value, however, does suggest that, for example, the major taxonomic categories of animals did arise separately within a very narrow window of geologic history. The absence of transitional precursors between the representatives of the new animal phyla strongly supports that impression (see Stephen C. Meyer, Marcus Ross, Paul Nelson, and Paul Chien's essay in this volume). Thus, Gould's discussion of "the extreme rarity of transitional forms" does bear on the question of the truth of universal common descent (evolution #5), and critics of evolution in this sense quite legitimately cite him on this point.

Third, in the passage cited, Gould is not in fact discussing "whether the rate of change of species is slow or gradual"; he is discussing "the extreme rarity of transitional forms in the fossil record." Because Gould accepts universal common descent and because he wants (as much as possible) to take the fossil evidence at face value, he assumes that a mechanism of morphological change exists that can produce change very rapidly. Gould's belief that morphological change must occur very rapidly constitutes part of his interpretation of why the fossil evidence looks as it does. Others, of course, might choose to interpret that same evidence differently. They might view morphologically disparate groups of organisms (such as the representatives of the new animal phyla that appear in the Cambrian) as having originated separately—that is, without having descended from a common ancestor. Yet the NAS booklet treats critics of evolution (presumably in the fifth sense) as ignorant or confused for failing to recognize "the" distinction between the fact and the mechanism of evolution. In fact, it is the NAS booklet that fails to make important definitional distinctions (between evolution #1–3 and #5—that is, between different senses of evolution that may or may not constitute facts, or between the different senses of evolution that might or might not have occurred).

Interestingly, Gould (one of the fifteen members of the NAS steering committee for its 1999 edition of *Science and Creationism*) also fell into this same rhetorical imprecision by treating the distinction between the fact and theory of evolution as if it constituted a unitary distinction. For example, in "Darwinism Defined: The Difference between Fact and Theory," Gould wrote:

> The fact of evolution is as well established as anything in science (as secure as the revolution of the earth about the sun), though absolute certainty has no place in our lexicon. Theories, or statements about the causes of documented evolutionary change, are now in a period of intense debate—a good mark of science in its healthiest state. Facts don't disappear while scientists debate theories. As I wrote in an early issue of this magazine (May 1981),

"Einstein's theory of gravitation replaced Newton's, but apples did not suspend themselves in mid-air pending the outcome."[26]

Here Gould argues that the occurrence of evolution is a fact and that scientists only theorize about *how* it happened. Yet clearly the sense of evolution that Gould means here to defend, namely, the theory of universal common descent, does not have the same epistemological status as observations of apples falling to the ground. No scientists can directly observe "evolution" (in this sense) occurring. No one can observe the history of life, or the pattern of a branching tree emerging, or the transitions between each of the major groups of organisms. In other places Gould himself speculates that evolution happened too fast for even the fossil record to preserve most of the transitional forms required by the theory of universal common descent.[27] Instead, as noted above, the *theory* of universal common descent was (and is) inferred (abductively) from many classes of presently observable phenomena: biogeographical distribution, fossil succession, homology, and the like. These latter phenomena are arguably facts akin to apples falling, but the theory or theories inferred from them are not.

The leadership of the National Association of Biology Teachers (NABT) has also recently adopted this same way of defining the issue in a policy statement about how evolution should be taught. The NABT published its "tenets of science, evolution and biology education" with the following introductory remarks:

> Modern biologists constantly study, ponder and deliberate the patterns, mechanisms and pace of evolution, but they do not debate evolution's occurrence. The fossil record and the diversity of extant organisms, combined with modern techniques of molecular biology, taxonomy and geology, provide exhaustive examples and powerful evidence for genetic variation, natural selection, speciation, extinction and other well-established components of current evolutionary theory. Scientific deliberations and modifications of these components clearly demonstrate the vitality and scientific integrity of evolution and the theory that explains it.[28]

The last phrase, "evolution and the theory that explains it," and the earlier phrase, "biologists . . . do not debate evolution's occurrence," both employ the word *evolution* in an alleged "fact" mode. But precisely which sense of "evolution" is said to be factual rather than theoretical? Like Gould, the NABT statement excludes mechanism (evolution #4 and #6) from the category of fact but lumps most of the other senses of the term into one mold. Thus, like Gould and the NAS statement, the NABT statement conflates evolution #1–3 with evolution #5. Yes, evolution in the sense of change has occurred, but has enough morphological change occurred to ensure that *all* organisms are related by common ancestry? That question is never seriously addressed, nor can it be, given the equivocal definitions in play.

3. Evolution as an "Unsupervised" and "Impersonal" Process: The Blind Watchmaker Thesis and the National Association of Biology Teachers

The NABT statement equivocates in other, arguably more significant, ways. For example, in 1995 the NABT issued the following statement: "The diversity of life on earth is the outcome of evolution: an unsupervised, impersonal, unpredictable and natural process of temporal descent with genetic modification that is affected by natural selection, chance, historical contingencies and changing environments."[29] Two years later the NABT deleted the words "unsupervised" and "impersonal" after two distinguished scholars, Alvin Plantinga and Huston Smith, wrote the NABT about the inappropriateness of those words: "Science presumably doesn't address such theological questions, and isn't equipped to deal with them. How could an empirical inquiry possibly show that God was not guiding and directing evolution?"[30]

The NABT Board of Directors took up that matter on 8 October 1997, voting unanimously to retain the objectionable wording. Wayne Carley, speaking for the board, said they felt "rather strongly" about keeping the statement unaltered. "We believe it. Evolution is real," he affirmed.[31] Carley did not say which meaning of the term *evolution* "is real," nor did he acknowledge that Plantinga and Huston accept evolution in most of the other senses of the word (#1–4 and/or #5) but were disputing the sixth blind watchmaker thesis as advanced by the NABT. On the last day of the 1997 annual NABT meeting, the board met again and voted to remove the two objectionable words, "unsupervised" and "impersonal," while maintaining: "The deletion of those two words would not affect the statement's accurate characterization of evolution, and affirmation of evolution's importance in science education."[32]

Here again, implicit definitions shift from phrase to phrase. Many scientists, and indeed Plantinga and Huston, would accept "evolution's importance to science" yet would not accept that scientific evidence has established that an "unsupervised" and "impersonal" (the two deleted words) mechanism is sufficient to explain the origin of every living system on Earth. But the NABT statement treats these two separate propositions as equivalent.

If the NABT story ended here, some might think that statements affirming evolution in the sixth sense are on their way out. But most prominent evolutionary biologists do not see the blind watchmaker thesis (as defined above) as an optional ideological add-on to neo-Darwinian evolutionary theory. Rather, they see it as a central part of the propositional content of neo-Darwinian theory, as indeed Darwin himself did. Thus, the NABT leadership did not really repudiate its commitment to evolution in the sixth sense. They were merely responding to what Eugenie Scott perceptively called "a communication problem" (a public relations crisis).[33]

The NABT's public relations campaign was soon challenged from the state of Tennessee. Massimo Pigliucci, assistant professor of ecology and evolution at the University of Tennessee, Knoxville, drafted "Defining Evolution: An Open Letter." His letter was posted on the Darwin Day website as part of a moderated discussion that included contributions from Berkeley law professor (now emeritus) Phillip Johnson and Eugenie Scott of the National Center for Science Education (NCSE). Pigliucci enlisted the signatures of an impressive array of scientists, including Harvard's Richard Lewontin, to support his rebuff of the NABT for their watering down of "evolution." The letter urges the NABT to reconsider its change to the classroom definition of evolution in the name of "scientific and educational principles." It argues that the NABT's two-word alteration to the definition of evolution "betrays" the "core" of "high ideals" such as "rationalism and open inquiry." What is this alleged core? The letter states:

> Science is based on a fundamental assumption: that the world can be explained by referring only to natural, mechanistic forces. [Phillip] Johnson is quite right in affirming that this is a philosophical position. He is wrong when he suggests that it is an unreasonable and unproven one. In fact, every single experiment conducted by any laboratory in any place on Earth represents a daily test of that assumption. The day in which scientists will be unable to explain natural phenomena without referring to divine intervention or other supernatural forces, we will have a major paradigm shift—of cataclysmic proportions.[34]

The letter affirms that "all we know so far about the evolutionary process tells us that there is no supervision except for the action of natural selection." Natural selection, for most evolutionary biologists, is the primary expression of the "blind watchmaker." Without foresight it molds existing biological structures into new ones.

Leading sociologist of science Steve Fuller, in a web-posted e-mail, "Why I Won't Sign the Open Letter," of 10 February 1998, wrote: "I found the Open Letter from the besieged biology teachers embarrassing. I'm sure there are some nasty things going on in Knoxville, but a petition of the sort circulating here is not the way to handle matters." Fuller explained his embarrassment in these words: "To describe evolution as 'impersonal' and 'unsupervised' is indeed ideological, especially when the people behind this petition themselves claim that evolution can neither prove nor disprove the existence of God. It's agnosticism upfront but atheism through the backdoor."[35]

Fuller's comment identifies the underlying reason for the public relations problem facing the science education establishment. On the one hand, for both public relations and constitutional reasons, public school science teachers and relevant professional societies must maintain ideological and religious neutrality. On the other hand, they are charged to teach a scientific theory that most prominent evolutionary biologists themselves understand to have decidedly metaphysical (indeed, antitheistic) implications.

Caught on the horns of this dilemma, what is a principled science teacher to do? Well, why not acknowledge the dilemma and teach the scientific and philosophical controversies that arise from the origins issue? On the one hand, teachers should explain that what we are calling "mere evolution" (evolution #1–4) *is* "one of the strongest and most useful scientific theories we have," to use NAS language. Mere evolution encompasses a vast number of specific cosmological, geological, and biological theories that "incorporate a large body of scientific facts, laws, tested hypotheses, and logical inferences." On the other hand, teachers should help students understand that a significant minority of scientists dissent on evidential grounds from the theory of universal common descent (evolution #5), and an even greater group dissents from the blind watchmaker hypothesis (evolution #6).[36] The equivocal use of the term *evolution* conceals this dissent and prevents open classroom discussion of legitimate scientific controversy and its associated evidential grounds.

Further, science teachers need not ignore the larger philosophical or worldview issues that arise from discussing, for example, the blind watchmaker thesis. The threat of ideological indoctrination does not come from allowing students to ponder the philosophical questions raised by the origins issue. Instead, it comes from force-feeding students a single perspective.

The best way to prevent indoctrination is to teach about the scientific controversies that surround the ideologically charged senses of the term *evolution*. But this can be accomplished only if teachers first define the "E" word precisely, distinguish its many distinct meanings (both uncontroversial and controversial), and allow dissenting scientific opinion about the latter meanings to have a voice in the classroom. Given the interest that such an approach would surely generate among students, one might wonder why informed biology teachers would do anything else.

Notes

1. Maynard M. Metcalf, quoted in *The World's Most Famous Court Trial: Tennessee Evolution Case* (Dayton, Tenn.: Bryan College, 1990), 139. A complete stenographic report of the trial; a reprint of the first edition published in Cincinnati by the National Book Company in 1925.

2. E. J. Larson, *Summer for the Gods: The Scopes Trial and America's Continuing Debate Over Science and Religion* (New York: Basic Books, 1997), 173–75.

3. K. S. Thomson, "The Meanings of Evolution," *American Scientist* 70 (1982): 529–31.

4. Ibid.

5. P. J. Bowler, "The Changing Meaning of 'Evolution,'" *Journal of the History of Ideas* 36 (1975): 99. The *Oxford English Dictionary* tipped Bowler to the fact that "since the seventeenth century, non-scientific authors had begun to use 'evolution' in a figurative sense, referring to almost any connected sequence of events." It is not surprising, therefore, that the word *evolution* is now often used across all scientific disciplines and in nonscientific literature as "change over time."

6. For an accessible introduction to this debate, compare these two sources (appropriate supplemental reading for biology courses): J. Coyne, "Not Black and White," review of *Melanism: Evolution in Action* by Michael Majerus, *Nature* 396 (1998): 35–36; J. Wells, "Second Thoughts About Peppered Moths," *Scientist* 13 (1999): 13. Because there is some debate as to whether one should apply the term *microevolution* (in contrast to *macroevolution*) to our evolution meaning #3, we have used the micro/macro "E" terms sparingly. Some prefer to reserve the term *microevolution* for strictly "evolution at or below the species level." See, for example, D. J. Futuyma, *Evolutionary Biology* (Sunderland, Mass.: Sinauer Associates, 1998), 447. Others find it

helpful to use the term for morphological divergence that generates differences (diversity) distinguishing not just varieties but also species, genera, and families—perhaps even orders, but certainly not the higher taxa disparity (major body plan differences) of classes, phyla, or kingdoms. In any case, *microevolution* is at least a fit term for shifts in gene frequencies within a species.

7. S. C. Meyer, "Of Clues and Causes: A Methodological Interpretation of Origin of Life Studies" (Ph.D. diss., Cambridge University, 1991); S. J. Gould, "Evolution and the Triumph of Homology, or Why History Matters," *American Scientist* 74 (1986): 60–69; W. M. Ho, "Methodological Issues in Evolutionary Theory" (Ph.D. diss., Oxford University, 1965); C. S. Peirce, *Collected Papers,* vols. 1–6, ed. C. Hartshorne and P. Weiss (Cambridge: Cambridge University Press, 1931); C. S. Peirce, "Abduction and Induction," in *The Philosophy of Peirce,* ed. J. Buchler (London: Routledge, 1956), 150–56; E. Sober, *Reconstructing the Past* (Cambridge: MIT Press, 1988).

8. S. C. Meyer, "Laws, Causes, and Facts: Response to Michael Ruse," in *Darwinism: Science or Philosophy?* ed. J. Buell and V. Hearn (Richardson, Tex.: Foundation for Thought and Ethics, 1994), 36.

9. C. Schwabe and G. W. Warr, "A Polyphyletic View of Evolution: The Genetic Potential Hypothesis," *Perspectives in Biology and Medicine* 27 (1984): 465–85; C. Schwabe, "On the Basis of the Studies of the Origins of Life," *Origins of Life* 15 (1985): 213–16; W. G. Inglis, "Evolutionary Waves: Patterns in the Origins of Animal Phyla," *Australian Journal of Zoology* 33 (1985): 153–78; P. Senapathy, *Independent Birth of Organisms* (Madison, Wisc.: Genome Press, 1994); M. S. Gordon, "The Concept of Monophyly: A Speculative Essay," *Biology and Philosophy* 14 (1999): 331–48; W. F. Doolittle, "Phylogenetic Classification and the Universal Tree," *Science* 284 (1999): 2124–28; W. F. Doolittle, "The Nature of the Universal Ancestor and the Evolution of the Proteome," *Current Opinion in Structural Biology* 10 (2000): 355–58; D. W. Thompson, *On Growth and Form* (Reprint; New York: Dover, 1992); P. A. Nelson, *On Common Descent* (Chicago: Evolutionary Monographs, 2004); D. T. Anderson, "Origins and Relationships among the Animal Phyla," *Proceedings of the Linnean Society of New South Wales* 106 (1982): 151–66; J. R. Nursall, "On the Origins of the Major Groups of Animals," *Evolution* 16 (1962): 118–23; G. Webster and B. C. Goodwin, "The Origin of Species: A Structuralist Approach," *Journal of Social and Biological Structures* 5 (1982): 15–47.

10. The primary purpose of definitional analysis is to make explicit how a term is actually used in particular semantic contexts. In our analysis of the "E" word, we are concerned with how prominent biologists and spokespersons for science actually use the term in scientific publications. Accordingly, the goal in evolution #6 is to capture one of the most pervasive meanings of the word as used within leading scientific publications, including biology textbooks. Had our goal been to render the results of a survey given to practicing biologists, the landscape of multiple meanings of evolution beyond evolution #5 would be more nuanced than our evolution #6. For example, a minority of biologists are convinced that divine providence, though beyond scientific detection, renders everything purposeful in nature, even mutation and natural selection. A recent survey shows that only a few biologists who are members of the National Academy of Sciences (an indication of prominence) hold such theistic views (5.5 percent of the NAS biologists surveyed professed belief in a "personal God"). See Edward J. Larson and Larry Witham, "Leading Scientists Still Reject God," *Nature* 394 (1998): 313.

11. R. Dawkins, *The Blind Watchmaker: Why the Evidence of Evolution Reveals a Universe without Design* (New York: W. W. Norton, 1986), 5.

12. M. Ruse, *Darwinism Defended: A Guide to the Evolution Controversy,* with a foreword by Ernst Mayr (Reading, Mass.: Addison-Wesley, 1982), xi–xii.

13. E. Mayr, "Darwin's Influence on Modern Thought," *Scientific American* 283 (2000): 81.

14. G. G. Simpson, *The Meaning of Evolution* (New Haven, Conn.: Yale University Press, 1967), 345.

15. K. Miller and J. Levine, *Biology,* 5th ed. (Upper Saddle River, N.J.: Prentice Hall, 2000), 658. This same textbook also contains these similar statements: "it is important to keep this concept in mind: *Evolution is random and undirected"* (658, emphasis in the original), and "It is important to remember that genetic variation is not controlled or directed toward a goal" (299). Miller and Levine have removed the claim that "evolution works without plan or purpose" in the 2002 edition of their textbook.

16. W. K. Purvis, G. H. Orians, and H. C. Heller, *Life: The Science of Biology,* 4th ed. (Sunderland, Mass.: Sinauer Associates, 1995), 14.

17. D. J. Futuyma, *Evolutionary Biology* (Sunderland, Mass.: Sinauer Associates, 1998), 5.

18. F. J. Ayala, "Darwin's Revolution," in *Creative Evolution?!* ed. J. H. Campbell and J. W. Schopf (Boston: Jones and Barlett, 1994), 5.
19. R. H. Brady, "Dogma and Doubt," *Biological Journal of the Linnean Society* 17 (1982): 79–96; D. Collingridge and M. Earthy, "Science Under Stress—Crisis in Neo-Darwinism," *History and Philosophy of the Life Sciences* 12 (1990): 3–26; G. de Beer, *Homology: An Unsolved Problem* (London: Oxford University Press, 1971); M. Denton, *Evolution: A Theory in Crisis* (Bethesda, Md.: Adler and Adler, 1986); N. Eldredge, *Time Frames: The Evolution of Punctuated Equilibria* (Princeton, N.J.: Princeton University Press, 1985); P. P. Grasse, *Evolution of Living Organisms* (New York: Academic Press, 1977); S. J. Gould, "Is a New and General Theory of Evolution Emerging?" *Paleobiology* 6 (1980): 119–30; M. W. Ho and P. T. Saunders, eds., *Beyond Neo-Darwinism* (London: Academic Press, 1984), ix; Ho, "Methodological Issues"; F. Hoyle and S. Wickramasinghe, *Evolution from Space* (London: J. M. Dent, 1981); S. Kauffman, "New Questions in Genetics and Evolution," *Cladistics* 1 (1985): 1247–65; S. Kauffman, *The Origins of Order: Self-Organization and Selection in Evolution* (Oxford: Oxford University Press, 1993); B. John and G. Miklos, *The Eukaryote Genome in Development* (London: Allen and Unwin, 1988); S. Løvtrup, *Darwinism: The Refutation of Myth* (London: Croom Helm, 1987); R. Lewin, *Bones of Contention* (New York: Simon and Schuster, 1987); P. S. Moorhead and M. M. Chaplain, *Mathematical Challenges to the Neo-Darwinian Interpretation of Evolution* (Philadelphia: Wistar Institute Press, 1967)—see especially the papers and comments from M. Eden, M. Schützenberger, S. M. Ulam, and P. Gavaudan; R. A. Raff and E. C. Raff, eds., *Development as an Evolutionary Process* (New York: Alan R. Liss, 1987), 84; A. Tetry, *A General History of the Sciences*, vol. 4 (London: Thames and Hudson, 1966)—see section on evolution, esp. 446; K. S. Thomson, *Morphogenesis and Evolution* (Oxford: Oxford University Press, 1988); D. B. Wake and G. Roth, eds., *Complex Organismal Functions* (New York: John Wiley, 1989); G. Webster, "The Relations of Natural Forms," in Ho and Saunders, *Beyond Neo-Darwinism*, 193–217; http://www.reviewevolution.com/pressRelease_100Scientists.php.
20. S. Gilbert, J. Opitz, and R. Raff, "Resynthesizing Evolutionary and Developmental Biology," *Developmental Biology* 173 (1996): 361.
21. Kauffman, *Origins of Order*.
22. F. Hoke, "Study Sees Alarming Science Undergrad Dropout Rate," *Scientist* 12, no. 5 (1993): 1.

23. National Academy of Sciences, *Science and Creationism: A View from the National Academy of Sciences* (Washington, D.C.: National Academy Press, 1999). The booklet is also available at http://www.nap.edu.

24. Ibid., 28.

25. Ibid.

26. S. J. Gould, "Darwinism Defined: The Difference between Fact and Theory," *Discover* (Jan. 1987): 64.

27. S. J. Gould, "Is a New and General Theory of Evolution Emerging?" *Paleobiology* 6 (1980): 127. Gould states: "perhaps, in many cases, the intermediates never existed. . . . I envisage a potential saltational origin for the essential features of key adaptations. Why may we not imagine that gill arch bones of an ancestral agnathan moved forward in one step to surround the mouth and form proto-jaws? Such a change would scarcely establish the *Baupläne* of the gnathostomes. So much more must be altered in the reconstruction of agnathan design—the building of a true shoulder girdle with bony, paired appendages, to say the least. But the discontinuous origin of a proto-jaw might set up new regimes of development and selection that would quickly lead to other, coordinated modifications. Yet Darwin, conflating gradualism with natural selection as he did so often, wrongly proclaimed that any such discontinuity, even for organs (much less taxa) would destroy his theory."

28. "NABT Unveils New Statement on Teaching Evolution," *American Biology Teacher* 58 (Jan. 1996): 61–62. The current NABT statement is at http://www.nabt.org/Evolution.html.

29. Ibid.

30. Quoted in Eugenie C. Scott, "NABT Statement on Evolution Evolves." Special report of the National Center for Science Education, at http://www.natcenscied.org/nabtart.htm.

31. Zondervan News Service (13 Oct. 1997). E-mail news from Zondervan Publishing House, http://www.zondervan.com, quoting a Religion News Service article, http://www.religionnews.com.

32. Scott, "NABT Statement."

33. Ibid.

34. http://fp.bio.utk.edu/darwin; http://fp.bio.utk.edu/darwin/Open%20 letter/letterhome.html.

35. http://vest.gu.se/vest_mail/0605.html.

36. http://www.reviewevolution.com/press/pressRelease_100Scientists. php; *New York Review of Books*, 1 Nov. 2001, 23.

The Deniable Darwin

David Berlinski

❖ ❖ ❖

Charles Darwin presented *On the Origin of Species* to a disbelieving world in 1859—three years after Clerk Maxwell had published "On Faraday's Lines of Force," the first of his papers on the electromagnetic field. Maxwell's theory has by a process of absorption become part of quantum field theory, and so a part of the great canonical structure created by mathematical physics. By contrast, the final triumph of Darwinian theory, although vividly imagined by biologists, remains, along with world peace and Esperanto, on the eschatological horizon of contemporary thought.

"It is just a matter of *time*," one biologist wrote recently, reposing his faith in a receding hereafter, "before this fruitful concept comes to be accepted by the public as wholeheartedly as it has accepted the spherical earth and the sun-centered solar system."[1] Time, however, is what evolutionary biologists have long had, and if general acceptance has not come by now, it is hard to know when it ever will.

In its most familiar, textbook form, Darwin's theory subordinates itself to a haunting and fantastic image, one in which life on Earth is represented as a tree. So graphic has this image become that some biologists have persuaded themselves they can *see* the flowering tree standing on a dusty plain, the mammalian twig obliterating itself by anastomosis into a reptilian branch and so backward to the amphibia and then the fish, the sturdy chordate line—our line, *cosa nostra*—moving by slithering stages into the still more primitive trunk of life and so downward to the single irresistible cell that from within its folded chromosomes foretold the living future.

This image is nonsense, of course. That densely reticulated tree, with its lavish foliage, is an intellectual construct, one expressing the *hypothesis* of descent with modification. Evolution is a process, one stretching over four billion years. It has not been observed. The past has gone to where the past inevitably goes. The future has not arrived. The present reveals only the detritus of time and chance: the fossil record and the comparative anatomy, physiology, and biochemistry of different organisms and creatures. Like every other scientific theory, the theory of evolution lies at the end of an inferential trail.

The facts in favor of evolution are often held to be incontrovertible; prominent biologists shake their heads at the obduracy of those who would dispute them. Those facts, however, have been rather less forthcoming than evolutionary biologists might have hoped. If life progressed by an accumulation of small changes, as they say it has, the fossil record should reflect its flow, the dead stacked up in barely separated strata. But for well over 150 years, the dead have been remarkably diffident about confirming Darwin's theory. Their bones lie suspended in the sands of time, theromorphs and therapsids and things that must have gibbered and then squeaked; but there are gaps in the graveyard, places where there should be intermediate forms but where there is nothing whatsoever instead.[2]

Before the Cambrian era, a brief 600 million years ago, very little is inscribed in the fossil record; but then, signaled by what I imagine as a spectral puff of smoke and a deafening *ta-da!* an astonishing number of novel biological structures come into creation, and they come into creation at once.

Thereafter, the major transitional sequences are incomplete. Important inferences begin auspiciously but then trail off, the ancestral connection between *Eusthenopteron* and *Ichthyostega,* for example—the great hinge between the fish and the amphibia—turning on the interpretation of small grooves within *Eusthenopteron*'s intercalary bones. Most species enter the evolutionary order fully formed and then depart unchanged. Where there should be evolution, there is *stasis* instead—the term is used by paleontologists Stephen Jay Gould and Niles Eldredge in developing their theory of "punctuated equilibria"—with the fire alarms of change going off suddenly during a long night in which nothing happens.

The fundamental core of Darwinian doctrine, philosopher Daniel Dennett has buoyantly affirmed, "is now beyond dispute among scientists."[3] Such is the party line, useful on those occasions when biologists must present a single face to their public. But it was to the dead that Darwin pointed for confirmation of his theory; the fact that paleontology does not entirely support his doctrine has been a secret of long standing among paleontologists. "The known fossil record," Steven Stanley observes, "fails to document a single example of phyletic evolution accomplishing a major morphologic transition and hence offers no evidence that the gradualistic model can be valid."[4]

Small wonder, then, that when the spotlight of publicity is dimmed, evolutionary biologists evince a feral streak, with Stephen Jay Gould, Niles Eldredge, Richard Dawkins, and John Maynard Smith abusing one another roundly like wrestlers grappling in the dark.

Pause for the Logician

Swimming in the soundless sea, the shark has survived for millions of years, sleek as a knife blade and twice as dull. *The shark is an organism wonderfully adapted to its environment.* Pause. And then the bright brittle voice of logical folly intrudes: *After all, it has survived for millions of years.*

That exchange should be deeply embarrassing to evolutionary biologists. Yet, time and again, biologists do explain the survival of an organism by reference to its fitness and the fitness of an organism by reference to its survival, the friction between concepts kindling nothing more illuminating than the observation that some creatures have been around for a very long time. "Those individuals that have the most offspring," writes zoologist Ernst Mayr, "are by definition . . . the fittest ones."[5] In *Evolution and the Myth of Creationism,* Tim Berra states that "fitness in the Darwinian sense means reproductive fitness—leaving at least enough offspring to spread or sustain the species in nature."[6]

This is not a parody of evolutionary thinking; it *is* evolutionary thinking. *Que será, será.*

Evolutionary thought is suffused in general with an unwholesome glow. "The belief that an organ so perfect as the eye," Darwin wrote, "could have been formed by natural selection is enough to stagger anyone."[7] It is. The problem is obvious. "What good," Stephen Jay Gould asked dramatically, "is 5 percent of an eye?" He termed this question "excellent."[8]

The question, retorted Oxford professor Richard Dawkins, the most prominent representative of ultra-Darwinians, "is not excellent at all": "Vision that is 5 percent as good as yours or mine is very much worth having in comparison with no vision at all. And 6 percent is better than 5, 7 percent better than 6, and so on up the gradual, continuous series."[9]

But Dawkins, replied Phillip Johnson in turn, had carelessly assumed that 5 percent *of* an eye would see 5 percent *as well as* an eye, and that is an assumption for which there is little evidence.[10]

Having been conducted for more than a century, exchanges of this sort may continue for centuries more; but the debate is an exercise in irrelevance. In sight, what is at work is a visual *system*, one that requires not only the anatomical structures of the eye and forebrain but the remarkably detailed and poorly understood algorithms required to make these structures work. "When we examine the visual mechanism closely," Karen K. de Valois remarked recently in *Science*, "although we understand much about its component parts, we fail to fathom the ways in which they fit together to produce the whole of our complex visual perception."[11]

Those facts suggest a chastening reformulation of Gould's "excellent" question, one adapted to reality: *Could a system we do not completely understand be constructed by means of a process we cannot completely specify?*

The intellectually responsible answer to this question is that we do not know—we have no way of knowing. But that is not the answer evolutionary theorists accept. According to Daniel Dennett, Dawkins is "almost certainly right" to uphold the incremental view because "Darwinism is basically on the right track."[12] In this, he echoes philosopher Kim Sterelny, who is also persuaded that "something like Dawkins's stories have *got* to be right" (emphasis added). After all, he asserts, "natural selection is the only possible explanation of complex adaptation."[13]

Dawkins himself has maintained that those who do not believe that a complex biological structure may be constructed in small steps are expressing merely their own sense of "personal incredulity."[14] But in countering their animadversions, he appeals to his own ability to believe almost anything. Commenting on the (very plausible) claim that spiders could not have acquired their web-spinning behavior by a Darwinian mechanism, Dawkins writes: "It is not impossible at all. That is what I firmly believe and I have some experience of spiders and their webs."[15] It is painful to see this advanced as an argument.

Unflagging Success

Darwin conceived of evolution as based on *small* variations among organisms, variations that by a process of accretion allow one species to change continuously into another. This suggests a view in which living creatures are spread out smoothly over the great manifold of biological possibilities, like colors merging imperceptibly in a color chart.

Life, however, is absolutely nothing like this. Wherever one looks there is singularity, quirkiness, oddness, defiant individuality, and just plain weirdness. The male redback spider (*Latrodectus hasselti*), for example, is often consumed during copulation. Such is sexual cannibalism—the result, biologists have long assumed, of "predatory females overcoming the defenses of weaker males." But it now appears that among *Latrodectus hasselti,* the male is complicit in his own consumption. Having achieved intromission, this schnook performs a characteristic somersault, placing his abdomen directly over his partner's mouth. Such is sexual suicide, awfulness taken to a higher power.[16]

It might seem that sexual suicide confers no advantage on the spider, the male passing from ecstasy to extinction in the course of one and the same act. But spiders willing to pay for love are apparently favored by female spiders, and female spiders with whom they mate, entomologists claim, are less likely to mate again. The male spider perishes; his preposterous line persists.

This explanation resolves one question only at the cost of inviting another: Why such bizarre behavior? In no other *Lactrodectus* species does the male perform that obliging somersault, offering his partner the oblation of his life as well as his love. Are there general principles that specify sexual suicide among this species but that forbid sexual suicide elsewhere? If so, what are they?

Once asked, such questions tend to multiply. If evolutionary theory cannot answer them, what, then, is its use? Why is the pitcher plant carnivorous but not the thorn bush, and why does the Pacific salmon require freshwater to spawn but not the Chilean sea bass? Why has the British thrush learned to hammer snails upon rocks but not the British blackbird, which often starves to death in the midst of plenty? Why did the firefly discover bioluminescence but not the wasp or the warrior ant? Why do the bees do their dance but not the spider or the flies? And why are women but not cats born without the sleek tails that would make them even more alluring than they already are?

Why? Yes, *why?* The question, simple, clear, intellectually respectable, was put to Nobel laureate George Wald. "Various organisms try various things," he finally answered, his words functioning as a verbal shrug. "They keep what works and discard the rest."[17]

But suppose the manifold of life were to be given a good solid yank, so that the Chilean sea bass but not the Pacific salmon required freshwater to spawn, or that ants but not fireflies flickered enticingly at twilight, or that women but not cats were born with lush tails. What then? An inversion of life's fundamental facts would, I suspect, present evolutionary biologists with few difficulties. *Various organisms try various things.* That idea is adapted to any contingency whatsoever, an interesting example of a Darwinian mechanism in the development of Darwinian thought itself.

A comparison with geology is instructive. No geological theory makes it possible to specify precisely a particular mountain's shape; but the underlying process of upthrust and crumbling is well understood, and geologists can specify something like a mountain's *generic* shape. This provides geological theory with a firm connection to reality. A mountain arranging itself in the shape of the letter "A" is not a physically possible object; it is excluded by geological theory.

The theory of evolution, by contrast, is incapable of ruling *anything* out of court. That job must be done by nature. But a theory that can confront any contingency with unflagging success cannot be falsified. Its control of the facts is an illusion.

Sheer Dumb Luck

"Chance alone," Nobel Prize–winning chemist Jacques Monod once wrote, "is at the source of every innovation, of all creation in the biosphere. Pure chance, absolutely free but blind, is at the very root of the stupendous edifice of creation."[18]

The sentiment expressed by those words has come to vex evolutionary biologists. "This belief," Richard Dawkins writes, "that Darwinian evolution is 'random,' is not merely false. It is the exact opposite of the truth."[19] But Monod is right and Dawkins wrong. Chance lies at the beating heart of evolutionary theory, just as it lies at the beating heart of thermodynamics.

The second law of thermodynamics holds dominion over the temporal organization of the universe, and what the law has to say we find verified by ordinary experience at every turn. Things fall apart. Energy, like talent, tends to squander itself. Liquids go from hot to lukewarm. And so does love. Disorder and despair overwhelm the human enterprise, filling our rooms and our lives with clutter. Decay is unyielding. Things go from bad to worse. And overall, they go *only* from bad to worse.

Those grim certainties the second law abbreviates in the solemn and awful declaration that the entropy of the universe is tending toward a maximum. The final state in which entropy is maximized is simply more *likely* than any other state. The disintegration of my face reflects nothing more compelling than the odds. Sheer dumb luck.

But if things fall apart, they also come together. *Life* appears to offer at least a temporary rebuke to the second law of thermodynamics. Although biologists are unanimous in arguing that evolution has no goal, fixed from the first, it remains true nonetheless that living creatures have organized themselves into ever more elaborate and flexible structures. If their complexity is increasing, the entropy that surrounds them is decreasing. Whatever the universe as a whole may be doing—time fusing incomprehensibly with space, the great stars exploding indignantly—biologically things have gone from bad to *better,* the show organized, or so it would seem, as a counterexample to the prevailing winds of fate.

How so? The question has historically been the pivot on which the assumption of religious belief has turned. How so? "God said: 'Let the waters swarm with swarms of living creatures, and let fowl fly above the earth in the open firmament of heaven.'" That is *how so.* Who on the basis of experience would be inclined to disagree? The structures of life are complex, and complex structures get made in this, the purely human world, only by a process of deliberate design. An act of intelligence is required to bring even a thimble into being. Why should the artifacts of life be different?

Darwin's theory of evolution rejects this counsel of experience and intuition. Instead, the theory forges, at least in spirit, a perverse connection with the second law itself, arguing that precisely the same force that explains one turn of the cosmic wheel explains another. Sheer dumb luck.

If the universe is for reasons of sheer dumb luck committed ultimately to a state of cosmic listlessness, it is *also* by sheer dumb luck that life first emerged on Earth, the chemicals in the prebiotic seas or soup illuminated and then invigorated by a fateful flash of lightning. It is again by sheer dumb luck that the first self-reproducing systems were created. The dense and ropy chains of RNA—*they* were created by sheer dumb luck, and sheer dumb luck drove the primitive chemicals of life to form a living cell. It is sheer dumb luck that alters the genetic message so that, from infernal nonsense, *meaning* for a moment emerges; and it is sheer dumb luck again that endows life with its *opportunities,* the space of possibilities over which natural selection plays: sheer dumb luck creating the mammalian eye and the marsupial pouch, sheer dumb luck again endowing the elephant's sensitive nose with nerves and the orchid's translucent petal with blush. Amazing.

Life, Complex Life

Physicists are persuaded that things are in the end simple; biologists, that they are not. A good deal depends on where one looks. Wherever the biologist looks, there is complexity beyond complexity, the entanglement of things ramifying downward from the organism to the cell. In a superbly elaborated figure, Australian biologist Michael Denton compares a single cell to an immense automated factory the size of a large city:

> On the surface of the cell we would see millions of openings, like the portholes of a vast space ship, opening and closing to allow a continual stream of materials to flow in and out. If we were to enter one of these openings we would find ourselves in a world of supreme technology and bewildering complexity. We would see endless highly organized corridors and conduits branching in every direction away from the perimeter of the cell, some leading to the central memory bank in the nucleus and others to assembly plants and processing units. The nucleus itself would be a vast spherical chamber more than a kilometer in diameter, resembling a geodesic dome inside of which we would see, all neatly stacked together in ordered arrays, the miles of coiled chains of the DNA molecule. . . . We would notice that the simplest of the functional components of the cell, the protein molecules, were astonishingly complex pieces of molecular machinery. . . . Yet the life of the cell depends on the integrated activities of thousands, certainly tens, and probably hundreds of thousands of different protein molecules.[20]

Whatever the complexity of the cell, it is insignificant in comparison with the mammalian nervous system; and beyond that, far impossibly ahead, there is the human mind, an instrument like no other in the biological world: conscious, flexible, penetrating, inscrutable, profound.

Here the door of doubt begins to swing. *Chance* and *complexity* are countervailing forces; they work at cross-purposes. English theologian William Paley (1743–1805) made this circumstance the gravamen of his well-known argument from design: "Nor would any man in his senses think the existence of the watch, with its various machinery, accounted for, by being told that it was one out of possible combinations of material forms; that whatever he had found in the place where he found the watch, must have contained some internal configuration or other, and that this configuration might be the structure now exhibited, viz., of the works of a watch, as well as a different structure."[21]

It is worth remarking, it is simply a *fact,* that this courtly and old-fashioned argument is entirely compelling. We *never* attribute the existence of a complex artifact to chance. And for obvious reasons: complex objects are useful islands, isolated amid an archipelago of useless possibilities. Of the thousands of ways in which a watch might be assembled from its constituents, only one is liable to work. It is unreasonable to attribute the existence of a watch to chance, if only because it is *unlikely.* An artifact is the overflow in matter of the mental motions of intention, deliberate design, planning, and coordination. The inferential spool runs backward, and it runs irresistibly from a complex object to the contrived artificial, circumstances that brought it into being.

Paley allowed the conclusion of his argument to drift from man-made to biological artifacts, a human eye or kidney falling under the same classification as a watch. "Every indication of contrivance," he wrote, "every manifestation of design, exists in the works of nature; with the difference, on the side of nature, of being greater or more, and that in a degree which exceeds all computation."[22]

In this drifting, Darwinists see dangerous signs of a non sequitur. There is a tight connection, they acknowledge, between what a watch is and how it is made. But the connection unravels at the human eye—or at any other organ, disposition, body plan, or strategy—if only because another and a simpler explanation is available. Among living creatures, say Darwinists, *the design persists even as the designer disappears.*

"Paley's argument," Dawkins writes, "is made with passionate sincerity and is informed by the best biological scholarship of his day, but it is wrong, gloriously and utterly wrong."[23] The enormous confidence this quotation expresses must be juxtaposed against the weight of intuition it displaces. It is true that intuition is often wrong—quantum theory is intuition's graveyard. But quantum theory is remote from experience; our intuitions in biology lie closer to the bone. We are ourselves such stuff as genes are made of, and although this does not establish that our assessments of time and chance must be correct, it does suggest that they may be pertinent.

The Book of Life

The discovery of the molecular structure of DNA by James D. Watson and Francis Crick in 1952 revealed that a living creature is an organization of matter orchestrated by a genetic text. Within the bacterial cell, for example, the book of life is written in a distinctive language. The book is read aloud, its message specifying the construction of the cell's constituents, and then the book is copied, passed faithfully into the future.

That striking metaphor introduces a troubling instability, a kind of tremor, into biological thought. With the discovery of the genetic code, every living creature comes to divide itself into alien realms: the alphabetic and the organismic. The realms are conceptually distinct, responding to entirely different imperatives and constraints. An alphabet, on the one hand, belongs to the class of finite combinatorial objects, things that are discrete and that fit together in highly circumscribed ways. An organism, on the other hand, traces a continuous figure in space and in time. How, then, are these realms coordinated?

I ask the question because in similar systems, coordination is crucial. When I use the English language, the rules of grammar act as a constraint on the changes that I might make to the letters or sounds I employ. That is something we take for granted, an ordinary miracle in which I pass from one sentence to the next, almost as if crossing an abyss by means of a series of well-placed stepping-stones.

In living creatures, things evidently proceed otherwise. There is *no* obvious coordination between alphabet and organism; the two objects are governed by different conceptual regimes, and that apparently is the end of it. Under the pressures of competition, the orchid *Orphrys apifera* undergoes a statistically adapted drift, some incidental feature in its design becoming over time ever more refined, until, consumed with longing, a misguided bee amorously mounts the orchid's petals, convinced that he has seen shimmering there a female's fragile genitalia. As this is taking place, the marvelous mimetic design maturing slowly, the orchid's underlying alphabetic system undergoes a series of *random* perturbations, letters in its genetic alphabet winking off or winking on in a way independent of the grand convergent progression toward perfection taking place out there where the action is.

We do not understand, we cannot re-create, a system of this sort. However it may operate in life, randomness in language is the enemy of order, a way of annihilating meaning. And not only in language, but in any language-*like* system—computer programs, for example. The alien influence of randomness in such systems was first noted by French mathematician M. P. Schützenberger, who also marked the significance of this circumstance for evolutionary theory. "If we try to simulate such a situation," he wrote, "by making changes randomly . . . on computer programs, we find that we have no chance . . . even to see what the modified program would compute: it just jams."[24]

Planets of Possibility

This is not yet an argument, only an expression of intellectual unease; but the unease tends to build as analogies are amplified. The general issue is one of size and space and the way in which something small may be found amid something very big.

Linguists in the 1950s, most notably Noam Chomsky and George Miller, asked dramatically how many grammatical English sentences could be constructed with 100 letters. Approximately 10 to the 25th power (10^{25}), they answered. A very large number. But a sentence is one thing; a *sequence,* another. A sentence obeys the laws of English grammar; a sequence is lawless and comprises *any* concatenation of those 100 letters. If there are roughly 10^{25} sentences at hand, the number of sequences 100 letters in length is, by way of contrast, 26 to the 100th power (26^{100})—an inconceivably greater number. The space of possibilities has blown up, the explosive process being one of combinatorial inflation.

Now, the vast majority of sequences drawn on a finite alphabet fail to make a statement: They consist of letters arranged to no point or purpose. It is the contrast between sentences and sequences that carries the full critical weight of memory and intuition. Organized as a writhing ball, the sequences resemble a planet-sized object, one as large as pale Pluto. Landing almost anywhere on that planet, linguists see nothing but nonsense. Meaning resides with the *grammatical* sequences, but they, those *sentences,* occupy an area no larger than a dime.

How on earth could the sentences be *discovered by chance* amid such an infernal and hyperborean immensity of gibberish? They cannot be discovered by chance, and, of course, chance plays no role in their discovery. Linguists or native English-speakers move around the place or planet with a perfectly secure sense of where they should go and what they are apt to see.

The eerie and unexpected presence of an alphabet in every living creature might suggest the possibility of a similar argument in biology. It is
DNA, of course, that acts as life's primordial text, the code itself organized
in nucleic triplets like messages in Morse code. Each triplet is matched to a
particular chemical object, an amino acid. There are twenty such acids in
all. They correspond to letters in an alphabet. As the code is read somewhere in life's hidden housing, the linear order of the nucleic acids induces
a corresponding linear order in the amino acids. The biological finger
writes, and what the cell reads is an ordered presentation of such amino
acids—a protein.

Like the nucleic acids, proteins are alphabetic objects, composed of discrete constituents. On average, proteins are roughly 250 amino acid
residues in length, so a given protein may be imagined as a long biochemical word, one of many.

The aspects of an analogy are now in place. What is needed is a relevant
contrast, something comparable to sentences and sequences in language.
Of course, nothing completely comparable is at hand: There are *no* sentences in molecular biology. Nonetheless, there is this fact, helpfully re-
counted by Richard Dawkins: "The actual animals that have ever lived on
earth are a tiny subset of the theoretical animals that *could* exist."[25] It follows that over the course of four billion years, life has expressed itself by
means of a particular stock of proteins, a certain set of lifelike words.

A combinatorial count is now possible. MIT physicist Murray Eden, to
whom I owe this argument, estimates the number of viable proteins at 10
to the 50th power (10^{50}). Within this set is the raw material of everything
that has ever lived: the flowering plants and the alien insects and the
seagoing turtles and the sad shambling dinosaurs, the great evolutionary
successes and the great evolutionary failures as well. These creatures are,
quite literally, composed of the proteins that over the course of time have
performed some useful function, with "usefulness" now standing for the
sense of sentencehood in linguistics.

As in the case of language, what has once lived occupies some corner in
the space of a larger array of possibilities, the actual residing in the shadow
of the possible. The space of all *possible* proteins of a fixed length (250
residues, recall) is computed by multiplying 20 by itself 250 times (20^{250}).
It is idle to carry out the calculation. The number is larger by far than sec-
onds in the history of the world since the big bang or grains of sand on the
shores of every sounding sea. Another planet now looms in the night sky,
Pluto-sized or bigger, a conceptual companion to the planet containing

every sequence composed by endlessly arranging the 26 English letters into sequences 100 letters in length. This planetary doppelgänger is the planet of all possible proteins of fixed length, the planet, in a certain sense, of every *conceivable* form of carbon-based life.

There the two planets lie, spinning on their soundless axes. The contrast between sentences and sequences on Pluto reappears on Pluto's double as the contrast between useful protein forms and all the rest. It reappears in the same dramatic difference in numbers, the enormous (20^{250}) overawing the merely big (10^{50}), the contrast between the two being quite literally between an immense and swollen planet and a dime's worth of area. That dime-sized corner, which on Pluto contains the English sentences, on Pluto's double contains the living creatures; and there the biologist may be seen tramping, the warm puddle of wet life achingly distinct amid the planet's snow and stray proteins. It is here that living creatures, whatever their ultimate fate, breathed and moaned and carried on, life evidently having discovered the small quiet corner of the space of possibilities in which things *work.*

It would seem that evolution, Murray Eden writes in artfully ambiguous language, "was directed toward the incredibly small proportion of useful protein forms," the word "directed" conveying, at least to me, the sobering image of a stage-managed search, with evolution bypassing the awful immensity of all that frozen space because in some sense evolution *knew* where it was going.[26]

Yet from the perspective of Darwinian theory, it is chance that plays the crucial—that plays the *only*—role in generating the proteins. Wandering the surface of a planet, evolution wanders blindly, having forgotten where it has been, unsure of where it is going.

The Artificer of Design

Random mutations are the great creative demiurge of evolution, throwing up possibilities and bathing life in the bright light of chance. Each living creature is not only what it is but what it might be. What, then, acts to make the possible palpable?

The theory of evolution is a materialistic theory. Various deities need not apply. Any form of mind is out. Yet a force is needed, something adequate to the manifest complexity of the biological world and something that in the largest arena of all might substitute for the acts of design, anticipation, and memory that are obvious features of such day-to-day activities as fashioning a sentence or a sonnet.

This need is met in evolutionary theory by natural selection, the filter but not the source of change. "It may be said," Darwin wrote, "that natural selection is daily and hourly scrutinizing, throughout the world, every variation, even the slightest; rejecting that which is bad, preserving and adding up all that is good; silently and insensibly working, whenever and wherever opportunity offers, at the improvement of each organic being in relation to its organic and inorganic conditions of life."[27]

Natural selection emerges from these reflections as a strange, forcelike concept. It is strange because it is unconnected to any notion of force in physics, and it is force*like* because natural selection *does* something; it has an effect and so functions as a kind of cause.[28] Creatures, habits, organ systems, body plans, organs, and tissues are *shaped* by natural selection. Population geneticists write of selection forces, selection pressures, and coefficients of natural selection. Biologists say that natural selection sculpts, shapes, coordinates, transforms, directs, controls, changes, and transfigures living creatures.

Natural selection, Richard Dawkins believes, is the artificer of design, a cunning force that mocks human ingenuity even as it mimics it: "Charles Darwin showed how it is possible for blind physical forces to mimic the effects of conscious design, and, by operating as a cumulative filter of chance variations, to lead eventually to organized and adaptive complexity, to mosquitoes and mammoths, to humans and therefore, indirectly, to books and computers."[29]

In affirming what Darwin showed, these words suggest that Darwin *demonstrated* the power of natural selection in some formal sense, settling the issue once and for all. But that is not true. When Darwin wrote, the mechanism of evolution he proposed had only life itself to commend it. But to refer to the power of natural selection by appealing to the course of evolution is a little like confirming a story in the *New York Times* by reading it twice. The theory of evolution is, after all, a *general* theory of change. If natural selection can sift the debris of chance to fashion an elephant's trunk, should it not be able to work elsewhere—amid computer programs and algorithms, words and sentences? Skeptics require a demonstration of natural selection's cunning, one that does not assume the phenomenon it is meant to explain.

No sooner said than done. An extensive literature is now devoted to what is optimistically called artificial life. These are schemes in which various programs generate amusing computer objects and by a process said to be similar to evolution show that they are capable of growth and decay and even a phosphorescent simulacrum of death. An algorithm called Face Prints, for example, has been designed to enable crime victims to identify their attackers. The algorithm runs through hundreds of facial combinations (long hair, short hair, big nose, wide chin, moles, warts, wens, wrinkles) until the victim spots the resemblance between the long-haired, big-nosed, wide-chinned portrait of the perpetrator and the perpetrator himself.

It is the presence of the *human* victim in this scenario that should give pause. What is *he* doing there, amid those otherwise blind forces? A mechanism that requires a discerning human agent cannot be Darwinian. The Darwinian mechanism neither anticipates nor remembers. It gives no directions and makes no choices. What is unacceptable in evolutionary theory, what is strictly forbidden, is the appearance of a force with the power to survey time, a force that conserves a point or a property because it will be useful. Such a force is no longer Darwinian. How would a blind force know such a thing? And by what means could future usefulness be transmitted to the present?

If life is, as evolutionary biologists so often say, a matter merely of blind thrusting and throbbing, any definition of natural selection must plainly meet what I have elsewhere called a rule against deferred success.[30] It is a rule that cannot be violated with impunity. If evolutionary theory is to retain its intellectual integrity, the rule cannot be violated at all.

But the rule is widely violated, the violations so frequent as to amount to a formal fallacy.

Advent of the Head Monkey

It is Richard Dawkins's grand intention in *The Blind Watchmaker* to demonstrate, as one reviewer enthusiastically remarked, "how natural selection allows biologists to dispense with such notions as purpose and design."[31] This he does by exhibiting a process in which the random exploration of certain possibilities, a *blind* stab here, another there, is followed by the filtering effects of natural selection, some of those stabs saved, others discarded. But could a process so conceived—a *Darwinian* process—discover a simple English sentence: a target, say, chosen from Shakespeare? The question is by no means academic. If natural selection cannot discern a simple English sentence, what chance is there that it might have discovered the mammalian eye or the system by which glucose is regulated by the liver?

A thought experiment in *The Blind Watchmaker* now follows. Randomness in the experiment is conveyed by the metaphor of the monkeys, perennial favorites in the theory of probability. There they sit, simian hands curved over the keyboards of a thousand typewriters, their long, agile fingers striking keys at random. It is an image of some poignancy, those otherwise intelligent apes banging away at a machine they cannot fathom; and what makes the poignancy pointed is the fact that the system of rewards by which the apes have been induced to strike the typewriter's keys is from the first rigged against them.

The probability that a monkey will strike a given letter is 1 in 26. The typewriter has twenty-six keys: the monkey, one working finger. But a letter is not a word. Should Dawkins demand that the monkey get two English letters right, the odds against success rise with terrible inexorability from 1 in 26 to 1 in 676. The Shakespearean target chosen by Dawkins—"Methinks it is like a weasel"—is a six-word sentence containing twenty-eight English letters (including the spaces). It occupies an isolated point in a space of 10,000 million, million, million, million, million, million possibilities.[32]

That is a very large number; combinatorial inflation is at work. These are very long odds. And a six-word sentence consisting of twenty-eight English letters is a very short, very simple English sentence.

Such are the fatal facts. The problem confronting the monkeys is, of course, a double one: they must, to be sure, find the right letters, but they cannot *lose* the right letters once they have found them. A random search in a space of this size is an exercise in irrelevance. This is something the monkeys appear to know.

What more, then, is expected; what more required? *Cumulative* selection, Dawkins argues—the answer offered as well by Stephen Jay Gould, Manfred Eigen, and Daniel Dennett. The experiment now proceeds in stages. The monkeys type randomly. After a time, they are allowed to survey what they have typed in order to choose the result "which *however slightly* most resembles the target phrase."[33] In Dawkins's experiment, a computer performs the crucial assessments, but I prefer to imagine its role assigned to a scrutinizing monkey, the Head Monkey of the experiment. The process under way is one in which stray successes are spotted and then saved. This process is iterated and iterated again. Variations close to the target are conserved *because* they are close to the target, the Head Monkey equably surveying the scene until, with the appearance of a miracle in progress, randomly derived sentences do begin to converge on the target sentence itself.

The contrast between schemes and scenarios is striking. Acting on their own, the monkeys are adrift in fathomless possibilities, any accidental success—a pair of English-like letters—lost at once, those successes seeming like faint untraceable lights flickering over a wine-dark sea. The advent of the Head Monkey changes things entirely. Successes are *conserved* and then conserved again. The light that formerly flickered uncertainly now stays lit, a beacon burning steadily, a point of illumination. By the light of that light, other lights are lit, until the isolated successes converge, bringing order out of nothingness.

The entire exercise is, however, an achievement in self-deception. A *target* phrase? Iterations that *most resemble* the target? A Head Monkey that *measures* the distance between failure and success? If things are sightless, how is the target represented, and how is the distance between randomly generated phrases and the targets assessed? And by whom? The Head Monkey? What of him? The mechanism of deliberate design, purged by Darwinian theory on the level of the organism, has reappeared in the description of natural selection itself, a vivid example of what Freud meant by the return of the repressed.

This is a point that Dawkins accepts without quite acknowledging, rather like a man adroitly separating his doctor's diagnosis from his own disease.[34] Nature presents life with no targets. Life shambles forward, surging here, shuffling there, the small advantages accumulating *on their own* until something novel appears on the broad evolutionary screen—an arch or an eye, an intricate pattern of behavior, the complexity characteristic of life. May we, then, see *this* process at work, by seeing it simulated? "Unfortunately," Dawkins writes, "I think it may be beyond my powers as a programmer to set up such a counterfeit world."[35]

This is the authentic voice of contemporary Darwinian theory. What may be illustrated by the theory does not represent a Darwinian mechanism; what would be a true Darwinian mechanism cannot be illustrated by the theory.

Darwin without Darwinism

Biologists often affirm that as members of the scientific community they positively welcome criticism. Nonsense. Like everyone else, biologists loathe criticism and arrange their lives so as to avoid it. Criticism has nonetheless seeped into their souls, the process of doubt a curiously Darwinian one in which individual biologists entertain minor reservations about their theory without ever recognizing the degree to which those doubts mount up to a substantial deficit. Creationism, so often the target of their indignation, is the least of their worries.

For many years, biologists have succeeded in keeping skepticism on the circumference of evolutionary thought, where paleontologists, taxonomists, and philosophers linger. But the burning fringe of criticism is now contracting, coming ever closer to the heart of Darwin's doctrine. In a paper of historic importance, Stephen Jay Gould and Richard Lewontin expressed their dissatisfaction with what they termed just-so stories in biology.[36] It is by means of a just-so story, for example, that pop biologist Elaine Morgan explains the presence in human beings of an aquatic diving reflex.[37] An obscure primate ancestral to humans, Morgan argues, was actually aquatic, having returned to the sea like the dolphin. Some time later, that primate, having tired of the water, clambered back to land, its aquatic adaptations intact. Just so.

If stories of this sort are intellectually inadequate—preposterous, in fact—some biologists are prepared to argue that they are unnecessary as well, another matter entirely. "How seriously," H. Allen Orr asked in a superb if savage review of Dennett's *Darwin's Dangerous Idea,* "should we take these endless adaptive explanations of features whose alleged Design may be illusory? Isn't there a difference between those cases where we recognize Design *before* we understand its precise significance and those cases where we try to make Design manifest *by* concocting a story? And isn't it especially worrisome that we can make up arbitrary traits faster than adaptive stories, and adaptive stories faster than experimental tests?"[38]

The camel's lowly hump and the elephant's nose—*these,* Orr suggests, may well be adaptive and so designed by natural selection. But beyond the old familiar cases, life may not be designed at all, the weight of evolution borne by neutral mutations, with genes undergoing a slow but pointless drifting in time's soft currents.

Like Orr, many biologists see an acknowledgment of their doubts as a cagey, a *calculated,* concession; but cagey or not, it is a concession devastating to the larger project of Darwinian biology. Unable to say *what* evolution has accomplished, biologists now find themselves unable to say *whether* evolution has accomplished it. This leaves evolutionary theory in the doubly damned position, of having compromised the concepts needed to make sense of life—complexity, adaptation, design—while simultaneously conceding that the theory does little to explain them.

No doubt, the theory of evolution will continue to play the singular role in the life of our secular culture that it has always played. The theory is unique among scientific instruments in being cherished not for what it contains but for what it lacks. There are in Darwin's scheme no biotic laws, no *Baupläne* as in German natural philosophy, no special creation, no élan vital, no divine guidance or transcendental forces. The theory functions simply as a description of matter in one of its modes, and living creatures are said to be something that the gods of law indifferently sanction and allow.

"Darwin," Richard Dawkins has remarked with evident gratitude, "made it possible to be an intellectually fulfilled atheist."[39] That is an exaggeration, of course, but one containing a portion of truth. The fact that Darwin's theory of evolution and biblical accounts of creation play similar roles in the human economy of belief is an irony appreciated by few biologists.

Notes

1. Tim M. Berra, *Evolution and the Myth of Creationism: A Basic Guide to the Facts in the Evolution Debate* (Stanford, Calif.: Stanford University Press, 1990), 144.

2. A. S. Romer, *Vertebrate Paleontology,* 3rd ed. (Chicago: University of Chicago Press, 1966).

3. Daniel C. Dennett, *Darwin's Dangerous Idea: Evolution and the Meanings of Life* (New York: Simon and Schuster, 1995), 20.

4. Steven Stanley, *Macroevolution: Pattern and Process* (San Francisco, Calif.: W. H. Freeman, 1979), 39.

5. Ernst Mayr, *Animal Species and Evolution* (Cambridge: Harvard University Press, 1963), 183.

6. Berra, *Evolution and the Myth of Creationism,* 68.

7. Charles Darwin, *On the Origin of Species* (Cambridge: Harvard University Press, 1964 [1859]), 204.

8. Stephen Jay Gould, *Ever Since Darwin: Reflections in Natural History* (New York: W. W. Norton, 1977), 107.

9. Richard Dawkins, *The Blind Watchmaker* (New York: W. W. Norton, 1986), 81.

10. Phillip E. Johnson, *Darwin on Trial,* 2d ed. (Downers Grove, Ill.: Inter-Varsity Press, 1993), 34–35. An emeritus professor of law at the

University of California at Berkeley, Johnson has a gift for appealing to the evidence when his opponents invoke theory.

11. Karen K. de Valois, review of *Foundations of Vision: Behavior, Neuroscience, and Computation,* by Brian A. Wandell, *Science,* 8 March 1996, 1371.

12. Dennett, *Darwin's Dangerous Idea,* 250.

13. Kim Sterelny, review of *The Blind Watchmaker,* by Richard Dawkins, *Australasian Journal of Philosophy* 66: 424.

14. Dawkins, *Blind Watchmaker,* 39.

15. Ibid.

16. The details have been reported in the *New York Times* and in *Science*— evidence that at least some entomologists have a good deal of time on their hands.

17. Wald's comments were made at a symposium held in 1966. The proceedings have been published by the Wistar Institute. See George Wald, discussion following "The Problems of Vicarious Selection" in *Mathematical Challenges to the Neo-Darwinian Interpretation of Evolution,* ed. Paul S. Moorhead and Martin M. Kaplan (Philadelphia: Wistar Institute Press, 1966), 70.

18. Jacques Monod, *Chance and Necessity* (New York: Vintage Books, 1971), 112.

19. Dawkins, *Blind Watchmaker,* 49.

20. Michael Denton, *Evolution: A Theory in Crisis* (Bethesda, Md.: Adler and Adler, 1986), 328–29.

21. William Paley, *Natural Theology* (New York: American Tract Society, 1850), 13.

22. Ibid., 24.

23. Dawkins, *Blind Watchmaker,* 5.

24. M. P. Schützenberger, *Mathematical Challenges to the Neo-Darwinian Interpretation of Evolution,* ed. Paul S. Moorhead and Martin M. Kaplan (Philadelphia: Wistar Institute Press, 1967), 74. Schützenberger's remarks, together with those of physicist Murray Eden at the same symposium, constituted the first significant criticism of evolutionary doctrine in recent decades.

25. Dawkins, *Blind Watchmaker,* 73.

26. Murray Eden, "Inadequacies of Neo-Darwinian Evolution as a Scientific Theory: Preliminary Working Paper" in *Mathematical Challenges to the Neo-Darwinian Interpretation of Evolution,* ed. Paul S. Moorhead and Martin M. Kaplan (Philadelphia: Wistar Institute Press, 1967), 109–11.

27. Charles Darwin, *On the Origin of Species,* 84.

28. Murray Eden is, as usual, perceptive: "It is as if," he writes, "some pre-Newtonian cosmologist had proposed a theory of planetary motion which supposed that a natural force of unknown origin held the planets in their courses. The supposition is right enough and the idea of a force between two celestial bodies is a very useful one, but it is hardly a theory." See "Inadequacies of Neo-Darwinian Evolution as a Scientific Theory" in *Mathematical Challenges to the Neo-Darwinian Interpretation of Evolution,* ed. Paul S. Moorhead and Martin M. Kaplan (Philadelphia: Wistar Institute Press, 1967), 5.

29. Richard Dawkins, "The Necessity of Darwinism," *New Scientist,* 15 April 1982, 130.

30. David Berlinski, *Black Mischief: Language, Life, Logic, and Luck* (New York: William Morrow, 1986).

31. Michael T. Ghiselin, review of *The Blind Watchmaker,* by Richard Dawkins, *New York Times,* 14 December 1986, sec. 7.

32. Dawkins, *Blind Watchmaker,* 47.

33. Ibid.

34. The same pattern of intellectual displacement is especially vivid in Daniel Dennett's description in *Darwin's Dangerous Idea* of natural selection as a force subordinate to what he calls "the principle of the accumulation of design." Sifting through the debris of chance, natural selection, he writes, occupies itself by "thriftily conserving the design work . . . accomplished at each stage" (68). But there is no such principle. Dennett has simply assumed that a sequence of conserved advantages will converge to an improvement in design. The assumption expresses a non sequitur.

35. Dawkins, *Blind Watchmaker,* 62. It is absurdly easy to set up a sentence-searching algorithm obeying purely Darwinian constraints. The result, however, is always the same: gibberish.

36. Stephen Jay Gould and Richard Lewontin, "The Spandrels of San Marco and the Panglossian Paradigm: A Critique of the Adaptationist Programme," in *Proceedings of the Royal Society of London,* ser. B, vol. 205, no. 1161 (1979), 581–598.

37. See Elaine Morgan, *The Aquatic Ape* (New York: Stein and Day, 1982) and her work, *The Scars of Evolution* (New York: Oxford University Press, 1994).

38. H. Allen Orr, "Dennett's Strange Idea," *Boston Review* (summer 1996), 30. See also http://bostonreview.mit.edu/br21.3/Orr.html.

39. Dawkins, *Blind Watchmaker,* 6.

Haeckel's Embryos and Evolution: Setting the Record Straight

Jonathan Wells

❊ ❊ ❊

In *The Origin of Species*, Charles Darwin wrote that "the embryos of mammals, birds, fishes, and reptiles [are] closely similar, but become, when fully developed, widely dissimilar." He inferred that all vertebrates "are the modified descendants of some ancient progenitor" and that "the embryonic or larval stages show us, more or less completely, the condition of the progenitor of the whole group in its adult state."[1] Darwin's contemporary, Ernst Haeckel, called this the "Biogenetic Law," according to which "ontogeny recapitulates phylogeny." To illustrate the law, Haeckel produced drawings of vertebrate embryos that have been widely used in biology textbooks ever since (figure 1).[2]

But Haeckel's Biogenetic Law was discredited by embryologists in Darwin's lifetime; recent work has shown that Haeckel's drawings misrepresent the embryos they purport to show; and Haeckel entirely omitted the earliest stages of development in which the various classes of vertebrates are morphologically very different.[3] Biology teachers should be aware that Haeckel's drawings do not fit the facts.

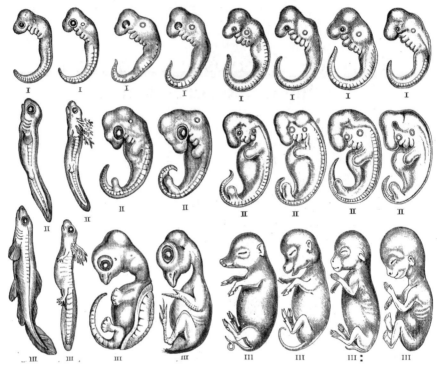

FIGURE 1. Haeckel's drawings, as reproduced by Romanes. The embryos are (left to right) fish, salamander, tortoise, chick, hog, calf, rabbit, and human. Note that only five of the seven vertebrate classes are represented and that half the embryos are mammals. G. J. Romanes, *Darwinism Illustrated* (Chicago: Open Court, 1892).

Haeckel's Discredited Biogenetic Law

Haeckel's Biogenetic Law maintains that vertebrate embryos pass through stages in which they exhibit adult features of their evolutionary ancestors. In its most famous example, the law teaches that "gill slits" in vertebrate embryos reveal their common aquatic ancestry. But human embryos do not really have gills or gill slits: Like all vertebrate embryos at one stage in their development, they possess a series of pharyngeal pouches, or tiny ridges in the neck region. In fish embryos, these actually go on to form gills, but in other vertebrates they develop into unrelated structures such as the inner ear or parathyroid gland. The embryos of reptiles, birds, and mammals never possess gills.[4]

The notion that vertebrate embryos transiently exhibit adult features of their evolutionary ancestors is false. Nineteenth-century embryologist Karl Ernst von Baer pointed out that although vertebrate embryos resemble each other at one point in their development, they never resemble the adult of any species, present or past.[5] Prominent twentieth-century embryologists have also criticized the Biogenetic Law: In 1922 Walter Garstang wrote that "the basis of this law is demonstrably unsound," and in 1958 Sir Gavin de Beer called it "a mental strait-jacket which has had lamentable effects on biological progress."[6]

Although vertebrate embryos never resemble the adults of any species, it is true that they pass through an intermediate stage in which some of them superficially resemble each other (Haeckel's first stage). Looking at development from this intermediate stage onward, von Baer concluded that early embryos exhibit features common to the phylum before developing the distinguishing characteristics of classes, genera, and species.[7]

Many twentieth-century biologists prefer von Baer's interpretation to Haeckel's. Early embryos may not possess ancestral *adult* structures, but their similarities are interpreted as vestiges of ancestral *embryonic* features. Since Haeckel's drawings can be used to illustrate von Baer's interpretation as well as Haeckel's, they have survived, even though Haeckel's interpretation has been discredited. Haeckel's embryos have thus become familiar to generations of biology students. Regrettably, his drawings misrepresent the facts.

Haeckel's Distorted Drawings

The version of Haeckel's drawings that has been widely used in textbooks (figure 1) omits two of the seven vertebrate classes (jawless fishes and cartilaginous fishes). It also uses a salamander rather than a frog to represent amphibians and placentals rather than monotremes or marsupials to represent mammals. Thus, it ignores groups that did not fit neatly into Haeckel's scheme.

Even worse, Haeckel's drawings distorted the embryos he selected. Embryologist Michael Richardson and his colleagues recently surveyed all seven classes of vertebrates and made drawings of actual embryos at the stage in which Haeckel claimed they were most similar. Their drawings, unlike Haeckel's, show significant differences among the various classes and even between marsupial and placental mammals (figure 2). Richardson and

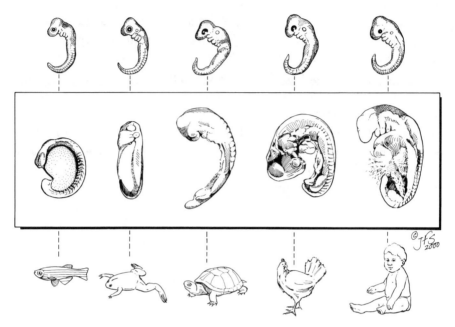

FIGURE 2. A comparison of Haeckel's drawings with actual vertebrate embryos. The embryos are (left to right): bony fish (zebrafish), amphibian (frog), reptile (turtle), bird (chicken), and a placental mammal (human). Illustration by Jody Sjogren © 2000. Used with permission.

his coworkers concluded that their survey "seriously undermines the credibility of Haeckel's drawings."[8]

Even if Haeckel's drawings were accurate, however, they would not justify the claim that vertebrate embryos are most similar in their earliest stages. This is because Haeckel omitted the earliest stages entirely.

Early Vertebrate Embryos Are Morphologically Dissimilar

After fertilization, an animal embryo first undergoes a process called cleavage, during which the fertilized egg subdivides into hundreds or thousands of separate cells. At the end of cleavage, those cells begin to rearrange themselves in a process known as gastrulation. During cleavage and gastrulation, the embryo establishes the general body plan (for example, shellfish, insect, or vertebrate) and generates basic types and organ systems (for example, skin, muscles, and gut). Only after cleavage and gastrulation does a vertebrate embryo reach the stage that Haeckel treated as the first step in development.

If it were true (as von Baer, Darwin, and Haeckel thought) that all vertebrates are most similar during the earliest stages of their development, the various classes would be most similar during cleavage and gastrulation. Yet a survey of only four classes (bony fish, amphibian, bird, and mammal) reveals that this is not the case (figure 3).

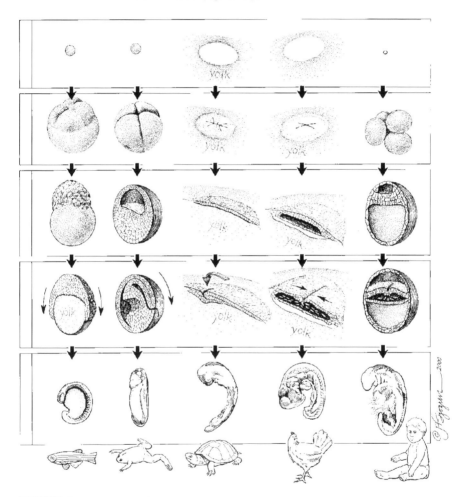

FIGURE 3. Drawings of early embryonic stages in five classes of vertebrates. The stages are (top to bottom): fertilized egg, start of cleavage, end of cleavage, gastrulation, and Haeckel's "first" stage. The fertilized eggs are drawn to scale relative to each other, while the scales of the succeeding stages are normalized to facilitate comparisons. The embryos are (left to right): bony fish (zebrafish), amphibian (frog), reptile (turtle), bird (chicken), and a placental mammal (human). Illustration by Jody Sjogren © 2000. Used with permission.

Differences among the four classes are evident even in the fertilized eggs: Zebrafish and frog eggs are approximately the same size (about 1 millimeter in diameter); the chick embryo is a disk 3–4 millimeters in diameter that sits on top of a large yolk; and the human embryo is only about 0.05 millimeter in diameter (figure 3, top row). The earliest cell divisions in zebrafish, frog, and chick embryos are similar except for the fact that they are unable to penetrate the yolk in fish and bird eggs; but the earliest cell divisions in humans (and all other mammals) are completely different from the other three, since one of the second cleavage planes is rotated 90 degrees relative to the other (figure 3, second row).

At the end of cleavage, the cells of the zebrafish embryo form a large cap on top of the yolk; in the frog, they form a ball with a cavity in one hemisphere; in the chick, they form a thin, two-layered disk on top of the yolk; and in humans, they form a disk within a ball (figure 3, third row).

Cell movements during gastrulation also differ among the four classes: In zebrafish, the cells migrate down the outside of the yolk; in frogs, they migrate through a pore into the inner cavity; and in chicks and humans, they move through a furrow into the hollow interior of the embryonic disk (figure 3, fourth row).

Although cleavage is somewhat similar in zebrafish and chick embryos and gastrulation somewhat similar in chick and human embryos, it is clearly not the case that vertebrate embryos are most similar in their earliest stages and diverge as they develop. This fact is well known to modern embryologists, many of whom have noted that it is inconsistent with the notions of von Baer, Darwin, and Haeckel. In 1976, William Ballard wrote that it is "only by semantic tricks and subjective selection of evidence" and by "bending the facts of nature" that one can argue that the cleavage and gastrulation stages of vertebrates "are more alike than their adults."[9] In 1991, Rudolf Raff and his colleagues confirmed that "eggs, cleavage, gastrulation and germ layer formation are very different in amphibians, birds, and mammals."[10]

Setting the Record Straight

If evolution is central to understanding biology, as many writers have argued, it is important that we give our students reliable information about it. Clearly, Haeckel's drawings are not reliable. Students who are taught that they constitute evidence for evolution and then later learn that they misrepresent the facts may feel betrayed by their former biology teachers and develop a distrust of science in general. Yet Haeckel's drawings are still featured prominently in some biology textbooks.

Of course, it would be illogical to conclude that Haeckel's distortions invalidate Darwin's theory. Although Darwin considered the embryological evidence "second to none in importance," he did not base his theory on that evidence alone.[11] Given the complexities of early vertebrate development, it might be better to look elsewhere for evidence of evolution, at least in an introductory course.

This does not mean that students interested in evolution should be discouraged from studying embryology. On the contrary, the interface between evolution and development is one of the most exciting research areas in biology today. According to evolutionary developmental biologist Rudolf Raff, "We are in a position to add to Darwin's synthesis by being able to probe more deeply into what were for him impenetrable laws of growth, reproduction, and inheritance."[12] Cell and developmental biologists John Gerhart and Marc Kirschner are equally optimistic: "Further study of the nature and modifiability of cellular and embryonic processes will help complete the explanation offered by Darwin for evolution as a process of descent with modification."[13]

The field of evolutionary developmental biology may provide us with many new insights. But these will surely come from facing the facts of nature, not from bending them to prop up old misconceptions.

Notes

1. C. Darwin, *The Origin of Species.* (New York: Modern Library, [1859] 1936), 338, 345.

2. E. Haeckel, *Anthropogenie, oder Entwicklungsgeschichte des Menschen* (Leipzig: Verlag von Wilhelm Engelmann, 1891).

3. P. J. Bowler, *Evolution: The History of an Idea,* rev. ed. (Berkeley: University of California Press, 1989); M. K. Richardson, J. Hanken, M. L. Gooneratne, C. Pieau, A. Raynaud, L. Selwood, and G. M. Wright, "There Is No Highly Conserved Embryonic Stage in the Vertebrates: Implications for Current Theories of Evolution and Development," *Anatomy and Embryology* 196 (1997): 91–106; R. P. Elinson, "Change in Developmental Patterns: Embryos of Amphibians with Large Eggs," in *Development as an Evolutionary Process,* ed. R. A. Raff and E. C. Raff, vol. 8 (New York: Alan R. Liss, 1987), 1–21.

4. G. Rager, "Human Embryology and the Law of Biogenesis," *Rivista di Biologia* 79, no. 4 (1986): 449–65.
5. K. E. von Baer, *Entwicklungsgeschichte der Thiere: Beobachtung und Reflexion* (Konigsberg: Bornträger, 1828); Bowler, *Evolution*, 129.
6. W. Garstang, "The Theory of Recapitulation: A Critical Restatement of the Biogenetic Law," *Journal of the Linnean Society (Zoology)* 35 (1922): 81; G. de Beer, *Embryos and Ancestors*, 3rd ed. (Oxford: Clarendon Press, 1958), 172.
7. von Baer, *Entwicklungsgeschichte*.
8. M. Richardson et al., "There Is No Highly Conserved Embryonic Stage," 91.
9. W. W. Ballard, "Problems of Gastrulation: Real and Verbal," *BioScience* 26 (1976): 38.
10. R. A. Raff, G. Wray, and J. J. Henry, "Implications of Radical Evolutionary Changes in Early Development for Concepts of Developmental Constraint," in *New Perspectives in Evolution*, ed. L. Warren and H. Koprowski (New York: Wiley-Liss, 1991), 189–207.
11. Darwin, *Origin*, 346.
12. R. A. Raff, *The Shape of Life: Genes, Development, and the Evolution of Animal Form* (Chicago: University of Chicago Press, 1996), 29.
13. J. C. Gerhart and M. Kirschner, *Cells, Embryos, and Evolution* (Malden, Mass.: Blackwell Science, 1997), 614.

Second Thoughts about Peppered Moths

Jonathan Wells

❈ ❈ ❈

Every student of biological evolution learns about peppered moths. During the industrial revolution, dark ("melanic") forms of this moth, *Biston betularia*, became much more common than light ("typical") forms, though the proportion of melanics declined after the passage of pollution-control legislation. When experiments in the 1950s pointed to cryptic coloration and differential bird predation as its cause, "industrial melanism" became the classical story of evolution by natural selection.

Subsequent research, however, has revealed major flaws in the classical story. It's time to take another look.

The Classical Story

In 1896, J. W. Tutt noted that typicals were well camouflaged against the light-colored lichens that grew on tree trunks in unpolluted woodlands; but in woodlands where industrial pollution had killed the lichens, exposing the bark and darkening the tree trunks, melanics were better camouflaged. Since conspicuous moths were more likely to be eaten by predatory birds, Tutt attributed the increase in the proportion of melanic forms to natural selection.

In the 1950s, Bernard Kettlewell tested the idea experimentally by marking several hundred peppered moths (typicals as well as melanics) and releasing them onto tree trunks in a polluted woodland near Birmingham, England. Kettlewell observed through binoculars that melanics seemed less conspicuous than typicals and that birds took conspicuous moths more readily than inconspicuous ones. That night he recaptured 27.5 percent of the melanics but only 13.0 percent of the typicals, suggesting that a much higher proportion of melanics had survived predation. Kettlewell later repeated this experiment in an unpolluted woodland in Dorset, England, where the recapture percentages were the opposite of those obtained in Birmingham. He concluded that "birds act as selective agents, as postulated by evolutionary theory" and that industrial melanism was "the most striking evolutionary change ever actually witnessed in any organism."[1]

Experiments conducted by other biologists seemed at first to corroborate Kettlewell's conclusions. When industrial melanism began to decline after the passage of antipollution legislation (presumably because pollution was no longer darkening the tree trunks), the decline seemed consistent with the theory that industrial melanism was due to cryptic coloration and differential bird predation.

Industrial melanism in peppered moths quickly became the standard textbook example of natural selection in action. Doubts about the classical story, however, began to emerge soon after Kettlewell's experiments, and it is now clear that those experiments were fundamentally flawed.

Problems with the Classical Story

When biologists looked beyond Birmingham and Dorset, where Kettlewell had conducted his experiments, they found discrepancies in the expected geographical distribution of melanic moths. For example, if melanic moths in polluted woodlands enjoyed as much of a selective advantage as Kettlewell's experiments seemed to indicate, they should have completely replaced typicals in heavily polluted areas such as Manchester. This never happened, however, indicating that factors other than selective predation must be affecting melanic frequencies.[2]

In rural East Anglia, where there was little industrial pollution and typicals seemed better camouflaged, melanics reached a frequency of 80 percent, prompting Lees and Creed to conclude that "either the predation experiments and tests of conspicuousness to humans are misleading, or some factor or factors in addition to selective predation are responsible for maintaining the high melanic frequencies."[3] Reviewing the geographical evidence in 1990, Berry concluded, "it is clear that melanic peppered moth frequencies are determined by much more than differential visual predation by birds."[4]

One notable discrepancy in the distribution of melanism was its lack of correlation with lichen cover on tree trunks. Even Kettlewell had observed that melanism began declining before lichens returned, and Lees and his colleagues found a lack of correlation with lichen cover which they considered "surprising in view of the results of Kettlewell's selection experiments."[5] According to Grant and Howlett, if the rise of industrial melanism had originally been due to the demise of lichens on trees, then "the prediction is that lichens should precede the recovery of the typical morph as the common form. That is, the hiding places should recover before the hidden. But, this is clearly not the case."[6]

In the United States, the frequency of melanics in southeastern Michigan dropped from over 90 percent to less than 20 percent between 1960 and 1995, thus paralleling the decline of melanism in the United Kingdom. Yet the decline in Michigan "occurred in the absence of perceptible changes in local lichen floras," prompting Grant and his colleagues to conclude that "the role of lichens has been inappropriately emphasized in chronicles about the evolution of melanism in peppered moths."[7] Recently, Sargent and his colleagues noted that "the recent declining frequency of melanism in *B. betularia* in North America, where the hypothesis of a cryptic advantage of melanism never seemed applicable," is "perplexing" in view of the classical story.[8] So the rise and fall of industrial melanism did not depend on lichens. Why, then, did lichens appear to be significant in Kettlewell's experiments?

The Normal Resting Places of Peppered Moths

In his experiments, Kettlewell released moths directly onto tree trunks and acknowledged that they "were not free to take up their own choice of resting site. . . . I admit that, under their own choice, many would have taken up position higher in the trees."[9] He assumed, however, that he could disregard this observation.

Before the 1980s, most investigators shared Kettlewell's assumption, and many of them found it convenient to conduct predation experiments using dead specimens glued or pinned to tree trunks. Some biologists who used dead moths suspected, however, that the technique was unsatisfactory. For example, Bishop and Cook noted discrepancies in their results that "may indicate that we are not correctly assessing the true nature of the resting sites of living moths when we are conducting experiments with dead ones."[10]

The figure accompanying that report showed live moths rather than dead ones, but the moths were placed manually on the desired backgrounds for the purpose of photographing them.[11] Most textbook pictures of peppered moths similarly show specimens that have been manually placed on tree trunks.[12]

Since 1980, however, it has become clear that peppered moths do not normally rest on tree trunks. Mikkola observed that "the normal resting place of the Peppered Moth is beneath small, more or less horizontal branches (but not on narrow twigs), probably high up in the canopies, and the species probably only exceptionally rests on tree trunks." He noted that "night-active moths, released in an illumination bright enough for the human eye, may well choose their resting sites as soon as possible and most probably atypically." Thus, "the results of Kettlewell (1955, 1956) fail to demonstrate the qualitative predation of the morphs of the Peppered Moth by birds or other predators in natural conditions."[13]

Mikkola used caged moths, but data on wild moths support his conclusion. In twenty-five years of fieldwork, Clarke and his colleagues found only one peppered moth on a tree trunk and admitted that they knew primarily "where the moths do *not* spend the day."[14] When Howlett and Majerus studied the natural resting sites of peppered moths in various parts of England, they found that Mikkola's observations on caged moths were valid for wild moths as well and concluded: "it seems certain that most *B. betularia* rest where they are hidden . . . [and] that exposed areas of tree trunks are not an important resting site for any form of *B. betularia*."[15] In a separate study, Liebert and Brakefield confirmed Mikkola's observations that "the species rests predominantly on branches. . . . Many moths will rest underneath, or on the side of, narrow branches in the canopy."[16]

In a recent book on melanism, Majerus criticizes the "artificiality" of much previous work in this area, noting that "in most predation experiments peppered moths have been positioned on vertical tree trunks, despite the fact that they rarely chose such surfaces to rest upon in the wild."[17] It seems that the classical example of natural selection is actually an example of unnatural selection!

Conclusion

The fact that peppered moths do not normally rest on tree trunks invalidates Kettlewell's experiments and poses a serious problem for the classical explanation of industrial melanism in peppered moths. Although cryptic coloration and selective predation have not been ruled out, one recent review concludes that "there is little persuasive evidence, in the form of rigorous and replicated observations and experiments, to support this explanation at the present time."[18]

Yet textbooks continue to present the classical story of industrial melanism in peppered moths as an example of evolution in action. Clearly, that is misleading. In particular, it is misleading to illustrate the story with photographs showing moths on tree trunks where they do not rest in the wild. Our students deserve better.

Notes

1. H. B. D. Kettlewell, "Selection Experiments on Industrial Melanism in the Lepidoptera," *Heredity* 9 (1955): 323–42; H. B. D. Kettlewell, "Further Selection Experiments on Industrial Melanism in the Lepidoptera," *Heredity* 10 (1956): 287–301.

2. J. A. Bishop and L. M. Cook, "Industrial Melanism and the Urban Environment," *Advances in Ecological Research* 11 (1980): 373–404; G. S. Mani, "Theoretical Models of Melanism in *Biston betularia*—A Review," *Biological Journal of the Linnean Society* 39 (1990): 355–71.

3. D. R. Lees and E. R. Creed, "Industrial Melanism in *Biston betularia:* The Role of Selective Predation," *Journal of Animal Ecology* 44 (1975): 67–83.

4. R. J. Berry, "Industrial Melanism and Peppered Moths (*Biston betularia* [L.])," *Biological Journal of the Linnean Society* 39 (1990): 301–22.

5. H. B. D. Kettlewell, *The Evolution of Melanism* (Oxford: Clarendon Press, 1973); D. R. Lees, E. R. Creed, and L. G. Duckett, "Atmospheric Pollution and Industrial Melanism," *Heredity* 30 (1973): 227–32.

6. B. S. Grant and R. J. Howlett, "Background Selection by the Peppered Moth (*Biston betularia* Linn.): Individual Differences," *Biological Journal of the Linnean Society* 33 (1988): 217–32.

7. B. S. Grant, D. F. Owen, and C. A. Clarke, "Parallel Rise and Fall of Melanic Peppered Moths in America and Britain," *Journal of Heredity* 87 (1996): 351–57.

8. T. D. Sargent, C. D. Millar, and D. M. Lambert, "The 'Classical' Explanation of Industrial Melanism: Assessing the Evidence," *Evolutionary Biology* 30 (1998): 299–322.
9. Kettlewell, "Further Selection Experiments."
10. J. A. Bishop and L. M. Cook, "Moths, Melanism and Clean Air," *Scientific American* 232, no. 1 (1975): 90–99.
11. L. M. Cook, University of Manchester, U.K., personal communication, 1998.
12. Sargent et al., "'Classical' Explanation."
13. K. Mikkola, "On the Selective Forces Acting in the Industrial Melanism of *Biston* and *Oligia* Moths (Lepidoptera: Geometridae and Noctuidae)," *Biological Journal of the Linnean Society* 21 (1984): 409–21.
14. C. A. Clarke, G. S. Mani, and G. Wynne, "Evolution in Reverse: Clean Air and the Peppered Moth," *Biological Journal of the Linnean Society* 26 (1985): 189–99.
15. R. J. Howlett and M. E. N. Majerus, "The Understanding of Industrial Melanism in the Peppered Moth (*Biston betularia*) (Lepidoptera: Geometridae)," *Biological Journal of the Linnean Society* 30 (1987): 31–44.
16. T. G. Liebert and P. M. Brakefield, "Behavioural Studies on the Peppered Moth *Biston betularia* and a Discussion of the Role of Pollution and Lichens in Industrial Melanism," *Biological Journal of the Linnean Society* 31 (1987): 129–50.
17. M. E. N. Majerus, *Melanism: Evolution in Action* (Oxford: Oxford University Press, 1998).
18. Sargent et al., "'Classical' Explanation."

Where Do We Come From? A Humbling Look at the Biology of Life's Origin

Massimo Pigliucci

❊ ❊ ❊

Life has to be given a meaning because of the obvious fact that it
has no meaning.

—Henry Miller, *The Wisdom of the Heart*

Science is a way of answering our questions about the natural world in a
rational manner. One fundamental of the scientific method is the repeatability of the phenomena under investigation. Here lies perhaps the
most difficult aspect of the endless quest for the origin of life on Earth. It
clearly is a question about the natural world, in fact one of the ultimate
questions (together with the origin of the universe itself). Yet the events
we are attempting to investigate are by definition unique. Life may well
have originated multiple times in the universe, including perhaps in our
galactic neighborhood. But so far we have only one example to go by.
Planet Earth is the only place that we know for certain harbors life as we
conceive it.

Before entering into a skeptical evaluation of the heart of the problem,
let us answer an even more fundamental question: Why do we care? Well,
I can come up with three orders of reasons. First, definitely ascertaining
that life originated by natural means would certainly have profound implications for any religious belief, further shrinking the role of any god in
human affairs. Second, should we arrive at the conclusion that life originated elsewhere in the universe and was then somehow "imported" to

Earth, this would automatically imply the existence of life as a widespread phenomenon in the universe and therefore the fact that living beings are not unique to our planet; it is hard to conceive of a more compelling blow to anthropocentrism since Copernicus and Galileo swept Earth away from the center of the universe a few centuries ago. Third, and perhaps more relevant, humankind would finally have a decent answer to the question "Where did we come from?" which, like it or not, has been vexing our philosophy, art, and science since the beginning of recorded history (and probably much earlier than that). If that doesn't sound to you like enough reason to ponder the controversy over the origin of life, the neurons in charge of your sense of curiosity are definitely in need of some repair.

Couldn't We Just Look at the Simplest Organism?

Let me start by clearing the field from one important misconception: There is no such thing as a modern-day "primitive" organism that we can examine to tell what our earliest ancestors looked like. True, there are plenty of "simple" organisms around today, from viruses to bacteria to slime molds. But slime molds are in fact eukaryotes (albeit of taxonomically very uncertain position); that is, their cellular structure and metabolism are basically not different from those of an animal or a plant (they actually look like fungi, though they are not even closely related to them). They are too complex for our purposes.

Bacteria are prokaryotes; that is, their cells are indeed simpler than most other living beings. Yet bacteria have been around for more than three billion years, and they have become perfect reproductive machines, characterized by an incredibly efficient metabolism and ability to withstand environmental changes. After all, it is not by chance that they have proliferated for so long. So that answer is unsuitable as well.

Finally, viruses are among the simplest living creatures in existence, so simple, in fact, that some biologists even doubt that they really qualify as "living." Evolutionarily speaking, however, viruses are late arrivals on the Darwinian stage. Viruses are short pieces of nucleic acids wrapped in a protein, they live only inside cells, they originated from preexisting cells, and they depend entirely on a host's metabolism to reproduce. Quite obviously, since our problem is to understand how the first living organisms came about, we cannot utilize as a model something that cannot survive outside an already existing cell. No, we are looking for something simple, yes, but self-sufficient, and really primitive.

The Alternative Answer: What about God?

No serious scientific discussion of any topic should include supernatural explanations, since the basic assumption of science is that the world can be explained entirely in physical terms, without recourse to godlike entities. Skepticism, however, has the flexibility of going beyond the strict scientific method—even though the two modes of inquiry are tightly connected. After all, as that fictional archetype of rationalism known as Sherlock Holmes said, "When you have eliminated the impossible, whatever remains, however improbable, must be the truth" (in Arthur Conan Doyle's *The Sign of Four*). It is ironic that Holmes's creator, Conan Doyle, believed in spirits and poltergeists, but that's another story.[1] Should it turn out that we really do not have a clue about the origin of life, we must entertain other, more esoteric possibilities, however unpleasant they may sound to a skeptical ear.

Further, in the specific case of the origin of life, even some scientists of decent reputation, such as British astrophysicist Fred Hoyle, have gone on record suggesting a supernatural beginning to all life on Earth. Hoyle, together with his colleague Chandra Wickramasinghe, suggested that a sort of silicon-chip creator actually goes around the universe sprinkling the seeds of life here and there, though for what purpose is not at all clear. An alternative scenario is the one advanced by creationists such as Duane Gish, in which the classical God of the Bible created the universe and humankind with a personal touch, and did so in the span of only six days. There is one crucial problem with both Hoyle's and Gish's positions, of course. There isn't a single shred of evidence supporting them. Further, at least Gish's claims are falsifiable and have been verified to be false. One of the cardinal points of his theory is that Earth is only a few thousand years old, whereas geology has long ago demonstrated that the real time frame is measured in billions of years. Hoyle's proposition suffers from the hallmark of all nonscientific statements: It is not disprovable. There isn't a single experiment that could reject the British physicist's hypothesis, which means that by definition it lies outside science's realm.

Should a skeptic then reject outright any possibility of the special creation of life? Well, no. As much as it is implausible, it is still possible. Two points must be borne in mind, however, before going for a Hoyle-like

explanation of the origin of us all. First, it has to be true that we really
don't have a clue about how life originated on Earth by natural means. As
we will see, although the situation is messy, it is not that desperate. Second, the mere fact that we cannot currently (or even ever) explain something does not constitute positive evidence for a supernatural explanation.
After all, for a long time we did not know what natural phenomena could
cause lightning, but eventually the theory based on the anger of Zeus did
turn out to be wrong. Consequently, even if we had no better answer, it is
still up to the "supernaturalists" to provide at least a shred of positive evidence. Without that, the next best position to hold on to would simply be
a provisional and salutary "I don't know."

Out of This World?

The next class of explanations about the ultimate provenance of life is
that—as any good old-fashioned science-fiction movie or magazine of the
1950s would have proclaimed—it is not of this world. Interestingly, Hoyle
and Wickramasinghe have made their contribution in this realm, too, by
suggesting that life was brought on this planet courtesy of an interstellar
cloud of gas and dust or perhaps by a comet.[2] Yet another British scientist
(and also an ex-physicist—but I'm sure this is a coincidence), Nobel laureate Francis Crick, joined the ranks of the extraterrestrialists. Crick suggested a scenario that envisions extraterrestrials "seeding" the galaxy,
much in the same fashion of Hoyle's silicon-chip creator.[3]

   Contrary to the supernatural explanations, the Hoyle-Wickramasinghe
theory (but not Crick's, for the same reasons seen above) is at least in principle open to experimental verification, in that it makes some relatively
precise predictions. For one thing, we should find plenty of organic compounds in interstellar clouds and/or inside comets. Both these expectations
have superficially been verified. I say superficially because the kind of
compounds found by astronomers in these media are very simple, much
too simple to provide any meaningful "seed" for the origin of carbon-based
life-forms on Earth. Further, extraterrestrial organic compounds have random chirality, unlike the organic compounds typical of living organisms.
Chirality is a property of any chemical structure that deals with the three-
dimensional arrangement of its atoms and molecules. All amino acids, for
example, the building blocks of proteins, can in theory come in two versions, which are mirror images of each other. These are called "left-" and
"right-" handed forms, and they are characterized by exactly the same

chemical properties, so that there is no physical-chemical reason for one form to be more abundant than the other. Accordingly, the organic compounds (which is a general term for carbon-based compounds and, contrary to the misleading name, does not necessarily imply the result of an organism's metabolism) found in space or in meteorites come in equal proportions of right- and left-handed forms.[4] Not so the compounds that are actually used by living organisms on Earth, which are found in only one version. If life had come from space, one would expect to find some sort of chiral asymmetry in space organic matter as well.

A second crucial objection to the life-from-space hypothesis is the solution of the continuity problem. If comets and meteors brought us, literally, to Earth a few billion years ago, why are they not doing it now? Meteors continue to bombard our planet and our neighbors in the solar system on a regular basis, yet so far not a single living organism or complex organic molecule has been found inside any of them. There is no reason to think that the primordial "shower of life" has ceased. Even though the conditions for the persistence of primordial life on our planet do not hold any longer (because of dramatic changes in the composition of the atmosphere or because of competition from "resident aliens," that is, from currently living organisms), presumably the space surrounding our solar system has not changed that much, leaving Hoyle, Crick, and the like with a major hole in their argument.

Another thought about extraterrestrial theories of life's beginning is that at a minimum they violate one of the most venerable principles of natural philosophy, namely Occam's razor. This is the idea that if two theories explain equally well a given problem, one should prefer the alternative that assumes the least number of entities (that is, makes the least gratuitous hypotheses). Since all extraterrestrial theories still rely on organic chemistry and since they require further assumptions, for example, the fact that the "seeds" found a safe passage through Earth's atmosphere without burning into nothingness as happens to most meteors, they violate Occam's rule. On the other hand, there is no real guarantee that the universe behaves as Occam suggested, so the razor can be invoked only as a provisional way of favoring simpler explanations, not as a definite argument against more complex or less likely alternatives.

Finally, it has to be realized that even if we do admit that life originated outside Earth and was then imported here, we really would not have an answer to how life started. We would have simply shifted the question to a remote and very likely inaccessible location.

The Chicken or the Egg in the Soup?

Having excluded, at least temporarily, gods and extraterrestrials, we are left with plain old biochemistry and biology to give us clues to the origin of life on our planet. The history of scientific research in this field is long and fascinating. It started in the 1920s with the Russian Alexander Oparin and his "coacervates," blobs of organic matter (mostly containing sugars and short polypeptides), supposedly the precursors of modern proteins. It was Oparin, together with British biologist J. B. S. Haldane, who came up with the idea of a "primordial soup," that is, the possibility that the ancient oceans on Earth were filled with organic matter formed by the interaction between the atmospheric gases and energy provided by volcanic eruptions, powerful electric storms, and solar ultraviolet radiation.[5]

We had to wait until the 1950s for Stanley Miller to attempt to reproduce the soup experimentally.[6] Miller started with a reasonable composition of the ancient atmosphere: mostly methane and ammonia, with no oxygen—since atmospheric oxygen, together with the ozone that blocks UV radiation, was in fact produced by the organic process of photosynthesis in blue-green algae. That happened much, much later than soup time (which is a fortunate coincidence, given that oxygen attacks and destroys—technically it "oxidizes"—organic compounds at a very fast rate).[7] Miller put the whole thing in a flask, gave it some electric charge, and waited. He did find that amino acids and other fundamental complex organic molecules were accumulating at the bottom of his apparatus. His discovery gave a huge boost to the scientific investigation of the origin of life. Indeed, for some time it seemed as if the re-creation of life in a test tube was within reach of experimental science. Unfortunately, Miller-type experiments have not progressed much further than their original prototype, leaving us with a sour aftertaste from the primordial soup.

Both Oparin and Miller, as well as other prominent researchers in the field up until the 1960s, thought that the problem was how to explain the appearance of proteins, since they must have caused the initial spark of life. (Another student of the problem, thinking along similar lines, was Sidney Fox, who discovered the possibility of forming "proteinoids," protein-like structures obtained by heating up mixtures of amino acids in a dry state—all in all, a very distant cousin of actual biological proteins). Any student of introductory biology today, however, knows that there are two major players inside every living cell: proteins and nucleic acids (DNA and RNA). The problem is that the structure of DNA was discovered only in

1953 (the year of Miller's experiment), and the nature of DNA as the information carrier of the cell was little appreciated before Watson and Crick unveiled the double-helix nature of this remarkable molecule.

The origin-of-life debate after the 1950s became decidedly slanted in favor of nucleic acids preceding proteins. The new discipline of molecular biology was making spectacular progress, first uncovering the universal code by which the instructions for making proteins are embedded in the nucleic acids; then by finding ways to extract and compare that information from different and distantly related species; and finally with the spin-off of modern genetic engineering and the ability to modify the genetic information directly, thereby transforming the characteristics of species more or less at will. Scientists such as Leslie Orgel, Walter Gilbert, and others therefore proposed that the egg, so to speak, came before the chicken. Some sort of primitive nucleic acid had appeared first, followed only later by proteins.

Now, in today's biochemically sophisticated cells, proteins and nucleic acids play very distinct roles. In fact, there are four fundamental activities that we need to discuss.

1. The DNA (deoxyribonucleic acid) encodes the information that eventually will give rise to proteins.
2. The "messenger" RNA (or mRNA, ribonucleic acid, similar to DNA but with an extra oxygen atom and a few other chemical differences) then carries the information to specialized structures known as ribosomes.
3. Inside the ribosomes (which are made of both nucleic acids and proteins), the message gets translated into proteins by virtue of a second type of RNA, known as "transfer" RNA (tRNA). The tRNA has the peculiar ability to attach itself to the mRNA on one side and to amino acids (the blocks that make up proteins) on the other side. This way, there is a chain of mRNA, which is paralleled by the forming chain of amino acids, which in turn will eventually result in a protein.
4. The proteins, most of which (but not all) are enzymes, are actually the "doers" of the cellular world. Some form the building blocks of cell structures and membranes; others are the builders themselves, in the form of enzymes capable of catalyzing all sorts of chemical reactions, including the replication of DNA and the transcription of its message into RNA—which, of course, closes the protein-nucleic acid circle!

It should be clear from the above extremely concise description of what goes on in a cell that we are indeed facing a classic chicken-and-egg

problem. If the proteins appeared first, so that they could eventually catalyze the formation of nucleic acids, how was the information necessary to
produce the proteins themselves coded? On the other hand, if nucleic acids
came first, thereby embodying the information necessary to obtain proteins, by which means were the acids replicated and translated into proteins? It seems to me pretty clear that the answer, as much as it is still very
much nebulous at the moment, must lie in the proverbial middle.[8] In fact,
the existence of tRNAs points to the distinct possibility of dual structures,
containing both RNA and amino acids. On a slightly different take, the discovery by Sydney Altman, Thomas Cech, and others, that some RNAs are
at least partially self-catalytic (that is, they can catalyze chemical reactions
onto themselves) lends support to the idea of a mixed origin of life in
which the original molecules were both replicators and enzymes, with the
two functions slowly diverging through evolutionary time and assigned to
distinct classes of molecules.[9] Most important, doesn't that appeal to your
sense of aesthetics as well?

Primordial Soup or Primordial Pizza?

There is one major problem with the Haldane-Oparin soup scenario: It
could get too watery. Since the organic compounds would be freely bumping into each other within the ocean, unless their concentration was extremely large, it is difficult to see how often dense-enough pockets of
organic molecules could have formed to allow some significant prebiotic
chemistry to occur.

This is more of a problem when we consider the question of the origin
of the first metabolic pathways. Metabolism requires protoenzymes to interact with their substrates so that a given reaction can take place. It was
unlikely, however, for enzymes and substrates to come close enough together in a three-dimensional space with no enclosing barriers (hence, several hypotheses about the formation of protocells with a lipid membrane).
Further, most of the necessary reactions for prebiotic chemistry, such as the
formation of polypeptides by aggregating individual amino acids, produce
water. This kind of reaction is difficult to have in an aqueous environment
because of thermodynamic considerations (it requires energy, and the
products are unstable and can be hydrolyzed back to their component
parts).

An alternative to the primordial soup has therefore been proposed, and
it has become known as the "primordial pizza."[10] The idea is that early

organic chemistry occurred on dry land, on the surface of minerals with physical properties conducive to accumulating and retaining organic molecules in place. Perhaps the best candidate for such a role is pyrite, fool's gold. On a two-dimensional surface, enzymes and substrates (or simply different amino acids or nucleotides without enzymes) would find themselves constrained with much less freedom of movement which, of course, would increase the chance of reciprocal encounters. Further, since the pyrite surface would have no water on it, the occurrence of water-producing reactions would be much facilitated. In fact, thermodynamic calculations show that these reactions would increase entropy and would therefore occur spontaneously.

Very little empirical research has been done on the concept of a primordial pizza, and other candidates are possible as material substrates besides pyrite, but the concept is appealing in its elegant solution of two major problems facing prebiotic chemistry. We should see some progress in this area in the next few years.

And Then What?
Hypercycles and Emerging Properties

I suggest that the problem of how complex organic compounds, the building blocks of life as we know it, might have formed on primordial Earth has been satisfactorily solved by Miller-type experiments or one of their variants. Further, there are good reasons to believe that the initial complex molecules that underwent chemical evolution were some sort of nucleic acid-protein mix such as modern day tRNAs or autocatalytic RNAs. But what happened after that? There is still a very large gap between a semicatalytic, semireplicating nucleo-protein and the first living "organism," whatever that may have been.

Moreover, the uncertainty about what the original organisms looked like is an important part of the problem. What exactly is life? That question was asked precisely in such fashion in 1947 by physicist Erwin Schrödinger.[11] Although Schrödinger's thinking led him to predict some of the properties of DNA as a necessary component of a living organism, we still have a vague notion of the boundary between life and inert matter. And so it should be, if we accept the idea that living organisms are made of inert matter that happens to acquire some "emergent properties" when assembled in particular manners. To put it in another fashion, living beings are not separated from the rest of the universe by some mysterious force or vital energy. At least, we have no reason to believe so.

How do we know, then, what is life from what is not? Well, we can come up with a list of attributes, some of which can be properties also of nonliving systems, but the ensemble of which defines a living organism:

Ability to replicate, giving origin to similar kinds (reproduction).

Ability to react to changes in the environment (behavior, not just limited to the special meaning that the word has in animals).

Growth (that is, reduction of internal entropy at the expense of environmental entropy—note that even single cells grow immediately after reproduction, so this is not a property restricted to multicellular life).

Metabolism (that is, capacity of maintaining lower internal entropy, including the ability of self-repair).

How did we get from a nucleo-protein to an entity capable of all of the above? And what did this entity (sometimes known as the progenote) look like? There are very few even tentative answers to these questions, and this, I think, is where the real problem of the origin of life lies. In Germany, Manfred Eigen has come up with one possible scenario, which invokes what he called "hypercycles." We can think of a hypercycle as a primitive biochemical pathway made up of self-replicating nucleic acids and semicatalytic proteins that happen to be found together in pockets within the primordial soup or on the primordial pizza.

It is possible to imagine that some of these hypercycles are made of elements that "cooperate" with each other—that is, the product of a component of the cycle can be the substrate for another one. Different hypercycles could have coexisted before the origin of life, and they would have competed for the ever-decreasing resources within the soup or pizza (the resources were decreasing because the hypercycles were using up some organic compounds at a higher rate than they were formed by comparatively inefficient inorganic processes). Eventually, such competition would have favored more and more efficient hypercycles, where the "efficiency" would be measured by the ability of these entities to survive and reproduce—that is, by the parameters of Darwinian evolution. Life as we know it (sort of) would have begun. Eigen and modern followers of complexity theory also expected these systems to become more complicated by addition of new components to the cycle. From time to time, the addition of one component would modify the whole system dramatically, giving it properties that the previous group did not possess (sort of like adding an atom of oxygen to two of hydrogen and suddenly getting something completely distinct and more complex: water). Complexity theorists such as Stuart Kauffman and Christopher Langton have already demonstrated on the basis of mathematical models that some self-replicating systems can display unexpectedly complex patterns of behavior.[12] The textbook examples of this phenomenon are the so-called cellular automata, mathematical entities first imagined by John von Neumann in 1940, which can now be studied at leisure by anybody who has a personal computer and a copy of a game aptly called "Life."[13] So, the general path leading to the origination of life seems to have been something like this:

Primordial soup or pizza (simple organic compounds formed by atmospheric gases and various sources of energy).

Nucleo-proteins (similar to modern tRNAs).

Hypercycles (primitive and inefficient biochemical pathways, emergent properties).

Cellular hypercycles (more complex cycles, eventually enclosed in a primitive cell made of lipids).

Progenote (first self-replicating, metabolizing cell, possibly made of RNA and proteins, with DNA entering the picture later on).

How plausible is all this? It is fairly conceivable as far as modern biology can tell. The problem is that each step is really difficult to describe in detail from a theoretical standpoint and so far (with the exception of the formation of organic molecules in the soup and of some simple hypercycles) has proven remarkably elusive from an empirical perspective. It looks as if we have several clues, but the puzzle may very well prove one of the most difficult for scientific analysis to solve. The reason for such difficulty could be, as pointed out at the beginning, that, after all, we have only one example to go by. Or it may simply be that the events in question are so far remote in time that there is very little we can be certain about. Consider that the fossil record shows completely formed, "modern-looking" bacterial cells a few hundreds of million years after the formation of Earth—that is, about 3.8 billion years ago. This tells us that whatever happened before that happened fast, but there is no record of it. Finally, it could very well be that we are missing something fundamental here. It may be that the origin-of-life field has not had its Einstein or Darwin just yet and that things are going to change just around the corner. Or never.

From Dust to Dust . . .

Contemporary discussion of the question of the origin of life cannot be complete without including A. G. Cairns-Smith's theory of clay crystals.[14] Briefly, the idea is that life did not originate with either nucleic acids or proteins (or, for that matter, with a combination of the two). No, the original replicator-catalyzing agents were actually crystals to be found everywhere in the clay that lay around primitive Earth. There are four cardinal points of the Cairns-Smith hypothesis. First, crystals are structurally much simpler than any biologically relevant organic molecule. Second, crystals grow and reproduce (that is, they can break because of mechanical forces, and each resulting part continues to "grow"). Third, crystals carry information, and this information can be modified. A crystal is a highly regular structure, which tends to propagate itself (therefore, it carries information). Further, the crystal can incorporate impurities while growing. These impurities alter the crystal's structure and can be "inherited" when the original piece breaks (hence, the information can be modified). Fourth, crystals have some minimum capacity of catalyzing (that is, accelerating) chemical reactions.

Cairns-Smith proposed that these very primitive "organisms" then started incorporating short polypeptides ("protoproteins") found in the environment, presumably in the soup or on the pizza, because they enhanced the crystals' catalyzing abilities. The road was then open for a gradual increase in the importance of proteins first, and then eventually of nucleic acids, until these two new arrivals on the evolutionary scene completely supplanted their "low-tech" progenitor and became the living organisms we know today.

What is wrong with this picture? First of all, Cairns-Smith seems to ignore what a living organism is to begin with. For one thing, crystals don't really have a metabolism, at least not in a sense even remotely comparable to what we find in actual living organisms. This may have something to do not only with the fact that crystals are structurally much less complex than a protein or a nucleic acid but also with their non-carbon-based chemistry, recognizably much simpler than the chemistry utilized by living organisms on Earth. The lower complexity and simpler chemistry may be insurmountable "hardware" obstacles to the origination of a true metabolism in clay matter.

Second, crystals don't really react to their environment either, another hallmark of every known living creature. Notice that this is a property distinct from metabolism, in that metabolism can be entirely internal, with no reference to the outside (except for some flux of energy that must come into the organism to maintain its metabolism). On the other hand, living organisms universally actively respond to changes in external conditions, for example, by seeking sources of energy or by avoiding dangers.

Further, an argument can be made that crystals are not actually capable of incorporating new information in their inherited "code," unlike what happens with mutations in living beings. True, they can assimilate impurities from the environment and "transmit" such "information" to their "descendents" for some time; but such impurities do not get replicated, they need continually to be imported from the outside, and they do not become a permanent and heritable part of the crystal. Moreover, impurities do not create new types of crystals, the way mutations eventually give rise to entirely new kinds of animals and plants.

Another colossal hole in the clay theory is, of course, that we have no clue of how the "mutiny" of nucleic acids and proteins actually occurred, and in fact we are given very faint hints about how a crystal could possibly co-opt a polypeptide to enhance its growth (which, by the way, should be something relatively easy to test in a modern biochemistry laboratory). It is true that the competing, more biologically traditional hypotheses also are at a loss providing detailed scenarios; but in the case of Cairns-Smith's suggestions, we don't simply miss the details, we literally have no idea how such a transition would come to pass. So, as much as creationists might like the flavor of a theory of the origin of life in which the first living beings came literally from dust (although Cairns-Smith is certainly no creationist), we are still left with ribonucleo-proteins as our best, albeit fuzzy, option. Skeptics and scientists will be pondering this question for some time to come.

Notes

1. M. Polidoro, "Houdini and Conan Doyle: The Story of a Strange Friendship," *Skeptical Inquirer* 22, no. 2 (1998): 40–46.
2. F. Hoyle and C. Wickramasinghe, *Lifecloud* (New York: Harper and Row, 1978).
3. F. Crick, *Life Itself* (New York: Simon and Schuster, 1981).
4. This particular statement may need to be modified because of recent research showing that cosmic radiation can in fact cause asymmetric chirality without the intervention of living organisms.

5. A. I. Oparin, *The Origin of Life on Earth* (New York: Macmillan, 1938); J. B. S. Haldane, "The Origin of Life," in *On Being the Right Size and Other Essays,* ed. J. M. Smith, (Oxford: Oxford University Press, 1985).

6. S. L. Miller, "A Production of Amino Acids under Possible Primitive Earth Conditions," *Science* 117 (1953): 528–29.

7. Recent research has questioned the notion of complete absence of oxygen from the primordial atmosphere, but the jury is still out on exactly how reducing or oxidizing the primordial conditions were. The alternative to the soup, the pizza proposed in the next section, would solve the problem by making the atmospheric conditions pretty much irrelevant.

8. S. L. Miller, "Peptide Nucleic Acids and Prebiotic Chemistry," *Nature Structural Biology* 4 (1997): 167.

9. G. Ertem and J. P. Ferris, "Synthesis of RNA Oligomers on Heterogeneous Templates," *Nature* 379 (1996): 238–40.

10. J. Maynard-Smith and E. Szathmary, *The Major Transitions in Evolution* (Oxford: Oxford University Press, 1995).

11. E. Schrödinger, *What Is Life?* (New York: Macmillan, 1947).

12. J. D. Farmer, S. A. Kauffman, and N. H. Packard, "Autocatalytic Replication of Polymers," *Physica* 22D (1986): 50–67; S. A. Kauffman, *The Origins of Order* (New York: Oxford University Press, 1993).

13. C. G. Langton, "Studying Artificial Life with Cellular Automata," *Physica* 22D (1986): 120–49.

14. A. G. Cairns-Smith, *Seven Clues to the Origin of Life* (Cambridge: Cambridge University Press, 1985); B. E. H. Maden, "No Soup for Starters? Autotrophy and the Origins of Metabolism," *Trends in Biochemistry* 20 (1995): 337–41.

Origin of Life and Evolution in Biology Textbooks: A Critique

Gordon C. Mills, Malcolm Lancaster, and Walter L. Bradley

❉ ❉ ❉

It has been noted by others that the states of Texas and California set textbook standards for the nation as a whole, primarily because of the large numbers of textbooks sold in those two states. The guidelines for textbook publishers in those states are Proclamation 66 (Texas) and the California Framework. Because of many differences in the two documents and because of the authors' participation in Texas adoptions, this critique will be limited to a comparison of Biology I textbooks with standards of Proclamation 66. We believe, however, that these criticisms should be pertinent to textbook evaluations nationwide. Criticisms are limited to chapters dealing with the origin of life and evolution. It should be noted that we are not critical of all portions of these chapters. For example, descriptions of the experiments of Pasteur and others regarding spontaneous generation are generally well written. Also, portions on paleontology and classification of species are in most cases to be commended.

The books critiqued are limited to 1991 editions of Biology I textbooks adopted by the state of Texas as listed below. The authors of this article recognize that textbook authors were given a mandate from the Texas State

207

Board of Education to deal with the topics of origin of life and evolution. Pertinent excerpts from Proclamation 66 that relate to these topics follow:

1. Scientific methods—under content: (1.4) scientific theories and laws based on existing evidence as well as new evidence; (1.6) problem-solving (data collection and analysis, conclusion).
2. Important scientific discoveries and theories of the past—under content: (2.2) Pasteur's discoveries (non-spontaneous generation, rabies vaccine, experiments with anthrax); (2.6) Darwin's theory of evolution.
4. Specialization and functions of cells and cellular organelles—under content: (4.2) theory of chemical origin of life.
6. Drawing logical inferences, predicting outcomes and forming generalized statements—under process skills: (6.2) deducing a biological hypothesis from experimental data; (6.3) examining alternative scientific evidence and ideas to test, modify, verify or refute scientific theories.
9. Theories of evolution—under content: (9.1) scientific theories of evolution; (9.2) scientific evidence of evolution and other reliable scientific theories, if any; (9.3) mechanisms of evolution; (9.4) patterns of evolution.

Have the textbook authors and editors clearly followed the above guidelines, such as item 6.3: "examining alternative scientific evidence and ideas to test, modify, verify or refute scientific theories"? That quotation is certainly an excellent expression of what constitutes valid science. Whether or not that guideline is followed is an important question for all biology teachers.

Origin of Life Hypotheses:
Credible or Beyond Credibility?

Despite an abundant use of leading questions and tentative terminology in their origin-of-life discussions, the majority of textbooks exude confidence that confirmation of a naturalistic model of life's origin is inevitable. The treatment in these textbooks stands in marked contrast to a review article by Klaus Dose summarizing origin-of-life research. In that thorough review, a strikingly different picture emerges of the current state of affairs regarding the origin of life. Dose, one of the best-known origin-of-life researchers for the past twenty years, provides the following summary in "The Origin of Life: More Questions than Answers": "More than 30 years of experimentation on the origin of life in the fields of chemical and molecular evolution have led to a better perception of the immensity of the problem of the origin of life on Earth rather than to its solution. At present all discussions on principal theories and experiments in the field either end in stalemate or in a confession of ignorance."[1]

First, we will consider the validity of the atmospheric models used for origin-of-life experiments, followed by whether data from these experiments are properly evaluated and interpreted.

Clinging to Outdated Atmospheric Models

Comments like that quoted above and the objective tone of the entire review article by Dose stand in sharp contrast to the optimism that colors the treatment of life's origin in most biology textbooks. The textbooks generally give the impression that the origin-of-life problem is nearly solved, since amino acids and other small building blocks have been produced using simulated atmospheres. In regard to composition of the early atmosphere, the following statements illustrate inaccuracies or overstatements in some texts. "The atmosphere had no free oxygen as it does today. Instead, the air was probably made up of water vapor, hydrogen, methane and ammonia."[2] "The Earth's first atmosphere most likely contained water vapor (H_2O), carbon monoxide (CO) and carbon dioxide (CO_2), nitrogen (N_2), hydrogen sulfide (H_2S) and hydrogen cyanide (HCN)."[3] It is unfortunate that only a few of the books acknowledge that it is not likely that the earth ever contained an atmosphere comparable to those used in simulation experiments.[4] The assumption that there was no oxygen in the early atmosphere is of crucial importance to the success of simulation experiments, yet there is no proof that oxygen was absent from that atmosphere.

Overstating Experimental Results

In several of the textbooks, inconsistencies and overstatements regarding the nature of compounds produced in simulation experiments pose a second problem. In some cases, false impressions are given because of what students are not told. Most texts fail to note that the compounds produced are markedly dependent on starting materials and experimental conditions. Some quotes follow: "They found amino acids, sugars and other compounds just as Oparin had predicted."[5] "Nucleic acids and ATP also have been formed."[6] "Their experiments have produced a variety of compounds, including various amino acids, ATP and the nucleic acids in

DNA."[7] "Similar mechanisms might have led to the formation of carbohydrates, lipids and nucleic acids."[8] "Thus, over the course of millions of years, at least some of the basic building blocks of life could have been produced in great quantities on early Earth."[9] The texts fail to note that most of the compounds produced in Stanley Miller and Harold Urey's original simulation experiment have no relevance to compounds found in living cells; that amino acids produced are always racemic (that is, D-, L-) mixtures; that carbohydrates and amino acids are never produced in the same experiment (they require different starting materials and different conditions); or that no one has produced any ATP or true nucleic acids using reasonable starting materials. As Dose notes: "Substantial amounts of biologically relevant sugars, including D, L-ribose, have never been produced in realistic prebiotic simulation experiments."[10]

The texts also neglect entirely the fact that compounds in cells have specific intramolecular bonds. Amino acids, carbohydrates, purines, and pyrimidines all have many possible isomers, and in most cases only one or at most very few of these isomers are found in living cells. In simulation experiments, mixtures of isomers would usually be produced.

In regard to formation of proteins from amino acids, several quotations follow: "Other scientists have shown that amino acids will link up when heated in the absence of oxygen gas."[11] Also, "amino acids tend to link together spontaneously to form short chains."[12] Neither of these texts notes that linkages occur only when amino acids are heated in the dry state; amino acids do not link together spontaneously in aqueous solution. Nor do these texts note that heating in the dry state produces some linkages that are not found in protein molecules, linkages that would prevent the formation of useful amino acid sequences.

Several quotations from the texts relating to membrane enclosures and/or cell formation are alive with expectation: "One process that must have occurred on the earth was the enclosure of nucleic acids in membranes. Once DNA was separated from the environment by some kind of boundary, it would be protected, and might be able to carry out the precise reactions of replication."[13] "Some of these droplets grow all by themselves, and others even reproduce."[14] These statements are pure speculation. Cell membranes usually contain lipids of various types, but they also contain proteins and carbohydrates. More important, membranes have very little to do with precise reactions of replication. Students are in no position to know it, but growth and division of coacervate droplets have no similarity to growth and reproduction of living cells.

The effect of the discussions in most of these texts is to make the emergence of life on Earth by chance appear to be highly probable. The following summary statement illustrates this:

> If we just said that life did arise from nonlife billions of years ago, why couldn't it happen again? The answer is simple: Today's Earth is a very different planet from the one that existed billions of years ago. On primitive Earth, there were no bacteria to break down organic compounds. Nor was there any oxygen to react with the organic compounds. As a result, organic compounds could accumulate over millions of years, forming that original organic soup. Today, however, such compounds cannot remain intact in the natural world for a long enough period of time to give life another start.[15]

It is not mentioned that degradation of organic compounds would occur in an early atmosphere as a result of electrical discharges, heat, ultraviolet light, and so forth, opposing any accumulations of relevant organic compounds. Nor is it mentioned that no geological evidence of an organic soup has ever been found. Coal, oil, and natural gas are all considered to be produced from ancient trees or organisms. For a critical evaluation of origin-of-life hypotheses, the reader is referred to two books that deal extensively with this topic.[16]

In closing this section, it should be noted that not all of the texts are equally careless in their statements regarding life's origin. Although all of the biology texts give the clear impression that the spontaneous origin of life on early Earth is very plausible, the degree to which erroneous statements are made in support of that view varies widely.

Neglect of the Central Problem,
Genetic Information

Although most of the texts deal with complex biochemical processes quite well in other chapters, none mentions the problem of the origin and transfer of genetic information in dealing with the origin of life. Moreover, the texts fail entirely to note that even if some complicated molecules were formed by chance, all of the machinery required to reproduce these molecules exactly must also be present in order for cells to survive and reproduce. Indeed, Harold Klein, chair of a National Academy of Sciences committee that recently reviewed origin-of-life research, notes that the simplest bacterium is so complicated from the point of view of a chemist that it is almost impossible to imagine how it happened.[17]

Instead, the textbooks' chapters on the origin of life uniformly disregard recent studies related to the complexity of origin-of-life requirements. Proteins in cells are made up of twenty different L-amino acids. The texts fail to note that unique linear sequences of those L-amino acids are required in protein molecules in order for those proteins to function. Unique amino acid sequences are required whether the protein is an enzyme, is a structural component, or is used for some other function. The unique sequence, in turn, is responsible for the three-dimensional structure of the protein, which is also essential to its function. Even though there may be some variability in amino acid sequence in some positions of a protein molecule, calculations with cytochrome c, a protein 104 amino acids long, indicate a 2×10^{-65} probability of achieving the linear structure of this one protein by chance.[18] Consequently, it is not surprising that the means of assembling such unique sequences during the process of protein synthesis in living cells is extremely complex.

The genetic information for such unique linear sequences is initially carried in sequences of nucleotides in the DNA of a gene in the nucleus of the cell. From there it is transferred to a nucleotide sequence in messenger RNA (or mRNA) in a process called transcription. Then the genetic information in mRNA is used to produce the sequence of amino acids in the final product, a protein molecule, in a process called translation. The latter process is so complex that even in the simplest organisms, as many as 200 different protein molecules are required. Altogether, the result of these different processes is an amazingly accurate transfer of information from the nucleotide sequence in DNA to the amino acid sequence in the protein.

In addition, the texts fail to note that most of the more complex biochemical reactions of cells require not only a protein enzyme, they also require an additional component (coenzyme, prosthetic group, and so forth). Examples of such groups are heme of various heme proteins and also the different vitamin coenzymes. These groups, which are often complex molecules, may be an integral part of the enzyme molecule (covalently bound), or they may freely dissociate from the protein. In the majority of cases, these organic components are absolutely essential to the catalytic function of the protein molecule. As a consequence, postulated scenarios for the origin of life must provide for the simultaneous formation of the essential coenzyme or prosthetic group and assembly of a specific linear amino acid sequence in the enzyme protein. They must, of course, also provide for the formation of many other complex macromolecules (nucleic acids, carbohydrates, lipids, and so forth) that are essential to the function and reproduction of the living cell. The failure to address these requirements shows even more fully the implausibility of the origin-of-life scenarios presented in the texts.

Of the important problems for origin-of-life models, Dose discusses the source of genetic information last, closing with a summary of few words: "The difficulties that must be overcome are at present beyond our imagination."[19] In regard to the chance hypothesis for the origin of genetic information, Kuppers notes: "The expectation probability for the nucleotide sequence of a bacterium is thus so slight that not even the entire space of the universe would be enough to make the random synthesis of a bacterial genome probable."[20]

Compare these statements with the easy confidence noted in the textbooks that a naturalistic explanation of life's origin is soon to be found. This confident tone, coupled with what students are not told, makes these chapters in the texts fall short of the guidelines: "examining alternative scientific evidence and ideas to test, modify, verify or refute scientific theories."

Definitions of Evolution

It should be evident that scientific terms, such as the word *evolution*, need to be clearly defined in high school biology textbooks. Such is not generally the case, however, as the books use that particular term in several senses without indicating that the meaning is changed. Keith Thomson, professor of biology at Yale University, indicates three commonly employed meanings of evolution:[21]

1. Change over time.
2. Relationships of organisms by descent through common ancestry.
3. A particular explanatory mechanism for the pattern and process of (1) and (2), such as natural selection.

Thomson notes that factual patterns of *change over time*, particularly as seen in the fossil record, can be studied in the absence of theories of how these patterns came to be. Thomson also emphasizes that the second meaning, *descent through common ancestry,* is a hypothesis, not a fact, and that it is derived from the twin premises that life arose only once on Earth and that all life proceeds from preexisting life. Cladistic analysis, championed currently by a number of biologists, has sought to evaluate relationships among organisms without regard to the twin premises cited above. In regard to the third meaning, a particular explanatory mechanism, there are currently many alternative hypotheses. Darwin insisted that changes had to be small and gradual. Gould and his associates, however, have proposed static intervals (stasis), followed by periods of rapid change (punctuated equilibrium).[22]

The biology texts, in general, do a poor job of distinguishing between these three different meanings of evolution. They generally fail to note that it is possible to accept the factual evidence for change over time while having a more restricted view of descent through common ancestry. For example, to speak of ancestral descent in regard to the relationship of an ancestral horse to a modern horse would be a very restricted use when compared to the relationship of an ancestral one-celled organism to a modern mammal. Likewise, accepting the factual evidence for change over time does not require the acceptance of a particular explanatory mechanism for these changes.

On another level, many scientists prefer to differentiate between microevolution and macroevolution: the former being the relatively small changes noted in the diversification of species, the latter being the changes required in the development of new phyla or possibly of new orders or classes. The term *macroevolution* has also been used in regard to development of new functions, such as vision or hearing. Many proponents of Darwinian natural selection have argued that processes demonstrated for microevolution may be extrapolated to account for macroevolution as well. When this type of extrapolation is used in an attempt to validate a theory, we have moved beyond the reasonable bounds of science. Scientifically, we should simply state that at present there is no satisfactory scientific explanation for macroevolutionary events. Those explanations that have been presented lie in the realm of philosophy.

Arguments for Biological Evolution

When we examine the arguments for biological evolution in the various high school texts, we find that marked differences exist between them and mainstream medical and biological science texts. The topics of structural homology (six texts), embryology (four texts), and vestigial organs (five texts) are treated with obsolete and erroneous discussions in the high school biology texts.

Structural Homology and Embryology

All of the high school textbooks confidently offer classic examples of structural homology as evidence of common ancestry, such as the similarity of bony structures of the five-digit forelimb in a variety of animals. Comments asserting or implying the common embryonic and genetic origin of homologous structures or their common ways of developing appear repeatedly in the discussions. Such an interpretation is clearly out of date and ignores a growing body of scientific data coming from prominent scientists. Sir Gavin de Beer, for example, poses important questions in his monograph titled *Homology: An Unsolved Problem.* For instance, homologous structures do not necessarily derive from similar positions in the embryo or parts of the egg, nor do they share the same organizer-induction processes, nor are they even necessarily controlled by corresponding genes.[23] The textbook authors should at least express the fact that this apparent argument for evolution, attractive as it sounds, is not without very significant problems and questions that remain to be answered. At least one of the textbooks points to Darwin's explanation of homology as the best one. Yet de Beer and others fault Darwin's concept of homology as "just what homology is not."[24] Goodwin adds that "homological equivalence is independent of history."[25] It is clear that there are important questions about the very notion of homology, but there is no suggestion of such questions in the textbooks.

Vestigial Structures

One would think that knowledgeable scientists would be extremely cautious about referring to vestigial structures in view of the fact that dozens of such structures were once thought to be present, but time and new scientific knowledge have removed almost every one from the list. A vestigial structure can be defined as a part or organ that was well developed in ancestral forms, but its size and structure have diminished until it currently has no function. Identification of a genuine vestigial structure requires that the part in question serve no contemporary useful purpose. The textbooks cite the coccyx (four texts), appendix (five texts), muscles that move the ears (three texts), canine tooth root structure (one text), wisdom teeth (one text), and the remnant of the third eyelid (one text) as vestigial organs. Space will not permit us to consider all of these, but two, the coccyx and the appendix, will be examined in some detail to demonstrate the fallacy of the textbook arguments.

The Coccyx. It is absolutely clear that the coccyx, or tailbone, is a functional unit and has been recognized as functional for many years. Examination of *Gray's Anatomy* will serve to indicate that the coccyx is one of four major points of attachment of the support of the perineal floor.[26] Also attached to the coccyx is the coccygeus muscle and a portion of sacrotuberous ligament, thus forming a significant portion of the posterior perineal support and adding stability to the pelvis via the interossical ligaments. The sequence of ossification of the coccygeal segments permits mobility of the coccyx during childbearing years and thus allows enlargement of the bony outlet of the birth canal during delivery of the baby. Expansion of the pelvic floor is minimized in other circumstances, however.

The Appendix. Today there is little doubt that the appendix contributes to human immune function. To its credit, one text gives at least a qualified acknowledgment of that role.[27] A journal discussion by Bjerke et al. notes the abundant content of organized lymphoid tissue in the appendix. The authors add:

> It seems justified to assume that the lymphoid follicles of the appendix are analogous to the Peyer's patches in having the capacity to generate IgA-cell precursors that migrate via lymph and blood to the distant gastrointestinal lamina propia. . . . We have found that normal human appendix mucosa contains relatively more IgC-producing cells than the colonic counterpart. This difference can be ascribed to preferential accumulation of IgG immunocytes adjacent to the numerous lymphoid follicles in the appendix.[28]

Kawanishi shares the view of the above authors regarding functionality of the appendix: "The human appendix, long considered only an accessory rudimentary organ, could possess a similar antigen uptake role prior to replacement by fibrosed tissue after repetitive subclinical infections or at least in early childhood when it is most prominent."[29]

The appendix is clearly a functional organ in humans and therefore cannot be considered as vestigial.

Sequence Similarities and Ancestral Descent

One of the major points made in many of the high school texts is that similarities of protein sequence provide strong support for evolution. These similarities are often used to indicate lines of ancestral descent of organisms. Protein sequence similarities can be used to indicate relationships among organisms, but whether those relationships indicate molecular homology (that is, ancestral descent) or whether there may be some other cause of the relationship is not always clear.

To give a specific example, rat and mouse cytochrome c molecules are identical in amino acid sequence, and the nucleotide sequences in the coding region of the cytochrome c genes differ in nine positions. With these very minor differences, the evidence is strong that a common rodent cytochrome c gene of the past is ancestrally related to the cytochrome c genes found at present in rats and mice. If, however, one compares mouse cytochrome c with cytochrome c of yeast (a unicellular eukaryotic organism), there are 37 differences in amino acid sequences of the two proteins and 118 differences in nucleotide sequences of the coding regions of the two genes.[30]

There is clearly similarity between the mouse and yeast genes, but is there an ancestral relationship of the yeast cytochrome c (or more properly of an earlier eukaryotic cytochrome c) to the mouse cytochrome c gene? Scientifically, we must say that there is insufficient evidence at present to make a firm statement. The obstacles to a step-by-step (that is, one nucleotide at a time) conversion in a hundred or more different nucleotide positions of an archetypal gene to form the present mouse gene are very great, since every intermediate would have to code for a functional cytochrome c molecule. Is this possible? If one postulates only chance conversions as a consequence of mutations, this conversion would seem to be beyond the realm of possibility. If one postulates that these nucleotide changes are under some type of control, the conversion might be more likely. But what is that control? Is it something built into the nature of molecules, or is it a consequence of an intelligent cause?

In seeking an answer to this question, we have moved to the border of science and philosophy, where premises and presuppositions are of primary importance. Honest scientists and students should recognize that there is room for differing opinions at this point.

Conclusion

We do not dispute the practice of teaching evolution to high school students. We think it should be made clear, however, that certain aspects of the theory of evolution are philosophical in nature. Evidence for the origin and evolution of life should be presented fairly and without distortion; but evidence that is not in accord with natural processes as an explanation should be clearly presented as well. When there are gaps or limitations in the data, they should be acknowledged. One of the outstanding biologists of the nineteenth century, Claude Bernard, noted: "when we have put forward an idea or a theory in science, our object must not be to preserve it by seeking everything that may support it and setting aside everything that may weaken it. On the contrary, we ought to examine with greatest care the facts that would overthrow it."[31]

We note that, contrary to Bernard's advice, the errors, overstatements, and omissions found in the high school biology texts we examined all tend to enhance the plausibility of hypotheses that are presented. Further, we do not regard the inclusion of outdated material and erroneous discussions as trivial. The items to which we have called attention in this essay mislead students and impede their acquisition of critical thinking skills.

If we fail to teach students to examine data critically, looking for points both favoring and opposing hypotheses, we are selling our youth short and mortgaging the future of scientific inquiry itself. We concur with the requirement that biology texts examine "alternative scientific evidence and ideas to test, modify, verify or refute scientific theories," but we think that the chapters on the origin of life and on evolution in most of the Biology I textbooks discussed here fall far short of meeting that requirement.[32]

Notes

1. K. Dose, "The Origin of Life: More Questions Than Answers," *Interdisciplinary Science Review* 13 (1988): 351.
2. A. L. Biggs, D. S. Emmeluth, C. L. Gentry, R. I. Hays, L. Lundgren, and F. Mollura, *Biology: The Dynamics of Life* (Columbus, Ohio: Merrill, 1991), 797.
3. K. R. Miller and J. Levine, *Biology* (Englewood Cliffs, N.J.: Prentice Hall, 1991), 343.
4. Dose, "Origin of Life," 351.
5. Biggs et al., *Biology*, 228.
6. Ibid.
7. A. Towle, *Modern Biology* (Orlando, Fla: Holt, Rinehart and Winston, 1991), 210.
8. Ibid.
9. Miller and Levine, *Biology*, 344.
10. Dose, "Origin of Life," 352.
11. Towle, *Modern Biology*, 210.
12. Miller and Levine, *Biology*, 344.
13. Towle, *Modern Biology*, 211.

14. Miller and Levine, *Biology,* 344.

15. Ibid., 346.

16. C. B. Thaxton, W. L. Bradley, and R. L. Olsen, *The Mystery of Life's Origin* (New York: Philosophical Library, 1984); R. Shapiro, *Origins* (New York: Summit Books, 1986).

17. Quoted in J. Horgan, "In the Beginning," *Scientific American* 264 (1991): 116–25.

18. H. P. Yockey, "A Calculation of the Probability of Spontaneous Biogenesis by Information Theory," *Journal of Theoretical Biology* 67 (1977): 377–98.

19. Dose, "Origin of Life," 355.

20. B. O. Kuppers, *Information and the Origin of Life* (Cambridge: MIT Press, 1990), 60.

21. K. Thomson, "The Meanings of Evolution," *American Scientist* 70 (1982): 529–31.

22. S. J. Gould, *The Panda's Thumb* (New York: W. W. Norton 1980).

23. G. de Beer, *Homology: An Unsolved Problem* (London: Oxford University Press, 1971), 13–15.

24. B. Goodwin, "Development and Evolution," *Journal of Theoretical Biology* 97 (1982): 51; C. Webster, *Beyond New Darwinism* (London: Academic Press, 1984), 193.

25. Goodwin, "Development," 51.

26. C. M. Goss, ed., *Gray's Anatomy,* 5th ed. (Philadelphia: Lea and Febiger, 1988).

27. Biggs et al., *Biology.*

28. K. Bjerke, P. Brandtzaeg, and T. O. Rognum, "Distribution of Immunoglobin Producing Cells in Normal Human Appendix and Colon Mucosa," *GUT* 27 (1986): 672–73.

29. H. Kawanishi, "Immunocompetence of Normal Human Appendicial Lymphoid Cells: In Vitro Studies," *Immunology* 60 (1987): 19.

30. G. C. Mills, "Cytochrome c: Gene Structure, Homology and Ancestral Relationships," *Journal of Theoretical Biology* 152 (1991): 177–90.

31. C. Bernard, *An Introduction to the Study of Experimental Medicine,* trans. H. C. Greene (New York: Henry Schuman, [1865] 1927), 40.

32. Textbooks examined but not cited specifically in this essay include: H. D. Goodman, L. E. Graham, T. C. Emmel, and Y. Shechter, *Biology Today* (Orlando, Fla.: Holt, Rinehart and Winston, 1991); J. E. McLaren, L. Rotundo, and L. Gurley-Digger, *Health Biology* (Lexington, Mass.: D. C. Heath 1991); W. D. Schraer and H. J. Stoltze, *Biology: The Study of Life* (Englewood Cliffs, N.J.: Prentice Hall, 1991).

※ Part III

The Theory of Intelligent Design:
A Scientific Alternative to Neo-Darwinian
and/or Chemical Evolutionary Theories

DNA and the Origin of Life: Information, Specification, and Explanation

Stephen C. Meyer

Theories about the origin of life necessarily presuppose knowledge of the attributes of living cells. As historian of biology Harmke Kamminga has observed, "At the heart of the problem of the origin of life lies a fundamental question: What is it exactly that we are trying to explain the origin of?"[1] Or as the pioneering chemical evolutionary theorist Alexander Oparin put it, "The problem of the nature of life and the problem of its origin have become inseparable."[2] Origin-of-life researchers want to explain the origin of the first and presumably simplest—or, at least, minimally complex—living cell. As a result, developments in fields that explicate the nature of unicellular life have historically defined the questions that origin-of-life scenarios must answer.

Since the late 1950s and 1960s, origin-of-life researchers have increasingly recognized the complex and specific nature of unicellular life and the biomacromolecules on which such systems depend. Further, molecular biologists and origin-of-life researchers have characterized this complexity and specificity in informational terms. Molecular biologists routinely refer to DNA, RNA, and proteins as carriers or repositories of "information."[3] Many origin-of-life researchers now regard the origin of the information in these biomacromolecules as the central question facing their research. As Bernd-Olaf Kuppers has stated, "The problem of the origin of life is clearly basically equivalent to the problem of the origin of biological information."[4]

This essay will evaluate competing explanations for the origin of the information necessary to build the first living cell. To do so will require determining what biologists have meant by the term *information* as it has been applied to biomacromolecules. As many have noted, "information" can denote several theoretically distinct concepts. This essay will attempt to eliminate this ambiguity and to determine precisely what type of information origin-of-life researchers must explain "the origin of." What follows will first seek to *characterize* the information in DNA, RNA, and proteins as an *explanandum* (a fact in need of explanation) and, second, to *evaluate* the efficacy of competing classes of explanation for the origin of biological information (that is, the competing *explanans*).

Part I will seek to show that molecular biologists have used the term *information* consistently to refer to the joint properties of *complexity* and functional *specificity* or *specification*. Biological usage of the term will be contrasted with its classical information-theoretic usage to show that "biological information" entails a richer sense of information than the classical mathematical theory of Shannon and Wiener. Part I will also argue against attempts to treat biological "information" as a metaphor lacking empirical content and/or ontological status.[5] It will show that the term *biological information* refers to two real features of living systems, complexity and specificity, features that jointly do require explanation.

Part II will evaluate competing types of explanation for the origin of the specified biological information necessary to produce the first living system. The categories of "chance" and "necessity" will provide a helpful heuristic for understanding the recent history of origin-of-life research. From the 1920s to the mid-1960s, origin-of-life researchers relied heavily on theories emphasizing the creative role of random events—"chance"—often in tandem with some form of prebiotic natural selection. Since the late 1960s, theorists have instead emphasized deterministic self-organizational laws or properties—that is, physical-chemical "necessity."

Part II will critique the causal adequacy of chemical evolutionary theories based on "chance," "necessity," and the combination of the two.

A concluding part III will suggest that the phenomenon of information understood as specified complexity requires a radically different explanatory approach. In particular, I will argue that our present knowledge of causal powers suggests intelligent design as a better, more causally adequate explanation for the origin of the specified complexity (the information so defined) present in large biomolecules such as DNA, RNA, and proteins.

I.

A. Simple to Complex:
Defining the Biological *Explanandum*

After Darwin published the *Origin of Species* in 1859, many scientists began to think about a problem that Darwin had not addressed.[6] Although Darwin's theory purported to explain how life could have grown gradually more complex starting from "one or a few simple forms," it did not explain, or attempt to explain, how life had first originated. Yet in the 1870s and 1880s, evolutionary biologists like Ernst Haeckel and Thomas Huxley assumed that devising an explanation for the origin of life would be fairly easy, in large part because Haeckel and Huxley assumed that life was, in its essence, a chemically simple substance called "protoplasm" that could easily be constructed by combining and recombining simple chemicals such as carbon dioxide, oxygen, and nitrogen.

Over the next sixty years, biologists and biochemists gradually revised their view of the nature of life. During the 1860s and 1870s, biologists tended to see the cell, in Haeckel's words, as an undifferentiated and "homogeneous globule of plasm." By the 1930s, however, most biologists had come to see the cell as a complex metabolic system.[7] Origin-of-life theories reflected this increasing appreciation of cellular complexity. Whereas nineteenth-century theories of abiogenesis envisioned life arising almost instantaneously via a one- or two-step process of chemical "autogeny," early twentieth-century theories, such as Oparin's theory of *evolutionary* abiogenesis, envisioned a multibillion-year process of transformation from simple chemicals to a complex metabolic system.[8] Even so, most scientists during the 1920s and 1930s still vastly underestimated the complexity and specificity of the cell and its key functional components—as developments in molecular biology would soon make clear.

B. The Complexity and Specificity of Proteins

During the first half of the twentieth century, biochemists had come to recognize the centrality of proteins to the maintenance of life. Although many mistakenly believed that proteins also contained the source of heredity information, biologists repeatedly underestimated the complexity of proteins.

For example, during the 1930s, English X-ray crystallographer William Astbury elucidated the molecular structure of certain fibrous proteins, such as keratin, the key structural protein in hair and skin.[9] Keratin exhibits a relatively simple, repetitive structure, and Astbury was convinced that all proteins, including the mysterious globular proteins so important to life, represented variations on the same primal and regular pattern. Similarly, biochemists Max Bergmann and Carl Niemann of the Rockefeller Institute argued in 1937 that the amino acids in proteins occurred in regular, mathematically expressible proportions. Other biologists imagined that insulin and hemoglobin proteins, for example, "consisted of bundles of parallel rods."[10]

Beginning in the 1950s, however, a series of discoveries caused this simplistic view of proteins to change. From 1949 to 1955, biochemist Fred Sanger determined the structure of the protein molecule, insulin. Sanger showed that insulin consisted of a long and irregular sequence of the various amino acids, rather like a string of differently colored beads arranged without any discernible pattern. His work showed for a single protein what subsequent work in molecular biology would establish as a norm: The amino acid sequence in functional proteins generally defies expression by any simple rule and is characterized instead by aperiodicity or complexity.[11] Later in the 1950s, work by John Kendrew on the structure of the protein myoglobin showed that proteins also exhibit a surprising three-dimensional complexity. Far from the simple structures that biologists had imagined earlier, an extraordinarily complex and irregular three-dimensional shape was revealed: a twisting, turning, tangle of amino acids. As Kendrew explained in 1958, "The big surprise was that it was so irregular . . . the arrangement seems to be almost totally lacking in the kind of regularity one instinctively anticipates, and it is more complicated than has been predicted by any theory of protein structure."[12]

By the mid-1950s, biochemists recognized that proteins possess another remarkable property. In addition to their complexity, proteins also exhibit specificity, both as one-dimensional arrays and three-dimensional structures. Whereas proteins are built from chemically rather simple amino acid "building blocks," their function (whether as enzymes, signal transducers, or structural components in the cell) depends crucially on a complex but specific arrangement of those building blocks.[13] In particular, the specific sequence of amino acids in a chain and the resultant chemical interactions between amino acids largely determine the specific three-dimensional structure that the chain as a whole will adopt. Those structures or shapes in turn determine what function, if any, the amino acid chain can perform in the cell.

For a functioning protein, its three-dimensional shape gives it a hand-in-glove fit with other molecules, enabling it to catalyze specific chemical reactions or to build specific structures within the cell. Because of its three-dimensional specificity, one protein can usually no more substitute for another than one tool can substitute for another. A topoisomerase can no more perform the job of a polymerase than a hatchet can perform the function of a soldering iron. Instead, proteins perform functions only by virtue of their three-dimensional specificity of fit, either with other equally specified and complex molecules or with simpler substrates within the cell. Moreover, the three-dimensional specificity derives in large part from the one-dimensional sequence specificity in the arrangement of the amino acids that form proteins. Even slight alterations in sequence often result in the loss of protein function.

C. The Complexity and Sequence Specificity of DNA

During the early part of the twentieth century, researchers also vastly underestimated the complexity (and significance) of nucleic acids such as DNA and RNA. By then, scientists knew the chemical composition of DNA. Biologists and chemists knew that in addition to sugars (and later phosphates), DNA was composed of four different nucleotide bases, called adenine, thymine, cytosine, and guanine. In 1909, chemist P. A. Levene showed (incorrectly as it later turned out) that the four different nucleotide bases always occurred in equal quantities within the DNA molecule.[14] He formulated what he called the "tetranucleotide hypothesis" to account for that putative fact. According to that hypothesis, the four nucleotide bases in DNA linked together in repeating sequences of the same four chemicals in the same sequential order. Since Levene envisioned those sequential arrangements of nucleotides as repetitive and invariant, their potential for expressing any genetic diversity seemed inherently limited. To account for the heritable differences between species, biologists needed to discover some source of variable or irregular specificity, some source of information, within the germ lines of different organisms. Yet insofar as DNA was seen as an uninterestingly repetitive molecule, many biologists assumed that DNA could play little if any role in the transmission of heredity.

That view began to change in the mid-1940s for several reasons. First, Oswald Avery's famous experiments on virulent and nonvirulent strains of *Pneumococcus* identified DNA as the key factor in accounting for heritable differences between different bacterial strains.[15] Second, work by Erwin Chargaff of Columbia University in the late 1940s undermined the "tetranucleotide hypothesis." Chargaff showed, contradicting Levene's earlier work, that nucleotide frequencies actually do differ between species, even if they often hold constant within the same species or within the same organs or tissues of a single organism.[16] More important, Chargaff recognized that even for nucleic acids of exactly "the same analytical composition"—meaning those with the same relative proportions of the four bases (abbreviated A, T, C, and G)—"enormous" numbers of variations in sequence were possible. As he put it, different DNA molecules or parts of DNA molecules might "differ from each other . . . in the sequence, [though] not the proportion, of their constituents." As he realized, for a nucleic acid consisting of 2,500 nucleotides (roughly the length of a long gene) the number of sequences "exhibiting the same molar proportions of individual purines [A, G] and pyrimidines [T, C] . . . is not far from 10^{1500}."[17] Thus, Chargaff showed that, contrary to the tetranucleotide hypothesis, base sequencing in DNA might well display the high degree of variability and aperiodicity required by any potential carrier of heredity.

Third, elucidation of the three-dimensional structure of DNA by Watson and Crick in 1953 made clear that DNA could function as a carrier of hereditary information.[18] The model proposed by Watson and Crick envisioned a double-helix structure to explain the Maltese-cross pattern derived from X-ray crystallographic studies of DNA by Franklin, Wilkins, and Bragg in the early 1950s. According to the now well-known Watson and Crick model, the two strands of the helix were made of sugar and phosphate molecules linked by phosphodiester bonds. Nucleotide bases were linked horizontally to the sugars on each strand of the helix and to a complementary base on the other strand to form an internal "rung" on a twisting "ladder." For geometric reasons, their model required the pairing (across the helix) of adenine with thymine and cytosine with guanine. That complementary pairing helped to explain a significant regularity in composition ratios discovered by Chargaff. Though Chargaff had shown that none of the four nucleotide bases appears with the same frequency as all the other three, he did discover that the molar proportions of adenine and thymine, on the one hand, and cytosine and guanine, on the other, do consistently equal each other.[19] Watson and Crick's model explained the regularity Chargaff had expressed in his famous "ratios."

The Watson-Crick model made clear that DNA might possess an impressive chemical and structural complexity. The double-helix structure for DNA presupposed an extremely long and high-molecular-weight structure, possessing an impressive potential for variability and complexity in sequence. As Watson and Crick explained, "The sugar-phosphate backbone in our model is completely regular but any sequence of base pairs can fit into the structure. It follows that in a long molecule many different permutations are possible, and it, therefore, seems likely that the precise sequence of bases is the code which carries genetic information."[20]

As with proteins, subsequent discoveries soon showed that DNA sequences were not only complex but also highly specific relative to the requirements of biological function. Discovery of the complexity and specificity of proteins had led researchers to suspect a functionally specific role for DNA. Molecular biologists, working in the wake of Sanger's results, assumed that proteins were much too complex (and yet also functionally specific) to arise by chance in vivo. Moreover, given their irregularity, it seemed unlikely that a general chemical law or regularity could explain their assembly. Instead, as Jacques Monod has recalled, molecular biologists began to look for some source of information or "specificity" within the cell that could direct the construction of such highly specific and complex structures. To explain the presence of the specificity and complexity in the protein, as Monod would later insist, "you absolutely needed a code."[21]

The structure of DNA as elucidated by Watson and Crick suggested a means by which information or "specificity" might be encoded along the spine of DNA's sugar-phosphate backbone.[22] Their model suggested that variations in sequence of the nucleotide bases might find expression in the sequence of the amino acids that form proteins. In 1955, Crick proposed this idea as the so-called sequence hypothesis. According to Crick's hypothesis, the specificity of arrangement of amino acids in proteins derives from the specific arrangement of the nucleotide bases on the DNA molecule.[23] The sequence hypothesis suggested that the nucleotide bases in DNA functioned like letters in an alphabet or characters in a machine code. Just as alphabetic letters in a written language may perform a communication function depending on their sequence, so, too, might the nucleotide bases in DNA result in the production of a functional protein molecule depending on their precise sequential arrangement. In both cases, function depends crucially on sequence. The sequence hypothesis implied not only the complexity but also the functional specificity of DNA base sequences.

By the early 1960s, a series of experiments had confirmed that DNA base sequences play a critical role in determining amino acid sequence during protein synthesis.[24] By that time, the processes and mechanisms by which DNA sequences determine key stages of the process were known (at least in outline). Protein synthesis or "gene expression" proceeds as long chains of nucleotide bases are first copied during a process known as transcription. The resulting copy, a "transcript" made of single-stranded "messenger RNA," now contains a sequence of RNA bases precisely reflecting the sequence of bases on the original DNA strand. The transcript is then transported to a complex organelle called a ribosome. At the ribosome, the transcript is "translated" with the aid of highly specific adaptor molecules (called transfer-RNAs) and specific enzymes (called amino-acyl tRNA synthetases) to produce a growing amino acid chain (figure 1).[25] Whereas the function of the protein molecule derives from the specific arrangement of twenty different types of amino acids, the function of DNA depends on the arrangement of just four kinds of bases. This lack of a one-to-one correspondence means that a group of three DNA nucleotides (a triplet) is needed to specify a single amino acid. In any case, the sequential arrangement of the nucleotide bases determines (in large part) the one-dimensional sequential arrangement of amino acids during protein synthesis.[26] Since protein function depends critically on amino acid sequence and amino acid sequence depends critically on DNA base sequence, the sequences in the coding regions of DNA themselves possess a high degree of specificity relative to the requirements of protein (and cellular) function.

D. Information Theory and Molecular Biology

From the beginning of the molecular biological revolution, biologists have ascribed information-bearing properties to DNA, RNA, and proteins. In the parlance of molecular biology, DNA base sequences contain the "genetic information" or the "assembly instructions" necessary to direct protein synthesis. Yet the term *information* can denote several theoretically distinct concepts. Thus, one must ask which sense of "information" applies to these large biomacromolecules. We shall see that molecular biologists employ both a stronger conception of information than that of mathematicians and information-theorists and a slightly weaker conception of the term than that of linguists and ordinary users.

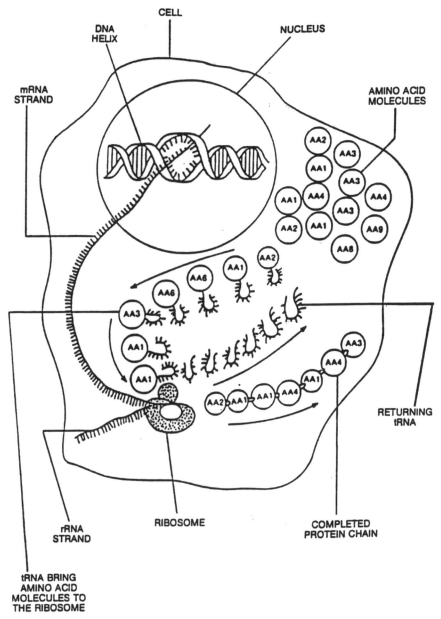

FIGURE 1. The intricate machinery of protein synthesis. The genetic messages encoded on the DNA molecule are copied and then transported by messenger RNA to the ribosome complex. There the genetic message is "read" and translated with the aid of other large biomolecules (transfer-RNA and specific enzyme) to produce a growing amino acid chain. Courtesy of I. L. Cohen of New Research Publications.

During the 1940s, Claude Shannon at Bell Laboratories developed a mathematical theory of information.[27] His theory equated the amount of information transmitted with the amount of uncertainty reduced or eliminated by a series of symbols or characters.[28] For example, before one rolls a six-sided die, there are six possible outcomes. Before one flips a coin, there are two. Rolling a die will thus eliminate more uncertainty and, on Shannon's theory, will convey more information than flipping a coin. Equating information with the reduction of uncertainty implied a mathematical relationship between information and probability (or its inverse, complexity). Note that for a die each possible outcome has only a one in six chance of occurring, compared to a one in two chance for each side of the coin. Thus, in Shannon's theory the occurrence of the more improbable event conveys more information. Shannon generalized this relationship by stating that the amount of information conveyed by an event is inversely proportional to the prior probability of its occurrence. The greater the number of possibilities, the greater the improbability of any one being actualized, and thus more information is transmitted when a particular possibility occurs.

Moreover, information increases as improbabilities multiply. The probability of getting four heads in a row when flipping a fair coin is $\frac{1}{2} \times \frac{1}{2} \times \frac{1}{2} \times \frac{1}{2}$, or $\left(\frac{1}{2}\right)^4$. Thus, the probability of attaining a specific sequence of heads and/or tails decreases exponentially as the number of trials increases. The quantity of information increases correspondingly. Even so, information theorists found it convenient to measure information additively rather than multiplicatively. Thus, the common mathematical expression ($I = -\log_2 p$) for calculating information converts probability values into informational measures through a negative logarithmic function, where the negative sign expresses an inverse relationship between information and probability.[29]

Shannon's theory applies most easily to sequences of alphabetic symbols or characters that function as such. Within any given alphabet of x possible characters, the placement of a specific character eliminates x-1 other possibilities and thus a corresponding amount of uncertainty. Or put differently, within any given alphabet or ensemble of x possible characters (where each character has an equi-probable chance of occurring), the probability of any one character occurring is 1/x. The larger the value of x, the greater the amount of information that is conveyed by the occurrence of a specific character in a sequence. In systems where the value of x can be known (or estimated), as in a code or language, mathematicians can easily generate quantitative estimates of information-carrying capacity. The greater the number of possible characters at each site and the longer the sequence of characters, the greater is the information-carrying capacity—or Shannon information—associated with the sequence.

The essentially digital character of the nucleotide bases in DNA and of the amino acid residues in proteins enabled molecular biologists to calculate the information-carrying capacity (or syntactic information) of those molecules using the new formalism of Shannon's theory. Because at every site in a growing amino acid chain, for example, the chain may receive any one of twenty amino acids, placement of a single amino acid in the chain eliminates a quantifiable amount of uncertainty and increases the Shannon or syntactic information of a polypeptide by a corresponding amount. Similarly, since at any given site along the DNA backbone any one of four nucleotide bases may occur with equal probability, the p value for the occurrence of a specific nucleotide at that site equals 1/4, or .25.[30] The information-carrying capacity of a sequence of a specific length n can then be calculated using Shannon's familiar expression ($I = -\log_2 p$) once one computes a p value for the occurrence of a particular sequence n nucleotides long where p = $(1/4)^n$. The p value thus yields a corresponding measure of information-carrying capacity or syntactic information for a sequence of n nucleotide bases.[31]

E. Complexity, Specificity, and Biological Information

Though Shannon's theory and equations provided a powerful way to measure the amount of information that could be transmitted across a communication channel, it had important limits. In particular, it did not and could not distinguish merely improbable sequences of symbols from those that conveyed a message. As Warren Weaver made clear in 1949, "The word *information* in this theory is used in a special mathematical sense that must not be confused with its ordinary usage. In particular, information must not be confused with meaning."[32] Information theory could measure the information-carrying capacity or the syntactic information of a given sequence of symbols but could not distinguish the presence of a meaningful or functional arrangement of symbols from a random sequence (for example, "we hold these truths to be self-evident" versus "ntnyhiznl-hteqkhgdsjh"). Thus, Shannon information theory could quantify the amount of functional or meaningful information that *might be present* in a given sequence of symbols or characters, but it could not distinguish the status of a functional or message-bearing text from random gibberish. Thus, paradoxically, random sequences of letters often have more syntactic information (or information-carrying capacity), as measured by classical information theory, than do meaningful or functional sequences that happen to contain a certain amount of intentional redundancy or repetition.

In essence, therefore, Shannon's theory remains silent on the important question of whether a sequence of symbols is functionally specific or meaningful. Nevertheless, in its application to molecular biology, Shannon information theory did succeed in rendering rough quantitative measures of the information-carrying capacity or syntactic information (where those terms correspond to measures of brute complexity).[33] As such, information theory did help to refine biologists' understanding of one important feature of the crucial biomolecular components on which life depends: DNA and proteins are highly complex, and quantifiably so. Yet the theory by itself could not establish whether base sequences in DNA or amino acid sequences in proteins possessed the property of functional specificity. Information theory helped establish that DNA and proteins *could* carry large amounts of functional information; it could not establish whether they did.

The ease with which information theory applied to molecular biology (to measure information-carrying capacity) has created considerable confusion about the sense in which DNA and proteins contain "information." Information theory strongly suggested that such molecules possess vast information-carrying capacities or large amounts of syntactic information, as defined by Shannon's theory. When molecular biologists have described DNA as the carrier of hereditary information, however, they have meant much more than the technically limited term *information*. Instead, as Sahotra Sarkar points out, leading molecular biologists defined biological information so as to incorporate the notion of specificity of function (as well as complexity) as early as 1958.[34] Molecular biologists such as Monod and Crick understood biological information—the information stored in DNA and proteins—as something more than mere complexity (or improbability). Their notion of information did associate both biochemical contingency and combinatorial complexity with DNA sequences (allowing DNA's carrying capacity to be calculated), but they also recognized that sequences of nucleotides and amino acids in functioning biomacromolecules possessed a high degree of *specificity* relative to the maintenance of cellular function. As Crick explained in 1958, "By information I mean the specification of the amino acid sequence in protein. . . . Information means here the *precise* determination of sequence, either of bases in the nucleic acid or on amino acid residues in the protein."[35]

Since the late 1950s, biologists have equated the *"precise* determination of sequence" with the extra-information-theoretic property of specificity or specification. Biologists have defined *specificity* tacitly as "necessary to achieve or maintain function." They have determined that DNA base sequences, for example, are specified not by applying information theory but by making experimental assessments of the function of those sequences within the overall apparatus of gene expression.[36] Similar experimental considerations established the functional specificity of proteins.

Further, developments in complexity theory have now made possible a fully general theoretical account of specification, one that applies readily to biological systems. In particular, recent work by mathematician William Dembski has employed the notion of a rejection region from statistics to provide a formal complexity-theoretic account of specification. According to Dembski, a specification occurs when an event or object (a) falls within an independently given pattern or domain, (b) "matches" or exemplifies a conditionally independent pattern, or (c) meets a conditionally independent set of functional requirements.[37]

To illustrate Dembski's notion of specification, consider these two strings of characters:

"iuinsdysk]idfawqnzkl,mfdifhs"
"Time and tide wait for no man."

Given the number of possible ways of arranging the letters and punctuation marks of the English language for sequences of this length, both of these two sequences constitute highly improbable arrangements of characters. Thus, both have a considerable and quantifiable information-carrying capacity. Nevertheless, only the second of the two sequences exhibits a specification on Dembski's account. To see why, consider the following. Within the set of combinatorially possible sequences, only a very few will convey meaning. This smaller set of meaningful sequences, therefore, delimits a domain or pattern within the larger set of the totality of possibilities. Moreover, this set constitutes a "conditionally independent" pattern. Roughly speaking, a conditionally independent pattern corresponds to a preexisting pattern or set of functional requirements, not one contrived after the fact of observing the event in question—specifically, in this case, the event of observing the two sequences above.[38] Since the smaller domain distinguishes functional from nonfunctional English sequences and the functionality of alphabetic sequences depends on the preexisting or independently given conventions of English vocabulary and grammar, the smaller set or domain qualifies as a conditionally independent pattern.[39] Since the second string of characters ("Time and tide wait . . .") falls within this smaller conditionally independent domain (or "matches" one of the possible meaningful sentences that fall within it), the second sequence exhibits a specification according to Dembski's complexity-theoretic account. That sequence therefore exhibits the joint properties of complexity and specification and possesses not just information-carrying capacity but both "specified" and, in this case, "semantic" information.

Biological organisms also exhibit specifications, though not necessarily semantic or subjectively "meaningful" ones. The nucleotide base sequences in the coding regions of DNA are highly specific relative to the independent functional requirements of protein function, protein synthesis, and cellular life. To maintain viability, the cell must regulate its metabolism, pass materials back and forth across its membranes, destroy waste materials, and do many other specific tasks. Each of these functional requirements in turn necessitates specific molecular constituents, machines, or systems (usually made of proteins) to accomplish these tasks. Building these proteins with their specific three-dimensional shapes requires specific arrangements of nucleotide bases on the DNA molecule.

Since the chemical properties of DNA allow a vast ensemble of combinatorially possible arrangements of nucleotide bases, any particular sequence will necessarily be highly improbable and rich in Shannon information or information-carrying capacity. Yet within that set of possible sequences a very few will, given the multimolecular system of gene expression within the cell, produce functional proteins.[40] Those that do are thus not only improbable but also functionally "specified" or "specific," as molecular biologists use the terms. Indeed, the smaller set of functionally efficacious sequences again delimits a domain or pattern within a larger set of combinatorial possibilities. Moreover, this smaller domain constitutes a conditionally independent pattern, since (as with the English sequences above) it distinguishes functional from nonfunctional sequences, and the functionality of nucleotide base sequences depends on the independent requirements of protein function. Thus, any actual nucleotide sequence that falls within this domain (or "matches" one of the possible functional sequences that fall within it) exhibits a specification. Put differently, any nucleotide base sequence that produces a functional protein clearly meets certain independent functional requirements, in particular, those of protein function. Thus, any sequence that meets such requirements (or "falls within the smaller subset of functional sequences") is again not only highly improbable but also specified relative to that independent pattern or domain. Thus, the nucleotide sequences in the coding regions of DNA possess both syntactic information and "specified" information.

A note of definitional clarity must be offered about the relationship between "specified" information and "semantic" information. Though natural languages and DNA base sequences are both specified, only natural language conveys meaning. If one defines "semantic information" as "subjectively meaningful information that is conveyed syntactically (as a string of phonemes or characters) and is understood by a conscious agent," then clearly the information in DNA does not qualify as semantic. Unlike a written or spoken natural language, DNA does not convey "meaning" to a conscious agent.

Rather, the coding regions of DNA function in much the same way as a software program or machine code, directing operations within a complex material system via highly complex yet specified sequences of characters. As Richard Dawkins has noted, "The machine code of the genes is uncannily computer-like."[41] Or as software developer Bill Gates has noted, "DNA is like a computer program, but far, far more advanced than any software we've ever created."[42] Just as the specific arrangement of two symbols (0 and 1) in a software program can perform a function within a machine environment, so, too, can the precise sequencing of the four nucleotide bases in DNA perform a function within the cell.

Though DNA sequences do not convey "meaning," they do exhibit specificity or specification. Moreover, as in a machine code, the sequence specificity of DNA occurs within a syntactic (or functionally alphabetic) domain. Thus, DNA possesses both syntactic and specified information. In any case, since the late 1950s, the concept of information as employed by molecular biologists has conjoined the notions of complexity (or improbability) and specificity of function. The crucial biomolecular constituents of living organisms possess not only Shannon or syntactic information but also "*specified* information" or "*specified* complexity."[43] Biological information so defined, therefore, constitutes a salient feature of living systems that any origin-of-life scenario must explain "the origin of." Further, as we will see below, all naturalistic chemical evolutionary theories have encountered difficulty explaining the origin of such functionally "specified" biological information.

F. Information as Metaphor: Nothing to Explain?

Though most molecular biologists would see nothing controversial in characterizing DNA and proteins as "information-bearing" molecules, some historians and philosophers of biology have recently challenged that description. Before evaluating competing types of explanation for the origin of biological information, this challenge must be addressed. In 2000, the late historian of science Lily Kay characterized the application of information theory to biology as a failure, in particular because classical information theory could not capture the idea of meaning. She suggests, therefore, that the term *information* as used in biology constitutes nothing more than a metaphor. Since, in Kay's view, the term does not designate anything real, it follows that the origin of "biological information" does not require explanation. Instead, only the origin of the *use* of the term *information* within biology requires explanation. As a social constructivist, Kay explained this usage as the result of various social forces operating within the "Cold War Technoculture."[44] In a different but related vein, Sarkar has argued that the concept of information has little theoretical significance in biology because it lacks predictive or explanatory power.[45] He, like Kay, seems to regard the concept of information as a superfluous metaphor lacking empirical reference and ontological status.

Of course, insofar as the term *information* connotes semantic meaning, it does function as a metaphor within biology. That does not mean, however, that the term functions *only* metaphorically or that origin-of-life biologists have nothing to explain. Though information theory has a *limited* application in describing biological systems, it has succeeded in rendering quantitative assessments of the complexity of biomacromolecules. Further, experimental work established the functional specificity of the sequences of monomers in DNA and proteins. Thus, the term *information* as used in biology does refer to two real and contingent properties of living systems: complexity and specificity. Indeed, since scientists began to think seriously about what would be required to explain the phenomenon of heredity, they have recognized the need for some feature or substance in living organisms possessing precisely these two properties together. Thus, Schrödinger envisioned an "aperiodic crystal"; Chargaff perceived DNA's capacity for "complex sequencing"; Watson and Crick equated complex sequences with "information," which Crick in turn equated with "specificity"; Monod equated irregular specificity in proteins with the need for "a code"; and Orgel characterized life as a "specified complexity."[46] Further, Davies has recently argued that the "specific randomness" of DNA base sequences constitutes the central mystery surrounding the origin of life.[47] Whatever the terminology, scientists have recognized the need for, and now know the location of, a source of complex specificity in the cell in order to transmit heredity and maintain biological function. The incorrigibility of these descriptive concepts suggests that complexity and specificity constitute real properties of biomacromolecules—indeed, properties that could be otherwise but only to the detriment of cellular life. As Orgel notes: "Living organisms are distinguished by their specified complexity. Crystals . . . fail to qualify as living because they lack complexity; mixtures of random polymers fail to qualify because they lack specificity."[48]

The origin of specificity and complexity (in combination), to which the term *information* in biology commonly refers, therefore does require explanation, even if the concept of information connotes only complexity in classical information theory and even if it has no explanatory or predictive value in itself. Instead, as a descriptive (rather than as an explanatory or predictive) concept, the term *information* helps to define (either in conjunction with the notion of "specificity" or by subsuming it) the effect that origin-of-life researchers must explain "the origin of." Thus, *only* where information connotes subjective meaning does it function as a metaphor in biology. Where it refers to an analog of meaning, namely, functional specificity, it defines an essential feature of living systems.

II.

A. Naturalistic Explanations for the Origin of Specified Biological Information

The discoveries of molecular biologists during the 1950s and 1960s raised the question of the ultimate origin of the specified complexity or specified information in both DNA and proteins. Since at least the mid-1960s, many scientists have regarded the origin of information (so defined) as the central question facing origin-of-life biology.[49] Accordingly, origin-of-life researchers have proposed three broad types of naturalistic explanation to explain the origin of specified genetic information: those emphasizing chance, necessity, or the combination of the two.

B. Beyond the Reach of Chance

Perhaps the most common popular naturalistic view about the origin of life is that it happened exclusively by chance. A few serious scientists have also voiced support for this view, at least, at various points in their careers. In

1954, biochemist George Wald, for example, argued for the causal efficacy
of chance in conjunction with vast expanses of time. As he explained,
"Time is in fact the hero of the plot. . . . Given so much time, the impossible becomes possible, the possible probable, and the probable virtually certain."[50] Later, in 1968, Francis Crick would suggest that the origin of the
genetic code—that is, the translation system—might be a "frozen accident."[51] Other theories have invoked chance as an explanation for the origin of genetic information, though often in conjunction with prebiotic
natural selection (see part C below).

Almost all serious origin-of-life researchers now consider "chance" an
inadequate causal explanation for the origin of biological information.[52]
Since molecular biologists began to appreciate the sequence specificity of
proteins and nucleic acids in the 1950s and 1960s, many calculations have
been made to determine the probability of formulating functional proteins
and nucleic acids at random. Various methods of calculating probabilities
have been offered by Morowitz, Hoyle and Wickramasinghe, Cairns-Smith,
Prigogine, Yockey, and, more recently, Robert Sauer.[53] For the sake of argument, these calculations have often assumed extremely favorable prebiotic conditions (whether realistic or not), much more time than was
actually available on the early earth, and theoretically maximal reaction
rates among constituent monomers (that is, the constituent parts of proteins, DNA, or RNA). Such calculations have invariably shown that the
probability of obtaining functionally sequenced biomacromolecules at random is, in Prigogine's words, "vanishingly small . . . even on the scale of
. . . billions of years."[54] As Cairns-Smith wrote in 1971: "Blind chance . . .
is very limited. Low-levels of cooperation he [blind chance] can produce
exceedingly easily (the equivalent of letters and small words), but he becomes very quickly incompetent as the amount of organization increases.
Very soon indeed long waiting periods and massive material resources become irrelevant."[55]

Consider the probabilistic hurdles that must be overcome to construct
even one short protein molecule of 100 amino acids in length. (A typical
protein consists of about 300 amino acid residues, and many crucial proteins are much longer.)

First, all amino acids must form a chemical bond known as a peptide
bond when joining with other amino acids in the protein chain. Yet in nature many other types of chemical bonds are possible between amino acids;
in fact, peptide and nonpeptide bonds occur with roughly equal probability.
Thus, at any given site along a growing amino acid chain, the probability of

having a peptide bond is roughly ½. The probability of attaining four peptide bonds is (½ × ½ × ½ × ½) = ¹⁄₁₆, or $(½)^4$. The probability of building a chain of 100 amino acids in which all linkages involve peptide linkages is $(½)^{99}$, or roughly 1 chance in 10^{30}.

Second, in nature, every amino acid found in proteins (with one exception) has a distinct mirror image of itself, one left-handed version, or L-form, and one right-handed version, or D-form. These mirror-image forms are called optical isomers. Functioning proteins tolerate only left-handed amino acids, yet the right-handed and left-handed isomers are produced in (amino acid–producing) chemical reactions with roughly equal frequency. Taking this "chirality" into consideration compounds the improbability of attaining a biologically functioning protein. The probability of attaining at random only L-amino acids in a hypothetical peptide chain 100 amino acids long is $(½)^{100}$ or again roughly 1 chance in 10^{30}. Starting from mixtures of DL- forms, the probability of building a 100-amino-acid-length chain at random in which all bonds are peptide bonds and all amino acids are L-form is, therefore, roughly 1 chance in 10^{60}.

Functioning proteins have a third independent requirement, the most important of all; their amino acids must link up in a specific sequential arrangement just as the letters in a meaningful sentence must. In some cases, changing even one amino acid at a given site results in loss of protein function. Moreover, because there are twenty biologically occurring amino acids, the probability of getting a specific amino acid at a given site is small—¹⁄₂₀. (Actually the probability is even lower because in nature there are also many nonprotein-forming amino acids.) On the assumption that all sites in a protein chain require one particular amino acid, the probability of attaining a particular protein 100 amino acids long would be $(¹⁄₂₀)^{100}$, or roughly 1 chance in 10^{130}. We know now, however, that some sites along the chain do tolerate several of the twenty amino acids commonly found in proteins, though others do not. Biochemist Robert Sauer of MIT has used a technique known as "cassette mutagenesis" to determine how much variance among amino acids can be tolerated at any given site in several proteins. His results imply that, even taking the possibility of variance into account, the probability of achieving a functional sequence of amino acids in several known (roughly 100 residue) proteins at random is still "vanishingly small," about 1 chance in 10^{65}.[56] (There are 10^{65} atoms in our galaxy).[57] Recently, Douglas Axe of Cambridge University has used a refined mutagenesis technique to measure the sequence specificity of the protein barnase, a bacterial RNase. Axe's work suggests that previous mutagenesis experiments actually underestimated the functional sensitiv-ity of proteins to amino acid sequence change because they presupposed (incorrectly) the context independence of individual residue changes.[58] If, in addition to the improbability of attaining a proper sequence, one consid-ers the need for proper bonding and homochirality, the probability of con-structing a rather short functional protein at random becomes so small (no more than 1 chance in 10^{125}) as to appear absurd on the chance hypothe-sis. As Dawkins has said, "We can accept a certain amount of luck in our explanations, but not too much."[59]

Of course, Dawkins's assertion begs a quantitative question, namely, "How improbable does an event, sequence, or system have to be before the chance hypothesis can be reasonably eliminated?" That question has re-cently received a formal answer. William Dembski, following and refining the work of earlier probabilists such as Emile Borel, has shown that chance can be eliminated as a plausible explanation for specified systems of small probability whenever the complexity of a specified event or sequence ex-ceeds available probabilistic resources.[60] He then calculates a conservative estimate for the "universal probability bound" of 1 in 10^{150} corresponding to the probabilistic resources of the known universe. This number provides a theoretical basis for excluding appeals to chance as the best explanation for specified events of probability less than $\frac{1}{2} \times 10^{150}$. Dembski thus an-swers the question of how much luck is—for any case—too much to in-voke in an explanation.

Significantly, the improbability of assembling and sequencing even a short functional protein approaches this universal probability bound—the point at which appeals to chance become absurd given the "probabilistic resources" of the entire universe.[61] Further, making the same kind of cal-culation for even moderately longer proteins pushes these measures of im-probability well beyond the limit. For example, the probability of generating a protein of only 150 amino acids in length (using the same method as above) is less than 1 chance in 10^{180}, well beyond the most con-servative estimates of the probability bound, given our multibillion year old universe.[62] Thus, given the complexity of proteins, it is extremely un-likely that a random search through the space of combinatorially possible amino acid sequences could generate even a single relatively short func-tional protein in the time available since the beginning of the universe (let alone the time available on the early earth). Conversely, to have a reason-able chance of finding a short functional protein in a random search of combinatorial space would require vastly more time than either cosmology or geology allows.

More realistic calculations (taking into account the probable presence of nonproteineous amino acids, the need for much longer proteins to perform specific functions such as polymerization, and the need for hundreds of proteins working in coordination to produce a functioning cell) only compound these improbabilities, almost beyond computability. For example, recent theoretical and experimental work on the so-called minimal complexity required to sustain the simplest possible living organism suggests a lower bound of some 250 to 400 genes and their corresponding proteins.[63] The nucleotide sequence-space corresponding to such a system of proteins exceeds $4^{300,000}$. The improbability corresponding to this measure of molecular complexity again vastly exceeds 1 chance in 10^{150} and thus the "probabilistic resources" of the entire universe.[64] When one considers the full complement of functional biomolecules required to maintain minimal cell function and vitality, one can see why chance-based theories of the origin of life have been abandoned. What Mora said in 1963 still holds: "Statistical considerations, probability, complexity, etc., followed to their logical implications suggest that the origin and continuance of life is not controlled by such principles. An admission of this is the use of a period of practically infinite time to obtain the derived result. Using such logic, however, we can prove anything."[65]

Though the probability of assembling a functioning biomolecule or cell by chance alone is exceedingly small, it is important to emphasize that scientists have not generally rejected the chance hypothesis merely because of the vast improbabilities associated with such events. Very improbable things do occur by chance. Any hand of cards or any series of rolled dice will represent a highly improbable occurrence. Observers often justifiably attribute such events to chance alone. What justifies the elimination of chance is not just the occurrence of a highly improbable event but also the occurrence of an improbable event that also conforms to a discernible pattern (that is, to a conditionally independent pattern; see part I, section E). If someone repeatedly rolls two dice and turns up a sequence such as 9, 4, 11, 2, 6, 8, 5, 12, 9, 2, 6, 8, 9, 3, 7, 10, 11, 4, 8, and 4, no one will suspect anything but the interplay of random forces, though this sequence does represent a very improbable event given the number of combinatorial possibilities that correspond to a sequence of this length. Yet rolling 20 (or certainly 200) consecutive sevens will justifiably arouse suspicion that something more than chance is in play. Statisticians have long used a method for determining when to eliminate the chance hypothesis; the method requires prespecifying a pattern or "rejection region."[66] In the dice example above, one could prespecify the repeated occurrence of seven as such a pattern in order to detect the use of loaded dice, for example. Dembski has generalized this method to show how the presence of any conditionally independent pattern, whether temporally prior to the observation of an event or not, can help (in conjunction with a small probability event) to justify rejecting the chance hypothesis.[67]

Origin-of-life researchers have tacitly, and sometimes explicitly, employed this kind of statistical reasoning to justify the elimination of scenarios relying heavily on chance. Christian de Duve, for example, has made the logic explicit in order to explain why chance fails as an explanation for the origin of life: "A single, freak, highly improbable event can conceivably happen. Many highly improbable events—drawing a winning lottery number or the distribution of playing cards in a hand of bridge—happen all the time. But a string of improbable events—drawing the same lottery number twice, or the same bridge hand twice in a row—does not happen naturally."[68]

De Duve and other origin-of-life researchers have long recognized that the cell represents not only a highly improbable but also a functionally specified system. For this reason, by the mid-1960s most researchers had eliminated chance as a plausible explanation for the origin of the specified information necessary to build a cell.[69] Many have instead sought other types of naturalistic explanations.

C. Prebiotic Natural Selection:
A Contradiction in Terms

Of course, even many early theories of chemical evolution did not rely *exclusively* on chance as a causal mechanism. For example, Oparin's original theory of evolutionary abiogenesis first published in the 1920s and 1930s invoked prebiotic natural selection as a complement to chance interactions. Oparin's theory envisioned a series of chemical reactions that he thought would enable a complex cell to assemble itself gradually and naturalistically from simple chemical precursors.

For the first stage of chemical evolution, Oparin proposed that simple gases such as ammonia (NH_3), methane (CH_4), water vapor (H_2O), carbon dioxide (CO_2), and hydrogen (H_2) would have existed in contact with the early oceans and with metallic compounds extruded from the core of the earth.[70] With the aid of ultraviolet radiation from the sun, the ensuing reactions would have produced energy-rich hydrocarbon compounds. They in turn would have combined and recombined with various other compounds to make amino acids, sugars, and other "building blocks" of complex molecules such as proteins necessary to living cells. These constituents would eventually arrange themselves by chance into primitive metabolic systems within simple cell-like enclosures that Oparin called coacervates. Oparin then proposed a kind of Darwinian competition for survival among his coacervates. Those that, by chance, developed increasingly complex molecules and metabolic processes would have survived to grow more complex and efficient. Those that did not would have dissolved.[71] Thus, Oparin invoked differential survival or natural selection as a mechanism for preserving complexity-increasing events, thus allegedly helping to overcome the difficulties attendant to pure-chance hypotheses.

Developments in molecular biology during the 1950s cast doubt on Oparin's scenario. Oparin originally invoked natural selection to explain how cells refined primitive metabolism once it had arisen. His scenario relied heavily on chance to explain the initial formation of the constituent biomacromolecules on which even primitive cellular metabolism would depend. Discovery during the 1950s of the extreme complexity and specificity of such molecules undermined the plausibility of his claim. For that and other reasons, Oparin published a revised version of his theory in 1968 that envisioned a role for natural selection earlier in the process of abiogenesis. His new theory claimed that natural selection acted on random polymers as they formed and changed within his coacervate protocells.[72] As more complex and efficient molecules accumulated, they would have survived and reproduced more prolifically.

Even so, Oparin's concept of *prebiotic* natural selection acting on initially unspecified biomacromolecules remained problematic. For one thing, it seemed to presuppose a preexisting mechanism of self-replication. Yet self-replication in all extant cells depends on functional and, therefore, (to a high degree) sequence-specific proteins and nucleic acids. Yet the origin of specificity in these molecules is precisely what Oparin needed to explain. As Christian de Duve has stated, theories of prebiotic natural selection "need information which implies they have to presuppose what is to be explained in the first place."[73] Oparin attempted to circumvent the problem by claiming that the first polymers need not have been highly sequence-specific. But that claim raised doubts about whether an accurate mechanism of self-replication (and thus natural selection) could have functioned at all. Oparin's latter scenario did not reckon on a phenomenon known as error catastrophe, in which small errors, or deviations from functionally necessary sequences, are quickly amplified in successive replications.[74]

Thus, the need to explain the origin of specified information created an intractable dilemma for Oparin. On the one hand, if he invoked natural selection late in his scenario, he would need to rely on chance alone to produce the highly complex and specified biomolecules necessary to self-replication. On the other hand, if Oparin invoked natural selection earlier in the process of chemical evolution, before functional specificity in biomacromolecules would have arisen, he could give no account of how such prebiotic natural selection could even function (given the phenomenon of error-catastrophe). Natural selection presupposes a self-replication system, but self-replication requires functioning nucleic acids and proteins (or molecules approaching their complexity)—the very entities that Oparin needed to explain. Thus, Dobzhansky would insist that, "prebiological natural selection is a contradiction in terms."[75]

Although some rejected the hypothesis of prebiotic natural selection as question-begging, others dismissed it as indistinguishable from implausible chance-based hypotheses.[76] The work of mathematician John von Neumann supported that judgment. During the 1960s, von Neumann showed that any system capable of self-replication would require subsystems that were functionally equivalent to the information storage, replicating, and processing systems found in extant cells.[77] His calculations established a very high minimal threshold of biological function, as would later experimental work.[78] These minimal-complexity requirements pose a fundamental difficulty for natural selection. Natural selection selects for functional advantage. It can play no role, therefore, until random variations produce some biologically advantageous arrangement of matter. Yet von Neumann's calculations and similar ones by Wigner, Landsberg, and Morowitz showed that in all probability (to understate the case) random fluctuations of molecules would not produce the minimal complexity needed for even a primitive replication system.[79] As noted above, the improbability of developing a functionally integrated replication system vastly exceeds the improbability of developing the protein or DNA components of such a system. Given the huge improbability and the high functional threshold it implies, many origin-of-life researchers came to regard prebiotic natural selection as both inadequate and essentially indistinguishable from appeals to chance.

Nevertheless, during the 1980s, Richard Dawkins and Bernd-Olaf Kuppers attempted to resuscitate prebiotic natural selection as an explanation for the origin of biological information.[80] Both accept the futility of naked appeals to chance and invoke what Kuppers calls a "Darwinian optimization principle." Both use computers to demonstrate the efficacy of prebiotic natural selection. Each selects a target sequence to represent a desired functional polymer. After creating a crop of randomly constructed sequences and generating variations among them at random, their computers select those sequences that match the target sequence most closely. The computers then amplify the production of those sequences, eliminate the others (to simulate differential reproduction), and repeat the process. As Kuppers puts it, "Every mutant sequence that agrees one bit better with the meaningful or reference sequence . . . will be allowed to reproduce more rapidly."[81] In his case, after a mere thirty-five generations, his computer succeeded in spelling his target sequence, "NATURAL SELECTION."

Despite superficially impressive results, such "simulations" conceal an obvious flaw: Molecules in situ do not have a target sequence "in mind." Nor will they confer any selective advantage on a cell, and thus differentially reproduce, until they combine in a functionally advantageous arrangement. Thus, nothing in nature corresponds to the role that the computer plays in selecting functionally nonadvantageous sequences that happen to agree "one bit better" than others with a target sequence. The sequence NORMAL ELECTION may agree more with NATURAL SELECTION than does the sequence MISTRESS DEFECTION, but neither of the two yields any advantage in communication over the other in trying to communicate something about NATURAL SELECTION. If that is the goal, both are equally ineffectual. Even more to the point, a completely nonfunctional polypeptide would confer no selective advantage on a hypothetical protocell, even if its sequence happened to agree "one bit better" with an unrealized target protein than some other nonfunctional polypeptide.

Both Kuppers's and Dawkins's published results of their simulations show the early generations of variant phrases awash in nonfunctional gibberish.[82] In Dawkins's simulation, not a single functional English word appears until after the tenth iteration (unlike the more generous example above that starts with actual, albeit incorrect, words). Yet to make distinctions on the basis of function among sequences that have no function is entirely unrealistic. Such determinations can be made only if considerations of *proximity to possible future function* are allowed, but that requires foresight, which natural selection does not have. A computer, programmed by a human being, can perform such functions. To imply that molecules can do so as well illicitly personifies nature. Thus, if these computer simulations demonstrate anything, they subtly demonstrate the need for intelligent agents to elect some options and exclude others—that is, to create information.

D. Self-Organizational Scenarios

Because of the difficulties with chance-based theories, including those relying on prebiotic natural selection, most origin-of-life theorists after the mid-1960s attempted to address the problem of the origin of biological information in a completely different way. Researchers began to look for self-organizational laws and properties of chemical attraction that might explain the origin of the specified information in DNA and proteins. Rather than invoking chance, such theories invoked necessity. If neither chance nor prebiotic natural selection acting on chance explains the origin of specified biological information, then those committed to finding a naturalistic explanation for the origin of life must necessarily rely on physical or chemical necessity. Given a limited number of broad explanatory categories, the inadequacy of chance (with or without prebiotic natural selection) has, in the minds of many researchers, left only one option. Christian de Duve articulates the logic: "a string of improbable events—drawing the same lottery number twice, or the same bridge hand twice in a row—does not happen naturally. All of which lead me to conclude that life is an obligatory manifestation of matter, bound to arise where conditions are appropriate."[83]

When origin-of-life biologists began considering the self-organizational perspective that de Duve describes, several researchers proposed that deterministic forces (stereochemical "necessity") made the origin of life not just probable but inevitable. Some suggested that simple chemicals possessed "self-ordering properties" capable of organizing the constituent parts of proteins, DNA, and RNA into the specific arrangements they now possess.[84] Steinman and Cole, for example, suggested that differential bonding affinities or forces of chemical attraction between certain amino acids might account for the origin of the sequence specificity of proteins.[85] Just as electrostatic forces draw sodium (Na+) and chloride (Cl-) ions together into highly ordered patterns within a crystal of salt (NaCl), so, too, might amino acids with special affinities for each other arrange themselves to form proteins. In 1969, Kenyon and Steinman developed that idea in a book entitled *Biochemical Predestination*. They argued that life might have been "biochemically predestined" by the properties of attraction existing between its constituent chemical parts, particularly among the amino acids in proteins.[86]

In 1977, another self-organizational theory was proposed by Prigogine and Nicolis based on a thermodynamic characterization of living organisms. In *Self Organization in Nonequilibrium Systems,* Prigogine and Nicolis classified living organisms as open, nonequilibrium systems capable of "dissipating" large quantities of energy and matter into the environment.[87] They observed that open systems driven far from equilibrium often display self-ordering tendencies. For example, gravitational energy will produce highly ordered vortices in a draining bathtub; thermal energy flowing through a heat sink will generate distinctive convection currents or "spiral wave activity." Prigogine and Nicolis argued that the organized structures observed in living systems might have similarly "self-originated" with the aid of an energy source. In essence, they conceded the improbability of simple building blocks arranging themselves into highly ordered structures under normal equilibrium conditions. But they suggested that, under nonequilibrium conditions, where an external source of energy is supplied, biochemical building blocks might arrange themselves into highly ordered patterns.

More recently, Kauffman and de Duve have proposed self-organizational theories with somewhat less specificity, at least with regard to the problem of the origin of specified genetic information.[88] Kauffman invokes so-called autocatalytic properties to generate metabolism directly from simple molecules. He envisions such autocatalysis occurring once very particular configurations of molecules have arisen in a rich "chemical minestrone." De Duve also envisions protometabolism emerging first with genetic information arising later as a byproduct of simple metabolic activity.

E. Order versus Information

For many current origin-of-life scientists, self-organizational models now seem to offer the most promising approach to explaining the origin of specified biological information. Nevertheless, critics have called into question both the plausibility and the relevance of self-organizational models. Ironically, a prominent early advocate of self-organization, Dean Kenyon, has now explicitly repudiated such theories as both incompatible with empirical findings and theoretically incoherent.[89]

First, empirical studies have shown that some differential affinities do exist between various amino acids (that is, certain amino acids do form linkages more readily with some amino acids than with others).[90] Nevertheless,

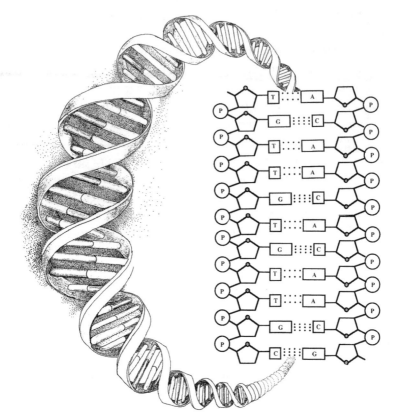

FIGURE 2. The bonding relationship between the chemical constituents of the DNA molecule. Sugars (designated by the pentagons) and phosphates (designated by the circled Ps) are linked chemically. Nucleotide bases (A's, T's, G's and C's) are bonded to the sugar-phosphate backbones. Nucleotide bases are linked by hydrogen bonds (designated by dotted double or triple lines) across the double helix. But no chemical bonds exist between the nucleotide bases along the message-bearing spine of the helix. Courtesy of Fred Heeren, Day Star publications.

such differences do not correlate to actual sequences in large classes of known proteins.[91] In short, differing chemical affinities do not explain the multiplicity of amino acid sequences existing in naturally occurring proteins or the sequential arrangement of amino acids in any particular protein.

In the case of DNA, this point can be made more dramatically. Figure 2 shows that the structure of DNA depends on several chemical bonds. There are bonds, for example, between the sugar and the phosphate molecules forming the two twisting backbones of the DNA molecule. There are bonds fixing individual (nucleotide) bases to the sugar-phosphate backbones on each side of the molecule. There are also hydrogen bonds stretching horizontally across the molecule between nucleotide bases, making so-called complementary pairs. The individually weak hydrogen bonds, which in concert hold two complementary copies of the DNA message text together, make replication of the genetic instructions possible. It is important to note, however, that there are *no* chemical bonds between the bases along the longitudinal axis in the center of the helix. Yet it is precisely along this axis of the DNA molecule that the genetic information is stored.

Further, just as magnetic letters can be combined and recombined in any way to form various sequences on a metal surface, so, too, can each of the four bases—A, T, G, and C—attach to any site on the DNA backbone with equal facility, making all sequences equally probable (or improbable). Indeed, there are no significant differential affinities between any of the four bases and the binding sites along the sugar-phosphate backbone. The same type of N-glycosidic bond occurs between the base and the backbone regardless of which base attaches. All four bases are acceptable; none is chemically favored. As Kuppers has noted, "The properties of nucleic acids indicate that all the combinatorially possible nucleotide patterns of a DNA are, from a chemical point of view, equivalent."[92] Thus, "self-organizing" bonding affinities cannot explain the sequentially specific arrangement of nucleotide bases in DNA because (1) there are *no* bonds between bases along the information-bearing axis of the molecule, and (2) there are no *differential* affinities between the backbone and the specific bases that could account for variations in sequence. Because the same holds for RNA molecules, researchers who speculate that life began in an RNA world have also failed to solve the sequence specificity problem—that is, the problem of explaining how information in functioning RNA molecules could have arisen in the first place.

For those who want to explain the origin of life as the result of self-organizing properties intrinsic to the material constituents of living systems, these rather elementary facts of molecular biology have decisive implications. The most obvious place to look for self-organizing properties to explain the origin of genetic information is in the constituent parts of the molecules that carry that information. But biochemistry and molecular biology make clear that forces of attraction between the constituents in DNA, RNA, and proteins do not explain the sequence specificity of these large, information-bearing biomolecules.

The properties of the monomers constituting nucleic acids and proteins simply do not make a particular gene, let alone life as we know it, inevitable. (We know this, in addition to the reasons already stated, because of the many variant polypeptides and gene sequences that exist in nature and that have been synthesized in the laboratory.) Yet if self-organizational scenarios for the origin of biological information are to have any theoretical import, they must claim just the opposite. And that claim is often made, albeit without much specificity. As de Duve has put it, "the processes that generated life" were "highly deterministic," making life as we know it "inevitable" given "the conditions that existed on the prebiotic earth."[93] Yet imagine the most favorable prebiotic conditions. Imagine a pool of all four DNA bases and all necessary sugars and phosphates; would any particular genetic sequence inevitably arise? Given all necessary monomers, would any particular functional protein or gene, let alone a specific genetic code, replication system, or signal transduction circuitry, inevitably arise? Clearly not.

In the parlance of origin-of-life research, monomers are "building blocks," and building blocks can be arranged and rearranged in innumerable ways. The properties of stone blocks do not determine their own arrangement in the construction of buildings. Similarly, the properties of *biological* building blocks do not determine the arrangement of functional polymers. Instead, the chemical properties of the monomers allow a vast ensemble of possible configurations, the overwhelming majority of which have no biological function whatsoever. Functional genes or proteins are no more inevitable, given the properties of their "building blocks," than, for example, the Palace of Versailles was inevitable, given the properties of the stone blocks that were used to construct it. To anthropomorphize, neither bricks and stone, nor letters in a written text, nor nucleotide bases "care" how they are arranged. In each case, the properties of the constituents remain largely indifferent to the many specific configurations or sequences they may adopt, nor do they make any specific structures "inevitable" as self-organizationalists must claim.

Significantly, information theory makes clear that there is a good reason for this. If chemical affinities between the constituents in the DNA determined the arrangement of the bases, such affinities would dramatically diminish the capacity of DNA to carry information. Recall that classical information theory equates the reduction of uncertainty with the transmission of information, whether specified or unspecified. The transmission of information, therefore, requires physical-chemical contingency. As Robert

Stalnaker has noted, "[information] content requires contingency."[94] If, therefore, forces of chemical necessity completely determine the arrangement of constituents in a system, that arrangement will not exhibit complexity or convey information.

Consider, for example, what would happen if the individual nucleotide bases (A, C, G, and T) in the DNA molecule *did* interact by *chemical* necessity (along the information-bearing axis of DNA). Suppose that every time adenine (A) occurred in a growing genetic sequence, it attracted cytosine (C) to it.[95] Suppose every time guanine (G) appeared, thymine (T) followed. If this were the case, the longitudinal axis of DNA would be peppered with repetitive sequences in which A followed C and T followed by G. Rather than a genetic molecule capable of virtually unlimited novelty and characterized by unpredictable and aperiodic sequences, DNA would contain sequences awash in repetition or redundancy—much like the arrangement of atoms in crystals. In a crystal, the forces of mutual chemical attraction do determine, to a very considerable extent, the sequential arrangement of its constituent parts. Hence, sequencing in crystals is highly ordered and repetitive but neither complex nor informative. In DNA, however, where any nucleotide can follow any other, a vast array of novel sequences is possible, corresponding to a multiplicity of possible amino acid sequences and protein functions.

The forces of chemical necessity produce redundancy (roughly, law- or rule-generated repetition) or monotonous order but reduce the capacity to convey information and express novelty. Thus, as chemist Michael Polanyi noted:

> Suppose that the actual structure of a DNA molecule were due to the fact that the bindings of its bases were much stronger than the bindings would be for any other distribution of bases, then such a DNA molecule would have no information content. Its code-like character would be effaced by an overwhelming redundancy. . . . Whatever may be the origin of a DNA configuration, it can function as a code only if its order is not due to the forces of potential energy. It *must be* as physically indeterminate as the sequence of words is on a printed page [emphasis added].[96]

In other words, if chemists had found that bonding affinities between the nucleotides in DNA produced nucleotide sequencing, they also would have found that they had been mistaken about DNA's information-bearing properties. Or, to put the point quantitatively, to the extent that forces of attraction between constituents in a sequence determine the arrangement of the sequence, to that extent will the information-carrying capacity of the system be diminished or effaced by redundancy.[97] As Dretske has explained: "As p(si) [the probability of a condition or state of affairs] approaches 1, the amount of information associated with the occurrence of si goes to 0. In the limiting case when the probability of a condition or state of affairs is unity [p(si) = 1], no information is associated with, or generated by, the occurrence of si. This is merely another way to say that no information is generated by the occurrence of events for which there are no possible alternatives."[98]

Bonding affinities, to the extent they exist, inhibit the maximization of information because they determine that specific outcomes will follow specific conditions with high probability.[99] Yet information-carrying capacity is maximized when just the opposite situation obtains, namely, when antecedent conditions allow many improbable outcomes.

Of course, as noted in part I, section D, the base sequences in DNA do more than possess information-carrying capacity (or syntactic information) as measured by classical Shannon information theory. These sequences store functionally specified information—that is, they are specified as well as complex. Clearly, however, a sequence cannot be both specified and complex if it is not at least complex. Therefore, self-organizational forces of chemical necessity, which produce redundant order and *preclude* complexity, also preclude the generation of specified complexity (or specified information) as well. Chemical affinities do not generate complex sequences. Thus, they cannot be invoked to explain the origin of information, whether specified or otherwise.

A tendency to conflate the qualitative distinctions between "order" and "complexity" has characterized self-organizational scenarios—whether those that invoke internal properties of chemical attraction or an external organizing force or source of energy. That tendency calls into question the relevance of these scenarios of the origin of life. As Yockey has argued, the accumulation of structural or chemical order does not explain the origin of biological complexity or genetic information. He concedes that energy flowing through a system may produce highly ordered patterns. Strong winds form swirling tornados and the "eyes" of hurricanes; Prigogine's thermal baths do develop interesting convection currents; and chemical elements do coalesce to form crystals. Self-organizational theorists explain well what does not need explaining. What needs explaining in biology is not the origin of order (defined as symmetry or repetition) but the specified information—the highly complex, aperiodic, and specified sequences that make biological function possible. As Yockey warns: "Attempts to relate the idea of order . . . with biological organization or specificity must be regarded as a play on words that cannot stand careful scrutiny. Informational macromolecules can code genetic messages and therefore can carry information because the sequence of bases or residues is affected very little, if at all, by [self-organizing] physicochemical factors."[100]

In the face of these difficulties, some self-organizational theorists have claimed that we must await the discovery of new natural laws to explain the origin of biological information. As Manfred Eigen has argued, "our task is to find an algorithm, a natural law, that leads to the origin of information."[101] Such a suggestion betrays confusion on two counts. First, scientific laws don't generally produce or cause natural phenomena, they describe them. For example, Newton's law of gravitation described, but did not cause or explain, the attraction between planetary bodies. Second, laws necessarily describe highly deterministic or predictable relationships between antecedent conditions and consequent events. Laws describe highly repetitive patterns in which the probability of each successive event (given the previous event) approaches unity. Yet information sequences are complex, not repetitive—information mounts as *improbabilities* multiply. Thus, to say that scientific laws can produce information is essentially a contradiction in terms. Instead, scientific laws describe (almost by definition) highly predictable and regular phenomena—that is, redundant order, not complexity (whether specified or otherwise).

Though the patterns that natural laws describe display a high degree of regularity, and thus lack the complexity that characterizes information-rich systems, one could argue that we might someday discover a very particular configuration of *initial conditions* that routinely generates high informational states. Thus, while we cannot hope to find a law that describes an information-rich *relationship* between antecedent and consequent variables, we might find a law that describes how a very particular set of initial conditions routinely generates a high information state. Yet even the statement of this hypothetical seems itself to beg the question of the ultimate origin of information, since "a very particular set of initial conditions" sounds precisely like an information-rich—a highly complex and specified—state. In any case, everything we know experientially suggests that the amount of specified information present in a set of antecedent conditions necessarily equals or exceeds that of any system produced from those conditions.

F. Other Scenarios and the Displacement of the Information Problem

In addition to the general categories of explanation already examined, origin-of-life researchers have proposed many more specific scenarios, each emphasizing random variations (chance), self-organizational laws (necessity), or both. Some of those scenarios purport to address the information problem; others attempt to bypass it altogether. Yet on closer examination, even scenarios that appear to alleviate the problem of the origin of specified biological information merely shift the problem elsewhere. Genetic algorithms can "solve" the information problem, but only if programmers provide informative target sequences and selection criteria. Simulation experiments can produce biologically relevant precursors and sequences, but only if experimentalists manipulate initial conditions or select and guide outcomes—that is, only if they add information themselves. Origin-of-life theories can leapfrog the problem altogether, but only by presupposing the presence of information in some other preexisting form.

Any number of theoretical models for the origin of life have fallen prey to this difficulty. For example, in 1964, Henry Quastler, an early pioneer in the application of information theory to molecular biology, proposed a DNA-first model for the origin of life. He envisioned the initial emergence of a system of unspecified polynucleotides capable of primitive self-replication via the mechanisms of complementary base-pairing. The polymers in his system would have, on Quastler's account, initially lacked specificity (which he equated with information).[102] Only later, when his system of polynucleotides had come into association with a fully functional set of proteins and ribosomes, would the specific nucleotide sequences in the polymers take on any functional significance. He likened that process to the random selection of a combination for a lock in which the combination would only later acquire functional significance once particular tumblers had been set to allow the combination to open the lock. In both the biological and the mechanical case, the surrounding context would confer functional specificity on an initially unspecified sequence. Thus, Quastler characterized the origin of information in polynucleotides as an "accidental choice remembered."

Although Quastler's way of conceiving of the origin of specified biological information did allow "a chain of nucleotides [to] become a [functional] system of genes without necessarily suffering any change in structure," it did have an overriding difficulty. It did not account for the origin of the complexity and specificity of the system of molecules whose association with the initial sequence gave the initial sequence functional significance. In Quastler's combination-lock example, conscious agents chose the tumbler settings that made the initial combination functionally significant. Yet Quastler expressly precluded conscious design as a possibility for explaining the origin of life.[103] Instead, he seemed to suggest that the origin of the biological context—that is, the complete set of functionally specific proteins (and the translation system) necessary to create a "symbiotic association" between polynucleotides and proteins—would arise by chance. He even offered some rough calculations to show that the origin of such a multimolecular context, though improbable, would have been probable enough to expect it to occur by chance in the prebiotic soup. Quastler's calculations now seem extremely implausible in light of the discussion of minimal complexity in part II, section B.[104] More significantly, Quastler "solved" the problem of the origin of complex specificity in nucleic acids only by transferring the problem to an equally complex and specified system of proteins and ribosomes. Whereas, admittedly, *any* polynucleotide sequence would suffice initially, the subsequent proteins and ribosomal material constituting the translation system would have to possess an extreme specificity *relative to the initial polynucleotide sequence* and relative to any protocellular functional requirements. Thus, Quastler's attempt to bypass the sequence specificity problem merely shifted it elsewhere.

Self-organizational models have encountered similar difficulties. For example, chemist J. C. Walton has argued (echoing earlier articles by Mora) that the self-organizational patterns produced in Prigogine-style convection currents do not exceed the organization or structural information represented by the experimental apparatus used to create the currents.[105] Similarly, Maynard-Smith, Dyson, and Shapiro have shown that Eigen's so-called hypercycle model for generating biological information actually shows how information tends to degrade over time.[106] Eigen's hypercycles presuppose a large initial contribution of information in the form of a long RNA molecule and some forty specific proteins and thus do not attempt to explain the ultimate origin of biological information. Moreover, because hypercycles lack an error-free mechanism of self-replication, the proposed mechanism succumbs to various "error-catastrophes" that ultimately diminish, not increase, the (specified) information content of the system over time.

Stuart Kauffman's self-organizational theory also subtly transfers the problem of the origin of information. In *The Origins of Order*, Kauffman attempts to leapfrog the sequence-specificity problem by proposing a means by which a self-reproducing and metabolic system might emerge directly from a set of "low specificity" catalytic peptides and RNA molecules in a prebiotic soup or "chemical minestrone." Kauffman envisions, as Iris Frey puts it, "a set of catalytic polymers in which no single molecule reproduces itself, but the system as a whole does."[107] Kauffman argues that once a sufficiently diverse set of catalytic molecules had assembled (in which the different peptides performed enough different catalytic functions) the ensemble of individual molecules would spontaneously undergo a kind of phase transition resulting in a self-reproducing metabolic system. Thus, Kauffman argues that metabolism can arise directly without genetic information encoded in DNA.[108]

Nevertheless, Kauffman's scenario does not solve, or bypass, the problem of the origin of biological information. Instead, it either presupposes the existence of unexplained sequence-specificity or it transfers such needed specificity out of view. Kauffman claims that an ensemble of relatively short and low specificity catalytic peptides and RNA molecules would suffice jointly to establish a metabolic system. He defends the biochemical plausibility of his scenario on the grounds that some proteins can perform enzymic functions with low specificity and complexity. He cites proteases such as trypsin that cleave peptide bonds at single amino acid sites and proteins in the clotting cascade that "cleave essentially single target polypeptides" to support his claim.[109]

Yet Kauffman's argument has two problems. First, it does not follow, nor is it the case biochemically, that just because *some* enzymes might function with low specificity, that *all* the catalytic peptides (or enzymes) needed to establish a self-reproducing metabolic cycle could function with similarly low levels of specificity and complexity. Instead, modern biochemistry shows that at least some, and probably many, of the molecules in a closed interdependent system of the type that Kauffman envisions would require high complexity and specificity proteins. Enzymatic catalysis (which his scenario would surely necessitate) invariably requires molecules long enough (at least 50-mers) to form tertiary structures (whether in polynucleotides or polypeptides). Further, these long polymers invariably require very specific three-dimensional geometries (which can in turn derive from sequence-specific arrangements of monomers) in order to catalyze necessary reactions. How do these molecules acquire their specificity of sequencing? Kauffman does not address this question because his illustration incorrectly suggests that he need not do so.

Secondly, it turns out that even the allegedly low specificity molecules that Kauffman cites to illustrate the plausibility of his scenario do not themselves manifest low complexity and specificity. Instead, Kauffman has confused the specificity and complexity of the parts of the polypeptides upon which the proteases act with the specificity and complexity of the proteins (the proteases) that do the enzymatic acting. Though trypsin, for example, acts upon (cleaves) peptide bonds at a relatively simple target (the carboxyl end of two separate amino acids, argenine, and lysine), trypsin itself is a highly complex and specifically-sequenced molecule. Indeed, trypsin is a non-repeating 200+ residue protein that possesses significant sequence-specificity as a condition of its function.[110] Further, it has to manifest significant three-dimensional (geometric) specificity to recognize the specific amino acids argenine and lysine—sites at which it cleaves peptide bonds. By equivocating in his discussion of specificity, Kauffman obscures from view the considerable specificity and complexity requirement of even the proteases he cites to justify his claim that low specificity catalytic peptides will suffice to establish a metabolic cycle. Thus, Kauffman's own illustration properly understood (that is, without equivocating about the relevant locus of specificity), shows that for his scenario to have biochemical plausibility it must *presuppose* the existence of many high complexity and specificity polypeptides and polynucleotides. Where does this information in these molecules come from? Kauffman, again, does not say.

Further, Kauffman must acknowledge (as he seems to in places),[111] that for autocatalysis (for which there is as yet no experimental evidence) to occur, the molecules in the "chemical minestrone" must be held in a very specific spatial-temporal relationship to one another. In other words, for the direct autocatalysis of integrated metabolic complexity to occur, a system of catalytic peptide molecules must first achieve a very specific molecular configuration, or a low configurational entropy state.[112] Yet this requirement is isomorphic with the requirement that the system must start with a highly specified complexity. Thus, to explain the origin of specified biological complexity at the systems level, Kauffman must presuppose the existence of highly specific and complex (i.e., information-rich) molecules as well as a highly specific arrangement of those molecules at the molecular level. Therefore, his work—if it has any relevance to the actual behavior of molecules—presupposes or transfers, rather than explains, the ultimate origin of specified complexity or information.

Others have claimed that the RNA-world scenario offers a promising approach to the origin-of-life problem and with it, presumably, the problem of the origin of the first genetic information. The RNA world was proposed as an explanation for the origin of the interdependence of nucleic acids and proteins in the cell's information-processing system. In extant cells, building proteins requires genetic information from DNA, but information on DNA cannot be processed without many specific proteins and protein complexes. This poses a chicken-or-egg problem. The discovery that RNA (a nucleic acid) possesses some limited catalytic properties similar to those of proteins suggested a way to solve that problem. "RNA-first" advocates proposed an early state in which RNA performed both the enzymatic functions of modern proteins and the information-storage function of modern DNA, thus allegedly making the interdependence of DNA and proteins unnecessary in the earliest living system.

Nevertheless, many fundamental difficulties with the RNA-world scenario have emerged. First, synthesizing (and/or maintaining) many essential building blocks of RNA molecules under realistic conditions has proven either difficult or impossible.[113] Further, the chemical conditions required for the synthesis of ribose sugars are decidedly incompatible with the conditions required for synthesizing nucleotide bases.[114] Yet both are necessary constituents of RNA. Second, naturally occurring RNA possesses very few of the specific enzymatic properties of proteins necessary to extant cells. Third, RNA-world advocates offer no plausible explanation for how primitive RNA replicators might have evolved into modern cells that do rely almost exclusively on proteins to process genetic information and regulate metabolism.[115] Fourth, attempts to enhance the limited catalytic properties of RNA molecules in so-called ribozyme engineering experiments have inevitably required extensive investigator manipulation, thus simulating, if anything, the need for intelligent design, not the efficacy of an undirected chemical evolutionary process.[116]

Most important for our present considerations, the RNA-world hypothesis presupposes, but does not explain, the origin of sequence specificity or information in the original functional RNA molecules. Indeed, the RNA-world scenario was proposed as an explanation for the functional interdependence problem, not the information problem. Even so, some RNA-world advocates seem to envision leapfrogging the sequence-specificity problem. They imagine oligomers of RNA arising by chance on the prebiotic earth and then later acquiring an ability to polymerize copies of themselves—that is, to self-replicate. In such a scenario, the capacity to self-replicate would favor the survival of those RNA molecules that could do so and would thus favor the specific sequences that the first self-replicating molecules happened to have. Thus, sequences that originally arose by chance would subsequently acquire a functional significance as "an accidental choice remembered."

Like Quastler's DNA-first model, however, this suggestion merely shifts the specificity problem out of view. First, for strands of RNA to perform enzymatic functions (including enzymatically mediated self-replication), they must, like proteins, have very specific arrangements of constituent building blocks (nucleotides in the RNA case). Further, the strands must be long enough to fold into complex three-dimensional shapes (to form so-called tertiary structures). Thus, any RNA molecule capable of enzymatic function must have the properties of complexity and specificity exhibited by DNA and proteins. Hence, such molecules must possess considerable (specified) information content. And yet explaining how the building blocks of RNA might have arranged themselves into functionally specified sequences has proven no easier than explaining how the constituent parts of DNA might have done so, especially given the high probability of destructive cross-reactions between desirable and undesirable molecules in any realistic prebiotic soup. As de Duve has noted in a critique of the RNA-world hypothesis, "hitching the components together in the right manner raises additional problems of such magnitude that no one has yet attempted to do so in a prebiotic context."[117]

Second, for a single-stranded RNA catalyst to self-replicate (the only function that could be selected in a prebiotic environment), it must find another catalytic RNA molecule in close vicinity to function as a template, since a single-stranded RNA cannot function as both enzyme and template. Thus, even if an originally unspecified RNA sequence might later acquire functional significance by chance, it could perform a function only if another RNA molecule—that is, one with a highly specific sequence relative to the original—arose in close vicinity to it. Thus, the attempt to bypass the need for specific sequencing in an original catalytic RNA only shifts the specificity problem elsewhere, namely, to a second and necessarily highly specific RNA sequence. Put differently, in addition to the specificity required to give the first RNA molecule self-replicating capability, a second RNA molecule with an extremely specific sequence—one with essentially the same sequence as the original—would also have to arise. Yet RNA-world theorists do not explain the origin of the requisite specificity in either the original molecule or its twin. Joyce and Orgel have calculated that to have a reasonable chance of finding two identical RNA molecules of a length sufficient to perform enzymatic functions would require an RNA library of some 10^{54} RNA molecules.[118] The mass of such a library vastly exceeds the mass of the earth, suggesting the extreme implausibility of the chance origin of a primitive replicator system. Yet one cannot invoke natural selection to explain the origin of such primitive replicators, since natural selection only ensues once self-replication has arisen. Further, RNA bases, like DNA bases, do not manifest self-organizational bonding affinities that could explain their specific sequencing. In short, the same kind of evidentiary and theoretical problems emerge whether one proposes that genetic information arose first in RNA or DNA molecules. The attempt to leapfrog the sequencing problem by starting with RNA replicators only shifts the problem to the specific sequences that would make such replication possible.

III.

A. The Return of the Design Hypothesis

If attempts to solve the information problem only relocate it, and if neither chance nor physical-chemical necessity, nor the two acting in combination, explains the ultimate origin of specified biological information, what does? Do we know of any entity that has the causal powers to create large amounts of specified information? We do. As Henry Quastler recognized, the "creation of new information is habitually associated with conscious activity."[119]

Experience affirms that specified complexity or information (defined hereafter as *specified* complexity) routinely arises from the activity of intelligent agents. A computer user who traces the information on a screen back to its source invariably comes to a *mind,* that of a software engineer or programmer. Similarly, the information in a book or newspaper column ultimately derives from a writer—from a mental, rather than a strictly material, cause.

Further, our experience-based knowledge of information-flow confirms that systems with large amounts of specified complexity or information (especially codes and languages) *invariably* originate from an intelligent source—that is, from a mind or a personal agent.[120] Moreover, this generalization holds not only for the semantically specified information present in natural languages but also for other forms of information or specified complexity whether present in machine codes, machines, or works of art.

Like the letters in a section of meaningful text, the parts in a working engine represent a highly improbable yet functionally specified configuration. Similarly, the highly improbable shapes in the rock on Mount Rushmore conform to an independently given pattern: the faces of American presidents known from books and paintings. Thus, both systems have a large amount of specified complexity or information so defined. Not coincidentally, they also originated by intelligent design, not by chance and/or physical-chemical necessity.

This generalization—that intelligence is the only known cause of specified complexity or information (at least, starting from a nonbiological source)—has received support from origin-of-life research itself. During the last forty years, every naturalistic model proposed has failed to explain the origin of the specified genetic information required to build a living cell.[121] Thus, mind or intelligence, or what philosophers call "agent causation," now stands as the only cause known to be capable of generating large amounts of information starting from a nonliving state.[122] As a result, the presence of specified information-rich sequences in even the simplest living systems would seem to imply intelligent design.[123]

Recently, a formal theoretical account of design reasoning has been developed that supports this conclusion. In *The Design Inference*, mathematician and probability theorist William Dembski notes that rational agents often infer or detect the prior activity of other minds by the character of the effects they leave behind. Archaeologists assume, for example, that rational agents produced the inscriptions on the Rosetta stone; insurance-fraud investigators detect certain "cheating patterns" that suggest intentional manipulation of circumstances rather than "natural" disasters; cryptographers distinguish between random signals and those that carry encoded messages. Dembski's work shows that recognizing the activity of intelligent agents constitutes a common and fully rational mode of inference.[124]

More important, Dembski identifies two criteria that typically enable human observers to recognize intelligent activity and to distinguish the effects of such activity from the effects of strictly material causes. He notes that we invariably attribute systems, sequences, or events that have the joint properties of "high complexity" (or low probability) and "specification" (see part I, section E) to intelligent causes—to design—not to chance or physical-chemical laws.[125] By contrast, he notes that we typically attribute to chance those low or intermediate probability events that do not conform to discernable patterns. We attribute to necessity highly probable events that repeatedly recur in a regular or lawlike way.

These inference patterns reflect our knowledge of the way the world works. Since experience teaches, for example, that complex and specified events or systems invariably arise from intelligent causes, we can infer intelligent design from events that exhibit the joint properties of complexity and specificity. Dembski's work suggests a comparative evaluation process for deciding between natural and intelligent causes based on the probabilistic features or "signatures" they leave behind.[126] This evaluation process constitutes, in effect, a scientific method for detecting the activity of intelligence in the echo of its effects.

A homespun example illustrates Dembski's method and criteria of design detection. When visitors first enter Victoria Harbor in Canada from the sea, they notice a hillside awash in red and yellow flowers. As they get closer, they reflexively, and correctly, infer design. Why? Observers quickly recognize a complex and specified pattern, an arrangement of flowers spelling "Welcome to Victoria." They infer the past activity of an intelligent cause—in this case, the careful planning of gardeners. Had the flowers been more haphazardly scattered so as to defy pattern-recognition, observers might have justifiably attributed the arrangement to chance—for example, to random gusts of wind scattering the seed. Had the colors been segregated by elevation, the pattern might have been explained by some natural necessity, such as certain types of plants requiring particular environments or soil types. But since the arrangement exhibits both complexity (the specific arrangement of flowers is highly improbable given the space of possible arrangements) and specificity (the pattern of flowers conforms to the independent requirements of English grammar and vocabulary), observers naturally infer intelligent design. As it turns out, these twin criteria are equivalent (or isomorphic, see part I, section E) with the notion of information as used in molecular biology. Thus, Dembski's theory, when applied to molecular biology, implies that intelligent design played a role in the origin of (specified) biological information.

The logical calculus underlying this inference follows a valid and well-established method used in all historical and forensic sciences. In historical sciences, knowledge of the present causal powers of various entities and processes enables scientists to make inferences about possible causes in the past. When a thorough study of various possible causes turns up only a single adequate cause for a given effect, historical or forensic scientists can make definitive inferences about the past.[127]

The Martian landscape, for example, displays erosional features—trenches and rills—that resemble those produced on Earth by moving water. Though Mars at present has no significant liquid water on its surface, some planetary scientists have nevertheless inferred that Mars did have a significant amount of water on its surface in the past. Why? Geologists and planetologists have not observed any cause other than moving water that can produce the kind of erosional features that we observe on Mars today. Since in our experience water alone produces erosional trenches and rills, the presence of these features on Mars allows planetologists to infer the past action of water on the surface of the red planet.

Or consider another example. Several years ago one of the forensic pathologists from the original Warren Commission that investigated the assassination of President Kennedy spoke out to quash rumors about a second gunman firing from in front of the motorcade. The bullet hole in the back of President Kennedy's skull apparently evidenced a distinctive beveling pattern that clearly indicated that it had entered his skull from the rear. The pathologist called the beveling pattern a "distinctive diagnostic" because the pattern indicated a single possible direction of entry. Since a rear entry was necessary to cause the beveling pattern in the back of the president's skull, the pattern allowed the forensic pathologists to diagnose the trajectory of the bullet.[128]

Logically, one can infer a cause from its effect (or an antecedent from a consequent) when the cause (or antecedent) is known to be necessary to produce the effect in question. If it's true that "where there's smoke there's fire," then the presence of smoke billowing over a hillside allows us to infer a fire beyond our view. Inferences based on knowledge of empirically necessary conditions or causes ("distinctive diagnostics") are common in historical and forensic sciences and often lead to the detection of intelligent as well as natural causes and events. Since criminal X's fingers are the only known cause of criminal X's fingerprints, X's prints on the murder weapon incriminate him with a high degree of certainty. Similarly, since intelligent design is the only known cause of large amounts of specified complexity or information, the presence of such information implies an intelligent source.

Indeed, since experience affirms mind or intelligent design as a necessary condition (and necessary cause) of information, one can detect (or retrodict) the past action of an intelligence from an information-rich effect—even if the cause itself cannot be directly observed.[129] Thus, the pattern of flowers spelling "Welcome to Victoria" allows visitors to infer the activity of intelligent agents even if they did not see the flowers planted or arranged. Similarly, the specified and complex arrangement of nucleotide sequences—the information—in DNA implies the past action of an intelligence, even if such mental activity cannot be directly observed.

Scientists in many fields recognize the connection between intelligence and information and make inferences accordingly. Archaeologists assume that a scribe produced the inscriptions on the Rosetta stone; evolutionary anthropologists establish the intelligence of early hominids from chipped flints that are too improbably specified in form (and function) to have been produced by natural causes; NASA's search for extraterrestrial intelligence (SETI) presupposes that any information embedded in electromagnetic signals coming from space would indicate an intelligent source.[130] As yet, however, radio-astronomers have not found any such information-bearing signals. But closer to home, molecular biologists have identified information-rich sequences and systems in the cell, suggesting, by the same logic, an intelligent cause for those effects.

B. Argument from Ignorance?
Or Inference to the Best Explanation?

Some would object that any such argument to design constitutes an argument from ignorance. Objectors charge that design advocates use our present ignorance of any sufficient natural cause of information as the sole basis for inferring an intelligent cause of the information present in the cell. Since we don't yet know how biological information could have arisen, we invoke the mysterious notion of intelligent design. On this view, intelligent design functions not as an explanation but as a placeholder for ignorance.

Although the inference to design from the presence of information in DNA does not qualify as a deductively certain proof of intelligent design (empirically based arguments in science rarely do), it does not constitute a fallacious argument from ignorance. Arguments from ignorance occur when evidence against a proposition X is offered as the sole (and conclusive) grounds for accepting some alternative proposition Y.

The inference to design as sketched above (see part III, section A) does not commit this fallacy. True, the previous section of this essay (see part II, sections A-F) argued that at present all types of natural causes and mechanisms fail to account for the origin of biological information from a prebiotic state. And clearly, this lack of knowledge of any adequate natural cause does provide part of the grounds for inferring design from information in the cell. (Though one could just as easily argue that even this "absence of knowledge" actually constitutes a knowledge of absence.) In any case, our "ignorance" of any sufficient natural cause is only part of the basis inferring design. We also *know* that intelligent agents can and do produce information-rich systems: we have positive experience-based knowledge of an alternative cause that is sufficient, namely, intelligence.

For this reason, the design inference defended here does not constitute an argument from ignorance but an inference to the best explanation.[131] Inferences to the best explanation do not assert the adequacy of one causal explanation merely on the basis of the inadequacy of some other causal explanation. Instead, they compare the explanatory power of many competing hypotheses to determine which hypothesis would, if true, provide the best explanation for some set of relevant data. Recent work on the method of "inference to the best explanation" suggests that determining which among a set of competing possible explanations constitutes the best depends on knowledge of the causal powers of competing explanatory entities.[132]

For example, both an earthquake and a bomb could explain the destruction of the building, but only a bomb could explain the presence of charring and shrapnel at the scene of the rubble. Earthquakes do not produce shrapnel, nor do they cause charring, at least not on their own. Thus, the bomb best explains the pattern of destruction at the building site. Entities, conditions, or processes that have the capability (or causal powers) to produce the evidence in question constitute better explanations of that evidence than those that do not.

It follows that the process of determining the best explanation often involves generating a list of possible hypotheses, comparing their known (or theoretically plausible) causal powers with respect to the relevant data, and then progressively eliminating potential but inadequate explanations, and finally, in the best case, electing the one remaining causally adequate explanation.

This essay has followed precisely this method to make a case for intelligent design as the best explanation for the origin of biological information. It has evaluated and compared the causal efficacy of four broad categories of explanation—chance, necessity, the combination of those two, and intelligent design—with respect to their ability to produce large amounts of specified complexity or information. As we have seen, neither scenarios based on chance nor those based on necessity (nor those that combine the two) can explain the origin of specified biological information in a prebiotic context. That result comports with our uniform human experience. Natural processes do not produce information-rich structures starting from purely physical or chemical antecedents. Nor does matter, whether acting at random or under the force of physical-chemical necessity, arrange itself into complex, information-rich sequences.

Nevertheless, it is not correct to say that we do not know how information arises. We know from experience that conscious intelligent agents can create informational sequences and systems. To quote Quastler again, the "creation of new information is habitually associated with conscious activity."[133] Further, experience teaches that whenever large amounts of specified complexity or information are present in an artifact or entity whose causal story is known, invariably creative intelligence—intelligent design—played a causal role in the origin of that entity. Thus, when we encounter such information in the biomacromolecules necessary to life, we may infer—based on our *knowledge* of established cause-effect relationships—that an intelligent cause operated in the past to produce the specified complexity or information necessary to the origin of life.

As formulated, this inference to design employs the same method of argumentation and reasoning that historical scientists use generally. Indeed, in the *Origin of Species,* Darwin himself developed his argument for universal common ancestry as an inference to the best explanation. As he explained in a letter to Asa Gray:

> I . . . test this hypothesis [common descent] by comparison with as many general and pretty well-established propositions as I can find—in geographical distribution, geological history, affinities &c., &c. And it seems to me that, *supposing* that such a hypothesis were *to explain* such general propositions, we ought, in accordance with the common way of following all sciences, to admit it till some *better* hypothesis be found out [emphasis added].[134]

Moreover, as formulated, the argument to design from the information in DNA also adheres to the standard uniformitarian canons of method employed within the historical sciences. The principle of uniformitarianism states that "the present is the key to the past." In particular, the principle specifies that our knowledge of present cause-effect relationships should govern our assessment of the plausibility of the inferences that we make about the remote causal past. Yet it is precisely such knowledge of cause-effect relationships that informs the inference to intelligent design. Since we know that intelligent agents do produce large amounts of information, and since all known natural processes do not (or cannot), we can infer design as the best explanation of the origin of information in the cell. Recent developments in the information sciences (such as Dembski's work in *The Design Inference*) help to define and formalize knowledge of such cause-effect relationships, allowing us to make inferences about the causal histories of various artifacts, entities, or events based on the complexity and information-theoretic signatures they exhibit.[135]

In any case, the inference to design depends on present *knowledge* of the demonstrated causal powers of natural entities and intelligent agency, respectively. It no more constitutes an argument from ignorance than any other well-grounded inference in geology, archaeology, or paleontology—where present knowledge of cause-effect relationships guides the inferences that scientists make about the causal past.

Objectors might still deny the legitimacy of inferring intelligent design (even as a best explanation) because we are ignorant of what future inquiry may uncover about the causal powers of other materialistic entities or processes. Some would characterize the design inference presented here as invalid or unscientific because it depends on a negative generalization—that is, "purely physical and chemical causes do not generate large amounts of specified information"—which future discoveries may later falsify. We should "never say never," they say.

Yet science often says "never," even if it can't say so for sure. Negative or proscriptive generalizations often play an important role in science. As many scientists and philosophers of science have pointed out, scientific laws often tell us not only what does happen but also what does not happen.[136] The conservation laws in thermodynamics, for example, proscribe certain outcomes. The first law tells us that energy is never created or destroyed. The second tells us that the entropy of a closed system will never decrease over time. Those who claim that such "proscriptive laws" do not constitute *knowledge,* because they are based on past but not future experience, will not get very far if they try to use their skepticism to justify funding for research on, say, perpetual motion machines.

Further, without proscriptive generalizations, without knowledge about what various possible causes cannot or do not produce, historical scientists could not make determinations about the past. Reconstructing the past requires making abductive inferences from present effects back to past causal events.[137] Making such inferences requires a progressive elimination of competing causal hypotheses. Deciding which causes can be eliminated from consideration requires knowing what effects a given cause can—and cannot—produce. If historical scientists could never say that particular entities lack particular causal powers, they could never eliminate them, even provisionally, from consideration. Thus, they could never infer that a specific cause had acted in the past. Yet historical and forensic scientists make such inferences all the time.

Moreover, Dembski's examples of design inferences—from fields such as archaeology, cryptography, fraud-detection, and criminal forensics—show that we often infer the past activity of an intelligent cause and do so, evidently, without worrying about committing fallacious arguments from ignorance. And we do so for good reason. A vast amount of human experience shows that intelligent agents have unique causal powers that matter (especially nonliving matter) does not. When we observe features or effects that we know from experience only agents produce, we rightly infer the prior activity of intelligence.

To determine the best explanation, scientists do not need to say "never" with absolute certainty. They need only say that a postulated cause is best, given what we know at present about the demonstrated causal powers of competing entities or agencies. That cause C can produce effect E makes it a better explanation of E than some cause D that has never produced E (especially if D seems incapable of doing so on theoretical grounds), even if D might later demonstrate causal powers of which we are presently ignorant.[138]

Thus, the objection that the design inference constitutes an argument from ignorance reduces in essence to a restatement of the problem of induction. Yet one could make the same objection against any scientific law or explanation or against any historical inference that takes present, but not future, knowledge of natural laws and causal powers into account. As Barrow and Tipler have noted, to criticize design arguments, as Hume did, simply because they assume the uniformity and (normative character) of natural law cuts just as deeply against "the rational basis of any form of scientific inquiry."[139] Our knowledge of what can and cannot produce large amounts of specified information may later have to be revised, but so might the laws of thermodynamics. Inferences to design may later prove incorrect, as may other inferences implicating various natural causes. Such possibilities do not stop scientists from making generalizations about the causal powers of various entities or from using those generalizations to identify probable or most plausible causes in particular cases.

Inferences based on past and present experience constitute knowledge (albeit provisional), not ignorance. Those who object to such inferences object to *science* as much as they object to a particular science-based hypothesis of design.

C. But Is It Science?

Of course, many simply refuse to consider the design hypothesis on grounds that it does not qualify as "scientific." Such critics affirm an extra-evidential principle known as methodological naturalism.[140] Methodological naturalism asserts that, as a matter of definition, for a hypothesis, theory, or explanation to qualify as "scientific," it must invoke only naturalistic or materialistic entities. On that definition, critics say, the intelligent design hypothesis does not qualify. Yet, even if one grants this definition, it does not follow that some nonscientific (as defined by methodological naturalism) or metaphysical hypothesis may not constitute a better, more causally adequate, explanation. This essay has argued that, whatever its classification, the design hypothesis does constitute a better explanation than its materialistic or naturalistic rivals for the origin of specified biological information. Surely, simply classifying an argument as metaphysical does not refute it.

In any case, methodological naturalism now lacks justification as a normative definition of science. First, attempts to justify methodological naturalism by reference to metaphysically neutral (that is, non-question-begging) demarcation criteria have failed.[141] Second, to assert methodological naturalism as a normative principle for all of science has a negative effect on the practice of certain scientific disciplines, especially the historical sciences. In origin-of-life research, for example, methodological naturalism artificially restricts inquiry and prevents scientists from seeking some hypotheses that might provide the best, most causally adequate explanations. To be a truth-seeking endeavor, the question that origin-of-life research must address is not "Which materialistic scenario seems most adequate?" but rather "What actually caused life to arise on Earth?" Clearly, one possible answer to that latter question is this one: "Life was designed by an intelligent agent that existed before the advent of humans." If one accepts methodological naturalism as normative, however, scientists may never consider the design hypothesis as possibly true. Such an exclusionary logic diminishes the significance of any claim of theoretical superiority for any remaining hypothesis and raises the possibility that the best "scientific" explanation (as defined by methodological naturalism) may not be the best in fact.

As many historians and philosophers of science now recognize, scientific theory-evaluation is an inherently comparative enterprise. Theories that gain acceptance in artificially constrained competitions can claim to be neither "most probably true" nor "most empirically adequate." At best, such theories can be considered the "most probably true or adequate among an artificially limited set of options." Openness to the design hypothesis would seem necessary, therefore, to any fully rational historical biology—that is, to one that seeks the truth, "no holds barred."[142] A historical biology committed to following the evidence wherever it leads will not exclude hypotheses a priori on metaphysical grounds. Instead, it will employ only metaphysically neutral criteria—such as explanatory power and causal adequacy—to evaluate competing hypotheses. Yet this more open (and seemingly rational) approach to scientific theory evaluation would now suggest the theory of intelligent design as the best, most causally adequate, explanation for the origin of the information necessary to build the first living organism.

Notes

1. Harmke Kamminga, "Protoplasm and the Gene," in *Clay Minerals and the Origin of Life*, ed. A. G. Cairns-Smith and H. Hartman (Cambridge: Cambridge University Press, 1986), 1.

2. Alexander Oparin, *Genesis and Evolutionary Development of Life* (New York: Academic Press, 1968), 7.

3. F. Crick and J. Watson, "A Structure for Deoxyribose Nucleic Acid," *Nature* 171 (1953): 737–38; F. Crick and J. Watson, "Genetical Implications of the Structure of Deoxyribose Nucleic Acid," *Nature* 171 (1953): 964–67, esp. 964; T. D. Schneider, "Information Content of Individual Genetic Sequences," *Journal of Theoretical Biology* 189 (1997): 427–41; W. R. Loewenstein, *The Touchstone of Life: Molecular Information, Cell Communication, and the Foundations of Life* (New York: Oxford University Press, 1999).

4. Bernd-Olaf Kuppers, *Information and the Origin of Life* (Cambridge: MIT Press, 1990), 170–72.

5. L. E. Kay, "Who Wrote the Book of Life? Information and the Transformation of Molecular Biology," *Science in Context* 8 (1994): 601–34; L. E. Kay, "Cybernetics, Information, Life: The Emergence of Scriptural Representations of Heredity," *Configurations* 5 (1999): 23–91; L. E. Kay, *Who Wrote the Book of Life?* (Stanford, Calif.: Stanford University Press, 2000), xv–xix.

6. Darwin's only speculation on the origin of life is found in an unpublished 1871 letter to Joseph Hooker. In it, he sketched the outlines of the chemical evolutionary idea, namely, that life could have first

evolved from a series of chemical reactions. As he envisioned it, "if (and oh! what a big if!) we could conceive in some warm little pond, with all sorts of ammonia and phosphoric salts, light, heat, electricity, etc., that a proteine compound was chemically formed ready to undergo still more complex changes." Cambridge University Library, Manuscripts Room, Darwin Archives, courtesy Peter Gautrey.

7. E. Haeckel, *The Wonders of Life,* trans. J. McCabe (London: Watts, 1905), 111; T. H. Huxley, "On the Physical Basis of Life," *Fortnightly Review* 5 (1869): 129–45.

8. A. I. Oparin, *The Origin of Life,* trans. S. Morgulis (New York: Macmillan, 1938); S. C. Meyer, "Of Clues and Causes: A Methodological Interpretation of Origin of Life Studies" (Ph.D. diss., Cambridge University, 1991).

9. W. T. Astbury and A. Street, "X-Ray Studies of the Structure of Hair, Wool and Related Fibers," *Philosophical Transactions of the Royal Society of London* A 230 (1932): 75–101; H. Judson, *Eighth Day of Creation* (New York: Simon and Schuster, 1979), 80; R. Olby, *The Path to the Double Helix* (London: Macmillan, 1974), 63.

10. Olby, *Path to the Double Helix,* 7, 265.

11. Judson, *Eighth Day,* 213, 229–35, 255–61, 304, 334–35, 562–63; F. Sanger and E. O. P. Thompson, "The Amino Acid Sequence in the Glycyl Chain of Insulin," parts 1 and 2, *Biochemical Journal* 53 (1953): 353–66, 366–74.

12. Judson, *Eighth Day,* 562–63; J. C. Kendrew, G. Bodo, H. M. Dintzis, R. G. Parrish, and H. Wyckoff, "A Three-Dimensional Model of the Myoglobin Molecule Obtained by X-Ray Analysis," *Nature* 181 (1958): 662–66, esp. 664.

13. B. Alberts, D. Bray, J. Lewis, M. Raff, K. Roberts, and J. D. Watson, *Molecular Biology of the Cell* (New York: Garland, 1983), 111–12, 127–31.

14. Judson, *Eighth Day,* 30.

15. Ibid., 30–31, 33–41, 609–10; Oswald T. Avery, C. M. MacCleod, and M. McCarty, "Induction of Transformation by a Deoxyribonucleic Acid Fraction Isolated from Pneumococcus Type III," *Journal of Experimental Medicine* 79 (1944): 137–58.

16. Judson, *Eighth Day,* 95–96; E. Chargaff, *Essays on Nucleic Acids* (Amsterdam: Elsevier, 1963), 21.

17. Chargaff, *Essays,* 21.

18. Crick and Watson, "Structure."

19. Judson, *Eighth Day*, 96.
20. Crick and Watson, "Genetical Implications," 964–67.
21. Judson, *Eighth Day*, 611.
22. Crick and Watson, "Structure"; Crick and Watson, "Genetical Implications."
23. Judson, *Eighth Day*, 245–46, 335–36.
24. Ibid., 470–89; J. H. Matthei and M. W. Nirenberg, "Characteristics and Stabilization of DNAase-Sensitive Protein Synthesis in *E. coli* Extracts," *Proceedings of the National Academy of Sciences, USA* 47 (1961): 1580–88; J. H. Matthei and M. W. Nirenberg, "The Dependence of Cell-Free Protein Synthesis in *E. coli* upon Naturally Occurring or Synthetic Polyribonucleotides," *Proceedings of the National Academy of Sciences, USA* 47 (1961): 1588–1602.
25. Alberts et al., *Molecular Biology*, 106–8; S. L. Wolfe, *Molecular and Cellular Biology* (Belmont, Calif.: Wadsworth, 1993), 639–48.
26. We now know, of course, that in addition to the process of gene expression, specific enzymes must often modify amino acid chains after translation in order to achieve the precise sequencing necessary to allow correct folding into a functional protein. The amino acid chains produced by gene expression may also undergo further modification in sequence at the endoplasmic reticulum. Finally, even well-modified amino acid chains may require preexisting protein "chaperons" to help them fold into a functional three-dimensional configuration. All these factors make it impossible to predict a protein's final sequence from its corresponding gene sequence alone. See S. Sarkar, "Biological Information: A Skeptical Look at Some Central Dogmas of Molecular Biology," in *The Philosophy and History of Molecular Biology: New Perspectives*, ed. S. Sarkar (Dordrecht, Netherlands: Boston Studies in Philosophy of Science, 1996), 196, 199–202. Nevertheless, this unpredictability in no way undermines the claim that DNA exhibits the property of "sequence specificity," or the isomorphic claim that it contains "specified information" as argued in part I, section E. Sarkar argues, for example, that the absence of such predictability renders the concept of information theoretically superfluous for molecular biology. Instead, this unpredictability shows that the sequence specificity of DNA base sequences constitutes a necessary, though not sufficient, condition of attaining proper protein folding—that is, DNA does contain specified information (part I, section E), but not enough to determine protein folding by itself. Instead, the presence of both

post-translation processes of modification and pretranscriptional genomic editing (through exonucleases, endonucleases, spliceosomes, and other editing enzymes) only underscores the need for other preexisting, information-rich biomolecules in order to process genomic information in the cell. The presence of a complex and functionally integrated information-processing system *does* suggest that the information on the DNA molecule is insufficient to produce proteins. It does not show that such information is *unnecessary* to produce proteins, nor does it invalidate the claim that DNA, therefore, stores and transmits specified genetic information.

27. C. Shannon, "A Mathematical Theory of Communication," *Bell System Technical Journal* 27 (1948): 379–423, 623–56.

28. F. Dretske, *Knowledge and the Flow of Information* (Cambridge: MIT Press, 1981), 6–10.

29. Ibid.; Shannon, "A Mathematical Theory."

30. B. Kuppers, "On the Prior Probability of the Existence of Life," in *The Probabilistic Revolution,* ed. Lorenz Kruger et al. (Cambridge: MIT Press, 1987), 355–69.

31. Schneider, "Information Content"; see also H. P. Yockey, *Information Theory and Molecular Biology* (Cambridge: Cambridge University Press, 1992), 246–58, for important refinements in the method of calculating the information-carrying capacity of proteins and DNA.

32. C. Shannon and W. Weaver, *The Mathematical Theory of Communication* (Urbana: University of Illinois Press, 1949), 8.

33. Schneider, "Information Content," 58–177; Yockey, *Information Theory,* 58–177.

34. See note 26. Sarkar, "Biological Information," 199–202, esp. 196; F. Crick, "On Protein Synthesis," *Symposium for the Society of Experimental Biology* 12 (1958): 138–63, esp. 144, 153.

35. Crick, "On Protein Synthesis," 144, 153.

36. Recall that the determination of the genetic code depended, for example, on observed correlations between changes in nucleotide base sequences and amino acid production in "cell-free systems." See Judson, *Eighth Day,* 470–87.

37. W. A. Dembski, *The Design Inference: Eliminating Chance Through Small Probabilities* (Cambridge: Cambridge University Press, 1998), 1–35, 136–74.

38. Ibid., 136–74.

39. Of the two sequences, only the second meets an independent set of functional requirements. To convey meaning in English one must employ preexisting (or independent) conventions of vocabulary (associations of symbol sequences with particular objects, concepts, or ideas) and existing conventions of syntax and grammar (such as "every sentence requires a subject and a verb"). When arrangements of symbols "match" or utilize these vocabulary and grammatical conventions (that is, functional requirements), meaningful communication can occur in English. The second sequence ("Time and tide wait for no man") clearly exhibits such a match between itself and preexisting requirements of vocabulary and grammar. The second sequence has employed these conventions to express a meaningful idea. It also, therefore, falls within the smaller (and conditionally independent) pattern delimiting the domain of all meaningful sentences in English and thus, again, exhibits a "specification."

40. J. Bowie and R. Sauer, "Identifying Determinants of Folding and Activity for a Protein of Unknown Sequences: Tolerance to Amino Acid Substitution," *Proceedings of the National Academy of Sciences, USA* 86 (1989): 2152–56; J. Reidhaar-Olson and R. Sauer, "Functionally Acceptable Solutions in Two Alpha-Helical Regions of Lambda Repressor," *Proteins, Structure, Function, and Genetics* 7 (1990): 306–10.

41. R. Dawkins, *River out of Eden* (New York: Basic Books, 1995), 11.

42. B. Gates, *The Road Ahead* (Boulder, Colo.: Blue Penguin, 1996), 228.

43. L. E. Orgel, *The Origins of Life on Earth* (New York: John Wiley, 1973), 189.

44. See note 5. Kay, "Who Wrote," 611–12, 629; Kay, "Cybernetics"; Kay, *Who Wrote*.

45. Sarkar, "Biological Information," 199–202.

46. E. Schrödinger, *What Is Life? And Mind and Matter* (Cambridge: Cambridge University Press, 1967), 82; Alberts et al., *Molecular Biology*, 21; Crick and Watson, "A Structure"; Crick and Watson, "Genetical Implications"; Crick, "On Protein"; Judson, *Eighth Day*, 611; Orgel, *Origins of Life*, 189.

47. P. Davies, *The Fifth Miracle* (New York: Simon and Schuster, 1998), 120.

48. Orgel, *Origins of Life*, 189.

49. Loewenstein, *Touchstone*; Davies, *Fifth Miracle*; Schneider, "Information Content"; C. Thaxton and W. Bradley, "Information and the Origin of Life," in *The Creation Hypothesis: Scientific Evidence for an Intelligent*

Designer, ed. J. P. Moreland (Downers Grove, Ill.: InterVarsity Press, 1994), 173–210, esp. 190; S. Kauffman, *The Origins of Order* (Oxford: Oxford University Press, 1993), 287–340; Yockey, *Information Theory,* 178–293; Kuppers, *Information and Origin,* 170–72; F. Crick, *Life Itself* (New York: Simon and Schuster, 1981), 59–60, 88; J. Monod, *Chance and Necessity* (New York: Vintage Books, 1971), 97–98, 143; Orgel, *Origins,* 189; D. Kenyon and G. Steinman, *Biochemical Predestination* (New York: McGraw-Hill, 1969), 199–211, 263–66; Oparin, *Genesis,* 146–47; H. Quastler, *The Emergence of Biological Organization* (New Haven, Conn.: Yale University Press, 1964).

50. G. Wald, "The Origin of Life," *Scientific American* 191 (August 1954): 44–53; R. Shapiro, *Origins: A Skeptic's Guide to the Creation of Life on Earth* (New York: Summit Books, 1986), 121.

51. F. Crick, "The Origin of the Genetic Code," *Journal of Molecular Biology* 38 (1968): 367–79; H. Kamminga, "Studies in the History of Ideas on the Origin of Life" (Ph.D. diss., University of London 1980), 303–4.

52. C. de Duve, "The Constraints of Chance," *Scientific American* (Jan. 1996): 112; Crick, *Life Itself,* 89–93; Quastler, *Emergence,* 7.

53. H. J. Morowitz, *Energy Flow in Biology* (New York: Academic Press, 1968), 5–12; F. Hoyle and C. Wickramasinghe, *Evolution from Space* (London: J. M. Dent, 1981), 24–27; A. G. Cairns-Smith, *The Life Puzzle* (Edinburgh: Oliver and Boyd, 1971), 91–96; I. Prigogine, G. Nicolis, and A. Babloyantz, "Thermodynamics of Evolution," *Physics Today* (23 Nov. 1972); Yockey, *Information Theory,* 246–58; H. P. Yockey, "Self-Organization, Origin of Life Scenarios and Information Theory," *Journal of Theoretical Biology* 91 (1981): 13–31; Bowie and Sauer, "Identifying Determinants"; Reidhaar-Olson et al., *Proteins;* Shapiro, *Origins,* 117–31.

54. Prigogine, "Thermodynamics."

55. Cairns-Smith, *Life Puzzle,* 95.

56. Reidhaar-Olson and Sauer, "Functionally Acceptable"; D. D. Axe, "Biological Function Places Unexpectedly Tight Constraints on Protein Sequences," *Journal of Molecular Biology* 301, no. 3: 585–96; M. Behe, "Experimental Support for Regarding Functional Classes of Proteins to Be Highly Isolated from Each Other," in *Darwinism: Science or Philosophy?* ed. J. Buell and V. Hearn (Richardson, Tex.: Foundation for Thought and Ethics, 1994), 60–71; Yockey, *Information Theory,* 246–58. Actually, Sauer counted sequences that folded into stable three-dimensional configurations as functional, though many sequences

that fold are not functional. Thus, his results actually underestimate the probabilistic difficulty.

57. Behe, "Experimental Support."

58. Axe, "Biological Function."

59. Dawkins, *Blind Watchmaker*, 54, 139.

60. Dembski, *Design Inference*, 175–223; E. Borel, *Probabilities and Life*, trans. M. Baudin (New York: Dover, 1962), 28. Dembski's universal probability bound actually reflects the "specificational" resources, not the probabilistic resources in the universe. Dembski's calculation determines the number of specifications possible in finite time. It nevertheless has the effect of limiting the "probabilistic resources" available to explain the origin of any *specified* event of small probability. Since living systems are precisely specified systems of small probability, the universal probability bound effectively limits the probabilistic resources available to explain the origin of specified biological information.

61. Dembski, *Design Inference*, 175–223. Cassette mutagenesis experiments have usually been performed on proteins of about 100 amino acids in length. Yet extrapolations from these results can generate reasonable estimates for the improbability of longer protein molecules. For example, Sauer's results on the proteins lambda repressor and arc repressor suggest that, on average, the probability at each site of finding an amino acid that will maintain functional sequencing (or, more accurately, that will produce folding) is less than 1 in 4 (1 in 4.4). Multiplying 1/4 by itself 150 times (for a protein 150 amino acids in length) yields a probability of roughly 1 chance in 10^{91}. For a protein of that length, the probability of attaining both exclusive peptide bonding and homochirality is also about 1 chance in 10^{91}. Thus, the probability of achieving all the necessary conditions of function for a protein 150 amino acids in length exceeds 1 chance in 10^{180}.

62. Dembski, *Design Inference*, 67–91, 175–214; Borel, *Probabilities*, 28.

63. E. Pennisi, "Seeking Life's Bare Genetic Necessities," *Science* 272 (1996): 1098–99; A. Mushegian and E. Koonin, "A Minimal Gene Set for Cellular Life Derived by Comparison of Complete Bacterial Genomes," *Proceedings of the National Academy of Sciences, USA* 93 (1996): 10268–73; C. Bult et al., "Complete Genome Sequence of the Methanogenic Archaeon, *Methanococcus jannaschi*," *Science* 273 (1996): 1058–72.

64. Dembski, *Design Inference*, 67–91, 175–223, 209–10.

65. P. T. Mora, "Urge and Molecular Biology," *Nature* 199 (1963): 212–19.

66. I. Hacking, *The Logic of Statistical Inference* (Cambridge: Cambridge University Press, 1965), 74–75.

67. Dembski, *Design Inference*, 47–55.

68. C. de Duve, "The Beginnings of Life on Earth," *American Scientist* 83 (1995): 437.

69. Quastler, *Emergence*, 7.

70. Oparin, *Origin of Life*, 64–103; Meyer, *Of Clues*, 174–79, 194–98, 211–12.

71. Oparin, *Origin of Life*, 107–8, 133–35, 148–59, 195–96.

72. Oparin, *Genesis*, 146–47.

73. C. de Duve, *Blueprint for a Cell: The Nature and Origin of Life* (Burlington, N.C.: Neil Patterson, 1991), 187.

74. G. Joyce and L. Orgel, "Prospects for Understanding the Origin of the RNA World," in *RNA World*, ed. R. F. Gesteland and J. J. Atkins (Cold Spring Harbor, N.Y.: Cold Spring Harbor Laboratory Press, 1993), 1–25, esp. 8–13.

75. T. Dobzhansky, "Discussion of G. Schramm's Paper," in *The Origins of Prebiological Systems and of Their Molecular Matrices*, ed. S. W. Fox (New York: Academic Press, 1965), 310; H. H. Pattee, "The Problem of Biological Hierarchy," in *Toward a Theoretical Biology*, ed. C. H. Waddington, vol. 3 (Edinburgh: Edinburgh University Press, 1970), 123.

76. P. T. Mora, "The Folly of Probability," in Fox, *Origins*, 311–12; L. V. Bertalanffy, *Robots, Men and Minds* (New York: George Braziller, 1967), 82.

77. J. Von Neumann, *Theory of Self-reproducing Automata*, completed and edited by A. Berks (Urbana: University of Illinois Press, 1966).

78. Pennisi, "Seeking"; Mushegian and Koonin, "Minimal Gene Set"; Bult et al., "Complete Genome Sequence."

79. E. Wigner, "The Probability of the Existence of a Self-reproducing Unit," in *The Logic of Personal Knowledge*, ed. E. Shils (London: Kegan and Paul, 1961), 231–35; P. T. Landsberg, "Does Quantum Mechanics Exclude Life?" *Nature* 203 (1964): 928–30; H. J. Morowitz, "The Minimum Size of the Cell," in *Principles of Biomolecular Organization*, ed. M. O'Connor and G. E. W. Wolstenholme (London: J. A. Churchill, 1966), 446–59; Morowitz, *Energy Flow*, 10–11.

80. Dawkins, *Blind Watchmaker*, 47–49; Kuppers, "On the Prior Probability."

81. Kuppers, "On the Prior Probability," 366.

82. Dawkins, *Blind Watchmaker,* 47–49; P. Nelson, "Anatomy of a Still-Born Analogy," *Origins and Design* 17 (3) (1996): 12.

83. de Duve, "Beginnings of Life," 437.

84. Morowitz, *Energy Flow,* 5–12.

85. G. Steinman and M. N. Cole, "Synthesis of Biologically Pertinent Peptides Under Possible Primordial Conditions," *Proceedings of the National Academy of Sciences, USA* 58 (1967): 735–41; G. Steinman, "Sequence Generation in Prebiological Peptide Synthesis," *Archives of Biochemistry and Biophysics* 121 (1967): 533–39; R. A. Kok, J. A. Taylor, and W. L. Bradley, "A Statistical Examination of Self-Ordering of Amino Acids in Proteins," *Origins of Life and Evolution of the Biosphere* 18 (1988): 135–42.

86. Kenyon and Steinman, *Biochemical Predestination,* 199–211, 263–66.

87. I. Prigogine and G. Nicolis, *Self-Organization in NonEquilibrium Systems* (New York: John Wiley, 1977), 339–53, 429–47.

88. Kauffman, *Origins of Order,* 285–341; de Duve, "Beginnings of Life"; C. de Duve, *Vital Dust: Life as a Cosmic Imperative* (New York: Basic Books, 1995).

89. C. Thaxton, W. Bradley, and R. Olsen, *The Mystery of Life's Origin: Reassessing Current Theories* (Dallas: Lewis and Stanley, 1992), v–viii; D. Kenyon and G. Mills, "The RNA World: A Critique," *Origins and Design* 17, no. 1 (1996): 9–16; D. Kenyon and P. W. Davis, *Of Pandas and People: The Central Question of Biological Origins* (Dallas: Haughton, 1993); S. C. Meyer, "A Scopes Trial for the '90's," *Wall Street Journal,* 6 Dec. 1993; Kok et al., "Statistical Examination."

90. Steinman and Cole, "Synthesis"; Steinman, "Sequence Generation."

91. Kok et al., "Statistical Examination"; B.J. Strait and G. T. Dewey, "The Shannon Information Entropy of Biologically Pertinent Peptides," *Biophysical Journal* 71: 148–155.

92. Kuppers, "On the Prior Probability," 64.

93. de Duve, "Beginnings of Life," 437.

94. R. Stalnaker, *Inquiry* (Cambridge: MIT Press, 1984), 85.

95. This, in fact, happens where adenine and thymine do interact chemically in the complementary base-pairing *across* the information-bearing axis of the DNA molecule. *Along* the message bearing axis, however, there are no chemical bonds or differential bonding affinities that determine sequencing.

96. M. Polanyi, "Life's Irreducible Structure," *Science* 160 (1968): 1308–12, esp. 1309.

97. As noted in part I, section D, the information-carrying capacity of any symbol in a sequence is inversely related to the probability of its occurrence. The informational capacity of a sequence as a whole is inversely proportional to the product of the individual probabilities of each member in the sequence. Since chemical affinities between constituents ("symbols") increase the probability of the occurrence of one, given another (i.e., necessity increases probability), such affinities decrease the information-carrying capacity of a system in proportion to the strength and relative frequency of such affinities within the system.

98. Dretske, *Knowledge and the Flow,* 12.

99. Yockey, "Self-Organization," 18.

100. H. P. Yockey, "A Calculation of the Probability of Spontaneous Biogenesis by Information Theory," *Journal of Theoretical Biology* 67 (1977): 377–98, esp. 380.

101. M. Eigen, *Steps Toward Life* (Oxford: Oxford University Press, 1992), 12.

102. Quastler, *Emergence,* ix.

103. Ibid., 1, 47.

104. Yockey, *Information Theory,* 247.

105. J. C. Walton, "Organization and the Origin of Life," *Origins* 4 (1977): 16–35.

106. J. M. Smith, "Hypercycles and the Origin of Life," *Nature* 280 (1979): 445–46; F. Dyson, *Origins of Life* (Cambridge: Cambridge University Press, 1985), 9–11, 35–39, 65–66, 78; Shapiro, *Origins,* 161.

107. Iris Fry, *The Emergence of Life on Earth* (New Brunswick, N.J.: Rutgers University Press, 2000), 158.

108. Kauffman, *Origins of Order,* 285–341.

109. Ibid., 299.

110. See Protein Databank at http://www.rcsb.org/pdb.

111. Kauffman, *Origins of Order,* 298.

112. Thaxton, et al., *Mystery of Life's Origin,* 127–43.

113. R. Shapiro, "Prebiotic Cytosine Synthesis: A Critical Analysis and Implications for the Origin of Life," *Proceedings of the National Academy of Sciences, USA* 96 (1999): 4396–4401; M. M. Waldrop, "Did Life Really Start Out in an RNA World?" *Science* 246 (1989): 1248–49.

114. R. Shapiro, "Prebiotic Ribose Synthesis: A Critical Analysis," *Origins of Life and Evolution of the Biosphere* 18 (1988): 71–85; Kenyon and Mills, "RNA World."

115. G. F. Joyce, "RNA Evolution and the Origins of Life," *Nature* 338 (1989): 217–24.
116. A. J. Hager, J. D. Polland Jr., and J. W. Szostak, "Ribozymes: Aiming at RNA Replication and Protein Synthesis," *Chemistry and Biology* 3 (1996): 717–25.
117. de Duve, *Vital Dust,* 23.
118. Joyce and Orgel, "Prospects for Understanding," 1–25, esp. 11.
119. Quastler, *Emergence,* 16.
120. A possible exception to this generalization might occur in biological evolution. If the Darwinian mechanism of natural selection acting on random variation can account for the emergence of all complex life, then a mechanism does exist that can produce large amounts of information—assuming, of course, a large amount of *preexisting* biological information in a self-replicating living system. Thus, even if one assumes that the selection/variation mechanism can produce all the information required for the macroevolution of complex life from simpler life, that mechanism will not suffice to account for the origin of the information necessary to produce life from nonliving chemicals. As we have seen, appeals to *prebiotic* natural selection only beg the question of the origin of specified information. Thus, based on experience, we can affirm the following generalization: "for all nonbiological systems, large amounts [note 118 below] of specified complexity or information originate only from mental agency, conscious activity, or intelligent design." Strictly speaking, *experience* may even affirm a less qualified generalization (such as "large amounts of specified invariably originate from an intelligent source"), since the claim that natural selection acting on random mutations can produce large amounts of novel genetic information depends on debatable theoretical arguments and extrapolation from observations of small-scale microevolutionary changes that do not themselves manifest large gains in biological information. Later in this volume (in "The Cambrian Explosion: Biology's Big Bang"), Meyer, Ross, Nelson, and Chien argue that neither the neo-Darwinian mechanism nor any other current naturalistic mechanism adequately accounts for the origin of the information required to build the novel proteins and body plans that arise in the Cambrian explosion. In any case, the more qualified empirical generalization (stated above in this endnote) is sufficient to support the argument presented here, since this essay seeks only to establish intelligent design as the best explanation for

origin of the specified information necessary to the origin of the *first* life.

121. K. Dose, "The Origin of Life: More Questions Than Answers," *Interdisciplinary Science Reviews* 13 (1988): 348–56; Yockey, *Information Theory*, 259–93; Thaxton et al., *Mystery*, 42–172; Thaxton and Bradley, "Information and the Origin," 193–97; Shapiro, *Origins*.

122. Of course, the phrase "large amounts of specified information" again begs a quantitative question, namely, "How much specified information or complexity would the minimally complex cell have to have before it implied design?" Recall that Dembski has calculated a universal probability bound of $1/10^{150}$ corresponding to the probabilistic/specificational resources of the known universe. Recall further that probability is inversely related to information by a logarithmic function. Thus, the universal small probability bound of $1/10^{150}$ translates into roughly 500 bits of information. Chance alone, therefore, does not constitute a sufficient explanation for the de novo origin of any specified sequence or system containing more than 500 bits of (specified) information. Further, since systems characterized by complexity (a lack of redundant order) defy explanation by self-organizational laws and since appeals to prebiotic natural selection presuppose but do not explain the origin of the specified information necessary to a minimally complex self-replicating system, intelligent design best explains the origin of the more than 500 bits of specified information required to produce the first minimally complex living system. Thus, assuming a nonbiological starting point (note 116 above), the de novo emergence of 500 or more bits of specified information will reliably indicate design.

123. Again, this claim applies at least in cases where the competing causal entities or conditions are nonbiological—or where the mechanism of natural selection can be safely eliminated as an inadequate means of producing requisite specified information.

124. Dembski, *Design Inference*, 1–35.

125. Ibid., 1–35, 136–223.

126. Ibid., 36–66.

127. Ibid.; E. Sober, *Reconstructing the Past* (Cambridge, Mass.: MIT Press, 1988), 4–5; M. Scriven, "Causes, Connections, and Conditions in History," in *Philosophical Analysis and History*, ed. W. Dray (New York: Harper and Row, 1966), 238–64, esp. 249–50.

128. *McNeil-Lehrer News Hour*, Transcript 19 (May 1992).

129. Meyer, *Of Clues*, 77–140.

130. Less exotic (and more successful) design-detection occurs routinely in both science and industry. Fraud-detection, forensic science, and cryptography all depend on the application of probabilistic or information theoretic criteria of intelligent design. Dembski, *Design Inference*, 1–35. Many would admit that we *may* justifiably infer a past human intelligence operating (within the scope of human history) from an information-rich artifact or event, but only because we already know that human minds exist. But, they argue, since we do not know whether an intelligent agent(s) existed prior to humans, inferring the action of a designing agent that antedates humans cannot be justified, even if we observe an information-rich effect. Note, however, that SETI scientists do not already know whether an extraterrestrial intelligence exists. Yet they assume that the presence of a large amount of specified information (such as the first 100 prime numbers in sequence) would definitively establish the existence of one. Indeed, SETI seeks precisely to establish the existence of other intelligences in an unknown domain. Similarly, anthropologists have often revised their estimates for the beginning of human history or civilization because they discovered information-rich artifacts dating from times that antedate their previous estimates. Most inferences to design establish the existence or activity of a mental agent operating in a time or place where the presence of such agency was previously unknown. Thus, to infer the activity of a designing intelligence from a time prior to the advent of humans on Earth does not have a qualitatively different epistemological status than other design inferences that critics already accept as legitimate. T. R. McDonough, *The Search for Extraterrestrial Intelligence: Listening for Life in the Cosmos* (New York: Wiley, 1987).

131. P. Lipton, *Inference to the Best Explanation* (New York: Routledge, 1991), 32–88.

132. Ibid.; S. C. Meyer, "The Scientific Status of Intelligent Design: The Methodological Equivalence of Naturalistic and Non-Naturalistic Origins Theories," in *Science and Evidence for Design in the Universe, The Proceedings of the Wethersfield Institute*, vol. 9 (San Francisco: Ignatius Press, 2000), 151–212; Meyer, "The Demarcation of Science and Religion," in *The History of Science and Religion in the Western Tradition: An Encyclopedia*, ed. G. B. Ferngren (New York: Garland, 2000), 17–23; E. Sober,

The Philosophy of Biology (San Francisco: Westview Press, 1993); Meyer, *Of Clues,* 77–140.

133. Quastler, *Emergence,* 16.

134. Francis Darwin, ed., *Life and Letters of Charles Darwin,* 2 vols. (London: D. Appleton, 1896), 1:437.

135. Dembski, *Design Inference,* 36–37, esp. 37.

136. Oparin, *Origin of Life,* 28; M. Rothman, *The Science Gap* (Buffalo, N.Y.: Prometheus, 1992), 65–92; K. Popper, *Conjectures and Refutations: The Growth of Scientific Knowledge* (London: Routledge and Kegan Paul, 1962), 35–37.

137. Meyer, *Of Clues,* 77–140; Sober, *Reconstructing the Past,* 4–5; de Duve, "Beginnings of Life," 249–50.

138. R. Harre and E. H. Madden, *Causal Powers* (London: Basil Blackwell, 1975).

139. J. Barrow and F. Tipler, *The Anthropic Cosmological Principle* (Oxford: Oxford University Press, 1986), 69.

140. M. Ruse, "*McLean v. Arkansas:* Witness Testimony Sheet," in *But Is It Science?* ed. M. Ruse (Amherst, N.Y.: Prometheus Books, 1988), 103; Meyer, "Scientific Status"; Meyer, "Demarcation."

141. Meyer, "Scientific Status"; Meyer, "Demarcation"; L. Laudan, "The Demise of the Demarcation Problem," in Ruse, *But Is It Science?* 337–50; L. Laudan, "Science at the Bar—Causes for Concern," in Ruse, *But Is It Science?* 351–55; A. Plantinga, "Methodological Naturalism?" *Origins and Design* 18, no. 1 (1986): 18–26; A. Plantinga, "Methodological Naturalism?" *Origins and Design* 18, no. 2 (1986): 22–34.

142. Bridgman, *Reflections of a Physicist,* 2d ed. (New York: Philosophical Library, 1955), 535.

Design in the Details:
The Origin of Biomolecular Machines

Michael J. Behe

❀ ❀ ❀

Darwinism's Prosperity

Within a short time after Charles Darwin published *The Origin of Species,* the explanatory power of the theory of evolution was recognized by the great majority of biologists. The hypothesis readily resolved the problems of homologous resemblance, rudimentary organs, species abundance, extinction, and biogeography. The rival theory of the time, which posited creation of species by a supernatural being, appeared to most reasonable minds to be much less plausible, since it would have a putative Creator attending to details that seemed to be beneath His dignity.

As time went on, the theory of evolution obliterated the rival theory of creation, and virtually all working scientists studied the biological world from a Darwinian perspective. Most educated people now lived in a world where the wonder and diversity of the biological kingdom were produced by the simple, elegant principle of natural selection.

However, in science a successful theory is not necessarily a correct theory. In the course of history there have also been other theories that achieved the triumph that Darwinism achieved, that brought many experimental and observational facts into a coherent framework, and that appealed to people's intuitions about how the world should work. Those theories also promised to explain much of the universe with a few simple principles. But, by and large, those other theories are now dead.

A good example of this is the replacement of Newton's mechanical view of the universe by Einstein's relativistic universe. Although Newton's model accounted for the results of many experiments in his time, it failed to explain aspects of gravitation. Einstein solved that problem and others by completely rethinking the structure of the universe.

Similarly, Darwin's theory of evolution prospered by explaining much of the data of his time and the first half of the twentieth century, but my essay will show that Darwinism has been unable to account for phenomena uncovered by the efforts of modern biochemistry during the second half of that century. I will do this by emphasizing the fact that life at its most fundamental level is irreducibly complex and that such complexity is incompatible with undirected evolution.

A Series of Eyes

How Do We See?

In the nineteenth century, the anatomy of the eye was known in great detail, and the sophisticated mechanisms it employs to deliver an accurate picture of the outside world astounded everyone who was familiar with them. Scientists of the nineteenth century correctly observed that if a person were so unfortunate as to be missing one of the eye's many integrated features, such as the lens, or iris, or ocular muscles, the inevitable result would be a severe loss of vision or outright blindness. Thus, it was concluded that the eye could only function if it were nearly intact.

As Charles Darwin was considering possible objections to his theory of evolution by natural selection in *The Origin of Species,* he discussed the problem of the eye in a section of the book appropriately entitled "Organs of extreme perfection and complication." He realized that if in one generation an organ of the complexity of the eye suddenly appeared, the event would be tantamount to a miracle. Somehow, for Darwinian evolution to be believable, the difficulty that the public had in envisioning the gradual formation of complex organs had to be removed.

Darwin succeeded brilliantly, not by actually describing a real pathway that evolution might have used in constructing the eye but rather by pointing to a variety of animals that were known to have eyes of various constructions, ranging from a simple light-sensitive spot to the complex vertebrate camera eye, and suggesting that the evolution of the human eye might have involved similar organs as intermediates.

But the question remains, how do we see? Although Darwin was able to persuade much of the world that a modern eye could be produced gradually from a much simpler structure, he did not even attempt to explain how the simple light-sensitive spot that was his starting point actually worked. When discussing the eye, Darwin dismissed the question of its ultimate mechanism by stating: "How a nerve comes to be sensitive to light hardly concerns us more than how life itself originated."[1]

He had an excellent reason for declining to answer the question: nineteenth-century science had not progressed to the point where the matter could even be approached. The question of how the eye works—that is, what happens when a photon of light first impinges on the retina—simply could not be answered at that time. As a matter of fact, no question about the underlying mechanism of life could be answered at that time. How do animal muscles cause movement? How does photosynthesis work? How is energy extracted from food? How does the body fight infection? All such questions were unanswerable.

The Calvin and Hobbes Approach

Now, it appears to be a characteristic of the human mind that when it lacks understanding of a process, then it seems easy to imagine simple steps leading from nonfunction to function. This can be seen in the popular comic strip *Calvin and Hobbes.* Little boy Calvin is always having adventures in the company of his tiger, Hobbes, by jumping in a box and traveling back in time, or grabbing a toy ray gun and "transmogrifying" himself into various animal shapes, or again using a box as a duplicator and making copies of himself to deal with worldly powers such as his mom and his teachers. A small child such as Calvin finds it easy to imagine that a box just might be able to fly like an airplane (or something), because Calvin doesn't know how airplanes work.

Scientists who were convinced of spontaneous generation during the nineteenth century reasoned in a similar manner. One of the chief proponents of the theory of spontaneous generation during the middle of the nineteenth century was Ernst Haeckel, a great admirer of Darwin and an eager popularizer of Darwin's theory. From the limited view of cells that nineteenth-century microscopes provided, Haeckel believed that a cell was a "simple little lump of albuminous combination of carbon," not much different from a piece of microscopic Jell-O.[2] Thus, it seemed to Haeckel that such simple life could easily be produced from inanimate material.

In 1859, the year of the publication of *The Origin of Species,* an exploratory vessel, the H.M.S. *Cyclops,* dredged up some curious-looking mud from the sea bottom. Eventually, Haeckel came to observe the mud and thought that it closely resembled some cells he had seen under a microscope. Excitedly, he brought this to the attention of no less a personage than Thomas Henry Huxley, Darwin's great friend and defender, who observed the mud for himself. Huxley, too, became convinced that it was Urschleim (that is, protoplasm), the progenitor of life itself, and Huxley named the mud *Bathybius haeckelii* after the eminent proponent of abiogenesis.

The mud failed to grow. In later years, with the development of new biochemical techniques and improved microscopes, the complexity of the cell was revealed. The "simple lumps" were shown to contain thousands of different types of organic molecules, proteins, and nucleic acids; many discrete subcellular structures; specialized compartments for specialized processes; and an extremely complicated architecture. Looking back from the perspective of our time, the episode of *Bathybius haeckelii* seems silly or downright embarrassing, but it shouldn't. Haeckel and Huxley were behaving naturally, like Calvin: since they were unaware of the complexity of cells, they found it easy to believe that cells could originate from simple mud.

Throughout history there have been many other examples, similar to that of Haeckel, Huxley, and the cell, where a key piece of a particular scientific puzzle was beyond the understanding of the age. In science, there is even a whimsical term for a machine or structure or process that does something but the actual mechanism by which it accomplishes its task is unknown: it is called a black box. In Darwin's time, all of biology was a black box: not only the cell, or the eye, or digestion, or immunity, but every biological structure and function because, ultimately, no one could explain how biological processes occurred.

Biology has progressed tremendously due to the model that Darwin put forth. But the black boxes Darwin accepted are now being opened, and our view of the world is again being shaken.

Take our modern understanding of proteins, for example.

Proteins

In order to understand the molecular basis of life, it is necessary to understand how things called proteins work. Proteins are the machinery of living tissue that builds the structures and carries out the chemical reactions necessary for life. For example, the first of many steps necessary for the conversion of sugar to biologically usable forms of energy is carried out by a protein called hexokinase. Skin is made in large measure of a protein called collagen. When light impinges on your retina, it interacts first with a protein called rhodopsin. A typical cell contains thousands and thousands of different types of proteins to perform the many tasks necessary for life, much like a carpenter's workshop might contain many different kinds of tools for various carpentry tasks.

What do these versatile tools look like? The basic structure of proteins is quite simple: they are formed by hooking together in a chain discrete subunits called amino acids. Although the protein chain can consist of anywhere from about 50 to about 1,000 amino acid links, each position can only contain one of twenty different amino acids. In this they are much like words: words can come in various lengths but they are made up from a discrete set of twenty-six letters.

Now, a protein in a cell does not float around like a floppy chain; rather, it folds up into a very precise structure which can be quite different for different types of proteins. Two different amino acid sequences—two different proteins—can be folded to structures as specific and different from each other as a three-eighths-inch wrench and a jigsaw. And like the household tools, if the shape of the proteins is significantly warped, then they fail to do their jobs.

The Eyesight of Humans

In general, biological processes on the molecular level are performed by networks of proteins, each member of which carries out a particular task in a chain.

Let us return to the question, how do we see? Although to Darwin the primary event of vision was a black box, through the efforts of many biochemists an answer to the question of sight is at hand.[3] The answer involves a long chain of steps that begin when light strikes the retina and a photon is absorbed by an organic molecule called 11-cis-retinal, causing it to rearrange itself within picoseconds. This causes a corresponding change to the protein, rhodopsin, which is tightly bound to it, so that it can react with another protein called transducin, which in turn causes a molecule called GDP to be exchanged with a molecule called GTP.

To make a long story short, this exchange begins a long series of further bindings between still more specialized molecular machinery, and scientists now understand a great deal about the system of gateways, pumps, ion channels, critical concentrations, and attenuated signals that result in a current to finally be transmitted down the optic nerve to the brain, interpreted as vision. Biochemists also understand the many chemical reactions involved in restoring all these changed or depleted parts to make a new cycle possible.

To Explain Life

Although space doesn't permit me to give the details of the biochemistry of vision here, I have given the steps in my talks. Biochemists know what it means to "explain" vision. They know the level of explanation that biological science eventually must aim for. In order to say that some function is understood, every relevant step in the process must be elucidated. The relevant steps in biological processes occur ultimately at the molecular level, so a satisfactory explanation of a biological phenomenon such as sight, or digestion, or immunity, must include a molecular explanation.

It is no longer sufficient, now that the black box of vision has been opened, for an "evolutionary explanation" of that power to invoke only the anatomical structures of whole eyes, as Darwin did in the nineteenth century and as most popularizers of evolution continue to do today. Anatomy is, quite simply, irrelevant. So is the fossil record. It does not matter whether the fossil record is consistent with evolutionary theory, any more than it mattered in physics that Newton's theory was consistent with everyday experience. The fossil record has nothing to tell us about, say, whether or how the interactions of 11-cis-retinal with rhodopsin, transducin, and phosphodiesterase could have developed, step by step.

"How a nerve comes to be sensitive to light hardly concerns us more than how life itself originated," said Darwin in the nineteenth century. But both phenomena have attracted the interest of modern biochemistry in the past few decades. The story of the slow paralysis of research on life's origin is quite interesting, but space precludes its retelling here. Suffice it to say that at present the field of origin-of-life studies has dissolved into a cacophony of conflicting models, each unconvincing, seriously incomplete, and incompatible with competing models. In private, even most evolutionary biologists will admit that they have no explanation for the beginning of life.[4]

The same problems that beset origin-of-life research also bedevil efforts to show how virtually any complex biochemical system came about. Biochemistry has revealed a molecular world that stoutly resists explanation by the same theory that has long been applied at the level of the whole organism. Neither of Darwin's black boxes—the origin of life or the origin of vision (or other complex biochemical systems)—has been accounted for by his theory.

Irreducible Complexity

In *The Origin of Species,* Darwin stated: "If it could be demonstrated that any complex organ existed which could not possibly have been formed by numerous, successive, slight modifications, my theory would absolutely break down."[5] A system that meets Darwin's criterion is one that exhibits irreducible complexity. By irreducible complexity I mean a single system that is composed of several interacting parts that contribute to the basic function and where the removal of any one of the parts causes the system to effectively cease functioning. An irreducibly complex system cannot be produced directly by slight, successive modifications of a precursor system, since any precursor to an irreducibly complex system is by definition nonfunctional.

Since natural selection requires a function to select, an irreducibly complex biological system, if there is such a thing, would have to arise as an integrated unit for natural selection to have anything to act on. It is almost universally conceded that such a sudden event would be irreconcilable with the gradualism Darwin envisioned. At this point, however, "irreducibly complex" is just a term, whose power resides mostly in its definition. We must now ask if any real thing is in fact irreducibly complex, and, if so, then are any irreducibly complex things also biological systems?

Consider the humble mousetrap (figure 1). The mousetraps that my family uses in our home to deal with unwelcome rodents consist of a number of parts. There are: (1) a flat wooden platform to act as a base; (2) a metal hammer, which does the actual job of crushing the little mouse; (3) a wire spring with extended ends to press against the platform and the hammer when the trap is charged; (4) a sensitive catch that releases when slight pressure is applied; and (5) a metal bar that holds the hammer back when the trap is charged and connects to the catch. There are also assorted staples and screws to hold the system together.

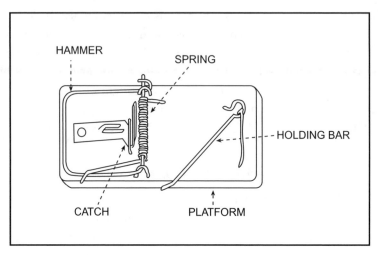

FIGURE 1: A household mousetrap. The working parts of the trap are labeled. If any of the parts are missing, the trap does not function.

If any one of the components of the mousetrap (the base, hammer, spring, catch, or holding bar) is removed, then the trap does not function. In other words, the simple little mousetrap has no ability to trap a mouse until several separate parts are all assembled.

Because the mousetrap is necessarily composed of several parts, it is irreducibly complex. Thus, irreducibly complex systems exist.

Molecular Machines

Now, are any biochemical systems irreducibly complex? Yes, it turns out that many are.

Earlier we discussed proteins. In many biological structures, proteins are simply components of larger molecular machines. Like the picture tube, wires, metal bolts, and screws that comprise a television set, many proteins are part of structures that only function when virtually all of the components have been assembled.

A good example of this is a cilium.[6] Cilia are hairlike organelles on the surfaces of many animal and lower plant cells that serve to move fluid over the cell's surface or to "row" single cells through a fluid. In humans, for example, epithelial cells lining the respiratory tract each have about 200 cilia that beat in synchrony to sweep mucus toward the throat for elimination.

A cilium consists of a membrane-coated bundle of fibers called an axoneme. An axoneme contains a ring of nine double microtubules surrounding two central single microtubules. Each outer doublet consists of a ring of thirteen filaments (subfiber A) fused to an assembly of ten filaments (subfiber B). The filaments of the microtubules are composed of two proteins called alpha and beta tubulin. The eleven microtubules forming an axoneme are held together by three types of connectors: subfibers A are joined to the central microtubules by radial spokes; adjacent outer doublets are joined by linkers that consist of a highly elastic protein called nexin; and the central microtubules are joined by a connecting bridge. Finally, every subfiber A bears two arms, an inner arm and an outer arm, both containing the protein dynein.

But how does a cilium work? Experiments have indicated that ciliary motion results from the chemically powered "walking" of the dynein arms on one microtubule up the neighboring subfiber B of a second microtubule so that the two microtubules slide past each other (figure 2). However, the protein cross-links between microtubules in an intact cilium prevent neighboring microtubules from sliding past each other by more than a

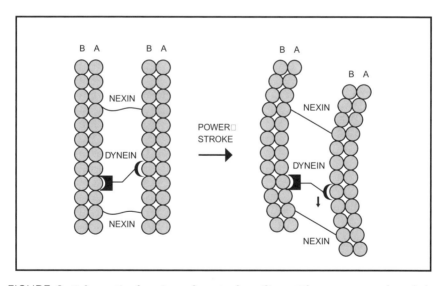

FIGURE 2: Schematic drawing of part of a cilium. The power stroke of the motor protein dynein, attached to one microtubule, against subfiber B of a neighboring microtubule causes the fibers to slide past each other. The flexible linker protein, nexin, converts the sliding motion to a bending motion.

short distance. These cross-links, therefore, convert the dynein-induced sliding motion to a bending motion of the entire axoneme.

Now, let us sit back, review the workings of the cilium, and consider what it implies. Cilia are composed of at least half a dozen proteins: alpha-tubulin, beta-tubulin, dynein, nexin, spoke protein, and a central bridge protein. These combine to perform one task, ciliary motion, and all of these proteins must be present for the cilium to function. If the tubulins are absent, then there are no filaments to slide; if the dynein is missing, then the cilium remains rigid and motionless; if nexin or the other connecting proteins are missing, then the axoneme falls apart when the filaments slide.

What we see in the cilium, then, is not just profound complexity, but it is also irreducible complexity on the molecular scale. Recall that by "irreducible complexity" we mean an apparatus that requires several distinct components for the whole to work. My mousetrap must have a base, hammer, spring, catch, and holding bar, all working together, in order to function. Similarly, the cilium, as it is constituted, must have the sliding filaments, connecting proteins, and motor proteins for function to occur. In the absence of any one of those components, the apparatus is useless.

The components of cilia are single molecules. This means that there are no more black boxes to invoke; the complexity of the cilium is final, fundamental. And just as scientists, when they began to learn the complexities of the cell, realized how silly it was to think that life arose spontaneously in a single step or a few steps from ocean mud, so, too, we now realize that the complex cilium cannot be reached in a single step or a few steps.

But since the complexity of the cilium is irreducible, then it cannot have functional precursors. Since the irreducibly complex cilium cannot have functional precursors, it cannot be produced by natural selection, which requires a continuum of function to work. Natural selection is powerless when there is no function to select. We can go further and say that if the cilium cannot be produced by natural selection or other similarly naturalistic mechanisms—and no other biochemically plausible mechanisms have been proposed—then the cilium was most probably designed.

A Nonmechanical Example

A nonmechanical example of irreducible complexity can be seen in the system that targets proteins for delivery to subcellular compartments.[7] In order to find their way to the compartments where they are needed to

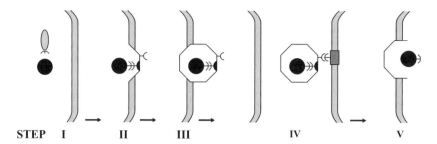

FIGURE 3: Transport of a protein from the ER to lysome. Step 1: A specific enzyme (gray oval) places a marker on the protein (black sphere). This takes place within the ER, which is delimited by a barrier membrane (cross-hatched bar with ends curving to the left). Step 2: The marker is specifically recognized by a receptor protein and the clathrin vesicle (hexagonal shape) begins to form. Step 3: The clathrin vesicle is completed and buds off from the ER membrane. Step 4: The clathrin vesicle crosses the cytoplasm and attaches through another specific marker to a receptor protein (dark gray box) on the lysosomal membrane (cross-hatched bar with ends curving to the right). Step 5: Through a series of several more steps the clathrin vesicle fuses with the lysosomal membrane and releases its cargo.

perform specialized tasks, certain proteins contain a special amino acid sequence near the beginning called a signal sequence.

As the proteins are being synthesized by ribosomes, a complex molecular assemblage called the signal recognition particle (SRP) binds to the signal sequence. This causes synthesis of the protein to halt temporarily. During the pause in protein synthesis, the SRP is bound by the transmembrane SRP receptor, which causes protein synthesis to resume and which allows passage of the protein into the interior of the endoplasmic reticulum (ER). As the protein passes into the ER, the signal sequence is cut off.

For many proteins, the ER is just a way station on their travels to their final destinations (figure 3). Proteins that will end up in a lysosome are enzymatically "tagged" with a carbohydrate residue called mannose-6-phosphate while still in the ER. An area of the ER membrane then begins to concentrate several proteins; one protein, clathrin, forms a sort of geodesic dome called a coated vesicle, which buds off from the ER. In the dome there is also a receptor protein that binds both to the clathrin and to the mannose-6-phosphate group of the protein, which is being transported. The coated vesicle then leaves the ER, travels through the cytoplasm, and binds to the lysosome through another specific receptor protein. Finally, in a maneuver involving several more proteins, the vesicle fuses with the lysosome, and the protein arrives at its destination.

During its travels, our protein interacted with dozens of macromolecules to achieve one purpose: its arrival in the lysosome. Virtually all components of the transport system are necessary for the system to operate, and therefore the system is irreducible. And since all of the components of the system are comprised of single or several molecules, there are no black boxes to invoke. The consequences of even a single gap in the transport chain can be seen in the hereditary defect known as I-cell disease. It results from a deficiency of the enzyme that places the mannose-6-phosphate on proteins to be targeted to the lysosomes. I-cell disease is characterized by progressive retardation, skeletal deformities, and early death.

The Study of "Molecular Evolution"

Other examples of irreducible complexity abound, including aspects of protein transport, blood clotting, closed circular DNA, electron transport, the bacterial flagellum, telomeres, photosynthesis, transcription regulation, and much more. Examples of irreducible complexity can be found on virtually every page of a biochemistry textbook. But if these things cannot be explained by Darwinian evolution, how has the scientific community regarded these phenomena of the past forty years?

A good place to look for an answer to that question is in the *Journal of Molecular Evolution* (*JME*), a journal that was begun specifically to deal with the topic of how evolution occurs on the molecular level. *JME* has high scientific standards and is edited by prominent figures in the field. In a recent issue, all eleven articles were concerned simply with the analysis of protein or DNA sequences. None of the papers discussed detailed models for intermediates in the development of complex biomolecular structures.

In the past ten years *JME* has published 886 papers. Of these, 95 discussed the chemical synthesis of molecules thought to be necessary for the origin of life, 44 proposed mathematical models to improve sequence analysis, 20 concerned the evolutionary implications of current structures, and 719 were analyses of protein or polynucleotide sequences. However, there weren't any papers discussing detailed models for intermediates in the development of complex biomolecular structures. This is not a peculiarity of *JME*. No papers are to be found that discuss detailed models for intermediates in the development of complex biomolecular structures in the

Proceedings of the National Academy of Science, Nature, Science, Journal of Molecular Biology, or, to my knowledge, any journal whatsoever.

Sequence comparisons overwhelmingly dominate the literature of molecular evolution. But sequence comparisons simply can't account for the development of complex biochemical systems any more than Darwin's comparison of simple and complex eyes told him how vision worked. Thus, in this area, science is mute.

Detection of Design

What's going on? Imagine a room in which a body lies crushed, flat as a pancake. A dozen detectives crawl around, examining the floor with magnifying glasses for any clue to the identity of the perpetrator. In the middle of the room next to the body stands a large, gray elephant. The detectives carefully avoid bumping into the pachyderm's legs as they crawl and never even glance at it. Over time, the detectives get frustrated with their lack of progress but resolutely press on, looking even more closely at the floor. You see, textbooks say detectives must "get their man," so they never consider elephants.

There is an elephant in the roomful of scientists who are trying to explain the development of life. The elephant is labeled "intelligent design." To a person who does not feel obliged to restrict his or her search to unintelligent causes, the straightforward conclusion is that many biochemical systems were designed. They were designed *not* by the laws of nature, not by chance and necessity. Rather, they were *planned.* The designer knew what the systems would look like when they were completed; the designer took steps to bring the systems about. Life on Earth at its most fundamental level, in its most critical components, is the product of intelligent activity.

The conclusion of intelligent design flows naturally from the data itself—not from sacred books or sectarian beliefs. Inferring that biochemical systems were designed by an intelligent agent is a humdrum process that requires no new principles of logic or science. It comes simply from the hard work that biochemistry has done over the past forty years, combined with consideration of the way in which we reach conclusions of design every day.

What is "design"? Design is simply the *purposeful arrangement of parts.* The scientific question is how we detect design. This can be done in various ways, but design can most easily be inferred for mechanical objects.

Systems made entirely from natural components can also evince design. For example, suppose you are walking with a friend in the woods. All of a sudden your friend is pulled high in the air and left dangling by his foot from a vine attached to a tree branch.

After cutting him down you reconstruct the trap. You see that the vine was wrapped around the tree branch, and the end pulled tightly down to the ground. It was securely anchored to the ground by a forked branch. The branch was attached to another vine—hidden by leaves—so that, when the trigger-vine was disturbed, it would pull down the forked stick, releasing the spring-vine. The end of the vine formed a loop with a slip-knot to grab an appendage and snap it up into the air. Even though the trap was made completely of natural materials, you would quickly conclude that it was the product of intelligent design.

Intelligent design is a good explanation for a number of biochemical systems, but I should insert a word of caution. Intelligent design theory has to be seen in context: it does not try to explain everything. We live in a complex world where lots of different things can happen. When deciding how various rocks came to be shaped the way they are, a geologist might consider a whole range of factors: rain, wind, the movement of glaciers, the activity of moss and lichens, volcanic action, nuclear explosions, asteroid impact, or the hand of a sculptor. The shape of one rock might have been determined primarily by one mechanism, the shape of another rock by another mechanism.

Similarly, evolutionary biologists have recognized that a number of factors might have affected the development of life: common descent, natural selection, migration, population size, founder effects (effects that may be due to the limited number of organisms that begin a new species), genetic drift (spread of "neutral," nonselective mutations), gene flow (the incorporation of genes into a population from a separate population), linkage (occurrence of two genes on the same chromosome), and much more. The fact that some biochemical systems were designed by an intelligent agent does not mean that any of the other factors are not operative, common, or important.

Conclusion

It is often said that science must avoid any conclusions that smack of the supernatural. But this seems to me to be both bad logic and bad science. Science is not a game in which arbitrary rules are used to decide what explanations are to be permitted. Rather, it is an effort to make true statements about physical reality. It was only about sixty years ago that the expansion of the universe was first observed. This fact immediately suggested a singular event—that at some time in the distant past the universe began expanding from an extremely small size.

To many people this inference was loaded with overtones of a supernatural event—the creation, the beginning of the universe. The prominent physicist A. S. Eddington probably spoke for many physicists in voicing his disgust with such a notion: "Philosophically, the notion of an abrupt beginning to the present order of Nature is repugnant to me, as I think it must be to most; and even those who would welcome a proof of the intervention of a Creator will probably consider that a single winding-up at some remote epoch is not really the kind of relation between God and his world that brings satisfaction to the mind."[8]

Nonetheless, the big bang hypothesis was embraced by physics and over the years has proven to be a very fruitful paradigm. The point here is that physics followed the data where it seemed to lead, even though some thought the model gave aid and comfort to religion. In the present day, as biochemistry multiplies examples of fantastically complex molecular systems, systems that discourage even an attempt to explain how they may have arisen, we should take a lesson from physics. The conclusion of design flows naturally from the data; we should not shrink from it; we should embrace it and build on it.

In concluding, it is important to realize that we are not inferring design from what we do not know but from what we do know. We are not inferring design to account for a black box but to account for an open box. A man from a primitive culture who sees an automobile might guess that it was powered by the wind or by an antelope hidden under the car, but when he opens up the hood and sees the engine he immediately realizes that it was designed. In the same way, biochemistry has opened up the cell to examine what makes it run, and we see that it, too, was designed.

It was a shock to the people of the nineteenth century when they discovered, from observations science had made, that many features of the biological world could be ascribed to the elegant principle of natural selection. It is a shock to us in the twenty-first century to discover, from observations science has made, that the fundamental mechanisms and systems of life cannot be ascribed to natural selection, but instead these mechanisms manifest a feature—irreducible complexity—that we know from experience only arises from intelligent design. But we must deal with our shock as best we can and go on. The theory of undirected evolution is already dead, but the work of science continues.

Notes

1. C. Darwin, *The Origin of Species,* 6th ed. (New York: New York University Press, 1988), 151.

2. J. Farley, *The Spontaneous Generation from Descartes to Oparin,* 2nd ed. (Baltimore: Johns Hopkins University Press, 1979), 73.

3. T. Devlin, *Textbook of Biochemistry* (New York: Wiley-Liss, 1992), 938–54.

4. University of Memphis rhetorician John Angus Campbell has observed that "huge edifices of ideas—such as positivism—never really die. Thinking people gradually abandon them and even ridicule them among themselves, but keep the persuasively useful parts to scare away the uninformed." J. A. Campbell, "The Comic Frame and the Rhetoric of Science: Epistemology and Ethics in Darwin's *Origin,*" *Rhetoric Society Quarterly* 24 (1994): 27–50.

5. Darwin, *Origin,* 154.

6. D. Voet and J. G. Voet, *Biochemistry* (New York: John Wiley and Sons, 1990), 1132–39.

7. Ibid., 297–304.

8. Cited in S. L. Jaki, *Cosmos and Creator* (Chicago: Gateway Editions, 1980), 5–6.

Homology in Biology: Problem for Naturalistic Science and Prospect for Intelligent Design

Paul Nelson and Jonathan Wells

Since 1859, the fundamental similarities between organisms—classically, at the level of gross anatomy; more recently, at the level of molecules—have been understood and explained according to the theory of common descent. That is, organisms are similar in various ways because they have descended from common ancestors (and, ultimately, from a single common ancestor) possessing the trait(s) in question. This explanation is widely seen as a fundamental aspect of the Darwinian revolution in biology.

Before Darwin, homology was defined morphologically and explained by reference to ideal archetypes—that is, to intelligent design. Darwin reformulated biology in naturalistic rather than teleological terms and explained homology as the result of descent with modification from a common ancestor.[1] Descent with modification, however, renders design unnecessary only if it is due entirely to naturalistic mechanisms. Two such mechanisms have been proposed, genetic programs and developmental pathways, but neither one fits the evidence. Without an empirically demonstrated naturalistic mechanism to account for homology, design remains a possibility that can be excluded only on the basis of questionable philosophical assumptions. Further, design uniquely explains patterns of homology difficult or impossible to reconcile with neo-Darwinian common descent.

Morphological and Phylogenetic Homology

From at least the time of Aristotle, people who study living organisms have noted some remarkable similarities among very diverse creatures. Bats and butterflies are quite different from each other, yet both have wings to fly. Bats fly and whales swim, yet the bones in a bat's wing and a whale's flipper are strikingly alike. The first kind of similarity refers to different structures that perform the same function; in 1843, anatomist Richard Owen called this analogy. In contrast, the second kind of similarity refers to similar structures that perform different functions; Owen called this homology. Owen (and other pre-Darwinian biologists) attributed homology to the existence of archetypes: that is, biological structures are similar because they conform more or less to preexisting patterns.[2]

In 1859, Charles Darwin offered a different explanation for homology. According to Darwin, bats and whales possess similar bone structures because they inherited them from a common ancestor—not because they were constructed according to the same archetype. By replacing archetypes (which imply design and intelligent agency) with a natural mechanism such as common descent, Darwin hoped to render idealistic explanations unnecessary and to place biology on a securely naturalistic basis.

Not all structural similarities, however, are inherited from a common ancestor (as Darwin and his followers recognized). For example, the eye of a mouse is structurally similar to the eye of an octopus, yet their supposed common ancestor did not possess such an eye. In 1870, Ray Lankester coined the term *homoplasy* to describe such features. Implicit in that distinction was a new definition of homology. As evolutionary biologist Ernst Mayr put it, after Darwin the "biologically most meaningful definition" of homology was: "A feature in two or more taxa is homologous when it is derived from the same (or a corresponding) feature of their common ancestor."[3] In other words, what Darwin proposed as the explanation for homology became its definition. For many biologists, the post-Darwinian (or phylogenetic) definition of homology has replaced the structural (or morphological) definition.[4]

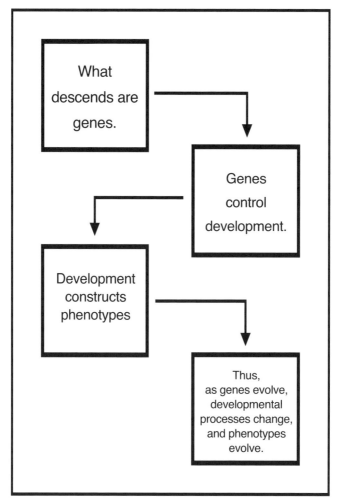

FIGURE 1. The neo-Darwinian picture (explanation) of homology.

Darwin's reform—explaining homology by material descent with modification—was incorporated into the neo-Darwinian synthesis of the mid-twentieth century with the discovery of the mechanisms of transmission genetics (that is, inheritance), about which Darwin knew nothing. Figure 1 displays a flow diagram with the key elements of the neo-Darwinian explanation of homology. The cardinal "explainer" (so to speak), or cause, that Darwin advocated classically in chapter 13 of the *Origin of Species* is material descent. Every organism in our experience has at least one parent. Thus, humans (for instance) possess two large bones, the radius and the ulna, in their forelimbs because, by hypothesis, their distant nonhuman primate ancestors also possessed two such bones, albeit with slightly different shapes—and so on, back to the primary progenitor that first evolved the radius-ulna pattern.

Neo-Darwinian biologists added to this the new causal dimension of the physical basis of heredity. In brief, at reproduction, each parent (in a sexually reproducing species) passes half of its genetic material (DNA) to its offspring. What descends from generation to generation, therefore, are genes: DNA. These genes in turn control the processes of development in the fertilized egg, as the phenotype (adult morphology) is being constructed. Evolution, or the adaptive modification of adult form, occurs because genes are subject to mutation. These modifications affect development; differing phenotypes are constructed among the offspring, which are then selected by their ability to compete and reproduce.

That explanation has a beautiful plausibility. It is also in very serious trouble. Within the past decade or so, a flood of new data on the genetic constituents of development, and the revisiting of older but still unsolved puzzles (see below), has battered the foundations of the neo-Darwinian explanation of homology. In a commentary on the troubled state of the concept, David Cannatella of the Department of Zoology at the University of Texas wrote: "Wake (1994) offered that homology is the central concept of all biology. If this is true, then a large group of comparative biologists lacks a guiding principle. One does not have to look very far to see that homology (and therefore homoplasy [convergence]) is not understood by many biologists."[5]

Despite the standard textbook claims, homology has never been adequately explained by neo-Darwinism. The time is ripe, we contend, to reconsider biology's exclusion of intelligent design as a possible cause.

The Need for a Naturalistic Mechanism

Ask your neighborhood evolutionary biologist how he or she knows that intelligent design is unnecessary to explain homology, and the odds are he or she will say something like, "Well, we have demonstrated a natural mechanism that accounts for the phenomenon." In actuality, however, the mechanism has not been demonstrated. Rather, homology is simply taken as prima facie evidence of descent, and design is excluded categorically. The problem is unintentionally illustrated by biologist Tim Berra in his

1990 book, *Evolution and the Myth of Creationism*. According to Berra, "If you look at a 1953 Corvette and compare it to the latest model, only the most general resemblances are evident, but if you compare a 1953 and a 1954 Corvette, side by side, then a 1954 and a 1955 model, and so on, the descent with modification is overwhelmingly obvious. This is what paleontologists do with fossils, and the evidence is so solid and comprehensive that it cannot be denied by reasonable people."[6]

As the title of his book indicates, Berra's primary purpose is to show that living organisms are the result of naturalistic evolution rather than of intelligent design. Structural similarities among automobiles, however, even similarities between older and newer models (which Berra calls "descent with modification") are due to construction according to preexisting patterns—that is, to design. Ironically, therefore, Berra's analogy shows that phylogenetic homology is not sufficient to exclude design-based explanations. In order to demonstrate naturalistic evolution, it is necessary to show that the mechanism by which organisms are constructed (unlike the mechanism by which automobiles are constructed) is not based on design.

One could simply postulate that the mechanism of biological evolution is naturalistic, arguing that the postulate is justified because science is limited to studying natural mechanisms. Although such a philosophical move may seem reasonable, it compromises the status of evolutionary biology as an objective science. Asserting that something is objectively true implies that it is based on empirical evidence, not merely assumed a priori on philosophical grounds. A methodological exclusion of design-based explanations constitutes a limitation on one's discipline, not a description of objective reality. If evolutionary biologists want to show that the actual mechanism of evolution does not involve intelligent design, they cannot merely exclude the possibility a priori but must take the more difficult approach of proposing and corroborating a naturalistic alternative.

This alternative must account naturalistically for what evolutionary biologist Leigh Van Valen has called "continuity of information."[7] According to Van Valen, homologous features are produced during the development of each individual organism by information that has been inherited, with modification, from the organism's ancestors. Thus, the first step toward understanding the mechanism of evolution would be to determine the nature of the information that controls the development of the embryo.

Homology and Genetics

One possibility is that the information that controls the development of the embryo is encoded in the organism's genes. In the 1930s, the synthesis of Darwin's theory and population genetics explained evolution as a change in gene frequencies. Several decades later, the discovery of the structure and function of DNA extended this explanation to the molecular level.

According to the neo-Darwinian synthesis, a genetic program encoded in DNA directs embryonic development. The process of reproduction transmits this program to subsequent generations, but mutations in the DNA sometimes modify it ("descent with modification"); thus, descendants of the original organism may possess structures that are similar but not identical ("homologies"). Neo-Darwinism asserts that if we find homologous adult structures in two or more groups—for instance, the paired limbs, dorsal nerve cord, and vertebral column of vertebrates—then those homologies were caused by the descent or transmission (from parent to offspring) of homologous genes and developmental processes. In short, homologous genes control homologous developmental processes, which construct homologous adult phenotypes. Thus, the neo-Darwinian theory of evolution predicts that if we find homologous structures we should also find homologous genes and developmental processes that produce those structures. Yet detailed studies at the molecular level fail to demonstrate the expected correspondence between changes in gene products and the sorts of organismal changes that constitute the "stuff of evolution."[8] According to Rudolf Raff and Thomas Kauffman, evolution by DNA mutations "is largely uncoupled from morphological evolution." The "most spectacular" example of this is the morphological dissimilarity of humans and chimpanzees despite a 99 percent similarity in their DNA.[9]

Some biologists have proposed that the remaining 1 percent consists of "regulatory genes," which have such profound effects on development that a few mutations in them could account for dramatic differences. For example, mutations in homeotic genes can transform a fly's antenna into a leg, or produce two pairs of wings where there would normally be only one, or cause eyes to develop on a fly's leg. Further, genes similar to the homeotic genes of flies have been found in most other types of animals, including mammals. Based on the profound developmental effects and almost universal occurrence of such genes, biologist Eric Davidson and his colleagues recently wrote that "novel morphological forms in animal evolution result from changes in genetically encoded programs of developmental regulation."[10]

According to the received neo-Darwinian view, homologous features are programmed by similar genes. Assuming that genes with similar sequences are unlikely to originate independently through random mutations, sequence similarity would indicate common ancestry. And, if this is so, the similar gene sequences should produce homologous anatomical and structural features.

The very universality of homeotic genes, however, raises a serious problem for that view since these homeotic genes are homologous and yet produce very different anatomical features in different organisms. Although mice have a gene very similar to the one that can transform a fly's antenna into a leg (Antennapedia), mice do not have antennae, and their corresponding gene affects the hindbrain. Although mice and flies share a similar gene that affects eye development (eyeless), the fly's multifaceted eye is profoundly different from a mouse's camera-like eye. In both cases (Antennapedia and eyeless), similar homeotic genes affect the development of structures that are nonhomologous by either the classical morphological definition or the post-Darwinian phylogenetic definition. If similar genes can "determine" such radically different structures, those genes aren't really determining structure at all. Instead, they appear to be functioning as binary switches between alternate developmental fates, with the information for the resulting structures residing elsewhere.[11]

Not only are nonhomologous structures produced by organisms with supposedly homologous genes, but organisms with different genes can also produce similar structures—again contradicting neo-Darwinian predictions. The most famous examples relate to the genes, mentioned above, that affect wing and eye development in flies. Fly embryos with a normal gene for wing development, when treated with ether, can be induced to grow a second pair, just as though they possessed the mutant form of the gene.[12] Flies with a mutant form of the eye gene fail to develop eyes; but if eyeless flies are bred for many generations, some of their descendents will develop eyes even though they still possess the mutant form of the gene. Such anomalies led embryologist Gavin de Beer to conclude that "homologous structures need not be controlled by identical genes" and that "the inheritance of homologous structures from a common ancestor . . . cannot be ascribed to identity of genes."[13]

The underlying assumption that a genetic program directs embryonic development has been seriously questioned by developmental biologists.[14] Sydney Brenner, who originally proposed genetic programs in 1970, repudiated the idea when he realized that the information required to specify the neural connections of even a simple worm far exceeds the information content of its DNA.[15] A decade later, developmental biologist Brian Goodwin noted that "genes are responsible for determining which molecules an organism can produce," but "the molecular composition of organisms does not, in general, determine their form."[16] In a 1990 critique of the notion of genetic programs, H. F. Nijhout concluded that "the only strictly correct view of the function of genes is that they supply cells, and ultimately organisms, with chemical materials."[17]

Clearly, the genetic explanation for homology is inadequate. As an alternative, some biologists have suggested that homology results from complex developmental mechanisms that are not reducible to a genetic program.

Homology and Developmental Pathways

Since homologies cannot be explained by equating developmental information with DNA sequences, some biologists have attempted to explain it by attributing it to similar developmental pathways. Although DNA determines the amino acid sequence of proteins essential for development, such pathways also require other factors, such as the localization of cytoplasmic constituents in the egg cell, physical constraints resulting from the size of the embryo, and so on.[18]

Efforts to correlate homology with developmental pathways, however, have been uniformly unsuccessful. First, similar developmental pathways may produce very dissimilar features. At the molecular level, it is well known that virtually identical inducers may participate in the development of nonhomologous structures in different animals.[19] At the multicellular level, the pattern of embryonic cell movements that generates body form in birds also generates body form in a few species of frogs.[20] Even at the organismal level, morphologically indistinguishable larvae may develop into completely different species.[21] Clearly, similar developmental pathways can produce dissimilar results.

Second, and more dramatically, similar features are often produced by very different developmental pathways. No one doubts that the gut is homologous throughout the vertebrates, yet the gut forms from different embryonic cells in different vertebrates. The neural tube, embryonic precursor of the spinal cord, is regarded as homologous throughout the chordates, yet in some of them its formation depends on induction by the underlying notochord while in others it does not.[22] Evidently, "structures can owe their origin to different methods of induction without forfeiting their homology."[23] As developmental biologist Pere Alberch noted in 1985, it is "the rule rather than the exception" that "homologous structures form from distinctly dissimilar initial states."[24]

Production of similar forms from dissimilar pathways is also common at later stages of development. Many types of animals pass through a larval stage on their way to adulthood, a phenomenon known as indirect development. For example, most frogs begin life as swimming tadpoles and only later metamorphose into four-legged animals. Many species of frogs, however, bypass the larval stage and develop directly. Remarkably, the adults of some of these direct developers are almost indistinguishable from the adults of species that develop indirectly. In other words, very similar frogs can be produced by direct and indirect development, even though the pathways are obviously radically different. The same phenomenon is common among sea urchins and ascidians.[25]

Even the classic example of vertebrate limbs shows that homology cannot be explained by similarities in developmental pathways. Skeletal patterns in vertebrate limbs are initially laid down in the form of cartilage condensations, which later ossify into bone. The sequence of cartilage condensation is the developmental pathway that determines the future pattern of bones in the limb. Yet similar bone patterns in different species (that is, homologies) arise from different sequences of cartilage condensation.[26] In the words of biologist Richard Hinchliffe: "Embryology does not contribute to comparative morphology by providing evidence of limb homology in the form of an unchanging pattern of condensation common to all tetrapod limbs."[27]

The constancy of final patterns despite varying pathways has prompted developmental biologist Günter Wagner to suggest that homology might be due to conserved developmental "constraints."[28] Wagner's critics, however, object that his notion is too vague to be useful.

Although developmental constraints emphasize the fact that embryos are capable of producing similar end-points by a variety of routes, such constraints do not constitute a naturalistic mechanism accessible to empirical investigation. So embryology has not solved the problem of homology. In 1958, Gavin de Beer observed that "correspondence between homologous structures cannot be pressed back to similarity of position of the cells in the embryo, or of the parts of the egg out of which the structures are ultimately composed, or of developmental mechanisms by which they are formed."[29] Subsequent research has overwhelmingly confirmed the correctness of de Beer's observation. Homology, whether defined morphologically or phylogenetically, cannot be attributed to similar developmental pathways any more than it can be attributed to similar genes. So far, the naturalistic mechanisms proposed to explain homology do not fit the evidence.

The Explanatory Promise of Design

In 1802, William Paley wrote that someone crossing a heath and finding a stone could reasonably attribute its presence to purposeless natural causes. On finding a watch, however, and seeing that "its several parts are framed and put together for a purpose," one could conclude that the watch had been designed. By analogy, Paley argued, one could also conclude that living things are designed.[30] In 1859, Charles Darwin argued that living things only appear to be designed and claimed that everything Paley attributed to design could be accounted for naturalistically, by descent with modification.

As Berra's automobile analogy shows, however, descent with modification is not enough to exclude design. It is necessary, in addition, to show that the mechanism of descent with modification is thoroughly naturalistic. Darwin thought he had done this with his theory of natural selection, but as the problem of homology demonstrates, he failed to accomplish his goal. Diverse organisms possess homologous features. Homology may or may not be due to inheritance from a common ancestor, but it is definitely not due to similarity of genes or similarity of developmental pathways. In 1971, de Beer wrote: "What mechanism can it be that results in the production of homologous organs, the same 'patterns,' in spite of their not being controlled by the same genes? I asked this question in 1938, and it has not been answered."[31] His question still has not been answered.

Without a naturalistic mechanism to account for homology, however, Darwinian evolution cannot claim to have demonstrated scientifically that living things are undesigned. The possibility remains that homologies are patterned after idealized archetypes. Without a demonstrated mechanism, naturalistic biologists are left with only one alternative: exclude design a priori on philosophical grounds.

Such an exclusion could be taken as a statement that intelligent design does not exist, or it could be taken as a statement that intelligent design is beyond the reach of empirical science. The first is a theological statement and warrants a theological response. The second is a methodological limitation that cannot be logically extrapolated to a limitation on reality. In other words, a scientist who makes the first move is engaging in theological disputation. A scientist who makes the second is declining to investigate a possible aspect of reality.

Regrettably, many biologists make both moves but fail to distinguish logically between them. While justifying their exclusion of intelligent design on methodological grounds, they act as though science has disproved its existence by providing a naturalistic explanation for homology. When confronted with the fact that science has failed in this regard, they reaffirm their methodological commitment and express faith that a naturalistic mechanism will someday be discovered.

And perhaps it will. But what if living things really are designed? Someone who finds a watch on the ground and wants to investigate its origin would be mistaken to rule out design a priori. Having already jumped to the wrong conclusion, that person might go on to waste an entire lifetime dabbling in spurious explanations. If science is truth-seeking, that is a strange way to do science.

So, how might intelligent design explain homology?

In the preceding sections, we discussed several patterns of biological evidence that are difficult to reconcile with neo-Darwinian common descent. Here, in this concluding section, we shall treat two of those patterns in somewhat more depth. Consider what follows as case studies in the explanatory tools that intelligent design uniquely brings to bear on open biological problems.

The first pattern concerns what is perhaps the most remarkable discovery of the past decade in developmental biology, namely, the surprising conservation of key embryonic regulators—homeobox genes—across wide taxonomic distances. Homeobox genes have been found in all animals examined, from flatworms to humans.[32] Their omnipresence and striking conservation have been taken by neo-Darwinians as powerful evidence that all animals arose by descent from a common multicellular ancestor, which itself possessed the genes in question.[33]

Yet on nearly any construal of common descent, those data should be deeply puzzling. To grasp the puzzle, think about the text you are now reading. Imagine comparing it to some other document you read recently—say, an advice column in this morning's newspaper. Suppose we asked you, "What makes this chapter different from the advice column you read this morning?" You would not answer by observing that both texts shared the words *the, this, we, you, all, question,* or any other shared strings of characters. This is a chapter about how intelligent design may explain homology; what you read this morning, on the other hand, was a bit of advice about how to get along with your spouse. The similarities between the words used in these different texts do not explain their higher-level differences—and that is what we wish to understand.

As biologists John Gerhart and Marc Kirschner have noted recently, if one wants to explain profound biological differences—such as exist between the animal phyla—to focus on what is conserved genetically among those phyla is to look in precisely the wrong place.[34] Other biologists have also shaken off the intoxicating wonder of the discovery of homeobox genes to ask about this puzzle, a puzzle perhaps first noticed by Miklos and John as they commented on the homeodomain itself, the DNA-binding protein domain.[35] Miklos and John noted that the homeobox domain itself (spanning sixty amino acids) was well conserved between "such organisms as yeast [a single-celled eukaryote] and man," creatures differing about as widely as one could imagine in their overall form and function. The homeobox itself, therefore, could not alone have been the relevant locus of the many changes (that is, differences) required between yeast and humans, just as the word *differences* in this sentence cannot alone explain the contrast in meaning between this sentence and another in the previous paragraph where *differences* also occurs. Several years later, surveying a much greater range of examples, Stanford University biologist Matthew Scott raised the same puzzle, albeit now referring to the conservation of Hox gene clusters: "Animal architecture is guided by many conserved regulators, among them homeobox genes that have related functions in mammals, insects, and worms. The surprising conservation of the regulators stands in stark contrast to the diversity of animal form. . . . However, if Hox genes are conserved, what is not conserved? What makes animals different, the regulation of Hox genes or their effects on the genes they control?"[36]

The problem can be grasped by lifting one's eyes from gene homology to the differences in development and form that first capture our attention as biological observers. What is it that makes the starfish a starfish or the worm a worm? As developmental biologist Eric Davidson notes, one cannot say "know one [pattern of development], know them all; the rest is just details."[37] A starfish is not a worm, and neither is a vertebrate. "Obviously," Davidson continues, "animals do develop differently," despite the many conserved genes they may share. Indeed, from a neo-Darwinian perspective, the conserved genes have become a paradox. As developmental biologists Denis Duboule and Adam Wilkins note, prior to the unanticipated discovery of conserved homeobox genes among the animal phyla, "most biologists . . . would probably have bet that diversity and difference in the underlying molecular systems was the general rule."[38] Neo-Darwinism predicts that differences in phenotypic form (such as characterize a starfish versus a worm versus a vertebrate) arise first in genetic mutations. "How have animals evolved to be so different?" asks Peter Lawrence of Cambridge University, when their key embryonic regulators are apparently so highly conserved?[39]

It is helpful to consider this puzzle first from the perspective of a naturalistic metaphysics of scientific explanation. Naturalism, as other authors in this volume note, limits one's explanatory tools fundamentally to natural regularities and chance (and their interaction). Thus, when biologists observe striking similarities among the genes isolated from very different organisms (for example, from a fruit fly and a mouse), those similarities must be explained either deterministically—by a natural regularity—or by chance. Chance can be eliminated immediately. Geneticist John Brookfield provides a wonderfully clear estimation of the likelihood that two gene sequences exhibiting high sequence similarity—call them p' and p"—arose by chance independently of each other. (This estimation, note carefully, presupposes the existence of the genetic code and other basic systems of cell biology; it is not an estimation calculated in a prebiotic milieu.) Brookfield begins with various facts about the genetic code:

> The genetic code indicates that long open reading frames are statistically improbable. If all bases are used equally and there is no correlation between successive bases, the probability that three successive bases form a stop codon is simply 3/64, or 0.0469. Starting from a methionine [start] codon, the number of codons before the next stop codon will be exponentially distributed, with a mean of 21.3.[40]

Brookfield continues:

> If a typical gene has, once spliced, an open reading frame of 500 amino acids [and let us suppose this is the case for p' and p"], the probability that an open reading frame this long or longer would exist by chance is 6×10^{-11}. . . . Thus, long open reading frames indicate either functional genes or their nonfunctional descendants.[41]

Thus, when we find in different species open reading frames—genes—that exhibit high sequence similarity, probability dictates that in the absence of a deterministic theory for the origin of similar gene sequences ab initio (and no such theory currently exists), high similarity can be explained only by the natural regularity of ordinary descent, or reproduction. In other words, the genes in question must share a common ancestor. As Colin Patterson observes, "Convergence [similarity without material descent] between molecular sequences is too improbable to occur, just as similarity between sequences is too improbable to be explained except by common ancestry. . . . This is the argument from complexity: if two structures are complex enough and similar in detail, probability dictates that they must be homologous rather than convergent."[42]

Hence, the puzzle outlined above. Very different organisms, placed in separate phyla, nevertheless exhibit highly similar genes that play important roles in development. But if their key development genes are similar, how did those organisms ever come to be different in the first place?

Intelligent design provides us with a third option. It does so uniquely (that is, when compared with all its theoretical competitors). An intelligent cause may reuse or redeploy the same module in different systems, without there necessarily being any material or physical connection between those systems. Even more simply, intelligent causes can generate identical patterns independently: We do so, for instance, every time we sign a bank check or credit card slip. Banks and other institutions that require a means of uniquely identifying individuals exploit the reuse of the same signature when verifying our identity.

How does that analogy bear on similar genes in different organisms? If we suppose that an intelligent designer constructed organisms using a common set of polyfunctional genetic modules—just as human designers, for instance, may employ the same transistor or capacitor in a car radio or a computer, devices that are not "homologous" as artifacts—then we can explain why we find the "same" genes expressed in the development of what are very different organisms. Here, the homology being explained is genetic, not morphological (for that pattern, see below). A particular gene, employed for its DNA-binding properties, finds its functional role in a higher-level system whose ultimate origin was intelligently caused. The overall system, not the gene itself, determines its functional role. And such systems, in our experience, can only be intelligently caused. We might give this a name: the organismal context principle (see figure 2).

Further, intelligent design explains why perturbations to key embryonic switches, such as homeobox genes, do not yield functional (or adaptive) consequences. All intelligently designed systems in our experience have delimited spheres of function. Put more simply, the relations of parts within a complex system constrain what "variations" on that system are

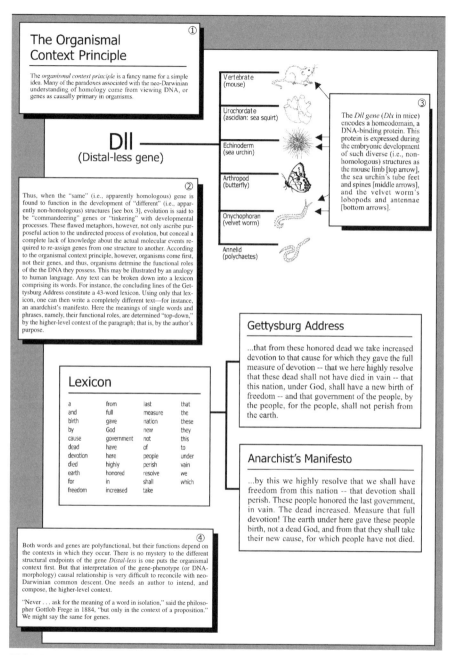

① The Organismal Context Principle

The *organismal context principle* is a fancy name for a simple idea. Many of the paradoxes associated with the neo-Darwinian understanding of homology come from viewing DNA, or genes as causally primary in organisms.

DII
(Distal-less gene)

Vertebrate (mouse)

Urochordate (ascidian: sea squirt)

Echinoderm (sea urchin)

Arthropod (butterfly)

Onychophoran (velvet worm)

Annelid (polychaetes)

③

The *Dll gene* (*Dlx* in mice) encodes a homeodomain, a DNA-binding protein. This protein is expressed during the embryonic development of such diverse (i.e., non-homologous) structures as the mouse limb [top arrow], the sea urchin's tube feet and spines [middle arrows], and the velvet worm's lobopods and antennae [bottom arrows].

②

Thus, when the "same" (i.e., apparently homologous) gene is found to function in the development of "different" (i.e., apparently non-homologous) structures [see box 3], evolution is said to be "commandeering" genes or "tinkering" with developmental processes. These flawed metaphors, however, not only ascribe purposeful action to the undirected process of evolution, but conceal a complete lack of knowledge about the actual molecular events required to re-assign genes from one structure to another. According to the organismal context principle, however, organisms come first, not their genes, and thus, organisms detrmine the functional roles of the the DNA they possess. This may be illustrated by an analogy to human language. Any text can be broken down into a lexicon comprising its words. For instance, the concluding lines of the Gettysburg Address constitute a 43-word lexicon. Using only that lexicon, one can then write a completely different text—for instance, an anarchdist's manifesto. Here the meanings of single words and phrases, namely, their functional roles, are determined "top-down," by the higher-level context of the paragraph; that is, by the author's purpose.

Lexicon

a	from	last	that
and	full	measure	the
birth	gave	nation	these
by	God	new	they
cause	government	not	this
dead	have	of	to
devotion	here	people	under
died	highly	perish	vain
earth	honored	resolve	we
for	in	shall	which
freedom	increased	take	

Gettysburg Address

...that from these honored dead we take increased devotion to that cause for which they gave the full measure of devotion -- that we here highly resolve that these dead shall not have died in vain -- that this nation, under God, shall have a new birth of freedom -- and that government of the people, by the people, for the people, shall not perish from the earth.

Anarchist's Manifesto

...by this we highly resolve that we shall have freedom from this nation -- that devotion shall perish. These people honored the last government, in vain. The dead increased. Measure that full devotion! The earth under here gave these people birth, not a dead God, and from that they shall take their new cause, for which people have not died.

④

Both words and genes are polyfunctional, but their functions depend on the contexts in which they occur. There is no mystery to the different structural endpoints of the gene *Distal-less* is one puts the organismal context first. But that interpretation of the gene-phenotype (or DNA-morphology) causal relationship is very difficult to reconcile with neo-Darwinian common descent. One needs an author to intend, and compose, the higher-level context.

"Never . . . ask for the meaning of a word in isolation," said the philosopher Gottlob Frege in 1884, "but only in the context of a proposition." We might say the same for genes.

FIGURE 2. The Organismal Context Principle.

possible. Your car will run on gasoline (or perhaps diesel fuel); it will not run on kerosene or fuel oil unless it is intelligently reengineered. Your laptop computer will not operate without its power supply, nor can you plug in your 110 volt electric shaver in Europe without the specific (intelligently engineered) device of a voltage converter. Designed systems are specified and as such have discoverable limits of function.

In precisely the same sense, organisms have discoverable limits of function and change. Biologists now know that mutations to homeobox genes in such model systems as mice or fruit flies yield severely crippled or (most often) dead organisms. The reason? "[I]t is important that the establishment of Hox expression domains be controlled faithfully as slight mistakes in this process will lead to the misidentification of the corresponding structures, an effect that is often referred to as homeotic transformation."[43]

Homeotic transformations in flies, as we have noted above, can be dramatic (two pairs of wings, instead of one; legs for antennae). What they are decidedly not is adaptive—that is, "fit" in the sense of being reproductively successful. *Drosophila* geneticists know that any homeotic mutant that manages to survive at all (in the laboratory) is a hopeless invalid, which must be isolated from other flies. In the wild, such organisms disappear more or less immediately. They are not candidates for future evolutionary change. Rather, homeotic mutants are life's proverbial born losers.

But if we suppose, as intelligent design theory hypothesizes, that discrete organismal systems are materially (historically) distinct from each other, having their origins in particular acts of intelligent causation, then we need not seek mechanisms of deep transformation for which—almost 150 years after Darwin—we still have no good evidence. Rather, we should expect— and for this we have mountains of evidence—that perturbing the development of complex animals will yield nonfunctional consequences, just as disabling the power supply of a computer yields a nonfunctional artifact.

The second pattern of homology to which we want to apply intelligent design theory is morphological: gross anatomical similarities, such as the pentadactyl limb (see figure 3). Here the situation is reversed from the one just considered. We observe a similar (rather than dissimilar) higher-level pattern, but its lower-level developmental constituents (for example, patterns of cartilage condensation) are different. Intelligent design uniquely affords us an explanation of this phenomenon.

Intelligent causes, unlike natural causes, can anticipate functional requirements. Consider a nonbiological example. Powered, controlled flight in the earth's atmosphere requires the presence of the following: a source

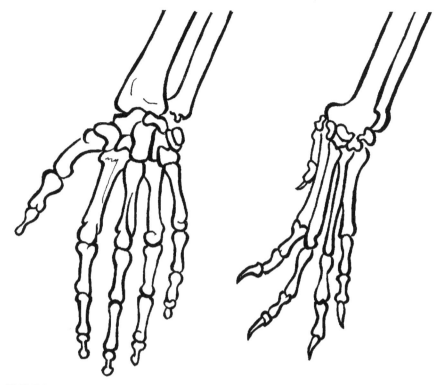

FIGURE 3. The pattern of the *pentadactyl* limb: the human hand and a dog's forelimb.

of lift, a source of thrust, and three-axis control (roll, pitch, and yaw). These are functional demands set by the task: "lift this heavier-than-air ob-ject from the ground, control its motion through the air, and set it down again on the ground." On visiting an aerospace museum, one will discover that these functional demands may be fulfilled in very different ways. The structure of a propeller power plant is "nonhomologous" with a jet engine. But even within structurally "homologous" systems, the particular materials constituting the relevant parts may differ. Thus, the surfaces that provide three-axis control—the ailerons, elevators, and rudder, on an alu-minum-skin, aluminum-frame turboprop passenger plane—will be similar in location and shape to those found on a prop-driven crop-dusting plane with a wooden frame and fabric skin.

Structural homology at a higher functional level, dictated by functional demands, may exist independently of its particular material substrate, because intelligent designers are not bound by the constraints of what might be called physical transmission or continuity. It would be nonsensical to try to "evolve" the aluminum-skin plane from its fabric-skin counterpart, maintaining continuity of materials. One must maintain three-axis control, to be sure, but that is a functional requirement, grasped abstractly. The requirement, however, can be satisfied by any number of different physical constituents.

In precisely the same way, diverse vertebrates exhibiting the pentadactyl pattern in their forelimbs and hindlimbs may possess that pattern not because they inherited it from a common ancestor—that is, not because of material continuity—but because there exists some functional requirement that the pattern satisfies. The lower-level developmental discontinuities we observe in building that pattern, however, may answer either to other (disparate) functional demands or may represent simply the freedom of the designer to employ different materials for the same functional end.

These are matters for further empirical investigation. But only intelligent design provides us the intellectual means even to begin explaining these phenomena. As such, the theory belongs in the toolkit of any biologist willing to grapple with the deep questions now raised by the phenomenon of homology.

Notes

1. In this essay, *naturalism* and *naturalistic* refer to the philosophical doctrine that nature is the whole of reality and that intelligent causation does not qualify as a scientific explanation.
2. Peter J. Bowler, *Evolution: The History of an Idea,* rev. ed. (Berkeley: University of California Press, 1989); Alec L. Panchen, "Richard Owen and the Concept of Homology," in *Homology: The Hierarchical Basis of Comparative Biology,* ed. Brian K. Hall (New York: Academic Press, 1994), 21–62.
3. Ernst Mayr, *The Growth of Biological Thought* (Cambridge, Mass.: Belknap Press, 1982).
4. Brian K. Hall, *Evolutionary Developmental Biology* (London: Chapman and Hall, 1992); Panchen, "Richard Owen."
5. David Cannatella, review of *Homology: The Hierarchical Basis of Comparative Anatomy,* ed. B. K. Hall, and *Homoplasy: The Recurrence of Similarity,* ed. M. J. Sanderson and L. Hufford, *Evolution in Systematic Biology* 46 (1997): 369.
6. Tim M. Berra, *Evolution and the Myth of Creationism* (Stanford, Calif.: Stanford University Press, 1990), 117.

7. Leigh M. Van Valen, "Homology and Causes," *Journal of Morphology* 173 (1982): 305–12.

8. R. C. Lewontin, *The Genetic Basis of Evolutionary Change* (New York: Columbia University Press, 1974), 160.

9. Rudolf A Raff and Thomas C. Kauffman, *Embryos, Genes, and Evolution* (New York: Macmillan, 1983), 67, 78.

10. E. H. Davidson, K. J. Peterson, and R. A. Cameron, "Origin of Bilaterian Body Plans: Evolution of Developmental Regulatory Mechanisms," *Science* 270 (24 Nov. 1995): 1319.

11. Jonathan Wells, "Unseating Naturalism: Recent Insights from Developmental Biology" (paper presented at the conference Mere Creation: Reclaiming the Book of Nature, Biola University, Los Angeles, 1996).

12. For a review, see Hall, *Evolutionary.*

13. Gavin de Beer, *Homology: An Unsolved Problem* (London: Oxford University Press, 1971), 15–16.

14. For a review, see Jonathan Wells, "The History and Limits of Genetic Engineering," *International Journal on the Unity of the Sciences* 5 (1992): 137–50.

15. Sydney Brenner, "The Genetics of Behaviour," *British Medical Bulletin* 29 (1973): 269–71.

16. Brian C. Goodwin, "What Are the Causes of Morphogenesis?" *BioEssays* 3 (1985): 32–36.

17. H. F. Nijhout, "Metaphors and the Role of Genes in Development," *BioEssays* 12 (1990): 444.

18. Wells, "History."

19. Scott F. Gilbert, *Developmental Biology,* 4th ed. (Sunderland, Mass.: Sinauer Associates, 1994).

20. Richard P. Elinson, "Change in Developmental Patterns: Embryos of Amphibians with Large Eggs," in *Development as an Evolutionary Process,* ed. Rudolf A. Raff and Elizabeth C. Raff (New York: Alan R. Liss, 1987), 1–21.

21. Gavin de Beer, *Embryos and Ancestors,* 3rd ed. (Oxford: Clarendon Press, 1958).

22. Gilbert, *Developmental Biology.*

23. de Beer, *Embryos,* 151.

24. Pere Alberch, "Problems with the Interpretation of Developmental Sequences," *Systematic Zoology* 34, no. 1 (1985): 51.

25. Rudolf A. Raff, *The Shape of Life: Genes, Development, and the Evolution of Animal Form* (Chicago: University of Chicago Press, 1996).

26. Neil H. Shubin, "The Implications of 'The *Baupläne*' for Development and Evolution of the Tetrapod Limb," in *Developmental Patterning of the Vertebrate Limb,* ed. J. R. Hinchliffe, J. M. Hurie, and D. Summerbell (New York: Plenum Press, 1991), 411–21.

27. Richard Hinchliffe, "Towards a Homology of Process: Evolutionary Implications of Experimental Studies on the Generation of Skeletal Pattern in Avian Limb Development" in *Organizational Constraints on the Dynamics of Evolution,* ed. J. Maynard Smith and G. Vida (Manchester: Manchester University Press, 1990), 121.

28. Günter Wagner, "The Biological Homology Concept," *Annual Review of Ecology and Systematics* 20 (1989): 51–69.

29. de Beer, *Embryos,* 152.

30. William Paley, *Natural Theology* (Houston: St. Thomas Press, [1802] 1972), 2.

31. de Beer, *Homology,* 16.

32. Frank H. Ruddle, Jane L. Bartels, Kevin L. Bentley, Claudia Kappen, Michael T. Murtha, and John W. Pendleton, "Evolution of Hox Genes," *Annual Review of Genetics* 28 (1994): 423–42.

33. Matthew P. Scott, "Intimations of a Creature," *Cell* 79 (1994): 1121–24.

34. John Gerhart and Marc Kirschner, *Cells, Embryos, and Evolution* (London: Blackwell Science, 1997).

35. G. L. G. Miklos and Bernard John, "From Genotype to Phenotype," in *Rates of Evolution,* ed. K. S. W. Campbell and M. F. Day (London: Allen and Unwin, 1987), 273.

36. Scott, "Intimations," 1121.

37. Eric Davidson, "Molecular Biology of Embryonic Development: How Far Have We Come in the Last Ten Years?" *BioEssays* 16 (1994): 610.

38. Denis Duboule and Adam S. Wilkins, "The Evolution of 'Bricolage,'" *Trends in Genetics* 14 (1998): 54.

39. Peter Lawrence, quoted in Michael Akam, "The Yin and Yang of Evo/Devo," *Cell* 92 (1998): 153–55.

40. John F. Y. Brookfield, "Genetic Redundancy," *Advances in Genetics* 36 (1997): 145.

41. Ibid.

42. Colin Patterson, "Homology in Classical and Molecular Biology," *Molecular Biology and Evolution* 5 (1988): 615.

43. Denis Duboule, "Hox Is in the Hair: A Break in Colinearity?" *Genes and Development* 12 (1998): 1.

The Cambrian Explosion: Biology's Big Bang

Stephen C. Meyer, Marcus Ross,
Paul Nelson, and Paul Chien

✠ ✠ ✠

I. Introduction: Design without a Designer?

Both Charles Darwin himself and contemporary neo-Darwinists such as Francisco Ayala, Richard Dawkins, and Richard Lewontin acknowledge that biological organisms appear to have been designed by an intelligence. Yet classical Darwinists and contemporary Darwinists alike have argued that what Francisco Ayala calls the "obvious design" of living things is only apparent. As Ayala, a former president of the American Association for the Advancement of Science, has explained: "The functional design of organisms and their features would therefore seem to argue for the existence of a designer. It was Darwin's greatest accomplishment to show that the directive organization of living beings can be explained as the result of a natural process, natural selection, without any need to resort to a Creator or other external agent."[1]

According to Darwin and his contemporary followers, the mechanism of natural selection acting on random variation is sufficient to explain the origin of those features of life that once seemed to require explanation by reference to an intelligent or purposeful designer. Thus, according to

323

Darwinists, the design hypothesis now represents an unnecessary and un-parsimonious explanation for the complexity and apparent design of living organisms. On these as well as methodological grounds contemporary biologists have generally excluded the design hypothesis from consideration as an explanation for the origin of biological form.

Yet does Darwinism, in either its classical or contemporary versions, fully succeed in explaining the origin of biological form? Can it explain *all* evidence of apparent design? Most biologists now acknowledge that the Darwinian mechanism of natural selection acting on random variations can explain small-scale microevolutionary changes, such as cyclical variations in the size of the beaks of Galapagos finches or reversible changes in the expression of genes controlling color in English peppered moths.[2] But what about the large-scale innovations in the history of life? What about the origin of completely new organs, body plans, and structures—the macroevolutionary innovation to which the fossil record attests? Does Darwinism, or neo-Darwinism, or any other strictly materialistic model of evolutionary change explain the origin of the basic body plans or structural "designs" of animal life, without invoking actual (that is, purposive or intelligent) design?

In this essay, we will test the claims of neo-Darwinism and two other materialistic models of evolutionary theory: punctuated equilibrium and self-organization. We will do so by assessing how well these theories explain the main features of the Cambrian explosion—a term that refers to the geologically sudden appearance of numerous new animal forms (and their distinctive body plans) 530 million years ago. We shall show that the Cambrian fossil record contradicts the empirical expectations of both neo-Darwinism and punctuated equilibrium in several significant respects. We further show that neither neo-Darwinism's selection/mutation mechanism nor more recent self-organizational models can account for the origin of the biological information necessary to produce the Cambrian animals and their distinctive body plans. Instead, we will argue that intelligent design explains both the pattern of the fossil record and the origin of new biological form and information better than the competing models of purposeless and undirected evolutionary change.

II. The Cambrian Explosion

The term *Cambrian explosion* describes the geologically sudden appearance of animals in the fossil record during the Cambrian period of geologic time. During this event, at least nineteen, and as many as thirty-five (of forty total), phyla made their first appearance on earth.[3] Phyla constitute the highest biological categories in the animal kingdom, with each phylum exhibiting a unique architecture, blueprint, or structural body plan. Familiar examples of basic animal body plans are cnidarians (corals and jellyfish), mollusks (squids and shellfish), arthropods (crustaceans, insects, and trilobites), echinoderms (sea star and sea urchins), and the chordates, the phylum to which all vertebrates including humans belong. The fossils of the Cambrian explosion exhibit several distinctive features.

A. Geologically Sudden Appearance and the Absence of Ancestral Precursors or Transitional Intermediates

First, as the name implies, the fossils of the Cambrian explosion appear suddenly or abruptly within a very brief period of geologic time (see figures 1 and 2). As recently as 1992, paleontologists thought the Cambrian period began 570 million years ago and ended 510 million years ago, with the Cambrian explosion itself occurring within a 20-to-40-million-year window during the lower Cambrian period. In 1993, radiometric dating of zircon crystals from formations just above and just below Cambrian strata in Siberia allowed for a precise recalibration of the age of Cambrian strata. Radiometric analyses of these crystals fixed the start of the Cambrian

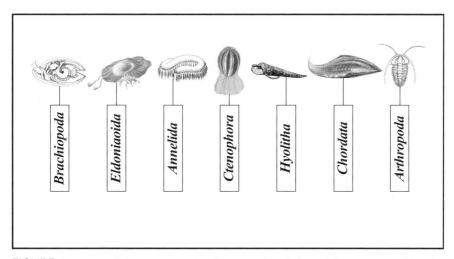

FIGURE 1. Some of the major animal groups (phyla) that first appeared in the Cambrian explosion. Artistic reconstructions of Cambrian fossils: *Brachiopoda* by Andrew Johnson, *Chordata* (*Myllokunmingia fengjiaoa*) courtesy of D. G. Shu, all other images courtesy of J. Y. Chen.

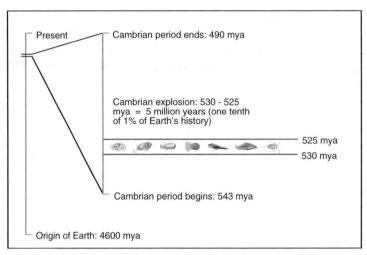

FIGURE 2. The Cambrian explosion occurred within a narrow window of geo-logic time. Artistic reconstructions of Cambrian fossils: *Brachiopoda* by Andrew Johnson, *Chordata* (*Myllokunmingia fengjiaoa*) courtesy of D. G. Shu, all other images courtesy of J. Y. Chen.

period at 543 million years ago and the beginning of the Cambrian explo-sion itself at 530 million years ago (see figure 2).[4] These studies also showed that the Cambrian explosion occurred within an exceedingly nar-row window of geologic time, lasting no more than 5 million years. Geo-logically speaking, 5 million years represents a mere 0.11 percent of Earth's history. As Chinese paleontologist Jun-Yuan Chen has explained, "com-pared with the 3-plus-billion-year history of life on earth, the period [of the explosion] can be likened to one minute in 24 hours of one day."[5] Yet most of the innovations in the basic architecture of animal forms occurred abruptly within just such a small fraction of the earth's history during the Cambrian. Due to the suddenness of the appearance of animal life in the Cambrian, the Cambrian explosion has now earned titles such as "The Big Bang of Animal Evolution" (*Scientific American*), "Evolution's Big Bang" (*Science*), and the "Biological Big Bang" (*Science News*).[6]

To say that the fauna of the Cambrian period appeared in a geologically sudden manner also implies the absence of clear transitional intermediates connecting the complex Cambrian animals with those simpler living forms found in lower strata. Indeed, in almost all cases, the body plans and struc-tures present in Cambrian period animals have no clear morphological antecedents in earlier strata. Some have argued that perhaps the Ediacaran (or Vendian) fauna hold some hope in this regard, but as we will show below, those hopes now seem unfounded.

B. Extensive Morphological Breadth and Representation of Phyla

Second, the Cambrian explosion exhibits an extraordinary morphological breadth and representation of the disparate animal phyla. Cambrian rocks display about half (or more) of the basic body plans or architectural designs of the animal kingdom. Representatives of nineteen of the forty known animal phyla definitely make their first appearance in the fossil record during the Cambrian explosion.[7] Three phyla appear in the Precambrian. Six animal phyla first appear in the fossil record after the Cambrian period, and twelve more are not represented in the fossil record. Nevertheless, for reasons described below, many paleontologists think that almost all of these additional eighteen phyla may well have originated during the Cambrian explosion. Some authorities even estimate that all animal phyla might have come into existence during the Cambrian explosion. As Valentine, Jablonski, and Erwin argue, "All living phyla may have originated by the end of the [Cambrian] explosion."[8]

An especially dramatic feature of the Cambrian explosion is the first appearance of all the invertebrate phyla (and subphyla) with mineralized exoskeletons, including the advanced metazoans such as Mollusca,

FIGURE 3. Fossil trilobite found in lower Cambrian strata near Chengjiang, China. Courtesy of J. Y. Chen.

Phylum: *Arthropoda*
Subphylum: *Trilobitomorpha*
Genus & species: *Eoredlichia intermedia*

FIGURE 4. Artistic reconstruction and fossil specimen of an *Anomalocaris* found near Chengjiang China. Courtesy of J. Y. Chen.

Phylum: *Arthropoda*

Subphylum: *Anomalocarida*

Genus & species: *Anomalocaris saron*

Echinodermata, and Arthropoda. Trilobites (see figure 3), a subphylum of Arthropoda, were highly complex animals whose thoraxes comprised three lobes or sections (a medial axial ring and two lateral pleurae). The bodies of trilobites were covered by a shieldlike, keratinized exoskeleton called a carapace, which covered both the head and thorax of these animals. Like modern arthropods, trilobites grew by shedding their carapaces, and these cast-off carapaces help to account for the abundance of trilobite fossils. The Chengjiang fauna also contains a number of fossils of now-extinct, top-of-the-food-chain predators with exotic names such as *Anomalocaris* (up to six feet in length; see figure 4), which indicates the presence of a complex food web and a diverse ecological community.

Shelled animals leave a far more durable and extensive record than their soft-bodied counterparts. Nevertheless, Cambrian fossil discoveries from both the Burgess shale in the Canadian Rocky Mountains and from

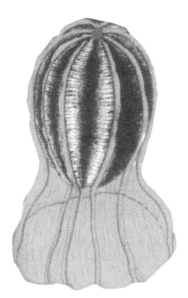

FIGURE 5. Artistic reconstruction and fossil specimen of a comb jelly found near Chengjiang, China. Courtesy of J. Y. Chen.

Phylum: *Ctenophora*

Genus & species: *Maotianoascus octonarius*

the lower Cambrian Yuanshan Formation near Chengjiang, China, have also shown exquisitely preserved soft-bodied fauna. The Chengjiang fauna even show many excellent examples of well-preserved animals with soft tissue (animals lacking even a keratinized exoskeleton), including members of phyla such as Cnidaria, Ctenophora (see figure 5), Annelida, Onycophora, Phoronida (see figure 6), and Priapulida. Burgess Shale fossils from the middle Cambrian (515 million years ago) confirm that many of these Cambrian organisms were long-lived and geographically widespread.

The lower Cambrian sediments near Chengjiang have preserved fossils of such excellent quality that soft tissues and organs, such as eyes, intestines, stomachs, digestive glands, sensory organs, epidermis, bristles, mouths, and nerves, can be observed in detail. Even fossilized embryos of sponges are present in the Precambrian strata near Chengjiang.[9] Cambrian-level strata show the soft body parts of jellyfish–like organisms (known as *Eldonia;* see figure 7), such as radiating water canals and nerve rings. These fossils even include the gut contents of several different kinds of animals and undigested food residue in their stools.[10]

FIGURE 6. Artistic reconstruction and fossil specimen of a phoronid found near Chengjiang, China. Courtesy of J. Y. Chen.

Phylum: *Phoronida*

Genus & species: *Iotuba chengjiangensis*

The Chengjiang fauna also confirms the presence of animals from the phylum Chordata. *Yunnanozoon lividum* is a fusiform eel-shaped animal with, among other features, a digestive tract, branchial arches, and a large notochord. *Yunnanozoon* has been interpreted as a primitive chordate.[11] Two possible cephalochordates have been identified from Cambrian deposits in both China and Canada: Paleontologists have found a single specimen of a possible cephalochordate, *Cathaymyrus,* from the lower Cambrian Qiongzhusi Formation near Chengjiang.[12] Additionally, the cephalochordate *Pikaia* is known from the middle Cambrian Burgess Shale.[13]

More important, several recent discoveries from China have surprised (if not shocked) the paleontological community regarding early chordates. Chen, Huang, and Li have recently reported the discovery of a sophisticated craniate-like chordate called *Haikouella lancelota* from the lower Cambrian Maotianshan Shale in China. According to Chen and his colleagues, *Haikouella* has many of the same features of the *Yunnanozoon lividum,* as well as several additional anatomical features including a "heart, ventral and dorsal aorta, an anterior branchial arterial, gill filaments, a caudal projection, a neural cord with a relatively large brain, a head with possible

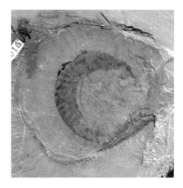

FIGURE 7. Artistic reconstruction and fossil specimen of an *Eldonia* found near Chengjiang, China. Courtesy of J. Y. Chen.

Phylum: *Eldoniaoida* (contested designation)

Genus & species: *Eldonia eumorpha*

lateral eyes, and a ventrally situated buccal cavity with short tentacles."[14] Also, D. G. Shu, Simon Conway Morris, and several Chinese colleagues have made a dramatic find of two small fish fossils, *Myllokunmingia fengjiaoa* and *Haikouichthys ercaicunensis* (see figures 8 and 9) suggesting a much earlier appearance for vertebrates than previously thought. Both of these taxa are jawless fish (agnathans) and are considered by Shu and his colleagues to be rather closely allied to lampreys.[15]

Lastly, a new paper by Shu and others reports the first convincing specimen of a urochordate (tunicate) from the Cambrian.[16] This specimen, *Cheungkongella ancestralis*, is likewise found from the early Cambrian shales (Qiongzhusi Formation) near Chengjiang. Remarkably, these recent finds now demonstrate that not only was the phylum Chordata present in the Cambrian but also that each one of the chordate subphyla (Cephalochordata, Craniata, and Urochordata) were present. Moreover, each of these chordate taxa displayed the morphological characteristics that place them securely within their respective subphyla. Indeed, many phyla such as arthropods, mollusks, and chordates include morphologically disparate subphyla that many paleontologists regard as separate body plans. If subphyla are included in the count of animal body plans, then at least thirty-two and possibly as many as forty-eight of fifty-six total body plans (57.1 to 85.7 percent) first appear on earth during the Cambrian explosion. Thus, depending on how one evaluates the data at either the phyla or

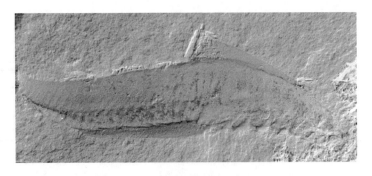

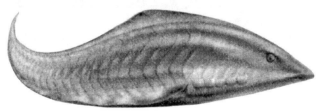

FIGURE 8. Artistic reconstruction and fossil specimen of a fish (similar to modern hagfish) found near Haikou, China. Courtesy of D. G. Shu.

Phylum: *Chordata*

Subphylum: *Vertebrata*

Genus & species: *Myllokunmingia fengjiaoa*

FIGURE 9. Fossil specimen of a fish (similar to modern lamprey) found near Haikou, China. Courtesy of D. G. Shu.

Phylum: *Chordata*

Subphylum: *Vertebrata*

Genus & species: *Haikouichthys ercaicunensis*

subphyla level, the Cambrian strata document the abrupt appearance of between 47.5 and 85.7 percent of all the animal body plans that have ever existed on earth.

C. Persistent Morphological Disparity or Isolation

A third feature of the Cambrian explosion (as well as the subsequent fossil record) bears mentioning. The major body plans that arise in the Cambrian period exhibit considerable morphological isolation from one another (or "disparity") and then subsequent "stasis." Though all Cambrian and subsequent animals fall clearly within one of a limited number of basic body plans, each of these body plans exhibits clear morphological differences (and thus disparity) from the others.[17] The animal body plans (as represented in the fossil record) do not grade imperceptibly one into another, either at a specific time in geological history or over the course of geological history. Instead, the body plans of the animals characterizing the separate phyla maintain their distinctive morphological and organizational features and thus their isolation from one another, over time. The body plans of animals exhibit what we are calling persistent morphological isolation or what others have called stasis (lack of directional change) during their time on earth.[18]

In one sense, of course, the stasis of the phylum as an abstract morphological unit is unremarkable, since phyla are defined for classificatory purposes by reference to an invariant set of anatomical characteristics. In another sense, however, body-plan stasis, as it finds expression in actual animals, is quite remarkable, precisely because actual animals naturally do fall within one, and only one, of a disparate but limited number of classificatory categories. While the phyla (as abstract classificatory units) must by definition exhibit stasis, the body plans of actual animals need not obey this definitional logic. As Jablonski has noted concerning the morphological disparity of the animal phyla, "[s]uch discordances are not simply an artifact of the greater inclusiveness of higher taxa . . . because similar patterns emerge from taxon-free analyses of multivariate morphological data."[19] In other words, the morphological distance between the Cambrian animals persists whether one uses a classical Linnean method to describe them or a taxonomy-free method of description in morphological space—suggesting that the persistence of morphological distance between Cambrian animals is not an artifact of a classification system.[20]

D. A "Quantum" or Discontinuous Increase in Specified Biological Information

Fourth, the sudden emergence of the various animals of the Cambrian explosion represents a dramatic discontinuous or "quantum" increase in the information content (or specified complexity) of the biological world. For 3 billion years, or five-sixths of the earth's history, the biological realm included little more than unicellular bacteria and blue-green algae. During this time, some significant increases in complexity did occur. About 2.7 billion years ago, more complex eukaryotic cells (cells with nuclei) emerged after nearly 1 billion years of earth's history in which only prokaryotic cells existed on the earth.[21] About 1 billion years ago, multicellular grade algae appeared. Then beginning about 565–570 million years ago in the late Precambrian (or Vendian), the first complex multicellular organisms appear in the rock record, including sponges, the peculiar Ediacaran biota, and perhaps some primitive worms or mollusks (see section IV.B; see figures 1 and 2). Forty million years later, the Cambrian explosion occurred. Relative to the rather modest increases in complexity that occurred between the origin of the first life (3.5 to 3.85 billion years ago) and the first appearance of multicellular algae (1 billion years ago), the emergence of the Vendian organisms (565–570 million years ago) and then, to a much greater extent, the Cambrian explosion (530 million years ago) represent steep climbs up the biological complexity gradient. Indeed, analyzed from an information-theoretic standpoint, the Cambrian explosion in particular represents a remarkable jump in the (specified) information content of the biological world.

Before proceeding, we must define the term *information* as used in biology. In classical Shannon information theory, the amount of information in a system is inversely related to the probability of the arrangement of constituents in a system or the characters along a communication channel.[22] The more improbable (or complex) the arrangement, the more Shannon information, or information-carrying capacity, a string or system possesses.

Since the 1960s, mathematical biologists have realized that Shannon's theory could be applied to the analysis of DNA and proteins to measure their information-carrying capacity. Since DNA contains the assembly instructions for building proteins, the information processing system in the cell represents a kind of communication channel.[23] Further, DNA conveys information via specifically arranged sequences of four different chemicals—called nucleotide bases—that function as alphabetic or digital characters in a linear array. Since each of the four bases has a roughly equiprobable chance of occurring at each site along the spine of the DNA molecule, biologists can calculate the probability, and thus the information-carrying capacity, of any particular sequence n bases long.

The ease with which information theory applies to molecular biology has created confusion about the type of information that DNA and proteins possess. Sequences of nucleotide bases in DNA, or amino acids in a protein, are highly improbable and thus have a large information-carrying capacity. But, like meaningful sentences or lines of computer code, genes and proteins are also *specified* with respect to function. Just as the meaning of a sentence depends upon the specific arrangement of the letters in the sentence, so, too, does the function of a gene sequence depend upon the specific arrangement of the nucleotide bases in the gene. Thus, as Sarkar points out, molecular biologists beginning with Francis Crick have equated *information* not only with complexity but also with "specificity," where specificity has meant "necessary to function."[24] Similarly, the Cambrian explosion represents not just an increase in complexity or Shannon information but an increase in the "specified complexity" or *specified* information of the biological world.

One way to measure the increase in specified information or specified complexity of the animals that appeared in the Cambrian is to assess the number of cell types that are required to build such animals and to compare that number with those creatures that went before.[25] Functionally more complex animal forms require more cell types to perform their more diverse functions. Compare, for example, a single-celled eukaryote and a trilobite or a mollusk. Although specialized internally, with a nucleus and various organelles, the single-celled eukaryote represents, obviously, a single type of cell. Not so with the trilobite or mollusk, where dozens of specific tissues and organs require "functionally dedicated," or specialized, cell types. But new cell types require many new and specialized proteins. For example, an epithelial cell lining a gut or intestine, which secretes a digestive enzyme, requires (minimally) structural proteins to modify its shape, regulatory enzymes to control the secretion of the digestive enzyme, and the digestive enzyme itself. New proteins in turn require new genetic information encoded in DNA. Thus, an increase in the number of cell types implies (at a minimum) a considerable increase in the amount of specified genetic information.

Molecular biologists have recently estimated that a minimally complex single-celled organism would require between 300 and 500 genes (or more

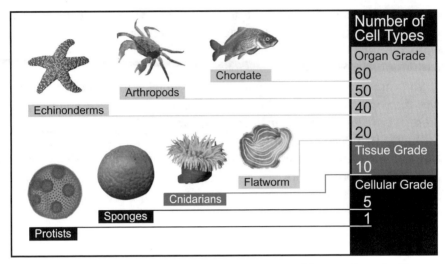

FIGURE 10. Biological Complexity Scale as measured by number of cell types per type of organism. Protist (Volvox) by John McWilliams, Flatworm by Wolfgang Seifarth, other images by Wernher Krutein.

precisely, between 318 and 562 kilobase pairs of DNA) to produce the proteins necessary to maintain life.[26] More complex single cells might require upward of 1 million base pairs. Yet to build the proteins necessary to sustain a complex animal would require orders of magnitude more coding instructions. For example, the genome size of the fly *Drosophila melanogaster* (an arthropod) is approximately 120 million base pairs.[27] Even *Caenorhabditis elegans,* a tiny worm about 1 millimeter long, has a genome of approximately 97 million base pairs.[28] Thus, transitions from a single cell to colonies of cells to complex animals represent significant (and in principle measurable) increases in specified complexity or information content.

The animal phyla represented in the top row of figure 10 (as depicted by modern representatives) first appeared in the Cambrian explosion. These highly complex animals typically had between forty and sixty different cell types. These new cell types would have required (at minimum) many new proteins and a correspondingly large complement of new genetic information encoded in DNA. Relative to the modest increases in specified complexity that occurred earlier in the Precambrian (see the bottom row of figure 10), the Cambrian explosion represents a steep climb up the biology complexity scale. Indeed, analyzed from an informational standpoint, the Cambrian explosion represents a remarkable jump in the specified information or specified complexity of the biological world.

III. Testing Neo-Darwinism and Punctuated Equilibrium against the Cambrian Fossil Record

In this section, we will test neo-Darwinism and punctuated equilibrium against the Cambrian fossil record. Both these theories envision mechanisms that produce biological change in a particular manner. As a result, both have implications for how life should develop over its history and what, therefore, the fossil record should generally look like. Further, both these theories, and neo-Darwinism in particular, purport to offer truly creative mechanisms of biological change. Since the Cambrian fossils attest not only to small-scale variations but also to large-scale innovations in basic body plans, the Cambrian data provide a key test to the efficacy of these mechanisms.

According to neo-Darwinism, biological change occurs as natural selection acts on small, random genetic changes and mutations (of various kinds), favoring those changes that enhance the survival of the organisms in which the changes occur. Over time, small-scale advantageous genetic changes accumulate, eventually resulting in large-scale changes in the morphology of organisms. Thus, according to neo-Darwinism, biological complexity should accumulate in a gradual bit-by-bit fashion over vast periods of geologic time.

A neo-Darwinian understanding of the mechanism that generates new biological structure generates three specific predictions or empirical expectations concerning the fossil record. Given the operation of the neo-Darwinian mechanism, the fossil record should show: (1) the gradual emergence of biological complexity and the existence of numerous transitional forms leading to new phylum-level body plans; (2) small-scale morphological diversity preceding the emergence of large-scale morphological disparity; and (3) a steady increase in the morphological distance between organic forms over time and, consequently, an overall steady increase in the number of phyla over time (taking into account factors such as extinction).

Alternatively, the theory of punctuated equilibrium envisions biological change occurring in larger, more discrete jumps as the result of natural selection acting primarily on whole species rather than on individuals within species. The theory of punctuated equilibrium, therefore, envisions a less gradual development of new living forms—it differs from neo-Darwinism in its understanding of the rate and mode of evolutionary development. Nevertheless, punctuated equilibrium implies that the fossil record should manifest many of the same general features that neo-Darwinism would predict. Thus, we consider each of the main neo-Darwinian predictions or expectations in turn and then compare them to the Cambrian fossil record as a way of testing both neo-Darwinism (and where applicable) punctuated equilibrium.

A. Prediction 1: The Gradual Emergence of Biological Complexity and the Existence of Numerous Transitional Forms Leading to Phyla-Level Body Plans

Charles Darwin regarded the sudden appearance of complex animals such as brachiopods and trilobites in the Cambrian strata (then called the Silurian) as a major challenge to his theory. Based on his theory, he "expected to find intervening strata showing fossils of increasing complexity until finally trilobites appeared."[29] Darwin realized that building highly complex animals such as trilobites from single-celled organisms by natural selection operating on minute, step-by-step variations would require a multitude of transitional forms and failed biological experiments over vast amounts of geologic time. Accordingly, he made the following prediction: "if the theory be true, it is indisputable that before the lowest [Cambrian] stratum was deposited, long periods elapsed, as long as, or probably far longer than, the whole interval from the [Cambrian] age to the present day; and that during these vast, yet quite unknown periods of time, the world swarmed with living creatures."[30]

Darwin's prediction is significant because he recognized the amount of time that his theory required. Geologists in Darwin's day employed relative dating methods. They did not yet have modern radiometric methods for determining the "absolute" date of rocks. Nevertheless, Darwin had a clear picture of what his postulated selection/variation mechanism implied about the history of life. On his theory, complex structures could only be built gradually, minute improvement by minute improvement. Thus, natural selection would require vast periods of time to create new biological forms and structures. Even in the nineteenth century, Darwin understood that this process would take many tens or hundreds of millions of years. Modern neo-Darwinists concur in this view. As noted above, neo-Darwinism envisions minute changes in gene sequences accumulating very slowly as the result of random mutations. Yet empirically derived estimates of mutation rates in extant organisms suggest that the kind of large-scale morphological changes that occurred in the Cambrian would have required far more time than the duration of the explosion (for further discussion, see section V.A.1).[31]

In addition to a pattern of gradual change, Darwinist theories anticipate a gradual increase in the complexity and morphological diversity of organisms over time. Clearly, the fossil record does (generally) show an overall increase in the complexity of organisms from Precambrian to Cambrian times. Nevertheless, the fossil record does not show that novel organisms arose gradually, nor does it document the existence of the many intermediate forms that Darwinian gradualism entails. Indeed, since the mutation/selection mechanism involves a trial and error process, both Darwinism and neo-Darwinism imply that the fossil record should show many transitional organisms and failed experiments (see figures 11 and

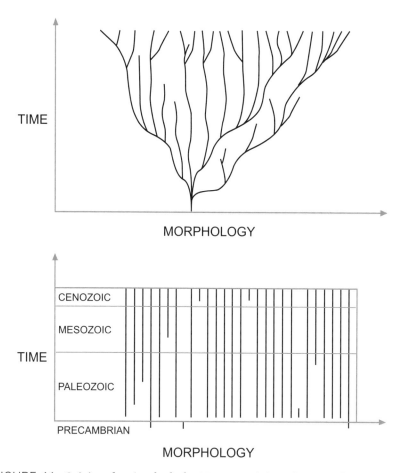

FIGURE 11. Origin of animal phyla: Neo-Darwinian theory (above) vs. fossil evidence (below).

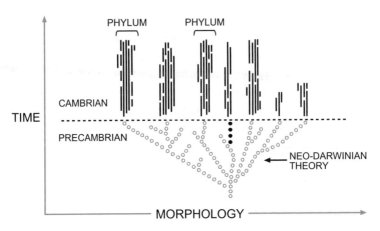

FIGURE 12. According to the theory of universal common descent (part of neo-Darwinian theory) the strata beneath the Cambrian rocks should evidence many ancestral and intermediate forms. Such forms have not been found for the vast majority of phyla. These anticipated and missing forms are represented by the gray circles. Lines and dark circles depict fossilized representatives of Phyla that have been found. Courtesy Art Battson.

12). Instead, organisms such as trilobites (phylum Arthropoda), with their articulated body plans, intricate nervous systems, and compound eyes, first appear fully formed at the beginning of the Cambrian explosion along with many other phyla of equal complexity. As Oxford zoologist Richard Dawkins acknowledges: "It is as though they [the invertebrate phyla] were just planted there, without any evolutionary history."[32]

Darwin was, of course, well aware even in the nineteenth century of the problem that the Cambrian explosion presented for his theory. He stated: "The case at present must remain inexplicable; and may be truly urged as a valid argument against the views here entertained."[33] Contrary to Darwin's hope, however, in the 150 years since the publication of the *Origin*, discoveries in paleontology have only made the puzzle of the Cambrian explosion more acute. Not only have expected transitional forms not turned up, but the pattern of the sudden appearance of novel structure has become more pronounced. Massive new fossil discoveries in the rocks of the Burgess Shale in Canada and in the Yuanshan Formation near Chengjiang, China, have documented many previously unknown Cambrian phyla, thus only increasing the number of expected and missing transitional intermediates required on a Darwinian account of the emergence of new living forms.

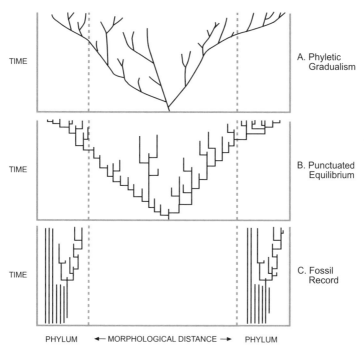

TIME

A. Phyletic
   Gradualism

TIME

B. Punctuated
   Equilibrium

TIME

C. Fossil
   Record

PHYLUM   ←— MORPHOLOGICAL DISTANCE —→   PHYLUM

FIGURE 13. Origin of animal phyla. Two interpretations of the history of life compared with the fossil record.

The difficulty posed by the absence of transitional intermediates for both neo-Darwinism and, to a lesser but still significant extent, punctuationalist evolutionary theories is illustrated in figure 13. The diagrams depict morphological change versus time. The first diagram shows the Darwinian and neo-Darwinian expectation that changes in morphology should arise gradually as minute microevolutionary changes accumulate. This Darwinian commitment to gradual change via microevolution produces the classic representation of the history of life as a branching tree (figure 13A).

The second diagram (figure 13B) represents another model of strictly naturalistic evolutionary change as advanced by Niles Eldredge and Stephen J. Gould. This model, known as punctuated equilibrium, was developed during the late 1960s in an attempt to explain (or describe) more accurately the pattern of sudden appearance and stasis that paleontologists had long observed in the fossil record. According to the punctuationalists, evolutionary change occurs rapidly often after long periods of what they called stasis, periods in which organisms manifest no directional change in their morphology. By repudiating Darwinian gradualism, this model specifically sought to account for the absence of transitional forms in the fossil record. Even so, insofar as this model maintained a commitment to the core Darwinian notion of common descent, it, too, implied that the fossil record should preserve many intermediate forms among higher-rank taxonomic levels. Figure 13B details how punctuationalists conceive of evolutionary change and thus also their expectations for what the fossil record ought to show. According to many punctuationalists, natural selection functions more as a mechanism for selecting the most fit species rather than the most fit individual among a species. Thus, morphological change should occur in larger, more discrete intervals than traditional Darwinism asserts. Nevertheless, as figure 13B shows, punctuationalists still envision many transitional forms as a result of a series of rapid evolutionary changes (albeit representing larger jumps in morphology).

Figure 13C shows the relationship between time and morphology in the actual fossil record. Note that, contrary to the predicted patterns above, the Cambrian radiation and subsequent variation occur after but not before the basic body plans appear in the fossil record. The fossil record also shows a dearth of transitional intermediates between Cambrian and Precambrian fauna.

Since the late 1960s, paleontologists have recognized that the general absence of transitional forms contradicts the picture of the history of life that neo-Darwinism implies, given its commitment to a gradualistic mechanism of evolutionary change (see figure 11). Fewer have recognized, however, that the absence of transitional forms also represents a severe (though relatively lesser) difficulty for punctuated equilibrium. Note that both standard neo-Darwinian and more recent punctuationalist versions of evolutionary theory predict (or expect) many more transitional intermediates than the fossil record actually preserves. This constitutes a particular difficulty because of the great number of new phyla represented in the Cambrian. At present, paleontologists lack clear ancestral precursors for the representatives of not just one new phylum but virtually all the phyla represented in Cambrian explosion (see section IV.B).

In a seminal paper titled "Interpreting Great Developmental Experiments: The Fossil Record" (after which figures 13A and 13B are patterned), paleontologists J. W. Valentine and D. H. Erwin question the sufficiency of both evolutionary models discussed above as explanations for the origin of body plans and higher-level taxa. They note that "transitional alliances are unknown or unconfirmed for any of the [Cambrian] phyla" and yet "the evolutionary explosion near the beginning of Cambrian time was real and produced numerous [new] body plans." Clearly, neo-Darwinism does not explain this pattern. But as Valentine and Erwin point out, neither does punctuated equilibrium. They note that the proposed mechanism of punctuated evolutionary change simply would have lacked the raw material upon which to work. As Valentine and Erwin note, the fossil record fails to document a large pool of species prior to the Cambrian. Yet the proposed mechanism of species selection requires just such a pool of species upon which to act. Thus, they conclude that "the probability that species selection is a general solution to the origin of higher taxa is not great."[34]

Recent work on statistical paleontology by Michael Foote of the University of Chicago reinforces this point. Foote develops a method by which evolutionary models can be tested against several variables. Foote shows that "given estimates of [a] completeness [of the fossil record], [b] median species duration, [c] the time required for evolutionary transitions, and [d] the number of ordinal- or higher-level transitions, we could obtain an estimate of the number of major transitions we should expect to see in the fossil record." His method provides a way to evaluate, as he puts it, "whether the small number of documented major transitions provides strong evidence against evolution."[35] Because estimates of the completeness of the fossil record, median species duration, and the number of ordinal- or higher-level transitions are reasonably well established, the time required for plausible mechanisms to produce macroevolutionary transitions, stands as the crucial variable in any such analysis. If the time required to produce major evolutionary change is high, as it is for neo-Darwinian mechanisms of change, then given current estimates of the completeness of the fossil record, median species duration, and the number of ordinal- or higher-level transitions, neo-Darwinism fails to account for the data of the fossil record. Conversely, for punctuated equilibrium to succeed as an explanation for the data of the fossil record, the time required for plausible mechanisms to produce macroevolutionary transitions must be very low. In other words, the explanatory success of punctuated equilibrium depends upon the existence of a mechanism that can produce rapid macroevolutionary change. As Foote and Gould note elsewhere, the punctuationalist model of Cambrian evolution requires a mechanism of unusual "flexibility and speed."[36] As yet, however, neither Foote nor Gould nor anyone else has identified such a mechanism with any genetic or developmental plausibility. Thus, given the current empirical climate, the logic of Foote's statistical methodology tends to reinforce the earlier work of Valentine and

Erwin, who concluded that "neither of the contending theories of evolutionary change at the species level, phyletic gradualism or punctuated equilibrium, seem applicable to the origin of new body plans," and thus we now require "a [new] theory for the evolution of novelty, not diversity."[37]

B. Prediction 2: Diversity Precedes Morphological Disparity (contra Completeness and Morphological Breadth)

The distinction between small-scale morphological diversity and large-scale morphological novelty (or what taxonomists call *disparity*) raises another key issue. Most biologists today believe that Darwinian mechanisms account for the great diversity of life, by which they often mean the vast numbers of different species in existence. Many fail to ask the question, "What produces novel morphology, and thus the *disparity* between forms, that we observe in the history of life?" By *disparity*, we mean the major differences in morphology, in contrast to minor variations. Specifically, paleontologists use the term *disparity* to measure the major morphological differences between the body plans that correspond to the higher-level taxonomic classifications, whereas they use *diversity* to describe the small-scale variations that correspond to lower-level taxonomic classifications such as species or genera. In other words, disparity refers to life's basic morphological themes, whereas diversity refers to the variations on those themes.[38]

According to neo-Darwinism, morphological distance between evolving organisms will increase gradually over time as small-scale variations accumulate by natural selection to produce increasingly complex forms and structures (including, eventually, new body plans). Thus, given the neo-Darwinian mechanism, one would expect that small-scale differences or "diversity" between species should precede the emergence of morphological disparity between body plans and phyla (see figures 13A and 14). As Richard Dawkins expresses the point: "What had been distinct species within one genus become, in the fullness of time, distinct genera within one family. Later, families will be found to have diverged to the point where taxonomists (specialists in classification) prefer to call them orders, then classes, then phyla. . . . Ancestors of two different phyla, say vertebrates and mollusks, which we see as built upon utterly different 'fundamental body plans' were once just two species within a genus."[39] Indeed, because the mutation/selection mechanism operates cumulatively and gradually, the novel body plans that define the different phyla must arise from numerous lower-level speciation events. For this reason, neo-

Darwinism expects a "cone of increasing diversity" in which large-scale morphological and taxonomic disparity results from the cumulative effects of many small-scale speciation events.

Darwin himself made this point in the *Origin*. Explaining his famous diagram (figure 14) illustrating the theory of common descent, Darwin described how higher taxa should emerge from lower taxa by the accumulation of numerous slight variations. As he said: "[T]he diagram illustrates the steps by which small differences distinguishing varieties are increased into larger differences distinguishing species. By continuing the process for a greater number of generations we get eight species." He went on: "I see no reason to limit the process of modification, as now explained, to the formation of [species and] genera alone. These two groups of genera will thus form two distinct families, or orders, according to the amount of divergent modification supposed to be represented in the diagram."[40] Thus, Darwin described small-scale variations producing new species, genera, and orders. This process would doubtless, on a Darwinian view, continue

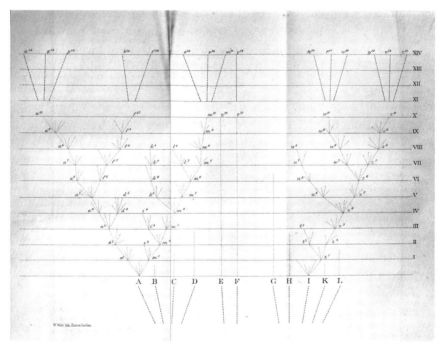

FIGURE 14. Darwin's theory of common descent illustrated here with his famous branching tree diagram, *Origin of Species*, 1859. Courtesy of the University of Oklahoma History of Science Collections.

until it produced new phyla as well. For both classical Darwinism and neo-Darwinism, diversity must precede disparity. Phyla-level differences in body plans must emerge, therefore, only after species-, genus-, and class-level differences appear.

Though advocates of punctuationalist change envision morphological distance arising in larger, more discrete intervals (due to species selection) than do classical neo-Darwinists, they, too, see phyla-level differences arising cumulatively starting from lower-level taxonomic differences between evolving forms. In other words, punctuated equilibrium also predicts morphological diversity preceding disparity (as figure 13B also shows). Thus, for both current evolutionary models, novel body plans are built "bottom-up" as the result of many smaller-scale genetic changes.

The actual pattern in the fossil record, however, contradicts this prediction (see figures 13C and 15). Instead of showing a gradual bottom-up origin of the basic body plans, where smaller-scale diversification or speciation precedes the advent of large-scale morphological disparity, disparity precedes diversity. Indeed, the fossil record shows a "top-down" pattern in which morphological disparity between many separate body plans emerges suddenly and prior to the occurrence of species-level (or higher) diversification on those basic themes. As science writer Roger Lewin has noted: "Several possible patterns exist for the establishment of higher taxa, the two most obvious of which are the bottom-up and the top-down approaches. In the first, evolutionary novelties emerge, bit by bit. The Cambrian explosion appears to conform to the second pattern, the top-down effect."[41] Or as Erwin, Valentine, and Sepkoski observe in their study of well-skeletonized marine invertebrates: "Most higher taxa were built from the top down, rather than from the bottom up. The fossil record suggests that the major pulse of diversification of phyla occurs before that of classes, classes before that of orders, orders before that of families. The higher taxa do not seem to have diverged through an accumulation of lower taxa."[42] In other words, instead of a multiplication of species and other representatives of lower-level taxa occurring first and the building to the disparity of higher taxa, the highest taxonomic differences such as those between phyla and classes appear first (instantiated by very few species-level representatives). Only later do lower-level taxonomic differences appear: different orders, families, genera, and so on. Yet we would not expect either the neo-Darwinian mechanism of natural selection acting on random genetic mutations or the mechanism of species selection to produce the top-down

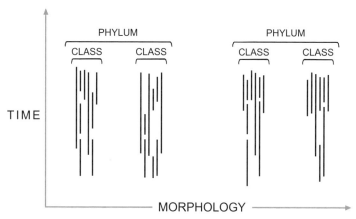

FIGURE 15. The top-down pattern of appearance in the fossil record: disparity precedes diversity.

pattern that we observe in the history of life following the Cambrian explosion.

C. Prediction 3: The Morphological Distance between Organic Forms and thus the Number of Phyla Will Increase Gradually over Time

According to neo-Darwinism and punctuated equilibrium, the fossil record should exhibit another feature. As we have seen, the neo-Darwinian mechanism and the punctuationalist mechanism (of species selection) imply that the morphological distance between organisms will increase gradually over time. Thus, both these mechanisms should produce a steadily increasing number of new body plans, or phyla, over time. Borrowing from Darwin's predictions on the emergence of species (see above), we can express graphically the idealized expectation of the neo-Darwinian (and the punctuationalist) model concerning the appearance of phyla over time (see figure 16). For both these evolutionary models, the number of new phyla should increase in a steady logarithmic fashion as members of one phylum diversify and give rise to new phyla.

Figures 17A and 17B depict numerically the first appearance of all animal phyla over geological time. Figure 17A shows the first appearance of animal phyla based solely on the present body of paleontological evidence. Figure 17B shows the total number of phyla that are often thought to have

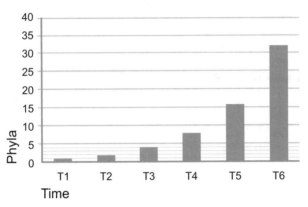

FIGURE 16. Animal phyla first appearances: idealized neo-Darwinism pattern.

made their first appearance in the Cambrian based on geological/environmental considerations as well as direct fossil evidence (see appendix E). Further, many of the phyla that first appear in the fossil record after the Cambrian are less complex than the phyla that first appear in the Cambrian. Since standard evolutionary reasoning assumes that complexity evolves from simplicity and not, generally, the reverse, both neo-Darwinists and punctuationalists often assumed that these simpler phyla must have been present in the Cambrian. Additionally, factors such as organism size, lifestyle, habitat, depositional environment, and the presence or absence of mineralized hard parts affect the likelihood of preservation. Many of the organisms representing phyla that first appear after the Cambrian, or those with no fossil record at all, have one or more of the above features that would have rendered their preservation unlikely, either in general or in specifically Cambrian conditions. Additionally, several phyla that do not appear in the fossil record—Dicymeda, Gastrotricha, Kinoryncha, and Platyhelminthes—have members with known parasitic or symbiotic relationships with a wide suite of animals representing specific phyla that did first appear in the Cambrian. Many of these organisms are small parasites that lived within the digestive systems of larger animals and would not have been good candidates for preservation (or discovery) in the fossil record. Thus, their absence in the fossil record does not necessarily indicate a recent first appearance. Instead, it seems likely that these parasitic organisms themselves may have first appeared as far back as the Cambrian coincident with host organisms of Cambrian age. Thus, several factors suggest reasons, independent of evolutionary assumptions, for suspecting a Cambrian appearance

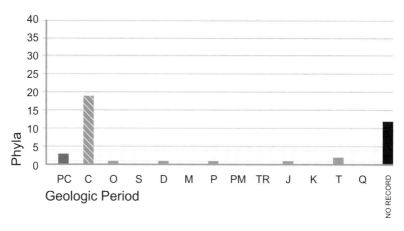

FIGURE 17A. Animal phyla first appearances: based on fossil data alone (see appendix C)

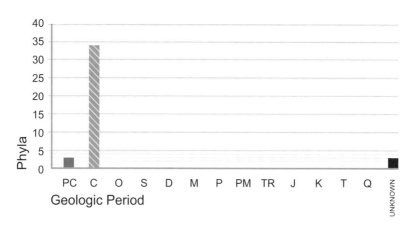

FIGURE 17B. Animal phyla first appearances: based on fossil data and other considerations (see appendix E)

for many of the eighteen phyla that either first appear in the fossil record after the Cambrian or that have no fossil record at all. Only three of these eighteen phyla can be excluded from a Cambrian first appearance given present knowledge (see the entries for Acanthocephala, Cycliophora, and Pentastoma in appendix E).[43]

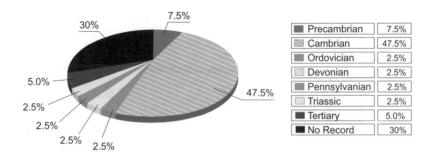

■ Precambrian	7.5%
▨ Cambrian	47.5%
■ Ordovician	2.5%
☐ Devonian	2.5%
■ Pennsylvanian	2.5%
▨ Triassic	2.5%
■ Tertiary	5.0%
■ No Record	30%

FIGURE 18A. Animal phyla first appearances: based on fossil data alone (see appendix C)

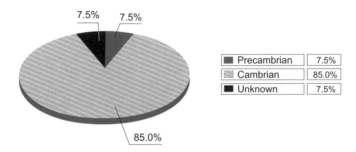

■ Precambrian	7.5%
▨ Cambrian	85.0%
■ Unknown	7.5%

FIGURE 18B. Animal phyla first appearances: based on fossil data and other considerations (see appendix E)

Of course, how one weighs and assesses these various factors will result in differing estimates for the number of phyla or phyla-subphyla body plans that first appear during the Cambrian. Values ranging from 47.5 to 85.7 percent are consistent with existing data. Though we are skeptical of strictly presuppositionally driven arguments based on the theory of universal common descent, we do favor, on geological and environmental grounds, estimates in the middle of this range (see appendix E).[44] Nevertheless, Figures 18A and 18B (or 19B) show body plan first appearances at both extremes of this range in order to show that, however one assesses the various factors discussed above, the empirical expectations of neo-Darwinism and punctuated equilibrium do not conform to paleontological evidence concerning body plan first appearance. Indeed, rather than conforming to neo-Darwinian and punctuationalist expectations of a steadily

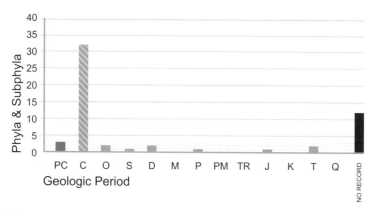

FIGURE 19A. Animal phyla and subphyla first appearances: based on fossil data alone (see appendix D)

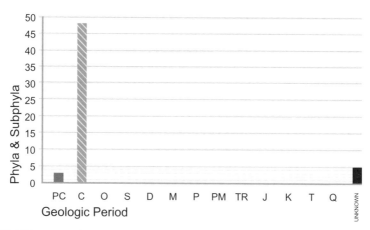

FIGURE 19B. Animal phyla and subphyla first appearances: based on fossil data and other considerations (see appendix E)

increasing number of phyla over geologic time, the fossil record shows a very different pattern; namely, a sudden burst of phyla first appearing in the Cambrian followed either by (as in 17A) a few small subsequent bursts or (as in 17B) a nearly complete absence of new phyla first appearing after the Cambrian.[45] Indeed, for 525 million years after the Cambrian explosion and for 3 billion years before it, the fossil record does not show anything like a steadily increasing number of new phyla. Nor does the sudden explosive appearance of between nineteen and thirty-five new phyla within a 5-million-year window fit the pattern of steady increase that one would expect given either of the two main evolutionary pictures of the history of life.

We have provided two other graphs that reinforce these points. Several animal phyla may be subdivided into a number of subphyla. These subphyla represent major morphological divisions within their respective phyla (distinctions even greater than those seen between classes). Since many paleontologists regard subphyla as equivalent, or nearly equivalent, to phyla, we have also presented graphs (figures 19A and 19B) to show the stratigraphic first appearance and presumed first appearance not only for all the animal phyla but also for the twenty-two animal subphyla.[46] Figure 19A graphs the first appearance of the phyla and subphyla on strictly empirical grounds. Figure 19B graphs the presumed first appearance of the phyla and subphyla based upon the most favorable estimates of the number (of phyla and subphyla) that may have been present in the Cambrian taking the other considerations discussed above into account. Note that representing the data in this way poses an even more severe challenge to the neo-Darwinian picture of the history of life.

Even conservative estimates based strictly on existing fossil evidence show that at least 47.5 percent of all known animal phyla and 57.1 percent of the known phyla and subphyla combined have their first appearance in the Cambrian. Estimates based on an analysis of the factors discussed above can raise these measures to as high as 85.7 percent or more. As mentioned above, we favor values in the middle of this spectrum. Figure 20 provides additional support for this judgment. This figure shows that 67.8 percent of the phyla that do appear in the fossil record appear first in the Cambrian. In other words, if we exclude for the sake of analysis those phyla that do not appear in the fossil record at all and only analyze those phyla that definitely do appear in the record, we arrive at a value near the middle of the extremes (as depicted in figures 18A, 18B, and 19B). This value may represent a very realistic, and perhaps even a lower bound, estimate of the percentage of phyla that first appear in the Cambrian. In any case, we see that however we analyze the data, the pattern of first appearance of the phyla (and subphyla) contradicts that predicted by both the neo-Darwinian and punctuationalist models.

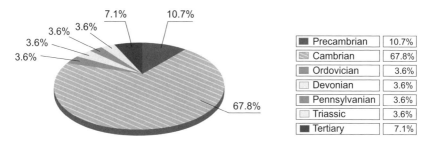

■ Precambrian	10.7%
▨ Cambrian	67.8%
■ Ordovician	3.6%
☐ Devonian	3.6%
■ Pennsylvanian	3.6%
☐ Triassic	3.6%
■ Tertiary	7.1%

FIGURE 20. Animal phyla first appearances: analysis based on fossilized phyla alone

D. Summary Assessment

When we compare the pattern of fossilization in the actual fossil record to the expected pattern given the neo-Darwinian mechanism, we encounter significant dissonance. Neither the pace nor the mode of evolutionary change match neo-Darwinian expectations. Indeed, the neo-Darwinism mechanism cannot explain the geologically sudden origin of the major body plans to which the term "the Cambrian explosion" principally refers. Further, the absence of plausible transitional organisms, the pattern of disparity preceding diversity, and the pattern of phyla first appearance all run counter to the neo-Darwinian predictions or expectations. Only the overall increase in complexity from the Precambrian to the Cambrian conforms to neo-Darwinian expectations. Although, as we have seen, the newer punctuationalist model of evolutionary change appears more consonant with some aspects of the Cambrian/Precambrian fossil record, it, too, fails to account for the extreme absence of transitional intermediates, the top-down pattern of disparity preceding diversity, and the pattern of phylum first appearance. Furthermore, punctuated equilibrium lacks a sufficient mechanism to explain the origin of the major body plans that appear in the Cambrian strata.

These problems underscore a more significant theoretical difficulty for evolutionary theory generally, namely, the insufficiency of attempts to extrapolate microevolutionary mechanisms to explain macroevolutionary development. As developmental biologists Gilbert, Opitz, and Raff have noted: "The Modern Synthesis is a remarkable achievement. However, starting in the 1970s, many biologists began questioning its adequacy in explaining evolution. Genetics might be adequate for explaining microevolution, but microevolutionary changes in gene frequency were not seen as able to turn a reptile into a mammal or to convert a fish into an amphibian. Microevolution looks at adaptations that concern only the survival of the fittest, not the arrival of the fittest."[47] Or as Roger Lewin stated in his summary of the historic Chicago "Macroevolution" conference in 1980: "The central question of the Chicago conference was whether the mechanisms underlying microevolution can be extrapolated to explain the phenomena of macroevolution. At the risk of doing violence to the position of some people at the meeting, the answer can be given as a clear, No."[48]

The origin of major innovations and complexity is increasingly recognized as an unsolved problem for all fully naturalistic versions of evolutionary theory, and biologists, especially developmental biologists, are beginning an intensive search for solutions.[49] Before considering whether the theory of intelligent design should be considered in this search, we will consider some objections to the paleontological arguments that we have marshaled against the adequacy of neo-Darwinism and punctuated equilibrium.

IV. Objections

A. The Artifact Hypothesis:
Is the Cambrian Explosion Real?

Many have argued that absence of Precambrian transitional intermediates does not disconfirm neo-Darwinian predictions but instead testifies only to the incompleteness of the fossil record. The difference between what the fossil record shows and what neo-Darwinism implies that it should show has led many to question not the neo-Darwinian mechanism or its picture of the history of life but the completeness of the fossil record.

Initially, however, Darwinists adopted a different approach. For many decades after the publication of the *Origin*, paleontologists sympathetic to Darwin's theory sought to find the missing ancestors of the Cambrian animals. The search for the missing fossils in Precambrian formations all over the world resulted in universal disappointment. Maintaining Darwin's theory, therefore, eventually required formulating ad hoc hypotheses to account for the absence of ancestral and transitional forms. Various so-called artifact hypotheses have been proposed to explain the missing ancestors. Artifact hypotheses hold that the fossil ancestors existed but for various reasons were not preserved in an "imperfect and biased" fossil record. On this view, the absence of the fossil ancestors represents "an artifact" of incomplete sampling of the fossil record and not an accurate representation of the history of life. Gaps in the fossil record are apparent, not real.

A popular version of the artifact hypothesis was proposed by the prominent American geologist Charles Walcott in the early 1900s. Taking his lead from Darwin, Walcott proposed a so-called Lipalian interval. According to Walcott, the ancestors of the trilobites first lived and evolved at a time when the Precambrian seas had receded from the land masses. Then, at the beginning of the Cambrian, the seas again rose, covering the continents and depositing recently evolved trilobites. According to Walcott, ancestral trilobites did exist but were not fossilized in terrestrial sediments until the beginning of the Cambrian. Before the Cambrian, during a period of recession of seas, trilobites (and their ancestral forms) were being deposited only in deep-sea sediments.[50] Thus, Walcott argued that paleontologists should not expect to find fossilized trilobites in terrestrial strata but only in the marine sediments that were, in Walcott's time, inaccessible to paleontology. The Lipalian interval hypothesis had the advantage of accounting for the sudden appearance of the trilobites and the absence of ancestral and transitional forms. Moreover, it could be tested, at least once offshore drilling technology advanced to allow for the sampling of the buried offshore Precambrian sedimentary rocks.

Walcotts's Lipalian interval hypothesis ultimately failed for two reasons. First, offshore drilling technology has now been developed, and offshore drilling cores have repeatedly failed to verify the existence of Walcott's predicted fossils in marine sediments.[51] Second, and more fundamentally, even if trilobite fossils had been found in the marine sediments, such fossils would not have confirmed the existence of Precambrian trilobite ancestors because Walcott incorrectly assumed that the oceanic crust included Precambrian sediments. At the time that Walcott proposed his version of the artifact hypothesis, geologists considered the oceanic and continental plates to be essentially stable and fixed with respect to one another. Mountain building, faulting, and other geologic events were thought to be caused by changes in eustacy (or other mechanisms favored at the time). The idea that lithospheric plates actually moved, recycling themselves through the process of plate tectonics, had not yet been proposed. According to modern estimations, the oldest section of oceanic crust is Jurassic (between 145 and 210 million years ago), far too young to contain the Precambrian fossil ancestors of the trilobites. Thus, the Lipalian interval was discarded (as a nonstarter) once geologists had accepted plate tectonic theory. Paleontologists today do not expect to find any Precambrian ancestors to the trilobites in oceanic sediments, since there are no Precambrian rocks in the ocean basins. Instead, if Precambrian ancestors of the trilobites (or any other Cambrian animals) did exist, then they would have to be found within Precambrian sedimentary rocks retained on the continental crust. Yet such Precambrian fossils have not been found.

Over the years, paleontologists have proposed various "missing strata" hypotheses to explain the missing ancestors. Some have suggested that rocks containing Precambrian transitional fossils were metamorphosed or melted beyond recognition. Others claimed that major evolutionary innovation occurred during periods in which sedimentary deposition had ceased. Advocates of these hypotheses abandoned them, however, once geologists began to uncover extensive Precambrian sedimentary deposits that again failed to document the existence of plausible ancestors for the complex Cambrian animals.[52]

Proponents of the artifact hypothesis have advanced other explanations. One asserts that the Precambrian ancestors of the Cambrian animals lacked hard parts such as shells and exoskeletons. Thus, according to this version of the artifact hypothesis, we should not expect to find remains of ancestral forms in the Precambrian fossil record since soft-bodied animals do not leave fossil remains.

Yet this idea has also met with difficulty. While clearly the fossil record does not preserve soft body parts of organisms as frequently as hard body parts, it has preserved enough soft-bodied animals and organs to render this version of the artifact hypothesis suspect. Indeed, entirely soft-bodied representatives of several phyla have been identified in the Cambrian.[53] Soft-bodied organisms are also preserved in Precambrian strata around the world. Even so, these Precambrian organisms do not represent plausible transitional intermediates to representatives of the Cambrian phyla. In each case, the jump in complexity (as measured by the number of cell types, for example) and the morphological disparity between the Precambrian and Cambrian organisms appear far too great (see section IV.B).

Furthermore, the postulation of exclusively soft-bodied ancestors for hard-bodied Cambrian organisms seems implausible on anatomical grounds.[54] Many phyla such as brachiopods and arthropods could have not evolved their soft parts first and then added shells later, since their survival depends in large part upon their ability to protect their soft parts from hostile environmental forces. Instead, soft and hard parts had to arise together.[55] As Valentine notes in the case of brachiopods, "the brachiopod

Baupläne cannot function without a durable skeleton."[56] To admit that hard-bodied Cambrian animals had not yet evolved their hard-bodied parts in the Precambrian effectively concedes that credible precursor animals themselves had not yet evolved.[57] As Chen and Zhou explain: "[A]nimals such as brachiopods and most echinoderms and mollusks cannot exist without a mineralized skeleton. Arthropods bear jointed appendages and likewise require a hard, organic or mineralized outer covering. Therefore the existence of these organisms in the distant past should be recorded either by fossil tracks and trails or remains of skeletons. The observation that such fossils are absent in Precambrian strata proves that these phyla arose in the Cambrian."[58]

Others have explained the absence of transitional organisms as the result of their putatively tiny size. Some have even suggested that transitionals only existed in the larval stage.[59] While possible perhaps, it should be noted that cells of filamentous microorganisms (interpreted as cyanobacteria) have been discovered and documented in the Warrawoona Group strata of western Australia. These microfossils, found in bedded carbonaceous cherts, are estimated to be between 3.3 billion to 3.5 billion years old.[60] Species of single-celled algae and the appearance of cells with a nucleus about 2.7 billion years ago have been well documented in the fossil record.[61] If paleontologists can find minuscule single cells in formations that are far older (and therefore far more rare due to the greater likelihood of tectonic destruction), it would seem that the allegedly tiny fossil precursors of the Cambrian animals should have been found somewhere in the over 500 million years of sedimentary strata below the Cambrian. Moreover, as already noted, the Precambrian rocks in China beneath the Chengjiang Cambrian biota reveal the presence of tiny sponge embryos at the very earliest stages of cell division.[62] If the fossil record has preserved such tiny organisms in Precambrian strata, why has it not preserved any of the allegedly miniature or soft-bodied ancestral forms of the animals that first appear in the Cambrian? If these strata can preserve embryos, then they should be able to preserve the ancestral animals to the new forms that arise in the Cambrian. But they do not.

Of course, there are conditions under which fossils are unlikely to be preserved. Nevertheless, the factors that generally make preservation unlikely do not help to account for the specific absence of Precambrian ancestral forms. We know, for example, that nearshore sands do not favor preservation of detail, let alone the fine detail of very small organisms a millimeter or less in length. Similarly, paleontologists rarely find the remains of parasites that live in the soft tissues of other organisms (indeed, parasitic organisms represent several of the phyla that have no fossil record).[63] Even so, such considerations do little to bolster the artifact hypothesis. The carbonates, phosphorates, and shales of the Precambrian strata beneath the Chengjiang fauna, for example, would have provided moderate to very favorable depositional environments in Precambrian times. Yet these strata do not preserve plausible ancestral forms for any of the animals in the Cambrian beds of the Chengjiang. Advocates of the artifact hypothesis need to show not just that certain factors discourage preservation in general (which is not disputed) but that these factors were ubiquitous in Precambrian depositional environments worldwide. If nearshore sands characterized all Precambrian sedimentary deposits, then paleontologists would not expect to find any ancestral, or at least any tiny ancestral, forms for the Cambrian animals. Yet clearly this is not the case. Precambrian strata include many types of sediments that can preserve—and in the case of sponge embryos, have preserved—animal remains in fine detail. Yet no forms plausibly intermediate to the metazoan animals have been found in such beds.

The implausibility of the artifact hypotheses in its various manifestations has been reinforced by recent work in statistical paleontology. Michael Foote has shown that new fossil discoveries have repeatedly fallen into existing taxonomic groups. This pattern of discovery suggests that the fossil record is, at best, curiously selective in its incompleteness. Though the record amply documents the organisms corresponding to the branches on the Darwinian tree of life, it inexplicably (from a neo-Darwinian point of view) fails to preserve the organisms required to connect the branches (that is, those corresponding to the nodes). As more and more fossil finds fall within existing higher taxonomic groups, it seems less and less likely that the absence of morphologically intermediate forms reflects a bias in sampling. In other words, Foote's analysis suggests the extreme improbability of discovering enough fossils representing previously unrepresented taxonomic categories to close the morphological distance between the Cambrian forms. Instead, based on sampling theory, Foote argues that "we have a representative sample of morphological diversity and therefore we can rely on patterns documented in the fossil record." As he concludes, "although we have much to learn about the evolution of form, in many respects our view of the history of biological diversity is mature."[64]

B. The Vendian Radiation

As we have seen above, some have attempted to defend neo-Darwinism by questioning the completeness of the fossil record. Nevertheless, others accept the testimony of the fossil record but then defend neo-Darwinism by suggesting that the fossil record does indeed document some of the transitional intermediate forms required by the theory and (to a lesser extent) by the theory of punctuated equilibrium. In particular, it has been suggested that a group of late Precambrian (Vendian) multicellular organisms might represent transitional intermediates to the Cambrian animals.

Paleontologists have made discoveries of Vendian fossils in England, Newfoundland, the White Sea in northwestern Russia, and the Namibian desert in southern Africa. While these fossils were originally dated at between 700 million and 640 million years old, volcanic ash beds both below and above the Namibian site have recently provided more accurate radiometric dates. These studies fix the date for the first appearance of the Vendian fossils at 565–570 million years ago and their last appearance at the Cambrian boundary about 543 million years ago.[65]

There are four types of Vendian fossils, all of which first appeared between 570 and 543 million years ago. The first includes the strange Ediacaran fauna named for their most notable locale in the Ediacara Hills in the outback of southwestern Australia. These include the flat, air mattress–like *Dickinsonia* and the enigmatic *Spriginna,* with its elongate and segmented body and possible head shield. These organisms are at least mostly soft bodied and large enough to identify with the naked eye. The second group consists of the Precambrian sponges, primitive animals that first arose 565–570 million years ago. The third group includes trace fossils (the possible remains of animal activity) such as tracks, burrows, and fecal pellets. These may represent the remains of primitive wormlike creatures or primitive mollusks. The fourth group of fossils may actually represent body fossils of primitive mollusks. Indeed, a recent discovery in the cliffs along the White Sea in northwest Russia provides support for the existence of mollusks in the Vendian. There, scientists have discovered thirty-five distinctive specimens of *Kimberella,* a simple animal form. These new White Sea specimens, dated at 550 million years ago, suggest that *Kimberella* "had a strong, limpet like shell, crept along the sea floor, and resembled a mollusk." Paleontologist Douglas Erwin of the Smithsonian Institution has commented that "it's the first animal that you can convincingly demonstrate is more complicated than a flatworm." Radula-style sea-floor tracks from Precambrian sediments in both Canada and Australia have been attributed to mollusks, and *Kimberella* may well be the track maker.[66] The authors of the original descriptive paper in *Nature*, Mikhail Fedonkin and Benjamin Waggoner, conclude on the basis of their finds that at least "'molluscan-grade bilaterians,' began to diversify before the beginning of the Cambrian."[67]

Though fascinating, the late Precambrian fossil record does not significantly diminish the difficulty of accounting for the Cambrian explosion on either a neo-Darwinian or punctuationalist model. First, with the exception of *Kimberella*, the body plans of visibly fossilized organisms (as opposed to trace fossils) bear no clear relationship to any of the new organisms that appear in the Cambrian explosion (or thereafter).[68] The Ediacaran organisms such as *Dickinsonia* and *Springinna* do not have eyes, mouths, or anuses. For this reason, many paleontologists doubt that these organisms even belong in the animal kingdom.[69] As Erwin, Valentine, and Jablonski have noted:

> Although the soft-bodied fossils that appear about 565 million years ago are animal-like, their classifications are hotly debated. In just the past few years these [Ediacaran] fossils have been viewed as protozoans; as lichens; as close relatives of the cnidarians; as a sister group to cnidarians plus all other animals; as representatives of more advanced, extinct phyla; and as representatives of a new kingdom entirely separate from the animals. Still other specialists have parceled the fauna out among living phyla, with some assigned to the Cnidaria and others to the flatworms, annelids, arthropods and echinoderms. *This confusing state of affairs arose because these body fossils do not tend to share definitive anatomical details with modern groups, and thus the assignments must be based on vague similarities of overall shape and form, a method that has frequently proved misleading in other cases* [emphasis added].[70]

Second, the late Precambrian strata document very few types of animals, three or at most four phyla (Cnidaria, Porifera, and possibly Mollusca and a worm phylum), even granting the most optimistic estimates of the significance of Vendian body and trace fossils.[71] Precambrian strata do reveal trace fossils consisting of surface tracks and burrows, along with fecal pellets. Though small, these could only have been made by organisms of a relatively high degree of differentiation. Thus, some have argued that these trace fossils suggest the existence of organisms with a head and tail, nervous systems, a muscular body wall allowing creeping or burrowing, and a gut with mouth and anus.[72] These inferred physical characteristics would indicate organisms of "organ grade" complexity, above that of flatworms. Some paleobiologists have, therefore, speculated that the tracks, burrows, and feeding trails indicate the existence of two (probably Mollusca and a worm phylum) or so types of animals prior to the Cambrian.[73]

Nevertheless, even on the most optimistic interpretation of these remains, Precambrian strata account for no more than four animal body plans (including some of largely unknown characteristics). Thus, neither the peculiar Ediacaran fauna nor the Precambrian fossil record taken as a whole establishes the existence of the wide variety of transitional intermediates that neo-Darwinism and punctuated equilibrium require. The Cambrian explosion attests to the first appearance of organisms representing at least nineteen phyla. Yet, Vendian organisms represent ancestral forms for, at most, four Cambrian phyla (granting ancestral status to a worm phylum and *Kimberella* as a mollusk). This leaves between 80 and 90 percent of the Cambrian phyla with no ancestors in the Precambrian rocks. Further, even if one grants that representatives of four phyla existed in the Precambrian, it does not follow that these forms were actually transitional intermediates. Some were, or may have been, representatives of known Cambrian phyla such as sponges (phylum Porifera), thus demonstrating not a gradual transformation but instead only the earlier appearance of a previously known phyla.

There is another reason that late Precambrian (or Vendian) fossils do not make it easier for neo-Darwinism to explain the pattern of appearance in the fossil record. The Vendian fossils themselves evidence a puzzling discontinuous increase in specified biological complexity, though not one nearly great enough (or of the right kind) to account for the Cambrian explosion. Prior to the appearance of organisms such as *Kimberella, Dickinsonia,* and sponges, the only living forms documented in the fossil record for over 3 billion years are single-celled organisms and colonial algae. The emergence of primitive mollusks, the two-dimensional animal-like *Dickinsonia,* sponges, and worms (as attested by trace fossils) represents, therefore, a significant discontinuous increase in the information content or specified complexity of the biological world, not unlike that evidenced in the Cambrian explosion itself (though of a much lesser degree).

Thus, the Ediacaran and other organisms in the Vendian may attest to a separate sudden increase in specified biological complexity within a short window of geological time (about 20 million years) following roughly 3 billion years in which only bacteria and algae inhabited the earth. The complexity jump required by the appearance of these organisms in this short period of time would seem to exceed the explanatory resources of either the selection/mutation or the species/selection mechanisms (see further discussion in section V.A). Thus, the appearance of the Vendian fossils does not solve the problem of the sudden increase in biological complexity during the Cambrian; at best it constitutes another, though lesser, manifestation of the same problem in older Precambrian strata.

Indeed, even if one regards the appearance of the Vendian fossils as evidence of a kind of "fuse" on the Cambrian explosion, the total time encompassed by the Vendian and Cambrian radiations still remains exceedingly brief relative to neo-Darwinian expectations and requirements.[74] Only 40–45 million years elapsed between the beginning of the Vendian radiation (565–570 million years ago) and the end of the Cambrian explosion (525 million years ago). This represents about 7 percent of the time that modern neo-Darwinists expect for the development of complex animals from their alleged common ancestor (see discussion of deep divergence in section IV.C) and, by nearly all accounts, far less time than the mutation/selection mechanism would require (see section V.A). Until recently, radiometric studies had estimated the duration of the Cambrian radiation itself at 40 million years, a period of time so brief, geologically speaking, that paleontologists had dubbed it an "explosion." The relative suddenness of this event, even on the earlier measure of its duration, had already raised serious questions about the adequacy of the neo-Darwinian mechanism. Treating the Vendian and the Cambrian radiations as one continuous evolutionary event (itself a dubious assumption) only returns the problem to its earlier (pre-Zircon redating) status—hardly a positive state of affairs for advocates of neo-Darwinism.

C. The Deep Divergence Hypothesis

Recently, evolutionary biologists have attempted to defend neo-Darwinism against the evidential challenge of the fossil record in another way. Some evolutionary biologists have denied the explosive character of the Cambrian radiation and postulated a long period of undetected or cryptic evolution in the Precambrian, beginning from a common ancestor, some 1.2 billion years ago. To support such claims, these biologists have asserted the primacy of molecular data over the evidence of the fossil record itself. In particular, a recent study of molecular sequence data by Wray, Levinton, and Shapiro, entitled "Molecular Evidence for Deep Precambrian Divergences among Metazoan Phyla," purports to provide compelling molecular evidence for a common ancestor of the Cambrian phyla dating from 1.2 billion years ago (or nearly 700 million years before the Cambrian radiation).[75] Wray, Levinton, and Shapiro suggest that the evolution of the

Cambrian phyla continued at a steady pace for nearly 700 million years from this "deep divergence" point until the Cambrian animals first appeared in the fossil record 530 million years ago. They then explain the absence of ancestral forms using a version of the artifact hypothesis, namely, that Precambrian ancestors existed in an exclusively soft-bodied form until the Cambrian explosion occurred.

Wray, Levinton, and Shapiro support their fundamental claim about the deep divergence of animal evolution 1.2 billion years ago on the basis of molecular sequence comparisons. Specifically, they compared the degree of difference between the amino acid sequences of seven proteins (ATP-ase, cytochrome c, cytochrome oxidase I and II, alpha and beta hemoglobin, and NADH I) derived from several different modern animals representing five Cambrian phyla (annelids, arthropods, mollusks, chordates, and echinoderms). They also compared the nucleotide base sequences of a ribosomal RNA (18S rRNA) from the same animal representatives of the same five phyla. Assuming that the degree of difference in sequencing reflects the amount of time that has elapsed since the ancestors of different animals began to diverge from each other, Wray, Levinton, and Shapiro determine a date for the common ancestor from which the evolution of the Cambrian animals began. Their analysis places the common ancestor from which all animal forms diverged at nearly 700 million years before the Cambrian explosion. Their analysis implies a very ancient or (stratigraphically) "deep" divergence of the animal forms, in opposition to those who claim that the Cambrian animals appeared suddenly. Indeed, a major purpose of their study was to disconfirm the traditional view "that the animal phyla diverged in an 'explosion' near the beginning of the Cambrian period." They argue instead that "all mean divergence time estimates between these four phyla and chordates, based on all seven genes, substantially predate the beginning of the Cambrian period." And they conclude, "Our results cast doubt on the prevailing notion that the animal phyla diverged explosively during the Cambrian or late Vendian, and instead suggest that there was an extended period of divergence during the mid-Proterozoic, commencing about a billion years ago."[76]

From a neo-Darwinian point of view, the results of Wray, Levinton, and Shapiro's study seem almost axiomatic, since the neo-Darwinian mechanism requires extensive amounts of time to produce the new form present in the Cambrian strata. As Andrew Knoll, a Harvard paleontologist, has stated, "The idea that animals should have originated much earlier than we see them in the fossil record is almost inescapable."[77]

Nevertheless, the "deep divergence" hypothesis suffers from several severe difficulties.

First, the postulation of an extensive 700-million-year period of undetectable evolution remains highly problematic from a paleontological point of view. The preservation of numerous soft-bodied Cambrian animals, as well as Precambrian sponge embryos and microorganisms, severely challenges those versions of the artifact hypothesis that invoke an extensive period of undetected soft-bodied evolution in the Precambrian. Further, the postulation of exclusively soft-bodied ancestors for hard-bodied Cambrian forms remains anatomically implausible, as noted earlier. A brachiopod cannot survive without its shell. Nor can an arthropod exist without its exoskeleton. Any plausible ancestor to such organisms would have needed hard body parts that could have been fossilized, yet none have been found in the Precambrian.

Second, Wray, Levinton, and Shapiro's results vary dramatically from other similar sequence comparisons. In a more recent publication, Ayala, Rzhetsky, and Ayala have recalculated the divergence times, using the same protein-coding genes as Wray, Levinton, and Shapiro (but eliminating 18S rRNA, an RNA-coding gene, because of problems with obtaining a reliable alignment) and adding an additional twelve protein-coding genes. Correcting what they argue are "a host of statistical problems" in the Wray, Levinton, and Shapiro study, Ayala, Rzhetsky, and Ayala found that their own estimates "are consistent with paleontological estimates"—not with the deep divergence hypothesis. "Extrapolating to distant times from molecular evolutionary rates estimated within confined data-sets," note Ayala and his colleagues, "are fraught with danger."[78] Nevertheless, to the extent that such estimates can be made, they contend, their results correspond with the standard paleontological estimates.

Third, Wray, Levinton, and Shapiro rely on the molecular clock data to estimate the point of deep divergence. Yet unlike radiometric clocks, molecular clocks depend upon a whole host of contingent factors, both biological and environmental, that render them unreliable. As Valentine, Jablonski, and Erwin note: "different genes in different clades evolve at different rates, different parts of genes evolve at different rates and, most importantly, rates within clades have changed over time."[79] Moreover, many environmental factors influence mutation rates, including catastrophic events that have often punctuated the geologic record. The mutation rate can greatly increase during the collapse of the magnetic field or following mass extinctions when new ecological niches open up. Further, mutations depend on biological processes that occur at different stages of cellular activity and development. They do not depend upon the physics of constant radiometric decay. In any case, without evidence from the fossil record (older than 565 million years ago) with which to calibrate the molecular clock, its reliability in dating the origin of the Cambrian animal phyla (at between 1 and 1.2 billion years ago) remains highly questionable. Thus, Valentine, Jablonski, and Erwin argue that "the accuracy of the molecular clock is still problematical, at least for phylum divergences, for the estimates vary by some 800 million years depending upon the techniques and or the molecules used . . . it is not clear that molecular clock dates can ever be applied reliably to such geologically remote events as Neoproterozoic branchings within the Metazoa."[80] Thus, as Simon Conway Morris concludes, "a deep history extending to an origination in excess of 1,000 Myr is very unlikely."[81]

Fourth, the basic housekeeping proteins (and ribosomal RNAs) that Wray, Levinton, and Shapiro analyzed would, in any case, have had little role in the origin of novel body plans. Nearly all of the proteins analyzed by Wray, Levinton, and Shapiro are found in any organism, from the simplest one-celled prokaryotes or protists (eukaryotes) to multicellular animals. Any evolution that these proteins might have undergone (over whatever duration of time) could not have caused higher-level body plans to differentiate, since such differentiation involves, at the very least, morphological regulator proteins (such as DNA binding proteins) that Wray, Levinton, and Shapiro did not analyze. As Johns and Miklos have noted elsewhere, "changes in . . . structural genes are unlikely to have anything to do with the production of [major] morphological change."[82] The kinds of proteins that Wray, Levinton, and Shapiro did analyze simply do not suffice to explain body-plan formation. Yet they use their analyses of the differences between these molecules to make, in effect, a claim about the time at which body plans began to diverge.

Finally, all analyses of sequence data make assumptions that raise serious questions about their reliability as indicators of very ancient common ancestors. All sequence analyses assume, rather than demonstrate, the doctrine of universal common descent. By assuming that sequence differences reflect the amount of time that has passed since different animals began to diverge from a common ancestor, molecular studies clearly presuppose that some such ancestor existed. Sequence analyses calculate how long ago a common ancestor for two (or more) organisms might have existed—*if one assumes* that some such organism must have existed. But whether the Cambrian animals had a common ancestor is part of the point at issue, or should be.[83] The fossil record taken at face value certainly provides no evidential basis for this claim. To invoke molecular analyses that presuppose a common ancestor as evidence for the existence of such an entity only begs the question. Perhaps the Precambrian rocks do not record transitional intermediates and ancestors for Cambrian animals because none existed. Citing sequence analyses that tacitly assume the existence of a common ancestor does not provide evidential support for the existence of such an ancestor. Certainly, it provides no reason for privileging molecular analyses over fossil evidence.

V. Evidence of Design?

Our discussion to this point has suggested that neither neo-Darwinism nor the theory of punctuated equilibrium adequately accounts for the pattern of fossil evidence surrounding the Cambrian explosion. Instead, both these theories rely on mechanisms that should produce new forms of life in a manner quite different than that evident in the Precambrian/Cambrian fossil record. In this section, we will now expand our critique by further challenging the efficacy of various undirected mechanisms of evolutionary change and by proposing an alternative causal explanation for both the origin of the new information that arises in the Cambrian and the other specific features of the explosion as described above.

Studies in the history and philosophy of science have shown that many scientific theories, particularly in the historical sciences, are formulated and justified as inferences to the best explanation.[84] Historical scientists, in particular, assess competing hypotheses by evaluating which hypothesis would, if true, provide the best explanation for some set of relevant data. Those with greater explanatory power are typically judged to be better, more probably true, theories. Darwin himself used this method of reasoning in defending his theory of universal common descent.[85] Moreover, contemporary studies on the method of inference to the best explanation have shown that determining which among a set of competing possible explanations constitutes the best depends upon judgments about the causal adequacy, or causal powers, of the competing explanatory entities.[86] Historical scientists reasoning in accord with uniformitarian canons of method judge the plausibility of causal explanations of past events against their knowledge of present cause-and-effect relationships—that is, against their knowledge of the present causal powers of various entities or processes.

In what follows, we shall make a case for intelligent design as the best—most causally adequate—explanation of the features of the Cambrian explosion. To do so, we will show that, in addition to the difficulties described above, the main materialistic mechanisms of evolutionary change are not sufficient to produce the new information and body plans that arise in the Cambrian. Yet we will not infer the activity of an intelligent designer just because known natural processes or mechanisms cannot explain the origin of the main features of the Cambrian explosion. Instead, we will show that intelligent agents possess precisely those causal powers that are needed to produce the unique features of the Cambrian explosion. In other words, we will show that the Cambrian explosion manifests hallmarks or positive indicators of intelligently designed systems—features that in any other realm of experience would trigger the recognition of purposive or intelligent activity. We now consider these features (in roughly the reverse order as they were discussed in Part II).

A. The "Quantum" Increase in Specified Biological Information

How can we best explain such a discontinuous or "quantum" increase in biological information that emerges during the Cambrian? Meyer argued, in a previous essay about the origin of life, that intelligent design provides a sufficient causal explanation for the origin of large amounts of information, since we have considerable experience of intelligent agents generating informational configurations of matter. To quote information theorist Henry Quastler, the "creation of new information is habitually associated with conscious activity."[87] Yet whether intelligent design constitutes a necessary or best causal explanation for the biological information that arises in the Cambrian depends upon whether other causally adequate explanations exist. In Meyer's previous discussion of the origin of genetic information in a prebiotic context, he argued against the sufficiency of three broad classes of naturalistic explanation for the origin of the genetic information required to make a cell in the first place. He argued that neither chance nor prebiotic natural selection acting on random variations nor physical-chemical necessity (that is, self-organization) can account for the origin of biological information starting from simple chemistry. Since only intelligent design is sufficient as a causal explanation for the origin of information, he concluded that intelligent design represents the best explanation for the origin of the information necessary to build the first living cell.

Nevertheless, the origin of information in the Cambrian fossils presents a different situation. Clearly, the amount of information represented by the many novel genes, proteins, and morphological structures that arise in the Cambrian defies the explanatory resources of chance, especially given the limited time involved in the explosion. Nevertheless, neo-Darwinists would argue that in a biological as opposed to a prebiotic context, the neo-Darwinian mechanism of natural selection acting on random variation does play a significant role in generating novel information. Further, self-organizational models for the origin of the Cambrian information explosion have been proposed.[88] Thus, for intelligent design to stand as *the best*, rather than just *a plausible*, explanation for the origin of the biological information that arises in the Cambrian, one must show the implausibility of both the neo-Darwinian and self-organizational mechanisms as explanations for the origin of the biological information that arises in the Cambrian. We shall do so below. (The theory of punctuated equilibrium offers no special mechanism for the origin of novel biological information beyond an appeal to macromutations. Since we critique this approach in our discussion of the neo-Darwinian and self-organizational mechanisms, we will offer no further critique of punctuated equilibrium.)

1. NATURAL SELECTION, GENES, AND PROTEINS

As noted above, one useful metric of complexity is number of cell types (see figure 10).[89] To build an animal requires, at a minimum, building many new types of cells. But cell types themselves require specialized proteins, and novel proteins require novel gene sequences—that is, new genetic information. The organisms that suddenly appeared in the Cambrian had many more novel and specialized cell types (and thus many more novel and specialized proteins) than the much more simple organisms found in the Precambrian. Hence, they would have required (at minimum) a vast amount of new genetic information. How did this information arise?

According to neo-Darwinism, novel genes and proteins arise as the result of natural selection acting on random variations or mutations in the genetic material of organisms. Yet since the 1960s a number of scientists and mathematicians have questioned the ability of mutation and selection to generate information in the form of novel genes and proteins. Their skepticism has derived from consideration of the extreme improbability (and specificity) of functional genes and proteins.

A typical gene contains over 1,000 precisely arranged bases. Yet for any specific arrangement of four nucleotide bases of length n, there are a corresponding number of 4^n possible arrangements of bases. For any protein, there are 20^n possible arrangements of protein-forming amino acids. A gene of 999 bases in length represents one of 4^{999} possible nucleotide sequences; a protein of 333 amino acids one of 20^{333} possibilities.

Since the 1960s, biologists have generally thought functional proteins to be rare among the set of possible amino acid sequences (of corresponding length). Some have used an analogy with human language to illustrate why. Michael Denton, for example, has shown that meaningful words or sentences are extremely rare among the set of possible combinations of English letters, especially as sequence length grows. (The ratio of meaningful 12-letter words to 12-letter sequences is $1/10^{14}$; the ratio of 100-letter sentences to possible 100-letter strings is $1/10^{100}$). Further, Denton shows that most meaningful sentences are *highly isolated* from one another in the space of possible combinations such that random substitutions of letters will, after a very few changes, inevitably degrade meaning. Apart from a few closely clustered sentences accessible by random substitution, the overwhelming majority of meaningful sentences lie, probabilistically speaking, beyond the reach of random search.

Denton and others have argued that similar constraints apply to genes. They have questioned, therefore, whether an undirected search via mutation/selection would have a reasonable chance of locating new islands of function—representing fundamentally new genes or proteins—within available time.[90] Some have also argued that alterations in sequencing would likely result in loss of protein function before fundamentally new function could arise. Nevertheless, neither the sensitivity of genes and proteins to functional loss as the result of sequence change nor the extent to which functional proteins are isolated within sequence space has been fully known.

Recently, experiments in molecular biology have shed light on these questions. A variety of "mutagenesis" techniques have shown that proteins (and thus the genes that produce them) are indeed highly specified relative to biological function.[91] Mutagenesis research tests the sensitivity of proteins (and, by implication, DNA) to functional loss as a result of alterations in sequencing. This research has shown that, though many proteins do tolerate a variety of amino acids at some sites without loss of function, amino acid residues at many key active sites cannot vary at all without functional loss.[92] Moreover, whereas proteins will admit some variation at some sites, even in these cases only a limited set of the twenty protein-forming residues will preserve function—that is, even at sites that admit variation not just any amino acid will do. Further, multiple as opposed to single amino acid substitutions generally result in rapid loss of protein function, even when these changes occur at sites that allow variation when altered in isolation.[93] Cumulatively, these constraints imply that proteins are highly sensitive to functional loss as a result of alterations in the sequencing and that functional proteins represent highly isolated and improbable arrangements of amino acids—arrangements that are far more improbable in fact than would be likely to arise by chance, even given our multibillion-year-old universe.[94]

Of course, neo-Darwinists do not envision a completely random search through the space of possible nucleotide sequences. They see natural selection acting to preserve small advantageous variations in genetic sequences and their corresponding protein products. Richard Dawkins, for example, likens an organism to a high mountain peak.[95] He compares climbing the sheer precipice up the front side of the mountain to building a new organism by chance. He acknowledges that this approach up "Mount Improbable" will not succeed. Nevertheless, he suggests that there is a gradual slope up the backside of the mountain that could be climbed in small, incremental steps. In his analogy, the backside up Mount Improbable corresponds to the process of natural selection acting on random changes in the genetic text. What chance alone cannot accomplish blindly or in one leap, selection (acting on mutations) can accomplish through the cumulative effect of many slight successive steps.

Yet the extreme specificity and complexity of proteins present a difficulty not only for the chance origin of specified biological information (that is, for random mutations acting alone) but also for selection and mutation acting in concert. Indeed, mutagenesis experiments cast doubt on each of the two scenarios by which neo-Darwinists envision new information arising by the mutation/selection mechanism. According to Neo-Darwinists, either new functional genes arise from noncoding sections in the genome or functional genes arise from preexisting genes. Both scenarios are problematic.

In the first scenario, neo-Darwinists envision new genetic information arising from those sections of the genetic text that can presumably vary freely without consequence to the organism. According to this scenario, noncoding sections of the genome, or duplicated sections of coding regions, can experience a protracted period of "neutral evolution" in which alterations in nucleotide sequences have no discernible effect on the function of the organism. Eventually, however, a new gene sequence will arise that can code for a novel protein. At that point, natural selection can favor the new gene and its functional protein product, thus securing the preservation and heritability of both.

This scenario has the advantage of allowing the genome to vary through many generations as mutations "search" the space of possible base sequences. The scenario has an overriding problem, however: the size of the combinatorial space and the extreme rarity of the functional sequences within that space of possibilities. Since natural selection can do nothing to help *generate* new functional sequences but rather can only preserve such sequences once they have arisen, chance alone—random variation—must do the work of information generation—that is, of finding rare functional sequences within a universe of combinatorial possibilities. Yet the probability of randomly assembling (or "finding," in the previous sense) a functional sequence is vanishingly small even on a scale of billions of years. Robert Sauer's mutagenesis experiments imply that the probability of attaining (at random) the correct sequencing for a short protein 100 amino acids long is about 1 chance in 10^{65}.[96] More recent mutagenesis research suggests that Sauer's methods imply probability measures that are, if anything, too optimistic.[97]

Other considerations imply additional improbabilities. First, new Cambrian animals would require proteins much longer than 100 residues to perform necessary specialized functions. Susumu Ohno has noted that Cambrian animals would have required complex proteins such as lysyl oxidase in order to support their stout body structures.[98] Lysyl oxidase molecules in extant organisms comprise over 400 amino acids. These molecules represent highly complex (nonrepetitive) and tightly specified arrangements of matter. Reasonable extrapolation from mutagenesis experiments done on shorter protein molecules suggests that the probability of producing functionally sequenced proteins of this length at random is far smaller than 1 chance in 10^{150}—the point at which, according to Dembski's calculation of the Universal Probability Bound, appeals to chance become absurd given the time and other probabilistic resources of the entire universe.[99] Second, the Cambrian explosion took far less time (5×10^6 years) than the duration of the universe as a whole (2×10^{10} years) that Dembski assumes in his calculation. Third, DNA mutation rates are far too slow to generate the novel genes and proteins necessary to building the Cambrian animals given the duration of the explosion. As Ohno has explained: "Assuming a spontaneous mutation rate to be a generous 10^{-9} per base pair per year and also assuming no negative interference by natural selection, it still takes 10 million years to undergo 1% change in DNA base sequences. It follows that 6–10 million years in the evolutionary time scale is but a blink of an eye. The Cambrian explosion denoting the almost simultaneous emergence of nearly all the extant phyla . . . within the time span of 6–10 million years can't possibly be explained by mutational divergence of individual gene functions."[100]

The mutation/selection mechanism faces another probabilistic obstacle. The animals that arise in the Cambrian exhibit structures that suggest many new *types* of cells, each of which would require many novel proteins to perform their specialized functions. Further, new cell types require *systems* of proteins that must, as a condition of function, act in close coordination with one another. The unit of selection in such systems ascends to the system as a whole. Natural selection selects for functional advantage. But new cell types require whole systems of proteins to perform their distinctive functions. In such cases, natural selection cannot contribute to the process of information generation until *after* the information necessary to build the requisite *system* of proteins has arisen. Thus, random variations must, again, do the work of information generation—and now not simply for one protein but for many proteins arising at nearly the same time. Yet the odds of this occurring by chance are far smaller than the odds of the chance origin of a single gene or protein (see above).

Richard Dawkins has acknowledged that "we can accept a certain amount of luck in our explanations, but not too much."[101] The neutral theory of evolution, which, by its own logic, prevents natural selection from playing a role in generating genetic information until after the fact, relies on entirely "too much luck." The sensitivity of proteins to functional loss, the need for long proteins to build new cell types and animals, the need for whole new *systems* of proteins to service new cell types, the brevity of the Cambrian explosion relative to mutation rates—all these factors suggest that the sequencing in many novel genes and proteins is too improbable (and tightly specified) to have a realistic chance of arising by chance unassisted by natural selection.

Yet the neutral theory requires novel genes and proteins to arise—essentially—by random mutation alone. Adaptive advantage accrues *after* the generation of new functional genes and proteins. Thus, natural selection cannot play a role *until* new information-bearing molecules have independently arisen. Thus, the neutral theory envisions the need to scale the steep face of a Dawkins-style precipice in which there is *no* gradually sloping backside—a situation that, by Dawkins's own logic, is probabilistically untenable.

In the second scenario, neo-Darwinists envision novel genes and proteins arising by numerous successive mutations in a preexisting genetic text that codes for proteins. To adapt Dawkins's metaphor slightly, this scenario envisions gradually climbing down one functional peak and then ascending another. Yet mutagenesis experiments again suggest a difficulty. Recent experiments performed by Douglas Axe at Cambridge University show that, even when exploring a region of sequence space populated by proteins of a single function, most multiple position changes quickly lead to loss of function.[102] Yet to turn one protein into another with *a completely novel* function requires vastly more changes than are typically sufficient to degrade function. Axe's results imply that, in all probability, random searches for novel proteins (through sequence space) will result in functional loss long before any novel functional protein will emerge.

Francisco Blanco at the European Molecular Biology laboratory has come to a similar conclusion. Using directed mutagenesis, his team has found that the sequence space between two natural protein domains is not populated by folded or functional confirmations (that is, proteins). Instead, mutant sequences "lack a well defined three-dimensional structure." They conclude: "The results obtained here show that both the hydrophobic core residues and the surface residues are important in determining the structure of the proteins, and suggest that the appearance of a completely new fold from an existing one *is unlikely to occur by evolution through a route of folded intermediate sequences*" (emphasis added).[103]

Thus, although this second neo-Darwinian scenario has the advantage of starting with functional genes and proteins, it also has a lethal disadvantage: any process of random mutation or rearrangement in the genome will almost inevitably generate nonfunctional intermediate sequences before any fundamentally new functional gene and protein would arise (see figure 21). Such sequences would thus confer no survival advantage on their host organisms. Yet natural selection favors *only* functional advantage. It cannot select or favor nucleotide sequences or polypeptide chains that do not yet perform biological functions, still less will it favor sequences that efface or destroy preexisting function.

Evolving genes and proteins must range through a series of nonfunctional intermediate sequences that natural selection will not favor or preserve but will, in all probability, eliminate.[104] When this happens,

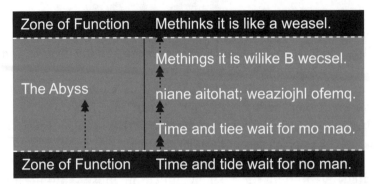

FIGURE 21. This diagram shows that multiple changes in the sequencing of letters in an English sentence inevitably degrade meaning before new meaning arises. A similar problem applies to sequence specific genes and proteins.

selection-driven evolution will cease. At this point, neutral evolution of the genome (unhinged from selective pressure) may ensue, but, as we have already seen, such a process faces immense probabilistic hurdles to generating new functional sequences even granting a cosmic time scale.

Thus, whether one envisions the evolutionary process beginning with a noncoding region of the genome or a preexisting functional gene, the functional specificity and complexity of proteins impose very stringent limitations on the efficacy of mutation and selection. In the first case, function must arise first before natural selection can act to favor a novel variation. In the second case, function must be continuously maintained to prevent deleterious (or lethal) consequences to the organism and to allow for the possibility of further evolution. Yet the complexity and functional specificity of proteins imply that both these conditions will be extremely difficult to meet. Therefore, the neo-Darwinian mechanism appears inadequate to generate the new information present in the novel genes and proteins that arise with the Cambrian animals.

2. NATURAL SELECTION AND NOVEL BODY PLANS

Problems with the neo-Darwinian mechanism run deeper still. To explain the origin of the Cambrian animals, one must account not only for new proteins and cell types but also for the origin of new body plans. Within the past decade, developmental biology has dramatically advanced understanding of how body plans are built during ontogeny. In the process, it has also uncovered a profound difficulty cutting to the core of neo-Darwinism.

To create significant changes in the form of organisms requires attention to timing. Mutations in genetic material that are expressed late in the development of an organism will not affect the body plan. Mutations expressed early in development, however, could conceivably produce gross changes in the morphology of an organism.[105] Thus, events expressed early in the development of organisms have the only realistic chance of producing large-scale macroevolutionary change.[106] As Miklos and Johns explain, macroevolutionary change requires changes in "very early embryogenesis."[107]

Yet recent studies in developmental biology make clear that mutations expressed early in development typically have deleterious (or at best neutral) effects, including mutations in the crucially important "master regulator," or hox, genes. For example, when early-acting body-plan molecules, or morphogens, such as bicoid (which helps set up the anterior-posterior head-to-tail axis in the fly *Drosophila*) are perturbed, development shuts down.[108] The resulting embryos die. Moreover, there is a good reason for this. If an engineer modifies the length of the piston rods in an internal combustion engine without modifying the crankshaft accordingly, the engine won't start. Similarly, processes of development are so tightly integrated spatially and temporally that changes early in development will require a host of other coordinated changes in separate but functionally interrelated developmental processes downstream. For this reason, as Stuart Kauffman explains, "A mutation disrupting formation of a spinal column and cord is more likely to be lethal than one affecting the number of fingers."[109]

This tight functional integration helps explain why mutations early in development inevitably result in embryonic death and why even mutations that are expressed somewhat later leave organisms crippled. For example, a regulative mutation in the bithorax gene (expressed midway in the development of a fly) does produce an extra pair of wings on a normally two-winged creature. Nevertheless, this "innovation" produces a cripple that cannot fly because it lacks, among other things, a musculature to support the use of its new wings. Since the developmental mutation was not accompanied by the many other coordinated developmental changes that would have been necessary to ensure the production of muscles at the appropriate place on the fly's body, the original mutation did not lead to a positive morphological change but to a strikingly deleterious one.

This problem has led to what geneticist John F. McDonald has called "a great Darwinian paradox." He notes that genes that vary within natural populations seem to affect only minor aspects of form and function—while genes that govern major changes, the very stuff of macroevolution, apparently do not vary or vary only to the detriment of the organism. As he puts it, "those [genetic] *loci* that are obviously variable within natural populations do not seem to lie at the basis of many major adaptive changes, while those *loci* that seemingly do constitute the foundation of many if not most major adaptive changes are not variable."[110] In other words, the kind of mutations that macroevolution needs (namely, *beneficial* regulatory or *Baupläne* mutations expressed during early development) don't occur; the kind it doesn't need (namely, viable genetic mutations in DNA expressed late in development) do occur, if infrequently.

Darwin wrote that "nothing can be effected" by natural selection "unless favorable variations occur."[111] Yet discoveries about the genetic regulation of development suggest that the kind of variations required by neo-Darwinism—favorable mutations that generate new body plans—do not occur.

Developmental biology has raised another formidable problem for the mutation/selection mechanism. Embryological evidence has long shown that DNA does not wholly determine morphological form, suggesting that mutations in DNA alone cannot account for the morphological changes required to build a new body plan.[112]

DNA directs protein synthesis. It also helps regulate the timing and expression of the synthesis of various proteins within cells. Nevertheless, DNA alone does not determine how individual proteins assemble themselves into larger systems of proteins, still less does it alone determine how cell types, tissue types, and organs arrange themselves into body plans.[113] Instead, other factors—such as the structure and organization of the cell membrane and cytoskeleton—play important roles in determining developmental pathways that determine body-plan formation during embryogenesis.

For example, the shape and location of microtubules in the cytoskeleton influence the "patterning" of embryos. Arrays of microtubules help distribute the essential proteins used during development to their correct location in the cell.[114] Of course, microtubules themselves are made of many protein subunits. Nevertheless, the protein subunits in the cell's microtubules are identical to one another. Neither they nor the genes that produce them account for the different shapes and locations of microtubule arrays that distinguish different kinds of embryos and developmental pathways. As Jonathan Wells explains, "What matters in development is the shape and location of microtubule arrays, and the shape and location of a micro-tubule array is not determined by its units."[115]

Two analogies may help. At a building site, builders will make use of many materials: lumber, wires, nails, drywall, piping, and windows. Yet building materials do not determine the floor plan of the house or the arrangement of houses in a neighborhood. Similarly, electronic circuits are composed of many components, such as resistors, capacitors, and transistors. But such lower-level components do not determine their own arrangement in an integrated circuit. Biological systems also depend on hierarchical arrangements of parts. Genes and proteins are made from simple building blocks—nucleotide bases and amino acids—arranged in specific ways. Cell types are made of, among other things, systems of specialized proteins. Organs are made of specialized arrangements of cell types and tissues. And body plans comprise specific arrangements of organs. Yet clearly the properties of individual proteins (or indeed the lower-level parts in the hierarchy generally) do not determine the organization of the higher-level structures and organizational patterns.[116] It follows, therefore, that the genetic information that codes for proteins does not determine these higher-level structures either.

These considerations pose another challenge to the sufficiency of the neo-Darwinian mechanism. Neo-Darwinism seeks to explain the origin of new information, form, and structure as the result of selection acting on randomly arising variation at a very low level within the biological hierarchy, namely, within the genetic text. Yet major morphological innovations depend on a specificity of arrangement at a much higher level of the organizational hierarchy that DNA alone does not determine. If DNA is not wholly responsible for body-plan morphogenesis, then DNA sequences can mutate indefinitely, without regard to realistic probabilistic limits, and still not produce a new body plan. Thus, the mechanism of natural selection acting on random mutations in DNA cannot *in principle* generate novel body plans, including those that first arose in the Cambrian explosion.

3. SELF-ORGANIZATIONAL MODELS AND NOVEL GENES AND PROTEINS

Of course, neo-Darwinism is not the only evolutionary model for explaining the origin of novel biological form in an undirected fashion. Stuart

Kauffman, for example, has recently advanced a self-organizational model to account for the emergence of form and presumably the information necessary to generate it. Whereas neo-Darwinism attempts to explain new form as the consequence of selection acting on random mutation, Kauffman suggests that selection acts not mainly on random variations but on emergent patterns of order that self-organize via the laws of nature.

Kauffman illustrates how this might work with various model systems in a computer environment. In one, he conceives a system of buttons connected by strings. Buttons represent novel genes or gene products, strings the lawlike forces of interaction that obtain between gene products—that is, proteins. Kauffman suggests that when the complexity of the system (as represented by the number of connected buttons and strings) reaches a critical threshold, new modes of organization can arise in the system "for free"—that is, without intelligent guidance—after the manner of a phase transition in chemistry. He explains that, "as clusters get larger, they begin to become cross-connected. Now the magic! As the ratio of threads to buttons passes the .5 mark, all of a sudden most of the clusters have become cross-connected into one giant structure." Kauffman then draws an analogy between the kind of cross-connected structures that arise spontaneously in his computer simulation and the web of interconnected chemical reactions that characterize stable metabolism in the living cell. As he puts it, "when a large enough number of reactions are catalyzed in a chemical reaction system, a vast web of catalyzed reactions will suddenly crystallize."[117]

Another model that Kauffman develops is a system of interconnected lights. Each light can flash in a variety of states—on, off, twinkling, and so forth. Since there is more than one possible state for each light and many lights, there are a vast number of possible states that the system as a whole can adopt. Further, in his system, rules determine how past states will influence future states. Kauffman asserts that, as a result of these rules, the system will soon, if properly tuned, produce a kind of order in which a few basic patterns of light activity recur with greater than random frequency. Further, insofar as these actual patterns of light activity represent a small portion of the total number of possible states in which the system can reside, Kauffman suggests that self-organizational laws might similarly find highly improbable biological outcomes—perhaps even sequences (of bases or amino acids) within a much larger sequence space of possibilities.

Do these simulations of self-organizational processes accurately model the origin of novel genetic information?

It's hard to think so.

First, in both examples, Kauffman presupposes but does not explain significant sources of preexisting information. In his buttons and strings system, the buttons represent proteins, themselves packets of information and the result of preexisting genetic information. Where does this information come from? Kauffman doesn't say, but the origin of such information is an essential part of what needs explanation in the history of life. Similarly, in his light system, the order that allegedly arises "for free"—that is, apart from an informational input by an agent—actually arises only if the programmer of the model system "tunes" it in such a way as to keep it from either generating an excessively rigid order or devolving into chaos.[118] Yet the tuning necessary to achieve this end involves an intelligent programmer selecting certain parameters and excluding others—that is, inputting information.

Second, Kauffman's model systems are not constrained by functional considerations and thus are not analogous to biological systems. A system of interconnected lights governed by preprogrammed rules may well settle into a small number of patterns within a much larger space of possibilities. But since these patterns have no function and need not meet any functional requirements, they have no specificity analogous to that present in actual organisms. Instead, examination of Kauffman's model systems shows that they do not produce sequences or systems characterized by specified complexity but instead by large amounts of symmetrical order or internal redundancy interspersed with aperiodicity or (mere) complexity.[119] Getting a law-governed system to generate repetitive patterns of flashing lights, even with a certain amount of variation, is clearly interesting but not biologically relevant. On the other hand, a system that generated the message "Eat at Joe's" would model a biologically relevant self-organizational process, at least, if the system produced such messages without agents having previously provided equivalent amounts of specified complexity. In any case, Kauffman's systems do not produce specified complexity and thus do not offer promising models for explaining an essential feature of the animals that arise in the Cambrian, namely, the specified information present in new genes and proteins.

4. SELF-ORGANIZATIONAL MODELS AND NOVEL BODY PLANS

Even so, Kauffman suggests that his self-organizational models can specifically elucidate aspects of the Cambrian explosion. According to Kauffman, new Cambrian animals emerged as the result of "long jump" mutations that established new body plans in a discrete rather than gradual fashion.[120] He also recognizes that mutations affecting early development are almost inevitably harmful. Thus, he concludes that body plans, once established, will not change and that any subsequent evolution must occur within an established *Baupläne*. And indeed, the fossil record does show a curious (from a Darwinian point of view) top-down pattern of appearance in which higher taxa (and the body plans they represent) appear first, only later to be followed by the appearance of lower taxa representing variations within those original body designs. Further, as Kauffman expects, body plans appear suddenly and persist without significant modification over time.

But here again Kauffman begs the most important question: What produced the new Cambrian body plans in the first place? Granted, he invokes "long jump" mutations to explain this, but he identifies no specific self-organizational process that can produce such mutations. Moreover, he concedes a principle that undermines the plausibility of his own proposal. Kauffman acknowledges that mutations that occur early in development are almost inevitably deleterious. Yet developmental biologists know that these are the only kind of mutations that have a realistic chance of producing large-scale evolutionary change—that is, the big jumps that Kauffman invokes. Though Kauffman repudiates the neo-Darwinian reliance upon random mutations in favor of self-organizing order, in the end he must invoke the most implausible kind of random mutation to provide a self-organizational account of the new Cambrian body plans. Clearly, his model is not sufficient.

5. INTELLIGENT DESIGN AND THE ORIGIN OF BIOLOGICAL INFORMATION

We have argued that the two most widely held materialistic mechanisms for generating biological form are not causally adequate to produce the discrete increases of specified complexity or information that would have been necessary to produce the new Cambrian animals. But do intelligent agents have causal powers sufficient to produce such increases in information, either in the form of sequence-specific lines of code or hierarchically arranged systems of parts? Clearly, they do.

In the first place, we know that intelligent human agents have the power to produce linear sequence-specific arrangements of characters. Indeed, experience affirms that specified complex information of this type routinely arises from the activity of intelligent agents. Human agents can generate information-rich lines of software and text. Further, whenever we encounter linear sequence-specific arrays of information and trace them back to their source, invariably we come to a mind—to that of a programmer or writer. In his essay, "DNA and the Origin of Life: Information, Specification, and Explanation," Meyer notes, "our experience-based knowledge of information-flow confirms that systems with large amounts of specified complexity (especially codes and languages) invariably originate from an intelligent source—that is, from a mind or personal agent." Clearly, intelligent agents have the causal powers to generate novel linear information-rich sequences of characters. To quote Henry Quastler again, the "creation of new information is habitually associated with conscious activity."[121] Experience teaches this obvious truth.

Further, intelligent agents have just those necessary powers that natural selection lacks as a condition of its causal adequacy. Recall that at several points in our previous analysis, natural selection lacked the ability to generate novel information precisely because it could only act after the fact of new functional information having arisen. Natural selection can favor new proteins and genes, but only after they provide some function. The job of generating new functional genes, proteins, and systems of proteins fell instead to entirely random mutations. Yet without functional criteria to guide a search through the space of possible sequences, random variation is probabilistically doomed. What is needed is not just a source of variation (that is, the freedom to search a space of possibilities) or a mode of selection that can operate after the fact of a successful search but instead a means of selection that (a) operates during a search—before success—and (b) is informed by knowledge of a functional target.

Demonstration of this requirement has come from an unlikely quarter: genetic algorithms. Genetic algorithms are programs that allegedly simulate the creative power of mutation and selection. Richard Dawkins and Bernd-Olaf Kuppers, for example, have developed computer programs that putatively simulate the production of genetic information by mutation and natural selection.[122] Nevertheless, as Meyer shows in his essay, "DNA and the Origin of Life: Information, Specification, and Explanation," these programs only succeed by the illicit expedient of providing the computer with a "target sequence" and then treating relatively greater proximity to *future* function (that is, the target sequence), not actual present function, as a selection criterion.[123] As David Berlinski has argued, genetic algorithms need something akin to a "forward looking memory" in order to succeed.[124] Yet such foresighted selection has no analogue in nature. In biology, where differential survival depends upon maintaining function, selection cannot occur before new functional sequencing arises. Natural selection lacks foresight.

What natural selection lacks, intelligent selection—that is, design—provides. Agents can arrange matter with distant goals in mind. In their use of language, intelligent human agents also routinely "find" highly isolated and improbable functional sequences within a vast space of combinatorial possibilities. Analysis of the problem of the origin of biological information exposes a deficiency in the causal powers of natural selection that corresponds precisely to powers that agents are uniquely known to possess. Agents do have foresight. Agents can also select functional goals *before* they exist. They can devise or select material means to meet those goals from among an array of other possible states and then actualize those goals in accord with a *pre*conceived design and independent set of functional requirements. The causal powers that natural selection lacks—almost by definition—are associated with the attributes of consciousness, rationality, and purposive intelligence. Thus, by invoking intelligent design to explain the origin of new information, design theorists are not positing an arbitrary explanatory element unmotivated by a consideration of the evidence. Instead, they are positing an entity with precisely the attributes and causal powers that the phenomenon in question requires as a condition of its production and explanation.

Second, the highly specified hierarchical arrangements of parts in animal body plans also bespeak design. At every level of the biological hierarchy, organisms require specified and highly improbable arrangements of lower-level constituents in order to maintain their form and function. Genes require specified arrangements of nucleotide bases; proteins require specified arrangements of amino acids; new cell types require specified arrangements of proteins and systems of proteins; new body plans require specialized arrangements of cell types and organs. Organisms not only contain information-rich components (such as proteins and genes), but they comprise information-rich arrangements of those components and the subsystems that comprise them.

Based on experience, we know that intelligent human agents have—by virtue of their rationality, consciousness, and foresight—the ability to produce information-rich arrangements of parts in which both individual modules and also the hierarchical arrangements of those modules exhibit complexity and functional specificity—information so defined. Individual transistors, resistors, and capacitors exhibit considerable complexity and specificity of design; at a higher level of organization, their specific arrangement and connection within an integrated circuit reflects further design. Conscious and rational human agents have, as a consequence of their powers of agency, the capacity to arrange parts in functionally specified, hierarchical patterns. Further, we know of no undirected process that has this capacity. Certainly, we have good reasons to doubt that either the mutation/selection mechanism or self-organizational processes can produce such information-rich hierarchies and structures. Instead, explaining the origin of biological information (at whatever level) requires causal powers that we uniquely associate with conscious and rational activity—with intelligent causes, not purely natural processes or material mechanisms. Thus, based on our experience and analysis of the causal powers of various explanatory processes and entities, we can infer the activity of a purposeful designing agent (with rational powers not unlike those of intelligent human beings) as the best, most causally adequate, explanation for the origin of the specified information required to build the Cambrian animals. In other words, intelligent design best explains the Cambrian information explosion.

B. Morphological Disparity Preceding Diversity: The Top-Down Pattern of Appearance

Design can also explain another feature of the Cambrian explosion: the so-called top-down pattern of appearance in which major morphological innovation and disparity precede minor variations of form (diversity) within those established body-plan designs. As noted above, the fossil record shows a hierarchical top-down pattern in which phyla-level morphological disparity appears first, followed only later by species-level diversity. This pattern suggests intelligent design for several reasons.

First, as noted earlier, standard materialistic models of evolutionary change are decidedly inconsistent with this pattern of fossil evidence since all such models employ what might be called bottom-up modes of causation. Neo-Darwinism, for example, seeks to explain the origin of novel body plans by starting with simpler animal forms and gradually assembling animals with more complex body plans via the gradual accumulation of small, successive material variations. Punctuated equilibrium employs a similar bottom-up strategy of explanation, albeit relying on larger jumps to move from simple to complex forms. Bottom-up models, generally, expect small-scale diversification to emerge first, followed later by enough large-scale morphological disparity to constitute a new body plan. (Self-organizational models partially avoid making this commitment but only at the cost of invoking biologically implausible "large jump," mutations as we have seen.) The bottom-up metaphor thus describes a kind of self-assembly in which the gradual production of the material parts eventually generates a new mode of organization for the whole. This approach suggests that the parts stand causally prior to the organization of the whole. As we have argued, however, this approach encounters both paleontological and biological difficulties: the fossil record leaves no evidence of the occurrence of such precursors, and the morphological transformations that the bottom-up approach requires are, in any case, biologically untenable. Further, the subsequent fossil record shows precisely a top-down pattern of appearance that is inconsistent with bottom-up models of evolutionary development. Bottom-up models do not produce top-down patterns. Thus, all such models lack causal adequacy as explanations for this feature of the Cambrian fossil record.

Second, the history of our own technological innovation manifests the same top-down pattern of appearance that we see in the Cambrian explosion (compare figures 15 and 22). As Stuart Kauffman has observed, "qualitative features of technological evolution appear rather strikingly like the Cambrian explosion . . . the 'taxa' fill in from the top-down."[125] Kauffman notes that in the history of human technological innovation with objects such as guns, bicycles, cars, and airplanes, "early diversity of forms appears more radical and then settles down to minor tuning" of the basic design plan.[126] Since the invention of the automobile, for example, all such systems have included four wheels, two axles, a drive shaft, and a motor. Though many new variations on the original model have arisen *after* the invention of the basic automobile design, all exemplify this same basic design plan. Curiously, we observe this pattern in the fossil record. In the Cambrian fossil record, morphological disparity precedes diversity. The major animal body plans appear first instantiated by only a single (or very few) species. Then later many other varieties arise with many new features, yet with all still exhibiting the same basic body plan. Phylogeny resembles technology.

But this suggests intelligent design in the history of life. The top-down metaphor implies the persistence of an organizational plan through generations of complex systems (whether technological or biological). Yet in such top-down sequences complex systems need not have any material connection to one another. Both the Model-T and the Ford Mustang instantiate the same basic automobile design (a motor, two axles, a steering

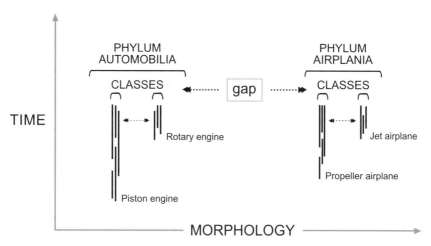

FIGURE 22. This hypothetical classification scheme suggests that the history of human technology manifests the same kind of top-down pattern of appearance and morphological isolation that is evident in the Cambrian fossil record.

column, a drive shaft, and so forth) though they share none of the same material parts. What, then, explains their continuity of organizational structure? Clearly, the answer is: an idea passed from one generation of engineers to another. In the case of different biological organisms that share a common body plan, evolutionary biologists would argue that the body plans remain constant even as the material systems instantiating them evolve gradually from one to another over many generations. Perhaps. But what explains the origin of the body plan itself that provides the pattern to which subsequent types animals will conform? We have seen that both neo-Darwinism and self-organizational mechanisms fail to explain the origin of the body plans that are necessary to establishing a top-down pattern of innovation. Further, the fossil record fails to attest to any material precursors (transitional intermediates) of these body plans. If this is so, if there are no material antecedents to the new body plans that arise in the Cambrian, could there have been a mental antecedent for them, as there most certainly has been in the case of the invention of the automobile and other technological systems that conform to the top-down pattern evident in the history of human technology?

    In the top-down patterns that we know from human technology, an idea (often represented as a blueprint) stands causally prior to the assembly and arrangement of the parts of the system. A blueprint or plan for the whole precedes and guides the assembly of parts in accord with that plan. But if novel body plans do not arise by the self-assembly of preexisting material constituents (as required by all bottom-up mechanisms of evolutionary development), where does the *plan* for the body plan come from? One possibility involves mental rather than material causation. We know from experience that intelligent agents often conceive of plans prior to the material instantiation of the systems that conform to the plans—that is, the intelligent design of a blueprint often precedes the assembly of parts in accord with a blueprint or preconceived design plan. In such systems, the parts do not generate the whole. Rather, an idea of the whole directs the assembly of the parts.

Could this form of causation explain the pattern in the fossil record? Critics of this idea could correctly point out that the fossil record can offer no direct evidence of the existence of mental cause—a preexisting design plan. Yet we lack similarly direct evidence of the ideas that shaped the assembly of parts in our own technology. An observer touring the assembly plant at General Motors plant will see no direct evidence of a prior plan (or even physical blueprint) for General Motors' new models but will perceive the basic design plan upon observing the finished product at the end of the assembly line. Such an observer will have no difficulty attributing this organizational plan to an intelligent source. Students of the history of technological systems may also perceive the activity of mind in the pattern of novel innovation followed by minor variations on an initial design concept. Indeed, we know that intelligent designers have produced precisely such top-down patterns of innovation in the history of designed systems. Thus, while the fossil record does not (and cannot) directly establish the prior existence of a mental rather than material cause, the preexistence of such a design plan could certainly explain the top-down pattern of morphological innovation evident in the fossil record. In other words, if the body plans of the Cambrian animals did arise as the result of an intelligent cause involving preconceived design plan, we would expect, from our experience of the histories of designed systems, to see precisely the kind of top-down pattern of innovation that we see in the fossil record.

Intelligent design, operating over time, often produces top-down patterns of innovation in technological systems. The Cambrian fossil record manifests such a top-down pattern. We know of no other type of cause that produces the kind of top-down patterns that are evident in both the fossil record and the history of human technology. Certainly, undirected bottom-up mechanisms of evolutionary development would not be expected to produce such top-down patterns. Thus, intelligent design provides a better, more causally adequate explanation of the pattern of morphological innovation in the fossil record than any of its materialistic bottom-up competitors.

C. Persistent Morphological Isolation or Disparity

The design hypothesis can also help explain why smaller-scale diversity arises *after,* and not before, morphological disparity in the fossil record and why this morphological disparity persists through geologic time.

Complex designed systems have a functional logic that makes their alteration difficult. Though the Model-A has been replaced by everything from the Yugo to the Honda Accord, the basic automobile "body plan" has remained unchanged from its first appearance in the late nineteenth century. Despite the appearance of many models, automobiles have also retained their "morphological distance" from other functionally distinct technological devices. Indeed, what we recognize as morphological disparity in biological systems has a direct analogue in our own technology. In biology, animals with different body plans differ fundamentally from each other in their overall organization. A starfish and a crab, for example, may exhibit some similarities in their low-level protein parts but they differ fundamentally in their digestive systems, their nervous systems, and in the overall organization of their organs and body parts. In the same way, automobiles and airplanes may have many similar parts, but they also differ in the composition of their distinguishing parts and in their overall organization. In both the biological and technological case, morphological discontinuities separate complex functionally integrated systems from one another.

Consider another example. The basic technology of the CD-ROM (as employed, for instance, in audio systems and computers) did not "evolve" incrementally from earlier technologies, such as magnetic media (for example, digital tape or disc storage) or analog systems such as the once-standard long-playing (LP) record. Indeed, it could not. In an analog recording, information is stored as three-dimensional microscopic grooves in a vinyl surface and is detected mechanically by a diamond stylus. This means of storing and detecting information differs fundamentally, *as a system,* from the digitally encoded pits storing data in the silvered surface of a CD-ROM, where information is detected optically, not mechanically, by a laser beam. Moreover, as a novel system, the CD-ROM had to be engineered from scratch, and, as a result, it displays a striking structural disparity or isolation from all other types of technological devices, even those that perform roughly the same function. As Denton expresses the point, "What is true of sentences and watches is also true of computer programs, airplane engines, and in fact of all known complex systems. Almost invariably, function is restricted to unique and fantastically improbable combinations of subsystems, tiny islands of meaning lost in an infinite sea of incoherence."[127]

Such morphological isolation represents a distinctive feature of designed systems and is a consequence of a deeper design logic that makes the modification of basic architectures difficult or even impossible. Airplanes do not change gradually or incrementally into automobiles, nor do LP records gradually become CDs. Nevertheless, the logic of designed systems does allow minor variations within a basic body-plan design, provided the fundamental organizational plan of the original system is not altered in a way that destroys function. Experience shows a certain hierarchical relationship between functionally necessary and functionally optional features in designed systems. An automobile cannot function without two axles, but it can function with or without twin I-beam suspension, antilock brakes, or "stereo surround-sound." This distinction between functionally necessary and optional features suggests the possibility of future innovation and variation on basic design plans, even as it imposes limits on the extent to which the basic designs themselves can be altered.

The logic of designed systems, therefore, suggests why we see the limited variability within body plans that we see in the history of life and why we also see the persistent isolation (disparity) in the morphology of animals that exemplify those basic body plans. In our experience, morphologically isolated systems that perform specialized functions invariably result from intelligent design. Thus, morphological disparity or isolation constitutes a kind of diagnostic of designed systems. Intelligent agents produce systems that have this feature. Yet neither the neo-Darwinian mechanism nor self-organizational processes can account for the body plan innovation that is a necessary condition of morphological disparity at the body-plan level. Nor would we expect such mechanisms to produce the pattern of persistent isolation that we observe between the separate phyla throughout the history of life. Thus, intelligent design can offer a more causally adequate explanation of the existence and persistence of the morphological disparity in the animal forms that first appear in the Cambrian.

D. Sudden Appearance and Absence
of Ancestral Precursors

Finally, intelligent design can also explain the sudden appearance of the animal body plans that arise in the Cambrian and the absence of ancestral precursors in the Precambrian. The materialistic models of evolution that we have examined generally envision the existence of transitional intermediates leading to the emergence of distinct body plans. Though they disagree about the increments of morphological change, these theories envision bottom-up modes of causation in which material parts, or materially instantiated intermediate forms of organization, necessarily precede the emergence of fully developed new body plans. On the other hand, if body plans arose as the result of an intelligent agent acting to actualize an immaterial plan or mental concept, then material precursors to the animal body plans need not exist in the fossil record. Thus, intelligent design would expect, and thus can explain, the absence of material antecedents in the fossil record. Immaterial plans need not leave a material trace. Yet given the problems with the artifact hypothesis, none of the materialistic evolutionary models can explain the dearth of material precursors and transitional intermediates in the Precambrian rocks.

Similarly, each of the models of undirected evolutionary change that we have examined has a difficult time explaining the geologically sudden appearance of the Cambrian fauna—neo-Darwinism in part because its mechanism requires vast amounts of time; self-organization and punctuated equilibrium because they lack efficacious mechanisms of any kind. Neo-Darwinism in particular would not expect a geologically sudden appearance of animal form. As Darwin himself insisted, *"natura non facit saltum"* (nature takes no leaps). Yet intelligent agents can act suddenly or discretely in accord with their powers of purpose and volition. Thus, the geologically discrete appearance of the various animal phyla in the Cambrian fossil record does suggest the possibility of the purposeful and volitional action of a conscious agent—an intelligent designer. Darwin himself regarded evidence of saltation (sudden appearance) as evidence for an act of special creation (though he denied evidence of a real, as opposed to a merely apparent, saltation). A discrete volitional act (or acts) of creation by a purposeful designer would, therefore, explain the sudden appearance of the Cambrian animals in the fossil record. By contrast, sudden appearance stands as a formidable challenge to neo-Darwinism and to all other bottom-up models of evolutionary change. Thus, intelligent design provides a better, more causally adequate, explanation of this feature of the Cambrian explosion as well.

VI. Conclusion

Of course, scientists wedded to a purely materialistic explanation will instinctively deny the very possibility of top-down intelligent causation. Yet we regularly employ precisely this mode of explanation, especially when we encounter the kinds of patterns and features that we see in the fossil record. Indeed, we see in the fossil record several distinctive features or hallmarks of designed systems, including: (1) a quantum or discontinuous increase in specified complexity or information; (2) a top-down pattern of innovation in which large-scale morphological disparity arises *before* small-scale diversity; (3) the persistence of structural (or "morphological") disparities between separate organizational systems; and (4) the discrete or simultaneous emergence of functionally integrated material parts within novel organizational body plans. When we encounter objects that manifest any of these several features and we know how they arose, we invariably find that a purposeful agent or intelligent designer played a causal role in their origin. Thus, when we encounter all these same features in the fossil record, we may infer—based upon established cause-and-effect relationships and uniformitarian principles—that the same kind of cause operated in the history of life. In other words, intelligent design constitutes the best, most causally adequate, explanation of the specific features of the Cambrian explosion, and the features of this explosion in turn attest to the activity and power of a purposeful intelligence.

Notes

The authors wish to thank John Wiester for inspiration and for sharing ideas that influenced the development of this article.

1. Francisco Ayala, "Darwin's Revolution," in *Creative Evolution?!*, ed. J. Campbell and J. Schopf (Boston: Jones and Bartlett, 1994), 4–5.
2. For a skeptical evaluation of the evolutionary significance of the classical Kettlewell experiments on industrial melanism: see Jonathan Wells, "Second Thoughts about Peppered Moths," *Scientist* (24 May 1999): 13.
3. Data regarding the first appearance of the animal phyla and references used in this compilation are included in appendixes C and D.

4. S. A. Bowring, J. P. Grotzinger, C. E. Isachsen, A. H. Knoll, S. M. Pelechaty, and P. Kolosov, "Calibrating Rates of Early Cambrian Evolution," *Science* 261 (1993): 1293–98.

5. Cui Lili, "Traditional Theory of Evolution Challenged," *Beijing Review* (31 March-6 April 1997): 10.

6. Jeffrey Levinton, "The Big Bang of Animal Evolution," *Scientific America* (Nov. 1992): 84–91; Richard A. Kerr, "Evolution's Big Bang Gets Even More Explosive," *Science* 261 (1993): 1274–75; R. Monastersky, "Siberian Rocks Clock Biological Big Bang," *Science News* 144 (4 Sept. 1993): 148.

7. See appendixes C and D.

8. J. W. Valentine et al., "Fossils, Molecules, and Embryos: New Perspectives on the Cambrian Explosion," *Development* 126 (1999): 851–59.

9. J. Y. Chen, C. W. Li, Paul Chien, G. Q. Zhou, and Feng Gao, "Weng'an Biota—A Light Casting on the Precambrian World" paper presented to the Origin of Animal Body Plans and Their Fossil Records conference, Kunming, China, 20–26 June 1999, sponsored by the Early Life Research Center and the Chinese Academy of Sciences; Paul Chien, J. Y. Chen, C. W. Li, and Frederick Leung, "SEM Observation of Precambrian Sponge Embryos from Southern China, Revealing Ultrastructures Including Yolk Granules, Secretion Granules, Cytoskeleton, and Nuclei" (paper presented to North American Paleontological Convention, University of California, Berkeley, 26 June-1 July 2001).

10. Cui Lili, J. Y. Chen, G. Q. Zhou, M. Y. Zhu, and K. Y. Yeh, *The Chengjiang Biota: A Unique Window of the Cambrian Explosion*, vol. 10 (Taichung, Taiwan: National Museum of Natural Science, 1997), is currently available only in the Chinese language. The translated English version is being completed by Paul Chien, University of San Francisco.

11. J. Y. Chen, J. Dzik, G. D. Edgecombe, L. Ramsköld, and G. Q. Zhou, "A Possible Early Cambrian Chordate," *Nature* 377 (1995): 720–22; J. Y. Chen and C. W. Li, "Early Cambrian Chordate from Chengjiang, China," *Bulletin of the National Museum of Science*, (1997): 257–73; J. Dzik, "*Yunnanozoon* and the Ancestry of Chordates," *Acta Palaeontologica Polanica* 40, no. 4 (1995): 341–60. Note, however, that the assertion that *Yunnanozoon* is a chordate has been challenged. See D. Shu, X. Zhang, and L. Chen, "Reinterpretation of *Yunnanozoon* as the Earliest Known Hemichordate" *Nature* 380 (1996): 428–30; D. G. Shu, S.

Conway Morris, and X. L. Zhang, "A Pikaia-like Chordate from the Lower Cambrian of China," *Nature* 384 (1996): 157–58.

12. Shu et al., "Pikaia-like Chordate," 157–58. Note, however, that the status of *Cathaymyrus* as a valid taxon has been challenged, with some paleontologists arguing that the single specimen of *Cathaymyrus* may actually be a dorso-ventrally compressed *Yunnanozoon;* see J. Y. Chen and C. W. Li "Early Cambrian Chordate," 257–72.

13. See Shu et al., "Pikaia-like Chordate," 157–58; S. Conway Morris, *The Crucible of Creation: The Burgess Shale the Rise of Animals* (New York: Oxford University Press, 1998). Simon Conway Morris is currently preparing a monograph redescribing *Pikaia.*

14. Jun-Yuan Chen, Di-Ying Huang, and Chia-Wei Li, "An Early Cambrian Craniate-like Chordate," *Nature* 402 (1999): 518–22.

15. D. G. Shu, H. L. Lou, S. Conway Morris, X. L. Zhang, S. X. Hu, L. Chen, J. Han, M. Zhu, Y. Li, and L. Z. Chen, "Lower Cambrian Vertebrates from South China," *Nature* 402 (1999): 42–46.

16. D. G. Shu, L. Chen, J. Han, and X. L. Zhang, "An Early Cambrian Tunicate from China" *Nature* 411 (2001): 472–73.

17. Brian Hall, "*Baupläne,* Phylotypic Stages, and Constraint: Why There Are So Few Types of Animal," *Evolutionary Biology* 29 (1996): 215–61.

18. James W. Valentine, "Why No New Phyla after the Cambrian? Genome and Ecospace Hypotheses Revisited," *Palaios* 10 (1995): 190–94. See also Jan Bergström, "Ideas on Early Animal Evolution," in *Early Life on Earth,* Nobel Symposium No. 84, ed. S. Bengston (New York: Columbia University Press, 1994), 460–66. "There is absolutely no sign of convergence between phyla as we follow them backward to the Early Cambrian. They were as widely apart from the beginning as they are today. Hierarchical levels apparently include a biological reality, not only classificatory convention. In fact, the overwhelming taxonomic difficulty is to recognize relationships between phyla, not to distinguish between them" (Bergström, "Ideas," 464).

19. D. Jablonski, "Micro- and Macroevolution: Scale and Hierarchy in Evolutionary Biology and Paleobiology," *Deep Time: Paleobiology's Perspective, Paleobiology* 26, supplement to no. 4 (2000): 15–52, esp. 24.

20. In any case, stasis is also a pervasive characteristic of individual genera and species. The trilobite specialist Niles Eldredge of the American Museum in New York, for example, describes commencing his work in the 1960s on the trilobite species *Phacops Rana.* Eldredge sampled Middle Devonian strata across the United States only to discover that

the trilobites did not vary smoothly and gradually between species as he had expected. They, too, exhibited stasis. Niles Eldredge and Stephen Jay Gould, "Punctuated Equilibria: An Alternative to Phyletic Gradualism," in *Models in Paleobiology,* ed. T. J. Schopf (San Francisco: Freeman, Cooper, and Company, 1972), 82–115, esp. page 107.

21. J. J. Brocks, G. A. Logan, R. Buick, and R. E. Summons, "Archean Molecular Fossils and the Early Rise of Eukaryotes," *Science* 285 (1999): 1033–36.

22. Claude Shannon, "A Mathematical Theory of Communication." *Bell System Technical Journal* 27 (1948): 379–423, 623–56.

23. Hubert P. Yockey, *Information Theory and Molecular Biology.* (Cambridge: Cambridge University Press, 1992), 110.

24. Sahotra Sarkar, "Biological Information: A Skeptical Look at Some Central Dogmas of Molecular Biology," in *The Philosophy and History of Molecular Biology: New Perspectives,* ed. Sahotra Sarkar (Dordrecht: Kluwer Academic Publishers, 1996), 191.

25. James W. Valentine, "Late Precambrian Bilaterians: Grades and Clades," in *Tempo and Mode in Evolution: Genetics and Paleontology 50 Years after Simpson,* ed. W. M. Fitch and F. J. Ayala (Washington, D.C.: National Academy Press, 1995), 87–107, esp. 91–93.

26. Mitsuhiro Itaya, "An Estimation of the Minimal Genome Size Required for Life," *FEBS Letters* 362 (1995): 257–60; Claire Fraser et al., "The Minimal Gene Complement of *Mycoplasma genitalium,*" *Science* 270 (1995): 397–403; Arcady R. Mushegian and Eugene V. Koonin, "A Minimal Gene Set for Cellular Life Derived by Comparison of Complete Bacterial Genomes," *Proceedings of the National Academy of Sciences USA* 93 (1996): 10268–73; Scott Peterson and Claire Fraser, "The Complexity of Simplicity," *Genome Biology* 2 (2001): 1–8.

27. John Gerhart and Marc Kirschner, *Cells, Embryos, and Evolution* (London: Blackwell Science, 1997), 121.

28. The *C. elegans* Sequencing Consortium, "Genome Sequence of the Nematode *C. elegans:* A Platform for Investigating Biology," *Science* 282 (1998): 2012–18.

29. P. Ward, *On Methuselah's Trail, Living Fossils and the Great Extinctions* (New York: W. H. Freeman, 1992), 29–30.

30. Charles Darwin, *The Origin of the Species* (Penguin Books, [1859] 1985), 313. See also Charles Darwin, *On the Origin of Species* (Cambridge: Harvard University Press, [1859] 1964), 307. Darwin's original quote used the "Silurian" rather than the "Cambrian" because in

Darwin's time, what we now label the Cambrian period was sub-
sumed within the concept of the lower Silurian.

31. Susumo Ohno, "The Notion of the Cambrian Pananimalia Genome,"
Proceedings of the National Academy of Sciences USA 93 (Aug. 1996):
8475–78.

32. Richard Dawkins, *The Blind Watchmaker: Why the Evidence of Evolution
Reveals a Universe without Design* (New York: W. W. Norton, 1986), 229.

33. Darwin, *Origin* (1985), 314; Darwin, *Origin* (1964), 308.

34. J. W. Valentine and D. H. Erwin, "Interpreting Great Developmental
Experiments: The Fossil Record," in *Development as an Evolutionary
Process,* ed. R. A. Raff and E. C. Raff (New York: Alan R. Liss, 1987),
74–77, 89, 96. See diagram on page 92.

35. Michael Foote, "On the Probability of Ancestors in the Fossil Record,"
Paleobiology 22 (1996): 141–51, 148.

36. Michael Foote and Stephen J. Gould, "Cambrian and Recent Morphological Disparity," *Science* 258 (1992): 1816.

37. Valentine and Erwin, "Interpreting," 74–77, 97. See diagram on page
92.

38. Stephen Jay Gould, *Wonderful Life: The Burgess Shale and the Nature of
History* (New York: W. W. Norton, 1989), 49.

39. Richard Dawkins, *Unweaving the Rainbow: Science, Delusion, and the Ap-
petite for Wonder* (Boston: Houghton Mifflin, 1998), 201.

40. Darwin, *Origin* (1985), 164, 168.

41. Roger Lewin, "A Lopsided Look at Evolution," *Science* 241 (1988):
292.

42. Douglas Erwin, James Valentine, and J. J. Sepkoski, "A Comparative
Study of Diversification Events: The Early Paleozoic versus the Mesozoic," *Evolution* 41 (1987): 1177–86.

43. *Cycliophora* is thus far a monospecific phylum containing the species
Symbion pandora. This organism is a small (about 350 μm in length),
baglike, ciliated metazoan that attaches itself to the mouthparts of the
Norway lobster, *Nephrops.* For a description of this new phylum, see P.
Funch, and R. M. Kristensen, "*Cycliophora* Is a New Phylum with
Affinities to *Entoprocta* and *Ectoprocta,*" *Nature* 378 (1995): 711–14.

44. Although the following considerations used for determining the possibility of a Cambrian origin for stratigraphically post-Cambrian phyla
(or phyla having no fossil record) are fairly subjective, they are
nonetheless a cautious inference based on important factors relevant
to preservation in the geologic record. Factors taken into account in

the determinations utilized for figures 17B, 18B, and 19B are: organism size, presence/absence of mineralized hard parts, mode of life, habitat/depositional environment, and trace fossil associations. Assumptions based on levels of complexity (that is, number of differentiated cell types) and evolutionary relatedness were not considered in the formulation of figures 17B, 18B, and 19B.

45. Of course, the pattern of body plan first appearance graphed in figures 17B, 18B, and 19B contradicts neo-Darwinism (and punctuated equilibrium) even more dramatically than the pattern graphed in figures 10A and 11A. As noted, evolutionary assumptions (about complex phyla necessarily evolving after simpler ones) provide one way of arriving at the higher estimates for the number of phyla present in the Cambrian as depicted in figures 17A, 18A, and 19A. Ironically, therefore, evolutionary assumptions lead to estimates for the number of phyla in the Cambrian that exacerbate the contradiction between current evolutionary models and the pattern of body plan first appearance. See appendixes C, D, and E.

46. Subphyla are included here for the following reasons: (1) subphyla represent major divisions within phyla that are nearly equivalent to phyla in terms of their morphological isolation relative to each other and to other phyla; (2) phyla containing subphyla are rare (only six animal phyla have subphyla: Arthropoda, Brachiopoda, Chordata, Echinodermata, Mollusca, and Porifera) and therefore worthy of special consideration.

47. S. Gilbert, J. Optiz, and R. Raff, "Review—Resynthesizing Evolutionary and Developmental Biology," *Developmental Biology* 173 (1996): 361.

48. Roger Lewin, "Evolutionary Theory under Fire," *Science* 210 (1980): 883.

49. Gilbert, Optiz, and Raff, "Resynthesizing," 357–72. See also Rudolf A. Raff, *The Shape of Life: Genes, Development, and the Evolution of Animal Form* (Chicago: University of Chicago Press, 1966); Wallace Arthur, *The Origin of Animal Body Plans: A Study in Evolutionary Developmental Biology* (Cambridge: Cambridge University Press, 1997).

50. Gould, *Wonderful Life*, 274–75.

51. Ibid., 272, 275–76.

52. Ibid., 272–76.

53. James W. Valentine, "The Macroevolution of Phyla," in *Origin and Early Evolution of the Metazoa*, ed. Jere H. Lipps and Phillip W. Signor

(New York: Plenum Press, 1992), 525–53, see section 3.2, "Soft-bodied Body Fossils," 529–31.

54. Bergström, "Ideas." "Animals such as arthropods and brachiopods cannot exist without hard parts. The absence of remains of skeletons and shells in the Precambrian therefore proves that the phyla came into being with the Cambrian, not before, even if the lineages leading to the phyla were separate before the Cambrian" (Bergström, "Ideas," 464).

55. Valentine and Erwin, "Interpreting," 74–77.

56. James W. Valentine, "Fossil Record of the Origin of *Baupläne* and Its Implications," in *Patterns and Processes in the History of Life,* ed. D. M. Raup and D. Jablonski (Berlin: Springer-Verlag, 1986), 209–22, esp. 215.

57. Moreover, even if advocates of this version of the artifact hypothesis are correct about the existence of soft-bodied Precambrian ancestral forms, they still must explain the origin of the distinctive and functionally necessary hard-bodied parts (such as the arthropod exoskeleton) that actually do appear in the Cambrian. At the very least, they must explain "an explosion" of hard-bodied parts in the Cambrian.

58. Lili et al., *Chengjiang Biota.*

59. Eric H. Davidson, Kevin J. Peterson, and R. Andrew Cameron, "Origin of Bilaterian Body Plans: Evolution of Developmental Regulatory Mechanisms," *Science* 270 (1995): 1319–24.

60. William J. Schopf and Bonnie M. Packer, "Early Archean (3.3-Billion to 3.5-Billion-Year-Old) Microfossils from Warrawoona Group, Australia," *Science* 237 (1987): 70.

61. Jochen J. Brocks, Graham A. Logan, Roger Buick, and Roger E. Summons, "Archean Molecular Fossils and the Early Rise of Eukaryotes," *Science* 285 (1999): 1033–36.

62. Chien et al., "SEM Observation." Sponges are assumed by most evolutionary biologists to represent a side branch, not a node on evolutionary tree of life leading to the Cambrian phyla. Thus, sponges are not regarded as plausible transitional intermediates between Precambrian and Cambrian forms (nor are they regarded as ancestral to the Cambrian phyla).

63. As noted, the geological record does preserve soft tissues but only infrequently. When it does, researchers fortunate enough to make such finds will rarely want to destroy important specimens (of soft-tissue organs) in order to examine them for traces of parasitic infection or

habitation. Not surprisingly, therefore, paleontologists have not found the remains of many parasitic organisms in the fossil record.

64. Michael Foote, "Sampling, Taxonomic Description, and Our Evolving Knowledge of Morphological Diversity," *Paleobiology* 23 (1997): 181.

In the same vein, paleontologist Michael J. Benton of the University of Bristol writes, "[I]t could be argued that there are fossils out there waiting to be found. It is easy to dismiss the fossil record as seriously, and unpredictably, incomplete. For example, certain groups of organisms are almost unknown as fossils. . . . This kind of argument cannot be answered conclusively. However, an argument based on effort can be made. Paleontologists have been searching for fossils for years and, remarkably, very little has changed since 1859, when Darwin proposed that the fossil record would show us the pattern of the history of life" ("Early Origins of Modern Birds and Mammals: Molecules vs. Morphology," *BioEssays* 21 [1999]: 1043–51, esp. 1046).

65. John P. Grotzinger, Samuel A. Bowring, Beverly Z. Saylor, and Alan J. Kaufman, "Biostratigraphic and Geochronologic Constraints on Early Animal Evolution," *Science* 270 (1995): 598–604. A few Ediacarans may have survived until the middle Cambrian. See Simon Conway Morris, "Ediacaran-like Fossils in Cambrian Burgess Shale-type Faunas of North America," *Paleontology* 36 (1993), part 3: 593–635.

66. R. Monastersky, "Ancient Animal Sheds False Identity," *Science News* 152 (30 Aug. 1997): 32.

67. Mikhail A. Fedonkin and Benjamin M. Waggoner, "The Late Precambrian Fossil *Kimberella* Is a Mollusc-like Bilaterian Organism," *Nature* 388 (1997): 868.

68. Another reason the Ediacaran body fossils cannot be assigned to the animal phyla in a decisive manner is because of the coarse grain size of the beds in which they occur. Details of body form are too vague to allow a clear decision, and until better means of analysis or new beds with finer grain texture are found, these fossils will remain as intriguing "problematica," problematic forms about which it is not possible to come to a decision. See G. L. Miklos, "Emergence of Organizational Complexities during Metazoan Evolution: Perspectives from Molecular Biology, Paleontology and Neo-Darwinism," *Mem. Ass. Australas. Palaeontols* 15 (1993): 7–41. See also J. Bergström, "Metazoan Evolution around the Precambrian-Cambrian Transition," in *The Early Evolution of Metazoa and the Significance of Problematic Taxa*, ed. A. M.

Simonetta and S. Conway Morris (Cambridge: Cambridge University Press, 1991), 25–34.

69. Some paleontologists have suggested that *Dickinsonia* and other similar Ediacarans are actually colonial prokaryotes. See Michael Steiner and Joachim Reitner, "What Are the Ediacara-type Fossils?" (paper presented to the Origin of Animal Body Plans and Their Fossil Records conference, Kunming, China, 20–26 June 1999), sponsored by the Early Life Research Center and the Chinese Academy of Sciences.

70. Valentine and Erwin, "Interpreting," 132.

71. Sponges (phylum Porifera) actually predate the first appearance of the other phyla present in the Ediacaran.

72. James W. Valentine, Douglas H. Erwin, and David Jablonski, "Developmental Evolution of Metazoan Body Plans: The Fossil Evidence," *Developmental Biology* 173 (1996): 373–81, article no. 0033, 375; B. Runnegar, "Evolution of the Earliest Animals," in *Major Events in the History of Life,* ed. J. W. Schopf (Boston: Jones and Bartlett, 1992).

73. B. Runnegar, "Proterozoic Eukaryotes: Evidence from Biology and Geology," in Bengston, *Early Life on Earth;* J. G. Gehling, "The Case for Ediacaran Fossil Roots to the Metazoan Tree," in *The World of Martin F. Glaessner: Memoir No. 20,* ed. B. P. Radhakrishna (Bangalore: Geological Society of India, 1991), 181–223.

74. The beginning of the Cambrian period (and the Paleozoic era) 543 million years ago is marked by the appearance of small shelly fossils consisting of tubes, cones, and possibly spines and scales of larger animals. These fossils, together with trace fossils, gradually become more abundant and diverse as one moves upward in the earliest Cambrian strata (the Manykaian Stage, 543–530 million years ago). The small shelly fossils, together with the tracks and burrows of the Vendian and earliest Cambrian, may be also be regarded, metaphorically, as part of the "burning fuse" of the forthcoming Cambrian explosion. Whether these or any of the fossils in the Ediacaran constitute true transitionals remains highly debatable.

75. Gregory A. Wray, Jeffrey S. Levinton, and Leo H. Shapiro, "Molecular Evidence for Deep Precambrian Divergences among Metazoan Phyla," *Science* 274 (1996): 568; for a similar study of molecular sequence data that comes to the same conclusion, see Daniel Y. C. Wang, Sudhir Kumar, S. Blair Hedges, "Divergence Time Estimates for the Early History of Animal Phyla and the Origin of Plants, Animals and Fungi,"

Proceedings of the Royal Society of London, Series B 266 (no. 1415): 163; see also Geerat J. Vermeij, "Animal Origins," *Proceedings of the Royal Society of London,* Series B 266 (no. 1415): 525–26; see also Richard A. Fortey, Erek E. G. Briggs, and Matthew A. Wills, "The Cambrian Evolutionary Explosion Recalibrated," *BioEssays* 19 (1997): 429–34.

76. Wray, Levinton, and Shapiro, "Molecular Evidence," 568.

77. R. L. Hotz, "Finding Turns Back Clock for Earth's First Animals," *Los Angeles Times,* 25 Oct. 1996.

78. Francisco José Ayala, Audrey Rzhetsky, and Francisco J. Ayala, "Origin of the Metazoan Phyla: Molecular Clocks Confirm Paleontological Estimates," *Proceedings of the National Academy of Sciences* 95 (1998): 606–611.

79. Valentine et al., "Fossils," 851–59, esp. 856.

80. Simon Conway Morris, "Evolution: Bringing Molecules into the Fold," *Cell* 100 (7 Jan. 2000): 5–6.

81. Simon Conway Morris, "Early Metazoan Evolution: Reconciling Paleontology and Molecular Biology," *American Zoologist* 38 (1998): 870.

82. Bernard Johns and George Miklos, *The Eukaryote Genome in Development and Evolution* (London: Allen and Unwin, 1988), 293.

83. For scientific challenges to the universal common ancestry thesis (that is, the monophyletic interpretation of the history of life), see Gerry Webster and Brian Goodwin, "The Origin of Species: A Structuralist Approach," *Journal of Social and Biological Structures* 5 (1982): 15–47; Christian Schwabe, "Theoretical Limitations of Molecular Phylogenetics and the Evolution of Relaxins," *Comparative Biochemistry and Physiology* 107B (1994): 167–77; Malcolm S. Gordon, "The Concept of Monophyly: A Speculative Essay," *Biology and Philosophy* 14 (1999): 331–48; Carl Woese, "The Universal Ancestor," *Proceedings of the National Academy of Sciences USA* 95 (1998): 6854–59.

84. Elliott Sober, *The Philosophy of Biology* (San Francisco: Westview Press, 1993), 44; Peter Lipton, *Inference to the Best Explanation* (New York: Routledge, 1991), 32–88; Stephen C. Meyer, "The Scientific Status of Intelligent Design: The Methodological Equivalence of Naturalistic and Non-Naturalistic Origins Theories," in *Science and Evidence for Design in the Universe: The Proceedings of the Wethersfield Institute* (San Francisco: Ignatius Press, 2000), 151–212; Stephen C. Meyer, "The Demarcation of Science and Religion," in *The History of Science and Religion in the Western Tradition: An Encyclopedia,* ed. G. B. Ferngren (New York: Garland, 2000), 17–23.

85. Francis Darwin, ed., *Life and Letters of Charles Darwin,* vol. 1 (London: D. Appleton, 1896), 437.
86. Lipton, *Inference,* 32–88.
87. Henry Quastler, *The Emergence of Biological Organization* (New Haven, Conn.: Yale University Press, 1964), 16.
88. Stuart Kauffman, *At Home in the Universe* (Oxford: Oxford University Press, 1995), 199–201.
89. Valentine, "Late Precambrian Bilaterians," 87–107.
90. M. Schützenberger, "Algorithms and the Neo-Darwinian Theory of Evolution," in *Mathematical Challenges to the Darwinian Interpretation of Evolution,* ed. P. S. Morehead and M. M. Kaplan, Wistar Institute Symposium Monograph (New York: Allen R. Liss, 1967); S. Løvtrup, "Semantics, Logic and Vulgate Neo-Darwinism," *Evolutionary Theory* 4 (1979): 157–72; David Berlinski, "The Deniable Darwin," *Commentary* (June 1996): 19–29; Michael Denton, *Evolution: A Theory in Crisis* (London: Adler and Adler, 1986), 308–24.
91. J. Bowie and R. Sauer, "Identifying Determinants of Folding and Activity for a Protein of Unknown Sequences: Tolerance to Amino Acid Substitution," *Proceedings of the National Academy of Sciences USA* 86 (1989): 2152–56; J. Reidhaar-Olson and R. Sauer, "Functionally Acceptable Solutions in Two Alpha-Helical Regions of Lambda Repressor," *Proteins, Structure, Function, and Genetics* 7 (1990): 306–16.
92. See also M. F. Perutz and H. Lehmann, "Molecular Pathology of Human Hemoglobin," *Nature* 219 (1968): 902–9.
93. Douglas D. Axe, "Extreme Functional Sensitivity to Conservative Amino Acid Changes on Enzyme Exteriors," *Journal of Molecular Biology* 301, no. 3 (2000): 585–96.
94. William A. Dembski, *The Design Inference: Eliminating Chance through Small Probabilities* (Cambridge: Cambridge University Press, 1998), 175–223; Denton, *Evolution,* 308–22; Kauffman, *At Home,* 44.
95. Richard Dawkins, *Climbing Mount Improbable* (New York: W. W. Norton, 1996).
96. Reidhaar-Olson and Sauer, "Functionally Acceptable Solutions," 306–16; Michael Behe, "Experimental Support for Regarding Functional Classes of Proteins to Be Highly Isolated from Each Other," in *Darwinism: Science or Philosophy,* ed. J. Buell and G. Hearn (Richardson, Tex.: Foundation for Thought and Ethics, 1992), 60–71.
97. Axe, "Biological Function," 585–96.
98. Ohno, "Notion," 8475–76.

99. Dembski, *Design Inference,* 175–223.

100. Ohno, "Notion," 8475–76.

101. Dawkins, *Blind Watchmaker,* 139.

102. Axe, "Biological Function," 585–96.

103. F. Blanco, I. Angrand, and L. Serrano, "Exploring the Conformational Properties of the Sequence Space between Two Proteins with Different Folds: An Experimental Study," *Journal of Molecular Biology* 285, no. 2 (1999): 741; E. Zuckerkandl, "The Appearance of New Structures in Proteins during Evolution," *Journal of Molecular Evolution* 7 (1975): 21.

104. Axe, "Biological Function," 585–96; Blanco, Angrand, and Serrano, "Exploring," 741–53; Miklos, "Emergence," 7–41; Zuckerkandl, "Appearance," 21.

105. Leigh Van Valen, "How Do Major Evolutionary Changes Occur?" *Evolutionary Theory* 8 (1988): 173–76, esp. 173.

106. Keith Stewart Thomson, "Macroevolution: The Morphological Problem," *American Zoologist* 32 (1992): 106–12, esp. 111; Kauffman, *At Home,* 200.

107. Johns and Miklos, *Eukaryote Genome,* 309.

108. C. Nusslein-Volhard and E. Wieschaus, "Mutations Affecting Segment Number and Polarity in Drosophila," *Nature* 287 (1980): 795–801; P. A. Lawrence and G. Struhl, "Morphogens, Compartments and Pattern: Lessons from Drosophila?" *Cell* 85 (1996): 951–61.

109. Kauffman, *At Home,* 200.

110. John F. McDonald, "The Molecular Basis of Adaptation: A Critical Review of Relevant Ideas and Observations," *Annual Review of Ecology and Systematics* 14 (1983): 77–102, 93.

111. Darwin, *Origin* (1964), 108.

112. Brian C. Goodwin, "What Are the Causes of Morphogenesis?" *BioEssays* 3 (1985): 32–36; Brian C. Goodwin, *How the Leopard Changed Its Spots* (New York: Scribner's, 1994); H. F. Nijhout, "Metaphors and the Role of Genes in Development," *BioEssays* 12 (1990): 441–46; Jonathan Wells, "Unseating Naturalism: Recent Insights from Developmental Biology," in *Mere Creation,* ed. William A. Dembski (Downer's Grove, Ill.: Intervarsity Press, 1998), 51–70; Jan Sapp, *Beyond the Gene* (New York: Oxford University Press, 1987).

113. Of course, many proteins bind chemically with each other to form complexes and structures within cells. Nevertheless, these "self-

organizational" properties do not fully account for higher levels of organization in cells, organs, or body plans.

114. Stephen L. Wolfe, *Molecular and Cellular Biology* (Belmont, Calif.: Wadsworth, 1993), 17–19.

115. Jonathan Wells, "Making Sense of Biology: The Evidence for Development by Design," *Touchstone* (July/Aug. 1999): 51–55, esp. 52.

116. Of course, many proteins do have binding affinities with other proteins, and these "self-organizational" properties do account for the structure of many protein complexes within cells. Nevertheless, these affinities do not fully account for (a) the structure of cells, (b) the structures formed by cells within organisms, or (c) the architecture of animal body plans. Wells, "Making Sense," 51–55, esp. 52.

117. Kauffman, *At Home,* 47–92, esp. 56, 58.

118. Ibid., 86–88.

119. Ibid., 53, 89, 102.

120. Ibid., 199–201.

121. Quastler, *Emergence,* 16.

122. Dawkins, *Blind Watchmaker,* 47–49; Bernd-Olaf Kuppers, "On the Prior Probability of the Existence of Life," in *The Probabilistic Revolution,* ed. Lorenz Kruger et al. (Cambridge: MIT Press, 1987), 355–69.

123. Stephen C. Meyer, "DNA by Design: An Inference to the Best Explanation for the Origin of Biological Information," *Rhetoric and Public Affairs* 1, no. 4: 532–33; Stephen C. Meyer, "The Explanatory Power of Design: DNA and the Origin of Information," in Dembski, *Mere Creation,* 127–28; Paul Nelson, "Anatomy of a Still-Born Analogy," *Origins and Design* 17, no. 3: 12.

124. David Berlinski, "On Assessing Genetic Algorithms" (public lecture, Science and Evidence of Design in the Universe Conference, Yale University, 4 Nov. 2000).

125. Kauffman, *At Home,* 202.

126. Ibid.

127. Denton, *Evolution,* 313.

Reinstating Design within Science

William A. Dembski

❊ ❊ ❊

Should design be permitted back into science generally and back into biology in particular? Scientists bristle at the thought. For those scientists who are atheists, design is an accident of natural history. With no divine architect to start creation on its course, they say, any designing agents, including ourselves, must result from a long evolutionary process that itself was not designed. For the atheist, design occurs at the end of an undesigned natural process and cannot be prior to it.

What about scientists who are not atheists? Sadly, most scientists who are theists agree with their atheist colleagues that design should be excluded from science. It's not that they agree with their atheist colleagues that the universe isn't designed. As good theists, they believe wholeheartedly that the universe is designed—and not just by any designer, but by the god of their religious creed. Nevertheless, as a matter of scientific integrity, they believe that science is best served by excluding design. The worry always is that invoking design will stifle scientific inquiry, substituting a supernatural cause where scientists should be seeking an ordinary natural cause.

Against this received view, I want to argue that design should be readmitted to full scientific status.

Design's Departure from Science

To make my argument, let me begin by briefly reviewing why design was removed from science in the first place. Design, in the form of Aristotle's formal and final causes, had after all once occupied a perfectly legitimate role within natural philosophy, or what we now call science. With the rise of modern science, however, those causes fell into disrepute.

We can see how that happened by considering Francis Bacon. Bacon, a contemporary of Galileo and Kepler, though himself not a scientist, was a terrific propagandist for science. Bacon concerned himself much about the proper conduct of science, providing detailed canons for experimental observation, recording of data, and inferences from data. What interests us here, however, is what he did with Aristotle's four causes. For Aristotle, to understand any phenomenon properly, one had to understand its four causes, namely its material, efficient, formal, and final causes.

A standard example philosophers use to illustrate Aristotle's four causes is to consider a statue, say Michelangelo's *David*. The material cause is what it's made of: marble. The efficient cause is the immediate activity that produced the statue: Michelangelo's actual chipping away at a marble slab with hammer and chisel. The formal cause is its structure: it's a representation of David and not some random chunk of marble. Finally, the final cause is its purpose: presumably, to beautify some Florentine palace.

Although much more can be said about Aristotle's four causes than is evident from that illustration, two points are relevant to this discussion. First, Aristotle gave equal weight to all four causes. In particular, Aristotle would have regarded any inquiry that omitted one of his causes as fundamentally deficient. Second, Bacon adamantly opposed including formal and final causes within science (see his *Advancement of Learning*). For Bacon, formal and final causes belong to metaphysics, not to science. Science, according to Bacon, needs to limit itself to material and efficient causes, thereby freeing science from the sterility that inevitably results when science and metaphysics are conflated. That was Bacon's line, and he argued it forcefully.

We see Bacon's line championed in our own day by atheists and theists alike. In *Chance and Necessity,* biologist and Nobel laureate Jacques Monod argues that chance and necessity alone suffice to account for every aspect of the universe. Now whatever else we might want to say about chance and necessity, they provide at best a reductive account of Aristotle's formal causes and leave no room whatever for Aristotle's final causes. Indeed, Monod explicitly denies any place for purpose within science.[1]

Monod is an outspoken atheist. Nevertheless, as outspoken a theist as Stanley Jaki will agree with Monod about the nature of science. Jaki is as theologically conservative a historian of science and Catholic priest as one is likely to find. Yet in his published work, he explicitly states that purpose is a purely metaphysical notion and cannot legitimately be included within science. Jaki's exclusion from science of purpose, and more generally of design, has practical implications. For instance, it leads him to regard Michael Behe's project of inferring biological design from irreducibly complex biochemical systems as hopelessly misguided.[2]

I don't want to give the impression that I'm advocating a return to Aristotle's theory of causation. There are problems with Aristotle's theory, and it needed to be replaced. My concern, however, is with what replaced it. By limiting scientific inquiry to material and efficient causes, Bacon fed into a mechanistic understanding of the universe that was soon to dominate science.

To be sure, mechanism has its advantages. Back in the seventeenth century, the French playwright Molière ridiculed Aristotelians for explaining the medicinal properties of opium in terms of its "dormitive power." Appealing to a formal cause like "dormitive power" is of course totally unenlightening. Much better is to know the chemical properties of opium and how those properties take advantage of certain nerve centers in the brain. Mechanistic explanations that describe how something works without speculating about its ultimate meaning or purpose seemed a much safer course for science, and one that promised to, and in fact did, yield much fruit.

Mechanism is still with us, though not the deterministic form that dominated from Newton to the quantum revolution. In our own day, scientists concentrate on undirected natural causes and take as their preferred mode of scientific explanation a combination of deterministic laws and chance processes. Chance and necessity, to use a phrase we've already seen, set the boundaries of scientific explanation, and woe to anyone who would reintroduce a sterile and moribund teleology into science.

Why Reinstate Design?

Faced with a discredited Aristotelian science, a marvelously successful modern science, and an entrenched opposition within the scientific community against design, why should anyone want to reintroduce design into science? The short answer is that chance and necessity have proven too thin an explanatory soup on which to nourish a robust science. In fact, by dogmatically excluding design from science, scientists are themselves stifling scientific inquiry. To many, this will no doubt seem counterintuitive. Nevertheless, the case for reintroducing design within science becomes compelling as soon as we attend to certain relevant facts.

The first glimmers that excluding design from science places an artificial restriction on science come from admissions by scientists opposed to design. Arch-Darwinist Richard Dawkins begins his book *The Blind Watchmaker* by stating that "biology is the study of complicated things that give the appearance of having been designed for a purpose."[3] Statements like his echo throughout the biological literature. In *What Mad Pursuit,* Francis Crick, Nobel laureate and codiscoverer of the structure of DNA, writes that "biologists must constantly keep in mind that what they see was not designed, but rather evolved."[4]

Granted, the biological community thinks that it has accounted for the apparent design in nature apart from any actual design (typically through the Darwinian mechanism of mutation and selection). The point to appreciate, however, is that in accounting for the apparent design in nature, biologists regard themselves as having made a successful *scientific* argument against actual design. Scientific refutation is a double-edged sword. Claims that are refuted scientifically may be wrong, but they are not necessarily wrong. Alternatively, for a claim to be scientifically falsifiable, it must have the possibility of being true.

To see this, consider what would happen if microscopic examination revealed that every cell was inscribed with the phrase "Made by Yahweh." Of course, cells don't have "Made by Yahweh" inscribed on them, but that's not the point. The point is that we wouldn't know it unless we actually looked at cells under the microscope.

Design always remains a live option in biology. A priori prohibitions against design are easily countered, especially in an age of diversity and multiculturalism where it is easy to ask, Who sets the rules for science? Nonetheless, once we admit that design cannot be excluded from science on first principles, a weightier question remains: Why should we want to admit design into science?

To answer this question, let us turn it around and ask instead, Why shouldn't we want to admit design into science? Leaving aside Aristotle's doctrine of causes, what's wrong with explaining something in terms of design by an intelligent agent? Certainly we explain many everyday occurrences by appealing to design. Moreover, in our workaday lives it is absolutely crucial to distinguish accident from design. We demand answers to such questions as, Did she fall or was she pushed? Did someone die accidentally or commit suicide? Was this song conceived independently or was it plagiarized? Did someone just get lucky on the stock market or was there insider trading?

Not only do we demand answers to such questions, but entire industries are devoted to drawing the distinction between accident and design. Here we can include forensic science, intellectual property law, insurance claims investigation, cryptography, and random number generation—to name but a few. Science itself needs to draw this distinction to keep itself honest. According to *Science,* a Medline websearch uncovered a "paper published in *Zentralblatt für Gynäkologie* in 1991 [containing] text that is almost identical to text from a paper published in 1979 in the *Journal of Maxillofacial Surgery.*"[5] Plagiarism and data falsification are more common in science than we would like to admit. What keeps those abuses in check is our ability to detect them.

If design is readily detectable outside the natural sciences, and if its detectability is one of the key factors keeping scientists honest, why should design be barred from the content of science? With reference to biology, why should we constantly have to remind ourselves that biology studies things that only appear to be designed but that in fact are not designed? Isn't it at least conceivable that there could be good positive reasons for thinking that biological systems are in fact designed?

The biological community's response to such questions has been to resist design at all costs. The worry is that for natural objects (unlike human artifacts), the distinction between design and nondesign cannot be reliably drawn. Consider, for instance, the following remark by Darwin in the concluding chapter of his *Origin of Species:*

> Several eminent naturalists have of late published their belief that a multitude of reputed species in each genus are not real species; but that other species are real, that is, have been independently created. . . . Nevertheless they do not pretend that they can define, or even conjecture, which are the created forms of life, and which are those produced by secondary laws. They admit variation as a vera causa in one case, they arbitrarily reject it in another, without assigning any distinction in the two cases.[6]

It's this worry of falsely attributing something to design (here identified with creation) only to have it overturned later that has prevented design from entering science proper.

That worry, though perhaps justified in the past, can now be dispatched. There does in fact exist a rigorous criterion for distinguishing intelligently caused objects from unintelligently caused ones. Many special sciences already use this criterion, though in a pretheoretic form (for example, forensic science, artificial intelligence, cryptography, archaeology, and the search for extraterrestrial intelligence).

The Complexity-Specification Criterion

What does that general criterion for detecting design look like? Although any detailed explanation and justification of the criterion are fairly technical, the basic idea is quite simple and easily illustrated.[7] Consider how radio astronomers in the movie *Contact* detected an extraterrestrial intelligence. That film, based on a novel by Carl Sagan, was an enjoyable piece of propaganda for the SETI (Search for ExtraTerrestrial Intelligence) research program. To make the movie interesting, the SETI researchers actually had to find an extraterrestrial intelligence. (The nonfictional SETI program has yet to be so fortunate.)

To increase their chances of finding an extraterrestrial intelligence, SETI researchers monitor millions of radio signals from outer space. Many natural objects in space produce radio waves (for example, pulsars). Looking for signs of design among all these naturally produced radio signals is like looking for a needle in a haystack. To sift through the haystack, SETI researchers run the signals they monitor through computers programmed with pattern-matchers. So long as a signal doesn't match one of the preset patterns, it will pass through the pattern-matching sieve (and will do so even if it has an intelligent source). If, on the other hand, it does match one of those patterns, then, depending on the pattern matched, the SETI researchers may have cause for celebration.

The SETI researchers in *Contact* did find a signal worthy of celebration, namely the following:

```
110111011111011111110111111111110111111111111110111111111111111
111101111111111111111111011111111111111111111111011111111111111
111111111111111111101111111111111111111111111111110111111111111
111111111111111111111111111101111111111111111111111111111111111
111111111101111111111111111111111111111111111111111111111011111
```

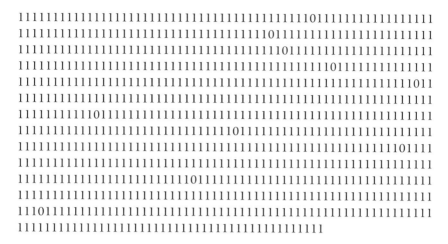

```
11111111111111111111111111111111111111111111011111111111111111
11111111111111111111111111111111111111011111111111111111111111
11111111111111111111111111111111111111011111111111111111111111
11111111111111111111111111111111111111111011111111111111111
11111111111111111111111111111111111111111111111111111111111011
11111111111111111111111111111111111111111111111111111111111111
11111111110111111111111111111111111111111111111111111111111111
11111111111111111111111110111111111111111111111111111111111111
11111111111111111111111110111111111111111111111111111111101111
11111111111111111111111111111111111111111111111111111111111111
11111111111111111111111011111111111111111111111111111111111111
11111111111111111111111111111111111111111111111111111111111111
11101111111111111111111111111111111111111111111111111111111111
1111111111111111111111111111111111111111111111
```

In that sequence of 1,126 bits, 1's correspond to beats and 0's to pauses. The sequence represents the prime numbers from 2 to 101, where a given prime number is represented by the corresponding number of beats (1's), and the individual prime numbers are separated by pauses (0's).

The SETI researchers in *Contact* took this signal as decisive confirmation of an extraterrestrial intelligence. What is it about this signal that decisively implicates design? Whenever we infer design, we must establish two things, *complexity* and *specification*. Complexity ensures that the object in question is not so simple that it can readily be explained by chance. Specification ensures that the object exhibits the type of pattern that signals intelligence.

To see why complexity is crucial to inferring design, consider the following sequence of bits:

110111011111

These are the first twelve bits in the previous sequence representing the prime numbers 2, 3, and 5, respectively. Now I can guarantee that no SETI researcher, if confronted with this twelve-bit sequence, is going to contact the science editor at the *New York Times,* hold a press conference, and announce that an extraterrestrial intelligence has been discovered. No headline is going to read, "Extraterrestrials Have Mastered the First Three Prime Numbers!"

The problem is that this sequence is much too short (that is, it has too little complexity) to establish that an extraterrestrial intelligence with knowledge of prime numbers produced it. A randomly beating pulsar might by chance just happen to output the sequence "110111011111." A sequence of 1,126 bits representing the prime numbers from 2 to 101, however, is a different story. Here the sequence is sufficiently long (that is, it has enough complexity) to establish that an extraterrestrial intelligence would have been required to produce it.

Even so, complexity by itself isn't enough to eliminate chance and implicate design. If I flip a coin a thousand times, I'll participate in a highly complex (or what amounts to the same thing, highly improbable) event. Indeed, the sequence I end up flipping will be one in a trillion trillion trillion . . . , where the ellipsis needs twenty-two more "trillions." That sequence of coin tosses won't, however, trigger a design inference. Though complex, the sequence won't exhibit a suitable pattern. Contrast this with the previous sequence representing the prime numbers from 2 to 101. Not only is that sequence complex, but it also embodies a suitable pattern. The SETI researcher who in the movie *Contact* discovered this sequence put it this way: "This isn't noise, this has structure."

What is a *suitable* pattern for inferring design? Not just any pattern will do. Some patterns can legitimately be employed to infer design, whereas others cannot. The basic intuition underlying the distinction between patterns that alternately succeed or fail to implicate design is, however, easily motivated. Consider the case of an archer. Suppose an archer stands 50 meters from a large wall with bow and arrow in hand. The wall, let's say, is sufficiently large that the archer can't help but hit it. Now suppose each time the archer shoots an arrow at the wall, he or she paints a target around the arrow so that the arrow is squarely in the bull's-eye. What can be concluded from this scenario? Absolutely nothing about the archer's ability as an archer. Yes, a pattern is being matched, but it is a pattern fixed only after the arrow has been shot. The pattern is thus purely ad hoc.

But suppose instead the archer paints a fixed target on the wall and then shoots at it. Suppose the archer shoots a hundred arrows and each time hits a perfect bull's-eye. What can be concluded now? Confronted with this second scenario, we are obligated to infer that here is a world-class archer, one whose shots cannot legitimately be referred to luck but rather must be referred to the archer's skill and mastery. Skill and mastery are, of course, special cases of design.

The type of pattern where the archer fixes a target first and then shoots at it is common to statistics, where it is known as setting a rejection region prior to an experiment. In statistics, if the outcome of an experiment falls within a *rejection region*, the chance hypothesis supposedly responsible for the outcome is rejected. A little reflection makes clear that a pattern need not be given prior to an event to eliminate chance and implicate design. Consider the following cipher text:

nfuijolt ju jt mjlf b xfbtfm

Initially, this looks like a random sequence of letters and spaces. You lack any pattern for rejecting chance and inferring design.

But suppose next that someone comes along, after you've seen this sequence, and tells you to treat it as a Caesar cipher, moving each letter one notch down the alphabet. Behold, the sequence now reads,

methinks it is like a weasel

Even though the pattern is now given after the fact, it still is the right sort of pattern for eliminating chance and inferring design. In contrast to statistics, which always tries to identify its patterns before an experiment is performed, cryptanalysis must discover its patterns after the fact. In both instances, however, the patterns are suitable for inferring design because the patterns exist independently of the events or entities that conform to them. English grammar and vocabulary exist independently of the encrypted sequences in which English words and grammatical structure are embedded. Similarly, the archer's arrow hits a target that existed independently of the arrow's final position on the wall.

Patterns divide into two types, those that in the presence of complexity warrant a design inference (those that manifest what I call "conditional independence") and those that despite the presence of complexity do not warrant a design inference. The first type of pattern is called a specification, the second a fabrication. Specifications are the independently existing (non–ad hoc) patterns that can legitimately be used to eliminate chance and warrant a design inference. In contrast, fabrications are the non-independent (ad hoc) patterns that cannot legitimately be used to warrant a design inference. This distinction between specifications and fabrications can be made with full statistical rigor.[8]

Why the Criterion Works

Why does the complexity-specification criterion reliably detect design? To see why this criterion is exactly the right instrument for detecting design, we need to understand what it is about intelligent agents that makes them detectable in the first place. The principal characteristic of intelligent agency is choice. Whenever an intelligent agent acts, it chooses from a range of competing possibilities.

This is true not just of humans but of animals in general as well as of extraterrestrial intelligences. A rat navigating a maze must choose whether to go right or left at various points in the maze. When SETI researchers attempt to discover intelligence in the extraterrestrial radio transmissions they monitor, they assume that an extraterrestrial intelligence could have chosen any number of possible radio transmissions, and then they attempt to match the observed transmissions with certain patterns as opposed to others. Whenever a human being utters meaningful speech, a choice is made from a range of possible sound-combinations that might have been uttered. Intelligent agency always entails discrimination, choosing certain things, ruling out others.

Given this characterization of intelligent agency, the crucial question is how to recognize it. Intelligent agents act by making a choice. How, then, do we recognize that an intelligent agent has made a choice? A bottle of ink spills accidentally onto a sheet of paper; someone takes a fountain pen and writes a message on a sheet of paper. In both instances ink is applied to paper. In both instances one among an almost infinite set of possibilities is realized. In both instances a contingency is actualized and others are ruled out. Yet in one instance we ascribe chance, in the other agency.

What is the relevant difference? Not only do we need to observe that a contingency was actualized, but we also need to be able to specify that contingency. The contingency must conform to an independently given pattern, and we must be able independently to formulate that pattern. A random inkblot is unspecifiable; a message written with ink on paper is specifiable.

Gibberish—the utterance of nonsense syllables uninterpretable within any natural language—always actualizes one utterance from the range of possible utterances. Nevertheless, gibberish, by corresponding to nothing we can understand in any language, also cannot be specified. As a result, gibberish is never taken for intelligent communication but always for what Wittgenstein calls "inarticulate gurgling."

Recognizing that one among many competing possibilities has been actualized, and then identifying a pattern to which the actualized possibility conforms, encapsulates how we recognize intelligent agency or, equivalently, how we detect design. Experimental psychologists who study animal learning and behavior have known this all along. To learn a task, an animal must acquire the ability to actualize behaviors suitable for the task as well as acquire the ability to rule out behaviors unsuitable for the task. Moreover, for a psychologist to recognize that an animal has learned a task, it is necessary not only to observe the animal making the appropriate discrimination but also to specify this discrimination.

Thus, to recognize whether a rat has successfully learned how to traverse a maze, a psychologist must first specify which sequence of right and left turns conducts the rat out of the maze. No doubt, a rat randomly wandering a maze also discriminates a sequence of right and left turns. But by randomly wandering the maze, the rat gives no indication that it can discriminate the appropriate sequence of right and left turns for exiting the maze. Consequently, the psychologist studying the rat will have no reason to think that the rat has learned how to traverse the maze.

Only if the rat executes the sequence of right and left turns specified by the psychologist will the psychologist recognize that the rat has learned how to traverse the maze. Now it is precisely the learned behaviors we regard as intelligent in animals. Hence, it is no surprise that the same scheme for recognizing animal learning recurs for recognizing intelligent agency generally, to wit: recognizing that one among several competing possibilities has been actualized, that others have been ruled out, and then specifying the one chosen (that is, matching it to an independently existing pattern).

Note that complexity is implicit here as well. To see this, consider again a rat traversing a maze, but now take a very simple maze in which two right turns conduct the rat out of the maze. How will a psychologist studying the rat determine whether it has learned to exit the maze? Just putting the rat in the maze will not be enough. Because the maze is so simple, the rat could by chance just happen to take two right turns and thereby exit the maze. The psychologist will therefore be uncertain whether the rat actually learned to exit the maze or whether this rat just got lucky.

But contrast this now with a complicated maze in which a rat must take a precise sequence of left and right turns to exit the maze. Suppose the rat must take a hundred appropriate right and left turns, and any mistake will prevent the rat from exiting the maze. A psychologist who sees the rat take no erroneous turns and in short order exit the maze will be convinced that the rat has indeed learned how to exit the maze and that this behavior was not dumb luck.

This general scheme for recognizing intelligent agency is but a thinly disguised form of the complexity-specification criterion. In general, to recognize intelligent agency we must observe a choice among competing possibilities, note which possibilities were not chosen, and then be able to specify the particular possibility that was chosen. Further, the competing possibilities that were ruled out must be live possibilities and sufficiently numerous so that specifying the possibility that was chosen cannot be attributed to chance. That is another way of saying that the range of possibilities is complex.

All the elements in this general scheme for recognizing intelligent agency (that is, choosing, ruling out, and specifying) find their counterpart in the complexity-specification criterion. It follows that this criterion formalizes what we have been doing right along when we recognize intelligent agency. The complexity-specification criterion pinpoints what we need to be looking for when we detect design.

As a postscript, it is worth pondering the etymology of the word *intelligent,* which derives from two Latin words, the preposition *inter,* meaning between, and the verb *lego,* meaning to choose or select. Thus, intelligence consists in *choosing between.* It follows that the etymology of the word *intelligent* parallels the formal analysis of intelligent agency inherent in the complexity-specification criterion.

So What?

There exists a reliable criterion for detecting design. The criterion detects design strictly from observational features of the world. Moreover, this criterion belongs to probability and complexity theory, not to metaphysics and theology. Further, this criterion can be applied to the analysis of biological systems. As I have argued elsewhere, Michael Behe's criterion of irreducible complexity constitutes a special case of specified complexity.[9] Thus my analysis reinforces Behe's judgment that irreducibly complex biochemical systems are best explained by intelligent design. My colleague Stephen C. Meyer shows in another essay in this book that the complexity-specification criterion also applies readily to the analysis of functional biomolecules such as DNA and proteins. He argues that these informational-rich (that is, complex and specified) macromolecules, upon which life itself depends, are also best explained by intelligent design. Thus, Richard Dawkins's claim that all biological design is only apparent needs therefore to be modified: "Biology is the study of complicated things that give the appearance of being designed because they actually are designed."

What are we to make of these developments? Many scientists remain unconvinced. So what if we have a reliable criterion for detecting design, and so what if that criterion tells us that biological systems are designed? How is looking at a biological system and inferring that it's designed any better than shrugging our shoulders and saying "God did it"? The fear is that design cannot help but stifle scientific inquiry.

But design is not a science stopper. Indeed, design can foster inquiry where traditional evolutionary approaches obstruct it. Consider the term, "junk DNA." Implicit in the term is the view that because the genome of an organism has been cobbled together through a long, undirected evolutionary process, the genome is a patchwork of which only limited portions are essential to the organism. Thus, by an evolutionary view, we expect a lot of useless DNA. If, on the other hand, organisms are designed, we expect DNA, as much as possible, to exhibit function. And indeed, the most recent findings suggest that designating DNA as "junk" merely cloaks our current lack of knowledge about function. For instance, in a recent issue of the *Journal of Theoretical Biology,* John Bodnar describes how "non-coding DNA in eukaryotic genomes encodes a language which programs organismal growth and development."[10] Design encourages scientists to look for function where evolution discourages it.

Or consider vestigial organs that later are found to have a function after all. Evolutionary biology texts often cite the human coccyx as a "vestigial structure" that hearkens back to vertebrate ancestors with tails. Yet if one looks at a recent edition of Gray's *Anatomy,* one finds that the coccyx is a crucial point of contact with muscles that attach to the pelvic floor. Now anatomy is nothing else than an exercise in design, studying the large scale design plan, or blueprints, for bodies. Thus, here again we find design encouraging scientists to look for function where evolution discourages it. Examples where the phrase "vestigial structure" cloaks our current lack of knowledge can be multiplied. The human appendix, formerly thought to be vestigial, is now known to be a functioning component of the immune system.[11]

Granted, once design is reinstated within science, it won't be business as usual. For instance, a lot of the unsubstantiated Darwinian just-so stories will go by the board (to which I say good riddance). But new questions will arise, and new research opportunities will present themselves.

Once we know that something is designed, we will want to know how it was produced, to what extent the design is optimal, and what its purpose is. Note that we can detect design without knowing what something was designed for. A room at the Smithsonian is filled with obviously designed objects for which no one has a clue about their purpose.

By reinstating design within science, we do much more than merely critique scientific reductionism. Scientific reductionism holds that everything is reducible to scientific categories. Scientific reductionism is easily seen to be self-refuting. The existence of the world, the laws by which the world operates, the intelligibility of the world, and the unreasonable effectiveness of mathematics for comprehending the world are issues raised by science that science is incapable of resolving.

To critique scientific reductionism, however, is not enough. Critiquing scientific reductionism does nothing to change science. Science must change because, by eschewing design, it has for too long operated with an inadequate set of conceptual categories. That inadequacy has led to a constricted vision of reality, skewing how science understands not just the world but also ourselves. Evolutionary psychology, which to some thinkers justifies everything from infanticide to adultery, is just one symptom of an inadequate conception of science. Barring design from science distorts science, making it a mouthpiece for materialism instead of a search for truth.

Martin Heidegger remarked in *Being and Time,* "A science's level of development is determined by the extent to which it is capable of a crisis in its basic concepts."[12] The basic concepts with which science has operated these last several hundred years are no longer adequate, certainly not in an information age, certainly not in an age where design is empirically detectable.

Science faces a crisis of basic concepts. The way out of this crisis is to expand science to include design. To reinstate design within science is to liberate science, freeing it from restrictions that were always arbitrary—restrictions that now encumber both the practice of science and science education.

Notes

1. Jacques Monod writes, "The cornerstone of the scientific method is the postulate that nature is objective. In other words, the systematic denial that 'true' knowledge can be got by interpreting phenomena in terms of final causes—that is to say, of 'purpose'" (*Chance and Necessity* [New York: Vintage, 1972], 21).

2. Jaki writes: "I want no part whatever with the position . . . in which science is surreptitiously taken for a means of elucidating the utterly metaphysical question of purpose" (*Chesterton: A Seer of Science* [Urbana: University of Illinois Press, 1986], 139–40, note 2).

3. Richard Dawkins, *The Blind Watchmaker: Why the Evidence of Evolution Reveals a Universe without Design* (New York: W. W. Norton, 1986), 1.

4. Francis Crick, *What Mad Pursuit* (New York: Basic Books, 1988), 138.

5. Eliot Marshall, "Medline Searches Turn Up Cases of Suspected Plagiarism," *Science* 279 (23 Jan. 1998): 473–74.

6. Charles Darwin, *On the Origin of Species* (Cambridge: Harvard University Press, [1859] 1964), 482.

7. For a full account, see William A. Dembski, *The Design Inference: Eliminating Chance through Small Probabilities* (Cambridge: Cambridge University Press, 1998).

8. Ibid., chap. 5.

9. William A. Dembski, *No Free Lunch: Why Specified Complexity Cannot Be Purchased without Intelligence* (Lanham, Md.: Rowman and Littlefield, 2001), 239–310.

10. John W. Bodnar, Jeffrey Killian, Michael Nagel, and Suniel Ramchandani, "Deciphering the Language of the Genome," *Journal of Theoretical Biology* 189 (1997): 183.

11. See Percival Davis and Dean Kenyon, *Of Pandas and People,* (Dallas, Tex.: Haughton, 1993), 128.

12. Martin Heidegger, "Being and Time," *Basic Writings,* ed. D. F. Krell, (New York: Harper and Row, 1977), 51.

Part IV

Critical Responses

The Rhetoric of Intelligent Design: Alternatives for Science and Religion

Celeste Michelle Condit

※ ※ ※

In public debate, the motives behind advocacy are always essential to analysis, because arguments are judged (and should be judged) by their combination of ethos, pathos, and logos. If we are to understand fully, and to assess fairly, the rhetorical debate over intelligent design, it is therefore essential to consider the fundamental motives of the advocates involved.

Most advocates of intelligent design seek to increase the scope of religious discourse, raising its social status compared to that of scientific discourse, especially by including it in the curricula of public schools. On the other side, the motive of most opponents of intelligent design is to protect the relative position of science in society and especially to protect whatever control scientists currently exert over school curricula.

Admitting to such motivations is crucial to analyzing this debate, because whether one finds the arguments in favor of intelligent design to be persuasive seems to be almost exclusively dependent on whether one already believes in an intelligent designer. Such a framework for interpretation also makes my own motives a relevant consideration. I am neither a scientist nor a religious advocate. I might best be described as an eclectic humanist, and in this essay I will suggest that it is not profitable for religious discourse to attempt to supplant scientific method—but that science in itself is not a complete and sufficient system of human thought. I will try to impugn simultaneously the appropriateness both of religious incursion into the realm of scientific explanation and of scientific explanation in the broader realm of human affairs by offering an alternative to either "God" (I use the scare quotation marks to remind us that there are widely varying notions of what such a "God" entity might be like) or to conventional scientific accounts of the origins of life.

Instead of the assumption that the intelligent designer specified by advocates of intelligent design is something like the Christian God, I will offer as a heuristic ploy the assumption that it is something more like a visit of aliens from another quadrant of the galaxy. Such a device will, I hope, reveal the inadequacy of the intelligent design argument as a stasis for the debate between science and religion and will thereby productively upset pat assumptions on both sides.

My argument proceeds by dealing in turn with each of the three major arguments for intelligent design: the origin of life, the origin of species, and Michael Behe's functionalism. It concludes with some thoughts about the proper character and role of science, religion, and the humanities in our society.

The Origin of Life

In the present volume, Stephen Meyer effectively reviews the intelligent design position on the origin of life. To develop his ethos and destroy that of his opponents, Meyer provides a history of the scientific search for the origins of life. In his narrative, scientists have successively offered first one and then another alternative to an intelligent designer, but each of their offerings has been found to be inadequate, leaving intelligent design as a kind of default option.

Meyer's first stopover on his review of scientific options for the origin of life is the "random chance" argument. Meyer argues that biological life could not have been created by random or chance combinations of the physical materials of the planet because there has been insufficient time in the earth's history to develop the available combinations. If we were to assume, however, that the intelligent designers of life on Earth were space-faring aliens, there would be no necessary conflict between random chance and the intelligent design hypothesis. There may have been plenty of time for life to originate by chance on the planets, galaxies, or universes from which our space-alien benefactors hail. Consequently, we could safely note in our children's textbooks that life on Earth was created by space-faring aliens *and* that life originated by chance combinations of the physical attributes in the universe.

Although many religious persons have long been content to reconcile religious and scientific explanations of life's origins, such a reconciliation may not be acceptable to many scientists, who really don't like my "space-alien hypothesis" because no material evidence exists of space aliens. Most scientists may still, therefore, prefer the other option that Meyer addresses—that life is the emergent product of loaded physical dice. Alas, Meyer's arguments on this contention are too seriously flawed to shake their faith.

The first problem is that Meyer commits the fallacy of composition and division when he complains that self-organization of DNA is impossible and so life could not have self-organized. No one that I know of thinks that DNA spontaneously self-organized from simple chemical elements. The general belief is that DNA evolved from simpler units, which themselves spontaneously (and then evolutionarily) organized.[1]

Meyer is correct, of course, that we do not have scientific evidence for what those simpler units were or what path their evolution might have taken. That does not, however, make space aliens a better hypothesis for the origin of life on Earth, when we don't have scientific evidence either for what those space aliens looked like or how they behaved. Meyer should not expect, therefore, that the lack of an empirically founded, well-developed, and precise scientific explanation of the origins of life from an earthly primordial soup will compel scientists to assume that no such account can be developed. The current lack of an explanatory model and evidence for it should compel good scientists to restrain themselves from unwarranted knowledge-claims. As good scientists, it will certainly also prompt them to continue to explore the possibilities latent in the soup as well as to search for extraterrestrials.

In contrast to empirically focused scientists, religious believers might find attractive the nonempirical (though still rational) argument offered by Meyer, which indicates that the character of DNA as a producer of information demonstrates evolution to be an impossible means for the origin of life. His protestations aside, however, Meyer's argument really does come down to an appeal to ignorance, because he makes crucial mistakes about the nature of information.

The problems with the scientific usages of the "information" metaphor with regard to genetics have been thoroughly dissected by critics in science studies, so it should not be surprising to find that these information metaphors do not provide an adequate defense against intelligent design: They do not provide an adequate account of biological processes in the first place.[2] Meyer and his colleague William Dembski do no better with these terms than do the scientists themselves. They muddle mechanistic and teleological visions of "information," producing a complicated but explicable error.

Meyer's and Dembski's arguments amount to the claim that information is a mental entity, and therefore any time we recognize "information" in nature, it stands as proof of an intelligent designer. Twenty-five hundred years of investigation into discourse systems, however, tell us quite clearly that "information" may be merely in the mind of the beholder, for something to be understood as "information" depends on the conventions applied and what a receiver of "information" already knows. Dembski admits as much, and Meyer notes that information is recognizable by its ability "to perform a (communication) function." Once we take into account the fact that communication is receiver-dependent, their examples prove the opposite of the point for which they use them.

If one does not speak English or understand the conventions of printed language, the squiggles on a page "Help! Our house is on fire!" (to use an example Meyer employs elsewhere) have no more specificity than "Abcd Qrtp~ 2@mnp rr t+ g*$4q."[3] Both sequences could easily be the product of the proverbial million monkeys typing. Dembski himself claims that Chinese is really no different from patterned vocal gibberish to those who do not understand Chinese. Thus, the *specification* that turns a pattern into meaningful "information" is as likely to be a product of a receiver as it is of a sender. Information is therefore information not because of specific, universal characteristics of its patterning (presumably generated by a Message Creator) but rather because of its structuration within a system of usage and within specific contexts (which may be fully human). The human tendency to read most patterns as "meaningful" (for example, tea leaves, astrology, weather-predicting) locates complexity and specification as a product of human pattern-reception, not as a sign of space-alien intelligence in action.

The same error undergirds Meyer's argument that DNA's double character as information and chemical material means that it cannot evolve, a claim he bases on the belief that "information content or message does not derive from the properties of the material medium."[4] In defending that claim, Meyer focuses on the channel as the relevant material medium, but a reception-sensitive understanding of communication would attend to the material composition of the receptor: the human interpreter. Here it matters very much that human minds have specific material characteristics, since the characteristics of the human brain do shape what we can count as information and how we can understand it.

Thus, the statement that "DNA provides information" is merely a metaphor that we may sometimes apply as a useful heuristic, but we should not take that to mean that cells "understand" the structure of DNA as "information," because cells are not capable of interpreting messages in a literal way. Consequently, Meyer's argument that DNA cannot evolve because its information content is separate from its material character is incoherent—built on false assumptions about the character of DNA (it is not disembodied "information") and about the relationship between materiality and information (the relevant relationship being in the receiver, not the channel).

Dembski and Meyer should take comfort that their errant tendencies to attribute an intelligent message-designer wherever they see information is not their unique failing but rather a species-wide tendency. The writings of Kenneth Burke long ago illuminated why we are prone to reverse the relationship between speaker and sender, imputing meaningful patterns to the world outside when they often emanate instead from the worldview inside us. Burke showed that human language features dramatism as a fundamental characteristic. That is, all natural human communication is structured to include an agent, act, agency, purpose, and scene.[5] Consequently, all human discourse tends to recount the world in terms that presuppose humanlike agents and purposes. Thus, most if not all so-called "primitive" tribes are animistic, attributing "spirits" (agents and agency) to natural objects.

Nonliterate human groups are not alone here; all humans easily infer design from pattern. Even scientists can routinely be caught in anthropomorphic talk (I remember my physics teacher offering an explanation like "The ball wants to get to the lowest possible energy state"). But such attribution of agency and purpose is as much about humans as speakers of natural languages as it is about the characteristics of the natural world. Thus, Burke argues, whether or not there is a God, our language would force us to invent one.[6] God is the linguistic embodiment of perfected agency, inevitably inhabiting our language because our language is hierarchical, demanding perfection, and because our language presupposes agency.

In some sense, then, science is the process of inventing languages that attempt to wring dramatism out of our perceptions and discourse. Intelligent design advocates attempt to co-opt this scientific approach by employing quantitative measures of information in order to circumvent the possibility that specification is simply a matter of human interpretation. Their measures, however, require prior (covert) humanly generated conventions embedded in dramatistic systems—specifically statistical thresholds chosen by experimenters and the covert blocking of measured units.

Therefore, while DNA clearly interacts with other chemicals in a patterned way, this does not mean that it inherently carries "meaning." The patterns are only meaningful, only a true code, once a function is assumed: the replication of the code. But DNA does not "intend" to replicate itself. It is not intelligent. It simply does replicate (in conjunction with the cell). That is the biophysical character of DNA, and that, therefore, is the nature of life. Once life—as the self-replication of a pattern—does come into being and does function in that fashion, we can circle back and talk about the code of life. But that is to say that life itself creates the possibility of meaning (that is, of "information").

To get to this point, however, no one had to intend it to function in this way (though it is still possible that the space aliens did so). It is possible that purpose is a product of life rather than life being the product of purpose. (This statement can be taken as true whether or not one believes in "God," at least if one believes that "God lives," for there is no reason to believe that purpose preceded "God." At best we could specify a draw, wherein "God" and purpose were simultaneous or are eternally co-present.)

Intelligent design theory simply repeats the pattern of the long history of rational advocacy for the existence of God; it constitutes a linguistic tautology. That tautology recurs because we are predisposed to see design in any pattern—our language systems put it there. We are a design-perceiving, designer-inferring species. The balance of proof in the intelligent design argument with regard to the origin of life thus rests today roughly where the creationist and creation-science debates always have. We place scientific speculations built on conjectures about what is likely, given the rest of the pattern of empirical findings about the material characteristics of life, against religious convictions about the existence of a nonmaterial realm and a supramaterial creator of material life. But arguments about the material character of life are unlikely to provide definitive proof that there is or is not a supramaterial entity at some other level. Unless our space aliens or other creators decide to make a material visit, religion will not be able to prove their existence materially, nor will science be able to prove definitively their nonexistence. Definitive proof of nonexistence of supramaterial entities is outside the realm of scientific practice.

The existence of supramaterial entities cannot be proven or disproven on material grounds by either scientists or religious rationalists. Science cannot, therefore, silence religion. But equally, religion cannot usurp science on these grounds. This does not mean that the two belief systems are practically incompatible, since belief in the coexistence of supramaterial and material realms has long held a foremost place in American public dogma. Even if "God" or our space-alien creators revealed his/her/themselves tomorrow in Madison Square Garden, science would not be done in. Scientists would immediately want to know "How did God come to be?" "What is the 'God' substance?" and "How did 'God' make life on Earth?" To put the "space aliens did it" answer into classroom textbooks would only sidestep the scientific issues. Scientific questions about the origins of life would still arise.

Speciation

Having briefly re-sorted the deck on the issue of the origin of life, I turn to the second major theme of the intelligent design advocates: that species have not evolved from each other or from a common source but rather that an alien life-form planted different species on Earth when they came on their flyby visit. Meyer, Ross, Nelson, and Chien here again take a page from the creationist and "creation-science" books, arguing that there are missing links in the tree of life. Those perceived gaps, they believe, cast definitive doubt on the possibility of evolutionary links between animal groupings. The intelligent design advocates add a set of putative functional gaps in the DNA record to the older concern about gaps in the fossil record. But again these arguments founder on linguistic problems.

First, let us explore the extent of the "gaps" that exist. It has become increasingly evident across the past century that "species" are partially arbitrary categories.[7] That is, boundaries between species have become so difficult to draw that it is problematic to find any definitive "gap" at all between many species. Reproductive isolation (the biological "gold standard" of speciation) is sometimes less than absolute and may vary over time. Moreover, in some species, recent DNA studies show greater variation within species across geographic ranges than variation between well-accepted species (for example, eastern and western gorillas differ more from each other than bonobos differ from common chimps).[8] It is odd to argue that definitive "gaps" exist in the evolutionary processes between species when scientists can't even draw clean boundaries between species and when species vary internally more than they do comparatively. "Tree diagrams" describing different species and their evolution are today generally drawn on the basis of statistical arguments rather than on absolute categorizations. Because the argument that there are gaps in the evolution between species so evidently fails, however, intelligent designers up the ante to the level of phyla.

The structure of the issue is the same at the level of phyla. The question remains, when are gaps really "too large" so that they constitute difference or isolation rather than simply being "neighborly"? The gaps at the level of phyla are, of course, apparently larger than those at the species level. That is the whole principle of the classification system, that phyla mark greater differences than do species. The problems of definition, however, recur here as well. When I studied high school biology, we were taught that there were ten phyla. A recent classification system lists thirty-five different phyla. Part of this difference in classification is change through time, part is high school versus specialized science, and part of it rests with differences of philosophy among the classifiers. Each of these causes emphasizes that even distinctions among phyla require partially artificial judgments of sameness and difference. So we ought not to take the "differences" among phyla too seriously. If we cannot even agree for all purposes and times and usages where the boundaries between these categories lie, it seems rather bizarre to argue that there are "gaps" between these groupings that are so great as to make evolutionary relationships among them impossible.

Again, it is the structure of language that misleads us. When we are playing with *similarity* and *difference*, we are always applying relative terms, so it is foolish to use those categorizations as proof of definitive boundaries. We are seduced to do so because the nature of language, the process of naming as an act of objectification, asks us to see and treat categories as discrete and isolated from each other. Such linguistically constructed isolation, however, should not then be interpreted to mean that the categories are too isolated to allow historical traverse between families of these entities. Measures of "gaps" should not, therefore, refer simply to verbal categorization but must consist in definitive sets of criteria—which intelligent design does not provide.

Meyer, Ross, Nelson, and Chien also try to buttress their argument with the theoretical claim that large gaps (the putative gaps between phyla) are difficult to traverse through mutation, since large gaps are hard to cross. I'm not sure where there are any large gaps between phyla, but if we were to assume for purposes of argument that such gaps exist, it is not at all clear that large gaps are mutationally prohibitive. As with small gaps, mutations that create largely different entities will most often fail, but they will sometimes succeed.[9] The fact that these successes are rare might account for the fact that there are (at most?) only thirty-five phyla; only thirty-five times has a differentiation at the level we identify as substantial phyletic change succeeded. It seems easy to imagine such successful mutations happening thirty-five times in all of the earth's history (though it is also still easy to imagine that space aliens brought just thirty-five basic types with them on their ship).

Of course, if jumps of this nature can be made, then one wouldn't expect to see intermediate forms in the fossil record, even if the fossil record were far more complete than it possibly could be over hundreds of millions of years—with most differences not manifested in ways that can be preserved through fossilization. For these reasons, therefore, the speciation and existence of multiple phyla on Earth do not require us to presume an intelligent designer of any sort. Space aliens may or may not be behind it all, but we cannot claim to need them in our textbooks.

Function, Evolution, and "Irreducible Complexity"

Public arguments of the intelligent design theorists about the origin and speciation of life on Earth are easy to defeat via the "space-alien" heuristic. If there is a lack of time on Earth and a gap in the fossil record, it is as reasonable to assume that space aliens brought life to Earth as it is to believe that a "God" created it. Neither "God" nor space aliens offer definitive physical records of their actions and existence. Michael Behe's functional argument, however, reaches to the nature of gods and space aliens themselves.

Behe argues that there are "irreducibly complex" biological systems and that such systems require a designer. If true, such a claim would privilege a nonbiological designer (presumably someone's version of "God") over alien biological designers (space aliens), at least somewhere in the universe. But irreducible complexity is chimerical. Although systems may appear to be

"irreducibly complex," based on a select function that is performed in a select way, multifunctionality is a general biological rule, and multifunctionality makes it easy to imagine how a complex interdependent system can
evolve without a designer.

Let us start the reimagination process with a simple case outside the biological world. Consider a so-called "natural bridge." A natural bridge can
be used in the same way as an artificial bridge, to cross over a valley, but
unlike an artificial bridge, no one had to design it. The natural arches of
rock that constitute natural bridges are interpretable on naive glance as "irreducibly complex." Because they have an arch structure, their formation
appears to entail a mutual support that can be gained in human architecture only through temporary bracing. Hence, we might assume that an intelligent designer would have had to construct natural arches using
temporary braces to hold the structure in place until the last, self-bracing
support (the top arch-stone) was in place. But natural bridges are neither
God's "bridges" (that purpose is imputed by humans) nor artificially constructed. Instead, geological processes form natural bridges. Rock beds are
laid down by sedimentary processes and then are selectively eroded from
below.

Similar reimagining works equally well with Behe's so-called irreducibly
complex biological machines. For example, it really doesn't take great
imagination to provide an account of how cilia might have evolved. The
original components served different isolated functions (as Behe notes that
scientists have already demonstrated). Some linking components brought
these components together so that they performed a new function. The architectural "brace" provided by earlier linking components was supplanted
by the evolution of other components that provided superior functions, so
the earlier braces "eroded." Today, to achieve functionality requires all of
the parts of the cilia to work in tandem.[10] But that doesn't mean that the
parts had to appear there simultaneously or that what we see today comprises anything like all of the historical components. The "braces" that constituted key steps in the evolution of cilia have been eroded by
evolutionary processes, but that does not mean it was impossible for them
to have been there.

Scientists may speculate about evolutionary pathways and even provide
models of them in the examples Behe gives, but often they cannot prove
them according to scientific criteria. The scientific discourse system requires experimental or empirical evidence of the existence of these components, and such evidence is unlikely to exist in many cases. Which is to say

that science is much better at describing current function than it is at providing histories, especially when the history is long term and refers to events that by their nature were unlikely to be recorded. Such methodological limitations do not constitute proof of the existence of an intelligent designer, especially when we have evolutionary histories that explain many apparently irreducible complexities. Most of the detailed work already done in evolutionary history, describing the development of various organs and features across species, is of that character; once we have an explanation, like the natural bridge, the organ or feature no longer appears to be "irreducibly complex." Irreducible complexity is, therefore, a statement about our ignorance of the history of something rather than a proof that it could not have evolved.

Once again, intelligent design advocates would have us believe that what science doesn't know constitutes proof of intelligent designers. But we don't face an either/or choice here. In the face of lack of evidence, the logical choice may well be to defer judgment. But if deferring judgment is not possible, we must choose the position with the greatest weight of evidence on its side. Given that evolutionary theory has amassed greater quantities of overall evidence by several orders of magnitude than has intelligent design (in either its space-alien or "God" versions), a forced choice would hardly favor the intelligent design hypothesis.

The Rhetorical Situation

This essay can be read as indicating that the major materialist arguments advanced on behalf of "intelligent design" do not carry a sufficient burden of proof to justify their inclusion in biology texts. I intend this as a serious answer to John Angus Campbell's serious plea for critical thinking in the science classroom. Campbell is, in part, correct when he asserts that science should not be taught dogmatically, as a series of truths to be memorized. But Campbell (like Steve Fuller) is wrong to want to reduce science education to nothing more than critical inquiry. Scientific method is, in crucial part, about the search for testable hypotheses and about the requirement that one attend to empirical data with as much honesty as can be humanly mustered.

Students should learn to do experiments, but they cannot do all the experiments or perform all the observations. The collective experience of the community of scientists must be passed on to them through authoritative reports, just as the collective experience of the moral community must be passed on to young people in discussion of values (the authority of experience being something Campbell advocates as an appropriate bastion against relativism in values but which he appears to want to rule out in science-teaching).

Science studies have, of course, documented the many ways in which scientists routinely (and probably inevitably) fail at full honesty in their empirical studies. That is why science must become more self-reflective and must include critical methods within its practice. But science would not be science if it were only critical discussion, and our social and material worlds would be impoverished if we denied the utility of empirical methods. Because curricular selection in science education requires that one attend to the relative weight and probity of the scientific evidence about evolution, the weight of the empirical evidence remains overwhelmingly in favor of the veracity of evolution as an account of how particular life-forms have developed. Perhaps the questions of the "origin" of life per se on Earth should be moved to a class in metaphysics, where speculations about divine guidance, space aliens, and molecular soups can vie as speculative systems. But the evidence and rationales offered by intelligent design are (currently at least) of such negligible weight that their inclusion in scientific courses about speciation and the evolution and integration of organismic components—even a properly critical discussion of such topics—is no more justifiable than inclusion of stories about space aliens.

The fact that there are a few creative alternative ideas and some passionate advocates of a particular view does not justify equal time for that view in schools, because school time is scarce. That scarcity requires that even critical discussions should focus on strongly supported alternatives, which is why critical ethical discussions of pederasty and organized criminality as a legitimate manifestation of capitalism are not priority topics for values-clarification courses either. If there is a place for critical discussion of religious beliefs in public schools, that place is not in the science curriculum.

My first conclusion, that a religiously generated doctrine does not constitute good science, should not be surprising, since religion cannot "do science" better than science does. Throughout history, every time religion has tried to argue on the terrain of science, it has failed.

A more important conclusion of this essay may be its less obvious suggestion that intelligent design does not do enough for religious purposes. The fact that space aliens also constitute a possible intelligent designer suggests that religious advocates who would place their rhetorical efforts behind a defense of intelligent design are misplacing their bets. Religious advocates who want to forward the goals of religion might be better served by efforts to expand the legitimacy of religious and ethical exploration and by efforts to keep science in its place rather than by efforts to infiltrate science with pseudoscientific doctrines.

This is to say that intelligent design is a bad argument for religious purposes because it accepts the criterion and worldview of science, which is the very metaphysical mind-set it would seek to deny. In the process, intelligent design advocates give up on exploring and advancing the kinds of discussion that are truly important for nonscientific discourse. That is an enormously consequential error. The implication to be drawn from the empirical, logical, and moral insufficiencies of religious texts to provide empirical accounts is *not* that science is an all-powerful and all-sufficient discourse.

One thing the intelligent design arguments and my "space-alien" heuristic should effectively accomplish is to point up that there remains much that scientists don't know and that one of those things is how life on Earth began. But even that question is not of first significance for religious discourse, because a properly scientific explanation of the origin of life could always be backstopped with a "because that is how God did it" that preserves a space for religious metaphysics. That space remains important since, in our society, religious discourse serves vital social functions that cannot be served by science. Religion provides humans a way of dealing with the realm of the humanly unknowable, a way of accepting the limits of human finitude, and a way to make valuations and judgments about the natural and human worlds that transcends immediate self-interest.

Religious discourse is therefore inherently nonliteral. It accepts the inevitability of human language's failure to encompass the universe totally. It helps us deal with things beyond our power to control and beyond our animal wants and desires. Religion is constantly frustrated by science, however, because science is constantly pushing back the zone of the unknown and the regions of what is beyond our power. If religion took itself more seriously—instead of mistaking itself for an empirical discourse—the continuing explorations of science would not constitute a problem; there is little danger that science will ever explain or control everything.

Beyond this universe of experience, there always lies another. If we explain this universe, we will want to know what lies beyond it. If we trace the origin of the universe back to the big bang, we will want to know what was before that? And outside of that? There will always be an "out there" for the scientific enterprise. Religion is one of the ways of getting at the important components of human life that transcend the natural world—for example, the difficult questions about what we should do with our power over the material universe.

Religion, like art, ethics, rhetoric, and the other humanities, addresses the realm of human values. For religious advocates, that realm is overdetermined by religious dictates. For humanists, that realm is an emergent product of human biology, the historical sedimentations of human culture, and human intellect and emotion. But in either case, providing guidance in the realm of human values is something the scientific method is ill-suited to do, a limitation that many scientists all too often forget. E. O. Wilson's book *Consilience: The Unity of Knowledge* pretends that science can answer all the important questions, including questions of human culture.[11] Wilson is right that scientific methods can be turned to answering some questions about human culture and even to elucidating some links between biology and culture. But Wilson is wrong, dreadfully wrong, when he implies that those are the only questions worth asking and that science offers the only valid way of answering them.

Science is constitutionally incapable of dealing with the nonmaterial realm, including the diversity and uniqueness within human culture.[12] If the only discourse shared within a polity were scientific, that polity would lack critical ingredients for coexistence and public concordances.

The old saw that both science and "religion" (a word I use loosely here to incorporate humanism) have important spheres in human life is thus a good one. This accommodationist approach does not require an impermeable boundary between the public and science, just as it does not require an impermeable boundary between religion and the public or between the humanities and the public. It does, however, require some respect for the rich and varying contributions that different ways of approaching questions have, and it requires that no one method and approach adopt an imperial stance. A mutual nonaggression pact might be in order. Scientists would agree to limit their pronouncements on human culture to the narrow facts they truly know as scientists (while in the persona of expert scientist), and religious advocates would stop trying to pretend that scientific methods can prove or disprove religious metaphysics. Humanists would limit their claims against science to the specific critical failings of science instead of pronouncing all science to be nothing more than a Eurocentric male fantasy imposed on powerless Others.

My plea for accommodation assumes, of course, that a totalized materialist philosophy is not essential for practicing science, an assumption that

Campbell seems to deny. Campbell uses the fact that "greater scientists" are almost all atheists in order to conclude that the endeavor of science is incompatible with nonmaterialist philosophies. I suggest that, more likely, "greater scientists" have become almost exclusively materialist (in the narrow sense) in their orientation because today they spend so much of their time doing science in a community isolated from the broader currents of contemporary life. "Greater scientists" tend, therefore, to have a generally impoverished view of the scope of human nature and the range of questions and methods for answering them that are available to our species.

In other words, it is not that science and religion (or the humanities) are inherently incompatible in any given society but rather that highly specialized individuals are not very good at recognizing anything outside their own specialties. On the other hand, consider the fact that John Campbell, a rhetorician, wants to remake science as primarily rhetorical, or that Steve Fuller, hermeneut, wants to remake science as exclusively hermeneutical. In an earlier era, scientists were less specialized and isolated and hence did not think that science was dealing with the only questions worth asking.

Kenneth Burke calls that outlook "trained incapacity."[13] The existence of "trained incapacities" in certain individuals does make it impossible to build a world in which we use appropriate methods for answering narrowly material questions and use other methods for answering other questions.[14] Different people provide different input to a social system, and hopefully, there are enough persons of a broader view to blend the answers in productive ways. John Campbell does not need to infiltrate science and turn it into something besides science. He just needs to help me keep science in its own very useful place.

Even with a general accommodation, there will remain grounds of legitimate contest between religion and science. Like any other set of communities, each wants a larger share of public resources and public space. Specific boundaries of science and the humanities (including religion) will need to be continuously negotiated. At least since the time of the Scopes trial, however, the dynamics of this rhetorical situation have led to the dominance of the accommodationist position, which renders unto Darwin that which is Darwin's and maintains religion in its own, more diffuse (but still powerful) sphere.[15]

The accommodationist position conceded that Darwin and the Bible could be reconciled. It is possible that science textbooks have violated that compact by teaching that science now knows what the origin of life on Earth was. My importation of space aliens in this essay should have made it clear that this is not yet the case. I hope that my use of this heuristic will also give scientists the space to admit ignorance without the immediate assumption that their ignorance implies a paralyzing religious hegemony. But I am not saying we ought to eliminate evolutionary theory from our textbooks or use science classrooms to give "equal time" to less plausible theories of speciation.

I understand the frustration of religious authorities with these limitations—it seems more difficult for religions to operate without state power than with it. Moreover, it is difficult to accept that scientific findings have a kind of incontestable validity (within their own sphere) that one's own religious beliefs lack. But such are the respective, perhaps ironic, characteristics of science and religion. Scientific methods deal with empirical objects that are accessible to shared observation and hence are amenable to producing relatively uniform conclusions within a scientific community that is even international in scope.

In contrast, true religious belief is about nonempirical objects that are transcendent and thus are not accessible to shared observation, or even to community dictation. Religious beliefs are effective only when they rest in the hearts of individuals, and to this point in history it appears that this means that they are too divergent in form for any large community to endorse or impose without violating the integrity of the heartfelt religious beliefs of other community members.

Science can trample on beliefs about the contents of the core of the earth without violating scientific assumptions because that is the nature of science: to use rigorous observation and experiment to check and revise our understandings of the material world. Religions, however, dare not trample on our heartfelt beliefs about the nature of the transcendent without losing their own essence, since personal commitment to a particular form of the transcendent is the goal of most modern religious practices.

Science is clearly an insufficient basis upon which to build a state, but science in its cupboard is useful indeed. Religious advocates need to recognize that the limitations on religion will be different from those on science, partially because religions are inherently schismatic and partially because religion has grander aspirations: to guide the course of human lives and aid in social reflection as well.

Given the breadth of religious concerns, religion is both powerful and dangerous. Its danger appears greatest when it turns from personal persuasion to public coercion. History and comparative cases around the world surely teach that the costs of a hegemonic theocratic state are at least as great as the costs of a social body where religious discourse must work without the coercive power of the state at its disposal.

   If religion is truly appropriate to humankind, it will survive without a space in the science classroom. It is possible to suggest, moreover, that a religion that requires such a space for survival is a religion that has lost its way—and may even deserve extinction.

Notes

1. It is precisely the separation between the physical variability of DNA and its functions that is consequential. That is, Meyer is wrong when he states that the medium of DNA can be separated from the information it contains, or that coding and information are "prior" to sequence specification. The fact that DNA's coding structure is variable, yet also induces the production of specified amino acid sequences, is what has allowed living organisms to exhibit evolutionary self-organization. The relative plasticity and mutability of DNA allow practically infinite options for the organization of the cell, and the self-organizing characteristics at the cellular/organismic/protocellular level determine which bodies of life replicate. Meyer routinely separates the facets of DNA as self-replicating and as cell-directing and argues that the unique characteristics of each half of these two items (or the tension between them) prove that DNA could not have provided an evolutionary basis for life. As I have elsewhere argued, it is the binding of these two characteristics in a "double coding" scheme that gives DNA a unique property in the physical world (the emergent characteristic we call "life"). Any argument against the physical/chemical sufficiency of DNA must deal with this holistic synergy, not with the mechanical parts in isolation. Meyer makes this error because his ontology and epistemology privilege "mindlike" entities (for example, information) over "matterlike" entities, but that is a circular argument. Of course, DNA did not spring into being as it is without transition from inert molecules, and even RNA is too complex to have formed spontaneously, but the DNA/RNA relationship makes it quite plausible to see these two as stair steps in a staircase on which the earlier steps are not visible to us. In fact, Meyer's argument proves too much. If the chemical world and physical properties of DNA were as isolated as he indicates, no useful mutation and evolution could be expected at all. If evolutionary processes are capable of making minor changes in the cell-DNA double-coded

specificity, which almost no one doubts, then there is simply no reason to believe that the protocell/DNA system is incapable of accumulating these changes through time to create something like modern, highly differentiated cell/organism systems. On the "double-coding" character of DNA, see Celeste Condit, "The Materiality of Coding: On Rhetoric, Genetics, and the Matter of Life," in *Rhetorical Bodies: Toward a Material Rhetoric,* ed. Jack Selzer and Sharon Crowley (Madison: University of Wisconsin Press, 1999).

2. Condit, "Materiality." The first detailed analysis of this metaphor occurs in Evelyn Fox Keller, *Refiguring Life: Metaphors of Twentieth-Century Biology* (New York: Columbia University Press, 1995). An attempt at a historically informed postmodern analysis is available in Lily E. Kay, "Who Wrote the Book of Life? Information and the Transformation of Molecular Biology, 1945–55," *Science in Context* 8 (1995): 609–34; Lily E. Kay, *The Molecular Vision of Life* (New York: Oxford University Press, 1993). A fully postmodern treatment is available in Richard Doyle, *On Beyond Living: Rhetorical Transformations in the Life Sciences* (Stanford, Calif.: Stanford University Press, 1997).

3. Stephen C. Meyer, "DNA by Design: An Inference to the Best Explanation for the Origin of Biological Information," *Rhetoric and Public Affairs* 1, no. 4 (1998): 519–56, esp. 539.

4. Ibid., 519–56, esp. 540.

5. Kenneth Burke, *A Grammar of Motives* (Berkeley: University of California Press, [1945] 1969).

6. Kenneth Burke, *The Rhetoric of Religion* (Berkeley: University of California Press, [1961] 1970).

7. The "partially" is key here. I am not arguing that the categories are constructed solely from human imagination and have no material components as referential base. Rather, the material (or "objective") base provides building materials that exert substantial constraints, but human language and agency carve their meanings from these blocks. The categories of species thus reflect both material features of the organisms being taxonomized and also human linguistic systems. See Condit, "Materiality"; Celeste Condit Railsback, "Beyond Rhetorical Relativism: A Structural-Material Model of Truth and Objective Reality," *Quarterly Journal of Speech* 69 (1983): 351–63.

8. Research by Maryellen Ruvolo, reported in Pat Shipman, "Does mtDNA Saw Neandertal Limb off Human Tree?" *Journal of NIH Research* 9 (1997): 30–31.

9. Of course, it is equally likely that these large gaps consist of multiple series of mutations that occurred relatively rapidly and were therefore not included in the fossil record. The fact that "we don't know" as an answer to any question supports neither the intelligent design nor the evolutionist perspective. "Don't knows" tend to get counted by members of each side as part of their own advantage because "don't knows" are interpreted in relation to the larger framework of beliefs held by an individual. Hence, scientists look for "don't knows" by seeking potential explanations consistent with the rest of the scientific explanatory framework, whereas intelligent design advocates understand "don't knows" as consistent with the rest of their religious framework.

10. Dembski's claim that "knock-out" experiments can be used to locate irreducible complexity is a good clue to the bankruptcy of the concept, given that knock-out mutations could result from a single-component system or an additive system as well as any complex one (whether additively or irreducibly complex).

11. Edward O. Wilson, *Consilience: The Unity of Knowledge* (New York: Alfred A. Knopf, 1998).

12. In my view, human culture is an emergent product of the material world and hence is influenced by that realm but holds characteristics unique to its own realm, just as life (biology) is an emergent product of the physical realm that holds characteristics based on that realm but also characteristics unique to its own realm. The argument here, however, is compatible with other religious views, which see human culture as wholly immaterial.

13. Duke borrows the concept from Veblen; see Kenneth Burke, *Permanence and Change: An Anatomy of Purpose,* 3rd ed. (Berkeley: University of California Press, [1954] 1984), 7–9.

14. I use the term "narrowly material" because I tend to espouse a "broadly material" worldview. The former is reductionistic, believing that items we identify as nonmaterial (such as "ideas") can be derived deterministically from the physical world. Instead, I believe that ideas are emergent properties of the physical world and therefore operate as a different category of being, though they are not "supernatural" in the old sense of the term, which denied the linkages between material elements and supramaterial elements such as ideas. See my "Materiality" and also "Crafting Virtue: The Rhetorical Construction of Public Morality," *Quarterly Journal of Speech* 73 (1987): 79–87. On other humanistic perspectives about the limitations of science, see Thomas B. Farrell and

G. Thomas Goodnight, "Accidental Rhetoric: The Root Metaphors of Three Mile Island," *Communication Monographs* 48 (1981): 271–300.

15. Lawrance Bernabo and Celeste Condit, "Two Stories of the Scopes Trial: Legal and Journalistic Articulations of the Legitimacy of Science and Religion," in *Popular Trials: Rhetoric, Mass Media, and the Law,* ed. Robert Hariman (Tuscaloosa: University of Alabama Press, 1990), 55–85.

Intelligent Design and Irreducible Complexity: A Rejoinder

David Depew

❈ ❈ ❈

In recent years, a new breed of scientific creationists has insisted that the supposed failures of Darwinism rest not so much on gaps in the fossil record and on other alleged epistemological inadequacies but more deeply on an overlooked fact about organisms. They are, says Michael Behe, "irreducibly complex" systems—systems "composed of several interacting parts that contribute to the basic function" in such a way that "the removal of any one of the parts causes a system to effectively cease functioning."[1] No such entity, it is claimed, can have come into existence bit by bit. Since Darwinian natural selection, the argument proceeds, is supposed to be committed to just such a bit-by-bit model of construction, it is ruled out as a likely origin of organic organization. Behe finds empirical support for this inference in molecular biochemistry.[2] Stephen C. Meyer, meanwhile, has taken this line of reasoning down to the most interesting level of all, the origin of life itself.[3] It is well known that origin-of-life research is stymied by the fact that nucleic acids specify proteins only if they are catalyzed by proteins. How could such an irreducibly complex system have come about? For Meyer, as for Behe, conscious design is the best explanation.

Arguments of this form go back a long way. Plato was so committed to a version of the argument from design (or rather to design) that he recommended executing any citizen who refused, after remonstration and demonstration, to acknowledge that mere matter cannot produce organic form and function.[4] Transmitted by the Stoics to modernity, the argument from design was so persuasively stated in William Paley's *Natural Theology* that Darwin devoted his entire life to refuting it.[5] Darwin was in turn challenged by William Whewell, Richard Owen, and Karl Ernst von Baer. When they asked questions such as "What's the good of half a wing?" they were putting forward versions of the irreducible complexity argument.

Why, I wonder, are arguments of this sort prominent at the present juncture in the history of evolution-creationism debates? What is the rhetorical exigency for their new urgency? Having speculated about answers to this question, I will go on, in the briefest compass, to assert that the kind of complexity envisioned by Behe is not in fact complex enough to describe organisms, or the process leading to their emergence, and so does not count as a compelling argument against commitment to a modest, and highly circumscribed, version of evolutionary naturalism.

Creationist arguments, like evolutionary arguments, are invented, deployed, received, and debated under particular discursive conditions, conditions that it behooves a rhetorical critic to reconstruct. In the 1970s and early 1980s, for example, one heard little of the argument from irreducible complexity, although it could readily have been formulated and deployed at that time, since the molecular biochemistry of the cell was already a highly developed science. Back then the stage was filled instead with fellows like Duane Gish, who terrorized Darwinians unskilled in the sly ways of the debater by pointing to gaps in the fossil record as a way of breaking the monopoly of evolutionary thought over school curricula. Still, after a while, that kind of argument became less prominent in mainstream venues, even as the fight for the schools continued—and continues still. Why?

One reason was that Gish's line of argument was too closely tied to a particular brand of creationism, young-earth creationism, and so to some old theological debates that have been reconstructed with great precision by Ronald Numbers.[6] But another reason was epistemological. As Charles Alan Taylor has pointed out, creationists of Gish's stamp tacitly relied on a radically inductivist, or so-called Baconian, conception of scientific method.[7] Baconian inductionism says that if you cannot point to facts as present to you as the sunshine outside my window on this fine day, and if

facts just that obvious do not add up to an exceptionless empirical generalization of the (admittedly false) "all-swans-are-white" variety, you presumably do not have a well-established scientific claim. By that standard, it was
pretty easy to find gaps in the fossil record. By the same standard, however, almost all of science becomes as questionable as scientific creationists
asserted evolution to be. So it was difficult for creationists who took that
line to point to paradigm cases of successful science as a touchstone against
which to indict what they took to be evolutionary theory's failures.

Baconian inductionism is more an invention of nineteenth-century positivists than of eighteenth-century Whigs, and of eighteenth-century Whigs
more than of sixteenth-century English chancellors like Francis Bacon. If it
is no longer a viable philosophy of science, that is because the problem
with the Baconian view lies in its presumption that as facts add up to empirical regularities—the old nineteenth-century notion of "laws"—they dis-
place "mere theories." It was on precisely this assumption that Ronald
Reagan, for example, could declare of evolution, "Well, it's just a theory."
Baconians like Reagan think of theories the same way as mystery writers
do. A theory is an appeal to something that has not been observed in order
to explain, by hypothetical reasoning, what one does observe but fails as
yet to understand because parts of the story are missing. If and when one
gets the missing pieces of evidence, led by the clues and predictions of the
theory, the theory itself disappears.

Historians of science have known for a long time, however, that this is
not what happened when Einstein's theory, for example, displaced Newton's. The triumph of Newtonian mechanics did not mean that Einstein's
mechanics was any less of a theory, or any more of a fact, after its universal acceptance than before. In science, theories forever mediate the com-
merce between humans and the world. The interesting questions are what
a theory is and when does it move from the status of a hypothesis to that
of a theory.

One highly influential set of answers to these questions is the "falsificationism" proposed by Karl Popper. Popper's idea was that what makes a
claim, or a whole theory, scientific is not that it is verifiable, as Baconian
inductionism—and positivism both logical and psychologistic—had it, but
that it is in principle *falsifiable*. For several decades, falsificationism has
been a shuttlecock batted back and forth between creationists and their
opponents.

Creationists, it seems, served first. Noting that Popper himself had at one
time agreed with an old sally to the effect that the principle of natural

selection is itself unfalsifiable, they attempted to turn the principle of non-falsifiability to their advantage by arguing that natural selection is explanatorily empty, since it rests on a circular definition of fitness. The fit are apparently defined as those that survive, the argument goes, so their survival cannot be appealed to as a reason for their fitness.[8] That defense of scientific creationism was certainly more effective than challenges based on radical inductivism. The effectiveness of that strategy was somewhat blunted, however, by the early intervention of philosophers of science in the debate. They showed that contemporary Darwinism (and probably Darwin's own brand) does not in fact define fitness in a tautological way.[9] Contemporary Darwinism is the Darwinism of population genetics, and population genetics is a statistical science through and through. It relies on expected fitness, rather than on realized or actual fitness, to constitute its *explanandum* and on the adapted properties of naturally selected populations to do the causal explaining.[10] When this fact about contemporary evolutionary theory was pointed out to Popper, he recanted. Popper, a great devotee of probabilistic thinking, knew very little about biology. Faced with the choice of affirming his commitment to the former or rejecting his claims about Darwinism, he quickly scurried down from his ill-formed views about evolutionary theory.

It was not long, in fact, before the weapon of falsification had been wrested entirely from the hands of creationists and placed firmly in the hands of their opponents. The high-water mark of this phase of the debate was Judge William Overton's decision in the Arkansas "creation science" case (*McLean v. Arkansas Board of Education* [1982]). As is well known, a number of philosophers of biology and philosophizing biologists descended on Little Rock to sell the judge on Popper's falsifiability criterion.[11] The upshot was that Overton was prevailed upon to declare that it was creationism, not Darwinism, that was not falsifiable and so should not be taught in the schools as an alternative scientific theory to Darwinism. That was supposedly because there was nothing that could count against so-called creation science. If, for example, radiometric dating had shown that dinosaurs did not live at the same time as Adam and Eve (let alone Fred and Wilma Flintstone), a creationist could always say that God had rigged the physical evidence to test our faith.

Creationists like Gish were rendered somewhat mute by such arguments. Nonetheless, a new breed of scientific creationists, notably Berkeley law professor emeritus Phillip Johnson, soon rose up to deploy the falsification ploy in a way that did not depend on the fate of the definition of natural selection. Johnson argued that by Overton's own Popperian standards, Darwinism was in worse shape than creationism. Darwinism, he claimed, does not relate to the facts it is supposed to explain in the same way that Newton's or Einstein's paradigmatic scientific theories do. Privately, physicists have all sorts of metaphysical interpretations of quantum mechanics. But what makes them professional physicists is their ability to wield the mathematical formalism of quantum mechanics and use it to interpret data. What makes one a Darwinian, by contrast, is said by Johnson to be the metaphysical materialism that many Darwinians flaunt, and not a theory like quantum mechanics. Moreover, differences between Darwinians—between the "selfish gene" theory of Richard Dawkins, for example, and the stress on the agency of organisms that Richard Lewontin regards as central, not to speak of the even greater differences between Darwinians and other evolutionary theorists—are formed along philosophical, not testably empirical, grounds. Since Popper named metaphysical ideas as his paradigm of nonfalsifiable statements, Johnson pointed a Popperian finger at Darwinism. It is not a scientific theory. It is a metaphysical research program.[12]

Predictably, some Darwinians responded to this argument by glorying in their infirmity. Dawkins, Daniel Dennett, and Michael Ruse, for example, have trumpeted their militant atheistic convictions, as if they were stunned refugees from the world of Voltaire who happened to find themselves in a late twentieth century in which, to their considerable surprise, religion still existed.[13] Even the brilliant Richard Lewontin stumbled rhetorically on this point—more out of frustration, I suspect, than Marxist militancy—by remarking in a now famous piece in the *New York Review of Books* that "we [Darwinians] have a prior commitment to materialism."[14]

Other contemporary Darwinians, however, such as Stephen Jay Gould (and, as the end of this essay will show, myself), have devoutly wished to evade this philosophical entanglement by blurring the line between the empirically falsifiable and the conceptually inventive. They can be thankful, accordingly, that few philosophers of science are strict Popperians any more. That is true largely because it turns out to be either too easy or too hard to falsify a theory. All theories, as Thomas Kuhn pointed out, are born in a sea of anomalies. Generally, they come trailing clouds of metaphysical glory almost until they are fully articulated. To wield the falsificationist ax too early, accordingly, means the premature extinction of research programs that, if the past is any guide to the future, might well go on to prove their worth. When, then, should one pull the plug on a good but underarticulated idea?

There does not seem to be any plausible systematic answer to that question. So falsificationism does not demarcate scientific rationality particularly well.

In part because of the rejection of falsificationism as a general account of theory formation and theory choice, as well as because the disciplines of history and sociology of science have by now done enough casework to show that working scientists actually spend little time attempting either to verify *or* falsify hypotheses, philosophers of science have in recent years begun in larger numbers to view science as an ongoing activity that is as constantly open to contest, debate, and revision as any other dimension of culture. In this process, research programs ebb and flow as they alternatively fail or succeed in solving the particular problems that excite a community of inquirers at any time. One good measure of success in this process is precisely the one invoked by Behe and Meyer: inference to the best causal explanation for a phenomenon, given the evidence that is contingently available at a given time.

Since this is the criterion that most intelligent design theorists wish to judge and be judged by, we may ask how the creationism-evolution debate stands when measured by this more reasonable, post-Popperian standard. Contemporary philosophers of biology who take a problem-oriented approach to science usually think of creationism as a genuine, but presently degenerative, research tradition. It is not to be dismissed because it is nonfalsifiable, or even because it has been decisively falsified, but because its rate of problem-solving success has been declining steadily since its golden day. That was probably in the 1840s, when most of the world's most prominent biologists and geologists—Cuvier, von Baer, Lyell, Owen, and Agassiz—cleaved to it. If the community of inquirers into organic origins suddenly shifted tomorrow to creationism, skeptics ask, what cascades of problem-solving could be expected to ensue? From the bottom of their sincere hearts, Darwinians of all stripes, materialist or no, theist or no, give the following answer: None.

Nor are Darwinians and philosophers who accept the problem-solving account of science much moved by accusations to the effect that Darwin himself could not explain such phenomena as speciation by appealing exclusively to natural selection. Darwinism, like scientific creationism, is a research tradition that has had a long and varied life. What Darwin could not explain is not what contemporary Darwinians cannot explain. Contemporary Darwinism is not limited to the same array of interpretive models and evolutionary agencies that Darwin himself had in hand. Accordingly, endless and obsessive reconstructions of Darwin's own doubts and worries, which seem so momentous to creationists whose own roots lie in a nineteenth-century ambiance, are, from the point of view of the conception of science shared by Behe, Meyer, Dembski, and other advocates of the intelligent design program, quite beside the point. That is not because Darwinism in some general sense has been confirmed or escaped falsification by retreating to deep metaphysical thickets but because it is a research tradition that has, up to the present, had a pretty good run. Creationism, by contrast, has been rather unfortunate in its lack of fecundity in the past century or so.

Intelligent design creationists are certainly to be commended for adopting views about how science actually works that are likely to be more illuminating than those that we have thus far reviewed. Having foresworn the easy but empty rhetorical victories that inductivism and falsificationism afford, they are certainly in a position to assert that, when one descends to the level of molecular biology and the origins of life, contemporary Darwinism is challenged. I do not think that it follows, however, that this fact means that the problem-solving prowess of scientific creationism is now in a position to claim a latter-day victory. I will try to explain why in what follows.

It is not odd, from a rhetorical point of view, to see why advocates of intelligent design are fond of the term *complexity. Complexity* has become a keyword both within contemporary science and among writers who employ the genre of *haut vulgarisation* to induce in the book-reading and PBS-watching public a "gee whiz" attitude toward contemporary trends in science.[15] One of the reasons that *complexity* has become an inviting keyword is that the rapid growth of computation, and especially the widespread and growing deployment of computer modeling, has begun to confer on scientific inquirers of all sorts analytical tools that can explore "complex systems." Such systems have hitherto consistently resisted understanding by way of the models of simple systems, whether mechanistic or probabalistic, that have virtually defined science since the seventeenth century. In such a discursive context, Behe and his colleagues can plausibly and relevantly assert that Darwinians have underestimated the intrinsic complexity of some of the phenomena their research tradition is supposed to explain, especially at the molecular level.

I could not agree more with the claim that contemporary Darwinism lacks models that can explain the evolution of cellular pathways and the problem of the origin of life. Meyer is correct to point out, for example, as my coauthor Bruce Weber and I have also done, that natural selection cannot in principle be the cause of life's origin. Natural selection is a phenomenon that depends for its operation on the very sort of variation and heredity that exists only in organisms and so can hardly be used to explain how organisms came into existence in the first place.[16]

Nor does Meyer miss the mark when he derides writers such as Francis Crick, Jacques Monod, and Dawkins, who appeal to sheer accident (including, in Crick's case, extraterrestrial intrusion) to explain the origin of life. That is no explanation at all. It is a confession of failure. In the face of the growing urgency of these problems, the inclinations of some Darwinian apologists to retreat to the high ground of metaphysical materialism can readily, and perhaps justly, be understood by hostile critics as an attempt, in the face of such inadequacies, to issue a philosophical guarantee that, in the absence of empirical proof, life will eventually be shown to be consistent with received Darwinian thought. But this is not science. It is scientistic ideology.

Still, I do not agree with the conclusions that Behe, Meyer, and others draw from reflections like these. In part, that is because I think Meyer too quickly dismisses the fact that even single-celled organisms, whatever else they may be, are self-organizing systems and that self-organization is not only an *explanandum*, something to be explained, but also an *explanans*, something that does the explaining, as the study of cellular automata and other complex systems has shown. I am suggesting, in other words, that there is a third way between intelligent design and natural selection and that this third way—the way of self-organization—is more likely than intelligent design to articulate itself, as science itself crosses the complexity barrier, into a productive, problem-solving research tradition.

The self-organization initiative begins from the perception that organisms are in the first instance thermodynamically open systems that spontaneously build internal structures (in the form of pathways) by drawing energy from their environments, using it to do work, and exporting workless energy, or entropy, to their environments. That is how organisms are coupled to their environments. But organisms are not only self-organizing, open, dissipative structures. They are *autocatalytic*, self-organizing, dissipative structures, structures that use the products and by-products of one cycle of energy and material processing to enhance the speed and efficiency of the next round. Such systems will certainly differ from one another in their rate of reconstructability in the next round. Those that feed off their environments more efficiently will proliferate at the expense of those that do it less well. This fact alone suggests, however, that there are forms of variation and selection that are not products of natural selection but that, on the contrary, are presupposed by it. It is precisely in autocatalytic dissipative systems, and in no other, that natural selection of the fit, rather than chemical selection of the merely efficient, eventually emerged.

In all probability this happened when a coevolving system of protein chains and nucleic acids had a positive effect on competition for energy fluxes among chemically selective systems—and not when some naked piece of RNA proceeded to decorate itself out with "survival machines." One implication of this picture is that the adaptations brought about by natural selection function to facilitate, coordinate, integrate, and regulate autocatalytic cycling of self-organizing, dissipative structures. Viewed from this perspective, natural selection is not called upon to bootstrap living things into existence. Rather, what needs to be explained is the emergence of natural selection itself by way of the progressive tightening of energetic cycles. One can see the results of this process at work in the cellular pathways that play such an important role in Behe's argument.

The approach briefly outlined above also requires us to see organisms as developmental processes rather than as decomposable, machinelike assemblies of discrete parts.[17] The latter may be irreducibly complex in the sense that the operation of each part depends on the operation of others, as Behe explains. But they are not irreducibly complex in this sense: They are, and result from, a complex self-organizing process, characterized as much by positive as by negative feedback, in which patterns of material cycling move toward adapted complexity by a process of ontogenetic bifurcation and division. The traits of organisms are mutually dependent, and irreducibly complex in the first sense, only *because* the self-organizing systems that are their foundation are already irreducibly complex in a deeper sense. Much of the puzzlement about the origins of such systems that has led intelligent people to have recourse to intelligent design disappears when one realizes that adaptive evolution does not consist of adding items agglutinatively, or even bit by bit, but by further differentiating an already given, even if wildly underarticulated, system that, by progressive articulation and stabilization by means of genes, comes to be less and less at the mercy of external conditions and more and more an agent in an environment that it constructs.

I take it, then, that there are two kinds of irreducible complexity. The first kind, Behe's kind, may be sufficient to rebut forms of Darwinism like those of Dawkins or Dennett, whose decompositional model of organisms as the "survival machines" of genes is, in essence, an attempt to "block the exits" to the supernatural while behavioral and cognitive traits are brought under the increasing control of materialist techno-science. It is a worthy task to blunt this enterprise. But I seriously doubt whether any creationist view that shares with its reductionist Darwinian opponents the assumption that organisms are widgets, rather than developmental systems, can be very effective against this reductionist, and mostly metaphysical, form of Darwinism or against the increasingly effective materialist techno-science that it shills for. The only way to do that, I believe, is to recognize that machines do not have ontogenies in the sense that organisms do and to insist, against utopian rhetoric, that on any reasonable problem-solving- and process-view of science, it is explanatorily irrelevant to assert that in the future they might.

The upshot of this argument is to reveal that intelligent design theorists and reductionistic Darwinians both miss the self-organizational alternative because they both assume that organisms are, or are like, machines. Like many analogies, this one generated some good science and, more recently, a biotechnological revolution. But this model shows its limitations precisely when its partisans, both Darwinian and creationist, show their common commitment to the claim that organisms express the property of designedness, which I believe screens off the developmental, as opposed to the machinelike, characteristics of organisms.

Within this framework, the intelligent design theorist argues that, where the property of designedness points to the mutually dependent complexity described by Behe, the most reasonable inference is that it comes from a designer, since natural selection as a progressive, bit-by-bit process seems incapable of explaining it. The Darwinian, by contrast, says that all objects with the property of designedness merely appear to be designed. In fact they come about by the "algorithmic" sorting of a "blind watchmaker."[18] It is just because both sides toil within the common assumption of designedness, however, that they take whatever analogy obtains between organisms and machines too far. "The cell is run by machines," writes Behe, "quite literally, molecular machines."[19] Would Dawkins disagree with that? Would he or Dennett be unhappy with Meyer's assumption that genes "contain" information in the same sense that modern computers do? Would he contest the implication that organisms are merely their "readouts"?

There are anti-Darwinian evolutionists who recognize the shared assumption about designedness that ties creationists and Darwinians into an eternally quarrelsome marriage. But in distancing themselves from the notion that the traits of organisms exhibit designedness, these "process

structuralists," as they are now known, also feel impelled to reject the notion that organisms are in any important way functional entities. Instead,
they think of species as arising from predictable mathematical permutations of a finite number of structural forms.[20] Evolutionists of this stripe
are at least as inimical to Darwinism as any fire-breathing creationist.[21]

It is important to note, accordingly, that the alternative approach I have
outlined retains the notion that the traits of organisms are functional, and
indeed adapted, without retaining design language in describing them. By
stressing that organisms are developmental systems that have evolved
from, and are undergirded by, autocatalytic chemically dissipative systems,
it becomes possible, in the course of explaining developmental phenomena
in a more convincing way than Darwinians have hitherto achieved, to
move the entire Darwinian tradition away from its roots in the argument
from design and toward a view of organisms as developmental systems.
Weber and I have expressed the moral of this story elsewhere. Complex
evolving developmental processes are not, in the final analysis, like designed entities at all. It doesn't matter whether the watchmaker is blind or
sighted, for in point of fact there is no watch.[22]

This argument reaffirms, in my judgment, what I will call a minimalist
naturalism. I take naturalism generally to mean that we should presume
that science, by shifting its conceptual structures as much as by marshaling
empirical evidence, will continue to solve baffling problems in ways that
do not depend on the supernatural. It means that we should not stand in
the path of science by invoking God too quickly. Even for theologians,
there is a good prudential reason for acceding to that policy while at the
same time hoping that science and the supernatural can live with one another on increasingly better terms. What usually becomes evident when
God is invoked prematurely is that someone's science was too limited, or
someone's God was too small, or both.

Admittedly, there is a historical connection between the naturalistic
heuristic that I commend and philosophical materialism. This intimate connection between naturalism as an explanatory strategy and materialism as
a metaphysical thesis, where it is not reducible to the claptrap of Enlightenment rhetoric, was formed by the perception that reductionistic methods
and atomistic ontologies have always facilitated the problem-solving
prowess of science better than holism. I think it unlikely, however, that
this dogma will stand up in the future. Indeed, I suspect that the old philosophical notion of materialism—the sort of thing we associate with Hobbes
or with Dawkins and Dennett—is likely to fall into virtual unintelligibility

long before science ceases to solve problems without appealing to the supernatural. It is true that by its very nature techno-science will always focus on what it can tear down, put back together again, and generally manipulate and mimic, and that its advocates will always tell us that their latest success shows that that's all there is. But creationists, who are interested in a far deeper, less manipulative inquiry into the nature of things than techno-scientists, should infer as little from this as I do.

Given my minimalist naturalism, it does not seem to be to the point when intelligent design theorists rebut the approach I have outlined by saying that they are merely trying to blunt the rhetorical efficacy of Darwinism and that attempts to find alternative evolutionary theories are irrelevant to this effort. In constructing a dichotomy that is supposed to lead from Darwinism to intelligent design, advocates of that position are logically committed to considering all other alternatives before they make this inference. That is especially so because they have adopted as their criterion "inference to the best explanation," and inference to the best explanation, particularly when it acknowledges that science goes on within problem-solving research traditions, requires all viable alternatives to be considered before judgment is reached. Approaches that unhinge the assumption that organisms are, or are like, machines seem to me far more likely to produce inferences to the best explanation than either Darwinism or design theory. Such approaches cannot be set aside in debates between creationists and Darwinians, except perhaps where such debates are little more than epideictic displays of argumentative virtuosity.

Some rather puzzling pedagogical implications flow from my position. If historical biology, and not just functional biology, is to be included in school curricula at all, the inclusion of intelligent design, as a version of creationism that is not narrowly sectarian, must also lead to including other viable alternatives. If it is a question of respecting the intelligence of students, they should be exposed to debates within Darwinism as well as to those between Darwinism and anti-Darwinian traditions in evolutionary theory, such as process structuralism, as well as to varieties of creationism. Whether this degree of contention will increase students' respect for science or lead to disgust with it is, however, very much an open question. Nonetheless, that is what is logically required by the criterion of inference to the best explanation to which intelligent design theorists subscribe. They must choose between that criterion and a suspiciously premature verdict, whether or not they want to do this, through—or more likely above—the heads of innocent students.

Notes

1. M. Behe, "Intelligent Design as an Alternative Explanation for the Existence of Biomolecular Machines," *Rhetoric and Public Affairs* 1, no. 4 (1998): 565.

2. M. Behe, *Darwin's Black Box: The Biochemical Challenge to Evolution* (New York: Free Press, 1996).

3. S. C. Meyer, "DNA by Design: An Inference to the Best Explanation for the Origin of Biological Information," *Rhetoric and Public Affairs* 1, no. 4 (1998): 519–56.

4. Plato, "Laws," in *Great Books of the Western World,* ed. Mortimer J. Alder (Chicago: University of Chicago Press, 1952), p. 770.

5. W. Paley, *Natural Theology: Evidences of the Existence and Attribute of the Deity: Collected from the Appearances of Nature* (Charlottesville, Va.: Lincoln-Rembrandt Publishing, [1802] 1986).

6. R. L. Numbers, *Darwinism Comes to America* (Cambridge: Harvard University Press, 1998).

7. C. A. Taylor, *Defining Science* (Madison: University of Wisconsin Press, 1996).

8. T. Bethell, "Darwin's Mistake," *Christianity Today* 21, no. 18 (17 June 1977): 12–15.

9. M. J. S. Hodge, "Natural Selection as a Causal, Empirical, and Probabilistic Theory," in *The Probabilistic Revolution,* ed. L. Kruger et al., vol. 2. (Cambridge: MIT Press, 1987), 233–70.

10. S. K. Mills and J. H. Beatty, "The Propensity Interpretation of Fitness," *Philosophy of Science* 46 (1979): 263–86. See also R. Brandon, "Adaptation and Evolutionary Theory," *Studies in History and Philosophy of Science* 9 (1978): 181–206.

11. M. Ruse, *But Is It Science?* (Buffalo, N.Y.: Prometheus Books, 1988).

12. P. Johnson, *Darwin on Trial* (Washington, D.C.: Regnery Gateway, 1991).

13. R. Dawkins, *The Selfish Gene,* 2nd ed. (Oxford: Oxford University Press, [1976] 1986); D. Dennett, *Darwin's Dangerous Idea* (New York: Simon and Schuster, 1995); M. Ruse, *Taking Darwinism Seriously* (London: Basil Blackwell, 1986).

14. R. Lewontin, "Billions and Billions of Demons," *New York Review of Books,* 9 Jan. 1997, 28–32.

15. For example, J. Gleick, *Chaos: Making a New Science* (New York: Viking, 1987).

16. D. Depew and B. Weber, *Darwinism Evolving: Systems Dynamics and the Genealogy of Natural Selection* (Cambridge: MIT Press, 1995).

17. P. Griffiths and R. Gray, "Developmental Systems and Evolutionary Systems," *Journal of Philosophy* 91 (1994): 277–304; S. Oyama, *The Ontogeny of Information* (Cambridge: Cambridge University Press, 1985).

18. Dawkins, *Selfish Gene.*

19. Behe, "Intelligent Design," 567.

20. B. Goodwin, *How the Leopard Changed Its Spots: The Evolution of Complexity* (London: Weidenfeld and Nicolson, 1994).

21. S. N. Salthe, *Development and Evolution* (Cambridge: MIT Press, 1993).

22. Depew and Weber, *Darwinism,* 7.

Biochemical Complexity:
Emergence or Design?

Bruce H. Weber

❈ ❈ ❈

In *Darwin's Black Box: The Biochemical Challenge to Evolution,* Michael Behe restates in modern biochemical terms William Paley's argument that there is an irreducible functional complexity to living beings that suggests the action of a designer-creator.[1] He repeats Paley's challenge for science to provide a naturalistic explanation that can account robustly for such complexity and adaptation. Darwin responded to Paley's challenge by suggesting that the mechanism of natural selection acting upon random, heritable variation could account for biological adaptation and descent with modification. But, Behe argues, Darwin could not have known what we now know about organisms and lineages of organisms at the biochemical and molecular level. This knowledge, he claims, stretches the explanatory power of Darwinian conceptions to and beyond their limit, leaving us only with the alternative of intelligent design to explain the emergence of novel and complex structures and phenomena in living systems.

I wish to question whether biochemical complexity, as Behe represents it, is indeed irreducible—and its emergence beyond scientific scrutiny. Behe does not deny that natural selection can act on populations to cause changes in gene frequencies. Nor does he deny the occurrence of mutations. He acknowledges that mutations in amino acid sequences of proteins provide evidence for descent with modification. To this extent, he agrees that biochemistry supports the fact of evolutionary change.

Behe, however, sees the systems of proteins and enzymes engaged in particular biological tasks, such as the bacterial flagellum, signal transduction at membranes, transport across membranes and within cells, blood clotting, the immune system, and the origin and regulation of metabolism, as having too many components that have to interact in precise ways for such systems to have evolved by a piecemeal, gradual process of natural selection. It is not that a primitive eye or flagellum might not have a selective advantage but rather that to get to even such primitive structures would require a large number of molecular changes that would not have any functional value until all the minimal molecular components were in place. Therefore, the complexity of the biochemical examples Behe cites could not have arisen except by design, any more than in the case of the mousetrap he uses as his analogy instead of Paley's watch, all other alternatives presumably being ruled out. He insinuates that this irreducible complexity is either ignored by contemporary evolutionists or is explained away by just-so stories in order to protect the Darwinian paradigm.

Behe makes much of the supposed lack of attempts by evolutionary biologists to provide credible causal explanations of the emergence of such complex adaptive systems. Nor does Behe give credit to what work has actually been done by the Darwinian research community. He virtually ignores a whole area of current research on self-organizing, emergent phenomena.

There have been many responses to Behe—some by biochemists, including one by me—that address how adequately he has represented the current literature with regard to the specific examples he cites.[2] There are in fact published attempts to address issues such as the origin of flagella, blood clotting, and the biochemical basis of vision. To outline how processes of gene duplication, domain and exon shuffling, and divergent evolution are suggested by current molecular data admittedly does not address how incomplete systems would have selective advantage. But we are at the point of accumulating enough data from DNA sequences and three-dimensional structures of proteins to make a number of tests of putative evolutionary explanations in the near future, not what would be expected of just-so stories.

For example, Behe argues that an account of the origin of the immune system is beyond the capacity of Darwinism, given the system's great complexity and the large number of genes required. A recent report, however, of the discovery of function of the RAG transposases and transposons in contemporary vertebrate immune systems, and of the possible role that introduction of such an activity could have had on the emergence of the vertebrate immune system, reveals the danger of assuming that the complexity of any system is not open to an evolutionary explanation.[3] A research program is now possible that can explore, by sequence analyses and computer simulations, putative routes of emergence of the immune system and hence of complex vertebrates that could not exist without their immune systems. If intelligent design were the prevailing paradigm, research would be stopped at delineating the function of these transposons/transposases.

When it comes to questions about the origin, or more correctly the emergence, of life, Behe says that little has actually been done and that what efforts have been made have been inadequate. Behe depends primarily on computer searches of the titles in the *Journal of Molecular Evolution* to argue that there is little effort by evolutionary biologists to address the problem. There are two difficulties here.

First, titles are not a sure guide to content. There have been papers on the origin of life published in the *Journal of Molecular Evolution* that eluded Behe's search because they do not have the word *origin* in their title, such as one on the role of membranelike structures and thermodynamic gradients in the origin of protocells.[4]

Second, most of the literature on origin of life is not published in the *Journal of Molecular Evolution* but rather in journals such as *Origins of Life and Evolution of the Biosphere, BioSystems, Journal of Theoretical Biology,* or *Nature,* in which Behe could have found a large number of both theoretical and experimental papers addressing the origin of life. Behe could have found papers, for example, that address how amphiphiles derived from carbonaceous chondrites can give rise to membranelike structures such as micelles and vesicles, how such structures show autocatalytic self-assembly and self-replication, and how polycyclic aromatic hydrocarbons, also derived from meteorites, can embed and orient in amphiphile bilayers in such a way that proton translocation, an important cellular energy-transducing mechanism, can occur.[5] Major works summarizing novel approaches to the problem of the origin of life are also missed, such as those of R. J. P. Williams and J. J. R. Frausto da Silva and of Harold Morowitz.[6] Whether or not Behe finds such work compelling, he at least owes it to his readers to report that such efforts in fact exist, since he makes much of their supposed absence.

One attempt to address the origin of life does receive some attention from Behe, that of Stuart Kauffman in his *Origins of Order*.[7] Behe argues that Kauffman can get self-organization to occur in his computer simulations only under specific initial and boundary conditions and that only certain types of interactions among the components of his models lead to organized behavior. Since self-organization does not arise by totally random chance events but requires certain "propensities" of interaction and, further, some type of selection, Behe concludes that Kauffman's approach can be safely dismissed as irrelevant to the problem of the emergence of living systems. Behe seems to miss the whole point of Kauffman's exercise.

What is extraordinary about Kauffman's models is that, although simple, they do capture a range of dynamical behavior of biological systems.[8] Of course, constraints have to be built in by the programmer. The question is whether those constraints are reasonable, reflecting at least by analogy the categories of local interaction between components and being away from equilibrium. That is, to the extent that Kauffman's models reflect the effect of built-in propensities of molecular properties and interactions, as well as the energy flow and entropy production of real physical and biological systems, they can be explored in simulations to give insight into possible large-scale events in natural systems. The propensities exist in nature; to model their existence the programmer must introduce some sort of similar constraint.[9] To demand that self-organization emerge from a totally ergodic system is to deny that there are propensities and initial and boundary conditions in the real world.

To state that they exist does not address the question of why there are such propensities for interaction and self-organization in nature. There could be an interesting argument for design with regard to setting the parameters, both in nature and in simulations. Those interested in exploring the emergence of life, however, are not concerned about the source of the propensities but the consequences of their existence.

I have argued that Kauffman's models do provide insight into what might have been important for the emergence of life.[10] His notions of protein-sequence phase space and how it might be explored, coupled with his concept of catalytic-task space, provide an approach to consider how ensembles of initially random sequences could, over time, be selected by chemical selection for catalytic and thermodynamic efficiency, to better fit various catalytic tasks. Another key insight is that of catalytic closure, by which ensembles of autocatalytic polymers of sufficient complexity can undergo a "phase transition" to a closed, emergent "protometabolism."

Natural physical and chemical systems under appropriate initial and boundary conditions of energy/matter gradients and flow show spontaneous self-organization, generating macroscopic ordered structure under thermodynamic imperatives of dissipation away from equilibrium. The approaches employed to describe such phenomena have been extended to biological systems, including the problem of the emergence of life.[11] Atomic and molecular properties and propensities could have interacted under thermodynamic constraints in the earth's early environment, working with physical and chemical selection to produce more complex emergent phenomena. This suggests that the chemistry envisioned by Kauffman could occur within a protocell and that life and its components emerged and became more articulate *as a whole* rather than sequentially, just as Kauffman's simulations suggest.

Such an account of the emergence of living systems suggests that biological selection (natural selection) of the reproductively fit, *as a phenomenon*, arose out of an earlier and ongoing action of physical selection for stable components and of chemical selection for energetic and catalytically efficient components as life and genetic information. This represents a recognition that there are various types of selection, that they themselves are emergent, and that these can interact with self-organizing properties of different types and levels of systems.[12] Selection may not have to do everything, or only in a gradual manner, since selection can be allied with self-organization to generate order and organization. Clearly, neither does self-organization have to do everything alone. Nor should any rational person expect that chance alone could generate order out of chaos. All three should be considered as acting together, to various degrees in specific instances, in order to generate robust explanations of emergence. The application of "complex systems dynamics" to biological problems is still in its infancy. Nonetheless, the point is that there is a research community, which includes some "card-carrying" Darwinians, that is attempting to address problems of emergence in general and especially in biological systems and thereby to give accounts of what Behe takes to be "irreducible complexity."

Thus, Behe's claim of irreducible complexity of biochemical systems is weakened by the actual scientific literature. But it is still an important issue that needs to be addressed. The application of complex systems dynamics may show how to understand the emergence of the type of functional complexity that concerns Behe. This is an incomplete work in progress, which is the characteristic of a living science that works with a human perspective. The demand for an immediate and complete explanation that can be satisfied only by a "God's-eye view" would not create a new paradigm so much as inhibit research on the problem of emergence. The very idea is inconsistent with the fundamentals of science.

Implied in Behe's account of the analogy of biological systems to a mousetrap, just as in Paley's to a watch, is the notion that organisms and their component parts either are artifacts, or are analogous to artifacts, or share some character with artifacts. But organisms have also been distinguished from artifacts ever since Aristotle wrote about the great difference between a house that had a designer and builder and an animal that is the product of a cycle of growth, development, and reproduction, whose parts can be defined, come into being, and indeed exist only in relation to the whole. Organisms are not assemblies of widgets.

Behe concedes that artifacts are a weak analogy to organisms in view of the fact that artifacts and organisms have different conditions of decomposition. But he claims that the part of an artifact's character that provides a robust analogy is that of irreducible complexity. Behe says we need to infer to the best argument. Since there are only two possible ways to deal with irreducible complexity, Behe argues, if the selectionist account is lacking, then intelligent design is demonstrated. But the supposed intractability of irreducible complexity may well be prematurely assumed for natural systems. Further, the fact that organisms arise through a developmental process, in which components needed for subsequent stages are brought into being during earlier stages, suggests that there can be mutually entailing roles for chance, selection, and self-organization. Any attempt to understand the emergence of complexity must address the reality of development.

The full integration of developmental biology with evolutionary theory is currently being explored in a number of ways. Behe is silent on these developments. As we understand development and evolution more deeply, we will probably see that developing organisms are as different from artifacts as they can be. So questions about the inseparability of organic structure from design, which are based on the analogy to artifacts, will be irrelevant. We will see that the proper study of biological complexity is its emergence, its developmental trajectories, and its evolutionary lineages. It may well be that, as the notions of complexity inform the sciences, we may need to recognize that even our earlier science is a relic of a crypto-theological age gone by—and that we need to find a richer and more nuanced theology as well as a more nuanced science.

Notes

1. M. J. Behe, *Darwin's Black Box: The Biochemical Challenge to Evolution* (New York: Free Press, 1996), and his discussion in this volume.

2. B. H. Weber, "Irreducible Complexity and the Problem of Biochemical Emergence," *Biology and Philosophy* 14, no. 4 (1999): 593–605.

3. A. Agrawal, Q. M. Eastman, and D. G. Schatz, "Transposition Mediated by RAG1 and RAG2 and Its Implications for the Evolution of the Immune System," *Nature* 394 (1998): 744–51.

4. H. J. Morowitz, B. Heinz, and D. W. Deamer, "Biogenesis as an Evolutionary Process," *Journal of Molecular Evolution* 33 (1991): 207–8.

5. D. W. Deamer and R. M. Pashley, "Amphiphilic Components of the Murchison Carbanaceous Chondrite: Surface Properties and Membrane Formation," *Origin of Life and Evolution of the Biosphere* 19 (1989): 21–38; P. A. Bachmann, P. L. Luisi, and J. Lang, "Autocatalytic Self-Replicating Micelles as Models for Prebiotic Structures," *Nature* 357 (1992): 57–79; D. W. Deamer and E. Harang, "Light-Dependent pH Gradients Are Generated in Liposomes Containing Ferrocyanide," *BioSystems* 24 (1990): 14.

6. R. J. P. Williams and J. J. R. Frausto da Silva, *The Natural Selection of the Chemical Elements* (Oxford: Oxford University Press, 1996); H. J. Morowitz, *Beginnings of Cellular Life: Metabolism Recapitulates Biogenesis* (New Haven, Conn.: Yale University Press, 1992).

7. S. A. Kauffman, *Origins of Order: Self-Organization and Selection in Evolution* (New York: Oxford University Press, 1993); Behe, *Darwin's Black Box*, 155–56, 178–79, 189–92.

8. D. J. Depew and B. H. Weber, *Darwinism Evolving: Systems Dynamics and the Genealogy of Natural Selection* (Cambridge: MIT Press, 1995).

9. R. E. Ulanowicz, "The Propensities of Evolving Systems," in *Evolution, Order and Complexity,* ed. E. L. Khalil and K. E. Bounding (London: Routledge, 1996), 217–33.

10. B. H. Weber, "Origins of Order in Dynamical Models," *Biology and Philosophy* 13 (1998): 133–44.

11. B. H. Weber, "Emergence of Life and Biological Selection from the Perspective of Complex Systems Dynamics," in *Evolutionary Systems,* ed. G. van de Vijver, S. S. Salthe, and M. Delpos (Dordrecht: Kluwer, 1998).

12. B. H. Weber and D. J. Depew, "Natural Selection and Self-Organization: Dynamical Models as Clues to a New Evolutionary Synthesis," *Biology and Philosophy* 11 (1996): 33–65.

Design Yes, Intelligent No:
A Critique of Intelligent Design Theory
and Neo-Creationism

Massimo Pigliucci

❊ ❊ ❊

A new brand of creationism has appeared on the scene in the last few years. The so-called neo-creationists largely do not believe in a young earth or in a too literal interpretation of the Bible. Although still mostly propelled by a religious agenda and financed by mainly Christian sources, the intellectual challenge posed by neo-creationism is sophisticated enough to require detailed consideration.

Among the chief exponents of intelligent design (ID) theory, as this new brand of creationism is called, is William Dembski, a mathematical philosopher and author of *The Design Inference*.[1] In that book, he attempts to show that there must be an intelligent designer behind natural phenomena such as evolution and the origin of the universe.[2] Dembski's argument is that modern science ever since Francis Bacon has illicitly dropped two of Aristotle's four types of causes from consideration altogether, thereby unnecessarily restricting its own explanatory power.[3]

Aristotle's Four Causes in Science

Aristotle identified *material* causes, what something is made of; *formal* causes, the structure of the thing or phenomenon; *efficient* causes, the immediate activity producing a phenomenon or object; and *final* causes, the purpose of whatever object we are investigating. For example, let's say we want to investigate the causes of the Brooklyn Bridge. Its material cause would be encompassed by a description of the physical materials that went into its construction. The formal cause is the fact that it is a bridge across a stretch of water and not either a random assembly of pieces or another kind of orderly structure (such as a skyscraper). The efficient causes were the blueprints drawn by engineers and the labor of people and machines that actually assembled the physical materials and put them into place. The final cause of the Brooklyn Bridge was the necessity for people to walk and ride between two landmasses while avoiding getting wet.

Dembski maintains that Bacon and his followers did away with both formal and final causes (the so-called teleonomic causes, because they answer the question of why something is) in order to free science from philosophical speculation and ground it firmly into empirically verifiable statements. That may be so, but things changed with the work of Charles Darwin.[4] Darwin was addressing a complex scientific question in an unprecedented fashion: He recognized that living organisms are clearly designed in order to survive and reproduce in the world they inhabit; yet as a scientist he worked within the framework of naturalistic explanations of such design. Darwin found the answer in his well-known theory of natural selection. Natural selection, combined with the basic process of mutation, makes design possible in nature without recourse to a supernatural explanation because selection is definitely nonrandom and therefore has "creative" (albeit nonconscious) power. Creationists usually do not understand this point and think that selection can eliminate only the less fit. Darwin's powerful insight was that selection is also a cumulative process, analogous to a ratchet, which can build things over time, as long as the intermediate steps are also advantageous.

For example, if we were to ask what are the causes of a tiger's teeth within a Darwinian framework, we would answer in the following manner. The material cause is provided by the biological materials that make up the teeth; the formal cause is the genetic and developmental machinery that distinguishes a tiger's teeth from any other kind of biological structure; the efficient cause is natural selection promoting some genetic variants of the tiger's ancestor over others; and the final cause is provided by the fact that having teeth structured in a certain way makes it easier for a tiger to procure its prey and therefore to survive and reproduce—the only "goals" of every living being.

Therefore, design is very much a part of modern science, at least whenever there is a need to explain an apparently designed structure (such as a living organism). All four Aristotelian causes are fully reinstated within the realm of scientific investigation, and science is not maimed by the disregard of some of the causes acting in the world.

What then is left of the argument of Dembski and of other proponents of ID? They, like William Paley well before them, make the mistake of confusing natural design and intelligent design by rejecting the possibility of the former and concluding that any design must by definition be intelligent.[5]

One is also left with the lingering feeling that Dembski is being disingenuous about ancient philosophy. It is quite clear, for example, that Aristotle himself never meant his teleonomic causes to imply intelligent design in nature.[6] Aristotle's mentor, Plato (in *Timaeus*), had already concluded that the designer of the universe could not be an omnipotent god but at most what he called a Demiurge, a lesser god who evidently messes around with the universe with mixed results. Aristotle believed that the scope of god was even more limited, essentially to the role of prime mover of the universe, with no additional direct interaction with his creation (that is, Aristotle was one of the first deists). In *Physics*, where he discussed the four causes, Aristotle treats nature itself as a craftsman, but clearly devoid of forethought and intelligence. A tiger develops into a tiger because it is in its nature to do so, and this nature is due to some *physical* essence given to it by its father (we would call it DNA) which starts the process. Aristotle makes clear this rejection of god as a final cause when he says that causes are not *external* to the organism (such as a designer would be) but *internal* to it (as modern developmental biology clearly shows).[7]

In other words, the final cause of a living being is not a plan, intention, or purpose but simply intrinsic in the developmental changes of that organism—which means that Aristotle identified final causes with formal causes as far as living organisms are concerned. He rejected chance and randomness (as do modern biologists) but did not invoke an intelligent designer in its place (contra Dembski). We had to wait until Darwin for a further advance on Aristotle's conception of the final cause of living organisms and for modern molecular biology to achieve an understanding of their formal cause.

Irreducible Complexity

ID theorists propose two additional arguments to demonstrate intelligent design in the universe: the concept of "irreducible complexity" and the "complexity-specification" criterion. "Irreducible complexity" is a term introduced in this context by molecular biologist Michael Behe in his book *Darwin's Black Box.*[8] The idea is that the difference between a natural phenomenon and an intelligent designer is that a designed object is planned in advance, with forethought. Although an intelligent agent is not constrained by a step-by-step evolutionary process, the latter is the only way nature itself can proceed—given that it has no planning capacity (this may be referred to as incremental complexity). Irreducible complexity then arises whenever all the parts of a structure have to be present and functional simultaneously for it to work, indicating that the structure was designed and could not possibly have been gradually built by natural selection.

Behe's example of an irreducibly complex object is a mousetrap. If you take away any of the minimal elements that make the trap work, it will lose its function; on the other hand, there is no way to assemble a mousetrap gradually for a natural phenomenon, because it won't work until the last piece is assembled. Forethought, and therefore intelligent design, is necessary. Of course it is. After all, mousetraps are human products; we *know* that they are intelligently designed. But what of biological structures? Behe claims that, although evolution can explain a lot of the visible diversity among living organisms, it is not enough when we come to the molecular level. The cell and several of its fundamental components and biochemical pathways are, according to Behe, irreducibly complex.

The problem with his statement is that it is at least partially contradicted by the available literature on comparative studies in microbiology and molecular biology, which Behe conveniently ignores.[9] For example, geneticists are continuously showing that biochemical pathways are partly redundant. Redundancy is a common feature of living organisms where different genes participate in the same or in partially overlapping functions. Although this may seem a waste, mathematical models show that evolution by natural selection has to imply molecular redundancy, because when a new function is necessary it cannot be carried out by a gene that is already doing something else without compromising the original function. On the other hand, if the gene gets duplicated (by mutation), one copy is freed from immediate constraints and can slowly diverge in structure from the original, eventually taking over new functions. This process leads to the formation of gene "families," groups of genes clearly originated from a single ancestral DNA sequence and that now are diversified and perform a variety of functions (for example, the globins, which vary from proteins allowing muscle contraction to those active in the exchange of oxygen and carbon dioxide in the blood).

As a result of redundancy, mutations can knock down individual components of biochemical pathways without compromising the overall function—contrary to the expectations of irreducible complexity. Notice that creationists have also tried to claim that redundancy is yet another evidence of intelligent design, because an engineer would produce backup systems to minimize catastrophic failures should the primary components stop functioning. Although very clever, that argument once again ignores the biology: the majority of duplicated genes end up as pseudogenes, literally pieces of molecular junk that are eventually lost forever to any biological utility.[10]

To be sure, in several cases biologists do not know enough about the fundamental constituents of the cell to be able to hypothesize or demonstrate their gradual evolution. But that is rather an argument from ignorance, not positive evidence of irreducible complexity. William Paley advanced exactly the same argument to claim that it is impossible to explain the appearance of the eye by natural means. Yet today biologists know of several examples of intermediate forms of the eye, and there is evidence that this structure evolved several times independently during the history of life on Earth.[11] The answer to the classical creationist question, "What good is half an eye?" is "Much better than no eye at all!"

Behe, however, does have a point concerning irreducible complexity. It is true that some structures simply cannot be explained by slow and cumulative processes of natural selection. From his mousetrap to Paley's watch to the Brooklyn Bridge, irreducible complexity is indeed the hallmark of intelligent design. The problem for ID theory is that there is no evidence so far of irreducible complexity in living organisms.

The Complexity-Specification Criterion

William Dembski uses an approach similar to Behe to back up creationist claims, in that he also wants to demonstrate that intelligent design is necessary to explain the complexity of nature. His proposal, however, is both more general and more deeply flawed. In *The Design Inference,* he claims that there are three essential types of phenomena in nature: "regular," random, and designed (which he assumes to be intelligent). A regular phenomenon would be a simple repetition explainable by the fundamental laws of physics—for example, the rotation of the earth around the sun. Random phenomena are exemplified by the tossing of a coin. Design enters any time that two criteria are satisfied: complexity and specification.[12]

First of all, leaving aside design for a moment, the remaining choices are not limited to regularity and randomness. Chaos and complexity theory have established the existence of self-organizing phenomena, situations in which order spontaneously appears as an emergent property of complex interactions among the parts of a system.[13] Far from being only a figment of mathematical imagination, as Behe maintains, this class of phenomena is real. For example, certain meteorological phenomena such as tornados are neither regular nor random but are the result of self-organizing processes.

But let us go back to complexity-specification and take a closer look at these two fundamental criteria, allegedly capable of establishing intelligent agency in nature. Following one of Dembski's examples, if SETI (Search for ExtraTerrestrial Intelligence) researchers received a very short signal that may be interpreted as encoding the first three prime numbers, they would probably not rush to publish their findings. That is because even though such a signal *could* be construed as due to some kind of intelligence, it is so short that its occurrence can just as easily be explained by chance. Given the choice, a sensible scientist would follow Occam's razor and conclude that the signal does not constitute enough evidence for ET. Also according to Dembski, however, if the signal were long enough to encode all the prime numbers between 2 and 101, the SETI people would open the champagne and celebrate all night. Why? Because such a signal would be both too complex to be explained by chance and would be specifiable, meaning that it is not just a random sequence of numbers, it is an intelligible message.

The specification criterion needs to be added because complexity by itself is a necessary but not sufficient condition for design. To see this, imagine that the SETI staff receives a long but random sequence of signals. That sequence would be very complex, meaning that it would take a lot of information actually to archive or repeat the sequence (you have to know where all the 0s and 1s are), but it would not be specifiable because the sequence would be meaningless.

Dembski is absolutely correct that plenty of human activities, such as SETI, investigations into plagiarism, or encryption, depend on the ability to detect intelligent agency. Where he is wrong is in assuming only one kind of design: For him, design equals intelligence and, even though he admits that such an intelligence may be an advanced extraterrestrial civilization, his preference is for a god, possibly of the Christian variety.

The problem is that natural selection, a natural process, also fulfills the complexity-specification criterion, thereby demonstrating that it is possible to have unintelligent design in nature. Living organisms are indeed complex. They are also specifiable, meaning that they are not random assemblages of organic compounds but are clearly formed in a way that enhances their chances of surviving and reproducing in a changing and complex environment. What, then, distinguishes living organisms from the Brooklyn Bridge? Both meet Dembski's complexity-specification criterion, but only the bridge is irreducibly complex. This has important implications for the consideration of design.

In response to some of his critics, Dembski claims that intelligent design does not mean optimal design.[14] The criticism of suboptimal design has often been advanced by evolutionists who ask why God would do such a sloppy job with creation that even a mere human engineer can easily determine where the flaws are. For example, why is it that human beings have hemorrhoids, varicose veins, backaches, and aching feet? If you assume that we were "intelligently" designed, the answer must be that the designer was rather incompetent—something that would hardly please a creationist. Instead, evolutionary theory has a single answer to all these questions: Humans evolved bipedalism (walking with an erect posture) only very recently, and natural selection has not yet fully adapted our body to the new condition. Our closest primate relatives, chimps, gorillas, and the like, are better adapted to their way of life, and therefore are less "imperfect" than ourselves!

Dembski is of course correct in saying that intelligent design does not mean optimal design. As much as the Brooklyn Bridge is a marvel of engineering, it is not perfect, meaning that it had to be constructed within the constraints and limitations of the available materials and technology, and it still is subject to natural laws and decay. The bridge's vulnerability to high winds and earthquakes and its inadequacy to bear a volume of traffic for which it was not built can be seen as similar to the back pain caused by our recent evolutionary history. The imperfection of living organisms, however, already pointed out by Darwin, does do away with the idea that they were created by an omnipotent and omnibenevolent creator, who surely would not be limited by laws of physics that he himself made up from scratch.

The Four Fundamental Types of Design and How to Recognize Them

Given the considerations above, I would like to propose a system that includes both Behe's and Dembski's suggestions, while at the same time showing why they are both wrong in concluding that we have evidence for intelligent design in the universe. Essentially, I think there are four possible kinds of design in nature which, together with Dembski's categories of "regular" and random phenomena and the addition of chaotic-self-organizing phenomena, exhaust all possibilities. Science recognizes regular, random, and self-organizing phenomena, as well as the first two types of design. The other two types of design are possible in principle, but I contend that there is neither empirical nor logical evidence that they actually occur.

The first kind of design is *non-intelligent-natural,* and it is exemplified by natural selection within Earth's biosphere (and possibly elsewhere in the universe). The results of this design, such as all living organisms on Earth, are not irreducibly complex, meaning that they can be produced by incremental, continuous (though not necessarily gradual) changes over time. These objects can be clearly attributed to natural processes also because of two other reasons: They are never optimal (in an engineering sense), and they are clearly the result of historical processes. For example, they are full of junk, nonutilized or underutilized parts, and they resemble similar objects occurring simultaneously or previously in time (see, for example, the fossil record). Notice that some scientists and philosophers of science feel uncomfortable in considering this "design" because they equate the term with intelligence. But I do not see any reason to embrace such limitation. If something is shaped over time—by whatever means—such that it fulfills a certain function, then it is designed, and the question is simply of how such design happened to materialize. The teeth of a tiger are clearly designed to cut efficiently into the flesh of its prey and therefore to promote survival and reproduction of tigers bearing such teeth.

The second type of design is *intelligent-natural.* These artifacts are usually irreducibly complex, such as a watch designed by a human. They are also not optimal, meaning that they clearly compromise between solutions to different problems (trade-offs), and they are subject to the constraints of physical laws, available materials, designer expertise, and so forth. Humans may not be the only ones to generate these objects, as the artifacts of any extraterrestrial civilization would fall into the same broad category.

The third kind of design, which is difficult, if not impossible, to distinguish from the second, is what I term *intelligent-supernatural-sloppy*. Objects created in this way are essentially indistinguishable from human or ET artifacts, except that they would be the result of what the Greeks called a Demiurge, a minor god with limited powers. Alternatively, they could be due to an evil omnipotent god that just amuses himself or herself with suboptimal products. The reason *intelligent-supernatural-sloppy* design is not distinguishable from some instances (but by all means not all) of *intelligent-natural* design is Arthur C. Clarke's famous law: From the point of view of a technologically less advanced civilization, the technology of a very advanced civilization is essentially indistinguishable from magic (such as the monolith in his *2001: A Space Odyssey*). I would be very interested if someone could suggest a way around Clarke's law.

Finally, we have *intelligent-supernatural-perfect* design, which is the result of the activity of an omnipotent and omnibenevolent god. These artifacts would be both irreducibly complex and optimal. They would not be constrained by either trade-offs or physical laws (after all, god created the laws themselves). While this is the kind of god many Christian fundamentalists believe in (though some do away with the omnibenevolent part), it's quite clear from the existence of human evil, as well as of natural catastrophes and diseases, that such a god does not exist. Dembski recognizes this difficulty and, in an article answering his critics, admits that his intelligent design could even be due to a very advanced extraterrestrial civilization and not to a supernatural entity at all.[15]

Conclusion

In summary, it seems to me that the major arguments of ID theorists are neither new nor compelling.

It is simply not true that science does not address all Aristotelian causes, whenever design needs to be explained.

Although irreducible complexity is indeed a valid criterion to distinguish between intelligent and nonintelligent design, those are not the only two possibilities, and living organisms are not irreducibly complex.[16]

The complexity-specification criterion is actually met by natural selection and cannot therefore provide a way to distinguish intelligent from nonintelligent design.

If supernatural design exists at all (but where is the evidence or compelling logic?), it is certainly not of the kind that most religionists would likely subscribe to, and it is indistinguishable from the technology of a very advanced civilization.

Therefore, Behe's, Dembski's, and other creationists' claims that science should be opened to supernatural explanations and that these should be allowed in academic as well as public school curricula are unfounded and based on a misunderstanding of both design in nature and of what the neo-Darwinian theory of evolution is all about.[17]

Notes

I would like to acknowledge Melissa Brenneman, Will Provine, and Niall Shanks for insightful comments on earlier versions of this article, as well as Michael Behe, William Dembski, Ken Miller, and Barry Palevitz for indulging in correspondence and discussions with me over these matters.

1. W. A. Dembski, *The Design Inference: Eliminating Chance through Small Probabilities* (Cambridge: Cambridge University Press, 1998).

2. M. Pigliucci, "Chance, Necessity, and the New Holy War against Science," review of *The Design Inference* by W. A. Dembski, *BioScience* 50, no. 1, (Jan. 2000): 79–81.

3. W. A. Dembski, "Reinstating Design within Science," *Rhetoric and Public Affairs* 1 (1998): 503–18.

4. C. Darwin, *The Origin of Species by Means of Natural Selection: Or, the Preservation of Favored Races in the Struggle for Life* (New York: A. L. Burt, [1859] 1910).

5. W. Paley, *Natural Theology: Or, Evidences of the Existence and Attributes of the Deity, Collected from the Appearances of Nature* (Boston: Gould, Kendall, and Lincoln, 1831).

6. S. M. Cohen, "The Four Causes" (2000). Accessed: ue255;}{\pard\plain 5/16/00), web page, faculty.washington.edu/smcohen.

7. Ibid.

8. M. J. Behe, *Darwin's Black Box: The Biochemical Challenge to Evolution* (New York: Free Press, 1996).

9. K. R. Miller, "The Biochemical Challenge to Evolution" (1996). Accessed: ue255;}{\pard\plain10/30/99), web page, biomed.brown.edu/faculty/M/Miller.

10. E. E. Max, "Plagiarized Errors and Molecular Genetics: Another Argument in the Evolution–Creation Controversy," *Creation/Evolution* 9 (1986): 34–46.

11. W. J. Gehring and K. Ikeo, "*Pax 6,* Mastering Eye Morphogenesis and Eye Evolution," *Trends in Genetics* 15 (1999): 371–77.

12. Dembski, "Reinstating Design."

13. S. A. Kauffman, *The Origins of Order* (New York: Oxford University Press, 1993); N. Shanks and K. H. Joplin, "Redundant Complexity: A Critical Analysis of Intelligent Design in Biochemistry," *Philosophy of Science* 66 (1999): 268–82.

14. W. A. Dembski, "Intelligent Design Is Not Optimal Design" (2000). Meta list accessed: ue255;}{\pard\plain2/3/00), web page, www.meta-list.org.

15. Ibid.

16. Shanks and Joplin, "Redundant Complexity."

17. P. Johnson, *Defeating Darwinism by Opening Minds* (Downers Grove, Ill.: InterVarsity Press 1997); E. Mayr and W. B. Provine, *The Evolutionary Synthesis: Perspectives on the Unification of Biology* (Cambridge: Harvard University Press, 1980).

On Behalf of the Fool

Michael Ruse

❇ ❇ ❇

Michael Ruse—whose style, person, and writings are a delight—invented the rationale of the Overton decision in the Arkansas creation-science trial to fit the criteria for a winning case as specified by his ACLU handlers. His position is a laughingstock among his professional peers and an ethical and conceptual embarrassment to his profession.[1]

Every scholar needs critics far more than he or she needs friends. Friends often accept signed copies of your books, promising to study them with care, and then all you get is silence. More than once I have found my gifts on the shelves of secondhand book shops, although my chagrin at finding my generosity thus misused is balanced by my delight at the marked-up prices of my old publications. Critics read one's work with care, keep one in the limelight, and help in the ongoing development and clarification of one's thinking. As a Darwinian and a Popperian, I think one's ideas are always in a state of flux, and critics are an absolutely essential part of the intellectual quest that makes life meaningful and worthwhile.

Thus stimulated by the comments and barbs of those whom I would call the New Creationists and who would probably prefer the label intelligent design theorists—people with whom I am glad to say I have the best of personal relations and long may they last—I welcome this opportunity to lay out my present thinking on those issues about the nature of science that bind us in interest and divide us in conclusion. Borrowing as my title Gaunilo's response to Anselm, and with about the same level of humility, like Gaul (and God) what I have to say is divided into three parts. I begin with some thoughts about the nature of science; I go on to make some comments about the connection between science and values; and I end with a few words on the question of science education. Entirely typically, I shall be dogmatic and avoid qualifications and the full and fair treatment of others. I want to get my ideas in front of you: to show you why I am right rather than why you are wrong. (In the same spirit I shall keep my references to a minimum and refer you to my recent books, *Monad to Man: The Concept of Progress in Evolutionary Biology; Mystery of Mysteries: Is Evolution a Social Construction?; Can a Darwinian Be a Christian? The Relationship Between Science and Religion;* and: *Darwin and Design: Does Evolution have a Purpose?*)

Science and Nonscience

First, let me speak to the nature of science. Historically and conceptually, I take the aim of science to be that of understanding the physical, empirical world around us—including here ourselves as part of that world. I take it that the aim of science is to go beyond the subjective and in some way to achieve objectivity, to "tell it like it is" in the words of the late Howard Cosell. I take it that over the years a number of criteria or norms have emerged or been developed that help one in the aim of objectivity. These are not written in stone, nor are they somehow distinct from everyday thought—science is not something set on one side, separate from everything else. Following the Catholic priest and philosopher and historian of science Ernan McMullin, I refer to these criteria as "epistemic norms" or "values," and I find it useful to use his list of what is to be included under this label.[2] There is *internal coherence* (the parts of science should not contradict each other); there is *external consistency* (two areas of science should get on with each other); important is *predictive accuracy* (science should help you forecast what is going to happen); even more significant is *fertility* (good science points you forward, giving interesting questions and guides for their solution); another norm is *unificatory power* (called the "consilience of inductions" by Victorian philosopher-historian of science, William Whewell; science binds together different areas of inquiry); and last but not least, though controversial in some respects, is *simplicity* (great science has a ring of truth or elegance to it).[3] You could add other epistemic values, but these will probably do. Popperian falsifiability, for instance, is covered by predictive accuracy and coherence/consistency.

Now I take it that, as years went by, scientists, if one may anachronistically so call them (the term was invented by Whewell in the 1830s), found that their epistemic norms revealed that the world is a world of a particular kind. It is not just a jumble of random events but something that goes along in a regular fashion: the world, to be blunt, is lawlike or law-governed. Moreover, getting good scientific pictures that conformed to the epistemic criteria meant paying attention to those laws and using them in one's theories or models or whatever. That was and is a back-and-forth process. As one aims for epistemic excellence, the laws become known and prominent. As one discovers and recognizes the laws, one achieves epistemic success. I do not think that this symbiotic relationship was something one could have worked out a priori. (In the culture of the philosophers, I am a follower of David Hume.) The world could have been punctuated by non-law-governed events. If we call the rule of law "natural," then what I am saying is that the world could have been punctuated by nonnatural or supernatural events (call them miracles, if you like). But the fact is that this did not prove to be so. The world runs on law-governed lines. Hence, as a matter of historical fact, what we call science—certainly what we call good or mature or professional science—came to be predicated on the exclusive rule of law. Whewell again illustrated this point; in 1837 (in *History of the Inductive Sciences*), in talking of organic origins, which he wanted to ascribe to miracles, he told us that science tells us nothing: it simply points upward.

What now is the status of belief in the rule of law? It is metaphysical in a sense. It is something about science rather than in science: it is a presupposition for the doing of science. That does not make it ipso facto beyond reason, a leap of faith. The fact is that making the assumption of lawfulness has yielded massive dividends, even when—especially when—at first it seems that law would not apply. So in a sense, one has a pragmatic justification for assuming law as the working background to science. Does this then rule out the supernatural, from science, that is? Could one have a science that included miracles? Well, I suppose logically one could, although today it might be better to use a qualifier; Alvin Plantinga speaks of "Augustinian science," a designation that Saint Augustine might or might not have appreciated.[4] But as I have just said, I do not think that such a science is reasonable or needed. Because I am a Humean and refuse to rule things out a priori, this does not mean that they are reasonable a posteriori.

I do not pretend that the epistemic criteria can give a sharp distinction on every occasion between science and nonscience or pseudoscience (a bit more on this point shortly), but I do think that they do a pretty good job. To pretend that something like astronomy is indifferent to the rule of law strikes me as slightly goofy. Modern physics is a paradigm of epistemic excellence. Creationism of the ilk to be found in John Whitcomb and Henry Morris's *Genesis Flood* is not.[5] (It was their kind of creationism that I had in my sights in Arkansas.) If you say that something like Freudian psychoanalytic theory sits on the borderline, I shall not be worried. I know the difference between men and women, even though the existence of hermaphrodites messes up the boundaries.

Two more points and I am done with this section. First, I take it that the way I have characterized science—the appeal to law, the use of epistemic norms—holds for all science, whether or not one believes in some ultimate reductive unity where all sciences would become one. In particular, it holds for Darwinian evolutionary theory (which for me means that it holds for the only genuine evolutionary theory around). It is true that Darwinism is historical, in the sense that it deals with events of the past, but one must distinguish between history and the science thereof. The extinction of the dinosaurs was a unique historical event, but the scientific explanation of such an extinction makes reference to laws just like any other scientific explanation. I myself think that Darwinism is teleological (unlike the physical sciences), in that it uses the language of final causes and the metaphor of design. Hence, in this respect I am a nonreductionist, but I do not see that this has any bearing on the required satisfaction of the criteria given above.

Second, I am not myself a Believer—I used to be, but now I would describe myself as a skeptic (about atheism, too, I would add)—but I feel neither threatened by nor hostile to religion as such. I think that some religions are pretty daft, Mormonism for instance; some religions are rather sad, Jehovah's Witnesses for instance; and some are downright dangerous, Northern Ireland Protestantism, to choose from many. But those views are in a way beside the point. I can see good reasons why someone might be a fairly traditional Christian (which is the religion I know best). I do not think that such a person is necessarily a wimp or has given up the right to intellectual integrity. I do think that, by and large, religion tries to tackle issues not in the realm of science and that such issues are important. I take very seriously the claim that Hitler's vile actions were the product of original sin. I do not therefore—as has been claimed by people like Stephen Jay Gould—think that you can or should keep science and religion entirely separate.[6] If you are an evolutionist, you must reject Augustine's account of original sin—located as it is in the Genesis story of Adam and Eve and the forbidden fruit. At the least, you must work toward some more modern understanding.

What about the specific issues of miracles and design? I do not see that my position renders miracles logically impossible or denies that they might have happened in the past. If they did, they lie outside science, and your reason for believing in them will be nonscientific. You will simply say that at this point you are not playing the game of science. You are making the traditional distinction between the "order of nature" and the "order of grace." I am not sure that your position will be particularly reasonable here, but I am not sure that reason is all there is to existence. (I have a sneaking sympathy for Luther and Kierkegaard at this point. Phillip Johnson finds it astonishing that an evolutionist as eminent as J. B. S. Haldane could have argued so modestly that our evolutionarily acquired powers of reason and sense might mean that the world is queerer than we can know, but I think that—as always—Haldane was on to something.)

As far as design is concerned, I take it that if you are a Christian you do think that God designed the world, including us, and that this bears testament to his glory. I have no problem with that. What worries me is when people start inferring God from the design. There are massive theological problems, the theodicy problem in particular. There are also scientific/philosophical problems. I am not an expert on physics, so I cannot speak authoritatively to the anthropic principle, but even if you allow that you cannot jiggle our laws of nature, I am not sure why that rules out other configurations. Rational numbers do not exhaust the range of natural numbers, but there is still an infinite number of them. Which being so, the fact that we have hit on one of an infinite number of possibilities seems a lot less impressive than that we have hit on the only possible one. In any case, as Hume pointed out, if things did not work and allow life, we would not be around to worry about them.

What really worries me is when people start putting up religion—design in particular—as a rival to science, which I think the New Creationists are doing. Quite apart from the scientific arguments that can be brought against this gambit—I and others have dealt with these matters elsewhere at length—history alone shows that this is a losing game for religion. And it is not necessary. You can have a good religion within the bounds of science.

To say that this is disproven by the fact that most scientists are not religious seems to me to take, at a minimum, a crude or ignorant view of history. The nineteenth century shows that scientists had to define and establish themselves against the forces of the religious (not religion as such). I would have been right there with Thomas Henry Huxley when he had to face William Wilberforce, the smarmy bishop of Oxford. Had history been otherwise, had the Church not been so determined to hold to power and privilege, the present might be otherwise. In any case, the real threat to traditional religion came from within, from things like the deconstructive power of Higher Criticism, rather than from without, from things like science. I would like to know how many members of university English departments today are religious. Yet I know that the hostility to science to be found in those quarters makes creationists look like boosters.

I might add, incidentally, that I am not convinced when people like Phillip Johnson protest that their appeal to design does not put them in competition with science because their position does not require an appeal to the supernatural, to the miraculous: Design and choice (although standing outside the causal nexus) are, thanks to us humans, already a commonplace in this world of ours. On the one hand, I am not convinced that we humans are outside the causal nexus. At the very least, I would follow Immanuel Kant in arguing that although we humans may be noumenally free, at the phenomenal level we are causally bound. On the other hand, I would question whether the Designer of the New Creationist is truly analogous to the human designer. If I design a table, I am part of this world. If the Designer designs a cell, then that Designer must at some level be intervening in the world's natural processes. At one point in time, you have uncoordinated bits and pieces; at a succeeding point you have an integrated functioning entity, and laws did not do it. Sounds like miracles to me. Or else you have to say that there was no supernatural occurrence (akin to the virgin conception of Jesus), in which case you are putting design one step back, which makes it all nonthreatening to the scientific commitment to a law-bound universe.

Science and Values

Move on now to the question of science and values. I am glad that my critics have picked up on my concern with values in science—with values in evolutionary biology in particular—recognizing that this concern is a challenge to the kind of epistemic stance I take on the nature of science and its distinction from nonscience. I am glad also that my critics appreciate that I have been working extensively on these issues for the past two decades—

since Arkansas in fact—although the republication of my *The Darwinian Revolution: Science Red in Tooth and Claw* reminds me that my concerns go back much farther, to when I first entered the profession in the 1960s. Let me tell you what I have found and what I now believe. (As I have said, I am an evolutionist, so my ideas develop. I am glad to say that detailed archival study has taught me things I did not know, and so although I certainly see a continuity with my self of two decades ago, I am supremely unconcerned if you say that not everything then was as it is now.)

I am not an "evolutionary epistemologist" of the kind that sees a direct analogy between the development of science and the development of organisms. I think that science has a direction that evolution does not.[7] But I do see science as evolving in a continuous fashion; I am not a follower of Thomas Kuhn in thinking that you get sharp breaks. I think that science— let me now restrict myself to evolutionary science—starts in a juvenile state (I would speak of it as a pseudoscience), which is not very epistemic, and at that point it is full of (and exists for and is justified by) social and cultural values. The early evolutionism of men like Erasmus Darwin and Jean Baptiste de Lamarck was full of social values, particularly the promotion and praise of progress—social progress in the social world and biological progress in the biological world: "Monad to man" as they used to call it and as I called my big book on the subject.[8]

Science matures, however, and what happens is that it becomes much more epistemic, as scientists work and discover and experiment and so forth. This happened to evolutionary theory, particularly thanks to Darwin and his successors. The theory of the *Origin of Species,* for instance, was built around a unification, a consilience: Accept evolution through natural selection and you will have an explanation of behavior, biogeography, paleontology, morphology, embryology, taxonomy, and much more. After Darwin, evolutionary thought was jacked right up—it was no longer a pseudoscience. And the improvement has continued down to today, where you find that the kind of work published in journals like *Evolution* is as epistemic—as professional or mature—as you could want.

But what about the values—meaning here the social or cultural values rather than the epistemic values? Where do they stand in the history of the theorizing, and most particularly where do they stand today? At one point I thought (following suggestions by McMullin) that, as science matures, the epistemic values expel the nonepistemic or cultural. No one today accepts Hitler's racial beliefs for the simple reason that they are incompatible with modern genetics. Evolutionary theory would seem to be a paradigmatic confirmation of this view of science. First Darwin's natural selection—resting as it does on the relativistic claim that what survives is what survives and that a winner at one time could be a loser at another—kills off the hope of progress, and then Mendel's genetics—which denies that the raw stuff, the mutations, of evolution are directed—hammers down the lid to the coffin.

Boy, did I get a surprise when I went to the sources. I found that Darwin was a progressionist, that post-Darwinians were progressionists, and that the coming of Mendel to evolutionary studies only confirmed the belief! If you doubt me, look at the writings of Sir Ronald Fisher or Theodosius Dobzhansky. (Better still, buy my most recent books and see what I have to say.)[9] More than this, I found that people—the chief force being Darwin's bulldog, Thomas Henry Huxley, together with his close chum, Herbert Spencer—positively pushed progress and other social values. They made of evolution a popular science, a science of the public domain, and they found their support in the temples of science, the new museums that were then being built. Both the British Museum (Natural History) and the American Museum of Natural History were headed by Huxley students. Far from the elimination of values from evolutionism, they were kept in and paraded. Evolution was even promoted as a secular religion, an alternative to Christianity both intellectually and socially. (To the sensitive reader, the clash between progress and the Christian doctrine of Providence will not go unnoticed. This is the real nub of the science/religion conflict, not Genesis.)

But there is more to the story than that. Evolution today—the evolution of the professional—is no longer a social-value-impregnated, secular substitute for Christianity. Around the 1930s, men like Fisher and Dobzhansky started to professionalize evolutionary thought. They realized that all of these social values were antithetical to their aims. So they then produced a purified evolutionism that was epistemic and social-value free. And this is what we have today. Or rather, this is one part of what we have today. Fisher and Dobzhansky still had their social values, and they still liked them in evolution. So they split the subject into two, the professional (which was new) and the popular (which was old). During the week, as it were, they did the professional—epistemic and value free—and on the weekend they did the popular. Or they got popularizers to work on the popular all week long, which is what we have to this day. We have popularizers like Gould and Dawkins. We have professionals like sociobiologist Geoff Parker and the late paleontologist Jack Sepkoski (if you say you have never heard of them, that proves my point). Then we have some people, my good friend Edward O. Wilson the best of the lot, who can be as professional as you like (look, for instance, at the work he did on island biogeography with the late Robert MacArthur) and who are also terrific at writing at the popular level. Here, Wilson presents evolutionary thinking that is absolutely dripping with social values. He is two Pulitzer Prizes down and still going.

So you see that ultimately I can have my cake and eat it, too. Darwinism is as epistemic as you like. It can keep its scientific head up proudly in any court of the land, even Arkansas (or as I write, Kansas). And Darwinism is as value laden as a religion. Indeed, it is a religion of a secular kind. Just look at Wilson's *On Human Nature* if you doubt me.[10]

Science and Education

So, finally, what about the classroom? I grew up in a country that had compulsory religious education; I live in a province that has a government-supported Catholic school system; and I have just (again) sent my kids off to a private, church-affiliated school. So you are not going to get much of a rise out of me if you start pushing for religious education. If everyone got taught by the Church of England I would be quite happy. (I grew up as a Quaker, but I will settle for the state system.) With Thomas Henry Huxley, I much regret the fact that today's schoolchildren do not know their Bible—and by the Bible I mean the King James Version. Tears well to my eyes when Ruth clings to Naomi, and I still envy the aged David his method of keeping warm in bed.

I understand, however, and respect the American system of keeping separate church and state, and if this is your way—and no bad way at that—then so be it. But so be it, both from the creationist and the evolutionist side. Darwinism as professional science is good-quality epistemic science and should be taught in biology classes. Dobzhansky was right: Nothing in biology makes sense except in the light of evolution. But remember, science and only science should be taught in science classes. Hence, on the one hand, it is quite wrong to teach creationism—call it intelligent design or what you will—in science classrooms. Keep it out and put it in the comparative religion or history classes.

I have great fun (meaning a good teaching experience) with Michael Behe and Phillip Johnson in my philosophy of science class. (I very much hope the U. S. Constitution does not stop things like that.) On the other hand, it is quite wrong to teach evolution as religion—call it "Darwin's dangerous idea" or what you will—in science classrooms. Keep it out and in the comparative religion or history classes. I have great fun (meaning a good teaching experience) with Richard Dawkins and Dan Dennett in my philosophy of science class. (I very much hope the Constitution does not stop things like that, either.)

So here I stand. You can separate out science from nonscience. Professional Darwinism is science, and intelligent design theory is not. Popular Darwinism is value impregnated. It is a form of secular religion in many respects. Professional Darwinism is not value impregnated. It is straight science. Evolution should be taught in biology classes, and intelligent design theory should not be taught. But science and only science should be taught in science classes, and popular Darwinism has no more place there than creationism.

Notes

1. J. A. Campbell, "Intelligent Design, Darwinism, and the Philosophy of Public Education," *Rhetoric and Public Affairs* 1, no. 1 (1998): 491.
2. E. McMullin, "Values in Science," in *PSA 1982*, ed. P. D. Asquith and T. Nickles (East Lansing, Mich.: Philosophy of Science Association, 1983), 3–28.
3. W. Whewell, *The History of the Inductive Sciences*, 3 vols. (London: Parker, 1837); W. Whewell, *The Philosophy of the Inductive Sciences*, 2 vols. (London: Parker, 1840).
4. A. Plantinga, "Methodological Naturalism," *Perspectives on Science and Christian Faith* 49, no. 3 (1997): 143–54.
5. J. C. Whitcomb and H. M. Morris, *The Genesis Flood: The Biblical Record and Its Scientific Implications* (Philadelphia: Presbyterian and Reformed Publishing, 1961).
6. S. J. Gould, *Rocks of Ages* (New York: W. W. Norton, 1999).
7. M. Ruse, 1998. *Taking Darwin Seriously: A Naturalistic Approach to Philosophy*, 2nd ed. (Buffalo, N.Y.: Prometheus, 1998).
8. M. Ruse, *Monad to Man: The Concept of Progress in Evolutionary Biology* (Cambridge: Harvard University Press, 1996).
9. M. Ruse, *The Darwinian Revolution: Science Red in Tooth and Claw* (Chicago: University of Chicago Press, [1979] 1999); M. Ruse, *Mystery*

of Mysteries: Is Evolution a Social Construction? (Cambridge: Harvard University Press, 1999); M. Ruse, *Can a Darwinian Be a Christian? The Relationship Between Science and Religion* (Cambridge: Cambridge University Press, 2000).

10. E. O. Wilson, *On Human Nature* (Cambridge: Harvard University Press, 1978).

Rhetorical Arguments and Scientific Arguments: Do My Children Have to Listen to More Arguments against Evolution?

Eugene Garver

❈ ❈ ❈

Intelligent design (ID) is a rhetorician's dream. Any scientific theory is part of a debate, not a revelation, and it is bad science, bad pedagogy, and bad politics to pretend otherwise. Reconstitute biology as a debate; see the rhetorical and persuasive and controversial nature of all thinking, all learning, all discussion; and many good things will follow. The clash between ID and evolution seems to be a dispute between incommensurables, so that if you think that evolution is bad science or antireligious, you will support ID; if you think that ID is bad science and is trying to eat its cake and have it, too, concerning whether it is religious, you will be unsympathetic.

Rhetorically, incommensurability appears as mutual suspicion. Each side sees itself as embattled by powerful enemies who don't play fair. Rhetoric, if not finding common ground, offers values and standards that are not themselves either scientific or religious and so not question-begging. ID is rhetorically attractive and promises many benefits. Teaching and learning will be improved, since students will come to see science as an activity, not an incontrovertible revelation. Moreover, science itself will be the better for it since, there, too, open-mindedness will be the norm, more hypotheses will flourish, and claims will be judged on the evidence instead of on metaphysical dogmas. Finally, the quality of public debate and democratic deliberation will be improved, as open-minded understanding replaces the clash of incommensurable ideologies. The wisdom and eloquence of John Stuart Mill's *On Liberty* will come alive:

> The greatest orator, save one, of antiquity, has left it on record that he always studied his adversary's case with as great, if not still greater, intensity than even his own. What Cicero practiced as the means of forensic success requires to be imitated by all who study any subject to arrive at the truth. He who knows only his own side of the case knows little of that. His reasons may be good, and no one may have been able to refute them. But if he is equally unable to refute the reasons on the opposite side, if he does not so much as know what they are, he has no ground for preferring either opinion. . . . So essential is this discipline [of attending equally and impartially to both sides and endeavoring to see the reasons of both in the strongest light] to a real understanding of moral and human subjects that, if opponents of all-important truths do not exist, it is indispensable to imagine them and supply them with the strongest arguments which the most skillful devil's advocate can conjure up.[1]

I believe that the project of making science more rhetorical, through consideration of ID, promises little benefit for education and less still for science and democracy. Unless, that is, one already assumes that ID has scientific and religious value—which begs the question.

I

The thesis that a confrontation between ID and evolutionary biology, or neo-Darwinism, or whatever it should be called, will make things better has its greatest plausibility in education. There it looks as though one could support the teaching of ID without thereby endorsing it as science or as religion. Some of the contributors to this volume testify to how lively their teaching becomes as students regard science as a form of debate.

Campbell offers an even better reason. Darwin himself developed his theory of evolution through a running debate between arguments from design and the alternatives he could imagine. Therefore, students will best learn evolution from a confrontation with those arguments from design. This further argument of Campbell's seems to me crucial. Otherwise, why not teach biology through a confrontation with Lysenko or Lamarck, which, religious feelings aside, are as intuitive as ID where Darwin is counterintuitive and so could sharpen the understanding of Darwin's innovations through these contrasts with beliefs that are as consonant with those of uneducated students as are beliefs about design. But I don't see anyone advocating the use of Lysenko or Lamarck to teach evolution by contrast.

But Campbell's narrative leads to several possibilities for teaching, and not only to the proposal to design ID alongside evolution. Rhetoric and revelation are not the only alternatives; evolution need not be taught as either revelation or as one half of a debate. One could teach evolution by teaching the conflict between it and ID, as Campbell suggests. One could teach it by teaching the *Origin of Species* and then showing how accounts of evolution have developed since Darwin. If one wants to teach science as a human activity, to trace the historical development of the things we now hold is often a good strategy. Or one could simply teach it dogmatically but intelligently, the option that seems not to have been considered here. Earlier in the paragraph that I quoted, Mill says: "Even in natural philosophy, there is always some other explanation possible of the same facts; some geocentric theory instead of heliocentric, some phlogiston instead of oxygen; and it has to be shown why that other theory cannot be the true one; and until this is shown, and until we know how it is shown, we do not understand the grounds of our opinion."[2]

Someone who has really learned and understood the Newtonian account of why the earth revolves around the sun and not the sun around the earth will have no trouble understanding why geocentrism must be false. A student who never considered geocentrism as an alternative is at no disadvantage. Fully understanding the current conception of evolution should include seeing why ID is false without having to consider ID itself. There is no reason to think that the teaching of science would be improved if heliocentrism were taught as an alternative to geocentrism or phlogiston theory as an alternative explanation to modern chemistry. Teaching ID then remains one strategic option among others. There are alternatives beyond either dogmatism or rhetorical debate.

If ID should be taught as an alternative to evolution in a stronger sense than geocentrism as a teaching device to make the meaning, the evidence for and against, of heliocentrism clearer, or phlogiston to bring out the strengths and weaknesses of oxygen, it is not for pedagogical reasons but because people think that ID itself has scientific or religious, not pedagogical, claims on us. The pedagogical appeal is thus a way of indirectly satisfying some nonpedagogical desire, whether scientific or religious.

What I find interesting in the discussion of ID is how easily it is assumed that if it is good to teach ID as an alternative to evolution, then the pedagogical situation is a good model both for how science should function and how democracy should work. In this case at least, I find no reason to believe those further conclusions. Even if in some circumstances to teach science rhetorically would be a good thing, there is little reason to think that either science or democracy would be improved by treating evolution and ID as alternatives. I believe that the implications of good teaching practice for both science and democracy are far more limited than the devotees of ID are maintaining.

II

I do not join in the hope that a debate between evolution and ID will improve scientific practice by making biologists more open-minded and democratic. When judged by the standards of the philosophy of science, there is good reason to be upset by the low level of the public statements of biologists and philosophers of science in the evolution/creationism debates. There is no reason to be disappointed or surprised, though. Public debate requires different skills, and different ways of reasoning, from scientific inquiry, unless one accepts the more imperialistic claims of rhetoric as a universal method. Public debate, whether in law courts or school boards, is rhetorical rather than scientific. Just as Aristotle says that the physician speaking for a crowd needs to argue rhetorically rather than medically, so the biologist or philosopher of science arguing about how to teach biology is in a rhetorical, not a scientific or a philosophical, situation. Therefore I do not see the performance of scientists and philosophers of science in these public forums as any evidence at all of their deficiency qua scientists and philosophers of science. Nor is there any reason to think that if they were better rhetoricians they would be better scientists or philosophers of science.

Evolutionary biology contains within itself competing hypotheses at every turn, and one of the unfortunate consequences of viewing it as one side in a debate is that it is treated, by partisans on both sides, as though it were a united front. This is no reason to be optimistic that biology itself will progress more if scientists divert attention to a confrontation with ID, unless, to beg the question, there are scientific merits to ID itself and not merely its predicted effects on biology or biologists. Ignoring the internal diversity of evolutionary biology is a normal rhetorical debating procedure. I am concerned that a confrontation between evolutionary biology and ID will *reduce* the internal diversity of biology itself by making scientists close ranks against an invader. It is one thing for scientists to act as rhetoricians in public debate, but it would not improve science for rhetoric to invade scientific practice itself.

For example, I see nothing wrong with biologists in public using the fact that creationism is not falsifiable as a grounds for dismissing its scientific pretensions. They are behaving as good rhetoricians. If I argue that creationism is not a science because it is not falsifiable, it does not follow that I am committed to falsifiability as a universal criterion for demarcating science. Why can't I say that creationism is not a science because it is not falsifiable but that in other cases something that is not falsifiable should be admitted to be science? Not all rhetorical major premises are universal. "I regard you as my friend because . . ." It doesn't follow that anyone else fitting that description would be or ought to be my friend. I think that so-and-so should be fired because of a weak publication record. Does it follow that I am committed to firing anyone with a comparable record? I deny it in all these cases.

Of course, I would then have to argue why falsifiability is the appropriate criterion for rejecting creationism even though it is not a universally applicable or relevant criterion. We make such arguments all the time in rhetoric. For example, given that creationism defines itself in opposition to evolutionary biology—which might itself be grounds for denying that it is a science; sciences don't define themselves by such opposition—its circumstances of affirmation might make falsification an especially relevant criterion for deciding whether it's a science. The reasons that creationism is not falsifiable might be especially damning and might not apply to scientific theories that are not falsifiable.

In the early battle over creationism, sometimes creationism was called bad science and sometimes not science at all. I am reminded of Aristotle's brief distinction between the rhetorician, who relies on argument, and the sophist, who will do anything to win. "Sophistry is not a matter of ability (*dynamis*) but of deliberate choice (*prohairesis*)." That is, sciences and arts succeed when their operations are explained through the methods and principles of that science or art, whereas failures consist in letting external desires and choices determine how one operates. It is not that sciences and arts have no external motivations and purposes but that those factors are not determinative. Creationism failed because it would do anything to win, and its ignoring of challenging evidence was in aid of winning, not of knowledge or of rational persuasion. Aristotle's distinction of rhetorician and sophist is so brief because there is no demarcation criterion. Judgments about whether one is arguing or merely *using* argument to win are always judgments in context and always judgments by a potential partisan, not the neutral referee that a demarcation criterion requires.

Paul Goodman's account of bad art makes sense here as an explanation for what is bad science, or not science at all: "The condition that seems essential to judge a work as 'bad' is . . . not incomprehension but comprehending only too well, seeing *through* it, we perceive enough formal combination to account for the parts that the poet has assembled and failed to integrate, and we understand the extrinsic social and psychological pressures that have made him attempt much and achieve little."[3]

The reasons creationism is not falsifiable are reasons that we can see through, whereas truly scientific theories might for good reason not be falsifiable. The same applies to other demarcation criteria, such as tentativeness and coherence.

Similarly, scientists might have religious or antireligious motivations, but only if those motives explain the activity is the activity thereby tainted. To attack evolution by observing that most scientists are atheists is completely irrelevant unless one can show that atheism diverts them from the avowed internal norms of science. Talk about "materialism" isn't any better, unless it can be shown to distort scientific practice.

This defense of the rhetoric of scientists in public debate shows that scientists, acting as rhetoricians and not as scientists, rightly respond to rhetorical and not to scientific standards of argument. I offer the defense to suggest that scientific and rhetorical standards of argument are distinct and that therefore the hope that as scientists become better rhetoricians they will become better scientists is a misguided hope.[4] I also think that there is no evidence that public debates about evolution versus creationism or evolution versus ID will make for a more informed, intelligent, or active public.

To quote Mill again, "As mankind improve, the number of doctrines which are no longer disputed or doubted will be constantly on the increase; and the well-being of mankind may almost be measured by the number and gravity of the truths which have reached the point of being uncontested."[5] Naturally, opinions that are uncontested today may be contested when there is new evidence, but that is not a reason to hold them as less than uncontested today.

III

I have been arguing that there is no reason to think that if scientists become better rhetoricians they will become better scientists. Nor do I see any reason to think that it will improve democracy or democratic deliberation to present ID as an alternative to evolutionary theory. Consider this thought-experiment:

A recent public opinion survey showed that 75 percent of Americans believe that the United States is larger and more populous than China. Powerful groups oppose the attempts of so-called geographic experts to impose their opinions on schoolchildren. The geographic orthodoxy is not only unproved—has anyone really *counted* all those Chinese?—but it offends deeply held beliefs that are essential to the functioning of the United States as the greatest country on Earth. These so-called experts force our children to recite back what they have been told and tell our children that their own beliefs are merely subjective prejudices that have to be abandoned in the light of truth. If one needed evidence for the corrosive effects of these geographical opinions, one need only look at how un-American the majority of professional geographers are. First, they deny that the United States is the biggest and most populous of nations, and then most of them deny American exceptionalism in other ways. Some of them actually travel outside the United States!

How should geography teachers respond to this difference between what students are told by other sources and the lessons the teachers want to teach? The fact that most people are said not to "believe in evolution" or believe that China is larger and more populated than the United States has to be taken into consideration to modify one's teaching. There is a difference between teaching a subject on which students have no prior opinions and a subject on which they have been forcefully told something contrary to what the teacher is trying to get across. But taking those initial beliefs into account is not a reason to defer to them or even respect them. It is probably, although not necessarily, a bad idea to be dismissive or even confrontational about such beliefs. One's teaching strategy would be affected by why these beliefs are held—among other things, whether there is supposedly a religious grounding or motivation for them—how widely they are held, how politically powerful the opposition is, and all sorts of other variables that are relevant to teaching but have no necessary bearing on either science or democracy.

My analogy is a bad one if one thinks that evolutionary biology is not a secure science. Once again, there is a circularity here. If ID is good science, it deserves a place in democratic deliberation. Not, however, because of arguments about democracy, free speech, or the rights of scientists, teachers, students, or parents—but because of those scientific merits. Rhetorical argument cannot construct a neutral forum in which the merits of evolution and ID can be debated. There is no such neutral forum because those merits are a scientific question.[6]

My analogy is also a bad one if one thinks that beliefs that are religiously motivated warrant special deference. Once again, there is a circularity. ID is supposed to be superior to creationism because it is not a matter of teaching religion. But if so, its relation to religion—which its partisans rightly do not deny—is irrelevant to its place in education. Religious motivation does not disqualify it from being science or from being taught. But then the greater harmony between ID and many theological beliefs than between evolution and religion is irrelevant to its place in education.[7]

The religious partisans of ID have a rejoinder. To require something other than evolution in the schools has nothing to do with the truth of Christianity but with the fact that it is so widely believed. I cannot improve on Mill's own response to this argument. "In the present age, which has been described as 'destitute of faith, but terrified at skepticism'—in which people feel sure, not so much that their opinions are true as that they should not know what to do without them—the claims of an opinion to be protected from public attack are rested not so much on its truth as on its public importance."[8] Religion is a bulwark of democracy, much as are our beliefs about the greatness of America. If evolution corrodes the belief in religion, then it is dangerous and should be suppressed or at least countered with healthier views of the subject.

The point here, we are told, is not to drive evolution away but to put it in its place. There is the hope that if evolution were presented to the public, as well as to students, alongside alternatives, its truth would shine through. Here is what Mill had to say about such hopes: "The dictum that truth always triumphs over persecution is one of those pleasant falsehoods which men repeat after one another till they pass into commonplaces, but which all experience refutes."[9] Given the current circumstances of the debates about teaching evolution, including the history of creationist interventions, it seems to me that the probability that truth will emerge, in the classroom or in public, from a confrontation between evolution and ID is extremely low.[10]

Let me return to my starting point. The scientific and religious merits of ID aside, its proponents offer a rhetorical vision of education, of science, and of democracy. Students of rhetoric have a vested interest in the triumph of that vision. I have presented some reasons for doubting these imperial aspirations of rhetoric. The rhetorical and political, as opposed to the scientific, debate over ID has been posed as a question of whether spokespersons for ID should be heard or silenced, in the classroom, in the lab, and in public. I suggest that that is too low a standard. The real question is not whether they have a right to speak but whether I have any reason to listen. Whether we should listen is simply a function of whether or not it is good science.

Notes

1. John Stuart Mill, *On Liberty*, ed. Currin V. Shields (New York: Macmillan/Library of Liberal Arts, [1859] 1956), 44–46.
2. Ibid., 44.
3. Paul Goodman, *The Structure of Literature* (Chicago: University of Chicago Press, 1954), 11.
4. "You may take Martin Luther or Erasmus for your model, but you cannot play both roles at once; you may not carry a sword beneath a scholar's gown, leading flaming causes from a cloister, Luther cannot be domesticated in a university. You cannot raise a standard against oppression, or leap into the breach to relieve injustice, and still keep an open mind to every disconcerting fact, or an open ear to the cold voice of doubt. I am satisfied that a scholar who tries to combine these parts sells his birthright for a mess of pottage; that when the final count is made, it will be found that the impairment of his powers far outweighs any possible contribution to the causes he has espoused. If he is fit to serve his calling at all, it is only because he has learned not to serve any other, for his singleness of mind quickly evaporates in the fires of passion, however holy" (Learned Hand, "On Receiving an Honorary Degree," in *The Spirit of Liberty*, ed. Irving Dillard, 3rd ed. [New York: Knopf, 1960], 138, quoted in Philip B. Kurland, "The True Wisdom of the Bill of Rights," in *The Bill of Rights in the Modern State*, ed. Geoffrey R. Stone, Richard A. Epstein, and Cass R. Sunstein [Chicago: University of Chicago Press, 1992], 8).
5. Mill, *On Liberty*, 53.

6. A brief scholarly note: In the *Topics,* Aristotle says that one of the functions of dialectic is to test the principles of the sciences, since no science can prove its own principles. He says frustratingly little about that testing procedure, and so one might hope that dialectic and rhetoric can offer non-question-begging ways of deciding between competing scientific principles such as evolution and ID. I doubt it. I think that the purpose of dialectic is to firm up one's principles and not to discover them or decide among competitors. It would be an Aristotelian use of dialectic to show students the truth of heliocentrism through a refutation of geocentrism or of evolution through a refutation of creationism or ID, but not to pretend or hope to discover which competing hypothesis is true using dialectic. This is a vexed issue in Aristotelian scholarship, and I do not claim to settle the issue in a footnote, but again I think the pedagogical value of ID does not carry over into a scientific value.

7. Unless ID is a stalking-horse for teaching religion, and I do not think that that is all that it is, I am mystified as to the supposed relevance of the claims about how atheistic most biologists are, which I tried to capture in the last sentence of my parable. Celeste Michelle Condit writes: "Whether or not one finds the arguments in favor of intelligent design to be persuasive seems to be almost exclusively dependent on whether one already believes in an intelligent designer" ("The Rhetoric of Intelligent Design: Alternatives for Science and Religion," *Rhetoric and Public Affairs* 1 [1998]: 593).

8. Mill, *On Liberty,* 27.

9. Ibid., 34. For a longer expression of the same sense of the limitations of democracy, see James Madison, letter to Edmund Randolph (10 Jan. 1788), in Robert Rutland and William M. E. Rachal, eds., *The Papers of James Madison,* vol. 10 (Chicago: University of Chicago Press, 1977), 355–56: "Whatever respect may be due to the rights of private judgment, and no man feels more of it than I do, there can be no doubt that there are subjects to which the capacities of the bulk of mankind are unequal, and on which they must and will be governed by those with whom they happen to have acquaintance and confidence. The proposed Constitution is of this description. The great body of those who are both for & against it, must follow the judgment of others not their own. Had the Constitution been framed and recommended by an obscure individual, instead of a body possessing public respect and confidence, can not be a doubt, that altho' it would have stood in identical

words, it would have commanded little attention from most of those who now admire its wisdom. . . . I infer from these considerations that if a Government be ever adopted in America, it must result from a fortunate coincidence of leading opinions, and a general confidence of the people in those who may recommend it."

10. For this reason, I do not understand Depew's greater dislike for selfish gene theory than his distrust of creationism. Given the mutual suspicion and feeling of being persecuted between biologists and creationists, I see no hope for useful discussion. Selfish gene theory, however, is inside the biologists' tent and therefore can be confronted scientifically and productively.

Design? Yes! But Is It Intelligent?

William Provine

❈ ❈ ❈

Intelligent design (ID) theory can be easily stated in four easy steps:

1. Observation and analysis of natural phenomena, from astrophysics to microorganisms here on Earth to subatomic chemistry.
2. Discovery that a structure is "irreducibly complex."
3. First conclusion: An intelligent designer created the "irreducibly complex" structure.
4. Second conclusion: The intelligent designer is the researcher's preferred deity or purposive force. Advocates of ID theory generally deny this step (since such discrimination is impossible), but they do make the conclusion anyway at a personal level.

The ID advocates in this volume believe that the Christian God created the "irreducibly complex" structures, which cannot occur naturally. Thus, they earn the title ID creationists, to be distinguished from young-earth (YE) creationists, who believe that the Christian God created "irreducibly complex" biological structures but also that the earth has a history of not more than 10,000 years. YE creationists base this view on their reading of the Bible, fossil evidence, geological indications of a Great Flood, and many objections to evolutionary biology. Both groups of creationists believe strongly that aspects of biological organisms were supernaturally, intelligently designed and that the existence of the Christian God can be deduced from the existence of "irreducibly complex" biological structures. Taken together, these groups of creationists are only a drop in the bucket of worldwide believers in ID.

Who believes in ID theory (or a less academic-sounding version)? Five times so far, Gallup has polled public beliefs about evolution, in 1982 (corresponding to the centenary of Charles Darwin's death), 1991, 1993, 1997, and 1999.[1] The results are close, almost indistinguishable statistically. These are the figures for 1999:

47 percent believe that God created man pretty much in his present form at one time in the last 10,000 years or so.

40 percent believe that human beings have developed over millions of years from less advanced forms of life, but God guided this process.

9 percent believe that human beings have developed over millions of years from less advanced forms of life. God had no part in this process.

4 percent gave no opinion.

The percentage for the third question is too large. When you subtract the "naturalists" who believe in some ID from sources other than "God" (Tao and so forth), the true naturalists shrink to around 5 percent. About 90 percent choose ID. So it goes for the USA.

What about the rest of the world? Virtually every place will have a lower percentage of late-arrival humans but will have a correspondingly higher percentage in the "God guides the process" idea (as long as other purposive intelligences are included), thus barely changing the vast majority who believe in the intelligent design of biological organisms.

ID thinking, or perhaps more accurately the feeling of ID, is the foundation stone of belief in a deity or at least in some kind of intelligent designer. No other argument for the existence of a deity is more accessible or persuasive. Examination of biological organisms, including humans, leads immediately to belief that they are intelligently designed.

That belief is only the first step. All else flows more easily from the existing belief in an intelligent designer, including life after death, ultimate foundations for ethics, ultimate meaning in life, and human free will. It's an attractive ball of wax, for sure.

Jehovah's Witnesses stopped by yesterday when I was away in town. They know that I am an atheist, but we have a very warm relationship. They usually stop when they have something for me. This time it was the

January 22, 2000 issue of their journal, *Awake!,* the cover showing a young girl holding out her hand, a lovely butterfly perched on her outstretched finger, with the title, "Life: A Product of Design." The first two articles in the issue give more detailed accounts of ID—for example, the skin of crocodiles, spider webs, woodpeckers surviving smashing their bills on trees, hummingbird thermal efficiency, production of firefly lights, and many more.[2]

What had produced these remarkable adaptations? The question is answered in the section, "Behind the Design—A Designer." Building on the work and authority of Michael Behe (including four quotes from his *Darwin's Black Box*), *Awake!* concludes: "Is it not reasonable, therefore, that this Agent also has a purpose, one that includes humans? If so, what is that purpose? And can we learn more about our Designer himself?"[3]

In section three, "The Great Designer Revealed," we discover (surprise!) a picture with an open Bible and two pictures of wild parrots and a tropical fish, with the heading, "The Bible and the book of nature reveal the Great Designer."[4] Jehovah's Witnesses resoundingly reject biological evolution but do believe in an old earth, distinguishing themselves from YE creationists. *Awake!* is printed in twenty million copies and in eighty–three languages.

ID theorists live in a highly receptive world. Walking through New York City, or Hong Kong, or local villages and towns, anywhere almost, at least nine of ten people think that organisms are intelligently designed. Advocates of the "new" ID argument in this book are not bucking the tide of opinion, they are riding the crest of overwhelming, worldwide support.

The current ID creationists wish to distance themselves from the vastly larger branch of YE creationists, but to the outsider, the two groups have more in common than differences. Both are ID creationists, but one group believes in an older earth and the other in a young earth. YE creationists also think they pay more attention to the Bible; so do the ID creationists, though somewhat more liberally (to this observer). Perhaps more pertinent, YE creationists also believe they can do science perfectly well. YE creationists are not pleased with the "superiority" attitude of the ID creationists.

ID creationists also generally reject evolution by descent, entirely apart from natural selection. Phillip Johnson, the acknowledged leader of the movement, in his most biological book, *Darwin on Trial,* spends five chapters (4–8) arguing against evolution by descent.[5] He attacks whale and wing evolution by descent, giving the impression that the Christian God made whales and wings. The Christian God could very well have guided every bit of the entire evolutionary process, but ID creationists require their intelligent designer to make "mousetraps" along the way. William Dembski, Jonathan Wells, Paul Nelson, and others in this volume reject evolution by descent and argue that evolutionists have no good evidence for it. ID creationists and YE creationists are not so far apart.

Why do advocates of the ID argument constantly paint themselves as a beleaguered minority? Perhaps the opinions of philosophers, evolutionary biologists, religious methodological naturalists (who act like naturalists when doing science but disbelievers in naturalism in their true selves), writers of science textbooks at all grade levels, NOMA (S. J. Gould's "Non-Overlapping Magisteria") believers, and liberal arts faculty generally count for more to the ID theorist than mere overwhelming popular support.

A View on Intelligent Design

I am very sympathetic to those who believe in ID. The sense of loss experienced by friends and students, after concluding that ID of biological organisms is nonexistent, is deep and sometimes very difficult. When belief in ID dies away, the other associated beliefs become tenuous: life after death, and so forth. I always recommend to students taking an evolution course to guard carefully their views of ID in biological organisms. Give it up, and the slide to naturalism flows quickly.

ID theory, in its ID movement garb, is basically a version of the "God of the Gaps." The standard problem is that this position is constantly retreating, as the "irreducible" structures become understood as "reducible." Plato's *Timaeus* is a direct argument for intelligent design of the heavens, Earth, and biological organisms. The organization and harmony of the heavens or organisms necessitated the existence of an intelligent creator. Galileo, Kepler, Newton, and so many other famous scientists used the same basic argument. Between Plato and Newton, the argument from ID could operate over a huge variety of celestial phenomena and organisms.

The retreat since Newton's day of the obvious examples of ID is striking. Now, Michael Behe has to plumb the depths of biochemical structures in the cell to find "irreducibly complex" mousetraps. Even in the fullness of time, many of his examples will never be completely solved from a naturalist perspective, simply because the structures are buried in some two to three and a half billion years of evolutionary history. Likely stories will abound, however, suggesting naturalistic ways the evolution could have happened.

I regularly read the following quotation to students in my evolution course for nonmajors in biology:

> The real difficulty for the mechanistic theory is that we are forced, on the one hand, to postulate that the germ-plasm is a mechanism of enormous complexity and definiteness, and, on the other, that this mechanism, in spite of its absolute definiteness and complexity, can divide and combine with other similar mechanisms, and can do so to an absolutely indefinite extent without alteration of its structure. On the one hand, we have to postulate absolute definiteness of structure, and on the other hand absolute indefiniteness.[6]

I then ask the students what is this material, and they shout in unison, DNA! The next paragraph continues:

> There is no need to push the analysis further. The mechanistic theory of heredity is not merely unproven, it is impossible. It involves such absurdities that no intelligent person who has thoroughly realised its meaning and implications can continue to hold it.[7]

Students are amazed. Who is this? The author is John Scott Haldane, renowned physiologist and father of the famous evolutionist J. B. S. Haldane, writing in 1914.

Beginning with the notion of genes in the first decade of the twentieth century, many scientists thought that heredity must be "irreducible." The problem was that nucleic acids were too boring in structure to be the hereditary material, and proteins were basically unsuited. Yet this material basis of heredity had to replicate like crazy (the hereditary material had to be simple to do that) and then transfer very complex information to the organism (the hereditary material must be very complex indeed). For more than forty years, J. S. Haldane's view was common among scientists.

Heredity probably would have been on Michael Behe's list had he worked in 1914. DNA turned out to be the basis of the most materialistic, mechanical system of inheritance, exactly what J. S. Haldane envisioned but considered impossible. An "irreducibly complex" phenomenon of nature became the materialistic science of today.

Perhaps someone can explain to me why I cannot see ID in biological organisms. I looked and looked and found no ID, which contributed strongly to my move to atheism. Yet ID creationists can see ID where I see none. If supernatural design is clear, why can I not see it? The examples given in *Rhetoric and Public Affairs* (vol. 1, no. 4, the journal on which this book is based) seem general and weak except for Behe's biomolecular machines. Advocates of ID end up citing Behe over and over again. One might think that a volume on ID would have lots and lots of robust examples.

Dembski claims that the ID argument gives good suggestions for research. His best example is the apparently selectively neutral DNA, the vast majority of which codes for nothing. Following ID, the researcher should proceed on the assumption that all the DNA is actually functional (the Creator creates nothing useless?). All ID advocates must oppose Kimura's neutral mutation/random drift theory or even Tomoko Ohta's nearly neutral theory of evolution. I consider those two revolutionary giants to have made the greatest contribution to evolutionary biology since the work of Charles Darwin, even if in mammals the proportion of selectively neutral DNA moves from about 95 percent of the total to 80 percent.

Incidentally, Charles Darwin might help to provide examples for ID theorists. His book *On the Various Contrivances by which British and Foreign Orchids are Fertilised by Insects* is jammed with examples of flower structures ensuring that insects are dusted with pollen, and later stripped of it, in cross-fertilizing plants of the same species.[8] Not only do many of the "contrivances" smack of mousetraps, but the entire system of particular insects adapted to fertilize only one species of orchids appears to be an "irreducibly complex" mechanism. Indeed, Darwin chose to study these plants precisely because botanists had traditionally described them as flowing from the intelligence of a creator. Of course, Darwin did have explanations. He described the contrivances as "beautiful adaptations": "When this or that part has been spoken of as adapted for some special purpose, it must not be supposed that it was originally always formed for this sole purpose. The regular course of events seems to be, that a part which originally served for one purpose, becomes adapted by slow changes for widely different purposes."[9]

The ID movement needs an expert in orchid fertilization to counter Darwin's naturalistic explanations. That particular advocate of ID will also have to deal with zoologist Douglas Gill (of the University of Maryland), an expert on insect fertilization of orchids.

In 1998, Edward Larson and Larry Witham conducted a poll of the National Academy of Sciences (USA); 95 percent of the biologists responding disbelieved in any kind of designing deity. Of scores of evolutionists around the world in my sphere, the great majority do not believe in ID. I am right in there with them. We can see no sign whatever of ID in biological organisms or of intelligent direction in evolution. Design, yes. Intelligent design, no.

For lack of space, I will give only one example of why I reject ID (there are many more). The intelligent designer isn't all that intelligent. I asked Dave Raup and Jack Sepkopski to estimate for me how many species of vertebrates existed at the end of the Cretaceous, about 70 million years ago. They said about 50,000. And how many exist now, I asked. They said about 100,000. Then the crucial question: How many of the species of vertebrates 70 million years ago gave rise to all that exist now? They said probably less than 20, but at the outside, 25. Then of the 50,000 or so species, all but 25 went extinct. And in the interval of 70 million years, most of the species of vertebrates that came into existence also went extinct. The inventions of the alleged intelligent designer are poor survivors.

What about natural selection? Natural selection is not a mechanism, does no work, does not act, does not shape, does not cause anything. Biologists are very lax in their language, and so was Charles Darwin. Natural selection is the outcome of a very complex process that basically boils down to heredity, genetic variation, ecology, and demographics. What emerges we call natural selection. The process yields organisms with adaptations, which help them to survive and flourish. The process also virtually guarantees extinction when the environment changes sufficiently, which it does. The intelligent designer appears to have no concept of environmental change. The pattern of extinction, however, is precisely what one would expect of the process producing adaptations. If one gets to Carnegie Hall by "practice, man, practice," then one understands natural selection as "demographics, man, demographics," followed by extinction.

Methodological Naturalism

First, I must clarify terminology. A "metaphysical" naturalist thinks that everything detected by humans is natural, not supernatural. This I will call All-Weather (A-W) naturalism. A "methodological" naturalist thinks that when doing science, make like an A-W naturalist; but in prayer, moral decisions, belief in gods, and so forth, reversion to supernaturalism is reasonable. This view I will call Fair-Weather (F-W) naturalism. When the going gets tough (will I survive death?), F-W naturalists take refuge in the supernatural. A-W naturalists just have to grit their teeth and meet the tough issues head-on.

Religious scientists have a problem. Scientists today, unlike the scientists of more than 150 years ago, generally dislike any presence of the supernatural in the natural. So to be accepted, religious scientists must conduct science without any mention of God or of religion generally. To escape this problem, lots of religious scientists adopt F-W naturalism. In science, F-W and A-W naturalists are indistinguishable.

F-W naturalists do not wish to be caught in the embarrassing position of finding evidence for ID and then having to take it back. They are also happy to end the special pleading from ID in nature to any particular deity, an embarrassing issue for advocates of ID. An added advantage for F-W naturalists is escape from the designation "creationist." The "God of the Gaps" disappears as a problem. So the attractions of F-W naturalism are great.

These advantages must be weighed against the downside of F-W naturalism. The argument from ID disappears. Hmmm. To give up that argument, used by the vast majority of people around the world, is quite a blow to religious thinking.

Is there a way out? Sure. F-W naturalists eschew the ID argument. Science is science. But this person discovers a deity or purpose in some other way, for example reading a religious text such as the Bible or Chuang Tsu, having a personal experience with the deity, believing on the authority of others, or using a tortuous academic argument for the existence of the deity. F-W naturalists, once belief in the deity is established, can then mysteriously detect the deity's handiwork in nature. This rationalization is a perfect example of having cake and eating it, too. Having ID and not having ID hardly seem compatible.

Another major problem with F-W naturalism is that it is plain old A-W naturalism. Everything that A-W naturalism applies to is something subject to F-W naturalism. Problem: Did Mary give virgin birth to baby Jesus? The A-W naturalist responds, "No, mammals don't have virgin births, but if they did, the offspring would have to be the same sex. Let's do a paternity test and find who actually was the father." The F-W naturalist says exactly the same thing! Problem: How can we explain the existence of highly religious people? The A-W naturalist says, "Probably religious persons grew up hearing every day about the deity. They think the deity speaks to them, or perhaps humans have an inborn need for a deity, and so forth." Again, the F-W naturalist says the same thing.

Or perhaps the F-W naturalist argues that a few, or many, miracles occur. The A-W naturalist says then to the F-W naturalist, "Please take the naturalist out of your name because you don't even pretend to believe in naturalism any more." No wonder I sympathize with ID theorists. If they are right, then the belief of the vast majority of people in the world is justified. If the F-W naturalists are right, then the vast majority of people around the world have been bamboozled, including most of the important characters in the great religious texts. The advocates of ID have a sea of popular support, and advocates of F-W naturalism have the support of some thoughtful college students and professors.

Stephen Jay Gould's Principle of NOMA

Steve Gould and I were friends since we met at Ernst Mayr's conference on the evolutionary synthesis in May 1974. Gould lauded much of my work in the history of modern evolutionary biology. In turn, I have long admired his scientific work and have been plenty irritated at the National Academy of Sciences for taking so long to send him an invitation to join. He was president of the American Association for the Advancement of Science (AAAS). I am also certain that he had been far and away the most influential and widely known historian of science in the world—although most of my fellow historians of science don't much like that observation. His popular essays are an international treasure.

On the issue of science and religion, however, we were poles apart. Gould's 1999 book, *Rocks of Ages: Science and Religion in the Fullness of Life*, announced his principle of NOMA.[10] Science and religion each has its own sphere of influence, and they do not overlap. Or rather, science and religion should stay apart, and thus all warring of science and religion will stop, and we will all live together in greater harmony. Problems in the relationship of science and religion are almost always, according to Gould, caused by a violation of NOMA. Almost everyone agrees that greater harmony in society is a fine goal.

One of Gould's favorite targets was belief in the intelligent design of biological organisms. Advocates of ID theory are directly violating NOMA. Thus, in one fell swoop Gould dismissed the favored view of some 90 percent of the population of the earth. I obviously agree with Gould about intelligent design in organisms, but I think also that a real disagreement exists. Gould's solution was to push NOMA in hopes of reaching harmony. I suggest rising above the real disagreement and aiming for more harmonious social relationships.

The biggest problem is that NOMA allows only certain kinds of religion. Nearly all of the religions around the world would have to give up crucial parts of their belief systems. Gould said it's fine to believe that God created all creatures through the laws of science but this is basically deism, considered atheism in Isaac Newton's day.

Gould described his own personal view as "agnostic," appropriately conciliatory in pursuit of NOMA. Did he treat his own scientific theories in a similarly agnostic way? Did he say he is an agnostic about the concept of punctuated equilibria, one of his favorite theories? No, after reviewing the evidence for a long time, he thought his theory was a darned good first guess, a null hypothesis. You assume the theory, but as a good scientist, you are prepared to change your mind when contrary evidence is produced. That is why I consider agnosticism to be a cop-out. Atheism is a robust null hypothesis but should be given up when evidence of a deity is clear. Gould, Thomas Henry Huxley (inventor of the term), and Charles Darwin all billed themselves as agnostics, although they somehow avoid being agnostic about natural selection. Gould appeared to be saying that religion is fine as long as it can't be distinguished from atheism in the natural world. Yet for many years, Gould bashed creationists. He wrote an editorial in *Science* magazine, the official journal of the AAAS, excoriating the Kansas State Board of Education for its 1999 decision to eliminate macroevolution from state testing standards.

In *Rocks of Ages*, Gould is almost completely intolerant of YE creationists. NOMA, a principle that, according to Gould, is respectful, loving, simple, humane, and rational, leads him to dismiss and denigrate half of the population in the United States. Gould nominates Charles Darwin for the most sensitive advocate of NOMA. For a very long time, Gould fought against scientists who try to pull moral conclusions out of the natural world: "One of the saddest chapters in the entire history of science records the extensive misuse of data to support the supposed moral and social consequences of biological determinism, the claim that inequalities based on race, sex, or class cannot be altered because they reflect the innate and inferior genetic endowments of the disadvantaged."[11]

In the *Descent of Man and Selection in Relation to Sex*, however, Darwin wrote extensively about social and moral faculties of humans, as affected by the process of natural selection, and about hereditary mental differences between men and women and between human races.[12] Darwin was vastly more a hereditarian about human social behavior than E. O. Wilson, often the target of Gould's barbs. Darwin violated NOMA flagrantly, in ways

Gould found particularly distressing, but in his mind, Darwin was the champion of NOMA.

Steve and I remained good friends despite these genuine differences of views on science and religion. Perhaps most importantly, we agreed that we need a more humane, kindly society. He wanted to rid the problems by his principle of NOMA, and I prefer to recognize the conflicts of life and try to work with others to give us a more caring way of life.

Pedagogy in the Teaching of Evolution

In 1999, the Kansas State Board of Education decided to eliminate macroevolution from state exams and gave local school boards the right to decide if macroevolution would be taught in district schools. Evolutionists have a central processing email site, called EvolDir.[13] Job announcements constitute over 90 percent of the announcements. The Kansas State Board of Education's decision, however, elicited lots of derisive messages on EvolDir. I sent the following message to the list:

> Dear kind members of EvolDir,
>
>   The Kansas decision is a gift to the teaching of evolutionary biology. At last we have begun to talk about including all students in high school biology classes, instead of limiting discussion only to naturalistic evolution.
>
>   Of the USA population, nearly 50 percent are YE creationists. Of those who do profess belief in evolution by descent, the vast majority believe that God guided the process and that some version of "design theory" is true. Other countries have at least sizeable minorities with similar views. Can it really be our aim to prevent students with such views from participating honestly in the discussion of evolution in high school biology classes? Do we really believe that students can be convinced of evolution while prevented from speaking their concerns about it?
>
>   We already have complete control of the evolution content of mainstream high school biology textbooks. Teachers bar most students from honest discussion of evolution in class, with the encouragement of the National Academy of Sciences, the National Center for Science Education (our watchdog), and the American Civil Liberties Union.[14]
>
>   The result is that students consider evolution perhaps the most boring subject of the biology class. But the evolution section of the course could be the most exciting, the most fun, and the most stimulating.
>
>   "Teaching" creationism or design theory is wholly unnecessary, and perhaps illegal in the USA. Students will raise all their issues related to evolution if invited and not put down. Nothing is illegal about such discussion in

the USA and probably elsewhere. Students will never forget the evolution section of the course, and will think about it for years, maybe for a lifetime.

Not much support for my contribution appeared on EvolDir, but some rather negative comments appeared there and others sent privately. Indeed, many evolutionists were appalled by my suggestion, though some were supportive.

In this volume, Eugene Garver gives a cogent argument for not introducing ID or creationism in the evolution class. Perhaps he has taught an evolution class and finds that suppressing most of the students from participating is a good approach. If I thought teaching were as he envisions it, I would instantly give up teaching. Without student participation, introducing their own views and being prepared for intense (but personally supportive) criticism, teaching is vacuous. Imparting knowledge is a bore. Give the students a book.

I have taught evolution everywhere from middle school (for two years) to high school (nine high schools in upstate New York, some every year) to college level, to graduate level, and to adult summer university. In every case, students have greatly enjoyed sharing and criticizing ideas and evidence concerning evolution. Even in a class of 400 or so, weekly sections of no more than 20 give students an opportunity for serious discussion. I think we learn a lot about evolutionary biology, from Darwin to the cutting edge, and have lots of fun doing it. Everyone from every perspective is heartily invited to participate. The goal is not to fill the student's noggin with what is believed about evolutionary biology now, but to leave the student with an interest in evolution for life. Let me depict a composite high school class.

Biology class in a small high school starts the section on evolution. The teacher follows Garver's advice. Jehovah's Witnesses in the class know far more than any other students in the class about evolution, and they are sure it did not occur. Witnesses begin thinking about evolution at a very early age. They are ready to talk about evolution in the class. The teacher forces these students to shut up, just as the students suspected. They must, the teacher says, learn the evolution presented in the textbook, approved by scientists at the National Academy of Sciences. They can believe whatever they wish but must learn the approved science. The approved science is the dull, certain, evolutionary biology presented in the biology textbook. Another biology class misses the excitement that free discussion of evolution promotes. And the unfairness is laid bare.

Let's try a different approach. The teacher thinks that evolution is an important subject but thinks that everyone in the class should participate. All views presented are subject to comment and criticism. The Witnesses present their views against evolution. The evolutionists who believe that God guided the evolutionary process and the naturalistic students and others of various beliefs join in the discussion. The teacher then says: "Good discussion so far about evolution by descent. Now go to the computer room and look up evolution on the Web and get more information in preparation for tomorrow's discussion"—on natural selection, or the concept of species, or geographical distribution, or random genetic drift, or whatever topic the teacher wishes to address. Students are delighted because they are heard and are taken seriously. The creationist student can go home and tell Mom and Dad, "You should have seen how I put down the evolutionists today." No parents will be disappointed if their children are given the opportunity to speak and participate.

Allowing all students to participate defuses the explosive possibility of investigating evolution in high school classes. Not one parent of a high school student, over three decades, has objected to this approach. The classes are exciting, and the students and high school teachers send enthusiastic notes of thanks.

Discussing ways to prevent participation of students in any class, while privileging some, is so deeply unfair. Many states have suggestions for keeping creationists from the discussions in biology classes. The National Academy of Sciences booklet mentioned above has some good hints. Viewing half or more of your students as "the enemy" is weird.

Creationists will have to speak louder. I continue to support those who would like to have their voices heard in biology classes. I encourage the effort to limit the teaching of evolutionary biology until such time as evolutionists encourage a more inclusive participation of students. The very idea of the American Civil Liberties Union conspiring with evolutionary biologists to limit the free speech of the majority of the high school students in this country is grotesque.

Notes

1. See http://www.gallup.com/poll/releases/pr990830.asp.
2. "Copying Life's Marvelous Designs,"*Awake!*, 22 January 2000, 6–7; "Learning from Designs in Nature," *Awake!*, 22 January 2000, 8–9.
3. "Learning from Designs in Nature," *Awake!*, 22 January 2000, 8–9.

4. "The Great Designer Revealed," *Awake!*, 22 January 2000, 10–11.

5. Phillip E. Johnson, *Darwin on Trial* (Downers Grove, Ill.: InterVarsity Press, 1993).

6. J. S. Haldane, *Mechanism, Life and Personality: An Examination of the Mechanistic Theory of Life and Mind* (London: John Murray, 1914), 58.

7. Ibid.

8. Charles Darwin, *On the Various Contrivances by which British and Foreign Orchids are Fertilised by Insects, and on the Good Effects of Intercrossing,* 2d ed. (London: John Murray, 1862).

9. Ibid., 282.

10. Stephen Jay Gould, *Rocks of Ages : Science and Religion in the Fullness of Life* (New York : Ballantine Publishing Group, 1999).

11. Ibid., 166.

12. Charles Darwin, *The Descent of Man, and Selection in Relation to Sex.* (London: John Murray, 1871).

13. http://life.biology.mcmaster.ca/~brian/evoldir.html.

14. See "Teaching About Evolution and the Nature of Science" at http://www.nap.edu/readingroom/books/evolution98/ and my review at http://fp.bio.utk.edu/darwin/NAS_guidebook/provine_1.html.

Creation and Evolution:
A Modest Proposal

Alvin Plantinga

❖ ❖ ❖

Should creationism be taught in public schools? That is an excellent and much debated question. I want to begin, however, by asking a complementary question before returning to that one: Should evolution be taught in public schools?

I'm not asking whether it is legally permissible to teach evolution in public schools; that matter has been long settled. I'm asking instead whether it *should* be taught. Given that it is permissible, is it also the right thing to do?

Why should that even be a question? Daniel Dennett thinks it a foolish question: "Should evolution be taught in the schools?" he asks. Well, "Should arithmetic? Should history?" Isn't it utterly obvious that evolution should be taught in public schools? I don't think so; the answer isn't nearly so simple. But we must initially specify the question a bit more closely.

First, I am asking whether evolution should be taught in the public schools of a country like the United States, one that displays the pluralism and diversity of opinion our country presently displays. Second, I am asking whether evolution should be taught as the sober truth, rather than as, for example, the best current scientific hypothesis or what accords best or is most probable (epistemically probable) with respect to the appropriate scientific evidence base.

The question is whether evolution should be taught in the way arithmetic and chemistry and geography are taught—as the settled truth.

Still another need for specification: The term *evolution* can expand and contract on demand. It covers a multitude of sins, as some might put it. First, there is the idea that at least some evolution has occurred, that there have been changes in gene frequencies in populations. I suppose everyone accepts this, so we can put it to one side. Second, there is the claim that the earth is very old, billions of years old, and that life has been present on the earth for billions of years. Third, there is the progress thesis, as we humans like to think of it. Initially there were prokaryotes, then single-celled eukaryotes, then increasingly more complex forms of life of great diversity, achieving a contemporary maximum in us. Fourth, there is the claim of universal common ancestry, the claim that any two living things, you and the poison ivy in your backyard, for example, share a common ancestor. Fifth, there is what I will call "Darwinism," the thesis that the cause of the diversity of forms of life is natural selection working on a source of genetic variation like random genetic mutation. Sixth and finally, there is the idea that life itself arose by purely natural means, just by the workings of the laws of physics and chemistry on some set of initial conditions or just by the workings of those laws together with what supervenes on their workings. This thesis is part of the contemporary scientific picture of the origin of life, although at present all such accounts of the origin of life are at best enormously problematic.[1]

Since the first thesis is accepted by everyone, we can set it aside and use the term *evolution* or "the theory of evolution" to refer to the conjunction of the remaining five theses or occasionally to the conjunction of the first four of these.

So why is there a question as to whether evolution should be taught in public schools? And if there is such question, what sort of question is it? I believe there *is* a question here, a question of justice or fairness. First, our society is radically pluralistic. I am thinking in particular of the plurality of religious and quasi-religious views our citizenry displays. I say "quasi-religious" because I mean the term to cover not only religious belief, as in Christianity, Islam, Judaism, Hinduism, Buddhism, and the like, but also other deep ways of understanding ourselves and our world, other deep ways of interpreting ourselves and our world to ourselves.

Thus, consider philosophical naturalism, the idea that there is no such person as God or anything or anyone at all like God. On this use, naturalism is or can be a quasi-religious view. Following John Rawls, let's call beliefs of this sort "comprehensive" beliefs. Now for many, perhaps most, citizens, these comprehensive beliefs are of enormous importance; for some, they are the most important beliefs of all. It is natural for these citizens to want their children to be educated into what they take to be true and correct comprehensive beliefs. So it is a matter of great importance to them which comprehensive beliefs their children adopt, some even thinking that people's eternal welfare depends on their accepting what are true comprehensive beliefs.

Next, we must think about the purpose of public schools. That purpose is somehow determined by or supervenes upon the purposes of the citizens who support and employ the staff of those schools. It is as if we are all party to a sort of implicit contract: We recognize the need to train and educate our children, but we don't have the time or competence to do it individually. We therefore get together to hire teachers to help instruct and educate our children, and together we pay for this service with our taxes.

What should we tell these teachers to teach? Of course, all the citizens party to the contract would prefer that their children be educated into their own comprehensive beliefs—that is, they are to be taught that those comprehensive beliefs are the sober truth. But that isn't feasible, because of the plurality of comprehensive beliefs. It would clearly be unfair and unjust for the school, which we all support, to teach one set of religious beliefs as opposed to another, to teach that evangelical Christianity, for example, is the truth. That would be unfair to those citizens who are party to the contract and whose comprehensive beliefs—Judaism, naturalism, Islam, whatever— are incompatible with evangelical Christianity. Because the teacher can't teach all or even more than one of those conflicting sets of beliefs as the truth, it would therefore be unfair to select any particular one and teach that one as the truth. More generally, fairness dictates that no belief be taught as the settled truth that conflicts with the comprehensive beliefs of some group of citizens party to the contract.

We can describe this as what I'll call the basic right (BR). All of the citizens party to the contract have the right not to have comprehensive beliefs taught to their children that contradict their own comprehensive beliefs.

Because our society is a pluralistic society, there are many mutually inconsistent sets of comprehensive beliefs. So no particular set of comprehensive beliefs can be taught without infringing on the BR. It is therefore unfair and unjust to teach one religious belief as opposed to others in the schools. It is improper and unjust to teach, for example, Protestant beliefs as opposed to Catholic, or Christian as opposed to Jewish or Hindu, or religious beliefs as opposed to naturalism and atheism.

More generally, for any group of citizens who are party to the contract, it would be unfair for public schools to teach beliefs inconsistent with their religious or comprehensive beliefs—unfair because it would go against BR. Of course, BR is a prima facie right. It is at least possible that special circumstances could arise, perhaps in wartime, in which this right would be overridden by other desiderata, for example, national security. The majority might also insist on teaching the denial of certain comprehensive views, Nazism, for example, in which case the fair thing to do would be to exclude Nazis from the contract (and also exclude them from the tax liability).

It is also easy to see how an issue of justice or fairness can arise over teaching evolution. As Robert Pennock points out, many American Indian tribes, for example, "have origin stories that, on their face, are antithetical to evolutionary theory and other scientific findings."[2] Consider a public school in an American Indian village of this sort, one where many or most of the citizens hold and are deeply committed to comprehensive beliefs that are contradicted by contemporary evolutionary theory. Perhaps they believe that the first human beings were specially created by God a hundred miles or so from their village, some thousands of years ago. Would it be fair or just to teach their children, in this public school, that these religious accounts of human origins are false? Would it be right to teach their children that their ancestors emerged on the Serengeti plains more than a million years ago and that they were not specially created at all, but descended from earlier, nonhuman forms of life? Would it be just to teach their children accounts of human origins that contradict their religious accounts? We can see that this would be unfair and unjust. These citizens are party to the implicit contract by which public education is founded; they support and help finance these schools.

By virtue of BR, then, they have a right not to have their children taught, in public schools, denials of their cherished religious beliefs. If their children are taught denials of these beliefs, these citizens' rights are being violated. They are being violated just as surely as if their children were taught, for example, that their religion is merely superstition and that evangelical Christianity is the truth of the matter.

The fact is that there is a substantial segment of the population, at least in certain states and certain parts of our country, whose comprehensive beliefs are indeed contradicted by the theory of evolution. Fundamentalist Christian, orthodox Jewish, and Muslim parents, and quite a few of them, think the earth is very young, perhaps only 10,000 years old. This is not a casual opinion with them, as might be their opinion that there are mountains on the far side of the moon. It is a part of their comprehensive belief. It is one of their religious beliefs that the Bible (the Hebrew scriptures, or the Koran) contains the truth on all the matters on which it speaks, and on this matter what it says is that the earth is young.

Others believe that the first human beings were created specially by God, so the theory of universal common ancestry is false. We may disagree with their beliefs here or even think them irrational—but that doesn't change matters. Even if their beliefs are irrational from our point of view, BR still applies. They have the right to require that public schools not teach as settled truths beliefs that are incompatible with their comprehensive beliefs.[3]

So we have a clear prima facie question of justice here. These citizens are party to the implicit contract; they pay their taxes; they support these schools and send their children to them. But then they have a prima facie right to have their children taught, as settled fact, only what is consistent with their comprehensive beliefs. This means that it is unfair or unjust to teach evolution—universal common ancestry, for example—in public schools, at any rate where the comprehensive beliefs of a substantial segment of the population are incompatible with evolution.

In the same way, of course, it would be unjust to teach creationism as the settled truth. Both doctrines conflict with the comprehensive beliefs of some of the parties to the contract.

Now for a reply. Doesn't truth have any rights here? Perhaps BR is a prima facie right, so runs the reply, but this right is overridden by the demands of truth. Robert Pennock, for example, "takes it for granted that one of the goals of education is to provide students a true picture of the natural world we share," which seems fair enough. He also takes it for granted that evolutionary theory is true, but then he concludes that evolutionary theory ought to be taught in public schools. "Matters of empirical fact," he says, "are not appropriately decided by majority rule, nor is it unfair to teach what is true, even though many people don't want to hear it."[4] That seems to suggest that if a proposition is true, it is fair to teach it in public schools even if it contradicts the comprehensive beliefs of citizens who are party to the contract and who support the public schools.

Pennock's reasoning seems deeply flawed. Suppose Christianity is in fact true, as I believe it is. Would that mean that it is fair to teach it in public schools where most of the citizens who support those schools are not Christians and reject Christian comprehensive beliefs? I think not. That would be unfair, and the fact that the belief system in question is true would not override the unfairness. We can't sensibly insist that what is true can properly be taught *even* if it contradicts the comprehensive beliefs of others party to the contract. After all, they also believe that their comprehensive beliefs are true, and that is why they hold them.[5]

Other things Pennock says suggest a different objection. According to Stephen J. Gould, there is a realm of values, and there is a realm of fact. Religion and comprehensive beliefs occupy the realm of values (hence the expression, "religious values"), and science occupies the realm of fact. Hence, when things are done properly, there can be no conflict. There are no properly religious beliefs on matters of fact.

Of course, that suggestion is much too strong. Clearly, most religions make factual claims: that there is such a person as God, that the world was created, that Mohammed was God's prophet and spokesman.

A slightly (but only slightly) more nuanced view, one that seems to me to be suggested by Pennock, can be put as follows.[6] When it comes to matters of empirical fact (however precisely that phrase is to be understood), scientific consensus trumps comprehensive belief. Questions of the origin of human beings and of life are factual questions, he says, questions of empirical fact. The proper way to deal with them, then, is by science; it is a matter of trespass for someone in the name of religion to propose an answer to such factual questions. So this fact of trespass means that BR is overridden in some cases.

If a factual question is at issue, the way to deal with it is by science. If you happen to have mistaken opinions about algebra or prime numbers (perhaps it is part of your comprehensive belief, somehow, that there is a greatest prime), that is your problem. You can't require public schools to respect your comprehensive opinion here and refrain from demonstrating to your children that in fact there is no greatest prime. Citizens do not have the right to object, on the ground of religious or comprehensive beliefs, to any scientific teaching. When it comes to issues that are dealt with by science, the prima facie claims of BR are overridden, and it is entirely right to teach denials of comprehensive beliefs in public schools, if those comprehensive beliefs are in fact contrary to contemporary scientific consensus.

But again, that point of view seems entirely mistaken. First, why should we think that scientific consensus overrides BR? Perhaps because we think that science is our best bet with respect to discovering truth or the approximate truth on the subjects on which it speaks. But if it is the truth we want taught to our children, it's far from clear that current science should be treated with so much deference. We all know how often scientific opinion has changed over the years. There is little reason to think that now it has finally arrived at the unrevisable truth, so that its current proposals are like the claim that there is no greatest prime.

According to Bryan Appleyard, "At Harvard University in the 1880's John Trowbridge, head of the physics department, was telling his students that it was not worthwhile to major in physics, since all the very important discoveries in the subject had now been made. All that remained was a routine tidying up of loose ends, hardly a heroic task worthy of a Harvard graduate."[7] Twenty years later the same opinion seemed dominant. For example, in 1902 Albert Michelson, of Michelson-Morley fame, declared that "the most important fundamental laws and facts of physical science have all been discovered and these are now so firmly established that the possibility of their ever being supplanted on consequences of new discoveries is remote."[8]

We all know of scientific theories that once enjoyed consensus but are now discarded: caloric theories of heat, effluvial theories of electricity and magnetism, theories based on the existence of phlogiston, vital forces in physiology, theories of spontaneous generation of life, the luminiferous ether, and so on.

There is another and even more important consideration. Pennock, we are supposing, thinks that the way to approach questions of empirical fact is through science, not through religion. Thus, scientific consensus trumps religious or comprehensive belief in such a way that the prima facie requirements of BR are overridden, and it is fair to teach evolution as settled fact, even if it conflicts with the religious beliefs of some of the citizens party to that implicit contract.

Now consider Pennock's Claim (PC). The right way to answer questions of empirical fact—for example, questions about the origin of life, the age of the earth, whether human beings have evolved from earlier forms of life—is through science or by the scientific method.

Note, first, that PC is not, of course, itself a question of empirical fact. Science itself does not decide between PC and other possibilities—for

example, the claim that the right way to approach certain empirical questions is not by scientific inquiry but by consulting the Bible or the elders of
the tribe. The question of whether the scientific epistemic or evidential
base is the right way to settle these issues is not itself to be settled with respect to the scientific epistemic base; this dispute is philosophical or religious rather than scientific.

Note, second, that there are many others, of course, who do not share
Pennock's opinion: They do not accept PC. Indeed, there are so many others
that a proposition incompatible with the PC opinion is part of their religious
or comprehensive beliefs. Perhaps PC is part of Pennock's comprehensive
beliefs, but its denial is part of the comprehensive beliefs of others who are
party to the contract. Clearly, it would be unfair to act on PC in opposition
to the other comprehensive beliefs that are incompatible with it.

Suppose, in fact, that fundamentalists are right: that the correct way to
determine the age of the earth is by consulting Scripture under a certain
literal construal of early Genesis. Would it follow that it was right in public
schools to teach as the settled truth that the age of the earth is some 10,000
years or so? I think not, and the same goes with respect to PC. PC may be
true, or (more likely, in my opinion) it may be false. Either way, it is just
one comprehensive belief among others. It would be unfair to teach comprehensive beliefs that entailed the denial of PC, but by the same token, it
would also be unfair to teach PC.

What we have seen so far, therefore, is that it is improper, unfair, to
teach either creationism or evolution in the schools. That is so, at any rate,
for areas where a substantial proportion of the parents hold religious or
comprehensive beliefs incompatible with either. Then what *can* be taught,
in public schools, about this crucial topic of origins, a topic deeply connected with our sense of ourselves, our sense of where we come from,
what our prospects are, what is "the good" for us, and the like? If we can't
teach either creationism or evolutionism, what can we teach in public
schools?

Well, possibly nothing. One answer in a pluralistic society like ours is to
say that there is no fair way to teach anything about origins. Hence, public
schools ought not to teach anything on that subject. They should instead
stick to subjects where there isn't disagreement at the level of religious or
comprehensive beliefs. To do so would just be a reflection of a more general
difficulty in having public schools at all in a pluralistic society. Perhaps when
the citizens get together to found a system of education, what they discover
is that there is too much diversity of opinion to make it feasible.

But that is a counsel of despair. I think perhaps we can do better. We can see somewhat more deeply into this question by turning to a bit of epistemology. We have already noted that different people accept different religious or comprehensive beliefs. More generally, for each person, P, there is an epistemic base, EBP, with respect to which the probability or acceptability of proposed beliefs is to be evaluated. That epistemic base includes, first, P's current beliefs. Since some beliefs are held more strongly than others, it includes, second, an index of degree of belief. Some beliefs, further, are of a slightly different form, "probably P." An epistemic base also includes, third, prescriptions as to how to conduct inquiry, how to learn more about the world, under what conditions to change belief, and the like. And finally, an epistemic base includes comprehensive beliefs. These comprehensive beliefs are not, of course, frozen in stone. They are not impervious to argument and reasoning, nor are they irrational or held in an irrational way.

A person's epistemic base is not static, of course; it constantly changes under the pressure of experience, what we are told by others, and the like. An epistemic base can also undergo sudden and drastic revision, as in a religious conversion, for example. (A proper characterization of the notion of an epistemic base would take us far afield, requiring an entire paper on its own. But I think the basic idea is fairly clear.)

What parents want, presumably, is that their children be taught the truth—which, of course, they take to be what is in accord with their own epistemic base. What is in accord with their own epistemic base, of course, is not just the propositions they themselves happen to accept. I may know or believe that there are people who hold lots of beliefs I don't hold—for example, about mathematics. I may also believe that their beliefs, whatever they are, are true, or likely to be true, or more likely to be true than the beliefs I actually hold; and I may therefore want my children taught those beliefs, even though they are not parts of my own epistemic base and even though some may conflict with beliefs in my own epistemic base. These beliefs, we may say, are in accord with my epistemic base although not contained in it.

That situation can happen with respect to religious or comprehensive beliefs too. I may be an American Indian who holds that the tribal elders know the truth about important matters of origin or about whatever; I may then want my children taught what these elders believe, even if I don't myself know precisely what it is that they believe.

We must note next that science, S, has its own epistemic base. Its base is presumably not identical with that of any of the citizens, although it overlaps in complex ways with those of some of the citizens. It is not important here to say precisely what goes into the scientific epistemic base (EBS) or how it is related to those of the citizens. Presumably, logic goes into it, together with prescriptions about how to conduct various kinds of inquiry, together with a host of commonsense beliefs, together with a good bit of firmly established current science.

But it is important to note certain beliefs that do not go into EBS, at least with respect to science as currently practiced. Among these would be the belief that there is such a person as God, that God has created the world, and that God has created certain forms of life specially—human beings, perhaps, or the original forms of life, or, for that matter, sparrows and horses. That is because science commonly respects what is often called methodological naturalism, the policy of avoiding hypotheses that mention or refer to God or special acts on the part of God or other supernatural phenomena, or hypotheses whose only support is the Bible or some other alleged divine revelation. There is dispute as to whether science by its very nature requires methodological naturalism, and there is also dispute as to whether science has a nature. But as commonly practiced, science does seem to be associated with methodological naturalism.

That means that EBS does not include any propositions of the above sort. It is not entirely clear whether EBS includes the denials of some propositions about God or rather just fails to include these propositions. It is also worth noting that a person could think that EBS is the proper epistemic base from which to conduct scientific inquiry, even if her or his own epistemic base contains some of those propositions excluded from EBS by methodological naturalism. Indeed, some persons might hold that a given proposition is a good scientific hypothesis even if it conflicts with one of their comprehensive beliefs and is therefore, as they see it, false. Thus, someone might think that a given scientific hypothesis—Darwinism, for example—is in fact false but nevertheless a source of fertile and useful hypotheses.

To return to our subject, then. We cannot in fairness teach evolution as the settled truth in public schools in a pluralistic society like ours, and of course we can't in fairness teach creationism either. But there is something we can do: We can teach evolution conditionally. That is, we can teach, as the sober truth, that from the vantage point of EBS the most satisfactory hypothesis is the ancient earth thesis, or universal common ancestry, or Darwinism, or even some hypothesis entailing naturalistic origins. We can also distinguish between the likelihoods of these EBS hypotheses. The ancient earth thesis is very nearly certain on the EBS basis; universal common ancestry much less certain, but still a very good bet; Darwinism still less certain; and naturalistic origins, or rather any particular current theory of naturalistic origins, unlikely, at least with respect to the current EBS.

We still must note one further complication: Given plausible views about EBS, it might be that a hypothesis is the best scientific hypothesis from the point of view of EBS, even though it is not, from that point of view, more probable than not. That might be, first, just because there are several conflicting hypotheses in the field, all of which enjoy substantial probability with respect to EBS, but none of which enjoys a probability as great as 50 percent. Second, it might be that a conjecture is a fine, fertile hypothesis such that inquiry pursued under its aegis is fruitful and successful, even though the hypothesis in question is unlikely with respect to EBS. Many more questions arise about EBS, but there is no space to explore them here.

Now, consider the claim that evolution is the best hypothesis (the one most likely to be true) or even that it is much more likely than not with respect to EBS. That claim, I take it, will be compatible with everyone's religious and comprehensive beliefs. There would then be no objection from the point of view of fairness to teaching this *claim* as the settled truth—while refraining, of course, from teaching evolution itself as the settled truth. Perhaps this is something like what the California Superior Court had in mind in *Segraves v. California,* when it declared that "any speculative statements concerning origins, both in texts and in classes, should be presented conditionally, not dogmatically."[9]

The same would go for creationism. With respect to certain widely shared epistemic bases, the most likely or satisfactory hypothesis will be the claim that God created human beings specially or even the claim that the earth is only 10,000 years old. Of course, the public schools will not, under this proposal, teach that only one epistemic base—either that of evangelical Christianity, for example, or of scientific naturalism—is in fact the correct or right or true epistemic base. The question of which epistemic base is the correct one is not a question on which public schools should pronounce, at least in areas where there is relevant religious disagreement. What public schools should teach as the sober truth is what is in accord with all the relevant epistemic bases; that is what should be taught unconditionally.

To return to our original question, then: Should creationism be taught in public schools? Should evolution? The answer is in each case the same. No, neither should be taught unconditionally; but yes, each should be taught conditionally.[10]

Notes

1. Robert Shapiro, *Origins* (New York: Summit Books, 1986).
2. Robert Pennock, "Should Creationism Be Taught in the Public Schools?" (paper presented at the American Philosophical Association Eastern Division Meeting, Dec. 1998), 9.
3. A slightly different issue: There are still others who believe, as part of their comprehensive belief, that God created the world and humankind one way or another, where one possibility is that he did it through an evolutionary process. These parents may very well believe that it is possible (epistemically possible) that human beings are genealogically related to earlier forms of life but that this suggestion is far from certain. They may therefore quite properly resist having it taught as settled truth, on a par with arithmetic and the proposition that there has been an American Civil War.
4. Pennock, "Should Creationism Be Taught," 26, 19, 18.
5. In the same vein, Pennock also holds that "parents certainly don't have a right to demand that teachers teach what is false"("Should Creationism Be Taught," 17). But this, too, seems to me mistaken: Didn't parents at the end of the last century have the right to demand that science teachers teach, for example, Newtonian mechanics, even though it doesn't work at the subatomic level? They also had a right to demand that science teachers teach that there is such a thing as the luminiferous ether, although that is false, at least by our current lights. Earlier parents had a similar right to demand that science teachers teach the caloric theory of heat, that there is such a thing as phlogiston, that electricity is a kind of fluid, that the sun goes around the earth, and so on.
6. Pennock, "Should Creationism Be Taught," 18–19.
7. Bryan Appleyard, *Understanding the Present* (New York: Doubleday, 1992), 110.
8. Quoted in Hanbury Brown, *The Wisdom of Science: Its Relevance to Culture and Religion* (Cambridge: Cambridge University Press, 1986), 66.
9. Pennock, "Should Creationism Be Taught," 14.
10. I'm grateful to Tom Crisp, Marie Pannier, and David VanderLaan for comments and criticism. This essay was originally presented at the American Philosophical Association Eastern Division Meeting (Dec. 1998).

Thinking Pedagogically about Design

John Lyne

❖ ❖ ❖

As human beings, we need to understand our position vis-à-vis the rest of nature, in ways that will permit us to recognize, and feel, that the world is our "home."

Stephen Toulmin, *The Return to Cosmology*

Living a purposeful life within a nature that is both blind and accidental is something humankind has not had much experience with. We can always unearth some ancient Greek who had that intuition, but this is mainly a twentieth-century phenomenon. Neither Newton nor Jefferson knew anything of it—and, if the polls are to be believed, neither do most Americans.

The "pieties of old" fit social understandings to the ways of a purposeful creation. Twenty-first-century scientific pieties seem to require, in an about-face, that we affirm purposelessness as the ground both of the cosmos and the life within it. That abrupt shift must put great pressures on the old pieties. I am speaking of piety here in Kenneth Burke's sense, as the longing to conform to the sources of one's being. How can we be at home in a place so apparently unlike us?

We continue to be uneasy about the wedge Darwin drove between science and the general culture. By and large, it is the morally threatening specter of biological evolution that has given us the image of science versus religion. Physics, by contrast, has not in recent centuries run afoul of religion and in fact sometimes makes good use of theistic rhetoric. Parents rarely worry that their children will learn something in physics or chemistry class that countermands their own beliefs. And physics itself extends an occasional open hand. The gurus of contemporary physics, such as Hawking and Weinberg, speak of their quest to "read the mind of God" (even though one suspects that phrase is less a theistic sentiment than a tactical ploy to put the reader in the proper state of awe before the throne of physics). The closest run-in of physics with religion is the big bang, and any alert theist can with little difficulty meet that challenge by pushing the question of origins one step further into regress. In any case, a cultural accommodation at this level is easier, because everything at issue seems (albeit deceptively) less related to our lives. Evolution, by contrast, speaks unflatteringly about our ancestors—and confusingly about us. It gives us a biological home only by evicting our angel half.

Michael Behe hits the nail on the head in saying that narratives about origins have a way of working themselves into a social agenda. That is certainly the case with the narrative about the beginnings of life, just as it is with the narrative about the origins of the cosmos. The rhetoric of science at these outer edges of the knowable needs to be examined in light of this, not just to help us understand how truth is spoken to power on cosmic issues but to illuminate how our positioning within the universe sets us up for very local dramas. Our cosmic myths, when functioning well, simultaneously satisfy our need to understand and our need to feel that things are as they should be, which is to say, natural. They undergird both our being and our knowing. They also lend themselves to strategic rhetorical deployment, which may or may not serve us well. When narratives of origin change, something is afoot.

I share William Dembski's suspicion of the evolutionary psychologists who explain our social and moral lives with reference to suppositions about how our distant precursors got along in the world. Likewise for the gene-talkers who extrapolate a social code from the genetic code. It should give us pause that such discourse moves so easily along the tracks of a currently dominant rhetoric of science. These moves entail powerful reconfigurations of who we (the long-term *we*) thought we were—as if piety and impiety had traded places. As naturalizing strategies, they are actually less de-mythifying than they appear, however. This form of naturalization has something in common with an appeal to natural law—that is, the attempt to ground culture in something primordial. It is ironic in the present context because Dembski and perhaps the others want to move to natural law via the bridge of intelligent design. As with the evolutionists, the appeal to nature becomes the trump card in matters of social consequence.

John Campbell has campaigned vigorously to create a forum for the critical examination of Darwinism, especially as it pertains to the classroom. Some of the fallout has already reached my classroom. For those who want to train better arguers, intelligent design theory does us the service in the pedagogical setting of taking the creationist argument out of the religious context. It permits us to switch attention from belief (which students always feel entitled to) to reasoning (where some skill must be demonstrated). Moreover, it brings into focus just what underpins the scientific discourses in question. I've found that a good many advocates of Darwinist principles have little idea what they really are.

I teach an undergraduate course in rhetoric of science, and one of the topics I have enjoyed using is the evolution-creation debate. Last time around, I used as a focal point the controversy stirred up by recent proposed changes in the textbook definition of evolution endorsed by the National Association of Biology Teachers (NABT). The key changes would essentially have made purposelessness a part of the very definition of evolution. Those changes struck some as a move from indifference to the design option to a position of overt hostility to it. Partly in response to a rhetorically effective challenge by advocates of intelligent design and advice from scholars with solid philosophy of science and rhetoric of science credentials, such as Alvin Plantinga and Houston Smith, the NABT backed down. That was either a victory for open debate or a dangerous sign of things to come, depending on your perspective.

A group of my students selected this topic for their main project, so they read a variety of viewpoints on the issue. Starting out, I tried to gauge where each student came into the conversation, and it turned out that there was a good mix of attitudes toward the question, ranging from the committed evolutionism of the biology major to the equally committed resistance of the outspoken Catholic student. The rest seemed somewhere in between.

What I had observed when I discussed the issue in other pedagogical contexts was that few students seemed to understand why the whole issue was considered a big deal. Many, regardless of their own beliefs, had apparently made some sort of mental accommodation whereby the two positions did not become mutually exclusive. Qua science, evolution was valid; qua religion or personal belief, it was not. Render unto Darwin what is Darwin's and unto God what is God's. These students had evidently escaped the modernist notion that knowledge should be unified. Either that or they were repressing an unresolved conflict.

At the end of the term, an interesting thing had happened. All of the students working on this topic had reached a similar conclusion: that both evolutionists and creationists had something worthwhile to say. Very democratic. This might be partly a reflection of the etiquette of letting everyone have their say, but I think the inquiry left them all with a better understanding of both positions and their entailments.

Of course, paying lip service to both positions is easier if one has no problem embracing a contradiction or if one has a loose grasp on the theoretical difficulties. It is also easier if one's conception of evolution is Lamarckian, as I believe it is in the general culture. The common assumption is that evolution is a quest to get better, "more highly evolved." Insofar as evolution is seen as a teleological process, the intelligent design theorists would appear to have an initial rhetorical advantage.

Having said this, I hope I will give no offense in aligning the intelligent design argument with theism. In the absence of any other nominee, I assume that the designer is God, although I understand that this view in no way commits the advocate to the Bible or, for that matter, to any other religion. I think that the position does perforce imply a kind of theism, however, and thus it inherits the windy political problem of how it can be taught—and of giving meaningful secular content to the idea of a Designer. Since this matter is normally handled not by physics but by metaphysics or revelation, one senses that for some of its advocates the deus ex machina is already waiting in the wings, textually and historically explained. It need not be so.

In trying to get some purchase on the Designer as *explanans,* one gets the sense that the theory is perhaps less an answer to the cosmic riddle than an opening to a whole new set of questions. It is not clear which of those questions could legitimately be discussed in public schools. Does the idea of intelligent design presuppose purposiveness? Is it outside the universe or immanent within it? Do time and historical sequence apply to the operation of this intelligence? Is the designing agent subject to the law of unintended consequences? Is the designer in any sense personal or accessible? Parenthetically, at a moment when rhetoric and related fields have put the whole notion of agency under critique, I don't think it would be entirely frivolous to consider how many of the arguments about individual agency could be resituated in the context of the Prime Agency—the matter of intentionality or of discursive formations, for instance, and the ways that our bias toward individualism predisposes our understanding of such things.

"Why," Dembski asks, "shouldn't we want to admit design into science?" I think I understand what he is saying here. But as a cultural proposition, I think the truth is that we do want to admit design into science. Agency and purpose are so much a part of how we make narrative sense of things that it makes Darwinian evolution an uphill struggle in capturing the hearts and minds of the people. Lamarckianism comes more naturally. Darwinism remains counterintuitive and runs so much against the grain of everyday thought that we almost have to force ourselves into the discipline of seeing it. Because the scope of the human experience is mainly within one's own lifetime and because things are done for reasons within that experience, we have to think differently than we normally do in order to grasp a nonteleological formative process. The intelligent design theorists are inviting us to consider the possibility that we need not do so.

The cultural problem remains: How should we narrate a story of intelligence in such a way that it is at home in the universe? Humans figure intelligence on the scale of problem-solving and reading-comprehension, of analytic and constructive skills. We have problems to solve, and we apply our intelligence to solving them. What in this is instructive in conceptualizing an analogous designing intelligence? In the Bible, God made himself manifest by speaking from time to time and showing some personality. It is very difficult to narrate a story of an implementing intelligence without representing it anthropomorphically—just as the spark of human consciousness cannot easily be understood without reference to the primal fire. This poses a problem for the design theorists. They are reaching for a universe that is more like us, but the constraints of scientific language preclude compelling narratives of design.

There is a corresponding difficulty on the other side. If we are to understand our own creative natures, or so Burke says, we need a representative anecdote of pure creation. The proposed language of the NABT definition suggests a very different representative anecdote, one of randomness, lack of supervision, and (closely trailing) absence of meaning. It wants an absence to be part of the strictly scientific picture, even while casting a penumbra that predisposes things against God. It's as if Occam's razor had left a five o'clock shadow.

Charles S. Peirce opined that God was the intelligibility of the universe. In one sense the theory of intelligent design is a stab at finding intelligibility in the universe, one that may place undue emphasis on origins. The idea of transmitted information, in contrast to mere order, gets us to intelligibility, but its relationship to origins is unclear. The design/information argument, as I understand it, applies only at the point of origin, because thereafter the mechanisms of replication presumably take over. Or do they?

Stephen C. Meyer's argument suggests either that nothing has changed much since the Day of Design or that there is intelligent intervention all along the way, perhaps at points of mutation. It seems to me that the intelligent design writers have been obscure about where they stand on this. Some of the arguments go to the origin of life; others suggest that designing continues with the production of each new case of irreducible complexity.

Or is the point that all irreducible complexities were present at the beginning? It looks to me as if we have a basic issue to resolve if we are to contemplate intelligent design. Are we speaking only of remote origins or of an ongoing inflow of information throughout the evolutionary trajectory? If self-replicating life appeared on this planet as a result of intelligently manipulated information, then that information produced the dodo bird and the dinosaur as well as the human. Is it being suggested that all this was preordained? If not, we start down the slippery slope of historicization, even to the point of suggesting an intermittent schedule of divine intervention.

Stephen C. Meyer, Marcus Ross, Paul Nelson, and Paul Chien highlight the challenges to gradualism that have been mounted in the scientific literature. Arguments of this general form have long been a staple of the anti-Darwinist rhetoric, but theirs is at least updated and beyond the anecdotal. I do not know what size leaps may occur in evolution or what would suffice definitionally as a leap, but I do know that gradualism is a relative thing. Thousands of generations of some species can pass in a geological instant, for instance, and the fossil record would suggest great suddenness if there were substantial changes within that time span. Evolutionary theory acknowledges great variations in the tempo of evolution. So—the counsel of the rhetorician—we must be careful not to read gradual as an absolute rather than a relative term. The punctuated equilibrium advocates, such as Stephen Jay Gould, emphasize the relatively sudden breaks with continuity that seem indicated by the fossil record, but these antigradualists are far from the design camp (even though their antigradualism has made them targets for kidnapping, so to speak, by the creation scientists).

All of this is to say that it seems worthwhile to probe some of the uses of good and reliable terms like *gradualism* and *function* in this context. Smoothly aligning "functions" with the features of organs and organisms, for instance, has the rhetorical effect of implying telic pressures on natural selection that may not be in evidence. For the benefit of the gentle reader—and I hope without being pedestrian—I would make the point this way: Our feet function to activate the accelerator and brake when we drive, but we would want to resist saying that this is "why" we have feet. I think that would be the case even in the commonsense narrative.

Let me now take a slightly different rhetorical turn by saying that as a person who has some sympathy with the "idealist" conception of the universe (where *idealist* means that the stuff of the universe is more analogous to mind than to traditionally conceived "matter"), it seems to me that Meyer has conceded to materialism some of its most questionable features.

One is that of brute matter, which, Meyer quite rightly observes, doesn't act in the ways we see things around us acting. That is in part because the very notion of brute matter is a relic of pre-twentieth-century physics and is living on in both common and academic superstition. It trades on the imagery of inertness, previously used as the defining contrast between matter and the "animated" aspects of the world. We now know that such a dichotomy is false. Matter is energy and anything but inert.

The second hostage given to materialism is the notion of determinism. The concept itself goes unexamined here. Yet it is posed as one of three obvious possibilities in the shaping of information, chance being the second. The third possibility, which Meyer advocates, is design, presumably the very antithesis of determinism. But is it conceptually distinct? One is tempted to argue that causal determination is not so much renounced as relocated as the product of the designing agency, itself a fully determining cause.

I am not sure I could make the argument here, but I have a hunch that the real generative power of historical process would be as much a casualty of an overly designing God as it is of determinism. The success of our public discussions of nature might well depend on whether we can find ways of speaking about the conceptual space that lies between mere chance and rigid determinism (*mutatis mutandis,* the same problem as in discussing the role of genes in human behavior). I am not sure if design occupies that space, but I suspect that it will offer little novelty as an explanation if it sticks to one end of the chance/no-chance continuum. The middle way is always better.

The design theorists might arguably be more persuasive with those who already have heightened sensitivities to the issue of religion in science if they cooked up science-fiction scenarios to help the secular-minded get a toehold in the design argument. I am thinking again about pedagogy. In

Stanley Kubrick's classic film *2001: A Space Odyssey,* for instance, the possibility of an intelligent intervention in the earthly order is raised, while finessing the question of what that intelligence is or what its relationship to origins is. The mysterious monolith that presents itself at the great threshold moments in our history is a blank canvas on which we can project either divinity, a more advanced species, or perhaps just an idea of progress. I would like to have students watch the film and then address that. They might be asked to consider the possibility that some cosmic Johnny Appleseed had scattered the seed we now call DNA far and wide, and in that prebiotic state of our earth it found fertile ground. Maybe the visitor even encoded messages that would take millennia to work their way to articulation by our DNA (perhaps borne along by the otherwise mysterious "junk" DNA). Maybe in the year 2020, say, the message will come through as plainly as the ear-piercing one emanating from monolith. This is science fiction, of course, but it does not conflict with anything we know about the mechanisms of evolution, and it lets us think of design without pressing the question of ultimacy (which is surely unknowable in the classroom).

As much as our still modernist sensibilities tell us that the scientific questions are separable from the cultural ones, the truth is more complicated. Debates about the origins of the big bang or DNA are also about the ground of our being and how we are to take our own measure in the world. And this is not to say that there are no ascertainable facts of the matter or that theories cannot be disproven. But it is partly a question of what feels right and natural.

An Intelligent Person's Guide to Intelligent Design Theory

Steve Fuller

❧ ❧ ❧

Public debates surrounding the legitimacy of intelligent design (ID) theory, popularly but incorrectly known as creationism, have so far been
limited to the United States. That, however, is not because America
uniquely suffers from antiscientific backlash. Such backlash is now fairly
widespread in the Western world, but usually it is driven by eco-warriors
who nevertheless share the creationists' holistic orientation to nature. In
fact, the controversial status of ID theory has very little to do with the relationship between science and religion, which, after all, has been largely
symbiotic in human history. Rather, it relates to the contingencies of
America's birth and the perverse twist that its founding myth has taken in
the development of the nation's legal system and political culture.

Why Americans Fear Creationism
More than Racism

Religious persecution endured by the early English-speaking settlers provided the background against which the much-vaunted separation of
church and state became the core of the Constitution's protection of civil

liberties, especially freedom of expression. The exclusion of religion from public school instruction was supposed to allow students the space to develop their own views without pressure to conform to a particular faith. Of course, in practice, one creed was given precedence, namely, belief in the USA itself, which remains emblazoned in the minds of all Americans over thirty as the Pledge of Allegiance that used to be recited at the start of each school day.

The idea of America as a secular faith became especially important in the second half of the nineteenth century, as waves of immigrants from outside northern Europe flowed into the country. In this context, religious difference was no longer seen as something the law should protect; rather, it became a potential source of divisiveness that demanded, in turn, an ideology that would enable Americans to transcend, if not eliminate, their religious differences in forging a world-class nation. This "melting pot" turned out to be mandatory education in the natural sciences, and the long-term effect has been to create a hostile public environment for views about the natural (and social) world that have affinities with religious modes of thought. For most of the twentieth century, in fact, when commentators have wanted to capture the "prescientific" character of religious thought, they would refer to its allegedly tribal qualities that obviously would inhibit the efforts needed to build a technologically advanced civilization.[1]

I have dredged up this ancient history because I believe that ID theory would appear much more benign today had the original settlers been escaping ethnic or racial, rather than religious, conflict. All else being equal, Americans would now be living under a Constitution that separates race and state, one that officially bans the teaching of racial hypotheses in public school science classes and unofficially discourages mainstream publication of works propounding racist theses. To be sure, we would be living in a land of political correctness but also one that probably would have never imported Africans as slaves or Asians as indentured servants or slaughtered most of the native inhabitants. In short, a USA founded on the separation of race and state, instead of church and state, would have probably had a morally more acceptable history.[2]

Considering the divisive role played by racism in American history, it is amazing that serious discussion continues to be given to books that allege a strong causal link between race and intelligence, even when they are written by behavioral psychologists and political economists—as opposed to people with the relevant expertise in physical anthropology or human genetics. I allude to *The Bell Curve*, 1994's contribution to a depressingly long line of prominently published books that desperately turn to race to explain persistent differences in the human condition.[3]

When raising these matters, it is customary to say that it is a testimony to America's liberal tradition that the book's authors have been able to push their views as far as they have. A blanket devotion to free speech, however, does not really provide the explanation, since a similar open-mindedness has not been extended to the much less socially disruptive ID theory. All that the free discussion of *The Bell Curve* proves is that the United States remains ideologically anchored in the values of the white middle-class individuals who constituted the nation's "founding fathers." Those men were much more comfortable talking publicly about differences in skin color than about spiritual persuasion, mainly because the former difference would concern the status of others, but the latter would concern themselves.

Creationism as the Abandoned Offspring of Lamarck

The relationship between America's tolerance of racism and intolerance of creationism in public intellectual life runs deeper than I have so far suggested. Racism and creationism can be seen as two lines of thought that were unwittingly revitalized with Darwin's triumph over Lamarck in the early twentieth century. Until Mendel's rediscovery gave natural selection a firm genetic basis, Darwinism could not adequately explain the transmission of adaptive traits without supposing that creatures had an uncanny ability to anticipate the future and then pass that knowledge to offspring in a more or less direct fashion so as to increase their fitness. Thus, Darwin remained wedded to Lamarck. In that context, racism amounted to a hardheaded acceptance of the doctrine of natural selection, according to which the environment is the nonnegotiable arbiter of an organism's fitness—no wishful thinking about the prospects for improvement, be it in the organism's own or its offspring's lifetimes.

Of course, racism does not strictly follow from Darwinism, since natural selection does not preclude "artificial" changes in the environment that end up "naturally" enhancing a population's fitness over time by protecting its members from hostile external forces. The idea, however, that organisms are flexible only at the level of entire populations (that is, their statistical propensity for variation), and not at the level of particular individuals, has given comfort to racists throughout the twentieth century.

For its part, creationism filled the vacuum left once Darwinism renounced the Lamarckian belief in the purposive unity of nature, a traditional component of evolutionary theory that was associated with all organisms inhabiting the same clearly bounded space (the planet Earth), which was thought to occupy a unique place in the universe. Here, creationism makes common cause with both the Gaia hypothesis, as originated by James Lovelock and developed by Lynn Margulis, and the Anthropic Principle associated with astronomers John Barrow and Frank Tipler.[4] Although none of these scientists has explicitly aligned themselves with creationism, their dissatisfaction with the current orthodoxies in biology and cosmology stems from the same sources as those of creationists. In short, then, the ascendancy of Darwinism in the twentieth century has had the effect of boosting the fortunes of racism and spurring creationists to don the mantle of the fallen Lamarck.

The idea that creationism has inherited Lamarck's charge may seem strange, until we consider particular articles in this volume. At least two of them, Stephen C. Meyer's and Michael J. Behe's, directly address ID theory's prospects as a strategy for unifying scientific knowledge, a goal traditionally of greater concern to Lamarckians than to Darwinians (though E. O. Wilson's sociobiology program has made a serious dent in this generalization).[5] A comparison of Meyer's and Behe's brief discussions of computers reveals that they hold rather different, perhaps even incompatible, views on the role of intelligent design in unification. Whereas Meyer says that design is largely independent of matter, for Behe design is inherent in matter.

Meyer stresses the familiar point from cognitive science that intelligence can be instantiated in many different ways, ranging from electronic circuitry to electrochemical neural impulses. More important, translation can occur between two such media without any loss in information. In that sense, then, mind would seem to transcend matter. It may be fair to Meyer's argument to say that he would reduce biology to a branch of informatics, which gives metaphysical precedence to the distinction intelligent/nonintelligent over living/nonliving. This move has potentially radical consequences that cannot be explored here, including the prospect that "biology" does not capture the causal dispositions of ultimate reality but rather reflects generalizations that are of specifically human interest—which is how many natural scientists currently think of the categories of social science.[6] In that case, Meyer may be read as claiming, in a fashion familiar to both Plato and Galileo, that God speaks the language of mathematics. In contrast, Behe conducts a scientifically updated version of the watchmaker argument for cosmic design that is more firmly planted in the Aristotelian tradition. Thus, today the imprint of divine intelligence is to be found in the biochemical detail of organic cell structure, just as the stamp of human intelligence can be seen in the microphysical structure of computers.[7]

The question begged in the previous paragraph is whether ID theory is indeed on a mission to unify scientific knowledge. Here it is worth recalling that ever since natural philosophy hemorrhaged into the natural science disciplines in the nineteenth century, the task of unification has been left largely to philosophers and theologians—to be sure, in decreasing numbers as the years have gone on. In Darwin's own lifetime, that disunified vision of scientific knowledge had already become evident when Lord Kelvin, the leading physicist of the day, declared that the earth was not old enough to allow natural selection to function as the incremental process by which primitive organisms could evolve to human beings. Of course, Kelvin turned out to be in error, but his objection draws attention to the fact that although Darwin operated in full knowledge of the biological and geological facts of his day, he did not make any special effort to render his theory compatible with the received wisdom on physical cosmology.[8]

In our own time, those intrepid scientists who have tried to square the demands of Darwinism and physics have come up with accounts that (perhaps unwittingly) appear friendly to ID theory. Although none of these scientists goes so far as to suggest that "natural selection" should be pictured as some superhuman agent literally selecting the course that nature should take, they acknowledge that there seem to be prior mathematically specifiable constraints on how organic development can occur.[9]

If we suppose that ID theory is, in some important sense, trying to unify scientific knowledge, then the difference between Meyer and Behe boils down to the levels at which they pitch their arguments. Meyer sees divine design as competing with natural selection at the metalevel of biological explanation. In other words, ID theory is meant to answer the question: Why is there something rather than nothing? It does not address the specific designs of particular organisms, which seem to be left to biology as it is normally practiced today. In contrast, Behe would have ID theory compete with natural selection at the object level of biological explanation, offering an alternative account of, say, an organism's cellular complexity.

Given those options, I would have to side with Meyer, whose arguments resemble the ones promoted by cognitive scientist Herbert Simon under the rubric of the "sciences of the artificial."[10] Although Simon does not deny the processes of natural selection, he nevertheless argues that if an ecosystem survives long enough, it will have developed sufficient means to maintain its basic structure despite ambient adversity. Resilience of form in the face of material changes is the mark of intelligence.[11] For example, whenever a natural disaster occurs, the surviving population manages to reconstitute itself into a functioning unit—perhaps without some of its previous members or amenities; but then again, the experience of the disaster may have enabled the emergence of more efficient means to satisfy the needs of those who remain.

My tentative approval notwithstanding, Meyer's view raises its own questions: one theological and the other more strictly scientific. Is it reasonable (or even nonblasphemous) to suppose that God is the Ultimate Artificer? Meyer's willingness to subvert the significance of the boundary between biological and mechanical forms of intelligence is intellectually bracing, but it also ends up suggesting that once we understand how humans construct stable environments that enable the steady transmission and accumulation of information over time and space, we have understood the basis of the divine plan (which, of course, occurs on a grander scale). Readers of a pious turn of mind can immediately appreciate how this argument from analogy might erase the ontological distance between God and his creatures. To be sure, this issue had already been a flashpoint for the medieval Scholastics; yet, it is surprising that the controversial implications of Meyer's proposal do not seem to have been registered in religious circles.

On the scientific side, the idea that the same information can be transmitted across different media intact is empirically disputable, notwithstanding the role it plays in many idealized mathematical models of physical reality. At the very least, Meyer would need to provide an account that enables one either to trace intermediary distortion or to show that any such distortion cancels out in the long term.[12]

To my mind, Behe seems too caught up in justifying specific patterns in nature. This opens him to the familiar charge of "perfectionism" that Stephen Jay Gould has lodged against creationists who suppose that there is a level of biological analysis—a "unit of creation," as it were—whose entities can be explained in terms of the specific function they were designed to perform.[13] Whereas Behe focuses on the organization of cells, earlier creationists typically focused on the morphology of entire plants and animals as the objects of design-based explanations. This understanding of ID theory presupposes that creation is modular, such that one can know the function of some things without knowing the function of others.

If, however, we take seriously that nature is a unified object in the mind of the Creator, then it is entirely possible—and I believe more plausible—to suppose that the purpose of specific entities, be they cells or species, cannot be discerned until at least the main contours of the entire world-picture are in place. On this more holistic view of creation, any given cell or species taken in isolation may seem the product of contingency, exactly as Darwinists suppose. But while Darwinists conclude their inquiry at that point, holistic creationists argue that the appearance of contingency merely reflects the incompleteness of our knowledge of the divine plan.

The model of the approach I urge here is the venerable field of *theodicy,* the explanation of divine justice in a world that permits monstrous births, dastardly deeds, and natural disasters. Theodicists from Saint Augustine to Leibnitz (and, in secular guise, Hegel) realized that much of creation was suboptimal, given the omnipotence, omniscience, and omnibenevolence of the Creator. This must mean (so theodicists conclude) that the divine plan involves a level of complexity that requires an understanding of more than simply the immediate causes and effects of particular events. For this reason, they concluded that an apparent evil or imperfection concealed a greater good.[14] At stake in the distinction I am drawing is no less than the way one conducts scientific inquiry. Are the objects of inquiry clarified one at a time or all at once? Call the former "atomistic" and the latter "hermeneutical." In the context of this discussion, the interesting point is that this choice is just as pertinent to the heterodox ID theory as to more orthodox versions of biology.

Conclusion: Creationism's Rhetorical Virtuosity

After reading various defenses of ID theory, I have no doubt that virtually any position in the philosophy of science can be used as a rhetorical resource to challenge the scientific establishment. Meyer, for example, appeals to an especially strong form of scientific realism—inference to the best explanation—to combat the evolutionists. Basically, he argues that the existence of a selector responsible for the workings of natural selection would be the best explanation of evolution, were it not ruled out of court a priori by scientists. In contrast, Jonathan Wells and Paul Nelson appropriate the opposing doctrine, instrumentalism, to undermine natural selection as an explanatory principle altogether.[15] At most, they claim, natural selection is a

redescription of the history of life-forms that, although suggestive and eco-
nomical, does not genuinely explain changes over time that are most naturally understood as "development." Clearly, the ideas of Meyer and those of
Wells and Nelson cannot both be correct. Moreover, Behe complains that
evolutionists seem to argue that all moral choice must be hardwired,
whereas Dembski suggests that God has already hardwired us to make
moral choices. Again, we are faced with a commitment to ID theory that
entails contradictory philosophical implications.

Finally, I would like to invoke *Fuller's Fairness Rule:* namely, if you appeal to metaphysical explanations at all, you must permit a plurality of
them—because metaphysical explanations are inherently totalizing in their
scope yet are ultimately unfalsifiable in their consequences. Since virtually
any metaphysical hypothesis can be maintained in the face of any negative
evidence, it is imperative that there be more than one in competition at
any point. Traditionally, philosophers have been prone to advocate extreme positions on this matter: either disallow metaphysical hypotheses altogether (instrumentalism) or allow only one metaphysical hypothesis
(realism), especially when scientific inquiry is identified with the single-
minded pursuit of a paradigm. Neither allows much of a sphere for the operation of rhetoric.

My own rule is based on a normative image of inquiry that I have developed as part of a critical history of the origins and reception of Thomas
Kuhn's *The Structure of Scientific Revolutions.* Starting with the work of William
Whewell, the Cambridge doyen who coined the word *scientist* in the 1830s, it
has become common to imagine the relationship between scientific discoveries and the received body of scientific knowledge as akin to tributaries issuing into a major river. I propose a reversal of that image, one presuming that
such discoveries are already biased and that the quest for science is to render
them compatible with the vast body of already existing local knowledges:
that is, a river that issues in a delta.[16] I heartily support the development of
ID theory as part of this general strategy of converting the dominant political
image of knowledge from that of tributaries to that of a delta. In that spirit,
ID theory's defenders should expect my support in the future.

Notes

1. A fair-minded account of the U.S. Constitution's historical bias against
   religion, including the vicissitudes of creationism, is Stephen Carter,
   The Culture of Unbelief (New York: Doubleday, 1993).

2. An interesting fictional account of a society founded on the separation of race and state, "Communitaria," is to be found in Steven Lukes, *The Curious Enlightenment of Professor Caritat* (London: Verso, 1996).

3. Richard Herrnstein and Charles Murray, *The Bell Curve: Race and Social Structure in American Life* (New York: Free Press, 1994).

4. James Lovelock, *Gaia* (Oxford: Oxford University Press, 1979); John Barrow and Frank Tipler, *The Anthropic Cosmological Principle* (Oxford: Oxford University Press, 1986).

5. See especially the roundly (and justly) criticized E. O. Wilson, *Consilience: The Unity of Knowledge* (New York: Alfred Knopf, 1998).

6. Here I would recommend that devotees of ID read Alexander Rosenberg, *Instrumental Biology, or the Disunity of Science* (Chicago: University of Chicago Press, 1994), which makes this argument from a rigorously realist standpoint that finds physics alone worthy of the mantle of science. Although Rosenberg probably regards himself as light years from ID theory, it is worth recalling that to set a standard of scientificity so high that it could be met only by a fully specified and mathematized form of inquiry is equivalent to doing the philosophy of science from the standpoint of an intelligent designer. At the start of his career, Rosenberg applied the same criteria to undermine the scientific status of social science. See Alexander Rosenberg, *Sociobiology and the Preemption of Social Science* (Baltimore: Johns Hopkins University Press, 1980).

7. One wonders what Behe would make of the thesis, nowadays most closely associated with mathematical physicist Roger Penrose, that argues that the acausal nature of quantum reality captures human consciousness and maybe even the moment of divine intervention, neither of which is characterizable in computational terms. Rather than positing an autonomous mental substance, however, Penrose believes that these quantum effects are transmitted and amplified through microtubules in the brain. See Roger Penrose, *The Emperor's New Mind* (Oxford: Oxford University Press, 1989); Roger Penrose, *Shadows of the Mind* (Oxford: Oxford University Press, 1986).

8. On this famous episode in the history of cross-disciplinary relations, see David Lindley, *The End of Physics* (New York: Basic Books, 1993), chap. 1.

9. Beyond the Gaia and Anthropic theorists mentioned earlier, I would add physicist Lee Smolin, biophysicist Stuart Kauffman, and biologist Brian Goodwin. All three are interviewed in John Brockman, *The Third*

Culture: Beyond the Scientific Revolution (New York: Simon and Schuster, 1995), 96–110, 286–302, 333–43.

10. Herbert Simon, *The Sciences of the Artificial* (Cambridge: MIT Press, 1977).

11. This definition is reminiscent of the criteria for life used by such early-twentieth-century experimental defenders of vitalism as Hans Driesch, who famously cut up urchins and worms, only to discover that they could maintain their vital functions in their materially diminished state. For a sympathetic but critical appraisal of Driesch's work, see Ernst Cassirer, *The Problem of Knowledge* (New Haven, Conn.: Yale University Press, 1950), 195 ff. An important difference between Driesch and ID theorists like Meyer is that the latter do not shy away from mathematical characterizations of what Driesch called "entelechy."

12. A kindred account inspired by chaos theory is the idea of "attractors" in nature, (that is, equilibria toward which disparate starting points tend to gravitate). The most interesting development of this line of thought in an anthropological context, as an antidote to cultural relativism, is Dan Sperber, *Explaining Culture: A Naturalistic Approach* (Oxford: Blackwell, 1996). Although Sperber fancies himself a hard-headed Darwinian, his distinctive use of chaos theory helps elaborate what it would mean for the same set of beliefs and values to be disseminated across vastly different material conditions without being completely lost in the process.

13. Stephen Jay Gould, *The Panda's Thumb: More Reflections in Natural History* (New York: W. W. Norton, 1980).

14. For more on the role of theodicy in the development of science, see Steve Fuller, *Science* (Minneapolis: University of Minnesota Press, 1997), 58–60.

15. Jonathan Wells and Paul Nelson, "Some Things in Biology Don't Make Sense in the Light of Evolution," *Rhetoric and Public Affairs* 1, no. 4 (1999): 557–64.

16. This point is developed in more detail in Steve Fuller, *Being There with Thomas Kuhn: A Philosophical History for Our Time* (Chicago: University of Chicago Press, 1999), Conclusion.

Creationism versus Darwinism: A Third Alternative

Brig Klyce and Chandra Wickramasinghe

※ ※ ※

In the highly polarized dispute between Darwinism and creationism, our position is unique. Although we do not align ourselves with either side, both sides treat us as opponents. Thus, we are outsiders with an unusual perspective—and our suggestion for a way out of the crisis has not yet been considered.

It must be unusual for the scientific community to be so strongly at odds with the general public on matters relating to evolution and the origin of life. Recent polls show that a clear majority of American adults do not accept the standard Darwinian account of evolution. A number of state legislatures and boards of education in the United States are now rewriting the rules in order at least to prevent Darwinism from being the only theory taught to pupils in their schools. In response, mainstream science sees no alternative but to mount a propaganda campaign advocating the standard Darwinian story in its narrowest and most restricted context.

The crisis is grave enough to precipitate a Kuhnian paradigm shift. The new paradigm we advocate would actually give some satisfaction to both sides, because, like John Lyne's students, we think that both sides have something worthwhile to say. But the relevant facts need to be distilled from the dogma.[1]

Creationists Are Right to Question Darwinism

The existing Darwinian account of evolution does not adequately explain sustained macroevolutionary progress, let alone the origin of life in the first place. That inadequacy must continue to be actively discussed and researched until a more satisfactory relationship between evidence and theory is established.

Probability arguments have been used for many years to demonstrate that the first origin of life from nonlife is an exceedingly improbable affair. The odds against such an origin can be measured in terms of numbers like $10^{40,000}$ to 1, truly superastronomical numbers. Darwinists scoff at these numbers and seldom consider them. Even so, the standard textbook story of a primordial soup on a primitive Earth leading to the emergence of life from nonliving matter is beginning to look more unlikely than ever. Consequently, new theories are continually being proposed. Among mainstream Darwinists today, there are half a dozen theories of the origin of life, including nucleotides first, proteins first, nucleotides and proteins simultaneously, containers first, and mineral scaffolds first. The proposed environments in which this origin is considered most likely to have taken place also range widely: near hot, undersea vents; in a cold, ice-covered sea; in tidal pools; deep underground; and in space. We welcome the growing acceptance that this last environment, space, could even harbor life and deliver it to Earth.

Besides the origin of life, there is equal trouble for Darwinian ideas of evolution, where the doubts are even older. Although sustained macroevolutionary progress, as evidenced in the geological record, must be accepted as an irrefutable fact, major questions remain in regard to the precise mechanisms by which evolutionary changes are wrought. Certainly, Mendelian genetics and modern gene-sequencing have offered much deeper insights into the mechanics of evolutionary change than Darwin and Wallace could have known about in the late nineteenth century. But a mechanism leading to truly innovative changes still continues to elude us. As Ernst Mayr wrote in 1988, "Unfortunately, the genetics of microevolutionary processes has been unable to provide a full explanation of macroevolution."[2] Whereas adaptation produced by small mutations is not in dispute, truly innovative change requires genes that do not appear to have been derived from prior genes by small mutations. As W. Ford Doolittle observes, "Many eukaryotic genes . . . seem to come from nowhere."[3]

Darwinists try to dismiss such observations with hand waving. But the ability of Darwinian evolution to produce sustained macroevolutionary progress cannot be firmly established without closed-system experiments. The ones that have been conducted so far do not sustain the theory. In a series of experiments with E. coli bacteria, no truly innovative changes were achieved even after 25,000 generations.[4] The fossil record, however, was generated in an open system, the biosphere. Here, just as cells from elsewhere may have seeded life on Earth originally, the genes that bring about the sustained macroevolutionary progress we observe may also come from elsewhere.

Until the origin of life and sustained macroevolutionary progress are demonstrated in closed-system experiments, the Darwinian account of them is on the same footing as Aristotle's theory of spontaneous generation before Pasteur. Darwinism should continue to be challenged to produce such evidence.

Darwinists Are Right to Defend Science

Science and religion are two great manifestations of the human spirit. Religious belief is essentially of a revelatory character, while scientific facts are the result of rigorous experiment and intellectual discipline. Scientific procedures are based on the assumption that no violations of physical law occur. When violations seem to occur, scientists may decide that the evidence was anomalous. Or perhaps the laws were not correctly understood and need to be amended. Of course, this process of amendment and reappraisal has not been completed.

Today, Darwinian theory extends well beyond the evidence, as creationists rightly notice. In this case, the details of the theory, not the underlying principles of science, should be challenged. But Phillip Johnson's attempt to overthrow "naturalism" does attack these very principles. As William Dembski complains, "For the sake of inquiry we are required to pretend that God does not exist."[5] Yes, that's how science is done. One may object to this principle, but it is the essence of science. Even if it were true that God, by a miracle, created life out of ordinary matter, it could not be established scientifically. Miracles are simply not amenable to scientific investigation, and scientists are right to dismiss them as unscientific.

How Can the Crisis Be Resolved?

A scientific solution is possible if Earth's biosphere is open to biological input from elsewhere. Within the last decade, mainstream science has admitted the possibility that life on Earth may have been seeded by germs from space—the basic panspermia theory. The first evidence of terrestrial life appears at about four billion years before the present, when the earth was being severely bombarded by comets and asteroids. This early start of life is well explained if life in the form of microorganisms was brought here along with the colliding comets.

If comets seeded Earth with microbial life some four billion years ago, that process must necessarily have continued to the present day. With cosmic microbes supplying a continual replenishment of genes, it would seem inevitable that Darwinian evolution, including the process of natural selection, must proceed in response to the arrival of new genes that serve as uncorrupted evolutionary potential. The details of the processes leading up to the accommodation of cometary genes within the genomes of evolving terrestrial life-forms is outside the scope of the present essay.

We note here, however, that several aspects of this general picture are in accord with recent data from molecular biology. First, horizontal gene transfer has recently been shown to play a major role in macroevolutionary progress.[6] Second, many genes appear to be older, when judged through sequence analysis and mutation rates, than they should be according to their position within geological strata in the fossil record.[7] Thus, the base of the microbial tree of life is looking more elusive that ever before, and the roots of the tree may well turn out to be firmly anchored, not on Earth but in the deep cosmos.

This expanded version of panspermia ("strong panspermia") is altogether different from the established Darwinian paradigm. It holds that, instead of sustained macroevolutionary progress, the history of life on Earth could actually be the development and sorting out, over many generations, of preexisting highly evolved cosmic life.

Must the Big Bang Rule Biology?

At this point, in our experience, creationists and Darwinists become aligned. They both argue that life on Earth, highly evolved or not, cannot simply descend from prior life ad infinitum, because there was a big bang. By logic, if the universe is a closed system that began in a lifeless state a finite time ago, then the origin of life and sustained macroevolutionary progress must have subsequently happened in it.

We are not surprised that creationists have adopted this account of creation. If the universe came from a big bang, preceded by nothing, it was in a sense a miracle. But we are puzzled that science, on debatable evidence and in violation of its own principles, seems to advocate a miracle. As John Maddox commented in 1998, "It is mystifying that a large part of the community of astronomers and astrophysicists around the world should regard the big bang as a good approximation of something called 'the truth' when they are aware of the empirical problems crying out for attention. Can we no longer live with the knowledge that we are ignorant of many things?"[8]

In our opinion, the standard big bang theory has enough problems of its own, and science should not ask it also to govern all of biology. In any case, if Darwinism can account for the origin of life and sustained macroevolutionary progress, it should be able to cite firmer and more immediate evidence than the big bang. Without the strict and narrow interpretation of the big bang, nothing says that life, even highly evolved life, could not come from the eternal past. That possibility allows for a fully scientific account of evolution and the origin of life on Earth—the strong version of panspermia. In this account, life descends only from prior life that was at least as highly evolved as its descendents.

What strong panspermia does not do is account for life "in the first place." Similarly, neither does the big bang, nor any theory, answer the question, "Why is there anything instead of nothing at all?" In our opinion, science has nothing to contribute on questions pertaining to the origin of physical reality or the origin of life. These matters are properly part of religion and not of science.

Meanwhile, What Should Be Taught in Our Schools?

We wish that science teachers would distinguish clearly between firmly established empirical facts concerning evolution and theories about mechanisms. They forget the fact that any theory of the world has at most a provisional, pro tem value. It is valid only until it is falsified or a better model is proposed. When the current favorite theory leaves as much unexplained as Darwinism does, students must learn that scientific alternatives exist. Failure to mention them is deceitful.

There are, of course, some problems in science for which a definite solution is possible, as, for instance, in the mathematics and the science of planetary motions. But the biggest problems about the ultimate origin of physical reality, or of life, clearly do not come under this heading. For them, science must remain silent.

Notes

1. John Lyne, "Intelligent Dasein," *Rhetoric and Public Affairs* 1, no. 4 (1999): 579–85.
2. Ernst Mayr, *Toward a New Philosophy of Biology* (Cambridge: Harvard University Press, 1988), 405.
3. W. Ford Doolittle, *Scientific American* 282, no. 2 (Feb. 2000): 90.
4. D. Papadopoulos et al., *Proceedings of the National Academy of Sciences USA* 96 (1999): 3807.
5. William A. Dembski, *Intelligent Design: The Bridge Between Science and Theology* (Downers Grove, Ill.: InterVarsity Press, 1999), 103.
6. Michael Syvanen and Clarence I. Kado, eds., *Horizontal Gene Transfer,* (Boston: Kluwer Academic Publishers, 1999).
7. Gregory A. Wray, Jeffrey S. Levinton, and Leo H. Shapiro, "Molecular Evidence for Deep Precambrian Divergences among Metazoan Phyla," *Science* 274 (25 Oct. 1996): 568–73.
8. John Maddox, *What Remains to Be Discovered* (New York: Free Press, 1998), 374–75.

The Rhetorical Problem of Intelligent Design

Phillip E. Johnson

❊ ❊ ❊

The greatest hurdle faced by the intelligent design (ID) movement is to overcome the prejudice that says that to attribute anything in biology to a Designer is to engage in "religion" rather than "science." To put the same prejudice in other words, Darwinists assume that ID amounts to "creationism," and therefore it must rest on a literal interpretation of the Bible rather than on empirical evidence. It matters not a whit that the advocates of ID talk of scientific evidence and that the Darwinists are the ones who want to bring the Bible into the discussion.

I have encountered that kind of response hundreds of times. After I have explained why the scientific evidence does not support Darwinian claims for the supposed vast creative power of natural selection, Darwinists typically respond by saying something about the need to keep religion and science separate. The bottom line is always the same: "ID violates the rules of the game no matter what the evidence, because an unyielding philosophical materialism is the basis of all science."

Of course, a "science" that is defined as applied materialist philosophy will always end up concluding that the apparent wonders of design in biology (whose existence everybody acknowledges) are actually produced by the operation of purposeless material processes such as random mutation and natural selection. As long as materialist prejudice bars the door, the advocates of ID cannot get a hearing regardless of how much evidence they have. But why does the prejudice have so much power, and how can it be overcome? I'll answer that question with specific reference to Stanley Fish's model of how liberal rationalism sets the boundaries of political and academic discussion, particularly with respect to claims in which God might lurk. Fish, who is not only a distinguished literary scholar but also a professor of law at Duke University, has set out his model in a 1997 article in the *Columbia Law Review* and also in an exchange with Richard John Neuhaus in *First Things*.[1]

Fish begins with John Locke's "A Letter Concerning Toleration" (1689), written after a century of religious conflict had shown the need for a formula that would enable conflicting religious factions to live together in peace while still providing the government with enough authority to rule. British Protestants had renounced the authority of the Pope and subsequently had beheaded one king (Charles I) and driven another into exile (James II). After these events, it was clear that no human authority could impose uniformity in religion at any acceptable cost.

Moreover, Locke's own theology taught him that every man should be left free to work out his own salvation as his conscience dictates. Locke therefore recognized that, because "every church is orthodox to itself," there can be no neutral vantage point from which one can judge which church is the true one, so the government's policy should be one of tolerance. On the other hand, there must be some limit to what is tolerated, or people would justify all sorts of crimes on the basis of religious motivation. Locke put the point in the form of a rhetorical question: "If some congregations should have in mind to sacrifice infants . . . or practise any other such heinous enormities, is the magistrate obliged to tolerate them, because they are committed in a religious assembly?"[2]

The answer, of course, is "no." As to matters that the civil government considers to be fundamental, religious dissidents, like everybody else, must conform to the law. The policy of tolerance applies only to matters that are properly for private decision, such as the form of worship. But of course this very division privileges the governing ideology, which sets the boundary between what is public and what is private and stigmatizes the outsiders. To believers in infant sacrifice—or in a right to abortion, to substitute a contemporary illustration—such killings are not heinous crimes but thoroughly proper behavior. If religious dissidents attain sufficient power, the magistrates may change their minds about what constitutes a heinous enormity. We have seen in our own time how abortion, previously regarded by apparent consensus as a felony, became by judicial mandate a constitutional right, so that now it is those who try to prevent abortions who find themselves stigmatized as criminals or oppressors.

But how does a government that lacks a supreme religious authority and admits that "every church is orthodox to itself" justify preferring one religious position over another?

Locke invoked a spurious consensus to justify the ruling orthodoxy, claiming that truly dangerous dissenting opinions are rare, because "no sect can easily arrive to such a degree of madness, as that it should think fit to teach, for doctrines of religion, such things as manifestly undermine the foundations of society, and are therefore condemned by the judgment of all mankind." (One of the manifestations of madness that Locke thus stigmatized was the opinion "that princes may be dethroned by those that differ from them in religion.") Fish comments that Locke's claim of nearly universal agreement on fundamental matters conceals some thorny questions. "How can there be something called 'the judgment of all mankind' if the entire project of toleration is a response to the bottom-line fact of plural judgments issuing from plural orthodoxies? How can you get to the judgment of all mankind, to what we now call 'common ground,' if you begin by declaring that differences are intractable because every church is orthodox to itself?"[3] I would add that an opinion can hardly threaten the foundations of society unless large numbers of people are attracted to it. Really crazy opinions marginalize themselves.

Fish's criticism exposes the central dilemma of an officially agnostic or relativist society, which is how to establish an orthodoxy for governmental purposes without seeming to be doing anything controversial. The time-honored liberal technique is to make it appear that what are actually highly partisan judgments come virtually from nowhere or from some abstract entity like universal reason. In Fish's words, "Each [rhetorical maneuver of this sort] achieves its apparent success only by performing a conceptual sleight of hand in which a distinction that is either debatable or permeable is passed off as perspicuous to everyone, usually by defining 'everyone' in a way that excludes (or marginalizes) those who would be likely to dispute either the fact or the shape of the distinction."[4] Fish criticizes the deception but not the practice, because there is no alternative. There must be a governing orthodoxy if there is not to be anarchy, and the power to govern includes the power to decide just how much tolerance to extend to dissidents.

In our own time, the conceptual sleight of hand is performed by designating the marginalized position as religious and the preferred position as an instance of the secular reasoning common to all humankind. If we look at a living organism and ask how it came to exist, some will say that God directed its making, and others will say that unintelligent material forces like mutation and selection were capable of doing the job without intelligent assistance. For modernists, the first alternative is a religious belief, and hence it may not be taught in the schools nor may it form the basis of public policy. It is roughly accurate to say that it is tolerated only on Sundays. The second alternative is science; as such, it must be taught as fact in the schools and for public purposes is the only legitimate assumption.

To make this distinction plausible, the rhetoricians must insist that "everybody knows" that belief in creation (theism) is purely subjective whereas belief in evolution (materialism) is based on scientific measurements and experiments, the kind of evidence we rely on to make things like airplanes and medicines. Anthropologist Donald Johanson can then settle all debate by proclaiming that "you can't accept one part of science because it brings you good things like electricity and penicillin and then throw away another part because it brings you some things you don't like about the origin of life."[5] That claim is as silly as saying that you can't accept one part of religion because it gives you the Sermon on the Mount while rejecting another part because it brings you the Spanish Inquisition. But few notice, because such statements tell us only what "everybody knows."

The rhetorical strategy of the ID movement is to break through the materialist prejudice by separating the two components of the contemporary definition of science. What if the study of the empirical evidence is leading us away from the dictates of materialist philosophy and toward recognition of the reality of the Designer? Which should we follow, the evidence or the philosophy? That is a question that the reigning scientific materialists cannot justify keeping off the intellectual agenda, nor can they afford to answer it. Once the right question is on the table, the ID position will eventually triumph. I know that not only because I have studied the evidence, but because I have seen how desperate the materialists are to keep the right question off the table. At some deep level, they know what I know.

Stanley Fish is critical of Christians (and of other theists, presumably) who attempt to participate in the liberal dialogue. He thinks that they are inherently totalitarians (God being an absolute authority) and that they therefore ought to want to put an end to the liberal debate rather than to join it. That attitude is on a par with geneticist Richard Lewontin's claim that allowing "the divine foot in the door" means the end of science, because then every event can potentially be attributed to miraculous intervention. Such "all or nothing" judgments reflect materialist propaganda rather than reality.

Recognizing the reality of God, the maker of natural laws, does not imply that there are no laws. If ID triumphs, science will go on—but some scientists will be interested in different questions. Chemical evolution will probably be abandoned for the same reasons that alchemy was abandoned, and Darwinism will join its cousins Marxism and Freudianism in the dustbin of intellectual history. But deciphering the genetic code will be more interesting than ever.

Likewise, recognizing the reality of a creator of human freedom does not make the liberal project any less necessary. The cultural consequences of God's reentry into reality will be significant, but the dialogue will go on. In universities, departments of gender studies may become less fashionable, and it may instead become intellectually respectable to endow professorships in theology. Physics will still be important because of what it can tell us about material causes, but few people will look to physics for a Theory of Everything. The human capacity for freedom and moral choice will have a much more secure metaphysical foundation in the divine mind than it has ever found in the Darwinian mechanism.

Changes like these affect the boundaries of the liberal dialogue but not its essence. Even if all rational people believed in God (as John Locke thought they should), there would still be many different interpretations of God's will, and each church would still be orthodox to itself. We can decide what is true for ourselves, but in the public realm we have to negotiate with others and persuade them if we can.

It is significant that the modern liberal project originated in a Christian realm, although one chastened by religious wars, and that the great totalitarian project of the twentieth century had its foundation in the Marxist version of scientific materialism.

Notes

1. Stanley Fish, "Mission Impossible: Setting the Just Bounds between Church and State," *Columbia Law Review* 97 (Dec. 1997): 2255; Stanley

Fish and Richard John Neuhaus, "Why We Can/Can't Just Get Along," *First Things* (18 Feb. 1996): 27.

2. Fish, "Mission Impossible," 2265.

3. Ibid., 2263.

4. Ibid.

5. Maitland A. Edey and Donald C. Johanson, *Blueprints: Solving the Mystery of Evolution* (Boston: Little and Brown, 1989), 2.

Appendix A
U.S. Commission on Civil Rights Hearing: On Curriculum Controversies in Biology, 21 August 1998

Transcribed by Laurie E. Heckel, court reporter

Panel Participants: Dr. Stephen C. Meyer, Dr. Eugenie Scott, and Richard Sybrandy

CHAIRPERSON BERRY: The meeting will come to order. The next panel is Curriculum Controversies in Biology. Could Mr. Stephen Meyer, Ms. Eugenie Scott, and Mr. Richard Sybrandy please come forward and take your seats? Thank you very much.

We very much appreciate your being here today and we apologize for starting a little bit late, and we would like to begin with you, Dr. Meyer, if you would please make an opening statement.

Dr. Meyer, Stephen Meyer, received his Ph.D. in history and philosophy of science from Cambridge in 1991. And he did a dissertation on origin-of-life biology and methodology of historical sciences. He was a geologist before that, and he is now director of the Center for Renewal of Science and Culture at the Discovery Institute and teaches philosophy at Whitworth College and he's contributed to several scholarly books and anthologies including *The History of Science and Religion in the Western Tradition*. He is currently working on a book formulating a scientific theory of biological design which looks specifically at the evidence for design in the encoded information in DNA.

Please proceed, Dr. Meyer.

MR. MEYER: Thank you. I would like to thank the commissioners for the opportunity to share my perspective on this important issue. Let me start with the scientific question as old as humankind: How did the astonishing diversity and complexity of life come to be? In particular, did a directing intelligence or mind have anything to do with the origin of biological organisms?

Darwinian evolutionary biologists say no. They contend that life arose and later diversified by entirely naturalistic processes such as natural selection acting on random variation. They say the scientific evidence weighs against the theory that a designing intelligence played a role in the history of life.

But if there can be evidence against a theory, it must be possible at least for there to be evidence for a theory as well. As Charles Darwin himself argued, both logic and intellectual honesty require consideration of both possibilities. He wrote in *The Origin of Species*, "A fair result can be obtained only by stating fully and balancing the facts and arguments on both sides of each question."

But is there any scientific evidence supporting the idea that intelligence played a role in the origin and development of life? In fact, there is. During the last forty years, evidence, much of which was unknown to Darwin, has come to light to support the design hypothesis: The breathtaking intricacy and complexity of even the simplest bacterial cell with its highly specified molecular machines and motors, the fossils of the Cambrian explosion which show all the basic forms of animal life appearing suddenly without clear precursors, and the encoded information in DNA which Bill Gates has recently likened to a software code. All these lines of evidence and many others suggest the prior action of a designing intelligence.

Is any of this evidence discussed in publicly-funded science classrooms? Almost never. As I have documented elsewhere, both high school and college biology textbooks make very selective presentations of the scientific evidence relevant to this question. For example, only one of the standard high school biology texts even mentions the Cambrian explosion, arguably the most dramatic event in the history of life. And not a single text discusses the challenge that Cambrian fossils pose to Darwinian evolutionary theory despite extensive discussions of this very point in technical paleontology journals and popular publications such as *Scientific American, Time* magazine and even, ironically, *Peoples Daily* in Communist China.

Why does this selective presentation of evidence persist in a nation known for its liberal intellectual traditions? Very simply, the opponents of full disclosure in science education insist, often backed by threat of lawsuit and other forms of social intimidation, that any deviation from a strictly neo-Darwinian presentation of origins constitutes an establishment of religion. They insist that the concept of design—intelligent design, that is—is inherently religious, whereas Darwinism, with its denial of intelligent design, is a strictly scientific matter.

But how can this be? Darwinism and design do not address two different subjects. They are two competing answers to the very same question: How did life arise and develop on Earth? Biology texts routinely recapitulate Darwinian arguments against intelligent design. Yet if these arguments are philosophically neutral and strictly scientific, why are evidential arguments for intelligent design inherently unscientific and religiously charged? The acceptance of this false asymmetry has justified an egregious form of viewpoint discrimination in American public science instruction.

I enclose a diagram showing the relationship between evidence, scientific interpretation, and the larger worldview considerations that inevitably come into play when discussing biological origins. This diagram and, to a much greater extent, published work in the philosophy of science suggest an equivalence in status between Darwinism and design theory. Both these theories are interpretations of biological data. Both, we must all admit, have larger philosophical or worldview implications. If design theory is religious, then so is Darwinism. If Darwinism is science, then so is design theory.

Despite this equivalence, the public school science curriculum generally allows students access to only one theoretical viewpoint and only to those evidences that support it. Students receive little exposure to scientific problems with neo-Darwinism and still less evidence that might support a contrary interpretation. Yet—and this is key—because origin theories have incorrigibly philosophical implications this imbalance in effect favors and promotes a naturalistic world view or philosophy over a theistic one.

Indeed, many texts openly explain the naturalistic and antitheistic implications of Darwinian theory. For example, in Douglas Futuyma's text, *Evolutionary Biology*, he writes, "by coupling the undirected purposeless variations to the blind uncaring process of natural selection, Darwin made theological or spiritual explanations of the life process superfluous." Purvis, Orians, and Heller tell students that, "the living world is constantly evolving without any goals. Evolutionary change is not directed."

Students skeptical about such overtly materialistic perspectives who wish to develop a view of the scientific evidence more consonant with a theistic worldview are often silenced. Indeed, the influential California Science Framework advises teachers to tell students to, "discuss the question further with their family or clergy."

For students and teachers wanting to consider or express a theistic viewpoint on this scientific subject—as opposed to advocating religion—(and this is a critical legal distinction) the present imbalance in public science instruction represents a clear form of viewpoint discrimination. In many cases, such discrimination has also entailed the abridgment of academic freedom for teachers and professors and the free speech rights of individual students.

I ask the commissioners to consider such practical measures as they have at their disposal to rectify this situation.

CHAIRPERSON BERRY: Thank you very much, Dr. Meyer.

Let me ask if anyone needs interpretation services, needs the skills of the interpreter. Could you please ask that? All right. I think the answer is no. Thank you very much.

Dr. Scott has a degree in biological anthropology. She has taught as a scientist for many years at various universities and she has been the executive director of the National Center for Science Education since 1987. The National Center for Science Education is a membership organization composed primarily of scientists with other interested citizens concerned with the teaching of evolution and the teaching of science in public schools. It is a nationally recognized clearinghouse for information and advice to keep evolution in the science classroom and scientific creationism out. NCSE is the only national organization that specializes on this issue.

Welcome and please proceed.

MS. SCOTT: Thank you very much. I have left red packets with you. They include background material for this really very complicated problem, and I hope you will have the leisure to take a look at it in the future. My statement, I'm obviously not going to read because it's too long. But I was asked by staffers to prepare some examples of what is going on in the creation/evolution controversy at the grass roots level around the country. And this is what I've done. I've tried to highlight some things so that we can go through them fairly quickly and we'll have more time for questions.

In the early part of this afternoon's session, I was pleased that the distinction was made between teaching about religion and advocating religion. So in my introductory paragraph what you will see, I agree with that point of view very strongly.

I will provide some case studies that demonstrate what's going on nationally, but I need to underscore three false claims that crop up all the time in the creation/evolution controversy: That evolution is a theory in crisis, that evolution is incompatible with religious belief, and that it is only fair in some fashion to present creationism or alternatives to evolution when evolution is taught. The book, *Voices for Evolution* consists of statements from scientific organizations, religious organizations, and education organizations that deal with all three of these issues. Evolution is not a theory in crisis. It is state-of-the-art science.

Let us move on to page 2 of the case studies. There are two manifestations of the creation/evolution controversy in American schools. One takes the form of equal time for creationism. I don't know if it's necessary to define creation science for you, but it's the idea that there is scientific evidence for a largely Biblical literalist interpretation of scripture, six twenty-four-hour days, special creation of all living things in the entire universe. And the claim to make this scientific creationism is that there is scientific data for this.

There were laws passed to require that creation science be taught when evolution is taught. These were overthrown by *Edwards v. Aguillard* in 1987. The court said that creationism is inherently a religious position and to advocate it as opposed to talk about it in a social studies class is unconstitutional. Creation science is a religious advocacy.

The other manifestation is alternatives to evolution, and my friend, Steve Meyer, and I disagree on intelligent design theory. I see it as a synonym for creation science. Abrupt appearance theory is another synonym for creation science. In fact, a recent U.S. District Court case, *Freiler v. Tangipahoa Parish* has recognized that curriculum proposals for intelligent design are equivalent to proposals for teaching creation science. Here are some examples of equal time in creationism in some form. We do get at the National Center for Science Education requests from districts, from teachers, because they are being asked to teach old-fashioned creation science even though it has been outlawed. There was current controversy in Post Falls, Idaho; a recent controversy in Merrimack, New Hampshire; Lake County, Florida; Salisbury, North Carolina. I won't reiterate these. They're bold-faced. You can recognize them.

In a number of communities, ministers have been invited to present creation science to students at school assemblies. This is clearly advocacy of religion. In some cases, students heard presentations on creationism from representatives of creationist ministries and this has occurred here in Washington, as well as in Peoria, and in Eads, Colorado. In the Eads situation, students were actually marched down the street to a church to hear a lecture on creation science.

There are many things that go on that are clearly religious advocacy in this context. There are teachers who decide to teach, to introduce creation science or an alternative on their own, even though courts have also addressed this issue.

Creation science may also be presented as intelligent design theory, or more vaguely as alternatives to evolution, or alternate theories to evolution, or a balanced treatment. These euphemisms have come up as a result of the Supreme Court case that has stated creation science is clearly religious advocacy. So new forms have evolved to take its place.

The other form that the creation/evolution controversy takes is on the bottom of page 3, anti-evolutionism itself. In addition to promoting creationism in its various forms, there is frank anti-evolutionary activity. Evolution is eliminated from the science curriculum in some places. Some districts and some teachers are encouraged, as it says on page 4, to teach evidence against evolution. And I assure you, the materials in this packet will—or should be reasonably persuasive, I hope, that there is no such thing as evidence against evolution. This is a euphemism again for creation science.

The idea is that evolution must be somehow disclaimed. It must be treated as theory, not fact. It must be treated as differently from all our scientific theories is another anti-evolution movement that has come up and is becoming more and more prevalent. Examples of the elimination of evolution, evidence against evolution disclaimers are presented in the following section on pages 4 and 5.

Textbook controversies also have sprung up around evolution and creationism. In Marshall County, Kentucky, a superintendent actually glued together the pages of a fourth grade book discussing the big bang because it didn't give equal time to creation, to the Bible, to the Biblical view of special creation.

State standards have also been weakened in terms of presenting evolution. A recent book by Lawrence Lerner published by the Fordham Foundation discusses evolution and state standards and criticizes a number of them for being deficient in this regard.

In conclusion, I would like to present a rather different view from my friend, Steve. I feel that the attack upon evolution and the promotion of creationism in its various forms at the K–12 school districts is an Establishment Clause problem under the First Amendment of the Constitution.

As a science educator, I'm also concerned about this being a problem for science literacy because whereas 79 percent of adults in the United Kingdom agree evolution took place, in the United States, only 47 percent. We have a major problem with science literacy as well as a First Amendment problem.

In the materials that I am leaving with you, I present some suggestions for how evolution may be taught without disrupting religious concerns of individuals. This will not be possible for all individuals. There are some individuals whose religious views are simply such that they will not be satisfied by any teaching of anything that goes against their religious views.

We cannot tailor the curriculum to suit all people, otherwise, we couldn't teach the germ theory to Christian Scientists. We have to make some decisions about what we teach, and I hope that I will be able to elaborate on this more.

Thank you.

CHAIRPERSON BERRY: There will be questions. Thank you very much. Mr. Richard Sybrandy—Sybrandy?

MR. SYBRANDY: That's correct.

CHAIRPERSON BERRY: —is an attorney with a general practice firm in Bellingham, Washington. He's worked at the National Legal Foundation on public school issues. And while at the National Legal Foundation, he compiled a parent and teacher's handbook on the rights of parents, teachers, and students in the public schools from a religious freedom perspective. From a referral from the Rutherford Institute, Mr. Sybrandy represents Roger DeHart, a biology teacher from Burlington, Washington. Mr. DeHart has for the past ten years included materials on intelligent design along with materials on evolution when teaching about the origin of life. The ACLU has threatened to sue in this case.

Please proceed, Mr. Sybrandy.

MR. SYBRANDY: Thank you. Again, I'd like to say it's an honor to speak here today and it's an honor to be with the esteemed members of this panel. Because I'm not a scientist, I'll be revising my remarks accordingly and leaving the science to the scientists. However, just as a means of introduction, judging from the remarks that we've heard so far, I think it would be a shame to deprive high school students in biology class from exposure to this type of debate. I would just say that as a means of introduction.

There are generally three points that I would like to make today and that is that, number one, the study of the origin of life—no matter what theory you favor—is a scientific theory that has religious implications. The second point I'd like to make is that simply because a scientific theory that's supported by fact has religious implications, that doesn't exclude it from being taught in the public schools. And the third point that I'd like to make is that excluding an alternative theory that is supported by science, simply on the basis that it may have a religious implication, is discrimination against religion. It could violate the teacher's rights to free speech. It could violate a student's right to know, and I'll explain later what I mean by a student's right to know.

Regardless of which theory is taught, there is going to be a religious implication. Darwin's theory of evolution says there is no creator. Life was the result of purely natural processes. As Carl Sagan once stated that there was nothing for the creator to do and every thinking person is forced to admit the absence of God. That's a religious implication to evolution.

You look at the flip side as well, the intelligent design theory which specifically Roger DeHart is exposing his students to, the intelligent design theory looks at the complex life that we see on earth and examines scientifically natural processes, what we know about natural processes, and it hypothesizes and says natural processes could not have resulted in life as we know it.

Well, then there must be a creator. Now, that's the implication. That's not what's taught, but that is certainly the clear implication behind intelligent design. Same implication as evolution. They're both religious, but that doesn't mean they should be excluded from the public schools. We all know that. I've been here today and I've heard the testimony. I'm sure this panel accepts that.

The real question is how legally to expose students to these issues. The evenhanded and objective instruction of intelligent design theory is not illegal. The Supreme Court in *Edwards v. Aguillard* addressed the issue of creation science, and I'd like to focus your attention on the specific facts of *Edwards v. Aguillard*. We had a situation where the stated legislative purpose of the act was to increase academic freedom. We have the religious right and fundamentalist Christians heavily advocating for the passage of this bill.

On the other hand, the court looked at what the bill actually did and mandated, and said this bill mandates that every time you teach evolution, you must give equal time to creationism. The court simply had a hard time figuring out how that increased academic freedom in the public schools.

I'd like to draw your attention to the quote in *Edwards v. Aguillard*, and the citation is 96 LED 2d at 525 and 526. "We do not imply that a legislature could never require that scientific critiques of prevailing scientific theories be taught. In a similar way, teaching a variety of scientific theories about the origins of humankind to schoolchildren might be validly done with the clear secular intent of enhancing the effectiveness of science instruction." And again, whether this enhances the effectiveness of science instruction, I'll leave to the scientists.

Again, in *Abington v. Schempp*, it has been made clear, and it's been quoted to the panel already, that basically you can present religious material as part of a secular program of education. It does not violate the Constitution.

Contrary to some assertions, intelligent design is not the study of the six-day theory of creation. Intelligent design simply looks at the evidence of life we have here. It looks at natural processes and says we believe evolution does not account for a lot of what we see here today.

From a scientific viewpoint, I don't think a court can find that there is any fact as to the origin of human life. There is no undisputed fact. And simply the discoveries, the recent discoveries about neutrino particles, the effect that has on the big bang theory, which is all part of the evolutionary process, it shows that evolution is a theory in crisis and theories are in a state of flux. Again, I would draw your attention to the July 20, 1998 cover story in *Newsweek* entitled "Science Finds God."

As a way of concluding, I would just say that students have a right to an unbiased instruction and when we deprive students of certain scientific facts and certain scientific theories merely on the basis that it happens to support a certain religious viewpoint—implicitly supports a religious viewpoint—that should not be excluded from children.

Mr. DeHart, when he teaches to his students, he uses the video, *Inherit the Wind*, and it's the video about the Scopes trial. It's the movie about the Scopes trial. And one of the telling parts in that trial is where they say it is the right to think that is on trial. And I think that's what we have in this issue as well, the right to think. Will we accept an orthodoxy or will we allow prevailing theories to be challenged by hard science? And I think that's the issue here today.

CHAIRPERSON BERRY: Thank you very much. Commissioners—questions for the panel?

VICE CHAIRMAN REYNOSO: I always have questions.

CHAIRPERSON BERRY: How about Mr. Anderson.

COMMISSIONER ANDERSON: Thank you. Dr. Meyer, would you tell us what your dissertation was on, the title, at Cambridge?

MR. MEYER: It was called "Of Clues and Causes: A Methodological Interpretation of Origin-of-Life Studies."

COMMISSIONER ANDERSON: And what was the scope of that?

MR. MEYER: It addressed the methodological ground rules of the origin-of-life debate and the nature of historical inference and historical discussion of the development of origin-of-life theories.

COMMISSIONER ANDERSON: And did it take into account intelligent design theory?

MR. MEYER: No, it did not.

COMMISSIONER ANDERSON: So it was involved primarily with what—evolution?

MR. MEYER: It analyzed the modes of explanation that are used in historical sciences such as evolutionary biology. It focused specifically on evolutionary, chemical evolutionary theory, and Darwin's theory of evolutionary biology.

COMMISSIONER ANDERSON: Was it a critical dissertation?

MR. MEYER: It was an analytical one. What I was attempting to establish there was that there are certain methodological canons in the historical sciences that actually legitimate alternative points of view. My research subsequent to my Ph.D. has—I've published a number of articles making the point that there is an equivalency of methodology in these two different strands of thought.

If you take the—you analyze evolutionary biology and analyze the rules of evidence and inference that are employed to decide what's a legitimate claim, you find that those same rules of evidence and inference can be used equally to legitimate alternative conclusions.

There has been a significant legal issue over the definition of science and this is known in arcane philosophy literature as the demarcation issue. And in the early '80s in the first of the creation trials in the South, in Arkansas, a definition of science was promulgated by Michael Ruse, a philosopher of science, a five-fold definition that Judge Overton accepted. This definition was immediately repudiated by other philosophers of science. And much of my work has been designed to show that the definition he used in order to exclude alternative points of views is philosophically tendentious and untenable.

And interestingly, in 1993, after actually Ruse and I spoke at a conference in Dallas, he repudiated that—his previous testimony—publicly. In an AAAS Meeting in Boston, he no longer asserted that there is a clear philosophical definition of science that can be used to make categorical exclusions of certain points of view. And this is a very significant development, both philosophically and legally.

COMMISSIONER ANDERSON: It seemed to be significant to the faculty in Cambridge.

MR. MEYER: Well, my initial research was at least—yeah.

COMMISSIONER ANDERSON: How would you describe the difference between creationism and intelligent design?

MR. MEYER: I have a slide I wish I had with me. There are—design has two crucial planks. One is that there is—that some sort of intelligent agent acted to create and that that action is detectable scientifically. For example, you have your big billboard here, but when you go into Victoria Harbor up north there, there is a mural of red and yellow flowers against the background of the harbor and it's a very specific arrangement. And as you get closer, you make a design inference. You can detect intelligence was involved in the arrangement of those flowers because they in effect spell a message—"Welcome to Victoria."

The theory of design stipulates that the presence of high information content is an indicator of intelligence so that design, an intelligent cause, is detectable by some clear probabilistic or information-theoretic criteria. So the idea is that a designer acted and that it is detectable in some way.

The theory of special creation stipulates a number of things. It is not strong on the idea of detectability. Oftentimes, creation is simply asserted as the result of a prior religious commitment. It's a deduction from religious authority rather than an inference from data. And it also stipulates a very specific tenet such as a six-day creation in six twenty-four-hour literal days, the reality of Noah's flood, a number of things that are drawn directly from the Genesis text.

Design theory has no truck with any of those matters.

COMMISSIONER ANDERSON: I think Sir Isaac Newton believed that there was an intelligent design behind physics. Would you say that teaching Newtonian physics is akin to teaching creationism?

MR. MEYER: Well, it's very interesting. I've just written an essay, and Newton's design arguments are actually quite extraordinary and very sophisticated. And he makes his arguments on the basis of the precise configuration of parts that you find, for example, in the eye or in the configuration of planets. And these kinds of arguments are coming back into currency.

I'm going to enter into evidence this book by Michael Behe called *Darwin's Black Box*, which is now in its twelfth or thirteenth printing. It's done very well. This is a photocopy enhancement of bacterial flagellum, a motor that is really an outboard motor on the back of a cell that powers—gives the cell its locomotion. It has fifty separate protein components. Each of these must work in precise coordination in order to attain any function. Behe argues, much as Newton did many centuries ago, that this system is irreducibly complex, that if you remove any of the components, you cease to get function. Now, he says, this type of system cannot be explained by Darwinian gradualistic evolution because to get any functional advantage, which is the stipulation of Darwinian theory, you have to have all the parts before you get any function. So you can't build this up gradually. If you have 50 percent of the parts, you don't have a motor that works half as well, you have a broken motor.

And so this kind of evidence in biology is resuscitating these kinds of design arguments. And this is part of the evidential basis for this theoretical approach.

COMMISSIONER ANDERSON: Thank you.

COMMISSIONER HORNER: I think that Dr. Scott might like to say something.

MS. SCOTT: I was going to ask you about protocol. Is it possible for us to comment?

CHAIRPERSON BERRY: Yes. If you'd like to say something, you may.

MR. MEYER: I knew she'd want to say something.

MS. SCOTT: We've done this before. I was interested in your bringing up Newton because Newton made a very clear distinction—as a very religious scientist, he made a very clear distinction about how science should work, which is directly relevant to what my two companions here have said about science in disagreement with it.

Newton's view was that we should understand the natural world solely by using natural processes. And he said this for religious reasons because he didn't want God's existence or God's transcendence, shall we say, to be tested by the base methods of science. There is—without getting into philosophers dancing on the heads of pins here, which we're dangerously close to doing, we have to distinguish between science as something that is naturalistic in a methodological sense. Yes, we explain the natural world restricting ourselves only to natural cause. This is what Darwin meant when he said, we will explain without recourse to the supernatural. This is what modern-day scientists say when they're studying any aspect of science. We're only talking about natural processes. Evolution is not inherently atheistic. It is methodologically naturalistic.

There is also, I will agree fully and I've criticized it myself, here something Steve and I can agree on, it is also the case that there are those who have taken evolution and made a philosophy of it. Now, I do not think that that should be—that philosophical views of evolutionary naturalism, if you will, should be promoted from the school room or from the college podium any more than should religious views. But I think it should be made very clear that evolution is not inherently a philosophical system as both of my companions have claimed.

MR. MEYER: May I come back on each of those three points.

COMMISSIONER HORNER: Sure, sure. I'll just hold my questions.

MR. MEYER: The historical point on Newton, I'm afraid, is just simply incorrect. If one opens to the *General Scholium*, the introduction to the *Principia*, arguably the greatest book of science ever written, one finds an exquisite design argument by Newton in which he makes clear that the arrangements of the planets can only be explained not, he says, by natural law, but only by the contrivance of a most wise artificer. He's very explicit about this. This is in the introduction to his *magnum opus*.

And you find these kinds of design arguments all throughout the scientific revolution from Boyle, from Kepler, from others. The convention of methodological naturalism to which Eugenie appeals is an entirely tendentious standard, and as Neal Gillespie establishes, a historian of biology, this was a result of the Darwinian polemic. Darwin established—in conjunction with other scientists who were like-minded in the late nineteenth century—this convention. It nowhere existed prior to the late nineteenth century. And the presence of these design arguments in the writing of the early scientific founders makes this clear.

We are, in addition to challenging the evidence—the Darwinian evidential claims—challenging the normative function of that convention, of methodological naturalism. That is up for grabs. We do not concede it.

And —this is one of the reasons that students are being limited from hearing this evidence because science has been defined, by definition, as an entirely naturalistic enterprise.

MS. SCOTT: That's right.

MR. MEYER: But that definition wins the debate by stipulation, and we don't want to allow that. We want a free and open discussion of the evidence and let the evidence lead us to the truth, no holds barred.

CHAIRPERSON BERRY: Let me say that Commissioner Horner is going to ask her questions. We are not going to have you go back and forth, and back and forth. Then we'll never get to all the questions. Then you'll have an opportunity for other exchanges as we go along.

COMMISSIONER HORNER: My question is for Dr. Meyer. Your chart has an arrow going from intelligent design and microevolution to a theistic worldview.

MR. MEYER: Yes.

COMMISSIONER HORNER: My question is, is it possible to have intelligent design without a theistic worldview?

MR. MEYER: Absolutely. The arrow there I intended—this is a fine point of logic, but an arrow of implication not entailment. For example, there are naturalistically-minded scientists. Scientists who hold a naturalistic worldview such as Fred Hoyle, for example, and perhaps—we don't know quite how to take Francis Crick on this point—but Crick and Hoyle have both suggested that perhaps the origin of life is such a difficult problem—and Crick says so many are the different conditions that have to come together—that perhaps the best explanation is that it was seeded here by intelligent beings from outer space.

COMMISSIONER HORNER: Is that the only alternative?

MR. MEYER: Well, no.

COMMISSIONER HORNER: Can you define intelligent designer—or intelligent design—without reference to a conscious deity, or without reference to an alien being?

MR. MEYER: Well, I think you can define it by reference to a conscious mind without stipulating the identity of that mind.

COMMISSIONER HORNER: Okay.

MR. MEYER: My point is that if a student is trying to integrate what he or she is learning into a worldview framework, they are often prevented in that process by this convention of methodological naturalism. And design theory, for obvious reasons, fits nicely in a theistic worldview, but it doesn't entail—it's not a proof of God's existence.

COMMISSIONER HORNER: And one last question for the philosophically illiterate of us on this panel, at least to me—are you repairing in your thinking to an older metaphysics that has been superseded in modern times or are you repairing to something entirely metaphysically new?

MR. MEYER: Personally, I'm more of a traditionalist. I think my—but this differs from scientist to scientist—my own metaphysical interests are more traditionally theistic. But there are others who have different points of view. We have some fellows in our Discovery Institute, David Berlinski, for example, basically a secular Jewish scholar who is very critical of Darwinism. And I frankly don't know what his metaphysical inclinations are, but he has scientific reasons for opposing neo-Darwinism, and he's done so with great elegance.

COMMISSIONER HORNER: But it is the case that almost all people who share your point of view are at least theistic.

MR. MEYER: Well, I get a lot of letters from pantheistic New Age sort of folk who think that this is kind of interesting, you know. And myself, I could make philosophical arguments against their position. I think, you know, this debate is, you know, what you make of this is in a sense your own—subject to your own philosophical consideration.

COMMISSIONER HORNER: I guess what I'm trying to get at is whether there is a very intimate, politically and philosophically intimate connection between intelligent design and believing in God in some traditional broad sense or whether there is a secular counterpart in support of intelligent design. I'm thinking of something, for instance, if you'll just bear with me just a moment.

MR. MEYER: Sure.

COMMISSIONER HORNER: This is very hard to talk about. About twenty years ago, I read some book by Teilhard de Chardin which seemed to suppose that over a period of millennia or millions of years—some period of time—all people would blend into one universal mind or something like that.

MR. MEYER: Right, right.

COMMISSIONER HORNER: Is it possible that there are people who believe in intelligent design from that point of view?

MR. MEYER: Yes, it is. Just as there are people who believe in evolution who find a way to merge that with a theistic worldview.

COMMISSIONER HORNER: It's a minority.

MR. MEYER: Right.

COMMISSIONER HORNER: It's a minority view, but there are—

MR. MEYER: Right. There are easier and harder kinds of inferences to make.

COMMISSIONER HORNER: Okay. That's enough. Thank you.

CHAIRPERSON BERRY: Okay. Other questions from other commissioners? Vice Chair.

VICE CHAIRMAN REYNOSO: I have a question for Dr. Scott. You mentioned, Dr. Scott, and the material that you gave us, indicates that you take a different view in terms of the melding of, or potential melding of science, even Darwinian theory, with religion. The implication is that there may not be any incongruity. Am I reading the material correctly?

MS. SCOTT: Could you restate the question, please. I'm not really sure what you're asking.

VICE CHAIRMAN REYNOSO: Can one accept a Darwinian theory of evolution and at the same time believe in God?

MS. SCOTT: Now I understand. Of course. And one of the articles that I've included in your packet is a review that I wrote for the *Annual Review of Anthropology* in which I represent the creation/evolution continuum. This is not a dichotomy where evolutionists line up on one side and creationists on another.

One reason why I would argue strongly against the presentation of creationism with evolution in the K–12 schools is because what creationism are you going to use? Are you going to use Catholic creationism? Are you going to use one of the many kinds of Protestant creationism, young-earth creationism, old-earth like Steve?

VICE CHAIRMAN REYNOSO: Native American creationism.

MS. SCOTT: And which Native American creationism are you going to use? You will remember that there are many, many different tribal groups with different traditions.

I think before we get bogged down in either philosophy or history, you forgot Laplace, by the way, if you're going to talk about Newton, I think— I'm sorry. I couldn't help that.

COMMISSIONER HORNER: It's all right. We didn't understand it.

(Laughter)

MS. SCOTT: That's okay. He understood.

I think it's important for us to remember how it is we determine what we teach at the K–12 level. And we don't determine what we teach at the K–12 level based upon a popularity contest. What we do is we look to see what is being taught at universities and what scholarship in that particular field, whether it's literature or geography or science or whatever, what the people who do that for a living consider to be state-of-the-art scholarship. So even though we find there is great enthusiasm for perpetual motion machines, and I can show you plenty of web sites that are promoting them—and that would be great because then we'd solve the energy problem—we don't teach perpetual motion machines because physicists have decided that's not going to work.

What Stephen is doing and his colleagues at the Discovery Institute and elsewhere in the country, a small group of people, they are going about trying to establish design theory in the right way. They are discussing this. They are holding conferences. They are writing papers and they have by and large, unfortunately for them, been met with a large thud. Design theory has been heard and it has at this point not yet been accepted.

There's an article in the packet by a man named Gilchrist who did a computer survey looking at scientific articles to see the place of intelligent design theory. This is an idea that is a contender in the world of science, and I think if you look at the article, you will see that he does not have any evidence for that at all.

Maybe intelligent design theory will someday prove to be a valid scientific alternative. I doubt it, and thus far, it isn't. And I don't think we should be presenting it to K–12 students until it has achieved its status within the world of science and scholarship as a whole.

If you go to Brigham Young or Baylor or Notre Dame, you will not be taught intelligent design theory. You will be taught evolution and you will be taught that evolution happened.

MR. MEYER: May I respond to that point?

CHAIRPERSON BERRY: Do we have questions from any of the other commissioners?

Yes, you may respond, and she may respond, and then you may respond.

(Laughter)

MR. MEYER: Using cultural hegemony in one domain as a justification for the continuance of cultural hegemony in another is tendentious. We in fact have some very cutting edge scholarship coming. Here is a brochure about a new book, *The Design Inference*, by Bill Dembski, double Ph.D., math and philosophy, University of Chicago. This is Cambridge University Press, 1998. A colleague in biology, Paul Nelson, has a book coming out in the distinguished Evolutionary Monograph Series at the University of Chicago Press. The book is . . . a design-based critique of Darwin's common ancestor thesis. We have a book, an anthology, coming out this fall with some fifteen design theorists.

It is indeed very difficult because of the convention of methodological naturalism, which Eugenie Scott cited before, for many of our people to make explicit the importance of their scientific research. Many of our people publish their research, the nuts and bolts of science, without making their theoretical point of view clear. But we have found that there is an openness with top-level academic publishers to our work and we're developing a very robust publishing program, and this is not something that's just taking place here in Seattle at Discovery. But there are many places. There are Germans, one at the Munich Institute of Technology. There are Israelis. There are people all around the world that hold this perspective who are finding ways to get their scientific case out.

So I think this is—again, I'd ask the commissioners to weigh the importance of this doctrine—which Eugenie mentioned before—this idea of methodological naturalism. This suppresses the free expression of scientific ideas that are contrary to the Darwinian perspective and that has to be taken into account in weighing the numbers game and counting heads. Even so, we have a very robust publishing program under works.

CHAIRPERSON BERRY: May I just make a minor intervention in the emphasis in fairness to Commissioner George. We heard what you said about the robust publishing program and all the rest of it and that's fine. But do you deny that there are distinguished organizations of academics who are scientists who still believe, and I don't just mean people who are against creationism philosophically, but most of the major scientific organizations still believe that evolution is a valid scientific theory and that the weight of the evidence is in support of it? Are you denying that this is the case, or are you saying that there is this developing field—

MR. MEYER: I would agree with you—yeah, I would agree with you about the majoritarian point.

CHAIRPERSON BERRY: You do agree with that. I'm just only doing it to balance it out.

MR. MEYER: No, sure, I understand. But I do not agree with the point about the weight of the evidence. I want to emphasize how important to this commission methodological naturalism is. This is a review I have quoted, a review of Michael Behe's book by Robert Shapiro, and he commends the book as a top-notch job of explaining one of the most vexing problems in biology, the origin of—the complexity of the—

CHAIRPERSON BERRY: Mr. Meyer, if I may –

MR. MEYER: Yes.

CHAIRPERSON BERRY: I'm not trying to engage you about the validity of the argument. I'm not even interested in that.

MR. MEYER: Oh, sorry. You just want a straight yes or no answer. Sorry.

CHAIRPERSON BERRY: No. I am simply putting in the record that there are many other scholars who have, you know—

MR. MEYER: Different claims?

CHAIRPERSON BERRY: —claims to distinction—

MR. MEYER: Yeah.

CHAIRPERSON BERRY: —who are in distinguished organizations of academics whose list of books I do not have here, and I don't know if Ms. Scott does so she can read all their latest works, that on balance there are scholars, many of them, who believe that the theory of evolution is a valid theory and that it is scientifically supported and that they have major works done by major publishers over the years and that the weight of scholarship is not all to the side of intelligent design.

MR. MEYER: Oh, no, I mean, I—

CHAIRPERSON BERRY: I'm only just stating that for the record.

MR. MEYER: I'm not making that point. The point is there is a debate here that's worth having in front of our students.

CHAIRPERSON BERRY: Right. And I don't know the answer. I'm just saying that that's covered my intervention, not to get into an argument over it.

MS. SCOTT: And that is exactly the point. Is this a debate worth having before our students?

CHAIRPERSON BERRY: Sure, any debate is worth it.

MS. SCOTT: Well, is it? I mean, no, that is an important issue because we could spend a lot of time at the K–12 level talking about many things that are debated in science. My suggestion—and one that I make in my article for our teachers on teaching evolution and avoiding the mine fields—is to encourage the teachers to have debates between students about actual scientific controversies.

Now, we've had a number of things jumbled together. We've had origin of life, which is not the same thing as descent with modification. Origin of life and actual common ancestry are different phenomena. We've had certain confusion about what is science and what is religion and does science have to be methodologically naturalistic and so forth.

There are many valid controversies in science that students could debate. Whether evolution took place is not one of them. We can debate how it took place.

CHAIRPERSON BERRY: Okay. Do you have something, Commissioner George?

COMMISSIONER GEORGE: I do have some questions, but I think Mr. Anderson—

CHAIRPERSON BERRY: Okay. Go right ahead.

COMMISSIONER ANDERSON: As I see the issue here for this panel, and maybe I'm just speaking for myself, is, number one, is any alternative to evolution so tainted by religion, that it constitutes the establishment of religion in the public schools and therefore cannot be taught? That's one issue. And the other issue is whether there is significant scientific literature and debate about the theory of evolution that alternative theories ought to be presented as good education policy.

Now, we can—I don't know how you measure the weight of the evidence, whether you weigh all the books on the one side, but I think at one point, a lot of books on one side and Galileo had—

(Laughter)

COMMISSIONER ANDERSON: So you can measure weight in different ways. But it seems to me that that ought to be the two issues, at least that I would see addressed here, number one, is there independent scientific grounds to see whether there's an alternative to the theory of evolution that ought to be discussed and, secondly, are those alternatives so tainted by religion as to be inappropriate in the public schools?

CHAIRPERSON BERRY: He's just simply stating, unless you want him to explicate again.

COMMISSIONER ANDERSON: Well?

MS. SCOTT: One place to look for the answer to the first question that you raised is at the National Academy of Sciences which consists of the most highly regarded scientists in the country. They advise Congress and groups like yourselves. They have recently published a book which I included in your red packets, except, unfortunately, you, Commissioner Lee and you, Commissioner Reynoso. I discriminated against my fellow Californians. I will get you your copies when I get back to my office. I didn't have enough to bring.

But in that book, which is teaching about evolution on the nature of science, they reiterate the fact that evolution is considered state-of-the-art science. Teachers need to teach it. And it's absolutely appropriate for the K–12 level.

CHAIRPERSON ANDERSON: I don't see anybody on this panel saying evolution ought not to be taught. I mean, that's not the issue we're discussing.

MS. SCOTT: This may not be what Steve and are I are discussing. But this certainly is happening out there in the big world, the grass roots examples that I gave you. There are many, many places where evolution is misunderstood to be antireligious, inherently antireligious, inherently a philosophical system such as ideas presented here, and therefore you can't teach it because you would be offending somebody's religion. And I think this is more the issue for —that the Commission would be concerned about rather than, you know, dancing on heads and pins over here.

CHAIRPERSON BERRY: We like dancing on heads and pins, but first let me see if Mr. Sybrandy—or Dr. Meyer, do you want to respond to what she said before I let Commissioner George ask questions?

MR. MEYER: I just wanted to make a point in response to Mr. Anderson's point which is that the detection of an intelligent cause is something which does not depend on a religious premise. We do it all the time. There are whole industries that are based on the ability to detect intelligence, cryptography, fraud detection in insurance work. I'm looking at a sign which I assume had an intelligent cause behind it because it has high information content.

I don't have to have a religious point of view in order to detect the effects of intelligence. And so I think the theory of design can be separated in a meaningful way from a prior religious commitment that's not incorrigibly tainted. And I forget what else is being discussed.

(Laughter)

CHAIRPERSON BERRY: You'll have another chance. Do you want to say anything, Mr. Sybrandy?

MR. MEYER: Let the lawyer get in.

MR. SYBRANDY: If I could address also Mr. Anderson's point as far as the first point you were making—is intelligent design so tainted by religious purpose or by religion that it constitutes an establishment? I think the weight of the cases that we've seen so far indicate that it is not. The *Freiler* case, which was discussed here earlier today, wasn't a case regarding whether intelligent design should be taught. It was a disclaimer case where every time someone mentioned evolution, the school, the biology teacher had to say, "And by the way, I'm not in any way trying to denigrate your belief in the six-day version, Genesis Biblical version of creation."

The court found that that disclaimer was unconstitutional because it had a sectarian purpose. And in fact, in *Freiler,* the court noted prior to this mandate of giving the disclaimer, the court stated that teachers had academic freedom to discuss all sorts of alternative theories in evolution. And the court mentioned that with approval, that you could mention alternatives to evolution. But they said in this case, we just don't see any secular purpose in doing this.

That's really where the court on every single creation and evolution case comes down. And I think it's important, instead of looking at the dicta of a case, to determine what is legal and what's not, they started to look at the holdings of the cases. Again, going back to *Edwards*, look at the holding of the case, look at exactly what the facts were and the *Lemon* prong of sectarian versus secular purpose.

CHAIRPERSON BERRY: Commissioner George.

COMMISSIONER GEORGE: Thank you, Madam Chair. As I understand the debate, there's a certain asymmetry here. Dr. Scott is taking the position not only that evolution must be taught in science curriculum in K–12, but also that alternatives or criticisms of evolution must not be taught.

Dr. Meyer by contrast, and here is the asymmetry, is not arguing that evolution may not be taught, but only arguing that criticisms of evolution must be taught along with evolution.

Now, let me just pause here to ask whether I've represented both of your points of view accurately.

MS. SCOTT: I'm afraid not in my case.

COMMISSIONER GEORGE: Okay. Could you correct me?

MS. SCOTT: Alternatives to evolution can certainly be taught if they, in the words of *Edwards v. Aguillard*, have a secular intent and are not religiously based. You have to teach secular alternatives to evolution, not religious alternatives. The problem is that Justice Brennan was a wonderful jurist, but he didn't know zip about science and there are no scientific alternatives to evolution that are recognized by scientists. Now, the whole history of the creation/evolution controversy from creation science to the recent alternatives to evolution—intelligent design theory or varieties—has always been, "Well, we're going to teach the evidence against evolution, and because evolution is not true, that means our position is true."

I congratulate Steve and his colleagues because they are at least attempting to come up with some sort of positive arguments for intelligent design. My personal opinion and that of most others is that they haven't succeeded. They may yet. If they do succeed, then they have a right to be taught. But they have to earn their spurs, so to speak, within the body of scholarship that decides what is state-of-the-art science.

I mean, we've all had papers rejected, right? I mean, we've all had our ideas; some are accepted, some aren't. I don't think that we should make a decision as to what to teach at the K–12 level until these issues have been decided at the level of scholarship that is most appropriate—the college and professional level.

COMMISSIONER GEORGE: Then I'm not sure that I did misrepresent your position.

MS. SCOTT: Well, maybe I was just unclear on what you said.

COMMISSIONER GEORGE: Let me try again. You take the view that at least for now students may not be presented with any putative reasons not to believe evolutionary theory.

MS. SCOTT: I think that students who are presented with these alternatives to evolution such as the ones discussed in my statement are receiving bad science. They may not be getting anything illegal, but it is definitely bad science. And if you look at the statements from the National Science Teachers Association and the National Association of Biology Teachers, they would agree with this.

As somebody who values scholarship and as a former academic, it pains me to rely upon authority for decision-making. This is not a comfortable feeling for me, but I think to some degree, we do. I don't know how many of you could tell me why perpetual motion machines don't work, but we all agree that we will not teach perpetual motion manufacturing in the schools.

COMMISSIONER GEORGE: Surely, Dr. Scott, you believe that competing accounts of evolution such as those given by Gould, say, on the one hand or my old colleague at New College Oxford, Richard Dawkins—

MS. SCOTT: Dawkins?

COMMISSIONER GEORGE: —ought to be taught although one side is plainly right and the other side plainly wrong.

MS. SCOTT: What you are talking about are debates about how evolution takes place. And I was saying before, if we were going to have debates among students as a critical thinking exercise, we should have them debating things that are validly considered—

COMMISSIONER GEORGE: But those are debates where there are minority and majority positions.

MS. SCOTT: Those are debates about how evolution takes place, not whether.

COMMISSIONER GEORGE: Oh, I understand that. But it's a ferocious debate, is it not?

MS. SCOTT: Uh-huh.

COMMISSIONER GEORGE: By which there have been claims of irrationality made by both sides against the other. And besides the fact that there are minority and majority positions, do you think it's a good thing to teach the conflict?

MS. SCOTT: Actually, I would be a little reluctant to have students engage in a "who will be the Dawkins side and who'll be the Gould side" debates, because they don't know enough about evolutionary theory to debate this issue.

COMMISSIONER GEORGE: Well, which do we teach them then? Do we teach them Dawkins's view or Gould's view?

MS. SCOTT: You know the irony of this is that students get so little evolution at all in school.

COMMISSIONER GEORGE: You're evading the question, Dr. Scott. Which would it be? Really, seriously, which should they be taught?

MS. SCOTT: How would you characterize Dawkins's view and Gould's view, because we may have a different understanding. The way I would look at it is they are both talking about natural selection, but they are both talking about difference of importance. The effect of natural selection in different kinds of contexts has different importance and explains different aspects of the fossil record.

COMMISSIONER GEORGE: Are we agreed that in speaking of evolution, we're speaking not only of descent from a common ancestor, but of a mechanism of random mutation and natural selection? Can we agree about that?

MS. SCOTT: And others, other mechanisms as well. The random mutation and natural selection is Darwinism. There are other mechanisms of evolution in addition.

COMMISSIONER GEORGE: In addition, or as competing accounts in the mechanism?

MS. SCOTT: In addition.

COMMISSIONER GEORGE: All right.

MS. SCOTT: Because nobody says natural selection doesn't work. That's a double negative, but you know what I mean.

COMMISSIONER GEORGE: Let me follow that nobody says natural selection—

MS. SCOTT: Everyone agrees evolution works. Everyone agrees natural selection is a major component.

COMMISSIONER GEORGE: Everybody who—everybody who both believes evolutionary theory and—well, that is just a tautology. People who believe in natural selection, believe in natural selection.

MS. SCOTT: No.

COMMISSIONER GEORGE: Or is it not true that there are some people who believe in descent from a common ancestor, but not in the mechanism of natural selection?

MS. SCOTT: I think there would be very few because natural selection—what natural selection does is shape groups within—populations within species. That, coupled with the phenomenon of reproductive isolation and speciation mechanisms, is what causes speciation.

Now, that basic picture is something I think you would find in all the textbooks and you'd get all the evolutionary biologists to agree with. Where these people square off and start arm wrestling is over the presence or absence of other factors such as reorganizations of the genome to various genetic processes, developmental biological processes, and these other—

CHAIRPERSON BERRY: Before you guys go too far afield from civil rights issues, let me just ask again—am I clear that you said that you didn't mind discussions of evolution and criticisms and different theories being presented so long as that they were not based on religion and so long as they were secular in nature?

Did I understand you to say that, quoting *Aguillard* when you first began there? You said you didn't mind the definition in *Aguillard*. That was before you complained about Brennan not knowing anything about science. And you were asked whether you thought people shouldn't discuss criticisms of evolution or different theories, and you said something about so long as they had a secular purpose and they were not based on religion. Did I hear you right or not? If I didn't, then tell me.

MS. SCOTT: Criticisms of evolution based on religion are unacceptable.

CHAIRPERSON BERRY: That's what I mean. Is that what you said?

MS. SCOTT: If there are solid scientific criticisms of evolution, of course, they can be heard.

CHAIRPERSON BERRY: I'll give it back to Commissioner George.

COMMISSIONER GEORGE: Let me take it back in a civil rights angle. Did I hear Dr. Scott right to say that she would object to criticisms such as those offered by Berlinski and Behe and Dembski and all these people. But she would not object to those criticisms being presented on grounds that they were religious, and therefore a violation or separation of church and state, but rather, that she would object to them on the grounds that they're bad science.

MS. SCOTT: You lumped a lot of people into the same hopper. Berlinski and Behe differ enormously in their attitude.

COMMISSIONER GEORGE: But they're critics of—

MS. SCOTT: The point is they're dealing with different matters completely.

COMMISSIONER GEORGE: But they're all critics of evolution.

MS. SCOTT: Yes. They're all critics of evolution.

COMMISSIONER GEORGE: And you wouldn't object to their views being presented on the grounds of separation of church and state or any constitutional issue. You would object to their criticisms to—they give reasons against believing at least certain theories of evolution.

MS. SCOTT: And some of these are religious reasons and some of these are secular reasons.

COMMISSIONER GEORGE: And say Berlinski's—you wouldn't object to Berlinski? Berlinski's not a believer. How are you going—

MS. SCOTT: Berlinski, if you read Berlinski's criticisms of evolution, he's just rehashing creation science except he leaves out the age of the Earth. He talks about the second law of thermodynamics.

COMMISSIONER GEORGE: Does he get excluded then on religious grounds? Are you going to say now you can't have students exposed to that, that's not only bad science, that's religion?

MS. SCOTT: He would be excluded on the grounds of bad science.

COMMISSIONER GEORGE: But not religion. So we don't have a civil rights—

MS. SCOTT: He's pretty careful about not mentioning religion.

COMMISSIONER GEORGE: Is that a hint about his motive or—

MS. SCOTT: Uh-huh.

COMMISSIONER GEORGE: So you're suggesting that his motive really is religious and therefore you're going to exclude him.

MS. SCOTT: No, no. I don't think either of us think that David is religious. I have other reasons for thinking—I think David is doing something different with this exercise.

COMMISSIONER GEORGE: But I want to get to the civil rights. In other words—

MS. SCOTT: It is a difficult issue because we are talking about civil rights and civil liberties. We're also talking—and I at least part of the time am talking about tautological issues, what's good science and science literacy.

COMMISSIONER GEORGE: Okay. If we could just keep it—

MS. SCOTT: And we may have slipped back and forth.

COMMISSIONER GEORGE: And I appreciate that in your unusual position because you are both a scientist and an advocate, a political advocate. But could we just stay on the civil rights dimension so that we could say that there are some people, as much as you might object to them on scientific grounds and object on straight-out school curricular grounds, you wouldn't object on civil rights/civil liberties grounds to their positions being presented in biology classes?

MS. SCOTT: I would not make a blanket statement.

COMMISSIONER GEORGE: Well, I'm not asking for a blanket statement. I'm not saying everybody. I'm saying there are some people like Berlinski's views.

MS. SCOTT: I don't know Berlinski's agenda. I think you're asking for a hypothetical that I'm reluctant to give you.

COMMISSIONER GEORGE: No. I'm asking for a specific. It's not a hypothetical. You know Berlinski's view very well. Okay. If Berlinski's view is to be excluded, but not on the grounds that it's religious, but on some other civil rights/civil liberties grounds, what are the civil rights/civil liberties grounds for excluding—

MS. SCOTT: Berlinski's view is not unique to him.

COMMISSIONER GEORGE: So.

MS. SCOTT: I mean, the position Berlinski advocates has been advocated by those who on the purpose prong of *Lemon* are definitely intending for religious establishment.

COMMISSIONER GEORGE: People argue for civil rights on the basis of religion and on the basis of secular things. Are we going to say because some people work for civil rights on religious grounds and invoke God and the brotherhood of man, that any advocacy of civil rights was itself a violation of civil rights?

MS. SCOTT: If you are familiar with the arguments that are raised in the creation science the vast majority of them never mention God. A lot of them have to do with supporting ideas like the whole world being supported by things, inundated by a flood, by evidence that the world is actually young, an awful lot of the literature, not the stuff—

COMMISSIONER GEORGE: But that's not Berlinski. If Berlinski's view were being presented to students, would there be anything objectionable on civil rights/civil liberties grounds?

MS. SCOTT: I would want to ask a lawyer.

COMMISSIONER GEORGE: Okay. Then, let me ask is it your position, Dr. Scott, that the evolution that you would like to see presented in schools without criticism—because, at least there's, at the moment, no criticism that would be sufficiently serious to put forward—is a view that has no preconditions or premises that are not themselves empirically verifiable. In other words, it rests on no questionable metaphysical assumptions. That's your view?

MS. SCOTT: My view is that science should be—evolution should be taught as science without metaphysical implications.

COMMISSIONER GEORGE: And that to believe in evolution with the mechanisms that we've discussed and perhaps additional mechanisms, say, natural selection, one can believe that without any nonempirical assumptions being made. In other words, to believe that does not presuppose as people like Phillip Johnson claim it does, certain assumptions that are not themselves empirically variable, certain assumptions that are metaphysical rather than—

MS. SCOTT: I think Phillip Johnson is dead wrong in his depiction of evolution as a fundamentally naturalistic philosophical system. It is no more naturalistic than heliocentrism. Excuse me. It is no more philosophically naturalistic than heliocentrism.

COMMISSIONER GEORGE: Dr. Meyer, would you like to comment?

MR. MEYER: One of the—let me first clarify my position and then come back. What we are advocating is teaching the controversy within the limits of the law. And there are legitimate scientific reasons for criticizing Darwinism. I started to point out Behe's molecular motor here. Some fifty book reviews have been written about Behe's book, many by scientists, most often conceding his point that there are no neo-Darwinian explanations for the origin of these motors. And so the grounds for exclusion of his view has been again this convention of methodological naturalism, it's against the ground rules which we have decided—

COMMISSIONER GEORGE: Can I just interrupt?

MR. MEYER: Yes, sure.

COMMISSIONER GEORGE: When you say, his view, I take it his view being the denial of the neo-Darwinian mechanism—

MR. MEYER: Right.

COMMISSIONER GEORGE: —not descent from a common ancestor, because as I understand Behe's position, he does not deny a common ancestor.

MR. MEYER: He's either in favor of that or agnostic about that.

COMMISSIONER GEORGE: Go ahead.

MR. MEYER: So my concern for science education has been rhetorically the same as Eugenie's. It's the bad science. We have a selective presentation of evidence going on. It's not fair to say that because you don't have a lot of people using the jargon, that there is not a significant scientific dispute here. Paleontology journals are full of discussions of the problem that the Cambrian explosion poses for the neo-Darwinian gradualistic model. Behe did a literature search in his book on systems like this and looked for neo-Darwinian explanations for their origin and found virtually none.

There is weighty evidence for this, and we want the evidence—students to be exposed to the evidence that supports these other viewpoints.

COMMISSIONER GEORGE: Now, do you take the view—contrary to Dr. Scott's view, do you take the view that in fact some nonempirical assumption must be made either way?

MR. MEYER: Yes.

COMMISSIONER GEORGE: So that there are metaphysical hypotheses not themselves empirically verifiable which must be made prior to one's adoption of either the design theory or evolutionary theory.

MR. MEYER: Right. In the diagram, I show a two-way arrow between worldview assumptions and theoretical viewpoints. The two can inform each other. And secondly, I think this is clearly the case by something that Eugenie has said already—that she accepts the principle of methodological naturalism. That's not an empirical or empirically verifiable principle. That is a philosophical principle. It's something that is a ground rule if you will—

MS. SCOTT: On both sides.

MR. MEYER: —which is not established by viewing nature. It's something which is only supported by rather dubious philosophical arguments.

COMMISSIONER GEORGE: Doctors of all science may take that to mean—

MS. SCOTT: Not just of evolution, of all science.

COMMISSIONER GEORGE: —that although it's a nonempirically verifiable assumption, it is nevertheless a noncontroversial one. I take it that your view, over Dr. Scott, is that it cannot be made in a way that does not shade over into a more comprehensive naturalism.

MR. MEYER: Correct.

COMMISSIONER GEORGE: So it looks to me—and then I'm going to let Dr. Scott come back and take a shot at me on it. It looks to me like your side has radicalized the discussion in such a way—radicalized meaning going to the root, in such a way as to drive the issue out of the realm of science precisely to the realm of philosophy where you make the orthodox scientists defend on philosophical grounds—

MR. MEYER: A latent philosophical principle of their whole enterprise, exactly.

COMMISSIONER GEORGE: Dr. Scott.

MS. SCOTT: I think the link between methodological naturalism and philosophical naturalism is faulty. One can be a methodological naturalist without being a philosophical naturalist.

COMMISSIONER GEORGE: Now, there you disagree—

MS. SCOTT: Absolutely.

COMMISSIONER GEORGE: —not only with people like Dr. Meyer, but also with people like Dawkins and Lewontin.

MS. SCOTT: Dawkins and Will Provine and others of that particular persuasion will admit that there are people who are methodological naturalists who are theists.

COMMISSIONER GEORGE: Oh that's a— we know that. But don't they take the view—and I can tell you they do because I had this discussion with Dawkins—that if you understand, if you have a correct understanding of evolution, you realize that there's no possibility of being a theist.

MS. SCOTT: I don't agree with Dawkins either. Philosophically, I'm more similar to him than—

COMMISSIONER GEORGE: So if we talk Dawkins's view—this I guess is the point—if we talk Dawkins's view in school, we'd be committing a civil liberties violation.

MS. SCOTT: Oh, absolutely, yeah. I have discouraged that. In fact, Will Provine and I have gone back and forth on this on a number of occasions.

COMMISSIONER GEORGE: So the *Blind Watchmaker* or Provine's works really shouldn't be taught—

MS. SCOTT: No, no, no. The philosophical views that they have— Provine has done very good work in *History of Science* and, you know, their reason to –

COMMISSIONER GEORGE: Not all his works, but, I mean, look at the *Blind Watchmaker*. Look at Dawkins's book. In Dawkins's book it quite exclusively—

MS. SCOTT: It had—

COMMISSIONER GEORGE: —adopts naturalist views so—

MS. SCOTT: It also presents a lot of straight science.

COMMISSIONER GEORGE: Well, yes, but I mean, are we going to permit it to be—wouldn't that be—

MS. SCOTT: We should not be advocating the view that evolution or science equates with disbelief because it's false and it also is an establishment problem or free exercise problem.

COMMISSIONER GEORGE: Just to conclude my line of questioning: So you both agree that there shouldn't be viewpoint discrimination, and Dr. Scott would say therefore Dawkins's comprehensive naturalism and Meyer's, Berlinski's and others' design theory ought to both be excluded?

It would be viewpoint discrimination to allow Dawkins's comprehensive naturalism a place, but not Meyer's design theory, but I take it the real difference is that just Dr. Scott says there are no legitimate scientific reasons that can be presented, at least for now, against evolution and therefore viewpoint discrimination isn't a problem between evolution and nonevolutionary views, at least at the moment, because there's no plausible nonevolutionary view.

MS. SCOTT: And you have to distinguish between keeping out Dawkins's metaphysics and intelligent design or creationist metaphysics, and whether or not you teach science as methodologically naturalist.

COMMISSIONER GEORGE: And your position you're trying to make out here is that I've got a view and we, the orthodox scientists and biologists, have a view that itself does not have any questionable metaphysical presuppositions.

MS. SCOTT: Not per se, although it certainly has implications. But it's clear that—I mean, look at something—look at an idea like natural selection. Natural selection was taken by Marx and modified to suit his agenda. It was taken by the Nazis and modified to suit their agenda. It was taken by the robber barons and modified to suit their agenda.

Now, you've got very, very different social and political ideas here, all claiming to be derived from natural selection. So clearly, I mean, I've often joked you could probably take photosynthesis and make a religion out of it if you wanted to. You should not confuse the philosophical implications or ideas people derived from a science with a science itself.

COMMISSIONER GEORGE: If something is random, it can't be directed, yes?

MS. SCOTT: Now, this is again a little bit of fancy footwork that goes on in this debate. When people who oppose evolution talk about randomness, they are generally using random in the sense that the man on the street is going to understand it, that there's nothing out there except just stuff falling into the place, and obviously you're not going to get a brick wall by all the bricks falling into their actual position, or the tornado that goes through the hangar and constructs the 727.

COMMISSIONER GEORGE: But on the other side, there's also Dawkins who says, yeah, random—

MS. SCOTT: But random as a concept important to evolution refers to the production of genetic variation, which is random in respect to the, quote, "needs of the organism." Now, evolution is not a random process, particularly, if natural selection is the mechanism that directs it, which most of us accept. Natural selection is the opposite of randomness. This is why this matter becomes so very complicated. We can get bogged down real fast at school board levels, in operations like this talking about very technical scientific elements.

What really matters I think is how do we decide what to teach in the curriculum. We can't make everybody happy. I suggest in an essay that I wrote to teachers ways that they could teach evolution without ruffling too many feathers. And I would encourage you to consider them when you make your report.

COMMISSIONER GEORGE: Thank you.

CHAIRPERSON BERRY: Thank you. I have considered this a wonderful discussion. I wish we could have had it in my seminar and taken all day and had lunch and then dinner.

And I must say, though, Dr. Meyer, I was so attracted to the intelligent design theory when I misunderstood it. And I thought you were going to say that the way the DNA particles encoded and so on that there had to be an intelligent, you know, workman up there and that it was God. And then I was going to say, hooray, I like that theory and it reinforces my beliefs. But then when you didn't want to concede that there was a being up there, God, or somebody—

MR. MEYER: I think the being was God and I think other arguments can be made for that. But it's a technical point as to whether you have an implication or a strict entailment, a proof of God's existence. I think the best explanation is that God is the designer, but it could be different.

COMMISSIONER GEORGE: A self-organizational pantheism, could it not?

CHAIRPERSON BERRY: I want God to be.

MS. SCOTT: Don't forget the extraterrestrials. That's it. We'll teach kids evolution, we'll teach them God, and we'll teach them extraterrestrials, and we'll teach them pantheism. Boy, wouldn't that go over well in the school districts.

CHAIRPERSON BERRY: I want to thank the panel very, very much. This is very illuminating. We have taken up our break with the discussion so we have to bring the next panel. So we thank you.

Note

This transcript has been edited for readability and to correct errors in transcription.

Appendix B
Helping Schools to Teach Evolution

Donald Kennedy

The noted geneticist Theodosius Dobzhansky once said that "nothing in biology makes sense except in the light of evolution." Most contemporary biologists would agree. We cannot answer the central questions about life—Why do so many species exist? Why do a few fundamental principles of biochemistry affect most of that extraordinarily diverse range of organisms? How do sudden changes, such as bacteria's resistance to drugs, spread rapidly through a population?—without referring to the theory of evolution. Evolution is as basic to the rest of biology as atomic structure is to physics.

Thus it is disheartening that in many parts of the United States, high school science classes do not teach about evolution at all or discuss it only briefly. In other countries, students in secondary and even elementary schools study evolution. But in the United States, religious opposition to teaching evolution is deeply rooted and growing stronger.

To help teachers confront the objections of fundamentalist Christians, the National Academy of Sciences (NAS) asked me to head a group of more than a dozen research scientists and high school teachers charged with producing material to help other teachers incorporate evolution into their science classes. Evolution is not an easy topic to teach well, and new information about it is accumulating rapidly. However, we all felt the need to deal with an increasingly intolerable situation in which access to the most important concept in biology was being compromised by a small but determined group of fundamentalists.

The result of our past two years of work is a booklet, "Teaching about Evolution and the Nature of Science," published in April.[1] The academy has printed 40,000 copies of the booklet and is making it available at no charge on the World Wide Web.[2] It includes careful descriptions of the evidence supporting the theory of evolution, but it does a great deal more. It attempts to provide answers to the questions about evolution that are commonly asked by students, especially those whose religious upbringing makes it difficult for them to accept what their teachers tell them in science class.

Creationists who object to teaching evolution can be divided into several groups. The most conservative creationists believe that the world is of recent origin and that God created all living things over six days, as described in Genesis. Other—perhaps most—creationists accept that evolution is responsible for small, gradual changes in organisms, but they are apt to deny the role of evolution in such larger-scale transformations as the development of whales from hoofed mammals. These creationists believe that God created the major categories of life but permitted natural changes to create minor variations. Another group of creationists accepts much of evolutionary theory but holds that the mechanisms at the most basic biological levels—the cellular and molecular—are so complex and elegant that some kind of "intelligent design" must have been involved in their creation.

Few scientists would object to creationist views expressed only from the pulpit. But many fundamentalist Christian groups have entered the political arena in search of equal time for "creation science" in the classroom. Several states passed laws during the 1980s requiring creationists' views to be presented in schools if the theory of evolution was taught. However, the Supreme Court held, in the 1987 case *Edwards v. Aguillard,* that a Louisiana statute prohibiting the teaching of evolution in the public schools unless accompanied by instruction in "creation science" constituted an impermissible endorsement of religion. That decision effectively banned such state restrictions on presenting evolution in the classroom. Nevertheless, some states' guidelines for teaching science in public schools now either omit evolution entirely or describe it as one of a number of possible theories to explain organic diversity. In several jurisdictions, Christian fundamentalists have won election to school boards and have influenced the content of local curricula.

The growth of the creationist movement in the 1980s and 1990s alarmed many American scientists. In 1984, the academy published a statement, "Science and Creationism: A View from the National Academy of Sciences." Unlike our new booklet, the 1984 statement was aimed at state and local policymakers and the public, not teachers in particular. A centerpiece of its argument was that science and religion represent different ways of knowing: Science is engaged in testing through experiments and research, whereas belief rests on spiritual convictions that, by their nature, resist such challenges. The statement argued that "creation science" was theology dressed up as science; it urged that science and religion not be considered as equivalent approaches to the same body of knowledge. The academy is updating the statement to include new evidence for evolution developed over the past fourteen years.

The academy understands that teachers in elementary and secondary schools need detailed help to present the subject effectively to their students. The difficulty is that the theory of evolution depends largely on inference: We know that many species have changed over time, but in only a few instances do we have a complete record of all the intermediate steps in the history of a present-day species. One resource for science teachers is the NAS's "National Science Education Standards," published in 1993. That document, the work of hundreds of scientists, sets standards for teaching, teacher preparation, and the content of science courses for all grades, in all fields—not just biology.

Our new booklet is another resource for teachers. We hope that teachers will use it to help answer objections from creationists to a unit on evolution or to show a student that the theory of evolution is compatible with most, though perhaps not all, religious views.

Besides presenting what we know about evolution, "Teaching about Evolution" describes how scientists test hypotheses and evaluate results. In the process, it debunks some common misunderstandings, such as the creationists' argument that evolution is "only" a theory, not a fact. The booklet explains that when the word *theory* is used in casual conversation, it may be little more than an idea, but that in science, a theory is an explanation supported by a variety of observations and tests. When I drop my pen, the fact is that the pen falls to the floor; the explanatory theory is gravity. We have no scientific doubts about gravity, but we still call it a theory.

I am optimistic that the new booklet will help teachers. Of the 40,000 copies that the NAS printed, 15,000 have been distributed to states, at no charge; the rest are selling fast. Besides my work on the booklet, my experiences since its publication have taught me a great deal about creationism and its impact on what our children are learning. Media interest in the booklet was intense, partly because of the prestige of the NAS, but mostly because the booklet suggested a continuing "hot" conflict between religion and science, with echoes of the Scopes trial. The publication was front-page news and the subject of editorials in several daily newspapers. I was asked to discuss the booklet on radio talk shows, in television interviews, and even in a debate on *The NewsHour with Jim Lehrer.*

I am now more worried about the chilling effect of creationism on teachers than I am about explicit bans by states or local school boards on teaching evolution. When I participated in a talk show on Wisconsin Public Radio, a high school teacher called in to say that, although he wasn't proud of his actions, he had decided to duck the whole issue by leaving evolution out of his course. He had a family, he told me, and they had to get along in a small community. Other callers spoke of trying to combine good teaching with a respect for the situations that many of their students were facing outside the classroom. I am full of admiration for most teachers and impressed, at the same time, with the seriousness of the problems they have to overcome.

The NewsHour with Jim Lehrer presented the issue as a debate: two biologists versus two creationists. One creationist was a very thoughtful young teacher from a Christian high school who professed admiration for the booklet and said that he had no problem with crediting small biological changes to evolution, but that he thought that evolutionists hadn't given satisfactory accounts of big biological changes. The other creationist, a dean at a fundamentalist Christian university, insisted on a literal biblical interpretation of creation and said that evolutionists were "brainwashing" their students while supported by tax dollars. I found particularly telling his charge that many evolutionary biologists are atheists; the claim that scientists (and thus science) are inherently antireligious is a perennial feature of the creationist case.

Perhaps the most useful lesson of these and other discussions is how important it is for scientists to treat religious conviction with respect—in particular, not to suggest, even indirectly, that science and religion are unalterably opposed. Most major religions have found ways to reconcile evolution and theology; a papal decree accepting evolution has made this absolutely clear for Catholics, for example. Indeed, the conflict between science and religion has surfaced only in one or two countries besides the United States. More important, most scientists have been able to combine their personal religious convictions and their work in science without difficulty. Obviously, some scientists have no formal religious commitments and do not worship. But others do, including colleagues of mine who engage the subject of evolution in their work—and they find no difficulty whatever in reconciling their beliefs with their science.

Scientists at colleges and universities have an important stake in the resolution of the conflict between creationism and evolution. Alabama—the state that gave us E. O. Wilson, perhaps the most important evolutionary biologist of his generation—recently refused to distribute the NAS's booklet to teachers in its schools. In many other states, students also are entering college with little knowledge of evolution and thus an incomplete under-standing of the natural world. Unless those of us in higher education begin to take an active role in shaping what elementary and secondary students learn about science—and in assisting local teachers who must walk a tightrope in even introducing the topic—a determined minority will con-tinue to deprive our future students of one of the foundations of scientific literacy.

Notes

1. [Both the NAS booklet and this essay were originally published in 1998. Ed.]
2. [The NAS booklet, "Teaching about Evolution and the Nature of Science," is available at http://www.nap.edu/readingroom/books/evolution98. Ed.]

Appendix C
Stratigraphic First Appearance of Phyla Body Plans

This appendix documents the stratigraphic first appearance of new body plans in the fossil record, treating the phylum as the unit of body-plan differentiation. The animal kingdom contains about forty phyla, six of which are further divided into subphyla. The subphyla are enumerated here but not treated as separate body plans for the purpose of this analysis. (We do treat the subphyla as separate body plans in our analysis in appendix D.) This appendix lists forty phyla and shows that three of these phyla first appear in the Precambrian era, nineteen in the Cambrian period, and six in later geologic periods, and twelve have no fossil history at all (see figure 17A in "The Cambrian Explosion: Biology's Big Bang"). The phyla are arranged here in alphabetical order within each successive geologic unit; the subphyla are indented and likewise arranged alphabetically within their respective phyla. The prefixes before the geologic periods are as follows: L = Lower; M = Middle; U = Upper. If a subphylum appears later than the first representative of the phylum to which it belongs, we note that separately in parentheses.

Precambrian: Three Phyla (possibility of a fourth)

Cnidaria[1]

Porifera[2]
  Gelatinosa (L. Cambrian)
  Nuda

Indeterminate track-making worm phylum (our figures in the essay "The Cambrian Explosion: Biology's Big Bang" include it as Precambrian only)

Kimberella[3]: Uncertain identity (Mollusc?) (our figures in the essay "The Cambrian Explosion: Biology's Big Bang" exclude it)

Cambrian: Nineteen Phyla

Annelida[4]

Arthropoda[5]

   Anomalocariida[6]

   Chelicerata[7]

   Crustacea[8]

   Hexapoda[9]   (U. Devonian)

   Myriapoda[10] (L. Silurian)

   Trilobita[11]

Brachiopoda[12]

   Craniiformea[13]

   Linguliformea[14]

   Rhynchonelliformea[15]

Chaetognatha[16]

Chordata[17]

   Cephalochordata[18]

   Craniata[19]

   Urochordata[20]

Coeloscleritophora[21]

Ctenophora[22]

Echinodermata[23]

   Asterozoa[24] (L. Ordovician)

   Blastozoa[25]

   Crinozoa[26]

   Echinozoa[27]

   Homalozoa[28]

Halkieriida[29]

Hemichordata[30]

Hyolitha[31]

Mollusca[32]

   Amphineura[33]

   Cyrtosoma[34]

   Diasoma[35]

Nematoda[36]

Onychophora[37]

Phoronida[38]

Pogonophora[39]

Priapula[40]

Tardigrada[41]

Tardipolypoda[42]

Later Geologic Periods: Six Phyla

Ordovician

Bryozoa/Ectoprocta[43]

Devonian

Echiura[44]

Pennsylvanian

Nemertina[45]

Jurassic

Entoprocta[46]

Tertiary

Nematomorpha[47]

Rotifera[48]

No Known Fossil Record: Twelve Phyla

Acanthocephala[49]

Cycliophora[50]

Dicyemida

Gastrotricha[51]

Gnathostomulida[52]

Kinoryncha[53]

Loricifera[54]

Orthonectida

Pentastoma[55]

Placozoa[56]

Platyhelminthes[57]

Sipuncula[58]

Notes

1. J. W. Valentine, D. Jablonski, and D. H. Erwin, "Fossils, Molecules, and Embryos: New Perspectives on the Cambrian Explosion," *Development* 126 (1999): 851–59; R. S. Boardman, A. H. Cheetham, and A. J. Rowell, eds., *Fossil Invertebrates* (Palo Alto, Calif.: Blackwell Science, 1987); S. C. Morris, "The Cambrian 'Explosion': Slow-fuse or Megatonnage?" *PNAS* 95 (2000): 4426–29.

2. Valentine, Jablonski, and Erwin, "Fossils, Molecules, and Embryos," 851–59; Morris, "Cambrian 'Explosion,'" 4426–29.

3. M. A. Fedonkin and B. M. Waggoner, "The Late Precambrian Fossil *Kimberella* Is a Mollusc-like Bilaterian Organism," *Nature* 388 (1977): 868–71.

4. Valentine, Jablonski, and Erwin, "Fossils, Molecules, and Embryos," 851–59; Morris, "Cambrian 'Explosion,'" 4426–29; J. Y. Chen and G. Q. Zhou, "Biology of the Chengjiang Fauna," in *The Cambrian Explosion and the Fossil Record*, ed. J. Y. Chen, Y. N. Change, and H. V. Iten, Bulletin of the National Museum of Science, no. 10 (Taichung, 1997), 11–105.

5. Valentine, Jablonski, and Erwin, "Fossils, Molecules, and Embryos," 851–59; Morris, "Cambrian 'Explosion,'" 4426–29; Chen and Zhou, "Biology of the Chenjiang Fauna," 11–105.

6. Morris, "Cambrian 'Explosion,'" 4426–29.

7. Boardman, Cheetham, and Rowell, *Fossil Invertebrates.*

8. Morris, "Cambrian 'Explosion,'" 4426–29; Chen and Zhou, "Biology of the Chenjiang Fauna," 11–105.

9. Boardman, Cheetham, and Rowell, *Fossil Invertebrates.*

10. Ibid.

11. Morris, "Cambrian 'Explosion,'" 4426–29; Chen and Zhou, "Biology of the Chenjiang Fauna," 11–105.

12. Valentine, Jablonski, and Erwin, "Fossils, Molecules, and Embryos," 851–59; Boardman, Cheetham, and Rowell, *Fossil Invertebrates;* Morris, "Cambrian 'Explosion,'" 4426–29; Chen and Zhou, "Biology of the Chenjiang Fauna," 11–105; E. N. K. Clarkson, *Invertebrate Paleontology and Evolution,* 4th ed. (Malden, Mass.: Blackwell Science, 1998).

13. Clarkson, *Invertebrate Paleontology.*

14. Ibid.

15. Ibid.

16. S. C. Morris, *The Crucible of Creation: The Burgess Shale and the Rise of Animals* (New York: Oxford University Press, 1998); J. Y. Chen and D. Y. Huang, "A Possible Lower Cambrian Chaetognath (Arrow Worm)," *Science,* 4 October 2002, 187.

17. Valentine, Jablonski, and Erwin, "Fossils, Molecules, and Embryos," 851–59; Boardman, Cheetham, and Rowell, *Fossil Invertebrates;* Morris, "Cambrian 'Explosion,'" 4426–29.

18. J. Y. Chen, J. Dzik, G. D. Edgecombe, L. Ramsköld, and G. Q. Zhou, "A Possible Early Cambrian Chordate," *Nature* 377 (1995): 720–22; J. Y. Chen and C. W. Li, "Early Cambrian Chordate from Chengjiang, China," in *The Cambrian Explosion and the Fossil Record,* ed. J. Y. Chen, Y. N. Change, and H. V. Iten, Bulletin of the National Museum of Science, no. 10 (Taichung, 1997), 257–73; D. G. Shu, S. C. Morris, and X. L. Zhang, "A Pikaia-like Chordate from the Lower Cambrian of China," *Nature* 384 (1996): 157–58.

19. D. G. Shu et al., "Lower Cambrian Vertebrates from South China," *Nature* 411 (2001): 42–46; J. Y. Chen, D. Y. Huang, and C. W. Li, "An Early Cambrian Craniate-like Chordate," *Nature* 411 (2001): 518–22.

20. D. G. Shu, L. Chen, J. Han, and X. L. Zhang, "An Early Cambrian Tunicate from China," *Nature* 411 (2001): 472–73.

21. Chen and Zhou, "Biology of the Chenjiang Fauna," 11–105; Morris, *Crucible of Creation.*

22. Valentine, Jablonski, and Erwin, "Fossils, Molecules, and Embryos," 851–59; Morris, "Cambrian 'Explosion,'" 4426–29; Chen and Zhou, "Biology of the Chenjiang Fauna," 11–105.

23. Valentine, Jablonski, and Erwin, "Fossils, Molecules, and Embryos," 851–59; Boardman, Cheetham, and Rowell, *Fossil Invertebrates;* Morris, "Cambrian 'Explosion,'" 4426–29.

24. Boardman, Cheetham, and Rowell, *Fossil Invertebrates.*

25. Ibid.

26. Ibid.

27. Ibid.

28. Ibid.

29. Morris, "Cambrian 'Explosion,'" 4426–29; Morris, *Crucible of Creation.*

30. Valentine, Jablonski, and Erwin, "Fossils, Molecules, and Embryos," 851–59; Boardman, Cheetham, and Rowell, *Fossil Invertebrates;* Morris, "Cambrian 'Explosion,'" 4426–29.

31. Boardman, Cheetham, and Rowell, *Fossil Invertebrates;* Chen and Zhou, "Biology of the Chenjiang Fauna," 11–105.

32. Valentine, Jablonski, and Erwin, "Fossils, Molecules, and Embryos," 851–59; Boardman, Cheetham, and Rowell, *Fossil Invertebrates;* Morris, "Cambrian 'Explosion,'" 4426–29.

33. Boardman, Cheetham, and Rowell, *Fossil Invertebrates.*

34. Ibid.

35. Ibid.

36. Morris, "Cambrian 'Explosion,'" 4426–29.

37. Valentine, Jablonski, and Erwin, "Fossils, Molecules, and Embryos," 851–59.

38. Valentine, Jablonski, and Erwin, "Fossils, Molecules, and Embryos," 851–59; Chen and Zhou, "Biology of the Chenjiang Fauna," 11–105.

39. Boardman, Cheetham, and Rowell, *Fossil Invertebrates.*

40. Valentine, Jablonski, and Erwin, "Fossils, Molecules, and Embryos," 851–59; Boardman, Cheetham, and Rowell, *Fossil Invertebrates;* Morris, "Cambrian 'Explosion,'" 4426–29; Chen and Zhou, "Biology of the Chenjiang Fauna," 11–105.

41. Valentine, Jablonski, and Erwin, "Fossils, Molecules, and Embryos," 851–59.

42. Chen and Zhou, "Biology of the Chenjiang Fauna," 11–105.

43. Valentine, Jablonski, and Erwin, "Fossils, Molecules, and Embryos," 851–59; Boardman, Cheetham, and Rowell, *Fossil Invertebrates;* Morris, "Cambrian 'Explosion,'" 4426–29; Chen and Zhou, "Biology of the Chenjiang Fauna," 11–105.

44. Boardman, Cheetham, and Rowell, *Fossil Invertebrates.*

45. Valentine, Jablonski, and Erwin, "Fossils, Molecules, and Embryos," 851–59; Boardman, Cheetham, and Rowell, *Fossil Invertebrates.*

46. Valentine, Jablonski, and Erwin, "Fossils, Molecules, and Embryos," 851–59.

47. Ibid.

48. Ibid.

49. Valentine, Jablonski, and Erwin, "Fossils, Molecules, and Embryos," 851–59; Boardman, Cheetham, and Rowell, *Fossil Invertebrates*.

50. P. Funch and R. M. Kristensen, "Cycliophora Is a New Phylum with Affinities to Entoprocta and Ectoprocta," *Nature* 378 (1995): 711–14.

51. Valentine, Jablonski, and Erwin, "Fossils, Molecules, and Embryos," 851–59; Boardman, Cheetham, and Rowell, *Fossil Invertebrates*.

52. Valentine, Jablonski, and Erwin, "Fossils, Molecules, and Embryos," 851–59; Boardman, Cheetham, and Rowell, *Fossil Invertebrates*.

53. Valentine, Jablonski, and Erwin, "Fossils, Molecules, and Embryos," 851–59; Boardman, Cheetham, and Rowell, *Fossil Invertebrates*.

54. Valentine, Jablonski, and Erwin, "Fossils, Molecules, and Embryos," 851–59.

55. Boardman, Cheetham, and Rowell, *Fossil Invertebrates*.

56. Valentine, Jablonski, and Erwin, "Fossils, Molecules, and Embryos," 851–59.

57. Ibid.

58. Ibid.

Appendix D
Stratigraphic First Appearance of Phyla-Subphyla Body Plans

This appendix documents the stratigraphic first appearance of new body plans in the fossil record, treating the subphylum as the unit of body plan differentiation. This is a special version of appendix C. As opposed to those who locate body plans at the phylum level, on the one hand, or the class level, on the other, we take the moderate position of identifying body plans with subphyla differences. The animal kingdom contains about forty phyla, six of which are further divided into subphyla. There are a total of twenty-two subphyla. If a phylum has no subphyla within it, we count the phylum as a single separate body plan. We do not count as an extra body plan the larger phylum to which each cluster of subphyla belongs. This method of counting produces a total of fifty-six body plans at the phyla-subphyla level. Our analysis of current paleontological literature indicates that three of these body plans first appear in the Precambrian era, thirty-two in the Cambrian period, and nine in later geologic periods, and twelve have no fossil history at all (see figure 19A in "The Cambrian Explosion: Biology's Big Bang").

Precambrian: Three Phyla-Subphyla Body Plans (possibility of a fourth)

Cnidaria[1]

Porifera: Nuda[2] (subphylum)

Indeterminate track-making worm phylum (our figures in the essay "The Cambrian Explosion: Biology's Big Bang" include it as Precambrian only)

Kimberella[3]: Uncertain identity (Mollusc?) (our figures in the essay "The Cambrian Explosion: Biology's Big Bang" exclude it)

Cambrian: Thirty-two Phyla-Subphyla Body Plans

Annelida[4]

Arthropoda: Anomalocariida[5] (subphylum)

Arthropoda: Chelicerata[6] (subphylum)

Arthropoda: Crustacea[7] (subphylum)

Arthropoda: Trilobita[8] (subphylum)

Brachiopoda: Craniiformea[9] (subphylum)

Brachiopoda: Linguliformea[10] (subphylum)

Brachiopoda: Rhynchonelliformea[11] (subphylum)

Chaetognatha[12]

Chordata: Cephalochordata[13] (subphylum)

Chordata: Craniata[14] (subphylum)

Chordata: Urochordata[15] (subphylum)

Coeloscleritophora[16]

Ctenophora[17]

Echinodermata: Blastozoa[18] (subphylum)

Echinodermata: Crinozoa[19] (subphylum)

Echinodermata: Echinozoa[20] (subphylum)

Echinodermata: Homalozoa[21] (subphylum)

Halkieriida[22]

Hemichordata[23]

Hyolitha[24]

Mollusca: Amphineura[25] (subphylum)

Mollusca: Cyrtosoma[26] (subphylum)

Mollusca: Diasoma[27] (subphylum)

Nematoda[28]

Onychophora[29]

Phoronida[30]

Pogonophora[31]

Porifera: Gelatinosa[32] (subphylum)

Priapula[33]

Tardigrada[34]

Tardipolypoda[35]

Later Geologic Periods:
Nine Phyla-Subphyla Body Plans

Ordovician
Bryozoa/Ectoprocta[36]
Echinodermata: Asterozoa[37] (subphylum)

Silurian
Arthropoda: Myriapoda[38] (subphylum)

Devonian
Arthropoda: Hexapoda[39] (subphylum)
Echiura[40]

Pennsylvanian
Nemertina[41]

Jurassic
Entoprocta[42]

Tertiary
Nematomorpha[43]
Rotifera[44]

No Fossil Record: Twelve Body Plans
See appendix C

Notes

1. J. W. Valentine, D. Jablonski, and D. H. Erwin, "Fossils, Molecules, and Embryos: New Perspectives on the Cambrian Explosion," *Development* 126 (1999): 851–59; R. S. Boardman, A. H. Cheetham, and A. J. Rowell, eds., *Fossil Invertebrates* (Palo Alto, Calif.: Blackwell Science, 1987); S. C. Morris, "The Cambrian 'Explosion': Slow-fuse or Megatonnage?" *PNAS* 95 (2000): 4426–29.
2. Valentine, Jablonski, and Erwin, "Fossils, Molecules, and Embryos," 851–59; Morris, "Cambrian 'Explosion,'" 4426–29.

3. M. A. Fedonkin and B. M. Waggoner, "The Late Precambrian Fossil *Kimberella* Is a Mollusc-like Bilaterian Organism," *Nature* 388 (1977): 868–71.

4. Valentine, Jablonski, and Erwin, "Fossils, Molecules, and Embryos," 851–59; Morris, "Cambrian 'Explosion,'" 4426–29; J. Y. Chen and G. Q. Zhou, "Biology of the Chengjiang Fauna," in *The Cambrian Explosion and the Fossil Record*, ed. J. Y. Chen, Y. N. Change, and H. V. Iten, Bulletin of the National Museum of Science, no. 10 (Taichung, 1997), 11–105.

5. Morris, "Cambrian 'Explosion,'" 4426–29.

6. Boardman, Cheetham, and Rowell, *Fossil Invertebrates*.

7. Morris, "Cambrian 'Explosion,'" 4426–29; Chen and Zhou, "Biology of the Chengjiang Fauna," 11–105.

8. Morris, "Cambrian 'Explosion,'" 4426–29; Chen and Zhou, "Biology of the Chengjiang Fauna," 11–105.

9. E. N. K. Clarkson, *Invertebrate Paleontology and Evolution*, 4th ed. (Malden, Mass.: Blackwell Science, 1998).

10. Ibid.

11. Ibid.

12. S. C. Morris, *The Crucible of Creation: The Burgess Shale and the Rise of Animals* (New York: Oxford University Press, 1998); J. Y. Chen and D. Y. Huang, "A Possible Lower Cambrian Chaetognath (Arrow Worm)," *Science*, 4 October 2002, 187.

13. J. Y. Chen, J. Dzik, G. D. Edgecombe, L. Ramsköld, and G. Q. Zhou, "A Possible Early Cambrian Chordate," *Nature* 377 (1995): 720–22; J. Y. Chen and C. W. Li, "Early Cambrian Chordate from Chengjiang, China," in *The Cambrian Explosion and the Fossil Record*, ed. J. Y. Chen, Y. N. Change, and H. V. Iten, Bulletin of the National Museum of Science, no. 10 (Taichung, 1997), 257–73; D. G. Shu, S. Conway Morris, and X. L. Zhang, "A Pikaia-like Chordate from the Lower Cambrian of China," *Nature* 384 (1996): 157–58.

14. D. G. Shu et al., "Lower Cambrian Vertebrates from South China," *Nature* 411 (2001): 42–46; J. Y. Chen, D. Y. Huang, and C. W. Li, "An Early Cambrian Craniate-like Chordate," *Nature* 411 (2001): 518–22.

15. D. G. Shu, L. Chen, J. Han, and X. L. Zhang, "An Early Cambrian Tunicate from China," *Nature* 411 (2001): 472–73.

16. Chen and Zhou, "Biology of the Chengjiang Fauna," 11–105; Morris, *Crucible of Creation*.

17. Valentine, Jablonski, and Erwin, "Fossils, Molecules, and Embryos," 851–59; Morris, "Cambrian 'Explosion,'" 4426–29; Chen and Zhou, "Biology of the Chengjiang Fauna," 11–105.
18. Boardman, Cheetham, and Rowell, *Fossil Invertebrates.*
19. Ibid.
20. Ibid.
21. Ibid.
22. Morris, "Cambrian 'Explosion,'" 4426–29; Morris, *Crucible of Creation.*
23. Valentine, Jablonski, and Erwin, "Fossils, Molecules, and Embryos," 851–59; Boardman, Cheetham, and Rowell, *Fossil Invertebrates;* Morris, "Cambrian 'Explosion,'" 4426–29.
24. Boardman, Cheetham, and Rowell, *Fossil Invertebrates;* Chen and Zhou, "Biology of the Chengjiang Fauna," 11–105.
25. Boardman, Cheetham, and Rowell, *Fossil Invertebrates.*
26. Ibid.
27. Ibid.
28. Morris, "Cambrian 'Explosion,'" 4426–29.
29. Valentine, Jablonski, and Erwin, "Fossils, Molecules, and Embryos," 851–59.
30. Valentine, Jablonski, and Erwin, "Fossils, Molecules, and Embryos," 851–59; Chen and Zhou, "Biology of the Chengjiang Fauna," 11–105.
31. Boardman, Cheetham, and Rowell, *Fossil Invertebrates.*
32. Valentine, Jablonski, and Erwin, "Fossils, Molecules, and Embryos," 851–59; Morris, "Cambrian 'Explosion,'" 4426–29.
33. Valentine, Jablonski, and Erwin, "Fossils, Molecules, and Embryos," 851–59; Boardman, Cheetham, and Rowell, *Fossil Invertebrates;* Morris, "Cambrian 'Explosion,'" 4426–29; Chen and Zhou, "Biology of the Chengjiang Fauna," 11–105.
34. Valentine, Jablonski, and Erwin, "Fossils, Molecules, and Embryos," 851–59.
35. Chen and Zhou, "Biology of the Chengjiang Fauna," 11–105.
36. Valentine, Jablonski, and Erwin, "Fossils, Molecules, and Embryos," 851–59; Boardman, Cheetham, and Rowell, *Fossil Invertebrates;* Morris, "Cambrian 'Explosion,'" 4426–29; Chen and Zhou, "Biology of the Chengjiang Fauna," 11–105.
37. Boardman, Cheetham, and Rowell, *Fossil Invertebrates.*
38. Ibid.
39. Ibid.
40. Ibid.

41. Valentine, Jablonski, and Erwin, "Fossils, Molecules, and Embryos," 851–59; Boardman, Cheetham, and Rowell, *Fossil Invertebrates*.
42. Valentine, Jablonski, and Erwin, "Fossils, Molecules, and Embryos," 851–59.
43. Ibid.
44. Ibid.

Appendix E
Probability of Other Body Plans Originating in the Cambrian Explosion

Appendixes C and D document the stratigraphic first appearance of animal body plans at the phyla and subphyla levels. These appendixes show that while fossil representatives of many phyla and subphyla first appear in the Cambrian period, some are not yet known to have been present then. This appendix analyzes the phyla and subphyla that do not presently have fossil representatives in the Cambrian period. Specifically, it assesses the likelihood that representatives of these phyla and subphyla might have originated in the Cambrian period based upon a variety of factors.

Six phyla appear in the fossil record after the Cambrian period. Twelve do not appear in the geologic record at all. Of these eighteen phyla, we judge a Cambrian first appearance probable in two cases, possible in thirteen, and unlikely in three.

When we add the thirteen possible, two probable, and nineteen documented phyla (see appendix C) that first appear in the Cambrian period, we get a total of thirty-four phyla out of the forty total animal phyla. This suggests that 85 percent of all animal phyla could have first appeared in the Cambrian explosion (see figures 17B and 18B in "The Cambrian Explosion: Biology's Big Bang").

If we consider also subphyla as representing body plans, then twenty-one new body plans either appear in the fossil record after the Cambrian period or have no representation in the fossil record at all. Of these twenty-one body plans (phyla or subphyla), we judge a Cambrian first appearance probable in three cases, possible in thirteen, and unlikely in five. When we add the thirteen possible, three probable, and thirty-two documented subphyla and phyla (see appendix D) that first appear in the Cambrian period, we get a total of forty-eight body plans (phyla-subphyla) out of the fifty-six, or 85.7 percent of all animal body plans (treating subphyla as a body plan) (see figure 19B in "The Cambrian Explosion: Biology's Big Bang"). Thus, both methods of body plan analysis produce approximately the same upper-end estimate for Cambrian first appearances: 85 percent.

These qualitative probability determinations are based on a number of factors that affect organismal preservation in the geologic record, including individual size, presence/absence of mineralized hard parts, mode of life, habitat/environment of deposition, and trace fossil associations. Evolutionary assumptions are not considered, though such considerations increase estimates of the number of body plans that probably originated in the Cambrian explosion (ironically posing a more acute evidential challenge to neo-Darwinism). Like appendixes C and D, this appendix lists animal body plans in alphabetical order within each successive geologic unit.

Body Plans Represented by Fossils in Geologic Periods since the Cambrian Period: Probability that They Originated in the Cambrian Explosion

Ordovician

Bryozoa / Ectoprocta[1]

Possible: The only well-skeletonized phylum not found in the Cambrian period. Partly because there are several extant groups of Bryozoa that lack skeletonized hard parts, it is possible that early representatives of this phylum were also soft bodied and thus so infrequently fossilized as to evade paleontologists studying Cambrian fauna. Most workers are confident that someday bryozoans will be found in the Cambrian period.

Echinodermata: Asterozoa[2] (subphylum)

Probable: Asterozoa (starfish and brittle stars) is the only echinoderm subphylum absent from the Cambrian period. It is present stratigraphically directly above, in the Lower Ordovician. Because asterozoans disintegrate quickly upon death, only catastrophically deposited strata are known to preserve them. Given that such depositional environments are rare in the Cambrian period (and thus Cambrian times have preferentially failed to preserve the organisms of asterozoan habitats), it is quite likely that asterozoans originated in the Cambrian period but simply were not fossilized in sufficient quantities to allow their detection.

Silurian

Arthropoda: Myriapoda[3] (subphylum)

Unlikely: This subphylum of Arthropoda represents such organisms as pill bugs, centipedes, and millipedes. As the fossil record of arthropods is excellent and there are no known fully aquatic myriapods, it is unlikely that myriapods existed in the Cambrian period.

Devonian

Arthropoda: Hexapoda[4] (subphylum)

Unlikely: This subphylum of Arthropoda contains insects. Because the arthropod fossil record is excellent and because there are no known fully aquatic insects, it is unlikely that hexapods existed in the Cambrian period.

Echiura[5]

Probable: Soft-bodied, unsegmented, burrowing worm. Some extant echiurans are known to build U-shaped burrows in soft marine substrate. Some paleontologists have compared these burrows to Cambrian ichnofossil *Skolithos*. Since it is likely that an echiuran is responsible for such *Skolithos,* it is quite reasonable to infer this phylum's existence in the Cambrian period.

Pennsylvanian

Nemertina[6]

Possible: Ribbon worms that live in the littoral zone of temperate oceans among rocks and algae or in mucous tubes in sand or mud. It is possible (though debated) that the fossil worm *Amiskwia* of the Burgess Shale is a nemertine. If so, then nemertines first appeared in the Cambrian period.

Jurassic

Entoprocta[7]

Possible: This phylum is quite small (only about 150 species), and consists of small (less than 5 millimeters long), V-shaped, filter-feeding marine organisms. They may be solitary or colonial and may attach to other organisms by a stalk. Due to their small size and lack of hard parts, it is quite possible that they existed in the Cambrian period but have eluded preservation or recognition.

Tertiary

Nematomorpha[8]

Possible: This phylum consists of long, thin, soft-bodied worms that dwell in freshwater ponds and soil (it also includes one marine genus, *Nectonema*). If the life habits of this group are relatively static through time, then it is not surprising that it has not been identified more often and in lower stratigraphic units. Because nematomorphs typically inhabit terrestrial/lacustrine environments, the rarity of these depositional units in the Cambrian period could help explain the absence of nematomorphs. As it is, their stratigraphic distribution is extremely limited (Tertiary), due to the exceptional conditions necessary to preserve soft tissue.

Rotifera[9]

Possible: Small (generally 0.2 to 0.5 millimeter long), soft-bodied phylum. Rotifers abound in moist soil and in freshwater streams and lakes. Their mouthparts are hard but so small that detection is quite unlikely. Due to their extremely small size and the general lack of paleosols and lacustrine and river deposits in the Cambrian period, rotifers easily could have evaded preservation or recognition.

Body Plans of Animals with No Fossil Record: Probability that They Originated in the Cambrian Explosion

Acanthocephala[10]

Unlikely: Gut parasites of vertebrates. As most vertebrates do not appear in the fossil record until well after the Cambrian period, it is unlikely that ancanthocephalans existed during the Cambrian period.

Cycliophora[11]

Unlikely: Monospecific phylum first identified in 1995. Lives on the mouthparts of the Norway lobster, *Nephrops*. Soft-bodied, less than 0.5 millimeter, and has a short free-living stage. The single species of this phylum, *Symbion pandora*, has yet to be discovered on contemporary crustaceans other than *Nephrops*. Because decapods (the order of crustaceans to which *Nephrops* belongs) first appear in the Triassic, it is unlikely that Cycliophora, an apparently decapod-dependent phylum, originated in the Cambrian period.

Dicyemida

Possible: Small, soft-bodied parasites of the excretory system of cephalopods. Dicyemids live most of their life in the kidneys of squids and octopi, with only a brief free-living adult phase. Due to their small size, lack of hard parts, and nearly lifelong residence in the soft tissue of other organisms, it is quite unlikely that dicyemids could be preserved, much less discovered and recognized.

Gastrotricha[12]

Possible: Extremely small (0.04 to 4.0 millimeters), soft-bodied, free-living worms. Marine forms of this phylum live on the surface of corals and in intertidal and subtidal sands. Their lack of hard parts and small size may account for their absence in the fossil record.

Gnathostomulida[13]

Possible: Small (0.3 to 1.0 millimeter) acoelomate worms. Members of this phylum live mainly between sand grains in shallow, salty waters. Their high-energy habitat, extremely soft bodies, and small size make preservation virtually impossible.

Kinoryncha[14]

Possible: Small, soft-bodied, burrowing, wormlike animals that live in muddy silts between high and low tidemarks or in shallow water mud. These marine environments are depositionally active and could possibly preserve specimens from this phylum. However, the extensive bioturbation that is characteristic of intertidal deposits throughout geologic time easily could have destroyed any remains or traces of kinorynchids.

Loricifera[15]

Possible: Small, soft-bodied, rotifer-like pseudocoelomate. Because this phylum is a recent discovery, paleontologists have not had many years to look specifically for its representatives in the fossil record (had it been preserved).

Orthonectida

Probable: Small, soft-bodied parasites of numerous invertebrate phyla, most of which first appear in the Cambrian period. It is highly unlikely that representatives of this phylum would be preserved.

Pentastoma[16]

Unlikely: All members of Phylum Pentastoma (tongue worms) are parasitic on terrestrial vertebrates (especially reptiles). Their nature as parasites makes fossilization virtually impossible, but the fact that they parasitize terrestrial vertebrates makes their presence in the Cambrian period unlikely.

Placozoa[17]

Possible: Monospecific marine phylum exclusively represented by *Tricoplax adhaerens*. Simplest of all animals; small (0.5 millimeter) and soft-bodied. Although known by zoologists for a century, their biology has been poorly explored. Thus, paleontologists have had little knowledge or motivation to discover it (had it been fossilized).

Platyhelminthes[18]

Possible: Flatworms; soft-bodied; simplest form of bilateria. Some free-living, some parasitic. Free-living forms prey on a number of phyla that first appear in the Cambrian period; parasitic forms parasitize vertebrates.

Sipuncula[19]

Possible: Unsegmented worm phylum. Some members have a calcerous anal shield. Though no body fossils of this phylum have been identified in the fossil record, sipunculids are known to produce traces similar to some Cambrian ichnofossils. Representatives of Sipuncula may have existed during the Cambrian period.

Notes

1. J. W. Valentine, D. Jablonski, and D. H. Erwin, "Fossils, Molecules, and Embryos: New Perspectives on the Cambrian Explosion," *Development* 126 (1999): 851–59; R. S. Boardman, A. H. Cheetham, and A. J. Rowell, eds., *Fossil Invertebrates* (Palo Alto, Calif.: Blackwell Science, 1987); S. C. Morris, "The Cambrian 'Explosion': Slow-fuse or Megatonnage?" *PNAS* 95 (2000): 4426–29; J. Y. Chen and G. Q. Zhou, "Biology of the Chengjiang Fauna," in *The Cambrian Explosion and the Fossil Record,* ed. J. Y. Chen, Y. N. Change, and H. V. Iten, Bulletin of the National Museum of Science, no. 10 (Taichung, 1997), 11–105.

2. Boardman, Cheetham, and Rowell, *Fossil Invertebrates.*

3. Ibid.

4. Ibid.

5. Ibid.

6. Valentine, Jablonski, and Erwin, "Fossils, Molecules, and Embryos," 851–59; Boardman, Cheetham, and Rowell, *Fossil Invertebrates.*

7. Valentine, Jablonski, and Erwin, "Fossils, Molecules, and Embryos," 851–59.

8. Ibid.

9. Ibid.

10. Valentine, Jablonski, and Erwin, "Fossils, Molecules, and Embryos," 851–59; Boardman, Cheetham, and Rowell, *Fossil Invertebrates.*

11. P. Funch and R. M. Kristensen, "Cycliophora Is a New Phylum with Affinities to Entoprocta and Ectoprocta," *Nature* 378 (1995): 711–14.

12. Valentine, Jablonski, and Erwin, "Fossils, Molecules, and Embryos," 851–59; Boardman, Cheetham, and Rowell, *Fossil Invertebrates.*

13. Valentine, Jablonski, and Erwin, "Fossils, Molecules, and Embryos," 851–59; Boardman, Cheetham, and Rowell, *Fossil Invertebrates.*

14. Valentine, Jablonski, and Erwin, "Fossils, Molecules, and Embryos," 851–59; Boardman, Cheetham, and Rowell, *Fossil Invertebrates.*

15. Valentine, Jablonski, and Erwin, "Fossils, Molecules, and Embryos," 851–59.

16. Boardman, Cheetham, and Rowell, *Fossil Invertebrates.*

17. Valentine, Jablonski, and Erwin, "Fossils, Molecules, and Embryos," 851–59.

18. Ibid.

19. Ibid.

Glossary

abiogenesis: the idea that, given the proper set of initial conditions, life can arise from nonliving organic matter.

allele: alternative forms of the same gene locus. An allele, therefore, is one pair of genes that occupy corresponding positions on homologous chromosomes and determine alternative expressions of a single trait.

amino acid: an organic compound that contains one or more amino groups and one or more acidic carboxyl groups; amino acids can be polymerized to form peptides and proteins.

analogy (analogous structure): a body part similar in function to that of another organism but only superficially similar in structure, at most. Such similarities are regarded not as evidence of inheritance from a common ancestor, as in homology, but as evidence only of similar function.

anastomosis: a union or interconnection of parts, especially as in branches, blood vessels, and so forth.

argument from ignorance: a charge that a lack of information or evidence for some point is being used as positive evidence for an opposing point.

artifact hypothesis: the idea that ancestors to the Cambrian phyla did exist but that their evolutionary history has been hidden by poor preservation, insufficient sampling, or a combination of the two.

autogeny: control of the expression of a gene by the product of that gene; or, in another context, the idea that life arose from self-organizing chemical reactions.

Baupläne: basic body plans.

biomacromolecules: high molecular weight substances of living matter, e.g., nucleic acids, proteins, complex carbohydrates.

Burgess Shale: a Middle Cambrian (ca. 515 million years ago) black shale in British Columbia that contains exquisitely preserved fossils, including many soft-bodied organisms.

cassette mutagenesis: a procedure in which molecular biologists systematically mutate or alter individual DNA codons in order to determine the effect of those alterations on protein folding or function.

chance: a form of explanation invoked when neither deterministic laws nor intelligent design accounts for an event or the behavior of a system. Chance processes are characterized by true contingency in which more than one possible outcome is allowed by physical law. Formally, chance is defined as the outcome of a process characterized by a probability distribution.

Chengjiang biota/fauna: a suite of fossils known from the lower Cambrian (530 million years ago) Maotianshan shale of China, known for their exquisite soft-body preservation.

chirality: the handedness of a molecule that can exist in two nonsuperimposable mirror images, like our left and right hands.

chromosome: compact threadlike structure in the nuclei of eukaryotic cells that consists of a single molecule of DNA and associated proteins.

cilia: short, cylindrical projections on living cells that typically function in locomotion.

cladistic analysis: a method of classifying organisms that arranges taxa according to their shared characters, i.e., synapomorphies.

coacervate: an aggregate of colloidal droplets held together by electostatic charges.

common ancestry: the idea that two or more organisms are biological descendants of a single organism in the past.

complexity: the degree of difficulty in solving a problem; a measure of the improbability of assembling a structure, system, or molecule. The most common forms of complexity are probabilistic (as in the probability of achieving some end) or computational (as in the memory or computing time needed for an algorithm to solve a problem).

complex specified information: information that is both complex and specified. Synonymous with specified complexity.

contingency: formally, a possibility whose complement is nonempty. An outcome is contingent if it could happen but if there were also other logically or physically possible outcomes that could have happened.

creation science: an approach to the origins of life question that looks for evidence consistent with the account of creation in the Book of Genesis. Unlike intelligent design theory, which starts from evidence (such as the fossil record or DNA), creation science hypothesizes that the account in Genesis is a historical account and then examines whether there is evidence to support this hypothesis.

cytochrome c: an iron-bearing molecule utilized in the electron transport chains of mitochondria and chloroplasts; cytochrome c is also used in protein comparison studies aimed at determining evolutionary relationships.

Darwinism: the theory that all living things descended from an original common ancestor through natural selection and random variation, without the aid of intelligence or nonmaterial forces.

Daubert v. Merrell Dow Pharmaceuticals, Inc. (1993): a decision by the U.S. Supreme Court that widened the scope of admissible scientific testimony. Previous standards had required "general acceptance" of a theory by the scientific community, but the new standard permits even minority theories so long as they are supported by competent evidence and a scientific methodology.

Deep Divergence hypothesis: the idea proposed by molecular biologists that divergence among many of the animal phyla occurred long before the Cambrian explosion, typically around one billion years ago.

demarcation arguments: attempts to "demarcate" or distinguish science from nonscience through criteria such as falsifiability, reliance on empirical data, repeatability, and so forth. A demarcation argument was adopted by the federal district court in *McLean v. Arkansas* (1982).

design inference: a form of inference in which design or intelligent agency is attributed to an event on the basis of its small probability and specification.

disparity: major variations in morphology or body plan.

diversity: minor variations within a basic body plan or biological form—e.g., a golden retriever and St. Bernard are variations of a basic form (dog).

DNA: deoxyribonucleic acid; the genetic code utilized by all organisms. It consists of two long, intertwined chains of nucleotide subunits that carry the pattern needed to specify the sequence of amino acids in proteins.

Ediacaran fauna: a suite of Precambrian (Vendian) multicellular organisms of uncertain affinities.

Edwards v. Aguillard (1987): A decision by the U.S. Supreme Court striking down a Louisiana statute that mandated the teaching of creation science as a condition for teaching evolution. The court found that the proposed curriculum was religion rather than science and, by restricting the teaching of evolution, did not advance the claimed purpose of the act, which was to enhance academic freedom.

embryo: the early developmental stage of a multicellular organism.

embryology: within biology, the study of the development of an organism from fertilization to the point that all major organ systems have formed.

entropy: a quantitative measure of the disorder of a system; inversely related to the amount of energy available to do work in a system. The more energy has become dispersed, the less work it can perform—and the greater the entropy. Biological systems have low entropy values as they are highly organized.

Establishment Clause: part of the First Amendment to the U.S. Constitution that prevents the government from establishing a preference for one religion over another or for religion as against nonreligion (or vice versa).

eukaryote: a cell that has membrane-bound organelles, including (and most important) a nucleus.

evolution: often defined as mere "change in living things over time" but variously meaning also descent with modification and particular mechanisms to account for change, such as natural selection and gene mutation.

fabrication: a pattern that is artificially concocted on the basis of an event and therefore cannot reasonably be used to attribute design to that event.

family: the level of classification midway between lower and higher taxon designations. A family is a more inclusive category than a genus and a less inclusive category than an order.

founder effect: reduction of the gene pool and alteration of gene frequencies resulting from the establishment, by two or a few organisms, of a new population isolated from the parental population.

gene: a unit of heredity located within a chromosome and composed of DNA.

gene flow: a loss or gain of alleles between two populations of a species.

gene pool: the total genetic material in the population of a species at a given point in time.

genetic drift: changes in gene frequencies of small populations that result from random mating.

genetic information: the specific linear sequences of subunits in DNA and RNA molecules that are required to sustain the living state by specifying the sequences of amino acids in proteins. Genetic information is both complex and specified.

genome: the total DNA for a given organism.

genotype: the combination of alleles inherited for a particular trait.

genus: a designation within the Linnean classification scheme. The second least general category after species; the level of classification between species and family.

homeobox gene: a gene containing a 180-base-pair segment (the "homeobox") that encodes a protein domain involved in binding to (and thus regulating the expression of) DNA. The homeobox is remarkably similar in many genes with different functions.

homeotic gene: a gene that affects embryo development by specifying the character of a body segment. The classic example is Antennapedia, a gene that, when mutated, causes a fly to grow a leg in place of an antenna.

homochirality: condition of a polymeric substance in which all the subunits (the monomers) are of the same handedness (mirror image form), i.e., either 100 percent left-handed or 100 percent right-handed.

homology: classically, similarity of structure and position ("structural homology"); thus the bones of vertebrate forelimbs were considered homologous even though the limbs function in different ways (e.g., for swimming, flying, running, or grasping). After Darwin, similarity due to inheritance from a common ancestor ("phylogenetic homology").

homoplasy: after Darwin, features that are structurally similar but thought not to be due to inheritance from a common ancestor.

hox gene: one of a cluster of homeotic genes. Many different types of animals have remarkably similar hox clusters.

hypercycles: theoretical prebiotic cycles of chemical reactions involving the autocatalytic amplification of substances thought to have been required for the presumed spontaneous origin of the first life forms.

improbability: the degree to which a probability is close to zero.

inference to the best explanation: a method of reasoning employed in the sciences in which scientists elect the hypothesis that would, if true, best explain the relevant evidence. Recent work in the philosophy of science has shown that those hypotheses that qualify as "best" typically provide simple, coherent, and causally adequate explanations of the evidence or phenomena in question.

information: related to the reduction of uncertainty. In classical information theory, the amount of information in a string of characters is inversely related to the probability of the occurrence of that string. The more improbable the string, the more uncertainty it reduces and the more information it conveys. Information defined in this mathematical way provides only a measure of improbability or complexity. It does not establish whether a string of characters conveys meaning (or performs a function). See also *complex specified information, semantic information, Shannon information, specified complexity,* and *syntactic information.*

intelligent design: the theory that certain features of the physical universe and/or biological systems can be best explained by reference to an intelligent cause (that is, the conscious action of an intelligent agent), rather than an undirected natural process or a material mechanism.

irreducible complexity: a single system composed of several well-matched, interacting parts that contribute to the basic function, wherein the removal of any one of the parts causes the system to effectively cease functioning.

law: a relation between antecedent conditions or causes and consequent events in which the antecedent either determines or renders probable the consequent (the former being a deterministic law, the latter being an inde-terministic law).

***Lemon* test**: named for a 1971 Supreme Court case interpreting the Estab-lishment Clause that holds state action unconstitutional if it fails to satisfy a three-pronged test: the action must have a secular purpose; it must have a primary effect that neither advances nor inhibits religion; and it must avoid excessive entanglement between the state and religion.

linkage: the tendency of genes located on the same chromosome to be in-herited together.

lipids: compounds such as fats, oils, or steroids that are insoluble in water.

macroevolution: large-scale changes in biological form, structure, or complexity. By all accounts, such changes are unobservable within the time scale of recorded human history.

melanism: an increased dark or black coloration of the skin, fur, or feath-ers due to a high occurrence of the pigment melanin.

metabolism: the ensemble of chemical processes that occur in living cells, including both biosynthetic and biodegradative pathways.

methodological naturalism: a rule or canon of method; methodological naturalism requires that scientists limit themselves to materialistic explana-tions when they seek to explain the nature and/or origin of natural phe-nomenon, objects, or processes. On this understanding of the "rules" of science, explanations that invoke intelligent causes or the actions of intelli-gent agents do not qualify as scientific.

microevolution: small-scale genetic changes. Such changes often are ob-servable in organisms.

minimal complexity: the simplest state, either genetic or metabolic, that is consistent with the viability of an organism.

monomer: a single, simple molecule that can link with others to form polymers.

mononucleotide: a single nucleotide.

monophyletic: an assemblage of organisms that share a common ancestor.

morphogenesis: development of the architectural features of organisms during ontogeny.

morphology: the form or structure of an organism.

mRNA: messenger RNA; the sequence of this RNA contains the same information as the DNA sequence in a "gene," specifying the order of amino acids in a protein; the sequence of mRNA is "read" by a ribosome to make the actual protein.

mutation: an alteration of the genetic material of a cell, which may be caused either by spontaneous changes or by external forces (such as radiation); mutations that occur in the gametes (sex cells) of an organism are heritable.

naturalism: the philosophical worldview that the physical or natural world (or the matter and energy that constitutes nature) is all that exists. Naturalism denies the existence of God.

natural selection: the natural process in which the fittest in a group of offspring survive to pass on their heritable traits to subsequent generations while those less fit may die off leaving no offspring—resulting in the termination of the traits characterizing the less fit organism. Darwin theorized that this process could account for changes in the characteristic traits of species over time and eventually produce wholly new species and types of organisms.

necessity: formally, a possibility whose complement is empty. An outcome is necessary if it had to happen and there were no other logically or physically possible options.

neo-Darwinism: the modern version of Darwinian evolutionary theory which postulates that natural selection acts on the heritable (genetic) variations within individuals in populations and where mutations provide the main source of these genetic variations; neo-Darwinism holds that the processes responsible for small-scale microevolutionary changes can be extrapolated indefinitely to produce large-scale macroevolutionary innovations in form. Also called the Modern Synthesis.

notochord: a flexible column located between the gut and nerve cord in the embryos of all chordates (a group of animals that includes the vertebrates, or animals with backbones).

nucleic acid: one of a class of molecules composed of joined nucleotides that allow an organism to reproduce (such as DNA and RNA).

nucleotide: the fundamental structural unit of a nucleic acid, or DNA, made up of a nitrogen-carrying base (purine or pyrimidine), a sugar molecule, and a phosphate group.

oligomers: short chains of molecular subunits (e.g., amino acids in proteins or nucleotides in DNA and RNA).

order: simple or repetitive patterns, as in crystals, that are the result of laws and cannot reasonably be used to draw a design inference. Alternatively, the level of classification above a family in generality and below a class.

pananimalian genome: hypothesis proposed by Susumo Ohno that the ancestor to the animal phyla contained a genome that could code for all the proteins necessary to build each of the animal phyla.

phylogenetic: referring to evolutionary history; based on descent with modification from a common ancestor.

phylogeny: the evolutionary history among a group of organisms.

phylum: the highest taxonomic rank of biological classification within a kingdom; a phylum classifies a group of organisms as sharing a fundamentally unique body plan.

polymer: a large molecule composed of repeated or similar structural units called monomers.

polynucleotides: a polymer of many mononucleotides combined (e.g., DNA and RNA).

polypeptide: a molecule consisting of many amino acids joined by peptide bonds, though not a molecule that necessarily performs a biochemical or biological function (as proteins do).

prebiotic: prior to the existence of biological life.

probabilistic resources: the number of opportunities for an event to occur or be specified. An event that seems quite improbable can become reasonably probable once all the probabilistic resources relevant to its occurrence are factored in.

prokaryote: an organism lacking membrane-bound organelles and in which the chromosomes are not contained within a membrane-bound nucleus.

protein: a three-dimensional macromolecule (polymer) composed of amino acids that performs a biological or biochemical function.

protein synthesis: the production of proteins on ribosomes in the cytoplasm. The process involves the assembly of specific linear chains of amino acids as directed by the sequences of nucleotides in messenger RNA molecules.

punctuated equilibrium: evolutionary theory that postulates that speciation occurs rapidly followed by prolonged periods of stasis; first proposed by Niles Eldridge and Stephen Jay Gould.

random variation: minor differences among the individual organisms in a population that are random with respect to the uses to which they may be put in the course of evolution.

reducing atmosphere: an atmosphere devoid of molecular oxygen but rich in hydrogen available for energy-storing in combination with other substances.

rejection region: a type of specification employed in Ronald Fisher's theory of significance testing in which a pattern is set up in advance of an experiment and a sample is then taken. Provided the sample falls within the rejection region, the chance hypothesis—i.e., the probability distribution said to be responsible for the sample—is then eliminated.

ribosome: an organelle composed of protein and ribonucleic acid that is manufactured in the nucleus and can be free in the cytoplasm or attached to the membranes of the (rough) endoplasmic reticulum; functions in protein synthesis.

Rosenberger v. Rector and Visitors of the University of Virginia (1995): a case brought by some students at the University of Virginia who were denied an allocation of student activity funds to promote their religious views. The university claimed their refusal was required by the Establishment Clause, but the U.S. Supreme Court ruled that if other student groups were able to promote their views, denial to a religious group was a form of viewpoint discrimination.

Scopes trial: the trial of John Scopes in 1925 that focused attention on whether a teacher had academic freedom to teach evolution. While Scopes lost the case, public sentiment turned against attempts to censor teachers.

self-organizational theories: theories ascribing to unassisted matter and energy the ability to organize themselves (e.g., on the prebiotic earth) into systems of increasing specified complexity culminating in the appearance of the first living cells.

semantic information: information that conveys meaning.

Shannon information: developed by Claude Shannon and Warren Weaver in the 1940s, Shannon information is concerned with quantifying information (usually in terms of bits) to keep track of information as it is communicated from a source to a receiver. The amount of Shannon information contained in a string of characters is inversely related to the probability of the occurrence of the string. Unlike specified complexity, Shannon information is solely concerned with the improbability or complexity of a string of characters rather than its meaning or patterning. See *specified complexity*.

small probability specification: a specification (conditionally independent pattern) that identifies an event of small probability.

speciation: the development of a new species by reproductive isolation of organisms from their ancestral population, resulting in the loss of interfertility with the ancestral population.

species: the taxonomic rank below genus; comprised of a group of organisms capable of interbreeding within the group but incapable of breeding with any other group of organisms.

specification: a conditionally independent pattern that in the presence of complexity can be employed to draw a design inference.

specified complexity: an event exhibits specified complexity provided the pattern to which it conforms identifies a highly improbable event (complexity) and the pattern itself is conditionally independent of the event. Specified complexity is a type of information.

syntactic information: information that is expressed in alphabetic character strings. Bits as represented on a computer and the four-character DNA code are examples. Syntactic information may or may not be specified. See *specification* and *specified complexity*.

theism: the worldview that posits a personal God as the creator and sustainer of the universe, who may also act as an agent within the universe.

therapsids: an extinct group of synapsid reptiles from which mammals are supposed to have evolved.

transcription: synthesis of RNA using a DNA template.

translation: synthesis of a protein using a messenger RNA template.

tRNA: transfer RNA; each tRNA attaches to a specific amino acid and guides the amino acid to its proper place (specified by mRNA) in the protein being assembled by the ribosome.

universal probability bound: a degree of improbability below which a specified event of that probability cannot reasonably be attributed to chance regardless of whatever probabilistic resources from the known universe are factored in. Universal probability bounds have been estimated anywhere between 10^{-50} (Emile Borel) and 10^{-150} (William Dembski).

vertebrates: chordates with a backbone; includes fish, amphibians, reptiles, birds, and mammals.

vestigial structures: features that apparently serve no function in an organism and are allegedly holdovers from an evolutionary past.

viewpoint discrimination: viewpoint discrimination occurs when a viewpoint is excluded from an otherwise public forum in which a wide variety of views may be expressed. Recent U.S. Supreme Court cases have ruled against public bodies (like schools) when they permit a facility to be used for a variety of different purposes but then exclude a viewpoint (often a religious viewpoint).

For Further Reading

Beckwith, Francis J. *Law, Darwinism, and Public Education: The Establishment Clause and the Challenge of Intelligent Design.* Lanham, Md.: Rowman and Littlefield, 2003.

Behe, Michael J. *Darwin's Black Box: The Biochemical Challenge to Evolution.* New York: Free Press, 1996.

Behe, Michael J., William A. Dembski, and Stephen C. Meyer. *Science and Evidence for Design in the Universe.* San Francisco: Ignatius Press, 2002.

Buell, Jon, and Virginia Hearn, eds. *Darwinism: Science or Philosophy?* Richardson, Tex.: Foundation for Thought and Ethics, 1994.

Craig, William Lane, and J. P. Moreland, eds. *Naturalism: A Critical Analysis.* New York: Routledge, 2000.

Darwin, Charles. *The Origin of the Species by Means of Natural Selection.* London: Penguin, 1985.

Davis, Percival, and Dean H. Kenyon. *Of Pandas and People: The Central Question of Biological Origins.* Edited by Charles B. Thaxton. Dallas: Haughton, 1990.

Dawkins, Richard. *The Blind Watchmaker: Why the Evidence of Evolution Reveals a Universe without Design.* New York: W. W. Norton, 1986.

Dembski, William A. *The Design Inference: Eliminating Chance through Small Probabilities.* Cambridge: Cambridge University Press, 1998.

———. *Intelligent Design: The Bridge between Science and Theology.* Downers Grove, Ill.: InterVarsity Press, 1999.

———. *No Free Lunch: Why Specified Complexity Cannot Be Purchased without Intelligence.* Lanham, Md.: Rowman and Littlefield, 2002.

———, ed. *Mere Creation: Science, Faith, and Intelligent Design.* Downers Grove, Ill.: InterVarsity Press, 1998.

Dembski, William A., and James M. Kushiner, eds. *Signs of Intelligence: Understanding Intelligent Design.* Grand Rapids, Mich.: Brazos Press, 2001.

Dembski, William A., and Michael Ruse. *Debating Design: From Darwin to DNA.* Cambridge: Cambridge University Press, forthcoming.

Denton, Michael. *Evolution: A Theory in Crisis.* Bethesda, Md.: Adler and Adler, 1986.

Depew, David J., and Bruce H. Weber. *Darwinism Evolving: System Dynamics in the Genealogy of Natural Selections.* Cambridge: MIT Press, 1995.

Desmond, Adrian, and James Moore. *Darwin.* London: Penguin, 1991.

Discovery Institute, *Getting the Facts Straight: A Viewer's Guide to PBS's "Evolution."* Seattle: Discovery Institute Press, 2001.

Ferngren, Gary B., Edward J. Larson, Darrel W. Amundsen, and Anne-Marie E. Makhla, eds. *History of Science and Religion in the Western Tradition: An Encyclopedia.* New York: Garland, 2000.

Giberson, Karl W., and Donald A. Yerxa. *Species of Origins: America's Search for a Creation Story.* Lanham, Md.: Rowman and Littlefield, 2002.

Gillespie, Neil C. *Charles Darwin and the Problem of Creation.* Chicago: University of Chicago Press, 1979.

Gould, Stephen Jay. *The Structure of Evolutionary Theory.* Cambridge: Harvard University Press, 2002.

_____. *Wonderful Life: The Burgess Shale and the Nature of History.* New York: W. W. Norton, 1989.

Hooper, Judith. *Of Moths and Men: An Evolutionary Tale: The Untold Story of Science and the Peppered Moth.* New York: W. W. Norton, 2002.

Hunter, Cornelius G. *Darwin's God: Evolution and the Problem of Evil.* Grand Rapids, Mich: Brazos Press, 2001.

Johnson, Phillip E. *Darwin on Trial.* 2d ed. Downers Grove, Ill.: InterVarsity Press, 1993.

_____. *Defeating Darwinism by Opening Minds.* Downers Grove, Ill.: InterVarsity Press, 1997.

_____. *Objections Sustained: Subversive Essays on Evolution, Law, and Culture.* Downers Grove, Ill.: InterVarsity Press, 1998.

_____. *Reason in the Balance: The Case Against Naturalism in Science, Law, and Education.* Downers Grove, Ill.: InterVarsity Press, 1995.

Johnson, Phillip E. and Denis O. Lamoureux, eds. *Darwinism Defeated?: The Johnson-Lamoureux Debate on Biological Origins.* Vancouver: Regent College Publishing, 1999.

Kauffman, Stuart A. *The Origins of Order: Self-Organization and Selection in Evolution.* New York: Oxford University Press, 1993.

Larson, Edward J. *Summer for the Gods: The Scopes Trial and America's Continuing Debate over Science and Religion.* New York: Basic Books, 1997.

_____. *Trial and Error: The American Controversy over Creation and Evolution.* New York: Oxford University Press, 1989.

Lenoir, Timothy. *The Strategy of Life: Teleology and Mechanics in Nineteenth Century German Biology.* Chicago: University of Chicago Press, 1982.

Mayr, Ernst. *Toward a New Philosophy of Biology: Observations of an Evolutionist.* Cambridge: Harvard University Press, 1988.

Mill, John Stewart. *On Liberty.* Harmondsworth, Eng.: Penguin, 1980.

Miller, Kenneth R. *Finding Darwin's God: A Scientist's Search for Common Ground between God and Evolution.* New York: Cliff Street Books, 1999.

Moreland, J. P., ed. *Creation Hypothesis: Scientific Evidence for an Intelligent Designer.* Downers Grove, Ill.: InterVarsity Press, 1994.

Newman, Robert C., and John L. Wiester. *What's Darwin Got to Do with It? A Friendly Conversation about Evolution.* Downers Grove, Ill.: InterVarsity Press, 2000.

Nord, Warren A., and Charles C. Haynes. *Taking Religion Seriously across the Curriculum.* Nashville, Tenn.: First Amendment Center, 1998.

Numbers, Ronald L. *The Creationists: The Evolution of Scientific Creationism.* New York: Knopf, 1992.

———. *Darwinism Comes to America.* Cambridge: Harvard University Press, 1998.

Pennock, Robert T., ed. *Intelligent Design Creationism and Its Critics: Philosophical, Theological, and Scientific Perspectives.* Cambridge: MIT Press, 2001.

Pera, Marcello. *The Discourses of Science.* Translated by Clarissa Botsford. Chicago: University of Chicago Press, 1994.

Ratzsch, Del. *Nature, Design, and Science: The Status of Design in Natural Science.* Albany: State University of New York Press, 2001.

Rea, Michael C. *World without Design: The Ontological Consequences of Naturalism.* New York: Oxford University Press, 2002.

Ruse, Michael. *Monad to Man: The Concept of Progress in Evolutionary Biology.* Cambridge: Harvard University Press, 1996.

———. *Darwin and Design.* Cambridge, Mass: Harvard University Press, 2003.

———, ed. *But Is it Science? The Philosophical Question in the Creation/Evolution Controversy.* Amherst, N.Y.: Prometheus, 1996.

Thaxton, Charles B., Walter L. Bradley, and Roger L. Olsen. *Mystery of Life's Origin: Reassessing Current Theories.* New York: Philosophical Library, 1984.

Wells, Jonathan. *Icons of Evolution: Science or Myth?: Why Much of What We Teach About Evolution is Wrong.* Washington, D.C.: Regnery, 2000.

Contributors

John Angus Campbell (Ph.D., rhetoric, University of Pittsburgh) is a professor and director of graduate studies in the Department of Communication at the University of Memphis. He has twice won the Golden Anniversary Award from the National Communication Association (1971 and 1987) for his scholarly essays and was a recipient of the Distinguished Teaching Award (1993) and the Dean's Recognition Award (1994) from the University of Washington. Most recently, he was named Communication Educator of the Year by the Tennessee State Communication Association (2001). In his research, he has specialized in the study of the rhetoric of science and is one of the founders of this increasingly important and growing academic subspecialty. He has published numerous highly regarded technical articles and book chapters analyzing the rhetorical strategy of Darwin's *Origin of Species*. He recently guest edited and contributed to a special issue on the intelligent design argument in the *Journal of Rhetorical & Public Affairs* (vol. 1, no. 4). He is at work on a scholarly book with the working title, *Charles Darwin: A Rhetorical Biography*.

Stephen C. Meyer (Ph.D., history and philosophy of science, University of Cambridge) is director of the Discovery Institute's Center for Science and Culture in Seattle, Washington and serves as University Professor, Conceptual Foundations of Science at Palm Beach Atlantic University in West Palm Beach, Florida. Meyer has worked previously as a geophysicist for the Atlantic Richfield Company and a professor of philosophy at Whitworth College. He is coauthor of the book, *Science and Evidence of Design in the Universe* (2002). Meyer has contributed to numerous scholarly books, including the forthcoming *Debating Design: From Darwin to DNA* (Cambridge University Press 2004). He has written for publications such as the *Wall Street Journal, Los Angeles Times, Chicago Tribune, National Review,* and *First Things.* He has appeared on television and radio programs such as Fox News, PBS's *TechnoPolitics* and *Freedom Speaks,* MSNBC's *Hardball with Chris Matthews,* and NPR's *Talk of the Nation* and *Science Friday.* He coauthored the film *Unlocking the Mystery of Life,* which has recently aired on PBS stations around the country. Meyer's testimony before the Ohio State Board of Education and his subsequent editorials in the *Cincinnati Inquirer* and the *Columbus Dispatch* influenced the Ohio State Board of Education's 2002 decision to require students to "critically analyze" evolutionary theory—the first statewide endorsement of the "teach the controversy" approach advocated by many of the contributors to this volume.

Michael J. Behe (Ph.D., biochemistry, University of Pennsylvania) is professor of biological sciences at Lehigh University in Pennsylvania. He has published extensively in both scholarly journals and publications such as the *New York Times, Boston Review, American Spectator,* and *National Review.* His book *Darwin's Black Box* (1996) was recently named by *National Review* and *World* magazine as one of the hundred most important books of the twentieth century.

David Berlinski (Ph.D., philosophy, Princeton) has taught philosophy, mathematics, and English at Stanford, Rutgers, the City University of New York, the University of Washington, the University of Puget Sound, San Jose State University, the University of Santa Clara, San Francisco State University, and the Université de Paris at Jussieu. He is the author of *A Tour of the Calculus* (1996), *The Advent of the Algorithm* (2000), and *Newton's Gift* (2001).

Walter Bradley (Ph.D., materials science, University of Texas at Austin) has been a principal investigator on research grants and contracts for the National Science Foundation, NASA, the U.S. Department of Energy, and private corporations. Bradley has coauthored several seminal works on the origin of life, including articles in the journal the *Origins of Life and Evolution of the Biosphere* and the book *The Mystery of Life's Origin,* which was republished in 1992.

Paul Chien (Ph.D., biology, University of California, Irvine) is professor (and ex-chair) in the Department of Biology at the University of San Francisco. Chien's work has been published in over a dozen technical journals, and he has spoken internationally—from Brazil to mainland China, where he has also been involved in cooperative research programs. Chien recently edited and translated *Darwin on Trial* into Chinese.

Celeste Condit (Ph.D., rhetorical studies, University of Iowa) is a research professor in the Department of Speech Communication at the University of Georgia. She is the author of *The Meanings of the Gene* (1999). Condit has published widely in publications ranging from the *Quarterly Journal of Speech* to the *American Journal of Human Genetics* to *Health Communication.* She has received the Douglas Ehninger Award for distinguished rhetorical scholarship from the National Communication Association as well as a Golden Anniversary Monograph Award.

Mark DeForrest (J.D., Gonzaga University) is an attorney residing in Spokane, Washington. He is currently employed as a legal writing and research instructor at Gonzaga. DeForrest has published several articles in venues as diverse as the *Harvard Journal of Law and Public Policy, Seattle Times, Gonzaga Law Review, Across Borders,* and *Utah Law Review.*

William A. Dembski (Ph.D., mathematics, University of Chicago; Ph.D., philosophy, University of Illinois, Chicago) is associate research professor in the conceptual foundations of science at Baylor University. He has published in such diverse publications as *Journal of Theoretical Probability, Nous, Scottish Journal of Theology,* and *Zygon*. He is also a regular contributor to *Meta* (www.metanexus.net). He is the author or editor of *The Design Inference* (1998), *Mere Creation* (1998), *Intelligent Design* (1999), *Unapologetic Apologetics* (with Jay Richards, 2001), *Signs of Intelligence* (with James Kushiner, 2001), *No Free Lunch* (2001), and *The Design Revolution* (2003).

David Depew is professor of communication studies and rhetoric of inquiry at the University of Iowa. He is associated with Iowa's internationally known Project on Rhetoric of Inquiry (POROI), an interdisciplinary research and teaching unit dedicated to applying rhetorical criticism and theorizing to scholarly and public controversies that involve claims to disciplinary knowledge. With Bruce H. Weber, he is coauthor of *Darwinism Evolving: Systems Dynamics and the Genealogy of Natural Selection* (1995). DePew and Weber also co-edited *Evolution and Learning: The Baldwin Effect Reconsidered.*

David K. DeWolf (J.D., Yale) is professor of law at the Gonzaga University Law School in Spokane, Washington. He has authored a number of books on the law, including *Washington Tort Law and Practice* (with K. W. Allen) and *Washington Contract Law and Practice* (with K. W. Allen and D. Barrier), as well as several technical and popular articles in publications such as *National Review* and the *Wall Street Journal.* He is a fellow of Discovery Institute's Center for Science and Culture. In 2000, DeWolf published (with Stephen Meyer and Mark DeForrest) an article in the *University of Utah Law Review* (republished in this volume). This article was cited by Senator Santorum of Pennsylvania in support of the provision that the Senator authored in support of a more scientifically inclusive and controversy-based approach to teaching biological evolution. This provision is now part of the report language of the "No Child Left Behind" federal education act.

Steve Fuller (Ph.D., history and philosophy of science, University of Pittsburgh) is professor of sociology at the University of Warwick, U.K. He is best known for his research program of "social epistemology," the subject of a journal he founded in 1987. His latest books include *The Governance of Science: Ideology and the Future of the Open Society* (2000) and *Thomas Kuhn: A Philosophical History for Our Times* (2000).

Eugene Garver (Ph.D., philosophy, University of Chicago) is Regents Professor of Philosophy at St. John's University, where he has been teaching since 1985. He is the author of *Machiavelli and the History of Prudence* (1987) and *Aristotle's Rhetoric: An Art of Character* (1994). He recently co-edited *Pluralism in Theory and Practice: Richard McKeon and American Philosophy* (2000) and was guest editor of a special issue of *Argumentation* called "Reasoning: Perspectives from the New Philosophy and History of Science."

Phillip E. Johnson (J.D., University of Chicago) was professor of law at the University of California at Berkeley for over twenty-five years. In addition to being a distinguished and widely published American legal scholar, he is a well-known critic of Darwinism. His provocative *Darwin on Trial* (1991) has inspired academic symposia at universities such as Stanford, Harvard, Chicago, Cornell, Southern Methodist University, and the University of Texas. His most recent books are *Defeating Darwinism by Opening Minds* (1997), *Objections Sustained* (1998), *The Wedge of Truth* (2000), and *The Right Questions* (2002).

Michael Newton Keas (Ph.D., history of science, University of Oklahoma) is associate professor of natural science at Oklahoma Baptist University (OBU) and a codesigner of the OBU Planetarium. He has contributed articles to scholarly anthologies and journals, including the American Chemical Society's *Nobel Laureates in Chemistry (1901–1992)* and the German centennial celebration of A. W. Hofmann's death, *Die Allianz von Wissenschaft und Industrie: August Wilhelm Hofmann (1818–1892): Zeit, Werk, Wirkung.*

Donald Kennedy (Ph.D., biology, Harvard University) served for a year as provost and for twelve years as president emeritus of Stanford University. During that time, he also continued his work on health and environmental policy issues as a member of the Board of Directors of the Health Effects Institute (a nonprofit research organization devoted to mobile source emissions), Clean Sites, Inc. (a similar organization devoted to toxic waste cleanup), and the California Nature Conservancy. Kennedy is a member of the National Academy of Sciences, the American Academy of Arts and Sciences, and the American Philosophical Society.

Brig Klyce studied English at Princeton University and received a Bachelor Architecture degree from the University of Tennessee in 1975. He began his study of panspermia as an avocation in 1981. After twenty years in the industrial laundry business, in 1995 he launched Acorn Enterprises LLC, a research and publishing company focused on panspermia. He maintains a website about the strong version of panspermia, which he hopes to rename "cosmic ancestry," at http://www.panspermia.org.

Malcolm Lancaster is a retired professor of clinical medicine from the University of Texas at San Antonio.

John Lyne (Ph.D., University of Wisconsin) is professor and chair of the Department of Communication at the University of Pittsburgh, where he is also a resident fellow at the Center for Philosophy of Science and a member of the graduate faculty in Bioethics and Health Law. Lyne's work has appeared in such journals as the *Quarterly Journal of Speech, Social Epistemology, Journal of Medical Humanities,* and *Cultural Studies.* He has coauthored a book with Henry F. Howe on sociobiology and evolutionary theory and was series editor-in-chief for the *Rhetoric of the Human Sciences* book series for the University of Wisconsin Press.

Gordon C. Mills (Ph.D., biochemistry, University of Michigan) spent thirty-five years on the medical school teaching and research faculty at the University of Texas Medical Branch, Galveston. For the past twelve years, he has applied his research training and experience to developing a theistic view of evolution and the origin of life that he refers to as a "Design Theory of Progressive Creation." Mills's work has been published in *Perspectives on Science and Christian Faith, Origins and Design,* and *Christian Scholar's Review.*

Paul Nelson (Ph.D., philosophy of biology, University of Chicago) is Senior Fellow at the Discovery Institute's Center for the Science and Culture. He has published articles in such journals as *Biology and Philosophy, Zygon, Rhetoric and Public Affairs,* and *Touchstone* and chapters in the anthologies *Mere Creation, Signs of Intelligence,* and *Intelligent Design, Creationism, and Its Critics* (MIT Press 2001). Nelson edits the journal *Origins and Design.*

Warren A. Nord (Ph.D., philosophy, University of North Carolina, Chapel Hill) has taught the philosophy of religion at the University of North Carolina—Chapel Hill and been director of the university's program in the Humanities and Human Values since 1979. Nord is the author of more than thirty articles and two books, *Religion and American Education: Rethinking a National Dilemma,* and (with Charles C. Haynes) *Taking Religion Seriously Across the Curriculum.*

Massimo Pigliucci (Doctorate in Genetics, University of Ferrara, Italy; Ph.D., botany, University of Connecticut) is an associate professor at the University of Tennessee in Knoxville, where he teaches ecology and evolutionary biology. He has published fifty technical papers and two books on evolutionary biology (*Phenotypic Evolution,* with Carl Schlichting, and *Phenotypic Plasticity: Beyond Nature vs. Nurture*). Pigliucci has been awarded several times the Oak Ridge National Labs award for excellence in research and has won the prestigious Dobzhansky Prize from the Society for the Study of Evolution, of which he is now vice president. As a skeptic, he has published in national magazines such as *Free Inquiry, Skeptic, Skeptical Inquirer, Philosophy Now,* and *Secular Nation.*

Alvin Plantinga (Ph.D., philosophy, Yale) is a founding member and past president of the Society of Christian Philosophers. He is the author of *God and Other Minds, The Nature of Necessity, Warrant: The Current Debate, Warrant and Proper Function,* and *Warranted Christian Belief.*

William Provine is professor in the Department of Ecology and Evolutionary Biology and in the Department of History at Cornell University; he is also the Charles A. Alexander Professor of Biological Sciences. He is a Fellow of the American

Association for the Advancement of Science and has held a Guggenheim Fellowship. In 1988, he won Cornell's Clark Distinguished Teaching Award.

Marcus Ross (M.S., paleontology, South Dakota School of Mines and Technology; Ph.D. candidate, University of Rhode Island) is a doctoral student in paleontology at the University of Rhode Island. In the summer of 1999, Ross traveled to southern China to study the famous Cambrian fossils near Chengjiang. He recently presented a poster at the Geological Society of America outlining a novel method for measuring increases in biological complexity as they arise the in fossil record.

Michael Ruse (Ph.D., philosophy of biology, University of Bristol) is the Lucyle T. Werkmeister Professor of Philosophy at Florida State University. He is a Fellow of the American Association for the Advancement of Science and has been awarded a Guggenheim Fellowship and a Killam Fellowship. He has written or edited several books, including *Can a Darwinian Be a Christian? The Relationship between Science and Religion,* and *Mystery of Mysteries: Is Evolution a Social Construction?* Ruse is the founding editor of *Biology and Philosophy.* He is the series editor of the *Philosophy and Biology* series for Cambridge University Press.

Bruce Weber (Ph.D., chemistry, University of California, San Diego) is Professor of Biochemistry Emeritus at California State University—Fullerton and Robert H. Woodworth Professor of Science and Natural Philosophy at Bennington College. He is an elected Fellow of the Linnean Society (London). He is coauthor, with David Depew, of *Darwinism Evolving: Systems Dynamics and the Genealogy of Natural Selection* (1995). He is also director of the Los Angeles Basin California State University Minority International Research Training Program.

Jonathan Wells (Ph.D., molecular and cell biology, University of California, Berkeley; Ph.D., religious studies, Yale University) has published articles in *Development, Proceedings of the National Academy of Sciences USA, BioSystems, Scientist,* and *American Biology Teacher.* He is also author of the book *Charles Hodge's Critique of Darwinism* (1988) and the book *Icons of Evolution: Why Much of What We Teach about Evolution Is Wrong* (2000).

Chandra Wickramasinghe (Sc.D., University of Cambridge) is professor at Cardiff University of Wales. Jointly with Sir Fred Hoyle, he was awarded the International Dag Hammarskjold Gold Medal for Science in 1986, and in 1992 he was decorated by the president of Sri Lanka with the titular honor of Vidya Jyothi. He was awarded the International Sahabdeen Prize for Science in 1996. He is a Fellow of the Royal Society of Arts and a Fellow of the Royal Astronomical Society.